Multidimensional Approach to Local Development and Poverty:

Causes, Consequences, and Challenges Post COVID-19

João Conrado de Amorim Carvalho
Centro de Ensino Superior Dom Bosco, Brazil

Francisco Espasandín Bustelo
Universidad de Sevilla, Spain

Emmanuel M. C. B. Sabino
Centro de Ensino, Formação e Pesquisa. Brazil

IGI Global
PUBLISHER of TIMELY KNOWLEDGE

A volume in the Advances in Electronic Government, Digital Divide, and Regional Development (AEGDDRD) Book Series

Published in the United States of America by
IGI Global
Information Science Reference (an imprint of IGI Global)
701 E. Chocolate Avenue
Hershey PA, USA 17033
Tel: 717-533-8845
Fax: 717-533-8661
E-mail: cust@igi-global.com
Web site: http://www.igi-global.com

Library of Congress Cataloging-in-Publication Data

Names: Carvalho, Joao Conrado de Amorim, 1959- editor. | Bustelo, Francisco Espasandin, 1964- editor. | Sabino, Emmanuel Carlos, 1960- editor.
Title: Multidimensional approach to local development and poverty : causes, consequences, and challenges post-COVID-19 / Joao Conrado de Amorim Carvalho, Francisco Espasandin Bustelo, and Emmanuel Carlos Sabino, editors.
Description: Hershey, PA : Information Science Reference, 2022. | Includes bibliographical references and index. | Summary: "This book offers various points of view within the different scientific areas, such as sociology, economics, management, entrepreneurship, marketing, education, among others, that can add to the efforts to combat poverty and current means and methods to modernize countries less developed"-- Provided by publisher.
Identifiers: LCCN 2021046477 (print) | LCCN 2021046478 (ebook) | ISBN 9781799889250 (hardcover) | ISBN 9781799889267 (paperback) | ISBN 9781799889274 (ebook)
Subjects: LCSH: Poverty--Developing countries. | COVID-19 (Disease)--Economic aspects. | Economic development--Developing countries.. | Organizational change--Developing countries. | Developing countries--Social policy--21st century. | Developing countries--Economic policy--21st century.
Classification: LCC HC59.72.P6 M85 2022 (print) | LCC HC59.72.P6 (ebook) | DDC 339.4/6091724--dc23/eng/20211108
LC record available at https://lccn.loc.gov/2021046477
LC ebook record available at https://lccn.loc.gov/2021046478

This book is published in the IGI Global book series Advances in Electronic Government, Digital Divide, and Regional Development (AEGDDRD) (ISSN: 2326-9103; eISSN: 2326-9111)

British Cataloguing in Publication Data
A Cataloguing in Publication record for this book is available from the British Library.

For electronic access to this publication, please contact: eresources@igi-global.com.

Advances in Electronic Government, Digital Divide, and Regional Development (AEGDDRD) Book Series

Zaigham Mahmood
University of Derby, UK & North West University, South Africa

ISSN:2326-9103
EISSN:2326-9111

Mission

The successful use of digital technologies (including social media and mobile technologies) to provide public services and foster economic development has become an objective for governments around the world. The development towards electronic government (or e-government) not only affects the efficiency and effectiveness of public services, but also has the potential to transform the nature of government interactions with its citizens. Current research and practice on the adoption of electronic/digital government and the implementation in organizations around the world aims to emphasize the extensiveness of this growing field.

The Advances in Electronic Government, Digital Divide & Regional Development (AEGDDRD) book series aims to publish authored, edited and case books encompassing the current and innovative research and practice discussing all aspects of electronic government development, implementation and adoption as well the effective use of the emerging technologies (including social media and mobile technologies) for a more effective electronic governance (or e-governance).

Coverage

- Citizens Participation and Adoption of E-Government Provision
- Adoption of Innovation with Respect to E-Government
- Public Information Management, Regional Planning, Rural Development
- Frameworks and Methodologies for E-Government Development
- Issues and Challenges in E-Government Adoption
- Knowledge Divide, Digital Divide
- Social Media, Web 2.0, and Mobile Technologies in E-Government
- ICT Infrastructure and Adoption for E-Government Provision
- Urban Development, Urban Economy
- Online Government, E-Government, M-Government

IGI Global is currently accepting manuscripts for publication within this series. To submit a proposal for a volume in this series, please contact our Acquisition Editors at Acquisitions@igi-global.com or visit: http://www.igi-global.com/publish/.

The Advances in Electronic Government, Digital Divide, and Regional Development (AEGDDRD) Book Series (ISSN 2326-9103) is published by IGI Global, 701 E. Chocolate Avenue, Hershey, PA 17033-1240, USA, www.igi-global.com. This series is composed of titles available for purchase individually; each title is edited to be contextually exclusive from any other title within the series. For pricing and ordering information please visit http://www.igi-global.com/book-series/advances-electronic-government-digital-divide/37153. Postmaster: Send all address changes to above address.

Titles in this Series

For a list of additional titles in this series, please visit: www.igi-global.com/book-series

Blockchain Technologies and Applications for Digital Governance
Pradeep Nijalingappa (Bapuji Institute of Engineering and Technology, India) and Mangesh Manikrao Ghonge (Sandip Foundation's Institute of Technology and Research Centre, India)
Information Science Reference • © 2022 • 266pp • H/C (ISBN: 9781799884934) • US $225.00

Advancements in Global Cyber Security Laws and Regulations
Shahid M. Shahidullah (Hampton University, USA) Zina McGee (Hampton University, USA) and Carla Miller Coates (North Carolina Agricultural and Technical State University, United States)
Information Science Reference • © 2022 • 305pp • H/C (ISBN: 9781799845850) • US $195.00

Handbook of Research on Nurturing Industrial Economy for Africa's Development
Frederick Muyia Nafukho (Texas A&M University, USA) and Alexander Boniface Makulilo (University of Dodoma, Tanzania)
Information Science Reference • © 2021 • 510pp • H/C (ISBN: 9781799864714) • US $245.00

Global Perspectives on the Impact of Mass Media on Electoral Processes
Stella Amara Aririguzoh (Covenant University, Nigeria)
Information Science Reference • © 2021 • 187pp • H/C (ISBN: 9781799848202) • US $195.00

Impact of Political Socialization on the Support for Democratic Principles Emerging Research and Opportunities
Allison Clark Ellis (University of South Carolina Upstate, USA)
Information Science Reference • © 2021 • 204pp • H/C (ISBN: 9781799842910) • US $175.00

Perspectives on ICT4D and Socio-Economic Growth Opportunities in Developing Countries
Patrick Ndayizigamiye (University of Johannesburg, South Africa) Glenda Barlow-Jones (University of Johannesburg, South Africa) Roelien Brink (University of Johannesburg, South Africa) Stella Bvuma (University of Johannesburg, South Africa) Rehana Minty (University of Johannesburg, South Africa) and Siyabonga Mhlongo (University of Johannesburg, South Africa)
Information Science Reference • © 2021 • 507pp • H/C (ISBN: 9781799829836) • US $195.00

Handbook of Research on Creative Cities and Advanced Models for Knowledge-Based Urban Development
Aly Abdel Razek Galaby (Faculty of Arts, Alexandria University, Egypt) and Amal Adel Abdrabo (Faculty of Education, Alexandria University, Egypt)
Information Science Reference • © 2021 • 388pp • H/C (ISBN: 9781799849483) • US $245.00

IGI Global
PUBLISHER of TIMELY KNOWLEDGE

701 East Chocolate Avenue, Hershey, PA 17033, USA
Tel: 717-533-8845 x100 • Fax: 717-533-8661
E-Mail: cust@igi-global.com • www.igi-global.com

Table of Contents

Detailed Table of Contents

There are two objectives that impel this work: first, to propose a valid, reliable, and parsimonious poverty index, named Municipal Poverty Index-Urban Audit (MPI-UA), and second, to describe the evolution of the multidimensional poverty risk of the Spanish municipalities according to C. For the construction of the MPI-UA, the information provided by the URBAN AUDIT database on Spanish municipalities with a population in excess of 20,000 inhabitants has been used. The validated data have been analyzed with the PLS technique to identify the variables that allow the establishment of the MPI-UA, although previously certain variables have had to be transformed. This chapter has valuable implications insofar as there is no known multidimensional poverty index for Spanish municipalities. Moreover, it may be of probable use for academics. In the case of local managers, the index can be useful both for the knowledge of the situation and for the design of public policies to reduce poverty.

The coronavirus has seriously affected the economy in general and tourism in particular. However, at the same time, it has been a great opportunity for rural tourism, as this type of tourism has been one of the beneficiaries of this health crisis. This is partly explained by the fact that travelers have turned to nature destinations and accommodation that guarantees social distance. Under the premise that tourism is a community product and that it is necessary to count on the community and local capacities, the aim of this research is to find out how the factors that make up the destination management models affect the development of rural tourism in a given region. It also seeks to know their influence on the results of rural accommodation companies in order to promote local development in this state of the pandemic. The work has been carried out with a total of 156 tourist accommodations. A total of eight management factors and five different clusters of companies were detected from the analysis of the dimensionality of the model.

Fair trade is a concept that is becoming increasingly ingrained in consumers. This means that companies that are committed to the development of fair-trade policies can find here a source of competitive advantage. Likewise, these practices will favour many producers in the primary sector, which could turn this into an effective way of fighting poverty. The aim of this research is to find out how fair trade has an impact

more interest in light beers than men, especially craft beer. It has also been found that differences in preferences between men and women are narrowing as opportunities to try beer increase. In this sense, younger age groups tend to show fewer differences. It was also observed that, during the period of social isolation, consumption habits were maintained, but purchases took place through a delivery system, which affected the performance of bars and restaurants.

This chapter aims to describe the role of intangible assets (trust, love, and well-being) in the development of organizations. After a first approach in which the authors point out distortions of the traditional organizational management models and politics in Brazil, they propose solutions adopted by several companies in construing of humanized models. Based on these successful experiences, they highlight several indicators that demonstrate the profitability of these organizations and their differentials in tackling the post-pandemic economic and social crisis.

For Mexican society it is relevant to know the prospects of well-being in an environment of instability and social insecurity; therefore, this research has the purpose of publicizing the health, economic, and social situation from COVID-19 in Mexico. The work has a qualitative, analytical, and descriptive research design considering current information from the Bank of Mexico with recent indicators of economic activity, The National Institute of Statistics and Geography (INEGI) with data on occupation and employment, as well as the National Council for the Evaluation of Social Development Policy (CONEVAL) regarding the consequences of poverty in Mexican society and other documents that refer to the problem, all this analysis in order to form an idea of the near future of Mexicans. Currently, there is an increase in poverty and inequality resulting from the mismanagement of government policies and the lack of proposals to improve the social sector.

Young people who are in a situation of residential care are considered to be in a condition of multidimensional poverty. Research aims to achieve the following general objectives: first, to identify the level of delinquency of young people and its determining factors and, second, to propose strategies and programs. This research will follow a two-stage research process in which different research methods will be applied. Along with the

Preface

It seems consensual that the phenomenon of poverty affects all countries, regardless of their stage of development. The causes of the problem are diverse and impacted by local peculiarities. In this sense, the consequences also differ from country to country, as do the means used to find solutions and reduce social impact.

Over the past two years, the problem of poverty has worsened with the onset of the Covid-19 pandemic. The need to interrupt the virus transmission mechanisms led to a series of social isolation measures, the establishment of curfews and lockdowns. Many companies were forced to suspend activities during the period in which the measures were imposed, resulting in unemployment, reduced production and, consequently, a low supply of products on the market, generating inflation.

Despite the scientific advances that provided the rapid genetic mapping of the virus and the development of vaccines, the outbreak of infections seriously affected some regions, resulting in a high number of hospitalizations and deaths. The publication of shocking images, the impossibility of health systems to serve everyone, the distrust of a large part of the population about the effectiveness of vaccines and the non-compliance with isolation rules to control the disease, delayed the effectiveness of the measures and helped to intensify the economic crisis that aggravated the problem of poverty.

Still, some interesting actions were registered to mitigate the negative effects of the Covid-19 crisis. Discussing these actions, the causes, consequences, and challenges brought to countries by Covid-19 is the main objective of this book. Researchers and authors strive to provide relevant and recent references in the fight against poverty. The focus is on how countries, companies and people became involved in a problem that was not detected on any radar in the strategic plans and which, arriving suddenly and without warning, caused widespread damage, requiring a great capacity for reaction. It is true that the pandemic cannot yet be considered over, and it is even likely that it will become endemic, reappearing in localized outbreaks. However, many adjustments have already been made to make it possible to live with the health crises that are reflected in the economy.

The first two chapters are devoted to describing the field of poverty research. Chapter 1 makes a bibliographical survey on the topic "extreme poverty", identifying the most relevant authors, journals, and descriptors, showing the evidence that allows researchers and other interested groups to improve the efficiency in the acquisition of high-impact knowledge on the topic. The bibliometric analysis was performed at the counting and Social Network Analysis technique, bringing an important contribution to the literature on "extreme poverty", as it is the first work that raises the intellectual structure of the topic in a multidisciplinary perspective.

Chapter 2 discusses the changes in the way of doing business during the COVID-19. The authors claim that there were speed gains not only due to technological evolution, but also due to the breaking of current market paradigms. The use of innovative dynamic capabilities is replacing individual organizational strategies with collective strategies that provide cooperative competition that generates mutual performance gains. The market now demands greater efficiency, quality, win-win partnerships, continuous learning, synergy, use of technologies, among others that have radically changed the way companies and entrepreneurs work towards achieving challenging goals and goals that provide better results and sustainability to the business. The overall aim of the chapter is to understand the relationship between coopetition and dynamic capabilities; relate collective strategies with dynamic capabilities; and verifying the degree of use of dynamic capabilities in cooperatives, according to a study carried out in cooperatives.

The third and fourth chapters deal with the situation of poverty. In Chapter 3, the authors discuss and propose a valid, reliable, and parsimonious poverty index, and then describe the evolution of the multidimensional poverty risk of Spanish municipalities. To construct the poverty index, they used the URBAN AUDIT database of Spanish municipalities with a population of over 20,000 inhabitants. The results achieved bring valuable implications, mainly because there is no multidimensional poverty index, which can be of use for academics, local managers and for the knowledge of the situation and the design of public policies for poverty reduction. Chapter 4 starts from the premise that Coronavirus has seriously affected the general economy and tourism, but, at the same time, it has been a great opportunity for rural tourism, as this type of tourism has been one of the beneficiaries of this health crisis. The authors believe travelers have turned to nature destinations and accommodations that ensure social distance. The work aims to verify how the factors that constitute the management models of tourist destinations affect the development of rural tourism in a given region and to know their influence on the results of rural accommodation companies, in order to promote local development in this pandemic state.

Chapters 6 through 9 discuss poverty, entrepreneurship, and finance. Chapter 6 seeks to identify the degree of knowledge that immigrant entrepreneurs in Portugal have about crowdfunding (CF) and their predisposition to use this financial mechanism, and the respective perceptions of benefits and risks. The results show that immigrant entrepreneurs have some knowledge about the general characteristics of CF, but most are not aware of the specifics of CF business models. The survey also reveals that although there is some predisposition, it is not very high among Brazilian immigrant entrepreneurs. The results also show that respondents recognize the benefits of CF, specifically the project visibility that the CF platform can provide. However, the main concern of immigrant entrepreneurs is essentially related to the fear of not being able to obtain the necessary pledge objective.

In Chapter 7, the authors intend to identify the level of entrepreneurial intention and multidimensional poverty of the population of a Spanish rural municipality; After this, they want to know the impact of the factors that, according to the theory of planned behavior, determine the entrepreneurial intention; they will also attempt to show the characteristics of the relationship between the entrepreneurial intention and multidimensional poverty and, in light of previously generated knowledge, strategies, programs, projects and / or actions that contribute to the reduction of multidimensional poverty will be proposed. They consider that this research provides social utility and is original to the extent that it remedies a weakness in the literature consulted: the deficit of studies that contemplate, from both the theoretical and empirical perspective, the relationship between entrepreneurial intention and multidimensional poverty.

Chapter 8 highlights microfinance as a tool to create opportunities for women and other underserved sections in India's formal financial structure. It also highlights the role of various institutions that play a significant role in providing rural credit through different channels. In this pandemic in which economies at the global level demand resilience strategies, microfinance can once again prove to be an effective strategy to recover in terms of improving the economic conditions of the poor and vulnerable – who have suffered most due to it. to blockades, especially in developing nations like India. Localization and promotion of local products can help drive business activities at multiple levels, which can slowly, gradually, but effectively improve the skewed global supply chain.

Chapter 9 examines the perspectives and challenges of using zakah as a source of funding in micro-enterprise support programs for refugees. According to the literature, lack of funds represents a fundamental obstacle in supporting refugee livelihoods, particularly in microenterprise programs. Zakat is one of the five pillars of Islam. All Muslims have to pay 2.5% of their wealth every year to the poor and needy. Refugees represent one of the main beneficiaries of zakah. Recently, UNHCR established zakah funds to mobilize zakah funds to help refugees. This article argues that rather than helping refugees with cash, the zakat fund or at least part of the zakat funds can be used to provide microcredit grants to support refugees and help them help themselves. Despite all the challenges of microfinance programs, particularly in the refugee context, well-designed microfinance programs can provide a more sustainable solution for refugees, particularly those trapped in protracted situations.

The Covid-19 issue, and poverty outcomes are discussed in chapters ten through fourteen. In Chapter 10, the author discusses the effects of Covid-19 in Turkey, one of the most affected countries. He claims that the effect of telecommuting, adopted during the pandemic, was tested on the anxiety levels of Turkish participants. The survey was conducted with white-collar employees working in the service sector. In the field study, the results revealed that telecommuting has a negative effect on individuals' anxiety levels, as predicted in the study. In Chapter 11, the authors present motivational factors that determine the behavior of beer consumers before and during the Covid-19 pandemic. The results showed that both before and during the pandemic, men consume more beer than women, however, women consume more expensive types of beer. Women are more likely to be influenced by their relatives, friends and social occasions. It was observed that during the period of social isolation, purchases took place through a delivery system, which affected the performance of bars and restaurants.

Chapter 12 aims to describe the role of intangible assets (trust, love and well-being) in the development of organizations. After a first approach in which distortions of traditional models and policies of organizational management in Brazil were pointed out, the authors propose solutions adopted by several companies in the construction of humanized models. From these successful experiences, several indicators were identified that demonstrate the profitability of these organizations and their differentials in facing the post-pandemic economic and social crisis.

The health, economic and social situation of COVID-19 in Mexico is dealt with in Chapter 13. The work is developed with current information from the Bank of Mexico using recent indicators of economic activity, the National Institute of Statistics and Geography (INEGI) with data on occupation and employment, as well as the National Council for the Evaluation of Social Development Policy (CONEVAL) on the consequences of poverty in Mexican society and other documents that refer to the problem. It concluded that there is an increase in poverty and inequality resulting from the mismanagement of government policies and the lack of proposals to improve the social sector.

Chapter 14 discusses whether the situation of young people who are in residential care are considered to be in a situation of multidimensional poverty in Spain. In this way, it seeks to identify the level of delinquency among young people and its determining factors and propose strategies and programs. It was noticed that the most frequent crimes refer to the involvement of these young people in gang fights; alcohol consumption; in attacking classmates, parents and teachers; they steal money and/or other objects from the Contributing Family; they consume pornography and go out to clubs, pubs and nightclubs. In the educational field, although they are dedicated to education, they get very low grades. They participate moderately in sporting activities and have very low participation in religious services; in addition, boys have a moderately high level of belief in the legal system.

The last two chapters are dedicated to describing suggestions for future research at an international level within the theme. Chapter 15 analyzes the regional imbalance of Foreign Direct Investment (FDI) in Mexico and its relationship with the poverty levels of the 32 states that comprise it. The period studied ranges from 1994 to 2020, taking as its starting point the entry into force of the North American Free Trade Agreement (NAFTA). From the 1980s to the early 1990s, FDI in Mexico maintained a tenuous growth and, from 1994 onwards, there was a considerable increase. The research concludes that poverty is a factor that prevents a symmetrical distribution of FDI across the entire Mexican territory.

Chapter 16 brings important findings. First, companies are being pressured by different interest groups to contribute to the achievement of the SDGs; second, a very high percentage of companies are not even sensitive to the fact that the SDGs are important for their sustainability; thirdly, researchers, especially those in the social sciences, did not generate knowledge about the state of the SDGs in companies; and fourth, the tourism sector is important for meeting the SDGs. The data collection method focuses on the material object "hotel companies" and uses secondary data available from different sources. Among the most relevant results of the survey, we highlight the following. First, the sample companies, although they do not appear to have a formal plan, implement one or more SDGs; in second place; the SDG implemented in the largest number of companies is Gender Equality; Thirdly, the least implemented SDGs are Quality Education, Clean Water and Sanitation, Affordable and non-polluting energy and Reduction of inequalities.

We are very grateful for the authors' dedication to producing relevant and up-to-date research to bring up the subject of the challenge of facing poverty and promoting local development, especially in a difficult time due to Covid-19.

This book is also dedicated to ASIBEAM – Associación Íbero-Americana de Economía, Administración y Marketing (Ibero-American Association of Economics, Administration and Marketing), dedicated to contributing to the reduction of poverty and hunger through applied research, generating and managing knowledge and relationships with interested groups. Some chapter authors in this book are affiliated with ASIBEAM and have dedicated research efforts to discuss the causes of poverty and ways to reduce its impact on society.

We editors hope that readers will find useful information and that they will be able to apply the examples and recommendations suggested in sustainable local development in their regions of origin.

Chapter 1
Intellectural Structure of the "Extreme Poverty" Research Field

Juan Ganaza Vargas
University of Sevilla, Spain

Francisco Espasandín-Bustelo
University of Sevilla, Spain

ABSTRACT

The main objective of this work is to know the situation of the intellectual structure of the scientific community researching "extreme poverty," especially to identify the most relevant authors, journals, and descriptors. In addition, the authors intend to present evidence that allows these researchers and other interested groups to improve the efficiency in acquiring high-impact knowledge on the topic. Through bibliometric analysis, both at the count and relationship levels (in this case with social network analysis [SNA] technique), they have carried out a study of the characteristics and intellectual structure of the academic and scientific network that has addressed the issue of extreme poverty. This work makes an important contribution to the literature on "extreme poverty" since it is the first known work that raises the intellectual structure of this topic from a multidisciplinary perspective.

INTRODUCTION

Poverty is, and has always been, a social problem. According to data from the World Bank (2020), the planet is home to around 7,550 billion inhabitants, of which 689 million live in conditions of extreme poverty and the effect of the COVID-19 pandemic will push about 150 million more people to extreme poverty.

Given the magnitude of this problem, the academic community reacts by generating scientific knowledge. In this sense, a search in the ISI Web of Science database with the topic "extreme poverty"

DOI: 10.4018/978-1-7998-8925-0.ch001

generates 2799 documents. Documents date of publication and their distribution by knowledge areas analysis reveals the following evidence.

Regarding the number of published documents (see Figure 1), we highlight that the first document was published in 1983 and, from that moment on, the number of documents followed an increasing evolution; reaching the figure of 297 in 2020.

Furthermore, Figure 2, which gathers the 25 knowledge areas with the highest number of documents, shows that the three most prolific areas are economy (335), health (279) and environment (214). The business area only offers 62 documents, which illustrates the need to increase the number of publications on this knowledge area over "extreme poverty" topic.

In the development and dissemination of this knowledge, the research communities play an essential role, given the marked social character that its enormous complexity requires (Espasandín-Bustelo, Palacios-Florencio and Sánchez-Rivas, 2020).

In words of Racherla & Hu (2010), intensity and scope of the relationships between researchers conditions the results obtained by these communities. The study of the relationships established in the research communities is, therefore, important to understand their structure and the invisible knowledge network (Ma, Lee & Yu, 2007; Pilkington & Teichert, 2006).

The main objective of this work is to know the situation of the intellectual structure of the scientific community that studies "extreme poverty", especially to identify the most relevant authors, journals and descriptors. In addition, it is intended to offer evidence that allows researchers and other interested groups to improve the efficiency in perceiving topic's high-impact knowledge.

This research, focused on the material object "scientific document" and on the formal object "social networks analysis", is classified as descriptive, exploratory and bibliometric.

Once the subject of study has been justified, the objectives, recipients and type of research have been established, this article presents the following structure. First, the literature is reviewed; second, the

Figure 1. Number of documents on the topic "extreme poverty per year
Source: Web of Science

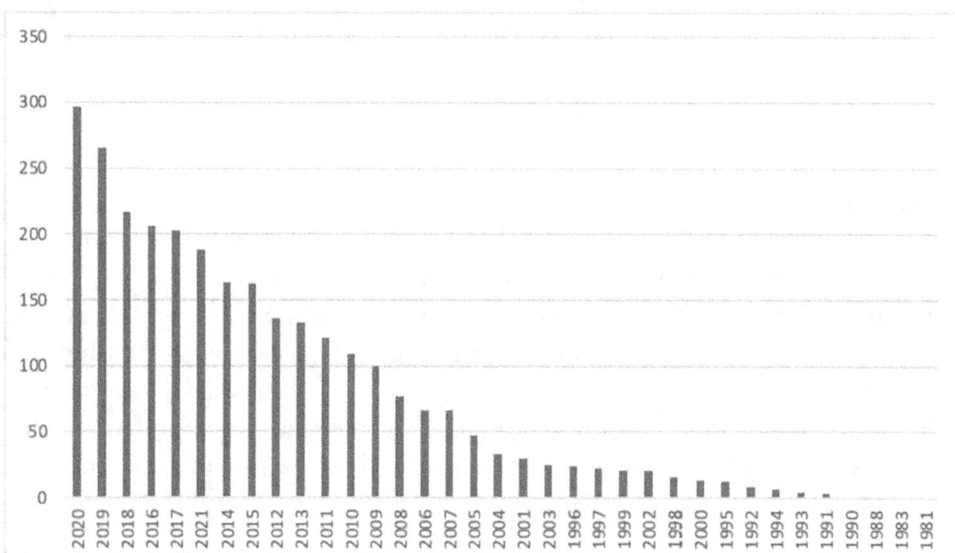

Figure 2. Number of documents on the topic "extreme poverty" by areas of knowledge
Source: Web of Science

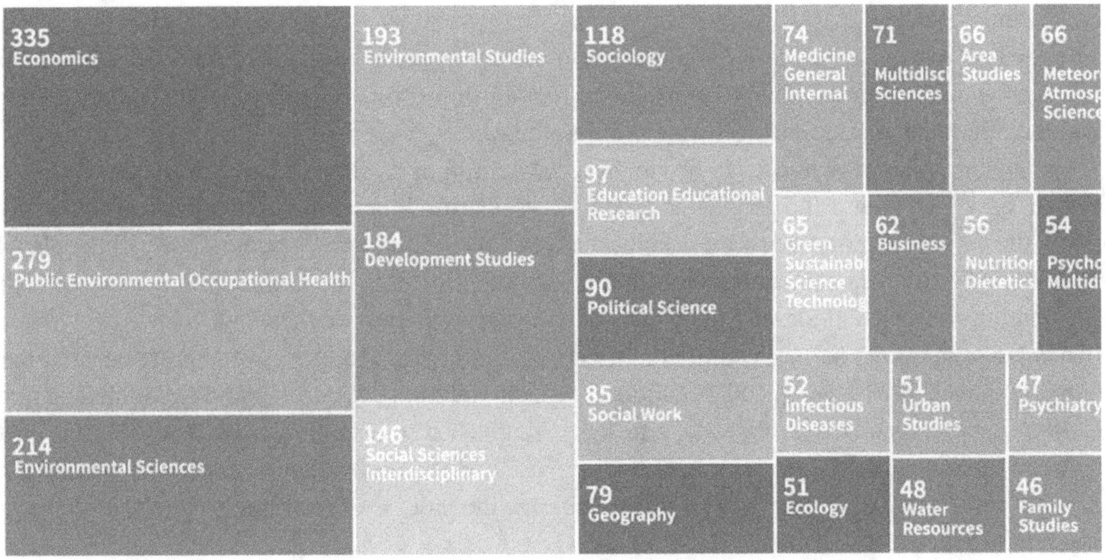

methods used are described; thirdly, the results are presented and, to conclude, the final considerations are offered, including implications, limitations and future lines of investigation.

LITERATURE REVIEW

General Aspects of Social Network Analysis (SNA)

The study of the relationships between different entities, both from the perspective of their nature and their role, has triggered a growing interest among scientists and academics in social networks analysis (Cross et al., 2002; Cross Prusak, 2002). In sociological field, a social network indicates, to a certain extent, a member of the network (represented by a node) capacity to influence other people or access certain resources (thanks to his contacts on the network). This is often known as social capital.

SNA origin is related to scientometrics or information science. This tool is integrated into bibliometric analysis or bibliometrics. Bibliometric analysis allows, using mathematical and statistical tools, to carry out an evaluation of documentary production based on a set of observable data: method used, authors characteristics, number of citations received, etc. (Benckendorff & Zehrer, 2013). New researchers can acquire, with this tool, a certain topic`s knowledge that lacks subjective bias (Benckendorff, 2009).

A social network is a structure made up of a set of different elements (individuals, documents, companies, pressure groups, ethnic groups, etc.) between which there is some type of relationship that allows identifying their connection. As Messner, Becker, Schaffer and Binder (2008) point out, a social network is an organization through which different autonomous entities are coordinated and voluntarily meet in order to achieve a common result by exchanging something (information, services, various goods, etc.).

Two elements make up a social network (Lozares, 1996; Scott, 1991): the nodes or vertices (network members) and the arcs or edges (links or connections between nodes). A vertex`s greater or lesser relevance depends on two factors: amount of information it can store and efficiency with which it processes that information. On the other hand, a relationship between nodes importance is a function of its intensity and frequency.

A social network graphic representation is made up by geometric figures (circles, rectangles, etc.), which represent the nodes, and arrows (when the relationship goes from one node to another) or edges (when the relationship is reciprocal), which represent links.

This work emphasizes knowledge networks idea. According to Beltrán and Castañeda (2003), it is a concept on which there is no consensus among the scientific literature on the topic. However, in our opinion, the definition proposed by these authors is relevant for this work: "a community of people who, formally or informally, occasionally, part-time or full-time, work in a common interest and base their actions on the construction, development and mutual sharing of knowledge".

Knowledge networks serve to stimulate information exchange, to share work practices and methodologies, as well as to develop collaboration in capacity building, research and development actions.

Three types of knowledge networks can be distinguished. Generation networks (focused on the knowledge creation process), transfer networks (focused on the dissemination process of research and its results) and assimilation networks (which emphasize the process of incorporation of knowledge into the system productive).

The State of the Art in the Area of Knowledge on Poverty

About knowledge area that studies poverty, García & Espasandín (2018) conclude the following evidences: there is no single poverty definition; most economic studies on poverty have focused on income; poverty is an epiphenomenon that accompanies or is governed by other phenomena and that presents various characteristics (complex, multidimensional, dynamic, adjustable and heterogeneous); poverty`s material objects are people, households / families, groups of people, and States; the formal object or the approaches or paradigms used are unidimensional and multidimensional approach, in which the needs and capabilities approaches are integrated. According to the one-dimensional approach, at the international level, a person is estimated to be poor when they have an income level of less than $ 2 per day. The needs approach points out poverty depends on unmet needs number. For the capabilities approach, poverty depends on the freedom to develop those capabilities.

On the other hand, Garcia & Espasandín (2018), argue that, in poverty measurement field, its incidence or extension, intensity, inequality and duration or dynamism can be measured. Likewise, can be used different measurement methods that can be classified as "direct and indirect", "objective and subjective" and "absolute and relative". Furthermore, measurements are made by multiple agents. Poverty analysis and research has been greatly marked by political connotations. Poverty measurement is usually cross-sectional, although there is more and more longitudinal data and the household / family is usually measured. An approximate number of 50 determinants of poverty are identified that are aggregated into three large groups (individual, household / family and environment).

Finally, there is evidence that the factors that lead a person or household down the path of poverty are multiple and varied. In the literature consulted, we have identified an approximate number of 50 determinants of poverty that, after analyzing them in detail, are added into three large groups: those related to the individual, those of the home / family and those that refer to the environment. In Tables 1 and 2 this chapter presents the poverty determinants for each group and the authors who study them.

Table 1. Individual and home / family as determinants of poverty

Typology			Dimension / Variable / indicator		Author and year of publication
Individual	Personal situation	Identification data	Age		Ribotta (2010)
					Valenzuela (2004)
					Aguirre (2010)
			Gender		Gutiérrez (2013)
					Larroza (2016)
					Valenzuela (2004)
			Ethnicity		Gallego (2014)
					Ribotta (2010)
		Emigration			Gallego (2014)
		Employment	Informal employment		Casanova & Dumas (2009)
					Gallego (2014)
					Pieck (1998)
			Salaries		Duryea, Jaramillo & Pagés (2002)
			Entrepreneurial activity		Degen (2008)
		Disability or illness			Castro & Cano (2013)
					Valenzuela (2004)
					Ribotta (2010)
					Ribotta (2010)
		Behaviors	Alcohol and/or drug abuse		Poverty & Human Development Initiative (2016)
			Mobility		Polanco (2013)
	Recursos personales	Capital intelectual	Human capital	Education	Retana (2015)
				Technological capital	Moreno (2011)
				Relational capital or social capital	Dalmasso (2008)
					Freyre (2013)
					Gutiérrez (2013)
		Financial capital	Financial resources		Pascual (2013)
	Personal capacities				García, Pupiales & Espitia (2013)
					Gallego (2014)
Home / Family	Family structure	Size			Méndez (2002)
	Home features	Demographic	Average age		Méndez (2002)
		Financial	Income		Méndez (2002)
		Employment situation	Economic sector		García Sainz (2017)
		Educational			Méndez (2002)
			Parents' education		Rúbies & Mendizàbal (2002)
					Retana (2015)
			Home education		Méndez (2002)
		Health	Serious illness or death of a family member		Castro & Cano (2013)
	Family crisis				Castro & Cano (2013)

Source: The Authors

Table 2. Environment as a determinant of poverty

Typology	Dimension / Variable / indicator	Author and year of publication
Climate	Climatic factors	Ribotta (2010)
National Culture	Social and cultural values	Dalmasso (2008)
Economy of the country	Average consumption	Chen & Ravallion (2013)
	Economic growth	Hernández (2008)
		Chen& Ravallion (2013)
		Neri et al. (2012)
		Gallego (2014)
	Income distribution	Méndez (2002)
	GDP	Méndez (2002)
		Castro & Cano (2013).
	Exchange rate	Méndez (2002)
	Inflation	Méndez (2002)
		Hernández (2008)
	Minimum salary	Méndez (2002)
	Labor productivity	Méndez (2002)
		Zuluaga (2009)
Environment	Environmental factors	Retana (2015)
Labour market	Unemployment	Feres & Villatoro (2012)
		Rúbies & Mendizàbal (2002)
		Valenzuela (2004)
	Ocupation rate	Méndez (2002)
Political-administrative and legal		Zurdo & López de la Nieta (2013)
	Wars and armed conflicts	Valenzuela (2004)
		Poverty & Human Development Initiative (2016)
	Commercial blockades	Ribotta (2010)
	Governance and transparency	Neri et al. (2012)
	Legal system	Minkler & Prakash (2017)
	Public spending	Valenzuela (2004)
		Hernández (2008)
		Castro & Cano (2013)
Sanitary and health		Driouchi, Zouag, & Boboc (2009)
	Diet	Piquer & Ordovás (2015)
Entrepreneurial system	Corporate Social Responsability	e
		Polanco (2013)

continued on following page

Table 2. Continued

Typology	Dimension / Variable / indicator		Author and year of publication
Society	Social climate		Ribotta (2010)
	Social violence		Gallego (2014
			Ribotta (2010)
	Demography		Zuluaga (2009)
	Inequality	Gini coefficient	Méndez (2002)
			Gentilini & Sumner (2012)
			Polanco (2013)
			Castro & Cano (2013)
			Marcón (2011)
Territory	Rural vs urban		Larroza (2016)
			Díaz (1993)
	Distance from most populated centers		Ribotta (2010)
Financial system			Casanova & Dumas (2009)
	Microcredits		Miguel et al (2011)
University			Marmolejo (2012)

Source: The Authors

METHODS

This study uses data on authors, articles, keywords, and citations. Based on the objectives of the study, the authors have analyzed scientific collaboration patterns and scientific research's intellectual structures for extreme poverty topic, although limited to certain fields of research (mainly, economics and business management). The main analysis methods used have been co-authorship, keyword co-occurrence and citation analysis. Authors have followed the steps suggested by Zupic & Cater (2015).

Data for the analysis have been obtained from Web of Science (WoS) database Social Sciences Citation Index (SSCI). This widely used database contains references and citations from more than 2,000 academic journals in social sciences field. Search was carried out on July 19, 2017 and the term "extreme poverty" was used. Were obtained 729 documents. Data was filtered to leave only scientific articles: a total of 692 useful documents were obtained.

These documents produced a total of 2,026 signatures, for a total of 1,889 different authors, 22,350 citations or references, 249 different publications and 2,665 descriptors (1,464 different).

Before analyzing the data, a considerable effort had to be made to normalize information and solve data inconsistencies. Specifically, authors names, institutional affiliation aspects and data on citations. The errors are due to several sources: WoS data capture process itself, modifications in titles abbreviations and original documents discrepancies and errors made by authors. Most common errors: authors' names arbitrarily including one or more initials or even the full name (eg.: Abbott, Pamela; Abbott, P), incomplete references, references with errors in any of the following fields (year, volume, initial and final pages number). To carry out this task, the SSCI data were imported into Excel spreadsheets and, after their classification, they were filtered by two independent researchers.

Documentary data treatment has been carried out with IBM SPSS 22 statistical package. Moreover, for relational data has been used SNA`s software NODEXL (Hansen, Shneiderman & Smith, 2010).

DISCUSSION OF RESULTS

WoS data were subjected to various analyzes. 26% of analyzed documents have not received any appointment within WoS; on the other hand, 83.7% of documents were cited less than 20 times, and, finally, only 7.6% received 50 or more citations. Results are presented in several sections, some with a double level of bibliometric analysis, both activity and relational. In the first section, this work studies the authors who have published articles on extreme poverty. The second section focuses on descriptors (keywords) analysis. In third section the authors analyze the journals, both those in which the documents included in our database have been published and those most cited (although the study is done only at the activity level without addressing the relational aspects). Finally, the chapter dedicates the last section to analyze documents` volume of citation, both original documents included in our database and most frequently referred documents among original documents.

Author Analysis

The 692 documents captured include a total of 2,026 signatures, although they are 1,889 different people. Only 103 authors have signed more than two different articles and the maximum number of articles signed by one author is 9. 94.6% of the authors have signed a single document. 20.8% of the signatories belong to North American institutions, otherwise Spanish signers represent 1.3%, English 5.1% and Brazilian 5%. Authors per document number is 2.9. 20 authors have signed 3 or more articles. Authors whose articles have had the highest number of citations in the WoS are Parry, Rosenzweig, Iglesias, Livermore and Fischer (with two articles with more than 100 citations). Most cited author has obtained more than 629 citations.

Now this chapter present and discuss relational data. First, Table 3 provides global data on co-authorship social network. Data show a low density and highly dispersed network, made up of 1,698 nodes (different authors). There are 405 different components: 150 pairs, 81 groups of three authors, 49 groups of 4 vertices, 36 of five, thirty-six of 6 authors, 11 septets, 13 groups of 8 authors, 5 groups with nine subjects, another 5 of 10 nodes, 8 clusters of 12 vertices, and clusters with a single appearance: of 13, of 15, of 18, 19, 20, 21, 24 and 28 authors (main component). The network is not very cohesive (density of 0.28%), the level of cooperation between extreme poverty`s authors is quite low. Average degree is 4.7 and betweenness centrality median is 0. Largest component is only made up of 28 subjects. All of this is shown graphically in Figure 3. Each quadrant of figure 3 shows one of the components identified in the network with all the authors that comprise it and the relationships between them. As there is a high number, only the most relevant have been tagged.

Table 4 shows the data on the authors with the highest number of articles published (only authors with 3 or more articles), specifically degree and betweenness centrality, and productivity (published articles). The author with the highest degree centrality, and therefore related to more people within the network, is Hotez, with a value of 23. However, the most influential authors, (those with the greatest betweenness centrality) are Peter Hotez, Mark Tomlinson and Leonor Pacheco. On the other hand, most productive authors are, among others, Spano, Bolland, Hotez, Ravallion and Rivera. The 5 authors who

Table 3. Extreme poverty co-authorship network indicators

Characteristics	Value
Nodes	1698
Number of links	4025
Isolated	0
Density	0,0028
Minimum degree	1
Maximum degree	23
Average degree	4,74
Diameter	3
Components	405
Main component (size)	28
Main component (percentage)	1,65
Clustering coefficient.	0,801

Source: The Authors

have received more than 100 citations in the considered data set are Ravallion, Hanjra, Qureshi, and Shaohua Chen. Three of them are found in Table 4. Therefore, our conclusion is that network`s most influential authors are Martin Ravallion and Shaohua Chen.

The following two figures (Figures 4 and 5) show the authors most closely related (higher degree centrality) and with the greatest intermediation capacity among network members (higher scores in betweenness centrality). The circles represent the authors and the lines their connections. Only the most relevant author networks are shown.

Descriptor Analysis

692 articles analyzed generate 1,464 unique descriptors. Data were examined to identify dominant themes about extreme poverty research included in our database. 40.9% of descriptors appear only once. Table 5 lists the 17 descriptors with highest frequency of appearance. It highlights that the word "poverty" is not the one that appears most frequently, occupying the ninth position. Three most common descriptors are "health", "children" and "growth".

A more in-depth explanation of the relationships between different descriptors can be seen across their co-occurrence network, which is shown in Figure 6. The 1,421 nodes make up a single network with a low density (0.88%), where the element with the highest degree centrality (health) is connected with 265 vertices and the most peripheral (for example, deficiency) with only 1 node. 16 different clusters of keywords can be identified: 7 clusters of two words, 4 clusters of three words, a quartet, 3 clusters with 10 descriptors, and finally the main cluster with 1,361 bound nodes. The latter group includes concepts such as health, children, impact, growth, countries, poverty, and prevalence. Only the most significant descriptors are tagged.

Figure 3. Extreme poverty co-authorship network
Source: The Authors

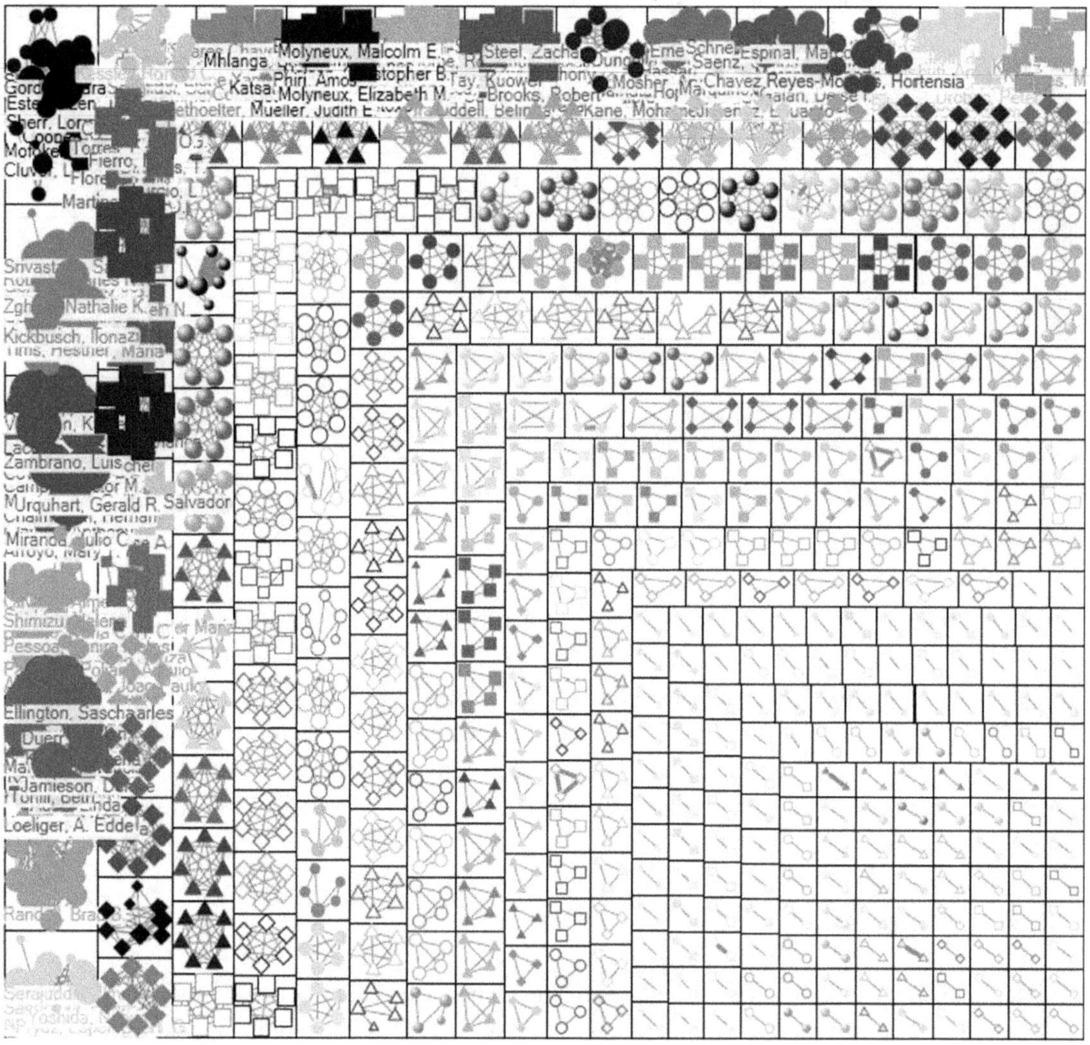

In relation to the individual values of the different descriptors within the co-occurrence network, as can be seen in Table 3, the most relevant and influential descriptors are the following: health, children, developing countries, impact and risk factors.

Journals Analysis

In this section we will use two perspectives of analysis. First, we will analyze the original documents, carrying out a count of the journals with the highest number of articles. In the second, we will perform an examination of the citations provided in the reference list of each article in order to determine which are the journals that receive the most citations. The 514 analyzed documents have generated 22,350 references or citations of other documents.

Table 4. Most relevant authors of the co-authorship network and their level of activity

Author	Degree centrality	Betweenness centrality	Published articles
Spano, Richard	6	9,500	9
Bolland, John M.	3	0,500	8
Hotez, Peter J.	23	129,750	4
Ravallion, Martin	1	13,000	4
Rivera, Craig	3	0,000	4
Casapia, Martin	4	0,000	3
Chen, Shaohua	13	35,000	3
Devereux, Stephen	2	4,000	3
Feldmeier, Hermann	5	0,000	3
Galasso, Emanuela	1	0,000	3
Gyorkos, Theresa W.	4	0,000	3
Hanjra, Munir A.	3	2,000	3
Jolliffe, Dean	11	0,000	3
Joseph, Serene A.	4	0,000	3
Pacheco Santos, Leonor Maria	19	73,333	3
Sabates-Wheeler, Rachel	4	6,000	3
Szwarcwald, Celia Landmann	4	0,000	3
Tomlinson, Mark	3	114,000	3
Vazquez, Jose Juan	1	0,000	3
Zanotti, Laura	2	0,000	3

Source: The Authors

Table 4 shows both the most productive original publications and those publications that are most cited in our database. Between the most productive journals we find titles such as "World Development", "Food Policy" and "Journal of Development Studies". In the table appear only the 12 journals with more than one article, it must be taken into account that there are 54 more publications. Most cited journals in analyzed original articles are, in descending order, "Journal of Development Economics", "Food Policy", "World Bank Research Observer", "World Development" and "Journal of Development Studies". On the other hand, it is necessary to point out that a journal of great importance is "Global Environmental Change-Human and Policy Dimensions", since the original article that has received the highest number of citations in the WoS belongs to it. The table also shows that the journals that occupy relevant positions in the two categories at the same time are: "Food Policy", "World Development", "American Journal of Agricultural Economics", "Global Environmental Change-Human and Policy Dimensions" and "Journal of Consumer Research".

Analysis of the Most Cited Documents

Finally, we analyze the most influential documents (those works that serve as a frame of reference for researchers on extreme poverty). This analysis has been carried out from a double perspective. On the

Figure 4. Co-authorship network on extreme poverty (authors with higher degree centrality)
Source: The Authors

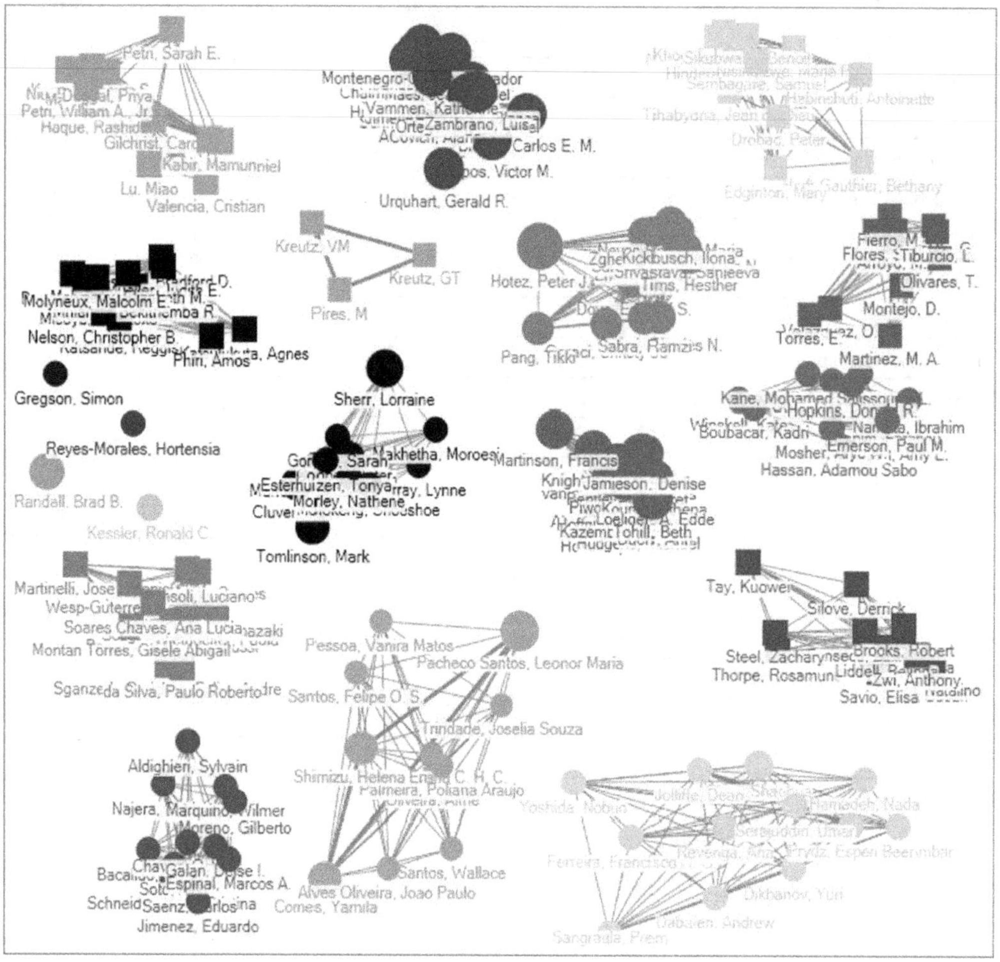

one hand, we have selected the original documents that have received the highest number of citations within the WoS. On the other hand, bibliographic references included in the our database original records have been analyzed to verify which documents appear the most in their bibliography. The data is shown in Table 7.

The data in Table 7 shows that no scientific work is present in both lists. It is important to note that Sen appears with 2 works among the list of most influential cited references, which makes him in a way one of the most influential authors on this topic.

CONCLUSION

Now this chapter expose conclusions, theoretical and empirical implications, limitations, and, lastly, future lines of research.

Figure 5. Co-authorship network on extreme poverty (authors with greater centrality of intermediation)
Source: The Authors

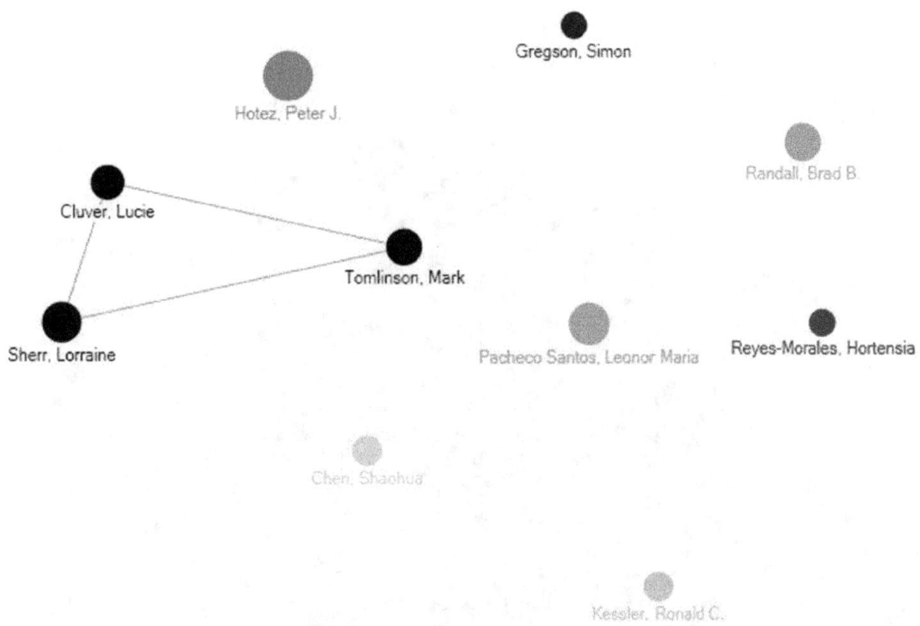

Table 5. Most frequent descriptors of extreme poverty

Descriptor	Frequency	Degree Centrality	Betweenness Centrality
Health	59	265	160457,751
Children	30	161	77438,503
Growth	29	143	54978,628
Countries	25	140	51977,757
Developing-countries	24	141	65736,566
Mortality	23	115	38058,857
Prevalence	23	146	50683,237
Impact	22	163	76758,527
Poverty	20	97	39428,376
Risk	18	92	26368,169
Africa	17	101	39652,323
Inequality	17	98	42459,288
Risk-factors	17	134	59145,113
South-Africa	16	103	42747,814
Income	15	66	16608,146
United-States	15	104	35108,479
Community	14	105	30649,380

Source: The Authors

Figure 6. Extreme poverty descriptors network
Source: The Authors

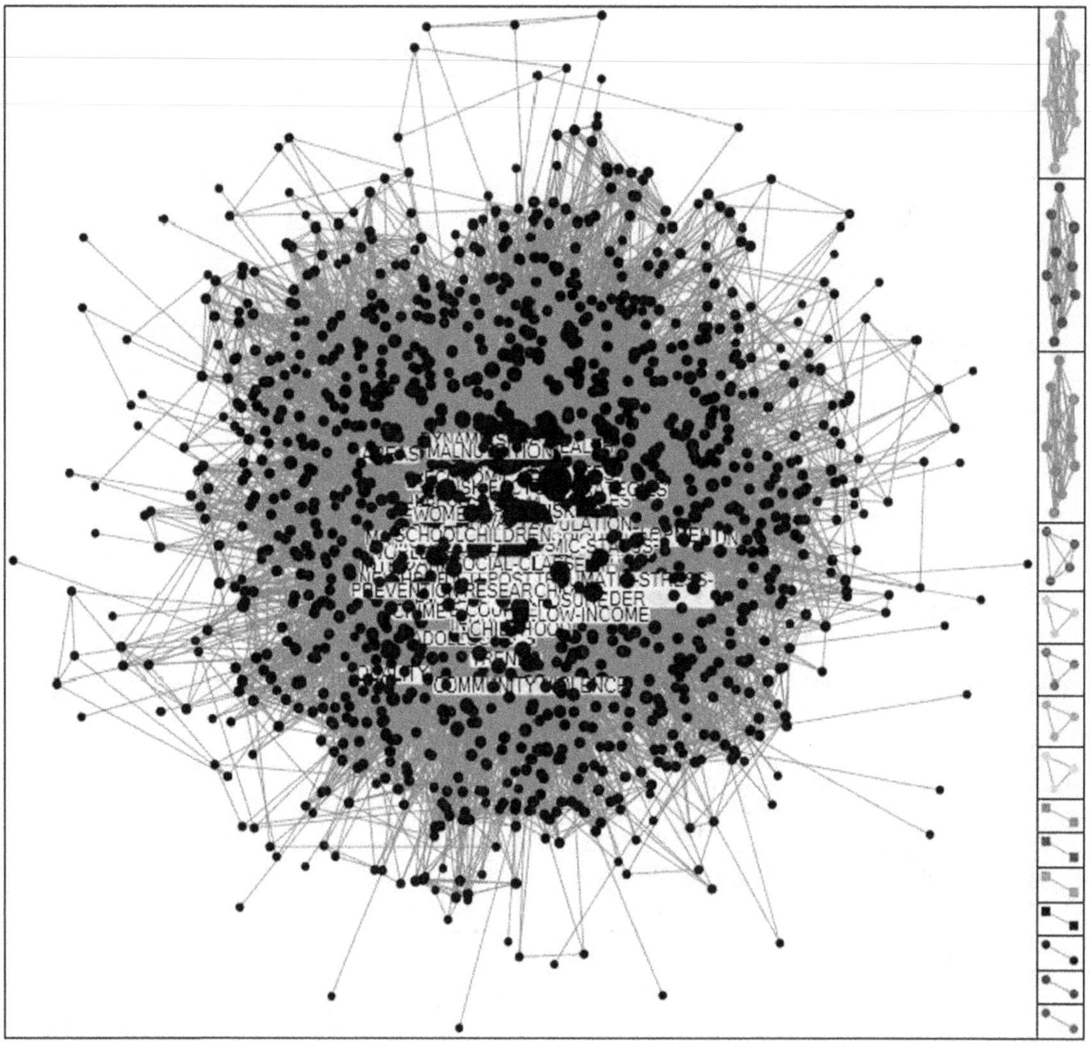

This chapter main conclusions are the following. In the first place, this study has made it possible to show the situation of extreme poverty`s research field from a relational perspective and for the set of research related to the journals included in social sciences area. Second, authors who write about extreme poverty in social sciences field are not highly cohesive, they show limited collaboration patterns. Third, the authors considered in the network do not seem to interact with other groups of researchers and there are situations of relative isolation between them: many islands and with little connection between them. Fourth, the analysis of the descriptors used in this research topic shows a very low density and the most common descriptors are "health" and "growth", while the descriptor "poverty" occupies a position that could be described as intermediate. Fifth, this work has found three journals relevant and influential in terms of productivity (number of articles found) and incidence (volume of citations): "World Development", "Food Policy" and "Journal of Development Studies". Finally, the most influential author, since

Table 6. Most cited journals analysis

Original journal	Articles number	Cited journal	Citations number
World Development	9	Journal Of Development Economics	274
Food Policy	5	Food Policy	180
Journal of Development Studies	4	World Bank Research Observer	165
Journal of African Economies	3	World Development	142
World Bank Research Observer	3	Journal Of Development Studies	44
Applied Economics	2	Journal Of Consumer Research	43
Estudios de Economia	2	Entrepreneurship Theory and Practice	42
Estudios de Economia Aplicada	2	Technological Forecasting and Social Change	34
Journal of Development Economics	2	World Bank Economic Review	30
Journal of Economic Inequality	2	European Review of Economic History	28
Technological Forecasting and Social Change	2	Health Economics	23
Tourism Economics	2	Harvard Business Review	19

Source: The Authors

he receives the greatest number of citations in his works, is Amartya Sen, although there are few works that have a relevant impact within the network.

This work has important implications for researchers, especially for those neophytes in the field, related to knowledge generation and dissemination. Throughout the process of generating knowledge, researchers will be able to know, after reading this article and efficiently, which are the main descriptors or topics of interest, the journals with the most impact and the most cited authors. Which undoubtedly increases scientific rigor and facilitates the researcher's first contact with this field of knowledge. In addition, the research also provides guidance when it comes to disseminating its results, since knowledge of the journals with the greatest impact becomes relevant for making publication decisions.

In addition, it should be added that this research also has implications for the network as a whole, since, as already indicated, it is a poorly cohesive network, with a shortage of researchers in the social sciences. To try to alleviate or resolve these weaknesses of the academic network in the field of "extreme poverty", measures could be implemented that facilitate contact between researchers, such as promoting the organization of research conferences on this field or promoting the creation of associations and networks of multinational and / or multidisciplinary researchers.

In this sense, Asibeam (Ibero-American Association of Economics, Administration and Marketing) could be a model to consider. This association arises as a consequence of the sensitivity of its members to the problem of poverty and the evident deficit of knowledge about the business-poverty relationship. It was created in the year 2017. It is made up of researchers from 26 universities from 16 Ibero-American countries. The association aims to contribute to the reduction of poverty and hunger through applied research, generating and managing knowledge and relationships with interested groups. Among its most relevant achievements are the holding of several congresses (with an average of 10 papers per congress), the publication of the book "Creation of Value for Poverty Reduction", the design of an award to recognize the best proposals to reduce poverty, an ongoing research on poverty and entrepreneurship in

Table 7. Most influential documents

Original Documents	Times cited	Bibliographic References
China's (uneven) progress against poverty	266	Sen, A. (2001). Development as freedom. Oxford Paperbacks.
Global water crisis and future food security in an era of climate change	180	Foster, J., Greer, J., Thorbecke, E. (1984). A class of decomposable poverty measures, Econometrica, 52(3): 761–766. DOI: 10.2307/1913475
How have the world's poorest fared since the early 1980s?	135	FILMER, D. & PRITCHETT, L. (2001). Estimating wealth effects without expenditure data-or tears: An application to educational enrolments in states of India. Demography, v.38, p. 115-132.
Microfinance and poverty in Bolivia	44	Wilson, W. J. (1987). The truly disadvantaged Chicago. IL: University of Chicago.
Life Satisfaction, Self-Determination, and Consumption Adequacy at the Bottom of the Pyramid	43	Black R, Allen Lh, Bhutta Za, Caulfield Le, De Onis M, Ezzati M, et al. (2008). Maternal and child undernutrition: global and regional exposures and health consequences. Lancet; 371 (9608):243-60. doi: 10.1016/S0140-6736(07)61690-0.
Delineating the Domain of Development Entrepreneurship: A Market-Based Approach to Facilitating Inclusive Economic Growth	42	Kellam, S. G. & Van Horn, Y. V. (1997). Life course development, community epidemiology, and preventive trials: A scientific structure for prevention research. American Journal of Community Psychology, 25(2), 177-188.
The future of the mobile phone business	34	Ostrom E. (1990). Governing the Commons: The Evolution of Institutions for Collective Action, Cambridge University Press, New York.
Globalization, poverty, and inequality: What is the relationship? What can be done?	32	Sachs, J. (2006). The End of Poverty: Economic Possibilities for Our Time. Penguin Books.
Social protection in a crisis: Argentina's Plan Jefes y Jefas.	30	Sen, A. (1976). Poverty: an ordinal approach to measurement. Econometrica: Journal of the Econometric Society, 219-231.
Inequality, poverty and the Kuznets curve in Spain, 1850-2000	28	Spano, R., Rivera, C. & Bolland, J. (2006). The impact of timing of exposure to violence on violent behavior in a high poverty sample of inner city African American youth. Journal of youth and adolescence, 35(5), 681-692.
Estimating the Short-Run Poverty Impacts of the 2010-11 Surge in Food Prices	27	Victora, C. G., Adair, L., Fall, C., Hallal, P. C., Martorell, R., Richter, L., ... & Maternal and Child Undernutrition Study Group. (2008). Maternal and child undernutrition: consequences for adult health and human capital. The Lancet, 371(9609), 340-357.
Are There Lessons for Africa from China's Success Against Poverty?	26	

Source: The Authors

all member countries, or the creation of an electronic magazine focused on the topics poverty (SDG1), hunger (SDG2), business and businessman (https://www.asibeam.org/).

In another vein, the research presents a series of limitations that are circumscribed to data collection and analysis. Regarding the limitations in data collection, the authors clarify, firstly, that it has not been possible to cover all the scientific production of the field of knowledge "extreme poverty", since only ISI database documents the have been considered and until 2017. Second, although the task of normalizing the information and solving the inconsistencies in the data has been quite exhaustive, as it has been executed and supervised by two researchers, it is possible that it may present errors and deficiencies. And, finally, keeping exclusively the first author is also considered a weakness, although the literature considers this option acceptable (Benckendorff and Zehrer, 2013). Regarding the limitations of data analysis, this chapter highlights firstly that institutional cooperation networks are not analyzed (Acedo et al., 2006); secondly, only data analysis tools derived from the analysis of social networks are used and, finally, a longitudinal analysis has not been carried out that allows to know how the academic network is evolving.

In order to correct these weaknesses, the following lines of investigation will be implemented: first, more documents will be searched in the Scopus and ProQuest databases; second, the most recent documents will be incorporated; thirdly, the controls that guarantee a better standardization of the information and the solution to the inconsistencies in the data will be increased, for which two researchers will be incorporated into the project; fourthly, all the signatory authors of the most influential documents will be included, to verify if there are important changes in the structure and content of the network; fifth, the analysis of the network will be expanded through invisible schools and patterns of institutional cooperation; sixth, the data will be analyzed using multidimensional scaling, factor analysis, and cluster analysis; and, finally, longitudinal analyzes will be carried out to compare the evolution of the field (Verspagen, 2007) and explain the changes that occur (Lu & Liu, 2014).

REFERENCES

Acedo, F. J., Barroso, C., Casanueva, C., & Galán, J. L. (2006). Co-authorship in management and organizational studies: An empirical and network analysis. *Journal of Management Studies*, *43*(5), 957–983. doi:10.1111/j.1467-6486.2006.00625.x

Aguirre, B. (2010). La multidimensionalidad de la pobreza: Una revisión de la literatura. *Revista Finanzas y Política Económica*, *2*(2), 101–113.

Banco Mundial. (2019). *La pobreza y la prosperidad compartida 2020. Un cambio de suerte*. Retrieved from https://www.un.org/es/global-issues/ending-poverty

Beltrán, R. M. & Galvis, S. C. (2003). Definición de un modelo de redes de conocimiento como soporte a la transferencia del conocimiento generado en clusters de investigación. *Revista GTI*, *2*(2).

Benckendorff, P. (2009). Themes and trends in Australian and New Zealand tourism research: A social network analysis of citations in two leading journals (1994–2007). *Journal of Hospitality and Tourism Management*, *16*(1), 1–15. doi:10.1375/jhtm.16.1.1

Benckendorff, P., & Zehrer, A. (2013). A network analysis of tourism research. *Annals of Tourism Research*, *43*, 121–149. doi:10.1016/j.annals.2013.04.005

Casanova, L., & Dumas, A. (2010). Corporate Social Responsibility and Latin American Multinationals: ¿Is Poverty a Business Issue? *Universia Business Review*, *25*, 132–145.

Castro Duran, L. I., & Cano Gonzalez, R. (2013). Poverty and vulnerability: Risk factors in the education of the borough. *Contextos Educativos-Revista de Educacion*, (16), 55–72.

Chen, S., & Ravallion, M. (2013). More relatively- poor people in a less absolutely- poor world. *Review of Income and Wealth*, *59*(1), 1–28. doi:10.1111/j.1475-4991.2012.00520.x

Cross, R., Borgatti, S. P., & Parker, A. (2002). Making invisible work visible: Using social network analysis to support strategic collaboration. *California Management Review*, *44*(2), 25–46. doi:10.2307/41166121

Cross, R., & Prusak, L. (2002). The people who make organizations go–or stop. *Networks in the Knowledge Economy*, *80*(6), 248–260. PMID:12048992

Dalmasso, M. B. E. (2008). Las ausencias en las producciones teóricas sobre la pobreza. ¿Una intervención Biopolítica? *Intersticios. Revista Sociológica de Pensamiento Crítico*, *2*(2).

Díaz, A. (1993). *Restructuring and the New Working Classes in Chile: Trends in Waged Employment, Informality and Poverty, 1973-1990*. UNRIS Discussion Paper No. DP47. Geneva: United Nations Research Institute for Social Development.

Driouchi, A., Zouag, N., & Boboc, C. (2009). Interdependencies of health, education and poverty: The case of South Mediterranean Economies. *Estudios de Economía Aplicada*, *27*(2), 523–543. doi:10.25115/eea.v27i2.4928

Duryea, S., Jaramillo, O., & Pagés, C. (2002). *Los mercados de trabajo en América Latina en los noventa: Descifrando la década*. Inter-American Development Bank.

Espasandin-Bustelo, F., Palacios-Florencio, B., & García, J. S. R. (2020). CSR intellectual structure in management and tourism. *The TQM Journal*, *32*(3), 521–541. doi:10.1108/TQM-06-2019-0173

Feres, J. C. & Villatoro, P. (2012). La viabilidad de erradicar la pobreza: un examen conceptual y metodológico. *CEPAL - Serie Estudios estadísticos y prospectivos*, 76.

Freyre, M. L. (2013). Labour Market and Career Paths in Contexts of Poverty. Challenges for Social Policy. *Gestión y Análisis de Políticas Públicas*, 10.

Gallego Duque, L. M. (2014). *Mecanismos causales de la educación y la pobreza. Aplicación a los casos de Medellín (Colombia) y BeloHorizonte (Brasil)* (Unpublished doctoral dissertation). Universitat Autònoma de Barcelona.

García, R. E. D., Pupiales, A. F. H., & Espitia, M. E. O. (2013). Relación entre la educación y los componentes del índice de pobreza de Amartya Sen: Un análisis en Colombia. *Revista CIFE: Lecturas de Economía Social*, *15*(23), 23–48. doi:10.153322248-4914.2013.0023.02

García del Junco, J., & Espasandín Bustelo, F. (2018). La pobreza: estado de la cuestión y situación en latinoamérica. *Proceedings I workshop internacional de ASIBEAM*.

Garcia Sainz, C. (2017). The impact of the economic crisis on time poverty and gender inequalities. *Arbor-Ciencia Pensamiento y Cultura, 193*(784).

Gentilini, U., & Sumner, A. (2012). What do national poverty lines tell us about global poverty? *IDS Working Papers, 2012*(392), 1-48.

Gutiérrez, J. P. (2013). Brechas en cobertura efectiva por nivel socioeconómico y condición de pobreza. *Salud Pública de México*, *55*(Supl.2), s106–s111. doi:10.21149pm.v55s2.5105 PMID:24626685

Hansen, D. L., Shneiderman, B., & Smith, M. (2010, August). *Visualizing threaded conversation networks: mining message boards and email lists for actionable insights*. In *International Conference on Active Media Technology* (pp. 47-62). Springer. 10.1007/978-3-642-15470-6_7

Hernández, A. J. (2008). Estudio de la progresividad del gasto público social y su impacto sobre la distribución del ingreso en Venezuela para los años 1997 y 2005. *Revista Venezolana de Análisis de Coyuntura*, *14*(2), 69–91.

Larroza, C. A. (2016). Pobreza en Paraguay: Contribución de la educación media en el acceso a las oportunidades para superar la pobreza. *Población y Desarrollo*, (43), 25–34.

Lozares Colina, C. (1996). La teoría de redes sociales. *Papers: Revista de Sociologia*, (48), 103–126.

Lu, L. Y. Y., & Liu, J. S. (2014). The knowledge diffusion paths of corporate social responsibility – From 1970 to 2011. *Corporate Social Responsibility and Environmental Management*, *21*(2), 113–128. doi:10.1002/csr.1309

Ma, Z., Lee, Y., & Yu, K. H. (2008). Ten years of conflict management studies: Themes, concepts and relationships. *International Journal of Conflict Management*, *19*(3), 234–248. doi:10.1108/10444060810875796

Marcón, O. A. (2011). De la pobreza a la exclusión: Implicancias teórico-prácticas pensadas desde Argentina. *Prospectiva*, (15), 207–234. doi:10.25100/prts.v0i15.1110

Marmolejo, A. M. (2012). Reflexiones Sobre Competitividad, Educación y Pobreza. *Revista Xihmai*, *1*(2).

Méndez, J. N. (2002). *Determinantes de la pobreza en Colombia: años recientes*. CEPAL.

Messner, M., Becker, C., Schäffer, U., & Binder, C. (2008). Legitimacy and identity in Germanic management accounting research. *European Accounting Review*, *17*(1), 129–159. doi:10.1080/09638180701819808

Miguel González, L. J., Candial Torres, A., Domenech Llorente, E., Ortega Salvador, Á., Pérez Miguel, L., Rodríguez Fernández, J. M., & Rodríguez López, F. (2011). *Microcréditos para combatir la pobreza: una introducción a los conceptos básicos de microfinanzas como instrumento alternativo para la financiación del desarrollo*. Retrieved from https://uvadoc.uva.es/bitstream/handle/10324/47443/MicrocreditosParaCombatirLaPobreza.pdf?sequence=1&isAllowed=y

Minkler, L., & Prakash, N. (2017). The role of constitutions on poverty: A cross-national investigation. *Journal of Comparative Economics*, *45*(3), 563–581. doi:10.1016/j.jce.2017.03.002

Moreno, J. A. D. (2011). *Informalidad laboral y pobreza urbana en Colombia*. CIDSE.

Neri, M., Oleas, S., Torrado, M. P., Vargas, C. P., Perticara, M., Lomelí, L. I. R., & Trujillo, J. D. (2012). *Pobreza, Desigualdad de Oportunidades y Políticas Públicas en América Latina*. Rio de Janeiro: Konrad-Adenauer-Stiftung Retrieved from https://scholar.google.es/scholar?hl=es&as_sdt=0%2C5&q=Pobreza%2C+Desigualdad+de+Oportunidades+y+Poli%CC%81ticas+Pu%CC%81blicas+en+Ame%CC%81rica+Latina&btnG=

Pascual, A. S. (2013). Marcos interpretativos de lo social en la vivencia de la «nueva pobreza» [Interpretative frameworks of the social in the living of the «new poverty»]. *Cuadernos de Relaciones Laborales*, *31*(2), 337–382.

Pieck, E. (2005). Work-related adult education: Challenges and possibilities in poverty areas. *International Journal of Lifelong Education, 24*(5), 419–429. doi:10.1080/02601370500169798

Pilkington, A., & Teichert, T. (2006). Management of technology: Themes, concepts and relationships. *Technovation, 26*(3), 288–299. doi:10.1016/j.technovation.2005.01.009

Piquer, D. C., & Ordovás, J. M. (2015). Relación entre el estado socioeconómico, la educación y la alimentación saludable. *Mediterráneo Económico*, (27), 283–306.

Polanco, Y. (2013). ¿Contribuyen las prácticas empresariales responsables a la reducción de la pobreza? [¿Do responsible business practices contribute to poverty reduction?]. *Contabilidad y Negocios, 8*(15), 43–56.

Poverty & Human Development Initiative. (2016). *Chad Multidimensional Deprivation and Vulnerability Survey*. OPHI Working Papers.

Racherla, P., & Hu, C. (2010). A social network perspective of tourism research collaborations. *Annals of Tourism Research, 37*(4), 1012–1034. doi:10.1016/j.annals.2010.03.008

Retana, C. S. (2015). Evaluación de impacto de la educación sobre la pobreza en Costa Rica (un análisis para educación secundaria y post-secundaria). *Revista de Ciencias Económicas, 33*(2), 9-23.

Ribotta, S. (2010). Pobreza, hambre y justicia en América Latina y el Caribe. Debatiendo sobre la justicia mientras 53 millones de latinoamericanos sufren hambre. *REIB: Revista Electrónica Iberoamericana, 4*(1), 144–180.

Rúbies, I. P., & Mendizábal, E. (2002). Pobreza y exclusión social en España. Una visión geográfica de las poblaciones de riesgo. *Revija za Geografijo*, 79–103.

Scott, J. (1991). *Social Network Analysis: A Handbook*. Sage.

Valenzuela, E., Hertel, T., Ivanic, M., & Nin-Pratt, A. (2004). *Evaluating poverty impacts of globalization and trade policy changes on agricultural producers*. Working Paper, Purdue University.

Verspagen, B. (2007). Mapping technological trajectories as patent citations networks: A study on the history of fuel cell research. *Advances in Complex Systems, 10*(1), 99–115. doi:10.1142/S0219525907000945

Zuluaga, I. A. (2009). Educación y pobreza. *Sotavento MBA*, (14), 72–79.

Zupic, I., & Čater, T. (2015). Bibliometric methods in management and organization. *Organizational Research Methods, 18*(3), 429–472. doi:10.1177/1094428114562629

Zurdo, Á., & López de la Nieta, M. (2013). Estrategias e imágenes sobre la crisis en el espacio social de la «nueva pobreza». Representaciones sociales y atribuciones causales. *Cuadernos de Relaciones Laborales, 31*(2), 383–433.

Chapter 2
Dynamic Capability and Coopetition:
A Strategic Alternative in the COVID-19 Era

Wlademir Leite Correia Filho
Universidade do Estado do Amazonas, Brazil

Daniel Knebel Baggio
https://orcid.org/0000-0002-6167-2682
UNIJUI, Brazil

ABSTRACT

The COVID-19 pandemic accelerated changes in company management, valuing coopetition as a collective strategy by strengthening the dynamic capabilities defined by Teece et al. as the firm's ability to integrate, build, and reconfigure external and internal competencies in rapidly changing environments. The adaptive capacity will prepare the company for adversity; the absorptive capacity favors the acquisition, assimilation, transformation, and application of external knowledge to create and maintain competitive advantages, and the capacity to innovate allows the identification of new business opportunities. The research showed that for the studied group, the good use of the dynamic absorption and adaptation capacities present in coopetition strongly contributes to the development of innovation competences, thus achieving and sustaining competitive advantage.

1. INTRODUCTION

Changes in the way business are made in the moment we're living, the COVID-19 pandemic, has gained greater speed not only due the technological evolution, but also to the breaking of current market paradigms. Nowadays focus is in seize opportunities with a different perspective at clients, suppliers and competitors looking for updates in increasingly shorter periods of time.

DOI: 10.4018/978-1-7998-8925-0.ch002

The use of innovative dynamic capabilities is making old paradigms of individual organizational strategies be replaced for collective strategies that provide cooperative competition that generate mutual gains in performance.

Market has become more selective, and entrepreneurs must focus more carefully on themes like efficiency, quality, win-win partnerships, continuous learning, synergy, technologies use, among others that has radically changed the way companies and entrepreneurs act seeking to achieve challenging goals and objectives that provide better results and business sustainability.

This article seeks to present how dynamic capabilities contribute to coopetition. Thus, in support to this general objective, we sought to understand the coopetition x dynamic capabilities relationship; relate collective strategies with dynamic capabilities; and verify the degree of use of dynamic capabilities in cooperatives, according to a study carried out in cooperatives.

2. THEORETICAL FRAMEWORK

Organizations need to change to be more sustainable in this highly competitive market. Some has understood that the client is the main focus meanwhile suppliers and competitors are partners in their marketing actions.

The most active companies, strategically, realized the cooperation bring synergy in their actions and increases results in a more efficient and effective way using theirs and their partner's dynamic capabilities.

2.1 Dynamic Capabilities

Teece et al. (2009) declare that dynamic capabilities are defined as the firm's ability to integrate, build and reconfigure external and internal competences in rapidly changing environments. Competencies are understood as the set of routines and organizational processes whose performance is provided by the possession of its own assets. Dynamic is understood as rapid changes situation in market environment that directly affect the organization.

For these authors, the approach of dynamic capabilities focuses on the process in which competences are developed and renewed. This process is conditioned by past choices and environment dynamism. Therefore, dynamic capabilities are based on the tripod: processes (routines or patterns of current practices and learning), positions (assets, governance structure, consumer bases and external relations with suppliers and partners), and trajectory (decision history and technological and market opportunities).

Camargo & Meireles (2012) propose that there are three capacities to support dynamic capabilities: (a) ability to feel the context of the environment; (b) ability to take advantage of opportunities; and (c) ability to manage threats and transformations.

Thus, it can be said that dynamic capabilities involve efforts of change and innovation through skills and competences or abilities, in order to identify market need and/or opportunities of idea generation; development of new products, services and better processes.

Wand and Ahmed (2007) point to the skills that support the three capabilities that compose dynamic capabilities: (a) adaptive capacity (the company's ability to identify and capitalize on emerging market opportunities); (b) absorptive capacity (company's ability in recognize the value of external information, assimilate it and apply it for commercial purposes); and (c) innovation capacity (company's ability in develop new products and markets through the orientation of strategic alignment for behaviors and innovation processes).

The development and application of there capacities favor the strategic effort to achieve better results in this troubled economic and social moment due to the COVID-19 pandemic.

2.1.1 Adaptive Capabilities

More and more organizations must use their dynamic capabilities to quickly adapt to the conditions of the environment, absorb and transform the knowledge in this environment, in addition to develop innovative skills to achieve and sustain competitive advantages.

Teece et al. (2008) affirm that the goal of adaptive capabilities is to prepare the company and align its dynamic capacity for internal and external adversities with adaptation in unusual scenarios.

Is not simple or easy for an organization to maintain or gain a competitive position, its complexity lies in market dynamic, which means suppliers, clients and competitors are factors that intervein in organizational process by multiple actions, relationships and combinations that occur day by day. Based on this assumption Coutinho & Ferraz (1994) understand that competitiveness can be better analyzed through the view of systemic competitiveness, which considers different factors and possibilities of articulation as determinants of the competitive advantage of organizations.

Having the organization open to changes is essential for competitiveness to be a major strategic differentiator. The faster the organization adapts to the new needs, the better conditions it will have to pursue new goals, its necessary to be able to relearn what it does and learn to do what it does not do.

2.1.2 Absorptive Capabilities

Dávila (2016) states that organizations with greater knowledge management skills tend to be more innovative and perform better. In a complementary way, innovation and sustainable competitiveness depend not only on an adequate execution of the organization's knowledge management processes, but also on how firms expand and reconfigure their knowledge base, adding new knowledge. Consequently, organizations that improve their abortion capacity (by investing in training, research and development, among other actions) will be more likely to be successful in innovation and competitiveness.

For Dávila (2016), knowledge management consists in creating, capturing, sharing and applying knowledge to create value through performance, learning and innovation results. And its success depends heavily on the knowledge sharing culture.

Absorptive capacity is a dynamic capacity by which organizations acquire, assimilate, transform and apply external knowledge to create and maintain competitive advantages (ZAHRA; GEORGE, 2002).

Firm's internal learning processes are the basic elements of the absorptive capacity, which is related to the continuous acquisition, distribution and use of relevant external knowledge within the company. This learning condition directly impacts the improvements required by the market in order to be constantly innovating its processes, products, services, marketing or its own organizational form.

2.1.3 Innovative Capabilities

Innovation drives changes that promote the development of organizations, ensuring that they achieve competitive advantage and guarantee their permanence and their development in competitive markets. For Wang and Ahmed (2007) innovation can occur in the product, market, behavior, process and strategy.

In this way, we can conceptualize innovative capabilities as the general ability of a company to act in the market focusing on its customer in order to introduce new products to the market or discover new markets to act, combining strategies with innovative behaviors and processes of entrepreneurs and managers.

An organization's ability to innovate allows it to identify new acting opportunities, growing the means of doing business and improving operational efficiency, using existing resources more efficiently and effectively. For this, it is necessary that organizations are creative entities capable of transforming their creativity into innovations so that they can effectively incorporate them in their products, processes, positions and paradigms (TIDD, BESSANT, & PAVITT, 2008).

The dynamic capacity to innovate and the management of its attributes of dispersion and interaction are, therefore, essential factors for the survival and success of a company in the 21st century when the intentional capacity to dynamically develop cooperative projects, in which the partners create and/or share technological and innovative resources for the sustainable generation of competitive advantages of innovation, which are distinctive and difficult to imitate, is at the apex of organizational strategies (COSTA & PORTO, 2015)

For these relational and cooperation capabilities to be successful, organizations must develop and systematize strategies, structures and administrative practices for the search, selection, implementation and management of cooperative relationships.

2.2 Collective Strategies

According to Ebers and Jarillo (1998, apud BALESTRIN et al, 2016) the adoption of collective strategies provides a series of advantages for participating companies: mutual learning, which will lead the company to better support the process of developing new products; co-specialty, as participating companies become profitable in new product and market niches; better information flow, facilitating the coordination of the resources flow between companies and reducing uncertainty in relationships, and economies of scale, the result of joint investments, such as, for example, in new products development projects.

For Mintzberg et al., (2000) the strategic focus now is to better meet customer needs, invest in innovation processes or establish synergy through collective strategies.

When developing collective strategies, companies obtain gains that can be observed from situations in the market environment that include positive sum growth. In a positive sum game, it is possible for all players to increase the size of the benefits they receive, that is, all players can win, which does not happen in other situations according to Nielsen (1988, APUD SILVA, 2017).

Companies that take part in collective strategies seek to obtain shared benefits, but that does not mean that they stop competing. According to Human and Provan (1997), companies obtain gains that are related to interorganizational exchanges when employing collective strategies.

Other advantages emerge from collective strategies so that companies can achieve and sustain collaborative differentials. The differentials can be mutual learning in the development of new products and processes, the co-specialty in the exploration of new market niches and better information flow. These differentials, furthermore, can promote gains both with the experiences of the partners, reduction of uncertainties levels and economies of scale and scope, as they develop joint actions that reduce costs and enhance the use of resources (GULATI; NOHRIA; ZAHEER, 2000; JARILLO, 1988; apud SILVA, 2017).

This fierce competition that is seen today in a market with operating restrictions for the part of the government due to the COVID pandemic19, in addition to similar products, cost reductions, increased quality, among others, it requires business strategies, with a focus on competitiveness, be innovative and move away from traditional approaches, as the number of company mergers is growing.

The establishment of partnerships and other forms of inter-business relationships, especially the productive arrangements, demonstrates the growing influence of external relations to companies, compared to internal constraints, in the establishment of competitive strategies and the achievement of results.

2.2.1 Coopetition

A collective strategy widely used in recent years is coopetition, a word that is formed by the verbs to compete and to cooperate and aims to enhance the competitive forces of the participants, as can be extracted from the concepts of several authors shown below.

Authors such as Verschoore (2010) and Maia & Maia (2011) list as benefits of cooptitive acting gains in scale and market power; learning and innovation; reducing costs and risks and sharing opportunities.

Coopetition has its roots in collaboration, as both arise from common interests that replace the maximization of individual economic and non-economic gain

Coopetition, therefore, implies thein sharing of objectives that induce agents to cooperate and compete to reduce risks, losses and uncertainties; expand its range of strategic options; leverage gains and outperform strategies based solely on competition or cooperation.

In the cooptitive view, cooperation and competition are complementary perspectives for obtaining competitive advantages (DELLA CORTE & ARIA, 2016).

Coopetition is a business strategy that is beyond current paradigms, as it sees interorganizational cooperation and competition seeking direct or indirect benefits for participants, therefore, it is a hybrid behavior (LUO, 2005).

The initial concept has evolved over the years with successful experiences, from a simple definition of 'competing + cooperating simultaneously', to a broad vision of a valuable network. Currently, coopetition is already pointed out as the formation of a new paradigm (DELLA CORTE & ARIA, 2016).

There are several advantages of coopetition, such as: sharing costs, resources, skills and knowledge; access to new technologies (which will allow the development of new products or the entry into new segments and new markets); increase the efficiency of company's actions; increase the initiative to seek opportunities and react to market threats; increase company's production; reduce company's effort and the risks associated to the investment; reinforce flexibility of its response to market demands; be more active in the acquisition of technological innovations; enhance your brands; increase the value perceived by customers; making gains with economies of scale; outperform competitors, etc.

3. METHODOLOGY

The present research is, according to Prodanov (2013), descriptive since the researcher only records and describes the facts observed without interfering with them. This type describes the characteristics of a given population or phenomenon or the establishment of relationships between variables. It involves the use of standardized data collection techniques: questionnaire and systematic observation.

Thus, a bibliographic research was used as the researcher resorted to materials already published, consisting mainly of books, magazines, publications in journals and scientific articles, dissertations and theses, with the aim of putting the researcher in direct contact with all the material already written research's subject.

It was a field research that aimed to obtain information and/or knowledge about the object of study.

Considering the accessibility and availability to contribute to the present study, a sample of 30 cooperatives was analyzed within the universe of 128 cooperatives registered with OCB / AM - Organization of Cooperatives in Brazil.

It was a quantitative research from the point of view of problem approach, according to Prodanov (2013) in a quantitative research everything is quantifiable, opinions and information are translated into numbers to classify and analyze them.

The information collection took place from August to December 2018, with a questionnaire being delivered to the management of the cooperative or association and 10 days after receipt the material was collected, on average.

To systematize the answers to the questions in the questionnaire, a scale was used to measure the current situation of the cooperative or association in the following order: 1 – None 2 – Rarely 3 – Sometimes 4 – Most of the time 5 – Always.

To assess the existence of a linear correlation between the variables, Spearman's correlation was used in order to identify whether there is any correlation between them.

To perform these analyzes, Microsoft® Word and Excell 2007 software, SPSS® (STATISTICAL PACKAGE FOR THE SOCIAL SCIENCES) version 17.0 for Windows was used.

4. RESULTS APRESENTATION AND ANALISYS

For the coopetition it was found that the cooperatives participating in the research know the following characteristics shown in Figure 1.

The following statements were researched:

There is trust and commitment among the participants that contribute to being coopetitive; The exchange of experiences and learning increases internal cohesion and stimulates generation and diffusion; The partners' ability to adapt and mobilize favors strategic alignment; The formalization of governance and the relationship between networked companies contribute to achieving goals; In coopetition, participants enhance identification, translation and conversion; In coopetition, benchmarking is strategic; We are coopetitive in our market.

Data shows that cooperatives understand that in a coopetitive relationship it is essential that there is trust between the participants once its roots are in collaboration, which leads to the identification of new opportunities for strategic actions shared by the partners.

Another fundamental point is related to the cooperative's dynamic capacities, since learning through the exchange of experiences and benchmarking strengthens the absorption capacity and the management of this acquired and shared knowledge leads to the acquisition of competitive advantages compared to competitors. The success of this strategy depends strongly on the culture of knowledge sharing, with no room for individual and opportunistic actions.

Figure 1. Coopetition: average of general data
Source: the author himself (2018)

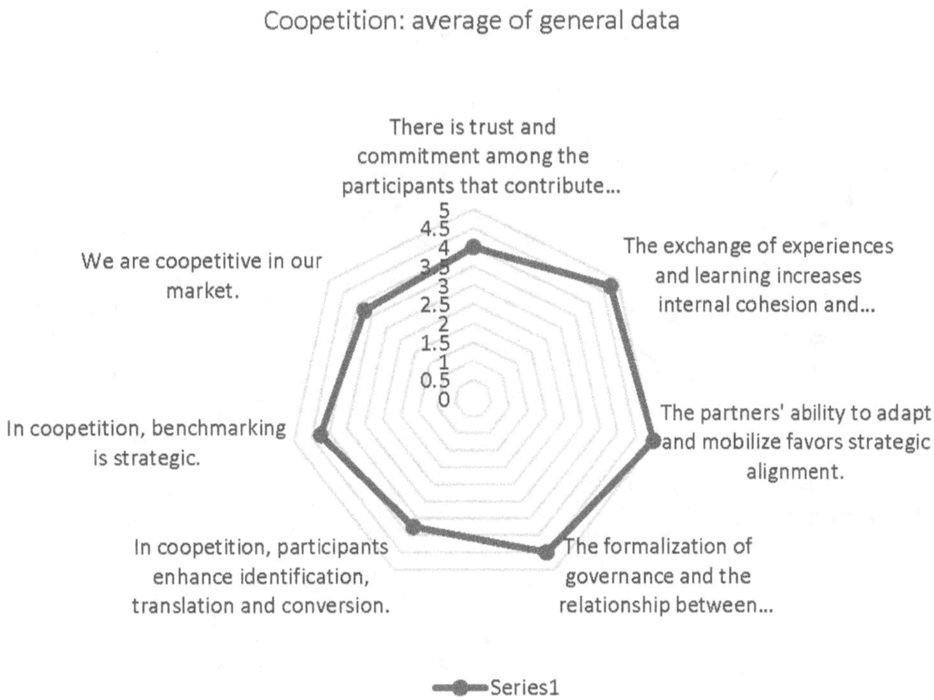

As for the ability capabilities, it appears that this acquired knowledge should serve to integrate, build and reconfigure organizational routines and processes, which generates greater external and internal competence in rapidly changing environments, as stated by Teece et al. (2009).

The good use of the absorptive and adaptative dynamic capacities present in the coopetition contributes strongly to develop innovative skills, and thus to achieve and sustain sustainable competitive advantages.

The indices presented by the group studied in this research can demonstrate that there is a possibility that there are gains such as reduction of risks, losses and reduction of uncertainties; expanding the range of strategic options; leveraging gains and obtaining superior performance in the market due to the use of coopetitiveness

Dynamic capabilities for Teece et al. (2009) are strengths for internal training to face the market and even support partners. These are based on the tripod: processes (routines or patterns of current practices and learning), positions (assets, governance structure, consumer base and external relations with suppliers and partners) and trajectory (decision history and technological and market opportunities).

To learn more about how cooperatives understand and use dynamic capabilities, the following statements were researched:

We carry out our actions solely because of our competencies and abilities; We are attentive to changes in the market; Our competitive advantages are based only on our skills; We always innovate before our competition; We seek the development of relational capabilities; We are always looking for new opportunities in the market; In our business relationships, we value adaptive capacity; In our business

Figure 2. Dynamic capacities: average of general data
Source: the author himself (2018)

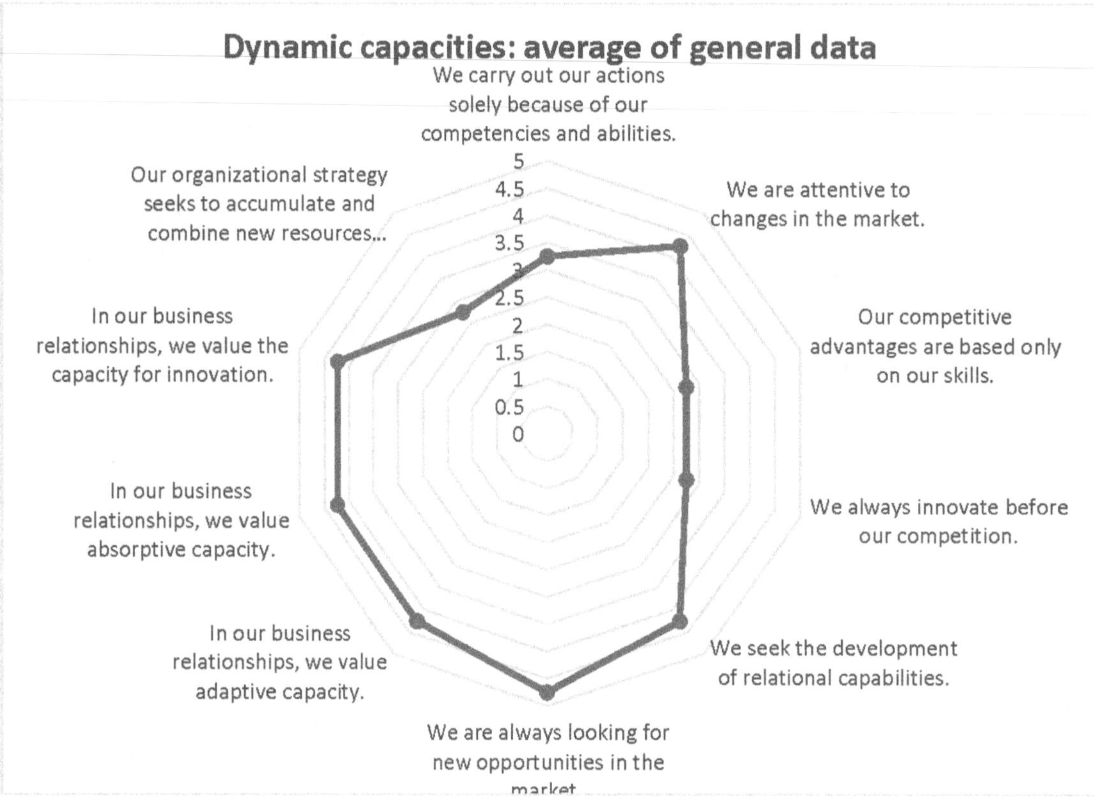

relationships, we value absorptive capacity; In our business relationships, we value the capacity for innovation; In our business relationships, we value the capacity for innovation.

Camargo & Meireles (2012) propose that there are three capacities to support dynamic capacities: (a) the ability to feel the context of the environment; (b) ability to take advantage of opportunities; and (c) ability to manage threats and transformations.

Thus, in this research it was found that there is an enabling environment for cooperatives to grow and develop, reach new markets, launch innovative products, but it is very clear that despite having strengths that provide conditions to have greater and better results we need to expand the relationship networks, learn from those who know how to do it and have a long-term collaborative thinking in actions that seek greater competitiveness, that is, there is a significant opening so that the coopetition strategy can be used more and better, which it will value more efficiently and effectively market actions.

It can be said that dynamic capabilities involves efforts for change and innovation, through skills and competences or capacities, in order to identify market needs and/or opportunities for generating ideas; development of new products, services and better processes.

Wang and Ahmed (2007) state that: adaptive capacity is the company's ability to identify and capitalize on emerging market opportunities, it refers to adaptation at the right time and is centered on routines and processes; absorptive capacity, on the other hand, is the company's ability to recognize the value of new external information, assimilate and apply it for commercial purposes, it refers to the use of external knowledge according to its previous level; and an organization's innovative capacity allows it to identify new opportunities for action, growing the means of doing new business and improving operational efficiency, using existing resources more efficiently and effectively.

Dynamic capabilities are especially relevant to innovation and coopetition, once, more important than the current resource base, is the ability to accumulate and combine new resources internally and externally, especially if these interactions contribute to the construction of distinctive competencies on topics such as Research and Development (R&D), new products and processes, new business models, among others (CHESBROUGH et al, 2008).

For Silva (2017) other advantages appear for the companies to reach and sustain collaborative differentials from the collective strategies, these are: the mutual learning in the development of new products and processes, the co-specialty in the exploration of new market niches, the better flow of information. These differentials can also promote gains with the experiences of partners, reducing the levels of uncertainties and economies of scale and scope, as they develop joint actions that reduce costs and enhance the use of resources.

Precisely, coopetition seeks to use more and better dynamic capabilities of partners and its own in order to be more competitive in this increasingly global market.

In this extremely open market for changes, those who are not able to perceive and adapt to new forms and requests will be left out of the competition. The proper use of dynamic capabilities makes the difference for successful companies.

4. CONCLUSION

Companies increasingly need to strengthen their internal capabilities in order to prepare themselves to face economic, social, legal, technological and political challenges, which end up interfering with their performance in the market.

A proposal for strengthening is in the coopetitive practice, in which competing companies cooperate in activities to strengthen their capabilities, thus allowing gains for all participants.

It is a paradigm shift in business management, which generally seeks only to compete with its competitors individually, spending efforts and resources in order to eliminate those others.

In cooperative practice, internal strengthening is sought through the development of dynamic capacities for absorption, adaptation and innovation, which allows for sustainable evolution.

Companies that already practice coopetition gain by reducing costs and increasing their efficiency in the market, through learning shared between partners that favor the strengthening of their competitive advantages collectively, identifying opportunities and seeking to strengthen their skills.

At a time when the world is going through the second wave of a pandemic known as COVID19, it is important that companies and entrepreneurs can evolve their way of operating in order not only to survive but to seek to evolve in this market highly troubled by limitations imposed by public administrators and for people's own health security.

REFERENCES

Balestrin, A. (2016). *Redes de Cooperação Empresarial: Estratégias de Gestão na Nova Economia*. Bookman Editora.

Camargo. (2012). *Capacidades Dinâmicas: o que são e como identificá-las? XXXVI Encontro da ANPAD*. Setembro de.

Chesbrough, H., Vanhaverbeke, W., & West, J. (2008). *Open innovation: researching a new paradigm*. Oxford University Press.

Costa & Porto. (2015). Capacidade dinâmica de cooperação nas multinacionais Brasileiras e seus fatores gerenciais determinantes. *Revista Eletrônica de Negócios Internacionais, 10*(1), 57-69.

Coutinho. (1994). *Estudo da competitividade da indústria brasileira* (4th ed.). Papirus.

Davila. (2016). *Relações Entre Práticas de Gestão do Conhecimento, Capacidade Absortiva e Desempenho*. Evidências do Sul do Brasil. Tese de Doutorado Universidade Federal de Santa Catarina. Centro Tecnológico. Programa de Pós Graduação em Engenharia e Gestão do Conhecimento.

Della Corte, V., & Aria, M. (2016). Coopetition and sustainable competitive advantage. The case of tourist destinations. *Tourism Management, 54*, 524–540. doi:10.1016/j.tourman.2015.12.009

Human & Provan. (1997). An emergent theory of structure and outcomes in small-firm strategic manufacturing network. Academy of Management Journal, 40(2), 368-403.

Luo, Y. (2005). Toward coopetition within a multinational enterprise: A perspective from foreign subsidiarie. *Journal of World Business, 40*(1), 71–90. doi:10.1016/j.jwb.2004.10.006

Maia, F. S., & Maia, T. S. T. (2011). Network training and strategic alliances in the civil construction sector. *Espacios Magazine., 32*, 38.

Mintzberg, H., & Ahlstrand, B. (2000). LAMPEL, J. Safári de estratégia. Porto Alegre. *The Bookman.*

Prodanov, C. C., & Freitas, E. C. (2013). *Metodologia do trabalho científico: Métodos e técnicas da pesquisa e do trabalho acadêmico* (2nd ed.). Universidade Feevale.

Silva. (2017). *A influência do pluralismo relacional nas estratégias coletivas de responsabilidade social corporativa de uma rede de pequenas empresas do setor hoteleiro. Tese (doutorado) na Universidade do Vale do Rio dos Sinos (Unisinos).* Programa de Pós-Graduação em Administração.

Teece, D. J. (2009). *Dynamic capabilities & strategic management.* Oxford University Press.

Tidd. (2008). *Gestão da Inovação. 3.* Bookman.

Verschoore, J. R. (2010). Programa Redes de Cooperação: Uma análise da política pública gaúcha de formação de redes. *Revista Pós Ciências Sociais., 7*, 101–116.

Wang, C. L., & Ahmed, P. K. (2007). Dynamic capabilities: A review and research. *International Journal of Management Reviews, Oxford, 9*(1), 31–51. doi:10.1111/j.1468-2370.2007.00201.x

Zahra, S. A., & George, G. (2002, April). Absorptive capacity: A review, reconceptualization, and extension. *Academy of Management Review, 27*(2), 185–203. doi:10.2307/4134351

Chapter 3
Proposal of a Multidimensional Poverty Index for Spanish Municipalities

Francisco Espasandin-Bustelo
Universidad de Sevilla, Spain

Juan Ganaza Vargas
Universidad de Sevilla, Spain

Julio García-del-Junco
Universidad de Sevilla, Spain

Jaime Ortega Gutierrez
Universidad de Sevilla, Spain

ABSTRACT

There are two objectives that impel this work: first, to propose a valid, reliable, and parsimonious poverty index, named Municipal Poverty Index-Urban Audit (MPI-UA), and second, to describe the evolution of the multidimensional poverty risk of the Spanish municipalities according to C. For the construction of the MPI-UA, the information provided by the URBAN AUDIT database on Spanish municipalities with a population in excess of 20,000 inhabitants has been used. The validated data have been analyzed with the PLS technique to identify the variables that allow the establishment of the MPI-UA, although previously certain variables have had to be transformed. This chapter has valuable implications insofar as there is no known multidimensional poverty index for Spanish municipalities. Moreover, it may be of probable use for academics. In the case of local managers, the index can be useful both for the knowledge of the situation and for the design of public policies to reduce poverty.

DOI: 10.4018/978-1-7998-8925-0.ch003

INTRODUCTION

Poverty has been recognised as a socioeconomic disease that affects peoples' capacity and productivity due to basic needs deprivation (Biswal, Mishra & Sarangi, 2020). According to Gentilini & Sumner (2012) 1500 million people lived in poverty, which is equivalent to more than a fifth of the world population (22.5%); although since the mid-1990's, poverty had decreased in all regions of the world (Fosu, 2017).

Regarding the geography of poverty, two portions of evidence stand out. Firstly, poverty affects all nations (Liu & XU, 2016) and more and more countries are paying attention to the poverty's alleviation (Wang, Gan, Chen & Voda, 2020). In the second place, world's most of poor do not live in low-income countries (LICs), as classified by the World Bank (Gentilini & Sumner, 2012). Conversely, 71% of multidimensionally poor people amount to close to 1 billion citizens who live in middle-income countries (MICs) (Alkire, Chatterjee, Conconi, Seth & Vaz, 2014).

According to estimations by various international organizations (Maqueda, 2021), millions of people could fall back into poverty due to the global pandemic. In the Spanish case, the pandemic increased poverty to the highest level since the great recession (Maqueda, 2021). In 2020, the AROPE rate of risk of poverty or social exclusion stood at 21%; which affects 3.3 million people and is equivalent to 7% of Spanish population.

On the other hand, United Nations 2030 Agenda for Sustainable Development first objective is to "End poverty in all its forms everywhere". The Agenda was adopted by all member states in 2015. According to Ari, Hariyani & Waloejo (2019), poverty reduction is the greatest challenge facing society and governments, and it has motivated some municipal authorities to generate programs and projects aimed at reducing it (Portales, 2019). Specifically, the international community is committed to reduce by at least half the number of men, women and children living in poverty in all its dimensions, according to national definitions of the term (Lanau, Mack & Nandy, 2020; Jindra & Vaz, 2019; Ambel, Mugera & Bain, 2020).

Assessing the success of policies and progress towards this commitment is particularly relevant in the context of the 2030 World Development Agenda to "leave no one behind" (Alkire, Roche & Vaz, 2017). In this domain, it is of paramount importance to identify the multiple dimensions of poverty (Salecker, Ahmadov & Karimli, 2020) and it is convenient to review the dimensions of the Multidimensional Poverty Indicator (MPI) to improve its alignment with the SDGs (Alkire, Oldiges & Kanagaratnam, 2020).

In order to precisely identify the situation of poverty, the need to project official measures of multidimensional poverty becomes necessary, so that they complement the income poverty measures (Alkire & Santos, 2013) and that show all the channels through which

poverty can manifest itself, its scope and the severity of deprivation (Bersisa & Heshmati (2021). In this domain, the situation varies from country to country. Consequently, there are countries that have already implemented a national or local MPI, and they have permanent official statistics to measure multidimensional poverty (Bhutan, 2010; Colombia and the European Union, 2011; Chile, El Salvador and Costa Rica, 2015; Maldives, Palestine, Ghana, and Angola, 2020); and other nations are in the process of reviewing the measurement method to determine national poverty lines (Gentilini & Sumner, 2012).

Poverty's multidimensional measurement plays an important role in its reduction or eradication (Salecker, Ahmadov & Karimli, 2020), since it can influence how it is understood, how it is analyzed or how policies are created in this sphere (Alkire & Foster, 2011). It has therefore been a hot topic in international poverty research for decades (Liu & Xu, 2016) to which scholars, policy makers and social planners have devoted great efforts (Bersisa & Heshmati, 2021).

The result of the efforts undertaken in the last decade is, in words of Datt (2019), a true explosion in the growth of the literature on multidimensional poverty measurement. Which has flourished in several different directions (Alkire & Foster, 2011).

This extensive literature has some flaws: lack of sufficient rigor as input for political interventions (Bersisa & Heshmati, 2021); does not systematically apply measurement theories and practices that have been shown to be successful in other fields (Najera & Gordon, 2020); often uses non-scientific frameworks based on ad hoc selection (Najera & Gordon, 2020); and few studies have compared monetary and multidimensional measures in depth (Salecker, Ahmadov & Karimli, 2020). In addition, the MPIs have been construed without reference to the theoretical framework (Alkire & Foster, 2011), they are prepared by experts and do not use citizen participation mechanisms in their construction (Galvez, Valdés & Castillo, 2019).

Consequently, much remains to be done in the development and application of multidimensional poverty indexes in various aspects: choice of dimensions and indicators, cut-off lines selection, and justification of the weights assigned to each dimension (Salecker, Ahmadov & Karimli, 2020).

Such is the relevance of measurement that, according to Ferreira & Lugo (2013), this purely academic debate has been transformed into a broad policy debate both within and between countries.

At political level, poverty reduction is unanimously acknowledged as a priority for all governments (Rimoldi, Arcagni, Fattore, di Belgiojoso, 2020). Authorities use topic's obtained information to: produce public policies (Alkire & Foster, 2011; Ferreira & Lugo, 2013), assess poverty alleviation policies impacts (Santos, 2013; Alkire & Seth, 2015), manage local development (Asselin, 2009), target poverty (Bersisa & Heshmati, 2021; Voronov, Ruza & Stasane, 2020) and, ultimately, reduce impoverished people's deprivation (Alkire, Roche & Vaz, 2017).

This research is longitudinal, qualitative, exploratory, normative and descriptive in nature and, in general, aims to contribute to the measurement of multidimensional poverty that will be useful for Spanish public managers. This general objective is specified in two specific objectives: firstly, to propose, based on the data available in the Urban Audit database, a valid, reliable and parsimonious index that measures the risk of municipal multidimensional poverty in Spain, and secondly, to analyse the dynamics of the risk of multidimensional poverty in Spanish municipalities in excess of 20,000 inhabitants.

To achieve these objectives, we propose the following structure. First, the literature on the topic of "measuring municipal multidimensional poverty" is reviewed, followed by a description of data collection and analysis methods used in the research, a discussion of the results, details of the theoretical and empirical implications and a synthesis of the main conclusions of the research, and finally, limitations and future lines of research.

LITERATURE REVIEW

Poverty concept is holistic (Gong, Kong & Tan, 2020), complex (Varela & Ocegueda, 2020), multifaceted (Silva, Bruno, Silva & Nascimento, 2020), unobserved or latent (Santos & Villatoro, 2020), dynamically evolving (Bersisa & Heshmati, 2021) and without consensus in its definition (Mora, Villafuerte & Martínez, 2020).

This research employs a poverty concept aligned with Bourguignon & Chakravarty (2003). So, poverty is the state in which "minimally acceptable" levels of different features, monetary and non-monetary, necessary for a subsistence standard of living are not achieved.

Poverty concept's another characteristic is that it cannot be properly understood with simple measures (Leu, Chen & Chen, 2016). In this sense, most of this topic's empirical work measures poverty with a unidimensional criterion, usually expenditure or income (Duclos, Sahn & Younger, 2006). In recent years there has been a growing consensus on unidimensional criterion inadequacy (Alkire & Santos, 2013): it does not show all the channels through which poverty manifests itself and does not reveal ambiguities and capacities (Bersisa & Heshmati, 2021) of this complex phenomenon (Galvez, Valdés & Castillo, 2019).

In terms of poverty measurement, it is worth noting that the most remote origin of indicators measuring multidimensional poverty is in the 1960s and focuses on human resource development (Pasha, 2017). Its subsequent development is later (Santos, 2014); along these lines Biswal, Mishra & Sarangi (2020) argue that multidimensional poverty's first measure dates to Townsend (1979), although the foundations of the MPI were established by Foster, Greer & Thorbecke (1984) and most of the pioneering work in the field was developed by the United Nations Development Programme (UNDP).

According to Pinilla-Roncancio, Mactaggart, Kuper, Dionicio, Naber, Murthy & Polack (2020), the literature proposes different approaches to measure poverty. In this sense, Voronov, Ruza & Stasane (2020) distinguish between absolute, relative and subjective poverty approaches; González & Santos (2020) differentiate between normative, semi-normative and non-normative approaches (the first two define the minimum standard of living to be met and the non-normative approach uses thresholds detached from the minimally acceptable standard of living); Bakar, Hamdan & Sani (2020) propose the existence of four approaches (monetary poverty, capability approach, social exclusion approach and participatory poverty assessment approach); Sanz, Peris & Escámez (2017) refer to Sen's (2000) welfare economics, Sachs's (2005) clinical economics, Stiglitz's (2015) approaches; and, finally, Codes (2008) refers to the subsistence or absolute poverty approach, the basic needs approach, the relative deprivation approach, the capability deprivation approach and the multidimensional poverty approach. According to Silva, Bruno, Silva & Nascimento (2020) multidimensional poverty approach is poverty measure's most robust.

As far as multidimensional poverty is concerned, although the literature offers several definitions, this research, as already indicated above, is based on the one proposed by Bourguignon and Chakravarty (2003), who define it as the deficit with respect to a threshold in each dimension of an individual.

Regarding theoretical approaches to multidimensional poverty measurement, Deutsch & Silber (2005) identify four approaches (fuzzy set theory, information theory, efficiency analysis and axiomatic poverty indexes). The capability approach (Sen, 1976) is the most widely accepted in the scientific community. According to Salecker, Ahmadov & Karimli (2020) this is because its measurements are more accurate, it is based on more realistic assumptions, it better captures the duration of poverty, it measures welfare outcomes rather than resource inputs, and it is no more problematic than unidimensional poverty measures when it comes to implementation.

Aligned with Sen (2001), capabilities denote a person's opportunity and ability to generate valuable outcomes, considering relevant personal characteristics and external factors. Capabilities are therefore an individual's freedoms or opportunities to choose to live a life at the height of human dignity. Sanz, Peris & Escámez (2017) argue that the minimum essential for a person's life to live up to human dignity is to comfortably surpass the threshold of these ten (10) core capabilities: to live to the end a human life of normal length; to be in good health; to be safe; to be able to use the senses (imagination, thought and reason); to be able to have attachments to things and people; to develop an idea about the good; to be able to live with others and have the social bases of self-respect and non-humiliation; to live with concern for and in relation to animals, plants and nature; to be able to laugh, play, enjoy recreational activities; and to have control over the political, material and working environment.

In relation to the properties that a multidimensional poverty indicator should have, several authors have addressed this issue (Chakravarty, Mukherjee & Ranade, 1998; Santos, 2013; Lanau, Mack & Nandy, 2020); and the approach of Najera & Gordon (2020) stands out for its clarity, proposing that an indicator should be suitable, valid, reliable, invariant in its measurement, additive and parsimonious.

According to Najera & Gordon (2020), the lack of consensus on the best way to measure multidimensional poverty gives rise to many different proposals. The literature consulted shows that the Multidimensional Poverty Index (MPI), designed by the UNDP, and the Alkire-Foster (AF) index are very important at the international level. In Europe, the AROPE rate, which measures the proportion of the total population at risk of poverty or social exclusion, is the main indicator for monitoring the EU 2030 target on poverty and social exclusion.

The standard conceptual framework for designing such multidimensional poverty indexes are counting-based methods (Alkire, Oldiges & Kanagaratnam, 2021; González & Santos, 2020) for the following reasons: their practicality and application in several recent research studies (Seth & Alkire, 2014); their frequent use for poverty policy design; and because they can be applied with precision using original and dichotomous data (Alkire, Oldiges & Kanagaratnam, 2021).

Several authors (Gallardo, 2020; Ambel, Mugera & Bain, 2020; Habtewold, 2021; Berenger, 2019) agree that counting methods follow a two-phase pattern in which, first, the poor are identified within a total population (identification phase) and, second, the multidimensional poverty index is constructed through an aggregation process (aggregation phase).

The identification of "who is poor" is a central issue in poverty measurement (Alkire & Santos, 2013) which consists of the following stages: selecting dimensions and indicators; weighting or assigning weights to each dimension and/or indicator; determining deprivation and poverty thresholds or cut-off lines.

The choice of the dimensions and indicators of a multidimensional poverty measure is a fundamental phase that requires the use of an explicit criterion (Santos, 2013). However, there is no consensus on the different dimensions and how they should be perceived in reality (Ponce, 2018). In principle, the number of possible dimensions seems inexhaustible, so it is very important to clarify the methods and criteria used for their selection. In this line, Alkire & Santos (2011) propose the following methods: deliberative participatory processes of a representative group of participants; regular feedback from communities; scientific literature on poverty; public consensus, for example with the SDGs, or data availability. Zavaleta (2017) argues that the most commonly used dimensions for measuring multidimensional poverty are: education, health, standard of living, employment and social protection. Regarding the selection of indicators, Najera & Gordon (2020) state that in multidimensional poverty measurement it is rare to have many indicators in each dimension and also there is no agreement on his number. In contrast, Asselin (2009) states that many indicators are generally used to measure multidimensional poverty and estimates the average at 44 indicators, which can be quantitative, qualitative or categorical in nature, and can be combinations of monetary and non-monetary indicators (González & Santos, 2020).

In the second phase, concerning each dimension and/or indicator's weighting, Ravallion (2011) argues that assigning weights to dimensions is as important as choosing dimensions, since multidimensional poverty measures are sensitive to each dimension's weight and the weighting structure plays an important role in measurement (Datt, 2019). Alkire & Foster (2011) propose assessing weights through recurrent participatory and deliberative processes or through a technical committee. Decancq & Lugo (2008) identify six methods for establishing weights: equal weights (most commonly used, although not entirely correct); frequency-based weighting, which sets weights in relation to the proportion of the population suffering deprivation in that dimension; more favourable weights, which are specific to each individual and maximise their well-being; regression based weights, which offer an interesting way to obtain weights; normative weighting, where each person is asked to weight each dimension according to its importance on a pre-determined scale and the average weight is considered; multivariate statistical weighting including structural equation modelling (SEM). Additionally, he proposes budget allocation, in which members of a representative group are asked to distribute a budget among several dimensions, paying more for those dimensions that are more relevant. In the same vein, Pasha (2017) proposes three different methods: normative weights, empirical or data-driven weights and hybrid weights. The application of the previous methods may result in dimension weights being equal (Santos, 2013; Catalán, Fifita & Faingaanuku, 2019; Yang & Fu, 2019; Bersisa & Heshmati, 2021) or different (Asselin, 2009; Ciani, Gagliardi, Riccarelli, & Betti, 2019; Gallardo, 2020; Wang, Gan, Chen & Voda 2020).

Finally, in the third phase, thresholds or cut-off lines are determined using the sequential "double cut" system, which clearly prioritizes people with multiple deprivation (Alkire & Foster, 2011). In the first cut-off, the deprivation index is calculated by setting a threshold for each dimension, and individuals, households or territories that do not reach that threshold are deprived in that dimension. In the second cut, the poverty rate is calculated, which involves counting the number of dimensions in which individuals, households or territories suffer deprivation (Santos, 2013). Alkire & Foster (2011) argue that a person is multidimensionally poor if he or she is deprived in at least one third of the weighted indicators and there is a large body of research that follows this criterion (Aslam, Kumar & Sorooshian, 2019; Bersisa & Heshmati, 2021; Datt, 2019; Loaiza, Muñetón & Vanegas, 2018; Mahrt, Rossi, Salvucci & Tarp, 2020; Torres, 2018; Ramírez, Díaz & Bedoya, 2017; Aslam, Kumar & Sorooshian, 2019).

Once the number of dimensions in which a person, household or territory is deprived is known, the literature offers two extreme approaches to identify who is poor: union and intersection methods. According to union approach (Habtewold, 2021) a person, household or territory is multidimensionally poor when it is deprived in at least one dimension. This approach has been criticised because it may identify people as poor who are not (Mideros, 2012). According to intersection approach, only individuals, households or territories deprived in all dimensions are considered poor (Alkire & Foster, 2011).

Once you know who is poor, you proceed to the aggregation phase, which consists of counting the people who are in multidimensional poverty (Alkire, & Santos, 2013).

Having presented the review of the literature on poverty measurement, and more specifically on multidimensional poverty, the methods used in the research are described below.

METHODOLOGY

This section describes the methods of data collection, data cleaning and data analysis.

Collection and Cleaning of Original Data

The information is taken from the Urban Audit database, which contains information on European municipalities with a population of more than 20,000 inhabitants; only data on Spanish municipalities is used in this paper.

The information contained in the database consists of the following variables: locality, year, resident population (number of persons), proportion of the population aged 0-14, proportion of the population aged 15-64, proportion of the population over the age of 65, average age of the population, proportion of nationals in the total population, proportion of native nationals in the total population, proportion of foreign-born in the total population, proportion of foreigners in the total population, total number of households, average household size, proportion of one-person households in total households, number of conventional dwellings according to land registry, number of conventional dwellings according to census, proportion of empty dwellings, crude birth rate (per thousand persons), crude death rate (per thousand persons), life expectancy at birth (years), unemployment rate (percentage), share of employed persons aged 20-64 in the labour force (percentage), activity rate (%), share of employment in services, share of employment in industry, average annual household income (euro), median annual income per inhabitant (euro), median annual income per consumption unit (euro), total area (Km^2), land use (%), continuous residential urban fabric, land use (%), continuous residential urban fabric, land use (%), discontinuous residential urban fabric, land use (%), industrial, commercial, public, military and private units land use (%), transport infrastructure land use (%), other artificial areas land use (%), urban green areas, sports and leisure facilities land use (%), agricultural areas land use (%), natural areas land use (%), proportion of children aged 0-4 years in day care out of population aged 0-4 years (%), proportion of population aged 25-64 years with highest level of education ISCED 0, 1 or 2 (%), proportion of population aged 25-64 years with highest level of education ISCED 3 or 4 (%), proportion of population aged 25-64 with highest level of education ISCED 5 or 6 (percentage), proportion of commuting to work by car (percentage), proportion of commuting to work on foot (percentage), proportion of commuting to work by public transport (percentage), average duration of commuting to work, number of annual tourist overnight stays, and, finally, accommodation capacity in tourist establishments. The data series retrieved includes information from 2010 to 2017.

Obtained information, prior to its analysis, has been cleaned in order to ensure that the data studied were homogeneous for all periods. This process has been carried out for each one of the years from 2010 to 2017, as follows. Firstly, the valid data for each of the variables in the database was considered, which led to the exclusion of the following variables from the final data to be processed: number of conventional dwellings according to the census, proportion of empty dwellings, life expectancy at birth (years), median annual income per inhabitant (euro), median annual income per consumption unit (euro), all land use variables, proportion of population aged 25-64 with highest level of education ISCED 0, 1 or 2 (%), share of population aged 25-64 with highest level of education ISCED 3 or 4 (%), share of population aged 25-64 with highest level of education ISCED 5 or 6 (%), share of commuting to work by car (%), proportion of people who walk to work (percentage), proportion of people who take a public transport to work (percentage) and average time to get to work. The data for the selected variables were then analysed for each locality and each year; as a result, we were only able to keep records for the years 2011, 2012, 2014 and 2015, and not for all localities.

In a third stage, it has been necessary to transform some of the original data so that all the indicators incorporated in the multidimensional poverty indexes are measured on a homogeneous scale and with the same meaning. Thus, firstly, data were converted into percentages: by multiplying the birth and death rates by 10 and calculating the percentage of household income in each locality with respect to each period's Spain median income. In a second stage, the meaning of the different indicators was analysed so that they all meant the same in poverty risk's terms, so that both mortality rate and unemployment rate were modified, obtaining the complementary value at 100.

Data Analysis

The PLS technique has been used to construct the multidimensional poverty indexes. PLS application, following Roldán and Cepeda (2018), has been done in several stages. A first stage aimed at identifying latent variables, made up of various individual indicators in the database, which we call first-order constructs (factors). All the first-order constructs considered were defined as B-mode or reflexive variables.

For the validation of constructs consisting of more than one item, the following process has been carried out: 1) first, we checked for the items multicollinearity's absence by calculating variance inflation factor (VIF), which has to be less than 3; 2) then, once necessary items have been removed, we analysed weights of each item in corresponding construct and remove those items without significant weight; and 3) finally, we determined each first-order factor's components and their corresponding weights. After identifying the first-order factors (specifically labelled as "income", "education", "health" and "employment") we proceeded to combine, using PLS technique, these first-order factors into one or two second-order constructs: those labelled as multidimensional poverty indicator numbers one (1) and two (2), respectively. The next step consisted of comparing the results obtained for the 3 poverty indicators for the last year analysed (2015) in order to try to identify the existence of a better poverty risk's indicator, which we call "Municipal Poverty Index-Urban Audit" (MPI-UA). Finally, we studied the evolution of this at-risk-of-poverty indicator at the municipal level over the time period considered (2011 to 2015).

DISCUSSION OF RESULTS

For results analysis, we have carried out the following steps. First, we expose the results obtained from the application of the PLS technique in the construction of the proposed poverty indicators.

The second phase consists of the presentation of the cross-sectional results (for 2015) obtained from the three poverty indicators used. Results are first offered at the level of various Spain's autonomous communities, highlighting for each of them the municipalities with poverty risk's highest and lowest. Then we present a comparison between municipalities at the national level. Finally, we highlight teratological situations.

Thirdly, the three municipal poverty indicators are compared in order to determine which of the three is the most valid, reliable and parsimonious.

Finally, a longitudinal study is presented (comparing the evolution over the four periods analysed), both at the level of autonomous communities and municipalities, and without forgetting teratological situations.

Construction of Indicators

The study of the indicators selected from the URBAN AUDIT database from a purely theoretical point of view suggests the existence of some aspects that affect local entities poverty risk. In first place, and as it is traditional in poverty's research, it is necessary to take into consideration variables related to family units income. In this database the measure is obtained from households' median annual net income (expressed in euro). As already specified, the indicator has been transformed into percentage terms by dividing each municipality's value by the value of the variable for Spain in each period.

A second aspect that conditions a country or municipality inhabitants' poverty risk, is its population's educational level: the only database indicator used is "proportion of children aged 0-4 years in day-care centers out of the population aged 0-4 years (Percentage)".

Information upon population health can also be poverty risk's indicative. Database collects information on the birth and death rates of each population, measured in per thousand people. These indicators were transformed into percentages, and then the mortality percentage was transformed again: subtracting this value from one hundred.

Finally, database provides information upon population's employment situation: activity rate, unemployment rate, percentage of employed over active population, percentage of jobs in the service sector and percentage of jobs in industry. Again, a change was made to unemployment rate indicator, so that its meaning would be similar to rest of indicators: therefore, the difference to one hundred of unemployment rate was obtained.

The information thus obtained was grouped in a single file, with values for the years 2011, 2012, 2014 and 2015. This file was processed using the PLS technique to obtain the relative weight of each variable in each of the constructs or factors indicated. It is important to point out that "income" and "education" factors, with a single indicator, are obtained directly with a weight equal to 1, while the other two factors have to be obtained from the weights of the variables that they are made up of.

The factor "income", as already indicated, is obtained as the percentage proportion that the family income of each population represents of the family income of the country.

The second construct ("education") corresponds to the percentage of the population under 4 years of age that is enrolled in kindergarten.

The "health" construct is obtained as a combination of the indicators birth rate (coefficient 0.529) and the difference to 100 of the mortality rate (coefficient 0.576), since there is no likelihood of multicollinearity between these variables.

The fourth factor identified, called "employment", was initially made up of the following variables: unemployment rate complementary to 100 (percentage), proportion of employed persons aged 20-64 in the labour force (percentage), activity rate (percentage), proportion of employment in services and, finally, proportion of employment in industry. VIF analysis results show, on the one hand, that unemployment rate complementary and proportion of employed persons are closely related variables and, therefore, unemployment rate complementary is dropped; on the other hand, there is a high collinearity between employment in the industrial sector and employment in the services sector, so we keep the latter variable.

Finally, this first-order construct is calculated by combining the following indicators with their corresponding coefficients: activity rate (0.259), percentage of employed over active (0.859) and percentage of employment in the services sector (0.372).

These weights were used to calculate the "health" and "employment" constructs by multiplying each indicator by its corresponding weight and adding or subtracting it (depending on its sign) with the other indicators that make up each construct.

The file obtained after the transformation of the above factors was again analysed with PLS to calculate two alternative multidimensional poverty indicators to the unidimensional indicator represented by income.

The first multidimensional poverty indicator (MPI1, from now on) has been obtained as a combination of the factors "health" (coefficient 0.872), "employment" (-0.154) and "education" (-0.275). The second multidimensional poverty indicator (MPI2) consists of 4 constructs, i.e., it involves adding the factor "income" to MPI1; it is thus defined by the indicated constructs with their corresponding coefficients: "income" (0.032), "health" (0.873), "employment" (-0.154) and "education" (-0.276).

Poverty Risk's Cross-Sectional Analysis in 2015

We calculated three municipal poverty indexes: unidimensional indicator represented by the ratio of the municipality's income to the national median income, MPI1 and MPI2.

Calculi were made for all Spanish municipalities with information in all 4 years and for the country as a whole. It is important to note that the three poverty indexes analysed (unidimensional, multidimensional 1 and multidimensional 2) have a negative relationship with population poverty risk, i.e., the higher the index value, the lower the poverty risk.

Based on this information, the different municipalities in the different years (2011, 2012, 2014 and 2015) have been ranked according to the three poverty indexes: unidimensional (income), MPI1 and MPI2. However, only last period's results (2015) are presented and commented, they are shown in Table 1. For 2015, results at Autonomous Community and municipal level will be commented. Furthermore, "most notable teratological situations" (those cases in which greater changes are observed in poverty risk indicators' classification) will be exposed.

At Autonomous Community (AC) level, it is important to note, firstly, the absence of data for the Basque Country and Navarre (a fact that is repeated in the other 3 years analysed).

Secondly, we find a considerable number of autonomous regions that are represented by less than 3 municipalities: Balearic Islands, Canary Islands, Murcia, Rioja, Extremadura, Cantabria, Asturias, Madrid, Aragon and, logically, the autonomous cities of Ceuta and Melilla.

In the case of autonomous regions with 3 or more municipalities and with respect to the unidimensional poverty indicator, several things should be noted. First, there are only two Autonomous Regions with more municipalities with incomes below the national median income, namely Andalusia and Valencian Community. Second, the remaining autonomous regions (Castilla y León, Catalonia, Castilla La Mancha and Galicia) have more municipalities with incomes above the median income in Spain.

At the level of local authorities by autonomous community we must highlight the following facts: a) Cadiz is the Andalusian locality with the highest income, Almeria occupies a medium position and, finally, Fuengirola has the lowest income; b) for the Valencian Community we have Valencia (highest income), Gandía (intermediate income) and Torrevieja (lower income); c) in Catalonia: best (Castelldefels); intermediate (Tarragona); worst (Lérida); d) highest poverty risk in Castilla y León community corresponds to Ponferrada, lowest to Burgos and average to Avila; e) in Castilla La Mancha: best situation (Toledo), average (Ciudad Real) and worst (Albacete); and f) for Galicia the data indicate that worst situation is in Orense, best in Santiago de Compostela and intermediate in Pontevedra.

In income terms, most unfavourable situations' municipalities in 2015 are mostly located in Andalusia (Fuengirola, Benalmádena, Torremolinos, Jerez de la Frontera, Marbella, Almería, Málaga and El Puerto de Santa María), followed by towns in Valencian Community (Torrevieja, Benidorm, Elche, Gandía and Alicante). In addition to these 13 towns, there are two more from Castilla y León: Ponferrada and Zamora. On the other hand, highest income levels cities are: Castelldefels, Madrid, Barcelona, Ceuta, Melilla, Toledo, Santiago de Compostela, Palma (de Mallorca), Tarragona and Zaragoza.

We briefly comment on the data provided in Table 1 for the two multidimensional poverty indexes, MPI1 and MPI2. In this exercise, the results of both indexes coincide fairly closely, so we comment on them together.

Autonomous Regions which show a situation that could be classified as positive (since they have more populations in positions behind those of Spain) are Andalusia, Valencian Community, Catalonia and Castilla La Mancha. Opposite situation occurs in Asturias, Galicia, Canary Islands and, lastly, Castilla y Leon.

Regarding the classification of the three municipalities for each Autonomous Community as being at poverty risk's lowest, highest and intermediate, there is absolute coincidence for both indicators. For Andalusia, these positions correspond to Cádiz (highest risk), Benalmádena (lowest) and Jerez de la Frontera (intermediate). For Castilla La Mancha: highest, Cuenca; lowest, Toledo; intermediate, Guadalajara. In Galicia, poverty risk´s lowest corresponds to Pontevedra, intermediate to Lugo and highest to Orense. In Castilla y León case, intermediate position is for Valladolid, most favourable for Avila and most unfavourable for Leon. For Valencian Community, Torrevieja (poverty risk's highes), Elche (lowest) and Alicante (medium) stand out. Finally, Catalonia region is characterised by Castelldefels' privileged situation, Barcelona's unfavourable situation and Lerida's intermediate situation.

All Spanish municipalities analysis highlights the following facts. Firstly, a relative concentration of populations with the poverty risk's highest in the Spain's northern territories: Gijon (first place in both indicators), León (second), Salamanca (3rd), Orense (fourth position), Santander (5th. place), Cádiz (6th.), Valladolid (7th.), Zamora (8th.), Corunna (9th. place), Oviedo (10th.), Lugo (11th.), Ponferrada (12th. and 16th.), Granada (13th. and 12th.), Barcelona (14th. and 19th.) and Santa Cruz de Tenerife (15th. and 14th.).

Second, poverty risk's lowest cities appear to be in coastal areas: Melilla has the best position (57th. place for both indicators), followed by Ceuta (56th.), Benalmadena (53rd.), Marbella (54th.), Toledo (52nd.), Murcia (55th.), Elche (52nd. and 51st.), El Puerto de Santa María (50th. and 49th.), Castelldefels (48th. and 50th.), Torremolinos (46th.) and Badajoz (47th.).

Finally, we comment on the most notable changes in Spanish localities positions in 2015. Changes most negative (or less favourable), which imply moving from a situation where there is no poverty risk to one where there is, are observed in the following cases: Barcelona (ranked 55th. in income and 14th. in MPI1 and 19th. in MPI2), Santiago de Compostela (51st., 12th. and 13th.), Oviedo (44th. and 10th.), Santander (from 43rd. to 5th. in MPI1 and MPI2), Coruña (42nd. and 9th.) and Valladolid (40th. and 7th.). Positive changes occur in the following cities: Benalmadena (4 in income; 53 in multidimensional), Elche (5; 52 and 51), Torremolinos (6; 46), Jerez de la Frontera (7; 49 and 48), Marbella (9; 54), Almería (10; 44 and 43) and El Puerto de Santa María (15; 50 and 49).

Choice of the Municipal Poverty Index-Urban Audit (MPI-UA)

Table 1 has revealed several things. Firstly, the existence of an almost absolute coincidence between MPI1 and/or MPI2 results. Secondly, that the inclusion of several dimensions in the municipal poverty index significantly influences Spanish municipalities situation in terms of their poverty level.

Poverty's academic literature has demonstrated clealy that multidimensional indicators (i.e., those that incorporate several dimensions made up of various elements and with differentiated weights) measure poverty risk with greater reliability and validity, both at individual and collective level. Therefore, of the three municipal poverty indicators analysed in this paper, we must first discard the unidimensional indicator, which only considers income level.

After unidimensional index deletion, it remains to be determined which of two multidimensional constructs is more appropriate. To do so, we have resorted to both constructs' reliability and validity

Table 1. Results of the poverty rates by autonomous community and municipality (2015)

CC. AA.	LOCALITY	ONE-DIMENSIONAL	ORDER	IPM1	ORDER	IPM2	ORDER
SPAIN	**SPAIN**	**100**	**16**	**12.52**	**27**	**15.72**	**27**
MURCIA	Cartagena	102.88	22	25.07	45	28.37	45
	Murcia	108.42	33	31.03	55	34.52	55
GALICIA	Coruña	115.53	42	-2.28	9	1.38	9
	Lugo	101.86	19	1.02	11	4.26	11
	Orense	101.10	18	-9.53	4	-6.34	4
	Pontevedra	107.30	31	9.02	22	12.44	23
	Santiago de Compostela	124.19	51	1.60	12	5.54	13
	Vigo	116.26	45	4.68	17	8.38	17
RIOJA	Logroño	111.29	38	8.84	21	12.39	22
CASTILLA LA MANCHA	Albacete	106.65	28	24.60	43	28.02	44
	Ciudad Real	114.59	41	12.89	29	16.54	29
	Cuenca	107.01	30	4.73	18	8.14	16
	Guadalajara	117.11	47	19.17	40	22.92	40
	Toledo	127.54	52	28.20	51	32.29	52
CANARY ISLANDS	Palmas de Gran Canaria, Las	109.27	34	7.14	20	10.62	20
	Santa Cruz de Tenerife	103.06	23	4.38	15	7.67	14
BALEARIC	Palma (de Mallorca)	120.59	50	22.56	42	26.43	42
EXTREMADURA	Badajoz	103.81	24	26.41	47	29.75	47
	Cáceres	106.77	29	18.64	39	22.05	39
CASTILLA Y LEÓN	Avila	102.03	21	16.68	37	19.94	37
	Burgos	116.39	46	10.31	25	14.03	26
	León	109.83	36	-13.78	2	-10.31	2
	Ponferrada	97.32	12	4.58	16	7.69	15
	Salamanca	100.82	17	-10.61	3	-7.42	3
	Valladolid	113.15	40	-3.36	7	0.23	7
	Zamora	97.55	13	-2.50	8	0.60	8
CATALONIA	Barcelona	136.47	55	4.27	14	8.62	19
	Castelldefels	147.05	57	26.70	48	31.42	50
	Lérida/Lleida	110.19	37	18.17	38	21.70	38
	Tarragona	119.96	49	20.17	41	24.01	41
VALENCIAN COMMUNITY	Alicante/Alacant	98.38	14	14.04	33	17.18	31
	Benidorm	78.56	2	10.43	26	12.94	24
	Castellón de la Plana/ Castelló de la Plana	103.81	25	13.89	32	17.21	32
	Elche/Elx	83.34	5	28.92	52	31.60	51
	Gandía	88.86	8	16.33	36	19.18	36
	Torrevieja	64.82	1	9.07	23	11.14	21
	Valencia	112.18	39	4.86	19	8.44	18
CANTABRIA	Santander	115.75	43	-9.05	5	-5.38	5

continued on following page

Table 1. Continued

CC. AA.	LOCALITY	ONE-DIMENSIONAL	ORDER	IPM1	ORDER	IPM2	ORDER
ASTURIAS	Gijón	106.32	27	-15.29	1	-11.92	1
	Oviedo	116.18	44	-0.85	10	2.85	10
MADRID	Madrid	144.18	56	13.18	30	17.78	34
ARAGON	Zaragoza	117.41	48	9.70	24	13.45	25
CEUTA	Ceuta	133.10	54	49.31	56	53.61	56
MELILLA	Melilla	131.67	53	71.50	57	75.79	57
ANDALUSIA	Almería	96.77	10	24.78	44	27.88	43
	Benalmádena	82.25	4	29.89	53	32.53	53
	Cádiz	109.79	35	-4.56	6	-1.04	6
	Córdoba	101.92	20	13.58	31	16.82	30
	Fuengirola	78.73	3	14.87	35	17.38	33
	Granada	105.89	26	1.93	13	5.29	12
	Jerez de la Frontera	87.58	7	27.58	49	30.39	48
	Málaga	96.98	11	14.69	34	17.79	35
	Marbella	89.51	9	30.74	54	33.62	54
	Puerto de Santa María, El	99.00	15	27.98	50	31.15	49
	Sevilla	107.94	32	12.79	28	16.23	28
	Torremolinos	86.89	6	26.32	46	29.11	46

analysis provided by PLS method. Specifically, we will compare for both indicators two reliability measures (composite reliability and rho A) and average variance extracted (AVE).

Results are given in Table 2 and show that MPI1 is better than MPI2, as it meets both criteria: reliability measure must be equal to or greater than 0.707 and average variance extracted has to be equal to or greater than 0.5. Table data indicate that MPI1 is valid and reliable and MPI2 is reliable, but not valid.

Another fact to consider that favours MPI1 over MPI2 is each index's number of dimensions. For MPI2 there are 4 (income, health, education and employment) while for MPI1 there are only three: employment, health and education. In other words, MPI1 is also more parsimonious than MPI2. Therefore, we chose a new poverty risk index at municipal level. We call this index Municipal Poverty Indicator-Urban Audit (MPI-UA), which is made up of dimensions and indicators shown in Chart 1, where are also included weights of each element and dimension.

Table 2. Multidimensional poverty constructs reliability and discriminant validity

CONSTRUCT	RELIABILITY		CONSTRUCT VALIDITY
	Composed	Rho A	Average variance extracted (AVE)
MPI1	0.659	0.836	0.513
MPI2	0.503	0.833	0.401

Table 3. Municipal Poverty Indicator-Urban Audit (MPI-UA) and its composition.

DIMENSION	DIMENSION WEIGHT	ELEMENT	ELEMENT WEIGHT
EDUCATION	-0.275	Proportion of 0–4-year-olds in childcare as a percentage of the 0–4-year-old population (percentage)	1
HEALTH	0.872	Birth rate (percentage)	0.529
		Mortality rate (complement to 100)	0.576
EMPLOYMENT	-0.154	Activity rate (percentage)	0.250
		Share of employed 20–64-year-olds in the labour force (%)	0.859
		Share of employment in services	0.372

Analysis of MPI-UA Longitudinal Evolution

In this section we present and comment MPI-UA evolution during time lapse analysed (2011, 2012, 2014 and 2015).

The results are presented by dividing the information into different sets and taking the situation in 2015 as a starting point. The data are presented as percentage variation of the MPI-UA of each population and each period with respect to the corresponding national average.

We start with cities that reach negative values in 2015 MPI-UA and, therefore, clearly they are below national average. As **Figure 1** shows, there are ten localities that show indicator's negative values for all the years studied. On the other hand, it should be noted that, in all cases, the distances from the national average tend to be greater in 2014 and 2015. As already noted in 2015 analysis, most of municipalities in this group are located in the country northwest: Gijón, Orense, Santander, Coruña and Oviedo. Next

Figure 1. Municipalities with negative UA-MPI values (2011-2015).

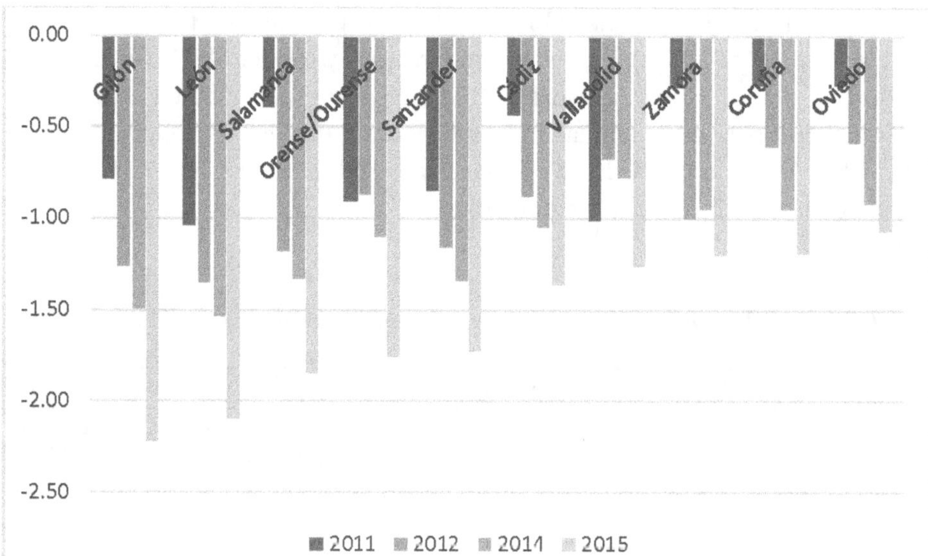

to them are Castilla y Leon's towns, such as León, Salamanca, Valladolid and Zamora. This trend only exception is Cádiz, located in the south of Spain and belonging to Andalusia.

Table 4 provides information about 2015 MPI-UA's municipalities that have a value up to 30% below national average. Data show that four of the five localities reach values below national average in all years. Logroño is the only exception, so that in 2012 and 2014 achieved lower poverty risk scores than national average. Furthermore, in these towns there is a reduction over time in the distance that separates them from the indicator at the national level, especially relevant in Benidorm and Zaragoza. Once again, except for Benidorm, this group's cities are located in country northern part: in addition to the aforementioned municipalities, we find Pontevedra and Burgos.

Figure 2 shows data for cities that in 2015 obtained positive MPI-UA values, but with negative differences respect to national average of 40% or more. Firstly, all the cities included obtain results with negative differences in all years, ranging from 17% for Ponferrada (and in 2011) to 92% for Lugo (year 2015). Secondly, the nine localities included in the figure are geographically distributed with a greater dispersion than in previous cases. Thus, together with the two Canary Islands towns (Santa Cruz de Tenerife and Las Palmas de Gran Canarias), we find 3 municipalities of Galicia (Lugo, Santiago de Compostela and Vigo), Ponferrada (Castilla y León) as well as Valencia, Barcelona and Granada.

Municipalities with MPI-UA values above national average have been divided into two groups. On the one hand, those who have achieved values below twice national average in 2015 -i.e., up to 99% above national average- (see Table 5). This group includes many Andalusian cities (Seville, Cordoba, Malaga, Fuengirola and Almeria), two Valencian Community towns (Alicante and Castellón de la Plana), Ciudad Real, the Spanish capital (Madrid), among others. A notorious case is Almería, which in the last three periods shows the greatest difference with respect to the Spanish average.

Finally, Figure 3 shows data for towns with a 2015 MPI-UA that at least doubles the national index. Firstly, there is only one municipality that achieves values above the Spanish average in all the years: Cartagena. Secondly, the two autonomous cities (Ceuta and Melilla) are the only ones that during 3 years obtain values that double national value. Other cities included in this figure are: Marbella, El Puerto de Santa María, Jerez de la Frontera and Torremolinos (Andaluian towns); Murcia Community cities (Cartagena and Murcia), Toledo, Castelldefels and Badajoz.

FINAL CONSIDERATIONS

In this section we highlight conclusions, implications, limitations and future lines of research.

Table 4. Municipalities with MPI-UA values positive and up to 30% below the national average (2011-2015).

Locality	2011	2012	2014	2015
Logroño	-0.27	0.17	0.06	-0.29
Pontevedra	-0.39	-0.13	-0.31	-0.28
Zaragoza	-0.51	-0.26	-0.29	-0.23
Burgos	-0.36	-0.11	-0.21	-0.18
Benidorm	-0.93	-0.49	-0.15	-0.17

These are the most relevant conclusions of this research. First, we propose the MPI-UA index (see Table 2), which measures the multidimensional poverty risk of Spanish municipalities with more than 20,000 inhabitants.

Secondly, in order to calculate the municipal multidimensional poverty risk, the counting approach has been considered and applied according to the following guidelines. First, dimensions and their respective indicators choice has been based on two main criteria: they are covered in scientific literature, and dimensions and/or indicators data exist in INE's Urban Audit database. Second, dimensions and/or indicators weighting has been data-driven (Pasha, 2017) and has resulted in different weightings across dimensions and indicators. Third, the MPI-UA index is calculated as the weighted sum of the values of each indicator and each dimension for each municipality. Fourth, municipal at-risk-of-poverty threshold is established based on the national MPI-UA. Fifth, to calculate each municipality's multidimensional poverty risk, each municipality's MPI-UA is compared with the threshold.

Thirdly, among MPI-UA index's characteristics we highlight the following: it is made up of three dimensions (education, health and employment) and six quantitative indicators (percentage of the population under 4 years of age who are enrolled in day care centers, birth rate, difference to 100 of mortality rate, activity rate, percentage of employed over active population, and percentage of employment in the service sector); and it is an "orthodox" multidimensional poverty indicator as it considers only dimensions and/or indicators of multidimensional poverty (health, education and employment).

Figure 3. Spanish municipalities with MPI-UA values 30% or more higher than in Spain (2011-2015).

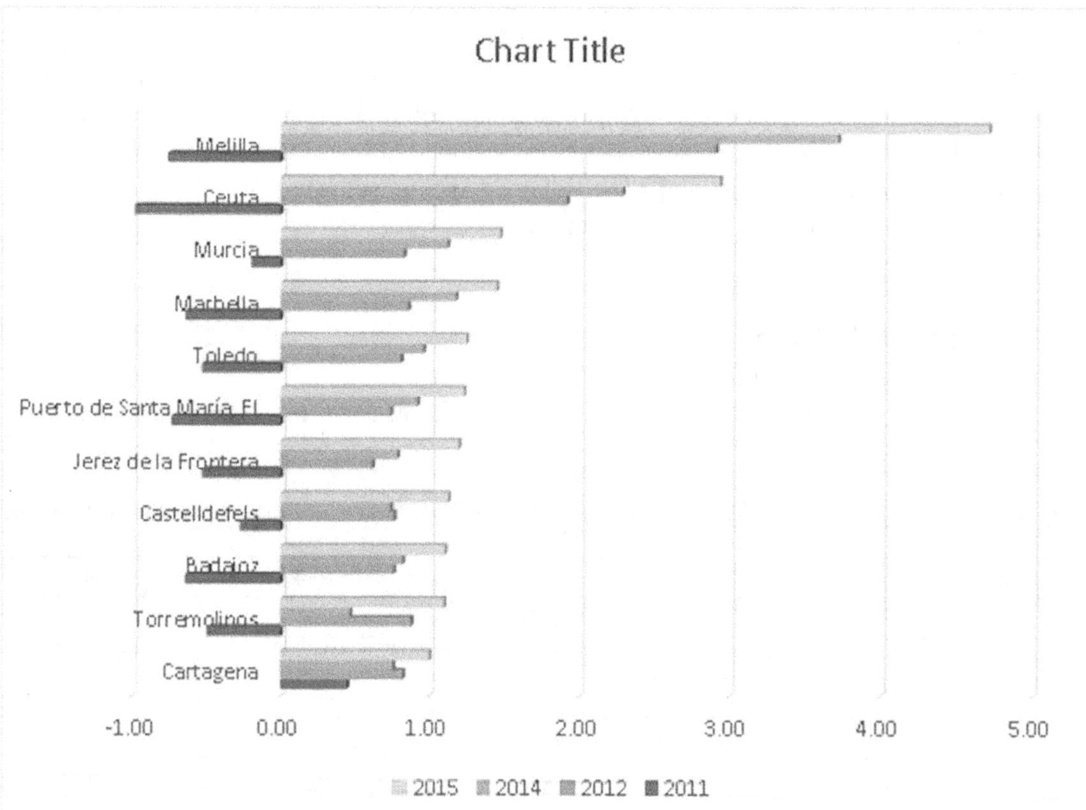

Figure 2. Spanish local authorities with positive MPI-UA values and 40% or more below national average (2011-2015).

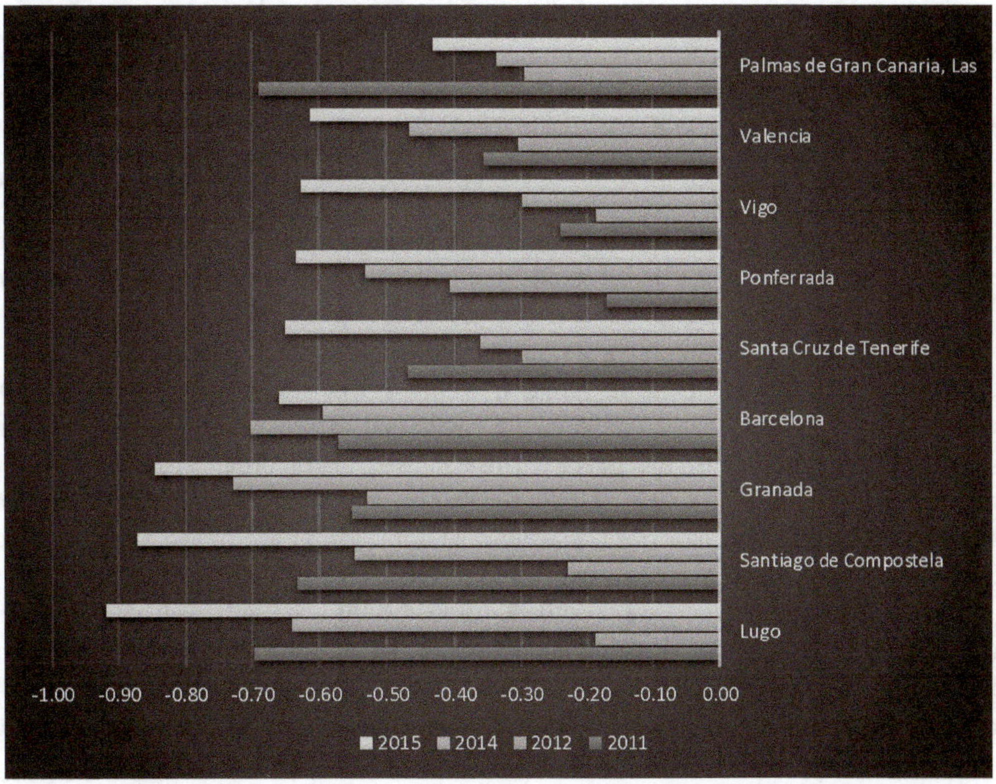

Table 5. Localities with MPI-UA values up to 99% above national average (2011-2015).

Locality	2011	2012	2014	2015
Seville	-0.55	-0.04	0.10	0.02
Ciudad Real	-1.00	0.32	0.13	0.03
Madrid	-0.74	0.00	0.03	0.05
Córdoba	-0.60	0.03	0.28	0.08
Castellón de la Plana/Castelló de la Plana	-0.82	0.36	0.20	0.11
Alicante/Alacant	-0.67	0.01	-0.07	0.12
Málaga	-0.66	0.22	0.19	0.17
Fuengirola	-0.22	0.30	0.27	0.19
Cáceres	-0.35	0.45	0.51	0.49
Tarragona	-0.66	0.53	0.65	0.61
Palma (de Mallorca)	-0.70	0.40	0.54	0.80
Albacete	-0.48	0.52	0.52	0.96
Almería	-0.74	0.55	0.98	0.98

Fourthly, the MPI-UA index fulfils at least five of the six properties that an indicator measuring multidimensional poverty should have according to Najera & Gordon (2020): it is, as can be seen in Table 2, a valid and reliable indicator; it is parsimonious, as it is made up of seven indicators, a figure far removed from the 44 indicators estimated on average by Asselin (2009); it is, as shown in the discussion of the results, invariant in its measurement and susceptible to being addictive.

In the fifth place, the municipalities with the highest risk of poverty, as the proposed MPI-UA values are below national average, are: Gijon, Orense, Santander, Coruña, Oviedo and Cádiz. Geographically, these municipalities are mostly concentrated in the northwest coast of Spain, except for Cadiz.

In sixth place, the municipalities with the lowest risk of poverty (MPI-UA values clearly above national average) are: Ceuta, Melilla, Marbella, El Puerto de Santa María, Jerez de la Frontera, Torremolinos, Cartagena, Murcia, Toledo, Castelldefels and Badajoz. These municipalities belong to autonomous communities bordering the Mediterranean Sea, except in Badajoz and Toledo's cases.

The main theoretical implication is the proposal of the MPI-UA (Municipal Poverty Index), which uses a solid scientific basis and which, consequently, can be considered by those researchers who intend to measure municipal multidimensional poverty. This addresses an important weakness in the literature on poverty in Spain, as there is no known indicator that measures municipal poverty from a multidimensional perspective; the indicator that is usually used to measure poverty in Spain and in Europe is AROPE, which measures the risk of poverty or social exclusion of its citizens.

Regarding empirical implications, we stress that in order to reduce the municipal poverty risk in Spain, the participation of various interest groups, including academics, public policy makers and private sector managers, is deemed necessary. The academic world should be more sensitive and assume a greater commitment to the generation of knowledge on poverty in Spain; with proposals for valid, reliable and parsimonious multidimensional poverty indicators, which allow for the identification of people at risk of poverty. Furthermore, the academy should provide descriptive, explanatory and predictive conceptual models on the poverty situation in Spanish municipalities.

On the other hand, policy makers must allocate resources to generate such knowledge, as well as design, implement and evaluate policies to reduce municipal poverty that go beyond the transfer of financial resources to the population at risk of poverty.

In the same manner, private sector must adopt a management model oriented towards Sustainable Development and focus its attention as a priority on SDG 1 "End poverty in all its forms everywhere". This will not be possible without partnerships between the stakeholders and the population at risk of poverty.

The limitations of the research can be categorised into two main groups: those inherent to collection of information and those derived from the process of calculating the municipal multidimensional poverty index.

Data collection limitations are the following. Firstly, the Urban Audit database is not designed to measure multidimensional poverty risk, as it collects information on living conditions in the main cities of the European Union and candidate countries; in this respect, Salecker, Ahmadov & Karimli (2020) state that multidimensional poverty measurement is often based on available information. Second, input for all indicators is not available for all years, which has made it necessary to consider only four years; in this regard, Alkire, Roche & Vaz (2017) note that like any other poverty measure, it has limited and imperfect records. Third, sample does not include all Spanish municipalities; only those with more than 20,000 inhabitants. Fourth, data are presented at municipal level; they are not disaggregated at neighbourhood, district, household or individual level. Fifth, information only refers to Spanish municipalities. And sixth, the most recent data available is from the year 2015.

Limitations derived from the process of calculating the municipal multidimensional poverty indicator are detailed below. Firstly, the MPI-UA does not include all the dimensions that can measure poverty, it only includes those included in the Urban Audit database; nor does it consider the ideal indicators. Secondly, although it has avoided weighting each dimension and indicator equally, dimensions and indicators' weighting, based on data analysis, can be questioned. Thirdly, the fact that the threshold that decides which municipalities are at risk of poverty is defined based on national input can also be questioned.

Despite these limitations, this exploratory research is considered to be the first step for a series of research to be developed in the future. Along these lines, we agree with Salecker, Ahmadov & Karimli (2020) that more research is needed on how to measure poverty, emphasising poverty's most extreme forms (Catalán, Fifita & Faingaanuku, 2019), chronic poverty (Thorat, Vanneman, Desai & Dubey, 2017) or rural poverty (Silva, Bruno, Silva & Nascimento, 2020).

Although, like Liu & Xu (2016), we recognise the difficulty in accessing the necessary information, future research will focus on overcoming these limitations. To this end, first, it will obtain information from all Spanish municipalities from various sources: panel data (Gallardo, 2020; Portales, 2019; Ogutu, Ochieng & Qaim, 2020; Alkire, Apablaza, Chakravarty & Yalonetzky; 2017); Big Data (Wang, Gan, Chen & Voda; 2020) or participatory and deliberative processes (Alkire & Foster, 2011); among other sources. Secondly, it will have a longitudinal character (Thorat, Vanneman, Desai & Dubey, 2017; Wang, Gan, Chen, & Voda, 2020; Santos & Villatoro; 2020), which will allow for the continuous revision and updating of the MPI-UA index. And third, in addition to measuring multidimensional poverty with the MPI-UA index, poverty's intensity and depth will be measured to provide more precise analyses, which are useful for public policies design (Alkire, Oldiges & Kanagaratnam, 2021).

Future research will also solve the technical problems of the construction of the MPI-UA index, according to the following guidelines. First, in line with Mitra, Posarac & Vick (2013) and Loaiza, Muñetón & Vanegas (2018), a sensitivity analysis of the MPI-UA will be conducted for different thresholds or cut-off lines. Second, the scope of the MPI-UA index will be extended beyond its basic dimensions (Salecker, Ahmadov & Karimli, 2020); since ignoring some dimensions may bias the evolution of poverty (Datt, 2019). Third, the relationship between dimensions will be assessed; since, as Ferreira & Lugo (2013) point out, the most interesting aspects of the multidimensionality of poverty arise from the interdependence between dimensions. Fourth, different definitions and combinations of indicators will be used (Alkire, Oldiges & Kanagaratnam, 2021). And fifth and finally, in line with Alkire & Seth (2016), the weights of the dimensions will be permitted to vary.

REFERENCES

Alkire, S., Chatterjee, M., Conconi, A., Seth, S. & Vaz, A. (2014). *Global multidimensional poverty index 2014*. Academic Press.

Alkire, S., & Foster, J. (2011). Counting and multidimensional poverty measurement. *Journal of Public Economics*, *95*(7), 476–487. doi:10.1016/j.jpubeco.2010.11.006

Alkire, S., Oldiges, C., & Kanagaratnam, U. (2021). Examining multidimensional poverty reduction in India 2005/6–2015/16: Insights and oversights of the headcount ratio. *World Development*, *142*, 105454. doi:10.1016/j.worlddev.2021.105454

Alkire, S., Roche, J. M., & Vaz, A. (2017). Changes over time in multidimensional poverty: Methodology and results for 34 countries. *World Development, 94*, 232–249. doi:10.1016/j.worlddev.2017.01.011

Alkire, S., & Santos, M. E. (2011). Acute Multidimensional Poverty: A New Index for Developing Countries. *Proceedings of the German Development Economics Conference, Berlin 2011, No. 3, ZBW - Deutsche Zentralbibliothek für Wirtschaftswissenschaften.* Leibniz-Informationszentrum Wirtschaft, Kiel und Hamburg.

Alkire, S., & Santos, M. E. (2013). A multidimensional approach: Poverty measurement & beyond. *Social Indicators Research, 112*(2), 239–257. doi:10.100711205-013-0257-3

Alkire, S., & Seth, S. (2015). Multidimensional poverty reduction in India between 1999 and 2006: Where and how? *World Development, 72*, 93–108. doi:10.1016/j.worlddev.2015.02.009

Alkire, S., & Seth, S. (2016). *Identifying destitution through linked subsets of multidimensionally poor: An ordinal approach.* OPHI Working Paper 99. University of Oxford.

Ambel, A. A., Mugera, H. K., & Bain, R. E. (2020). Accounting for drinking water quality in measuring multidimensional poverty in Ethiopia. *PLoS One, 15*(12), e0243921. doi:10.1371/journal.pone.0243921 PMID:33320919

Ari, I. R. D., Hariyani, S., & Waloejo, B. S. (2019, October). Neighbourhood Relationship among Villages in Gedangan District: Multidimensional Poverty Approach. *IOP Conference Series. Earth and Environmental Science, 328*(1), 012043. doi:10.1088/1755-1315/328/1/012043

Aslam, M., Kumar, S., & Sorooshian, S. (2019). Social Versus Financial Performance of Microfinance: Bangladesh Perspective. *Review of World Economics, 10*(3), 263–272.

Asselin, L. M. (2009). *Analysis of multidimensional poverty: Theory and case studies* (Vol. 7). Springer Science & Business Media. doi:10.1007/978-1-4419-0843-8

Bakar, A. A., Hamdan, R., & Sani, N. S. (2020). Ensemble Learning for Multidimensional Poverty Classification [Pembelajaran Ensembel untuk Pengelasan Kemiskinan Pelbagai Dimensi]. *Sains Malaysiana, 49*(2), 447–459. doi:10.17576/jsm-2020-4902-24

Bérenger, V. (2019). The counting approach to multidimensional poverty. The case of four African countries. *The South African Journal of Economics, 87*(2), 200–227. doi:10.1111aje.12217

Bersisa, M., & Heshmati, A. (2021). A Distributional Analysis of Uni-and Multidimensional Poverty and Inequalities in Ethiopia. *Social Indicators Research, 155*(3), 1–31. doi:10.100711205-021-02606-w

Biswal, S. N., Mishra, S. K. & Sarangi, M. K. (2020). Feminization of multidimensional poverty in rural Odisha. *Rupkatha Journal on Interdisciplinary Studies in Humanities, 12*(5).

Bourguignon, F., & Chakravarty, S. R. (2003). The measurement of multidimensional poverty. *The Journal of Economic Inequality, 1*(1), 25–49. doi:10.1023/A:1023913831342

Catalán, H. E. N., Fifita, V. K., & Faingaanuku, W. (2019). Small-Area Multidimensional Poverty Estimates for Tonga 2016: Drawn from a Hierarchical Bayesian Estimator. *Applied Spatial Analysis and Policy*, 1–24.

Ciani, M., Gagliardi, F., Riccarelli, S., & Betti, G. (2019). Fuzzy measures of multidimensional poverty in the Mediterranean Area: A focus on financial dimension. *Sustainability*, *11*(1), 143. doi:10.3390u11010143

Codes, L. (2008). A trajetória do pensamento científico sobre a pobreza: em direção a uma visão complexa. Brasília, DF: Ipea.

Datt, G. (2019). Distribution-sensitive multidimensional poverty measures. *The World Bank Economic Review*, *33*(3), 551–572. doi:10.1093/wber/lhx017

Decancq, K., & Lugo, M. A. (2008). *Setting weights in multidimensional indices of well-being*. Oxford Poverty & Human Development Initiative OPHI Working Paper 18.

Deutsch, J., & Silber, J. (2005). Measuring multidimensional poverty: An empirical comparison of various approaches. *Review of Income and Wealth*, *51*(1), 145–174. doi:10.1111/j.1475-4991.2005.00148.x

Duclos, J. Y., Sahn, D. E., & Younger, S. D. (2006). Robust multidimensional poverty comparisons. *Economic Journal (London)*, *116*(514), 943–968. doi:10.1111/j.1468-0297.2006.01118.x

Ferreira, F. H., & Lugo, M. A. (2013). Multidimensional poverty analysis: Looking for a middle ground. *The World Bank Research Observer*, *28*(2), 220–235. doi:10.1093/wbro/lks013

Foster, J., Greer, J., & Thorbecke, E. (1984). A class of decomposable poverty measures. *Econometrica*, *52*(3), 761–766. doi:10.2307/1913475

Fosu, A. K. (2017). Growth, inequality, and poverty reduction in developing countries: Recent global evidence. *Research in Economics*, *71*(2), 306–336. doi:10.1016/j.rie.2016.05.005

Gallardo, M. (2020). Measuring vulnerability to multidimensional poverty. *Social Indicators Research*, *148*(1), 67–103. doi:10.100711205-019-02192-y

Galvez, M. O., Valdés, B. C., & Castillo, V. P. (2019). Pobreza y autopercepción de salud: Contraste entre pobreza multidimensional y pobreza por ingresos. *Atencion Primaria*, *51*(8), 513–514. doi:10.1016/j.aprim.2018.07.013 PMID:30992153

Gentilini, U., & Sumner, A. (2012). What do national poverty lines tell us about global poverty? *IDS Working Papers*, *2012*(392), 1-48.

Gong, Z., Kong, Q., & Tan, J. (2020). Analysis on multidimensional poverty reduction of industrial structure upgrading based on provincial panel data and spatial Durbin model. *International Journal of Sustainable Development and Planning*, *15*(8), 1197–1204. doi:10.18280/ijsdp.150806

Habtewold, T. M. (2021). Impact of climate-smart agricultural technology on multidimensional poverty in rural Ethiopia. *Journal of Integrative Agriculture*, *20*(4), 1021–1041. doi:10.1016/S2095-3119(21)63637-7

Ignacio-González, F. A., & Santos, M. E. (2020). Multidimensional poverty in urban Argentina: Reduction of disparities between the Norte Grande Argentino and Centro-Cuyo-Sur? (2003-2016). *Cuadernos de Economía (Santiago, Chile)*, *39*(81), 795–822. doi:10.15446/cuad.econ.v39n81.76486

Jindra, C., & Vaz, A. (2019). Good governance and multidimensional poverty: A comparative analysis of 71 countries. *Governance: An International Journal of Policy, Administration and Institutions*, *32*(4), 657–675. doi:10.1111/gove.12394

Lanau, A., Mack, J., & Nandy, S. (2020). Including services in multidimensional poverty measurement for SDGs: Modifications to the consensual approach. *The Journal of Poverty and Social Justice: Research, Policy, Practice*, *28*(2), 149–168. doi:10.1332/175982720X15850580703755

Leu, C. H., Chen, K. M., & Chen, H. H. (2016). A multidimensional approach to child poverty in Taiwan. *Children and Youth Services Review*, *66*, 35–44. doi:10.1016/j.childyouth.2016.04.018

Liu, Y., & Xu, Y. (2016). A geographic identification of multidimensional poverty in rural China under the framework of sustainable livelihoods analysis. *Applied Geography (Sevenoaks, England)*, *73*, 62–76. doi:10.1016/j.apgeog.2016.06.004

Loaiza Quintero, O. L., Muñetón Santa, G., & Vanegas López, J. G. (2018). An exploratory assessment of the relationship between multidimensional poverty and armed conflict: The case of Antioquia, Colombia. *Desarrollo y Sociedad*, (80), 11–51. doi:10.13043/DYS.80.1

Mahrt, K., Rossi, A., Salvucci, V., & Tarp, F. (2020). Multidimensional poverty of children in Mozambique. *Child Indicators Research*, *13*(5), 1675–1700. doi:10.100712187-019-09696-6

Maqueda, A. (2021). *La pandemia elevó la pobreza en 2020 al mayor nivel desde la Gran Recesión.* Disponible en https://elpais.com/economia/2021-07-15/la-pandemia-elevo-la-pobreza-en-2020-al-mayor-nivel-desde-la-gran-recesion.html

Mideros, A. (2012). Ecuador: definición y medición multidimensional de la pobreza, 2006-2010. *Revista Cepal*.

Mora, C., Yahevh, O., Villafuerte, L. F., & Sinforoso Martinez, S. (2020). Factors Derived from Multidimensional Poverty That Affect the Usability of E-Government in Mexico. *Braz. J. Pub. Pol'y*, *10*, 69.

Nájera Catalán, H. E., & Gordon, D. (2020). The importance of reliability and construct validity in multidimensional poverty measurement: An illustration using the multidimensional poverty index for Latin America (MPI-LA). *The Journal of Development Studies*, *56*(9), 1763–1783. doi:10.1080/00220388.2019.1663176

Ogutu, S. O., Ochieng, D. O., & Qaim, M. (2020). Supermarket contracts and smallholder farmers: Implications for income and multidimensional poverty. *Food Policy*, *95*, 101940. doi:10.1016/j.foodpol.2020.101940

Pasha, A. (2017). Regional perspectives on the multidimensional poverty index. *World Development*, *94*, 268–285. doi:10.1016/j.worlddev.2017.01.013

Pinilla-Roncancio, M., Mactaggart, I., Kuper, H., Dionicio, C., Naber, J., Murthy, G. V. S., & Polack, S. (2020). Multidimensional poverty and disability: A case control study in India, Cameroon, and Guatemala. *SSM - Population Health*, *11*, 100591. doi:10.1016/j.ssmph.2020.100591 PMID:32405529

Ponce, M. G. (2018). Medición de pobreza multidimensional de la iniciativa en pobreza y desarrollo humano. *Revista de Ciencias Sociales*, *24*, 98–113.

Portales, L. (2019). Reducción de la pobreza multidimensional y fortalecimiento de la inclusión social a través de un programa municipal El caso de la evaluación de impacto del programa «Un Solo San Pedro». *Revista Iberoamericana de Estudios de Desarrollo*, *8*(2), 108–139. doi:10.26754/ojs_ried/ijds.327

Ramírez, J. M., Díaz, Y., & Bedoya, J. G. (2017). Property tax revenues and multidimensional poverty reduction in Colombia: A spatial approach. *World Development*, *94*, 406–421. doi:10.1016/j.worlddev.2017.02.005

Ravallion, M. (2011). Mashup indices of development. *The World Bank Research Observer*, *27*(1), 1–32. doi:10.1093/wbro/lkr009

Rimoldi, S. M., Arcagni, A., Fattore, M., & di Belgiojoso, E. B. (2020). Targeting policies for multidimensional poverty and social fragility relief among migrants in Italy, using F-FOD analysis. *Social Indicators Research*, 1–19.

Roldán, J. L., & Cepeda, G. (2018). Curso sobre PLS-SEM (6ª ed.) Universidad de Sevilla.

Sachs, J. (2005). *The end of poverty: How we can make it happen in our life time*. Penguin Books.

Salecker, L., Ahmadov, A. K., & Karimli, L. (2020). Contrasting monetary and multidimensional poverty measures in a low-income Sub-Saharan African Country. *Social Indicators Research*, *151*(2), 547–574. doi:10.100711205-020-02382-z

Santos, M. E. (2013). *Measuring multidimensional poverty in Latin America: Previous experience and the way forward.* OPHI Working Paper 66.

Santos, M. E. (2014). *Measuring multidimensional poverty in Latin America: previous experience and the way forward. Oxford Poverty & Human Development Initiative*. OPHI. doi:10.35648/20.500.12413/11781/ii040

Santos, M. E., & Villatoro, P. (2020). The importance of reliability in the multidimensional poverty index for Latin America (MPI-LA). *The Journal of Development Studies*, *56*(9), 1784–1789. doi:10.1080/00220388.2019.1663177

Sanz, R., Peris, J. A., & Escámez, J. (2017). Higher education in the fight against poverty from the capabilities approach: The case of Spain. *Journal of Innovation & Knowledge*, *2*(2), 53–66. doi:10.1016/j.jik.2017.03.002

Sen, A. (1976). Poverty: An ordinal approach to measurement. *Econometrica*, *44*(2), 219–231. doi:10.2307/1912718

Sen, A. (2000). A decade of human development. *Journal of Human Development*, *1*(1), 17–23. doi:10.1080/14649880050008746

Sen, A. (2001). *Desigualdade reexaminada*. Record.

Seth, S., & Alkire, S. (2014). Did poverty reduction reach the poorest of the poor? Assessment methods in the counting approach (No. ophiwp077). Queen Elizabeth House, University of Oxford.

Silva, J. J. D., Bruno, M. A. P., Silva, D. B., & Nascimento, D. (2020). Multidimensional poverty in Brazil: Analysis of the period 2004-2015. *Brazilian Journal of Political Economy*, *40*(1), 138–160. doi:10.1590/0101-31572020-2924

Stiglitz, J. E. (2015). *New theoretical perspectives on the distribution of income and wealth among individuals: Part IV: Land and credit (No. w21192)*. National Bureau of Economic Research.

Sumner, A. (2012). Where do the poor live? *World Development*, *40*(5), 865–877. doi:10.1016/j.worlddev.2011.09.007

Thorat, A., Vanneman, R., Desai, S., & Dubey, A. (2017). Escaping and falling into poverty in India today. *World Development*, *93*, 413–426. doi:10.1016/j.worlddev.2017.01.004 PMID:28966435

Torres Penagos, M. F. (2018). Índice de pobreza multidimensional oculta para la localidad de Teusaquillo (Bogotá): Propuesta metodológica a partir de percepciones ciudadanas. *Cuadernos de Economía (Santiago, Chile)*, *37*(74), 555–588. doi:10.15446/cuad.econ.v37n74.56164

Townsend, P. (1979). *Poverty in the United Kingdom*. Allen Lane and Penguin Books. doi:10.1525/9780520325760

Varela Llamas, R., & Ocegueda Hernández, J. M. (2020). Multidimensional poverty and the labor market in Mexico. *Cuadernos de Economía (Santiago, Chile)*, *39*(79), 139–165.

Voronov, V.V., Ruza, O.P. & Stasane, S. J. (2020). Multidimensional poverty in the Baltic States in the EU context: theoretical and practical aspects. *Baltic Region*, *12*(3).

Wang, K., Gan, C., Chen, L., & Voda, M. (2020). Poor Residents' Perceptions of the Impacts of Tourism on Poverty Alleviation: From the Perspective of Multidimensional Poverty. *Sustainability*, *12*(18), 7515. doi:10.3390u12187515

Yang, Y., & Fu, C. (2019). Inclusive financial development and multidimensional poverty reduction: An empirical assessment from rural China. *Sustainability*, *11*(7), 1900. doi:10.3390u11071900

Zavaleta, D. (2017) *¿Cuáles son las dimensiones y los indicadores más usados por los países en sus IPM nacionales?* Disponible en https://mppn.org/es/what-are-the-dimensions-and-indicators-most-commonly-used-by-countries-in-their-national-mpis/

Chapter 4
Study of Success Factors in Rural Tourism to Promote Local Development in the Most Forgotten Regions

Beatriz Palacios-Florencio
Universidad Pablo de Olavide, Spain

Juan Manuel Berbel-Pineda
Universidad Pablo de Olavide, Spain

Elena García-de-Soto-Camacho
https://orcid.org/0000-0001-7439-7336
Universidad de Huelva, Spain

ABSTRACT

The coronavirus has seriously affected the economy in general and tourism in particular. However, at the same time, it has been a great opportunity for rural tourism, as this type of tourism has been one of the beneficiaries of this health crisis. This is partly explained by the fact that travelers have turned to nature destinations and accommodation that guarantees social distance. Under the premise that tourism is a community product and that it is necessary to count on the community and local capacities, the aim of this research is to find out how the factors that make up the destination management models affect the development of rural tourism in a given region. It also seeks to know their influence on the results of rural accommodation companies in order to promote local development in this state of the pandemic. The work has been carried out with a total of 156 tourist accommodations. A total of eight management factors and five different clusters of companies were detected from the analysis of the dimensionality of the model.

DOI: 10.4018/978-1-7998-8925-0.ch004

INTRODUCTION

The coronavirus has generated significant economic effects. The tourism sector has been particularly affected by the pandemic. According to data from the UNCTAD report (2021), the fall in international tourism derived from the coronavirus could represent a loss of more than 4 trillion dollars in global GDP during the years 2020 and 2021. This report also indicates a 74% decrease in the number of tourist arrivals in 2020 in relation to 2019. However, this unfavorable situation for international tourism in turn represents an opportunity for the development and growth of rural tourism, supported by national travelers and tourists.

Rural areas, because of globalization, have experienced important social and economic changes, which have particularly affected traditional rural industries (such as agriculture and / or forestry). Given this, tourism and its related services appear as a substitution industry for rural communities (Lane, 1994; Ohe. 2020; Xu, Wang, Wu, Liang, Jiao & Nazneen, 2018), becoming an important element or the only engine of growth in many regions that do not have a developed primary or secondary sector. nor with an important offer of the so-called "sun and beach tourism" (Saarinen, 2007).

Under the "community approach" to tourism development, which promulgates that rural tourism development and entrepreneurship cannot function without the participation and collaboration of entrepreneurs directly and indirectly involved in tourism (Murphy 1985; Ohe, 2020), this work analyzes the phenomenon of rural tourism, studying different aspects that can guarantee its correct development (Li-Chan et al., 2013; Correia-Loureiro, 2014), such as the need to undertake in this subsector of the economy (Dias, González-Rodríguez & Patuleia, 2020; Lanfranchi et al. al., 2014), the importance of proper tourism planning (Fotiadis et al., 2016; Healy et al., 2016), the role played by the entrepreneur (Dias, Silva, Patuleia & González-Rodríguez, 2020; Xu, Wang, Wu, Liang, Jiao & Nazneen, 2018; Zampetakis & Kanelakis, 2010) or the importance of accepting the residents for tourism development (Brida et al., 2011).

The challenge posed by the situation created by the coronavirus for rural tourism has led us to present the results of our research on the development of rural tourism in Andalusia (Spain). In this region, although it leads the "sun and beach tourism" (Andalusian Tourism, 2014), rural tourism has become both a complement to it, contributing to reduce its seasonality, and a type of substitute tourism, in addition to be a benchmark in rural tourism in Spain. Therefore, it seems essential to analyze the factors that facilitate the rise of rural tourism in Andalusia and study how its development is being carried out, as it is a reference that can serve for the development of this type of tourism in other regions, both in Spain and in Spain. other countries, especially in local communities with important natural resources and in a situation of poverty.

Therefore, the objective of this work is to examine the characteristics of rural tourism in Andalusia, identifying the existing destination management models in it, as well as the influence that proper destination management has on business results, examining the key factors that contribute to the success of this type of business. And this with the purpose of offering a series of recommendations that may be useful for the development of this type of activity in less developed regions.

It is structured as follows. First, a literature review is made to see what factors determine the correct development of rural tourism. Next, the work methodology carried out is shown and an empirical study is carried out to determine the existing destination management models and make explicit the constitutive factors of such models that affect the development of this type of tourism in Andalusia and in the results achieved by rural accommodation units. Finally, the conclusions, limitations and practical applications of this research will be presented.

CONCEPTUAL FRAMEWORK

The decade of the eighties represents perhaps the starting point for rural tourism. The crisis in the agricultural sector led to a reconsideration of the exploitation of this economic activity. Non-traditional strategies began to be produced for the sustenance of agricultural operations, one of which was tourism, associated with business opportunity (Ohe, 2020; Wilson et al, 1991). Accommodations that combine agricultural and tourist activities entered the tourism market by offering, on a small scale, high-quality accommodation and / or developing specific activities for visitors (Dieguez-Castrillon et al., 2009). This diversifying strategy requires fewer economic resources, being easier to articulate than other development strategies such as, for example, industrial-scale production. It can be developed, in a more domestic environment, with the participation of the local government through small companies, not requiring large foreign firms to invest capital. Tourism can generate significant complementary income for agricultural holdings, in addition to providing benefits both for companies directly related to it (establishments that offer accommodation) and for those indirectly related (gas stations, shops, restaurants, etc.). It should be noted, however, that despite being one of the most viable options for rural communities, disadvantages have also been detected in this type of activity (low wages and seasonal employment, for example). And, although rural tourism is not the only means of revitalizing rural areas, it has undoubtedly become one of the main alternatives for their development, which ensures their future sustainability through preservation and opening up new employment opportunities, increasing the diversity of occupations, conserving the landscape and nature, as well as supporting rural handicrafts and tourist attractions (Helgadóttir & Dashper, 2021; Maksimović et al., 2015).

Like other economic development strategies, rural tourism requires several components to be successful. Tourism development involves (1) attractions: the natural and man-made features both within and adjacent to a rural community; (2) promotion: the commercialization of a rural community and its tourist attractions; (3) tourist infrastructure: access facilities (roads, airports, trains, and buses), water and electricity services, parking, signs, and recreational facilities; (4) services: lodging, restaurants, and various retail businesses necessary to serve the needs of tourists; and (5) hospitality: the way tourists are treated both by residents of the rural community and by employees of tourist businesses and attractions (Gunn, 1988). However, it should be noted that, although the above elements and the assets of a community are important for the development of tourism, only the broad participation and collaboration of rural tourism entrepreneurs can guarantee an adequate basis for the success of tourism development (Ohe, 2020; Wilson et al., 2001).

Thus, the community approach to tourism development and entrepreneurship holds that tourism is a community product and that, together with entrepreneurial skills and the presence of tourism companies, it is also necessary to have the community and local capacities (for example, leadership local and formal and informal networks), which should be directly involved in tourism development and promotion (Murphy 1985). From this perspective, ten groups of factors of vital importance for tourism development in rural areas are identified: (1) a complete tourism package, (2) effective community leadership, (3) support and participation of the local government, (4) sufficient funds for tourism development, (5) strategic planning, (6) coordination and cooperation between entrepreneurs and local leaders, (7) coordination and cooperation between rural tourism entrepreneurs, (8) information and technical assistance for the development and promotion of tourism, (9) information to visitors and organization of conferences and events, and (10) widespread support from the local community (Wilson et al., 2001; Fotiadis et al., 2013, 2016; Villanueva-Álvaro, Mondéjar-Jiménez & Sáez-Martínez, 2017; Dias, González-Rodríguez & Patuleia, 2020; Dias, Silva, Patuleia & González-Rodríguez, 2020).

Therefore, and as indicated in the objective of this work, it is a question of determining which are the factors that motivate to bet on rural tourism (in the specific case of the Andalusian community), as well as the key dimensions of the model of management that affect the relevant business results of the entrepreneurs involved in this economic activity.

METHODOLOGY

In order to analyze the success factors in the development of rural tourism in Andalusia, from the community approach to tourism development, we used a questionnaire based on previous research focused on examining this type of factors, on the destination and destination management model. business effectiveness, which analyzes the following dimensions (Wilson et al., 2001; Fotiadis et al., 2013):

1. Organization of the tourist offer
2. Leadership
3. Local government: support and participation
4. Financing for tourism development
5. Coordination and cooperation between investors and local authorities
6. Strategic planning
7. Coordination and collaboration between tourism entrepreneurs for the activation of the regions
8. Technical assistance and information on tourism development and promotion
9. Support from the local community for tourism development
10. Information to visitors and organization of conferences and events

The target population is made up of all the rural accommodation companies located in the mountain areas of the Andalusian natural parks. The data on these organizations have been obtained from two sources: the website of the Andalusian rural accommodation network and the Toprural website. The choice of these entities has been based on the fact that they have adequate tourism development management models, which, on the other hand, guarantee the success and sustainability of the businesses. The population is made up of 624 rural accommodation tourism companies. Telephone contact was made with the owners and managers of the entities in order to inform them about the research, request the possibility of participating and provide them with the option of completing the survey, online or via email. We obtained a sample of 156 companies, which represents a response rate of 25%.

The questionnaire used contains a total of 81 questions, divided into different sections. The first section focuses on the descriptive elements of the surveyed company. The second focuses on understanding the reasons for engaging in rural tourism, as well as the factors that contribute to the success of rural tourism companies. The third section is made up of questions related to the tour package that is offered to tourists. The fourth part of the questionnaire aims to analyze the dimensions of the target management and business efficiency measurement model. In the last part of the questionnaire, performance variables of the analyzed companies are included: occupancy rate, performance obtained with respect to their competitors and the sector, degree of satisfaction with the results of the establishment, among others. We adopt a five-point Likert scale to assess the sections and the overall satisfaction rates.

The determination of the dimensionality of the destination management and business effectiveness model, previously exposed, has been carried out through an exploratory factor analysis with which factorial extractions of main components with varimax rotation have been carried out and the basic tests of factorial analysis (Kaiser Mayer Olkin, Bartlett's test, determinant of the correlation matrix, Cronbach's alpha and parallel analysis), using the statistical software SPSS version 23. In addition, we carried out the analysis in parallel by Horn (1965) in order to clarify which factors, have to be conserved, using the FACTOR 10.3.01 program.

Finally, based on the dimensions found with the factor analysis, a hierarchical cluster analysis has been performed. This technique has been used in order to identify the existing destination management archetypes in the group of rural Andalusian companies. To ratify this grouping, a discriminant analysis has been used. The determination of statistically significant differences between the conglomerates based on the volume of sales and profitability has been established using the non-parametric Kruskal-Wallis test.

RESULTS

The identification data of the surveyed entities indicate that most of them are rural houses (48.7%) or are included in other categories (32.1%), such as rural apartments. Furthermore, most of the accommodations are small in size (71.8%), with no more than 18 beds in the unit. Almost all accommodations have an annual opening period (93.6%).

Regarding the factors that led entrepreneurs to participate in this type of tourism, respondents stated that their main motivation was the reinforcement of income (53.8%), establishing a main source of income (16.7%), emotional reasons, for example, the family business. tradition (11.5%) and other causes (7.7%).

As can be seen in Table 2, the respondents believe that the quality of the accommodation is the main reason for their success. Other important success factors are the personal ability in the management of the tourist unit and the power of attraction of the offer, based on a great variety of activities and services.

In relation to the dimensionality of the destination management and business effectiveness model, the results of the exploratory factor analysis conclude the existence of eight main factors that explain 71.15% of the total variance, an acceptable value in the social sciences (Hair et al., 2006). Horn's (1965) parallel analysis supports the existence of four explanatory dimensions of 43.47% of the total variance,

Table 1. Data sheet

Sample	156 valid questionnaires (25% response rate)
Questionnaire Dimensions	10 (81 questions)
Measurement Scale	Likert (5 points)
Statistical Techniques	Exploratory Factor Analysis with Principal Component Analysis Hierarchical Cluster Analysis
Statistical Software	SPSS v.23

Source: Own elaboration

Table 2. Main success factors in rural tourism

What are the main reasons for your success?	N	1	2	3	4	5	Average
Personal skills of the entrepreneur in the management of the tourist unit	156	2 (1.3%)	-	16 (10.3%)	64 (41.0%)	74 (47.4%)	4.33
Quality of accommodation (in., Comfort and cleanliness)	156	2 (1.3%)	-	4 (2.6%)	36 (23.1%)	114 (73.1%)	4.67
Attractiveness of the tourist offer (eg, variety of activities and services)	156	2 (1.3%)	4 (2.6%)	8 (5.1%)	82 (52.6%)	60 (38.5%)	4.24
Specialized employee training	156	4 (2.6%)	8 (5.1%)	44 (28.2%)	64 (41.0%)	36 (23.1%)	3.77
Others	156	40 (25.6%)	8 (5.1%)	36 (23.1%)	30 (19.2%)	42 (26.9%)	3.17

so we opted to keep the eight dimensions obtained with the exploratory factor analysis, which yields greater explanatory power than the analysis parallel. The dimensions identified and the elements that make them up are offered in Table 2.

Based on the eight factors or dimensions that make up the tourist destination management model, a hierarchical cluster analysis has been carried out, using the squared Euclidean distance as a measure of dissimilarity and Ward's method as a conglomeration method. The technique has made it possible to identify five clearly differentiated management archetypes within the group of companies analyzed. In the process, two observations representing isolated groups have been eliminated in order to improve the results and their interpretation. The discriminant analysis technique applied to the 5 clusters detected allowed to ratify the grouping obtained, since all the cases were correctly classified. Table 3 shows the standardized values obtained in each dimension for each cluster and the number of companies included (in parentheses). Based on these results, the characteristics for each of the identified clusters are set out below in order to try to describe and explain the corresponding destination management model.

The first conglomerate, identified with the number 1, is the most numerous, with a total of seventy companies (45% of the total). This group of companies presents relatively unremarkable standardized values in seven of the eight dimensions. The defining characteristic of this group is its negative score (-0.8154) corresponding to dimension 5: "Coordination and collaboration between tourism entrepreneurs for the activation of the regions". It is also the only group with a negative score in this dimension. So we can affirm that this conglomerate is characterized by a "low business associationism" for the development and promotion of tourism.

Cluster two, made up of twenty-six companies, stands out for the high scores achieved in dimensions 2 ("Leadership" with the highest value of the 5 clusters: 1.1488) and 7 ("Support from the local community for tourism development", Also with the highest score: 0.905). In addition, it is a group of companies with the lowest values in dimensions 3 ("Local government: support and participation") and 6 ("Technical assistance and information on tourism development and promotion"). We are, therefore, with a model characterized by active leadership, where it is perceived that leaders understand the im-

Table 3. Exploratory Factor Analysis Dimensions

Dimensions	Variable encoding	Description of the destination management and business efficiency variable
1. Organization of the tourist offer	ORGOFER1	Institutions invest in the development of tourist sites in order to make them more attractive to visitors
	ORGOFER2	Our tourist offer involves the local community, the region and the investors and entrepreneurs who collaborate in planning it.
	ORGOFER3	Tourist areas are effectively promoted through special events and through the promotion of the local community
	PLAEST2	Thanks to planning, it is possible to achieve the support of entrepreneurs for the development and promotion of tourism
2. Leadership	LIDER1	Our leaders are active, understand the importance of tourism, create perspectives and promote tourism
	LIDER2	We have qualified leaders who manage the available resources well and guarantee the correct management of social capital and sources of financing.
	LIDER3	Our leaders have learned to face the gaps and problems that arise
3. Local government: support and participation	GOBLOC1	There is financing for the development and promotion of tourism
	GOBLOC2	There is a specific active presence for the construction and maintenance of tourist infrastructure
	GOBLOC4	Support, experience and training are provided to people working in the tourism sector
	GOBLOC5	The local government provides support through financial resources for the creation of tourist brochures, as well as through actions that guarantee accessibility to the destination and the improvement of the region's landscapes
	FINANC1	Individual investors are encouraged and supported with financing programs (e.g. European funds, development investment programs, etc.)
	FINANC2	There is coordination between the local public sector and financial entities to support investors in the tourism sector.
4. Coordination and cooperation between investors and local authorities	CINVAUT1	The local government provides assistance and cooperation to tourism companies
	CINVAUT2	Local authorities identify investors' needs
	CINVAUT3	Local leaders assume that tourism depends on collaboration between investors and local organizations
	FINANC3	Financing is reinforced for works related to the development and promotion of the tourism product
	FINANC4	Local taxes are used to support tourist activities
	PLAEST3	All agents (employees, managers, authorities, local community ...) participate in the planning process
	PLAEST4	There is coordination between all agents to achieve common objectives
	ASITEC1	There is collaboration with universities and tourism agents that enables technical assistance and information
	ASITEC3	Technical assistance and information comes from conferences, professional meetings, and exhibitions and meetings in other regions
	ACOMLOC1	Residents are informed about the positive impact of tourism, and this is the result of a successful information policy for residents.
5. Coordination and collaboration between tourism entrepreneurs for the activation of the regions	CEMPTUR3	There are business associations for tourism development
	CEMPTUR4	Business associations allow the incorporation of new companies in these associations
6. Technical assistance and information on tourism development and promotion	GOBLOC3	Maintenance and cleanliness are emphasized in order to maintain the attractiveness of the offer for visitors
	ASITEC2	To obtain subsidies related to tourism financing, we turn to consultants and professionals
7. Support from the local community for tourism development	ACOMLOC2	Locals support tourism because it has more positive consequences (job creation, infrastructure improvement ...) than negative ones (alters traditional values, increased crime, increased population ...)
	ACOMLOC4	Older residents support tourism development in the region
8. Information to visitors and organization of conferences and events	INFOR1	Visitor information centers are efficient and effective
	INFOR2	We collaborate with local professional chambers
	INFOR3	The organization of events (for example, trade fairs) that attract visitors to the region is promoted.
	INFOR4	Conference and event organizers support and coordinate collaboration between investors and local authorities

Table 4. Average values in the factors per cluster.

DIMENSION	CLUSTER 1 (70)	2 (26)	3 (12)	4 (32)	5 (14)
1. Organization of the tourist offer	,1269237	-,0696690	1,1488192	-,6657599	-,2744358
2. Leadership	-,3597560	1,1488283	-,6754760	,3007680	-,1816074
3. Local government: support and participation	,0667838	-,4807244	,0162335	,1829025	,1930749
4. Coordination and cooperation between investors and local authorities	-,0257839	-,2343381	-1,0240453	,5872521	-,4450018
5. Coordination and collaboration between tourism entrepreneurs for the activation of the regions	-,8153730	,1282100	1,3108728	,6563501	,9563471
6. Technical assistance and information on tourism development and promotion	,0312141	-,5666242	,5208965	,2230929	-,1644881
7. Support from the local community for tourism development	-,0684182	,9046761	,1354224	,1155963	-1,7853471
8. Information to visitors and organization of conferences and events	,0077185	-,5206230	1,1578464	,5600066	-,8717188

portance of tourism, creating perspectives and promoting it, and also carry out a correct management of the available resources, both of the available social capital. as well as accessible sources of financing. On the other hand, in this management model the support that the local community provides to the tourism development of the region is of vital importance, assuming that the positive consequences of it (creation of jobs, improvement of infrastructures ...) are greater to negative ones (alteration of traditional values, increase in crime, increase in population ...). We could say that it is a model of "strong leadership with support from the local community". The two negative dimensions show, on the one hand, notable shortcomings in relation to the existing financing for the development and promotion of tourism, as well as the financial support provided by the local government (for example, European funds, development investment programs, etc.); and, on the other, the lack of a specific active presence for the construction and maintenance of tourism infrastructure and the low rates of support, experience and training provided to people who work in the tourism sector. In short, the rural organization in this model has to assume a leadership role in the absence of institutional support.

In relation to the third conglomerate, made up of twelve rural accommodation units, it should be noted that it is characterized by the highest and positive levels in three dimensions ("Organization of the tourist offer", "Coordination and collaboration between tourism entrepreneurs for the activation of the regions "and" Information to visitors and organization of conferences and events ") and a highly negative one in dimension 4 (" Coordination and cooperation between investors and local authorities "). Therefore, this model is characterized by the high investment of the institutions in the development of tourist places and in their promotion, involving the local community, the region and the investors and entrepreneurs who collaborate in the tourist planning of the area. In this conglomerate there is a high level of business associations, which allows for tourism promotion and development initiatives, supported by efficient and effective information centers. Events (for example, trade fairs), organized jointly by local businessmen and with little participation from public authorities, are encouraged and attract an acceptable number of visitors to the region. We can classify this group as "creators of tourism offer".

Cluster four, the second most populous (32 companies), can be characterized by the following features. First, it shows the highest score (and the only one that is positive) of the five groups based on dimension 4 ("Coordination and cooperation between investors and local authorities"). Second, it is the conglomerate with the worst "Organization of the tourist offer" (value of -0.666). Finally, regarding the dimension "Local government: support and participation", the conglomerate is characterized by the existence of a moderately favorable situation. The companies of this conglomerate are aware of the importance that collaboration between investors and local organizations has for the tourism development of the region, of the existence of a certain degree of associationism between companies, of the need for the support of governments. local. It seems that all this arises as a consequence of the absence of an adequate organization of the tourist offer. We can say that it is a conglomerate "promoter of local institutional collaboration".

The last conglomerate, made up of fourteen companies, is characterized by offering negative normalized values in six of the dimensions and especially low in two of them: "Information to visitors and organization of conferences and events" and "Support of the local community for the Touristic development". On the other hand, in the two remaining factors ("Coordination and collaboration between tourism entrepreneurs for the activation of the regions" and "Local government: support and participation") the values are positive and relatively high compared to the other conglomerates. Therefore, one might think that the scant support of the locals leads to a lower predisposition to organize tourist events that increase the number of tourists visiting the region. The group can be labeled as "moderate associations and local government support".

Table 5 shows the distribution of the different types of accommodation among the five identified clusters. The data indicate, firstly, that rural hotels are not creators of tourist offer or promoters of institutional collaboration. Secondly, there is a certain tendency of concentration of rural houses and of the category "others" (mainly rural apartments and tourist houses of rural accommodation) in the groups "under business associationism" and "promoters of institutional collaboration". Finally, it seems that rural complexes are not committed to being "creators of tourism offer".

In order to offer recommendations to the most disadvantaged regions with regard to the development of rural tourism and the creation of wealth, the following paragraphs offer an analysis of the relationships between each of the 5 management models identified (the conglomerates) and the different outcome variables included in the measurement instrument.

Table 5. Distribution among clusters by type of accommodation

		GROUP				
		1 ("Low business associations")	2 ("strong leadership with support from the local community")	3 ("creators of tourist offer")	4 ("promoter of local institutional collaboration")	5 ("moderate associationism and support from the local government")
		Count	Count	Count	Count	Count
Type of accommodation	Rural Hotel	4	4	0	0	2
	Rural Complex	6	4	2	4	2
	Rural House	34	12	6	18	6
	Others	26	6	4	10	4

Table 6 shows the average values obtained by each conglomerate with respect to the 5 outcome variables considered: reputation, sales volume, profitability, costs and market share. The data presented in Table 7 highlight the following: 1) absence of differences in the reputation variables (all indicate being above expectations) and market share (all groups reach the expected level); 2) an advantageous position of conglomerate 3 ("creators of tourism offer") based on the volume of sales that indicate that they are above expectations; 3) the low volume of sales reached by conglomerate 5 ("moderate associationism and support from the local government"), as they indicate that they are below expectations; and 4) the

Table 6. Average values of results by cluster

	GRUPO				
	1 ("Low business associations")	2 ("strong leadership with support from the local community")	3 ("creators of tourist offer")	4 ("promoter of local institutional collaboration")	5 ("moderate associationism and support from the local government")
	Average	Average	Average	Average	Average
Reputation	4	4	4	4	4
Sales volume	3	3	4	3	2
Profitability	2	3	3	2	3
Costs	3	4	4	3	4
Market share	3	3	3	3	3

*Table 7. Contingency Sales volume * Cluster*

			GROUP					Total
			1	2	3	4	5	
Sales volume	Far below expectations	Count	0	2	0	0	4	6
		% Within group	0,0%	7,7%	0,0%	0,0%	28,6%	3,9%
	Lower than expected	Count	28	6	0	16	2	52
		% Within group	40,0%	23,1%	0,0%	50,0%	14,3%	33,8%
	The expected	Count	28	6	6	12	6	58
		% Within group	40,0%	23,1%	50,0%	37,5%	42,9%	37,7%
	Above what is expected	Count	14	12	4	4	2	36
		% Within group	20,0%	46,2%	33,3%	12,5%	14,3%	23,4%
	Far above the expected	Count	0	0	2	0	0	2
		% Within group	0,0%	0,0%	16,7%	0,0%	0,0%	1,3%
Total		Count	70	26	12	32	14	154
		% Within group	100,0%	100,0%	100,0%	100,0%	100,0%	100,0%

unfavorable situation shown in terms of profitability (below expectations) two groups: "low business associationism" (1) and "promoter of local institutional collaboration" (4).

To check whether the results shown in Table 5 are statistically significant, we have carried out the non-parametric Kruskal-Wallis test. The results of this test confirm the existence of statistically significant differences between the clusters in terms of sales volume (significance level: 0.003) and profitability (significance level: 0.020).

We offer the results on sales volume in Table 7. In view of the results produced by said contingency table, we verify that 100% of the rural accommodation units belonging to conglomerate three ("creators of tourist offer") present a high level of satisfaction with the results in relation to the volume of sales, being more than 50% in satisfaction levels higher or much higher than expected. Regarding conglomerate five ("moderate associations and support from the local government"), despite the fact that 57% of rural accommodation units have acceptable levels of satisfaction (expected and above expectations) with respect to sales, notes that 28.6% of them have sales levels well below expectations, far exceeding the dissatisfaction values of the rest of the conglomerates

Regarding profitability, as Table 8 illustrates, cluster four ("promoter of local institutional collaboration") seems to obtain the worst results, with almost 69% of the companies below expectations (62, 5% obtain returns below those expected and 6.3% well below). Along the same lines, 48.6% of the companies in conglomerate one ("under business associationism") obtain lower returns than expected. Once again, the group with the most favorable results in terms of profitability is the third ("creators of tourism offer"), 50% of cases at the expected level and 33.4% above said level.

*Tabla 8. contingency Profitability * Cluster*

			GROUP					Total
			1	2	3	4	5	
Profitability	Far below expectations	Count	6	2	0	2	4	14
		% Within group	8,6%	7,7%	0,0%	6,3%	28,6%	9,1%
	Lower than expected	Count	28	8	2	20	4	62
		% Within group	40,0%	30,8%	16,7%	62,5%	28,6%	40,3%
	The expected	Count	34	16	6	8	2	66
		% Within group	48,6%	61,5%	50,0%	25,0%	14,3%	42,9%
	Above what is expected	Count	2	0	2	2	2	8
		% Within group	2,9%	0,0%	16,7%	6,3%	14,3%	5,2%
	Far above the expected	Count	0	0	2	0	2	4
		% Within group	0,0%	0,0%	16,7%	0,0%	14,3%	2,6%
Total		Count	70	26	12	32	14	154
		% Within group	100,0%	100,0%	100,0%	100,0%	100,0%	100,0%

CONCLUSION

The development of rural tourism, as well as its diversification, depends on multiple factors. On the one hand, there are external factors, such as aspects of the socio-economic and physical environment (macroeconomic trends, social movements, behavior of public and private institutions, etc.). On the other, internal issues must be taken into account: structural and management characteristics of the establishment (or business).

From the internal perspective of rural tourism development, the management model applied by rural tourism organizations is of vital importance. One of the proposals to analyze these entities is the destination management and business effectiveness model (Wilson et al, 2001). As in previous studies (Fotiadis et al., 2013), a redefinition of this model has been carried out through an exploratory factor analysis and it has been concluded that there are eight relevant dimensions for managing rural destinations. From these dimensions, five conglomerates or management models have been identified, characterized by the different weights that the management dimensions have in them.

The largest group in the sample, rural houses, tends to opt for the management models "under business associationism" and "promoter of local institutional collaboration". In other words, they do not maintain relationships with other entrepreneurs and prefer collaboration with local authorities. On the other hand, rural apartments and rural accommodation tourist homes show a similar trend to rural houses, since they are concentrated in the same management modalities. Modalities that, on the other hand, are the ones that bring together the largest number of businesses: 70 and 34.

Rural hotels are concentrated in clusters one ("low business association") and two ("strong leadership with support from the local community"), highlighting the importance of leadership for these companies, as well as the support of the local community. . This type of accommodation is usually larger than the rest of those contemplated in the study and can have a greater impact, so it is important for them to have significant support from the local population.

The data provided by the cluster analysis and the Kruskal-Wallis non-parametric test, focusing on the influence that each dimension of the destinations model may have on sales volume and profitability, show that organizations that adopt the management model number 3 (called "creators of tourism offer") are those that obtain the best results in terms of sales volume and profitability. It is a management model that places special emphasis on several dimensions, among which are the organization of the tourist offer, the promotion of business associations, the use of technical and informational means for the development and promotion of tourism and, finally, a clear commitment to holding information days and informative events.

On the other hand, the less favorable positions differ according to the variable considered. Thus, from the sales point of view, the worst-placed group is group 5 ("moderate associationism and local government support"). Rural institutions that trust everything to moderate levels of collaboration with other companies and moderate support from local authorities. In the case of profitability, we find two management conglomerates that present unfavorable data: the fourth ("promoter of local institutional collaboration") and the first ("under business associationism"). The collective "promoter of local collaboration" adopts a management system that is highly focused on collaboration with all the groups involved (investors, local authorities and other businesses), although it lacks concern for aspects related to the organization of the tourist offer. Group one, characterized by low collaboration with other entrepreneurs, also shows unremarkable levels in the remaining seven dimensions.

From the above, it can be inferred that for better tourism development in rural areas it is essential that institutions invest in the development of tourist sites in order to make them more attractive to visitors and promote them effectively. It is also essential that they carry out good tourism planning involving both the local community and the investors and entrepreneurs who collaborate in it.

Business associationism becomes another essential aspect for the correct development of tourism, being equally important that existing business associations allow the incorporation of new companies in them.

In the same way, efficient and effective tourist information centers, collaboration with local professional chambers and the organization of events, with the collaboration between investors and local authorities, increase the arrival of tourists with a direct impact on the income statement of rural accommodation companies.

Finally, it is essential for companies to obtain good results, the support of the local community for tourism development, an aspect to be taken into consideration by managers in order to develop a good information policy for the local community and involve it in the tourist planning of the territory, so that it does not represent a brake on the tourist development of the region.

REFERENCES

Brida, J. G., Osti, L., & Faccioli, M. (2011). Residents' perception and attitudes towards tourism impacts. *Benchmarking*, *18*(3), 359–385. doi:10.1108/14635771111137769

Correia-Loureiro, S. (2014). The role of the rural tourism experience economy in place attachment and behavioral intentions. *International Journal of Hospitality Management*, *40*, 1–9. doi:10.1016/j.ijhm.2014.02.010

Dias, Á., González-Rodríguez, M. R., & Patuleia, M. (2020). Developing poor communities through creative tourism. *Journal of Tourism and Cultural Change*, 1–21. doi:10.1080/14766825.2020.1775623

Dias, Á., Silva, G. M., Patuleia, M., & González-Rodríguez, M. R. (2020). Developing sustainable business models: Local knowledge acquisition and tourism lifestyle entrepreneurship. *Journal of Sustainable Tourism*, 1–20. doi:10.1080/09669582.2020.1835931

Dieguez-Castrillon, M. I., Gueimonde-Canto, A., & Sinde-Cantorna, A. (2009). Rural Tourism as diversification strategy: Determinants and performance in Galicia. *Cuadernos de Gestión*, *9*(2), 31–54.

Fotiadis, A., Vassiliadis, C., & Piper, L. (2013). Measuring dimensions of business effectiveness in Greek rural tourism areas. *Journal of Hospitality Marketing & Management*, 1–28.

Fotiadis, A., Yeh, S., & Huan, T. C. (2016). Applying configural analysis to explaining rural-tourism success récipes. *Journal of Business Research*, *69*(4), 1479–1483. doi:10.1016/j.jbusres.2015.10.128

Gunn, C. A. (1988). *Tourism Planning* (2nd ed.). Taylor and Francis.

Healy, N., Van Riper, C., & Boyd, S. W. (2016). Low versus high intensity approaches to interpretive tourism planning: The case of the Cliffs of Moher, Ireland. *Tourism Management*, *52*, 574–583. doi:10.1016/j.tourman.2015.08.009

Helgadóttir, G., & Dashper, K. (2021). 20 years of Nordic rural tourism research: A review and future research agenda. *Scandinavian Journal of Hospitality and Tourism*, *21*(1), 60–69. doi:10.1080/15022250.2020.1823246

Lane, B. (1994). What is rural tourism? *Journal of Sustainable Tourism*, *2*(1), 7–21. doi:10.1080/09669589409510680

Lanfranchi, M., Giannetto, C., & De Pascale, A. (2014). Rural tourism: A kind of sustainable tourism in the face of global economic crisis. *International Journal for Responsible Tourism*, *3*(2), 15–28.

Li-Chan, Ch., Shang-Ping, L., & Chun-Min, K. (2013). Rural tourism: Marketing strategies for the bed and breakfast industry in Taiwan. *International Journal of Hospitality Management*, *32*, 278–286. doi:10.1016/j.ijhm.2012.07.005

Maksimović, M., Urošević, S., & Mihajlović, D. (2015). The effects of the development of rural tourism on stara planina. *ЕКОНОМИКА*, *61*(2), 83–91. doi:10.5937/ekonomika1502083M

Murphy, P. E. (1985). *Tourism: A Community Approach*. Methuen.

Ohe, Y. (2020). *Community-based rural tourism and entrepreneurship*. Springer. doi:10.1007/978-981-15-0383-2

Saarinen, J. (2007). Contradictions of Rural Tourism Initiatives in Rural Development Contexts: Finnish Rural Tourism Strategy Case Study. *Current Issues in Tourism*, *10*(1), 96–105. doi:10.2167/cit287.0

UNCTAD. (2021). *Covid-19 and tourism an update. Assessing the economic consequences*. Consultado en julio de 2021 en la siguiente direccion de internet: https://unctad.org/system/files/official-document/ditcinf2021d3_en_0.pdf

Villanueva-Álvaro, J. J., Mondéjar-Jiménez, J., & Sáez-Martínez, F. J. (2017). Rural tourism: Development, management and sustainability in rural establishments. *Sustainability*, *9*(5), 818. doi:10.3390u9050818

Wilson, S., Fesenmaier, D., Fesenmaier, J., & Van Es, J. (2001). Factors for Success in Rural Tourism Development. *Journal of Travel Research*, *40*(1), 132–138. doi:10.1177/004728750104000203

Xu, H., Wang, C., Wu, J., Liang, Y., Jiao, Y., & Nazneen, S. (2018). Human poverty alleviation through rural women's tourism entrepreneurship. *Journal of China Tourism Research*, *14*(4), 445–460. doi:10.1080/19388160.2018.1507860

Zampetakis, L., & Kanelakis, G. (2010). Opportunity entrepreneurship in the rural sector: Evidence from Greece. *Journal of Research in Marketing and Entrepreneurship*, *12*(2), 122–142. doi:10.1108/14715201011090594

Chapter 5
Fair Trade Practices for Fighting in Emerging Countries:
A Business-Centred Approach

Sergio De-la-Piedra-Vindrola
Universidad de Lima, Peru

Juan Manuel Berbel-Pineda
https://orcid.org/0000-0002-4783-9749
Universidad Pablo de Olavide, Spain

Beatriz Palacios-Florencio
Universidad Pablo de Olavide, Spain

ABSTRACT

Fair trade is a concept that is becoming increasingly ingrained in consumers. This means that companies that are committed to the development of fair-trade policies can find here a source of competitive advantage. Likewise, these practices will favour many producers in the primary sector, which could turn this into an effective way of fighting poverty. The aim of this research is to find out how fair trade has an impact on company results. To this end, managers from 102 companies in an emerging economy (Peru) are analysed. PLS-SEM is used for this analysis. The results indicate that there is a mediating effect of fair trade on the relationship between corporate social responsibility and company performance. However, significant differences have been found compared to developed economies. These results provide insight into emerging economy managers' assessments of responsible business practices.

INTRODUCTION

Fair trade (FT) is a social movement whose objective is to improve the conditions of workers in developing countries (Oosterveer et al., 2014, Hainmueller et al., 2015; Naylor, 2018). Its strategy is to ensure that producers receive a fair price for their certified-origin products and to apply the "Fairtrade" mark to

DOI: 10.4018/978-1-7998-8925-0.ch005

these products. In less than 25 years, this type of trade has reached significant market shares in European countries (Oosterveer et al., 2014, Raynolds & Greenfield, 2015; David, 2016; Geysmans et al., 2017). However, the market shares of these products are still generally low (Brunner, 2014, Argade & Singh, 2016; Möckel, 2019; Ciambotti et al., 2019).

FT represents one of the possible ways to alleviate poverty in developing countries (Tovernić, 2017; Klammer & van den Anker, 2018; Overbeek, 2019). The funds received go directly to the producers, who receive an adequate amount for their work, which contributes to improve their situations (Navrátilová et al., 2019). This trading system implies that the individual purchase choice of final consumers influences the power and wealth distribution in world trade (Anderson, 2018; Sama et al., 2018; Gillani et al., 2019).

On the other hand, in an increasingly global context in which consumers are interconnected, both the literature and business practice highlight the importance of developing management systems based on corporate social responsibility (CSR) (e. g., Hickle, 2017; Brunton et al., 2017), as a sign of the organization commitment towards economic, social and environmental sustainability (Porter and Kramer, 2011). In addition, many works have shown a direct relation between CSR and company results (performance) (Lai et al., 2010; Kumar et al., 2016; López-Pérez et al., 2017).

The literature reveals previous studies related to the FT background and prior knowledge for consumers (Pérez and De los Salmones, 2018). Another group of studies have examined the determinant elements of this type of consumption (Ríos et al., 2015). Some authors such as Lin et al. (2011) took as a reference the justice framework to structure their study. From the marketing point of view in the FT, the trust value that FT generates among consumers has been demonstrated (Andorfer and Liebe, 2015).

However, despite the relevance of this phenomenon, the literature review brought us to determine that there is still scarce research that has addressed the real impact of FT on business results. The vast majority of these works consider the customer perception in developed economies where a large percentage of the population has their basic needs covered. However, studies that have addressed the phenomenon in the emerging country context have not been found. Therefore, we can affirm that, until now, there is no clear evidence of empirical research on a possible mediating effect of FT between CSR and business performance variables in emerging economies, becoming this research pioneering in this regard.

Once this gap in the literature has been identified, this research aims to find out whether there is a mediating effect of the FT between CSR and enterprise performance. The relevance of the study lies in the fact of analyzing the context of an emerging economy from the perspective of managers of retailing companies, in such a way that, indirectly, we are capturing consumers' attitude and predisposition to consume fair trade products. We understand that the result obtained could immensely contribute not only to retailing companies, but also to producers, local communities, environment and society in general.

To respond to the above objectives, a causal model that explores the mediation of the FT in the relation between CSR and performance applying the PLS-SEM technique is proposed. This model is submitted to the case of an emerging economy (Peru).

To do this, in the following section, the bibliographic review of the concepts related to the object of study is presented. Below, the hypotheses that make up the reference model are shown. Thereupon, the field work and data validation are developed, taking as a reference a sample of more than 100 managers from the retailing field in Peru. Finally, the results are exposed and the main theoretical implications of the study are discussed.

CONCEPTUAL FRAMEWORK

Fair Trade

Apparently, the term "fair trade" was first used in 1985 as a "*commitment to transparency and accountability to provide greater benefits to small producers*" (Anderson, 2018; Jones et al., 2019). This does not imply that the concept had not been used before, although implicitly, so it is uncertain to establish a more specific date. For Low and Davenport (2005), in addition to religious charities and the recovery effort after World War II, there were several movements that influenced the start of the FT, highlighting among them: opposition to capitalism, decolonization, alternative lifestyles and the emergence of indigenous initiatives that were empowering producers in the southern hemisphere. Therefore, this concept groups several local initiatives emerged in a decentralized manner and without communication between them (Gendron et al., 2009).

However, from 1946, the FT takes shape (Kocken, 2006) from various initiatives in America and Europe. The foundation of SERRV International established in 1949 the first formal FT store in the USA. According to Stenn (2013), at the end of the 1980s, the first formal partnerships focused on the cause were born, such as the European Fair Trade Association (EFTA) in 1987 and the International Fair Trade Association (IFAT) in 1989. In 1994, the FT Federation and the International Fairtrade Labeling Organization (FLO International) were created.

"Fair trade" is described as an "*innovative network that challenges conventional trade, as well as forms the basis of the links between producers and consumers*" (Bacon et al., 2008; Jaffee, 2014). Raynolds (2012) points out that fair trade is used as a tool to assess the possibilities of market social returning. However, when examining fair trade as a practice based on social relations, the discussion about the real elective level it has in trade arises (Howard and Jaffee, 2013).

Organizations that practice FT participate in supporting producers, raising awareness and launching campaigns for standard changes and the practice of international trade (Castaldo et al., 2009). Nevertheless, it is important to note that other authors such as Argenti (2004) and De Pelsmacker and Janssen (2007) complement the definition of fair trade according to their experience basis. Respect to the concept presence in academic literature, Bossle and Pedrozo (2012) present a bibliometric study where the relative novelty of the concept is observed. To that end, they analyze its presence in relevant publications and events. In this regard, they comment that there are few mentions to the countries of Latin America even when many producers in this region would benefit from the FT.

Corporate Social Responsibility (CSR)

In the last two decades, CSR has become an important element in both academic literature and business practices. In this regard, Porter and Kramer (2011) widely describe the economic, social and environmental dimension of CSR. Furthermore, from a business point of view, organizations should be concerned with knowing the main interests of their stakeholders. CSR becomes a key indicator of companies' concern for the sustainability of their activity.

In the management field, the CSR literature addresses various disciplines: strategy, accounting, finance, marketing, human resources, operations and marketing; besides, more recently, it advocates for an interdisciplinary and transversal management. For example, in the marketing field, many authors have focused on analyzing how stakeholders perceive CSR activities (Yim et al., 2019). In our study we adopt a regulatory approach to CSR, that is, whether a company should participate in CSR activities, and whether these activities have any influence on its financial performance.

To understand the effects of CSR, it is important to analyze the perception of immediate stakeholders (Brown and Dacin, 1997; Sen and Bhattacharya, 2001; Ramasamy and Yeung, 2009). A specific case is the managers' growing interest of the phenomenon, due to the possible significant influence of the concept on consumer responses (Bhattacharya and Sen, 2004). In many cases, consumers do not only value the main attributes, price and quality of a product (Gupta and Hodges, 2012). Now companies must worry about offering an image that reflects a responsible and sincere relation with their environment. This is precisely the reason why this study is important for managers: knowing to what extent FT and CSR interact to generate better results.

Business Profitability

In this study, business profitability will be used as the key concept to understand the success or failure of business management (REF). It determines the economic return with respect to the effort made at a given time, and its analysis allows resources to be assigned substantially more efficiently. Over time, the academic literature has stated that this magnitude has been measured both with objective parameters (REF) and with subjective indicators based on the perception of those responsible (Torugsa et al., 2012; Lai et al., 2010) or in a mixed way (Hurghis, 2017). In this sense, the comments of Homburg et al. (1999) that defend the validity of subjective measures based on perception metrics to measure this construct are particularly interesting. Hence, in the field of CSR, for example, the recent works of Flores et al. (2020) or López-Pérez et al. (2018) have used subjective measures of profitability to measure the relation between CSR and performance.

Model and Hypothesis

Based on these three variables and the literature analyzed, below we can show a model that, although it seems simple, relates the concepts and ideas presented here and, therefore, will serve as a reference for our empirical study. First of all, we propose an initial model that poses a direct and positive relation between CSR and profitability. Subsequently, in the second place, another model is introduced that includes the fair trade effect and that reinforces the explanatory capacity of the phenomenon. Hence, the first model links the CSR with the performance and the second model presents the mediation of fair trade between these two variables.

CSR actions impact various organization areas. For example, it improves the competitive advantage of companies in different domains (Melo & Garrido-Morgado, 2012). CSR can help improve the efficiency of internal processes by improving employee motivation, relationships with supplier and productivity (Lund-Thomsen and Nadvi, 2010; Barrena-Martínez et al., 2015; Ferri et al., 2016), introducing more efficient and environmentally friendly production techniques (Orlitzky et al., 2011) and facilitating access to better funding sources (Doh et al., 2010; Torres et al., 2012). Additionally, Kim et al. (2012) suggest that these companies tend to behave more ethically and may achieve a more favorable attitude from consumers towards their products (Torres et al., 2012). Consequently, we can say that markets reward socially and environmentally responsible corporations (Flammer, 2013; López-Pérez et al., 2018).

Figure 1. CSR, fair trade and performance: managers' perception

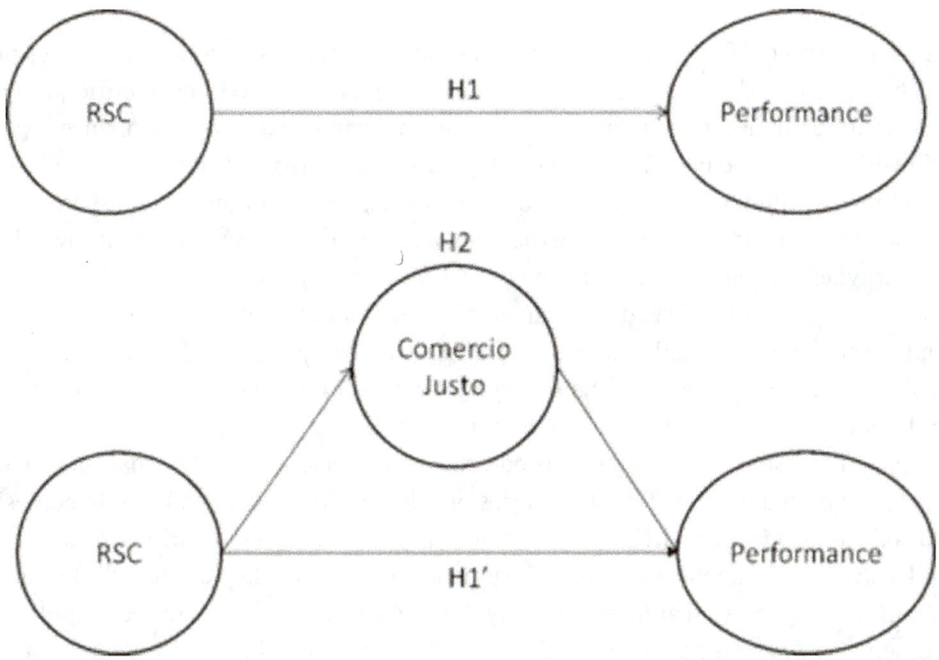

Furthermore, we observe that the new social challenges impact on organizations' management and that entrepreneurs no longer measure profitability only in numerical terms, but consider other social variables that affect the company performance. Hence, organizations are motivated to implement CSR practices as a means to be rewarded and preserve their legitimacy. Based on all these arguments, the following hypothesis is proposed:

Hypothesis 1: *There is a positive relation between CSR and performance.*

Additionally, the FT represents a very specific way of planning and executing the business activity (REF). It is directly related to the social dimension of CSR, since it is committed to offering fair treatment to raw material suppliers and, thus, helps the economic and social development of local communities (REF). The FT has an impact on the image that the company transmits towards the market and its stakeholders, in such a way that increases trust towards the brand and reinforces its commercial positioning (REF). Some authors (e. g. Low and Davenport, 2005; Anderson, 2018: Jones et al., 2019) indicate that there is a direct correlation between this variable and the CSR and the performance of the company. Precisely, an added value of this research lies in analyzing the possible mediation of the FT in the relation between CSR and performance. In this way, we propose:

Hypothesis 2: *There is a mediating effect between CSR and performance.*

METHODOLOGY AND DATA

To achieve the research objectives, an empirical analysis was carried out based on surveys of Peruvian managers. The survey used in this research is based on works published in scientific journals (name) and responds to different questions related to CSR, fair trade and business performance.

The fieldwork was carried out through an on line survey in February 2019. Intentional sampling was followed, looking for similarity in the distribution of managers according to industrial sector (coffee companies and others in this area), small, medium and large companies with high turnover. For this, the database of Peruvian companies and contact networks was used.

The fieldwork began with the sending of an email briefly presenting the study objective, the survey duration and the researcher's email contact, in case of doubts or questions. Thereupon, the survey link was attached to be completed on line. The survey took about 3 minutes to complete and was available in Spanish. Previously, managers had to give their permission for the study.

Subsequently, the results have been proposed descriptively and a profile of managers and the theoretical model have been drawn up. Finally, a series of relations have been made for hypothesis testing.

For data collection, questionnaires were distributed among managers of various Peruvian companies involved in FT activities. The measurement instrument was completed by a total of 102 subjects.

The data in Table 1 shows that approximately 70% of the respondents are men and the remaining 30% are women. Nearly all respondents are Peruvian. The educational profile indicates that all of them have technical and/or university studies. The average age of the respondents is around 40 years old. Although these people have worked in their current company little more than 5 years, they have been committed to fair trade for a longer time. On the other hand, the organizations in which they work are highly involved in fair trade activities, for an average of almost 30 years. Respect to the data distributed by sex, women are younger and have less work experience in the companies they work in, although they have been participating in fair trade activities for longer.

RESULTS AND DISCUSSION

For the data analysis, we have used the Partial Least Squares (PLS) technique, which allows the analysis of structural equation models based on variance. The measurement model used in this work is composite and reflective (Mode A), so that the use of traditional PLS is viable (Sarstedt et al., 2016). We have used PLS SmartPLS 3.2.8 software (Ringle, Wende & Becker, 2015).

The use of a single questionnaire in a self-report format to obtain the data of the latent variables (corporate social responsibility and fair trade) requires to verify the existence of common variance between them. In line with Huber & Power (1985) and Podsakoff et al. (2003), we have followed the procedural steps related to the design of questionnaires. We separate the different measures and guarantee the anonymity of the respondents. The presence of common influence in the responses was measured with the Harman test (1967). The 31 questionnaire elements assessed have been grouped into a total of 7 factors, and the largest of them explains 35% of the variance. Therefore, according to Podsakoff and Organ (1986), we can point out the absence of a common factor of influence between these items.

The latent model perspective (MacKenzie, Podsakoff and Jarvis, 2005; Real, Leal & Roldán, 2006) was used when analyzing the relations between the different constructs of the model and its indicators. Conversely, two alternative models have been compared. The first model shows a direct relation between

Table 1. Respondent characteristics

	Absolute frequencies		
	Global	**Woman**	**Man**
Participants	102	32	70
Nationality			
Peruvian	99	32	68
Other	3	0	2
Education level			
Elementary school	1	0	1
Technical college	7	5	2
University	38	15	23
Master	55	10	45
Doctor	2	0	2
	Averages		
	Global	**Woman**	**Male**
Age	39.70	36.83	40.94
Working years	6.42	5.83	6.68
Company experience in fair trade	29.40	15.00	35.44
Manager's experience in fair trade	8.69	10.31	7.98

Source: Own elaboration

the independent variable (corporate social responsibility) and the dependent variable (company performance). The second model consists of including a third variable (fair trade) and measuring its effect on the dependent variable, as well as its ability to mediate between CSR and performance.

Measurement Model

Table 2 collects the needed data to begin with the validation of the measurement model: determine the reliability of the individual items. We have measured all latent variables (constructs) in mode A (reflective). Although not all the factorial loads of the items exceed the minimum criterion of 0.707 (Carmines and Zeller, 1979), those elements that reach values higher than 0.650 have been retained, following the recommendations of Hair et al. (2014). Several items have been removed from the total of 36 in the original questionnaire: 11 items from CSR, 3 of fair trade construct and none of the Performance variable.

In order to measure the constructs reliability, composite reliability indices (ρc) have been calculated (Werts, Linn and Jöreskog, 1974). In all cases, we observe the fulfillment of the minimum requirement: a composite reliability greater than 0.7 (Nunnally, 1978). Regarding convergent validity, as Table 3 illustrates, all latent variables exceed the minimum level of 0.5 (Fornell and Larcker, 1981) in the AVE.

The analysis of the discriminant validity of the various constructs (latent variables) has been performed based on two criteria: Fornell-Larcker and Heterotrait-Monotrait ratio (HTMT). The data is collected in Tables 3 and 4. The Fornell-Larcker criterion is strictly met among all latent variables. In relation to

Table 2. Individual reliability, composed reliability and average variance extracted for the constructs

Construct and indicator	Loading	Cronbach alpha	Composed reliability	AVE
CSR		0.931	0.940	0.547
Makes donations to charity.	0.702			
Supports non-governmental organizations (NGOs) that work in problem areas.	0.792			
Contributes to campaigns and projects that promote social welfare.	0.822			
Participates in activities whose objective is to protect and improve the natural environment quality.	0.758			
Makes investments to improve the future generations lives.	0.683			
Implements special programs to minimize its negative impact on the environment.	0.678			
Protects consumer rights beyond legal requirements.	0.675			
Encourages their employees to participate in volunteer activities.	0.666			
Mainly concerned with their employees' needs and wishes.	0.666			
Has a specific budget to carry out social and humanitarian activities.	0.800			
Does altruistic activities on a regular basis.	0.759			
Has personnel in charge of carrying out altruistic activities.	0.772			
Cooperates with non-governmental organizations (NGOs) to perform social and humanitarian activities.	0.813			
FAIR TRADE (FT)		0.775	0.851	0.590
Concerned about labor issues that affect people in developing countries around the world.	0.704			
Believes in fair trade goals.	0.862			
Thinks consumers buy fair trade products because they want to be more socially responsible.	0.772			
Thinks consumers are willing to pay more for items that they know they are produced under fair trade standards.	0.725			
PERFORMANCE (PERF)		0.952	0.963	0.840
Economic profitability.	0.928			
Financial profitability.	0.934			
Sales growth.	0.891			
Net contribution margin.	0.908			
Market share.	0.920			

the HTMT ratio, the data meets the criterion, since all values are less than 0.85. For all these reasons, it can be affirmed that there is discriminant validity among the constructs.

Diagonal elements (bold figures) are the square root of the variance shared between the constructs and their measures. Off-diagonal elements are the correlations among constructs. For discriminant validity, diagonal elements should be larger than off-diagonal.

Table 3. Averages, typical deviations and construct correlations

Constructs	CSR	FT	PERF
CSR	**0.740**		
FT	0.363	**0.768**	
PERF	0.660	0.465	**0.917**

Table 4. Discriminant validity (HTMT ratio)

	CSR	FT
FT	0.381	
PERF	0.682	0.518

Structural Model

In the case of the structural model, we have proceeded to the analysis of the sign, size and significance of the path coefficients, the R2 values and the Q2 test. According to Hair Hult, Ringle and Sarstedt (2017), we have used the bootstrapping technique with 5000 samples to determine the t statistics and the confidence intervals, with the goal of obtaining the relation significance. Table 5 offers the direct effects (path coefficients), the t statistic value and the corresponding confidence intervals, together with the R2 and Q2 values. All the direct effects are significant and positive and, therefore, all the hypotheses of the proposed model are supported by the data. The R2 values show an appropriate predictive level for

Table 5. Direct effects on endogenous variables (models without and with mediation)

Effects on endogenous variables	Direct effects	t Value (bootstrap)	Percentile 95% confidence interval	Correlations	Explained variance
MODEL WITHOUT MEDIATION					
PERFORMANCE ($R^2 = 0.435$ / $Q^2 = 0.364$)					
H1: CSR	0.664***	12.685	[0.533; 0.751] Sig	0.664	43.50%
MODEL WITH MEDIATION					
PERFORMANCE ($R^2 = 0.484$ / $Q^2 = 0.406$)					
H1': CSR	0.566***	10.998	[0.364; 0.715] Sig	0.660	37.36%
H3: FT	0.259*	2.139	[0.003; 0.483] Sig	0.465	12.04%
FAIR TRADE ($R^2 = 0.123$ / $Q^2 = 0.055$)					
H2: CSR	0.363***	4.494	[0.131; 0.502] Sig	0.363	12.30%

***p<0.001, **p<0.01, *p<0.05, ns: not significant.

t (0.05; 4999) = 1.645; t (0.01; 4999) = 2.327; t (0.001; 4999) = 3.092. One-tailed test.

Table 6. Summary of mediating effects

	Coefficient	Bootstrap 95% CI			
	Point estimate	Percentile		BC	
Individual indirect effects					
CSR -> TF -> PERF	0.094	0.006	0.230	0.004	0.223
Total indirect effects					
CSR -> PERF	0.094	0.006	0.230	0.004	0.223

ns: not significant.

all its variables: confidence, internal motivation and commitment. The Q2 values also reveal the model predictive relevance, since they are all greater than 0.

Table 6 shows the values of the indirect effects of the CSR variable on the endogenous performance variable. The results indicate that the total effect is significant, since the value 0 is not included between the two ends of the confidence interval. Thus, it is a partial and complementary mediation, since both the direct and indirect effects have the same sign.

CONCLUSION

Hitherto, there is no evidence of empirical research on the existence of a potential mediating effect of the FT between the CSR and business performance variables in emerging economies. For this reason, the main objective of this study was to find out whether there was such a mediating effect between these variables, considering an emerging economy. To do this, based on the existing literature, the relations between the variables and their influence have been studied. Part of the development of the research

Figure 2. Model with total effect

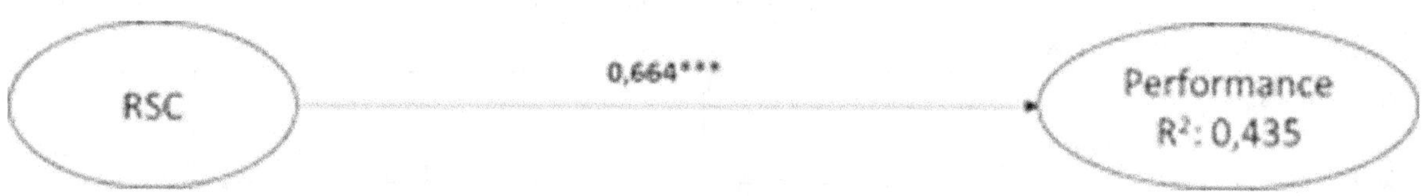

Figure 3. Model with mediation

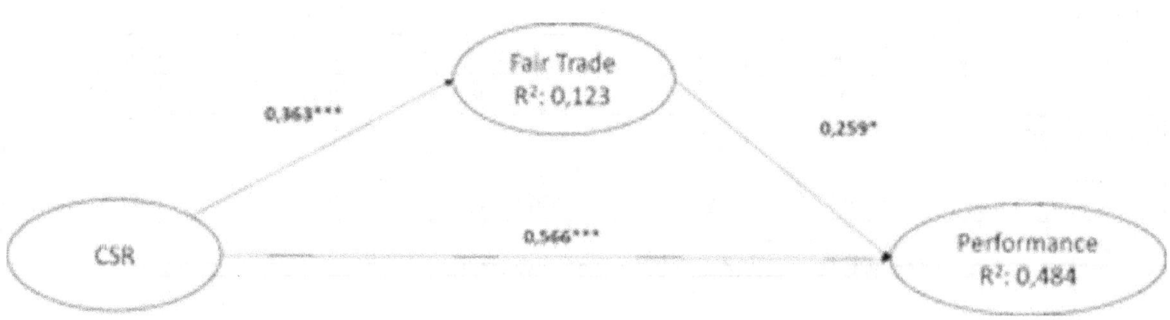

was to choose an adequate sample to measure the variables. An important group of Peruvian managers represented the sample. Hence, knowing their perception and opinion on CSR, performance and FT issues can be regarded as an excellent instrument for the design of strategies adapted to new social demands.

On the one hand, the research conceptually examines what position fair trade has in the relation between CSR and business performance. The first concepts are considered as tools to promote persistent changes in market conditions. Currently, sustainability and value creation, which are directly related to the management capacity to meet the needs of the present and future generation without compromising it, assume high significance.

On the other hand, after analyzing the results, we can verify that, as well as mediating in the relation between CSR and performance, the FT does it in a positive and significant way. The results indicate that aspects such as FT and CSR have an impact on business profitability, which can help to reinforce the positioning of certain products in the field of retailing. Taking into account this revelation, the enterprises should boost this value and promote awareness campaigns that provide support to companies committed to FT among consumers. It is for this reason that managers should raise their voices and draw the attention of the business community to support the design and application of new strategies to this situation and, especially considering that, currently, there is no mandatory standard on these practices, but its importance is overwhelming.

These fair trade practices can be favored with the current context we are facing: the health and economic crisis caused by COVID-19. This crisis is promoting strong government measures to support the local product trade and, in some way, awareness campaigns for consumers towards the consumption of products related (directly or indirectly) to the concept of FT. In addition, a change in habits among costumers themselves towards the purchase of products that include the so-called FT is perceived in recent times. Therefore, find out the perception of consumers towards FT both before and after this crisis could be an interesting idea for future research.

The work presents the following main limitations. On the one hand, the reference model. Although it may seem simple (based only on two hypotheses), we wanted to present the idea and the relation in a simple way, without the intermediation of more variables. Therefore, this relation between CSR and performance and the effect of the FT are clearly exposed. Another limitation may be derived from the sample size. Although there are 102 respondents, we must consider that the sample is comprised of company managers (so smaller sample sizes are generally accepted) and, in this case, belonging to a certain sector (retailing).

In conclusion, we understand that the results obtained could immensely contribute not only to retailing companies, but also to producers, local communities, environment and society in general. The study findings have significant implications for the management of the FT and CSR by public and private organizations in the communication and production field as well as in labor, industrial and retail relations.

REFERENCES

Anderson, M. (2018). Fair trade and consumer social responsibility: Exploring consumer citizenship as a driver of social and environmental change. *Management Decision*, *56*(3), 634–651. doi:10.1108/MD-01-2017-0013

Andorfer, V. A., & Liebe, U. (2015). Do information, price, or morals influence ethical consumption? A natural field experiment and customer survey on the purchase of fair trade coffee. *Social Science Research*, *52*, 330–350. doi:10.1016/j.ssresearch.2015.02.007 PMID:26004466

Argadc, A., & Singh, S. (2016). Seeking Markets in Production Fields: An Assessment of the Potential for Fair Trade in India. *Millennial Asia*, *7*(2), 131–152. doi:10.1177/0976399616655028

Argenti, P. A. (2004). 'Collaborating with activists: How Starbucks works with NGOs'. *California Management Review*, *47*(1), 91–115. doi:10.2307/41166288

Bacon, C. M., Mendez, V. E., & Gliessman, S. R. (2008). *Confronting the Coffee Crisis: Fair Trade, Sustainable Livelihoods and Ecosystems in Mexico and Central America*. MIT Press. doi:10.7551/mitpress/9780262026338.001.0001

Barrena-Martínez, J., López-Fernández, M., Márquez-Moreno, C., & Romero-Fernández, P. (2015). Corporate social responsibility in the process of attracting college graduates. *Corporate Social Responsibility and Environmental Management*, *22*(6), 408–423. doi:10.1002/csr.1355

Bhattacharya, C. B., & Sen, S. (2004). Doing better at doing good: When, why and how consumers respond to corporate social initiatives. *CA Management Review*, *47*(1), 9–24. doi:10.2307/41166284

Bossle, M. B., & Pedrozo, E. A. (2012). Comércio Justo: Em que estágio estamos? *Revista de Gestão Social e Ambiental*, *6*(2), 33–44. doi:10.24857/rgsa.v6i2.428

Brown, T. J., & Dacin, P. A. (1997). The company and the product: Corporate associations and consumer product responses. *Journal of Marketing*, *61*(1), 68–84. doi:10.1177/002224299706100106

Brunner, T. A. (2014). Applying neutralization theory to fair trade buying behaviour. *International Journal of Consumer Studies*, *38*(2), 200–206. doi:10.1111/ijcs.12081

Brunton, M., Eweje, G., & Taskin, N. (2017). *Communicating corporate social responsibility to internal stakeholders: walking the walk or just talking the talk? Business Strategy and the Environment*. Early View.

Castaldo, S., Perrini, F., Misani, N., & Tencati, A. (2009). The missing link between corporate social responsibility and consumer trust: The case of fair trade products. *Journal of Business Ethics*, *84*(1), 1–15. doi:10.100710551-008-9669-4

Ciambotti, G., Sottini, A., & Sydow, A. (2019). *Scaling strategies of social enterprises in fair-trade markets: Meru herbs in Kenya*. SAGE Publications.

David, C. B., & Kim, H. S. (2016). Developing Markets, Building Networks: Promoting Fair Trade in Asia. In *Fair Trade, Corporate Accountability and Beyond*. Routledge.

De Pelsmacker, P., & Janssens, W. (2007). A model for fair trade buying behaviour: The role of perceived quantity and quality of information and of product-specific attitudes. *Journal of Business Ethics*, *75*(4), 361–380. doi:10.100710551-006-9259-2

Doh, J., Howton, S., Howton, S., & Siegel, D. (2010). Does the market respond to an endorsement of social responsibility? The role of institutions, information and legitimacy. *Journal of Management*, *36*(6), 1461–1485. doi:10.1177/0149206309337896

Ferri, L., Oelze, N., Habish, A., & Molteni, M. (2016). Implementation of responsible procurement management: An institutional perspective. *Business Strategy and the Environment*, *25*(4), 261–276. doi:10.1002/bse.1870

Flammer, C. (2013). Corporate social responsibility and shareholder reaction: The environmental awareness of investors. *Academy of Management Journal, 56*(3), 758–781. doi:10.5465/amj.2011.0744

Flores-Hernández, A., Cambra-Fierro, J., & Vázquez-Carrasco, R. (2020). Sustainability, brand image, reputation and financial value: Manager perceptions in an emerging economy context. *Sustainable Development, 28*(4), 935–945. doi:10.1002d.2047

Gendron, C., Bisaillon, V., & Rance, A. I. (2009). The institutionalization of fair trade: More than just a degraded form of social action. *Journal of Business Ethics, 86*(1), 63–79. doi:10.100710551-008-9758-4

Geysmans, R., de Krom, M. P., & Hustinx, L. (2017). "Fairtradization": A performative perspective on fair trade markets and the role of retail settings in their enactment. *Consumption Markets & Culture, 20*(6), 539–558. doi:10.1080/10253866.2017.1331909

Gillani, A., Kutaula, S., Leonidou, L. C., & Christodoulides, P. (2019). The impact of proximity on consumer fair trade engagement and purchasing behavior: The moderating role of empathic concern and hypocrisy. *Journal of Business Ethics*, 1–21.

Gupta, M., & Hodges, N. (2012). Corporate social responsibility in the apparel industry: An exploration of Indian consumer perceptions and expectations. *Journal of Fashion Marketing and Management, 16*(2), 216–233. doi:10.1108/13612021211222833

Hainmueller, J., Hiscox, M. J., & Sequeira, S. (2015). Consumer demand for fair trade: Evidence from a multistore field experiment. *The Review of Economics and Statistics, 97*(2), 242–256. doi:10.1162/REST_a_00467

Hickle, G. (2017). Extending the boundaries: An assessment of the integration of extended producer responsibility within corporate social responsibility. *Business Strategy and the Environment, 26*(1), 112–124. doi:10.1002/bse.1908

Homburg, C., Krohmer, H., & Workman, J. Jr. (1999). Strategic Consensus and Performance: The Role of Strategy Type and Market-Related Dynamism. *Strategic Management Journal, 20*(4), 356–357. doi:10.1002/(SICI)1097-0266(199904)20:4<339::AID-SMJ29>3.0.CO;2-T

Howard, P. H., & Jaffee, D. (2013). Tensions between firm size and sustainability goals: Fair trade coffee in the United States. *Sustainability, 5*(1), 72–89. doi:10.3390u5010072

Hurghis, R. (2017). Integrated reporting and board features. *Audit Francier, 15*(1), 21–30.

Jaffee, D. (2014). Brewing Justice: Fair Trade Coffee, Sustainability, and Survival. University of California Press. doi:10.1525/9780520957886

Jones, E., Tiffen, P., Balfour, S., & Mayo, E. (2019). Celebrating the life and work of Fair Trade pioneer, Robin Murray, 1940–2017. *Journal of Fair Trade, 1*(1), 6–12. doi:10.13169/jfairtrade.1.1.0006

Khalid, R. U., Seuring, S., Beske, P., Land, A., Yawar, S. A., & Wagner, R. (2015). Putting sustainable supply chain management into base of the pyramid research. *Supply Chain Management, 20*(6), 681–696. doi:10.1108/SCM-06-2015-0214

Kim, Y., Park, M. S., & Wier, B. (2012). Is earnings quality associated with corporate social responsibility? *The Accounting Review*, *8*(3), 761–796. doi:10.2308/accr-10209

Klammer, J., & van den Anker, F. W. (2018). A Platform to Connect Swiss Consumers of Fair Trade Products with Producers in Developing Countries*: Needs and Motivations. In International Conference of Design, User Experience, and Usability* (pp. 664-681). Springer. 10.1007/978-3-319-91806-8_52

Kocken, M. (2006). Introduction. In A. Osterhaus (Ed.), Business Unusual: Success and Challenges of Fair Trade (pp. 5–6). Academic Press.

Kumar, K., Boesso, G., & Michelon, G. (2016). How do strengths and weaknesses in corporate social performance across different stakeholder domains affect company performance? *Business Strategy and the Environment*, *25*(4), 277–292. doi:10.1002/bse.1874

Lai, C., Chiu, C., Yang, C., & Pai, D. (2010). The effects of corporate social responsibility on brand performance: The mediating effect of industrial brand equity and corporate reputation. *Journal of Business Ethics*, *95*(3), 457–469. doi:10.100710551-010-0433-1

Lin, H.-H., Wang, Y. S., & Chang, L. K. (2011). Consumer responses to online retailer's service recovery after a service failure. *Managing Service Quality*, *21*(5), 511–534. doi:10.1108/09604521111159807

López-Pérez, M., Melero-Polo, I., & Sesé, J. (2017). Management for Sustainable Development and Its Impact on Firm Value in the SME Context: Does Size Matter? *Business Strategy and the Environment*, *26*(7), 985–999. doi:10.1002/bse.1961

López-Pérez, M., Melero-Polo, I., Vázquez, R., & Cambra-Fierro, J. (2018). Sustainability and Business Outcomes in the Context of SMEs: Comparing Family Firms vs. Non-Family Firms. *Sustainability*, *10*(11), 4080–4090. doi:10.3390u10114080

Low, W., & Davenport, E. (2005). Postcards from the edge: Maintaining the 'alternative' character of fair trade. *Sustainable Development*, *13*(3), 143–153. doi:10.1002d.275

Lund-Thomsen, P., & Nadvi, K. (2010). Global value chains, local collective action and corporate social responsibility: A review of empirical evidence. *Business Strategy and the Environment*, *19*(1), 1–13. doi:10.1002/bse.670

Maaya, L., Meulders, M., Surmont, N., & Vandebroek, M. (2018). Effect of environmental and altruistic attitudes on willingness-to-pay for organic and fair trade coffee in Flanders. *Sustainability*, *10*(12), 4496–4510. doi:10.3390u10124496

Melo, T., & Garrido-Morgado, A. (2012). Corporate reputation: A combination of social responsibility and industry. *Corporate Social Responsibility and Environmental Management*, *19*(1), 11–31. doi:10.1002/csr.260

Möckel, B. (2019). Dilemmas of Moral Markets: Conflicting Narratives in the West German Fair Trade Movement. In *Moralizing Capitalism* (pp. 267–292). Palgrave Macmillan. doi:10.1007/978-3-030-20565-2_12

Navrátilová, M., Abrhám, J., Beranová, M., & Brož, D. (2019). Fair Trade Products And Sustainable Consumer Behaviour. *Journal of Security & Sustainability. Issues (Chicago, Ill.)*, *8*(4), 34–43.

Naylor, L. (2018). Fair trade coffee exchanges and community economies. Environment and Planning A. *Economy and Space*, *50*(5), 1027–1046.

Oosterveer, P., Rossing, G., Hendriksen, A., & Voerman, K. (2014). Mainstreaming fair trade: the role of retailers. *Sustainability: Science, Practice and Policy*, *10*(2), 4–13.

Orlitzky, M., Siegel, D., & Waldman, D. (2011). Strategic corporate social responsibility and environmental sustainability. *Business & Society*, *50*(1), 6–27. doi:10.1177/0007650310394323

Overbeek, A. (2019). Examining the Efficacy of Fair Trade and Alternative Consumption on Environmental Sustainability and Human Rights in Developing Countries. *Consilience*, (21), 158–171.

Pelham, A. M. (1997). Mediating Influences on the Relationship between Market Orientation and Profitability in Small Industrial Firms. *Journal of Marketing Theory and Practice*, *5*(3), 55–77. doi:10.1080/10696679.1997.11501771

Pérez, A., & de los Salmones, M. D. (2018). Information and knowledge as antecedents of consumer attitudes and intentions to buy and recommend fair-trade products. *Journal of Nonprofit & Public Sector Marketing*, *30*(2), 111–133. doi:10.1080/10495142.2017.1326358

Porter, M., & Kramer, M. (2006). Strategy and society: The link between competitive advantage and CSR. *Harvard Business Review*, *84*, 78–92. PMID:17183795

Porter, M., & Kramer, M. (2011). Creating shared value. *Harvard Business Review*, *89*, 62–77.

Ramasamy, B., & Yeung, M. (2009). "Chinese consumers" perception of corporate social responsibility (CSR). *Journal of Business Ethics*, *88*(1), 119–132. doi:10.100710551-008-9825-x

Raynolds, L. T. (2012). Fair trade: Social regulation in global food markets. *Journal of Rural Studies*, *28*(3), 276–287. doi:10.1016/j.jrurstud.2012.03.004

Raynolds, L. T., & Greenfield, N. (2015). Fair trade: movement and markets. Handbook of research on Fair Trade, 24-41.

Rios, K., Finkelstein, S. R., & Landa, J. (2015). Is there a "fair" in fair-trade? Social dominance orientation influences perceptions of and preferences for fair-trade products. *Journal of Business Ethics*, *130*(1), 171–180. doi:10.100710551-014-2221-9

Sama, C., Crespo-Cebada, E., Díaz-Caro, C., Escribano, M., & Mesías, F. J. (2018). Consumer Preferences for Foodstuffs Produced in a Socio-environmentally Responsible Manner: A Threat to Fair Trade Producers*? Ecological Economics*, *150*, 290–296. doi:10.1016/j.ecolecon.2018.04.031

Stenn, T. (2013). Fair Trade and Justice: An examination of fair trade. *The Review of Radical Political Economics*, *20*(10), 1–12.

Torres, A., Bijmolt, T., Tribó, J., & Verhoef, P. (2012). Generating global brand equity through corporate social responsibility to key stakeholders. *International Journal of Research in Marketing*, *29*(1), 13–24. doi:10.1016/j.ijresmar.2011.10.002

Torugsa, N., O'Donohue, W., & Hecker, R. (2012). Capabilities, proactive CSR and financial performance in SMEs: Empirical evidence from an Australian manufacturing industry sector. *Journal of Business Ethics*, *109*(4), 483–500. doi:10.100710551-011-1141-1

Tovernić, I. (2017). *Fair trade in response to the problems of agricultural production of developing countries* (Doctoral dissertation). Ekonomski fakultet, Sveučilište u Zagrebu.

Yim, S., Bae, Y. H., Lim, H., & Kwon, J. (2019). The role of marketing capability in linking CSR to corporate financial performance: When CSR gives positive signals to stakeholders. *European Journal of Marketing*, *53*(7), 1333–1354. Advance online publication. doi:10.1108/EJM-08-2017-0526

Chapter 6
Brazilian Immigrant Entrepreneurs in Portugal and the Challenges of Crowdfunding

Susana Bernardino
https://orcid.org/0000-0002-1639-3553
Polytechnic of Porto, Portugal

J. Freitas Santos
https://orcid.org/0000-0001-8233-5039
Polytechnic of Porto, Portugal

Eliane Casarin
Polytechnic of Porto, Portugal

ABSTRACT

The objective of the study is to understand the degree of knowledge that immigrant entrepreneurs in Portugal have about crowdfunding and the predisposition they have for using this financial mechanism, and the related perceptions about benefits and risks. The chapter uses a quantitative approach, based on an online survey sent to immigrant entrepreneurs in Portugal. The results show that immigrant entrepreneurs have some knowledge about the general features of CF. However, most of them are not aware of the specificities of CF business models. Regarding the predisposition for using CF, the research reveals that although there is some predisposition, it is not very high among Brazilian immigrant entrepreneurs. The results also show that the respondents recognise the benefits of CF, specifically the project's visibility that the CF platform can offer. However, immigrant entrepreneurs' main concern is essentially related to the fear of not being able to obtain the necessary pledging goal.

DOI: 10.4018/978-1-7998-8925-0.ch006

INTRODUCTION

Entrepreneurship is an important instrument for promoting economic growth, job creation, income generation and the improvement of individuals' skills and abilities, especially for immigrants who could face special economic and socio-cultural integration difficulties in the hosting country (García-Cabrera et al., 2020). For immigrants, entrepreneurship can be a way of empowerment and of breaking the risk of economic and social exclusion to which they are exposed, especially in time of pandemic or economic and social crises.

Nevertheless, when launching their social ventures, entrepreneurs face some challenges, especially the capacity to mobilise the financial resources necessary for the venture, mainly in the initial stages (Belleñamme et al., 2010). Immigrant entrepreneurs, who launch projects in other markets than their own country of origin, face increased challenges, which they need to overcome for the venture to succeed (Jiang et al., 2016).

The COVID-19 pandemic is leading to a severe deterioration of economic and social conditions, making the poverty and social exclusion risk increasingly higher, especially for more susceptible groups, such as immigrants. Further, the Post-COVID-19 period will face significant challenges related to the resources available to create new ventures, where immigrant entrepreneurs, will once again face difficulties in obtaining funding for their projects.

Over the last few years, new forms of financing have been developed. Collaborative funding, or crowdfunding (CF), is one of these new fundraising tools that are especially promising for small start-up ventures and has experienced strong growth as a source of financing for the entrepreneurial activity in the economic-financial crisis that arose in 2008 (Kuti & Madarász, 2014; Stemler, 2013).

Despite its potential as an alternative funding source, CF is still a not very explored area. Indeed, crowdfunding is so far scarcely known by the general population, and even by some of the publics who might be most interested in using this type of funding, such as entrepreneurs.

This research aims to understand the level of knowledge that Brazilian immigrant entrepreneurs in Portugal have about crowdfunding and their propensity to use this alternative funding source.

This study is justified by the academic relevance that crowdfunding and immigrant entrepreneurship have acquired in literature, as well as the practical importance that the exploitation of new forms of funding has for immigrant entrepreneurship. Moreover, in this turbulent and challenging environment, it is crucial to discover new paths to reduce the obstacles to immigrant entrepreneurship and find new funding sources for those who want to develop an entrepreneurial activity to improve their economic and social condition.

The chapter begins with a literature review on the concept of immigrant entrepreneurship and its implications, and then it advances to the presentation of the crowdfunding concept and the existing business models. Next, follows the description of the methodology used in the study, the results and conclusions

BACKGROUND

Immigrant Entrepreneurship

According to the International Organization for Migration (2019, p. 103) immigration is "the act of moving into a country other than one's country of nationality or usual residence, so that the country of destination effectively becomes his or her new country of usual residence". The term immigrant entrepreneurship, in turn, refers to the portion of immigrants who opt for entrepreneurship, i.e., for the creation of their own business that allows them to exploit a market opportunity (Shane & Venkataraman, 2000), driven either by their own choice or just by necessity (Baggio & Baggio, 2015; Zolfagharian & Iyer, 2020).

As a result, immigrants who are being entrepreneurs by choice seek better living conditions for themselves and their families, aiming to grow economically through their own business. On the other hand, entrepreneurship driven by necessity is directly linked to the scarcity of opportunities and create their own business to obtain sources of income due to the difficulty of accessing work in the host country (Van Auken et al., 2006; Zolfagharian & Iyer, 2020).

The Organization for Economic Co-operation and Development (OECD, 2019) defines immigrant entrepreneurs as foreign-born who seek to generate value through the creation or expansion of economic activity, through the identification of new products, processes, or markets.

As Azmat (2010) emphasises, immigrant entrepreneurship is related to the search for opportunities across borders, or the exercise of the same entrepreneurial activity in several countries, highlighting some points in common with the theme of internationalisation. The phenomenon of immigrant entrepreneurship has attained great relevance worldwide, in several areas of study (Cruz & Falcão, 2017). For Lintner (2015), entrepreneurial immigrants are seen as agents of territorial development and can be seen as a new and important space for social, economic and political development.

According to existing research, immigrants are more likely to create a new business and work as self-employed people than natives with the same skills (Sahin et al., 2007; Mestres, 2010; Stakanov, 2016; Brzozowski et al., 2017). For this reason, entrepreneurship often becomes an instrument for the labor integration of immigrants in the host country, especially when it is considered an alternative to the lack of employment opportunities and potential exploitation by employers (Coutinho et al., 2008).

According to OECD (2019), immigrants are another rapidly growing group of entrepreneurs. The number of self-employed immigrants in the European Union has nearly doubled since 2002, increasing from 1.9 million to 3.6 million in 2018. Consequently, immigrant entrepreneurship has a vital role in the country's economy, by making use and taking advantage of the immigrants' resources and skills, for economic and social development (Stakanov, 2016). As a consequence, immigrant entrepreneurship has an important role in the country's economy, by making use of immigrants' resources and abilities. This impulse is also felt in the origin countries by promoting trade and leveraging companies' internationalisation. According to Sahin, Nijkamp and Baycan (2007) high unemployment rates, low participation rates and low status are the main determinants that lead immigrants to become entrepreneurs in many European countries, especially in cities.

The research of Dabić et al. (2020) highlights that one of the main reasons for immigrant entrepreneurship are the entrepreneurial motivation. However, other reasons also coexist such as i) theory of disadvantage, and ii) cultural theory.

The theory of disadvantage claims that immigrant entrepreneurship is the only way for immigrants to survive in the host country, considering that the need for subsistence forces immigrants to open their own businesses (Dabić et al., 2020). Oliveira (2019) further adds that the theory of disadvantage takes into account the constraint and exclusion situations felt by immigrants. Cultural theory, in turn, refers to the cultural background that is found in the immigrants' characteristics, which sometimes drives entrepreneurial motivation (Dabić et al., 2020). Oliveira (2019) shows that discrimination in the labor market and the barriers that the immigrant community faces in accessing social mobility, contribute to foster entrepreneurial activity. In this sense, entrepreneurial initiatives emerge as responses to the constraints immigrants experience when entering the host country's working labor market (Ulceluse, 2020).

Accordingly, among the various factors that drive immigrants to be entrepreneurs are the desire to get better-paid jobs, the identification of business opportunities in the host country, the lack of economic opportunities, and the instability found in the country of origin (Jiang *et al.*, 2016).

There are several difficulties that immigrants face when they are looking for better living conditions in other countries (Sah, 2019; García-Cabrera et al., 2020), such as language abilities, knowledge about the local culture, understanding of laws, norms, institutions, as well as the business and economic world of the country in which they are entering (Dabić *et al.*, 2020; Golob *et al.*, 2020). Jiang *et al.* (2016), also highlight the need to survive in the initial stage of the new business, especially due to the numerous difficulties related to the acquisition of human, financial and social capital, as well as the barriers faced in the institutional environment of the host country, which is different from those of the country of origin.

Another critical factor that immigrant entrepreneurs face refers to access to finance and the necessary financial instruments to invest in the business, since entrepreneurs may not have enough resources or networks to provide them with the required funding, nor have information on existing financial support tools to entrepreneurs (Coutinho *et al.*, 2008; Tengeh & Nkem, 2017; Muchineripi et al., 2019; Dabić *et al.*, 2020). Therefore, when launching a new project, entrepreneurs often face major difficulties, including in attracting external financial resources, in the various early stages of the project (Belleñamme et al., 2010; Silva & Monteiro, 2014; Blaseg et al., 2020).

The investigation on the main barriers faced by immigrant entrepreneurs living in Portugal, conducted by Paço and Ramos (2018) indicates the access to credit, untruth, lack of initiative, cultural differences, polarity, mentality, lack of knowledge, language and bureaucracy. However, for Coutinho *et al.* (2008), the major challenges of immigrant entrepreneurship is the absence of knowledge of the dynamics needed to create and manage a new business, especially access to credit.

Crowdfunding

Crowdfunding (CF) is an Anglo-Saxon term that means collaborative funding. By the combination of the words "crowd" and "funding", the concept intends to convey funding through the crowd (Shneor & Vik, 2020). The CF system has its origin in crowdsourcing which, in a broad sense, uses the "crowd" to obtain ideas, feedback and solutions to develop corporative activities (Belleñamme et al., 2010). In particular, crowdfunding consists of the practice of involving the crowd to raise funds, finance entities or their activities and projects, usually obtained through the internet (Belleflamme et al., 2014). Through the use of digital platforms, crowdfunding enables the collection of financial resources provided by a large group of people, which together allow the funding of an idea or venture (Wang *et al.*, 2020). To believe in the project or organisation and having the spirit of cooperation are some of the factors that have supported the crowdfunding system since its origins (Dresner, 2014). A more comprehensive definition is that provided by Mollick(2014) for whom the crowdfunding refers to the efforts of individuals and entrepreneurial groups to finance their ventures through the relatively small contributions of a relatively large number of individuals using the internet, without conventional financial intermediaries.

The development of the crowdfunding system has occurred impressively over the past few years, primarily due to technological advancements and the boom in social media. These factors have enabled the entrepreneur to access more people (potential investors and also possible future customers), who can raise the necessary resources to implement the entrepreneurial ideas or products, especially in the start-up phase (Pierrakis & Collins, 2012; Cumming & Johan, 2020). In this sense, crowdfunding has revolutionised traditional funding methods, such as loans granted by banks, lenders and other financial entities. Therefore, as Mollick (2014) argues, crowdfunding represents a potentially disruptive change in how new ventures are financed.

CF represents an alternative for obtaining financial resources, which is critical for developing economic or social activities. Agrawal et al. (2013) emphasise that entrepreneurs are particularly interested in crowdfunding when traditional financing mechanisms have very high capital costs and also when ventures can derive additional benefits from CF resources, such as interaction with different potential investors who are located in other geographic areas.

Indeed, despite the external financing requirements that new businesses may face, startups generally have difficulty accessing bank credit due to the high requirements imposed by this funding method (Blaseg et al., 2020). This difficulty is one of the main reasons why young businesses are significantly more likely to use crowdfunding (Blaseg et al., 2020).

Crowdfunding encompasses four main modalities of funding, which are donation, reward, loan and equity. As mentioned by Bernardino and Santos (2020), the different CF modalities can be grouped into i) non-investment models and ii) investment models. Thus, the donation and reward modalities do not allow the offer of a monetary reward as a counterpart to the financing obtained; differently, the CF modalities based on loan and shares are classified as investment, since they financially benefit the investors who have supported the campaigns (Belleflamme et al., 2015).

As mentioned by Cumming and Johan (2020), the CF-based donation modality does not involve any type of obligation for the entity seeking financing, as a counterpart to the resources received. For this reason, the campaigns of this modality are usually associated with social causes, in which people donate resources without being interested in obtaining a return; nevertheless, many organisations symbolically offer rewards to the supporters of the campaign, to acknowledge the support provided.

Unlike those of donations, people who invest their financial resources on reward-based CF platforms expect to receive some compensation in return. This modality is important because it serves as a test of the product to be launched in the market (Cumming & Johan, 2020).

According to Mollick (2014), the loan-based crowdfunding is the one where the funds are offered in the form of a loan, with the expectation of some return rate on the capital invested. The loan based crowdfunding is the one where the funds are offered in the form of a loan, with the expectation of some return on the capital invested (Mollick, 2014). It consists of a credit-based funding option, which involves pre-established interest at the time of resource mobilisation, which is done through a large number of individuals who make the loan directly to the organisation or project (Moura, 2017; Cumming & Johan, 2020).

Equity-based crowdfunding, in turn, represents the riskiest and mots complex CF modality (Cumming & Johan, 2020). Therefore, investors who choose to adhere to this financing model are more likely to show a low aversion to risk. By participating in a CF campaign they are acquiring part of the business idea or company. Thus, by creating a campaign in this type of financing, the entrepreneur is abdicating part of the company to allow the increase in equity capital, achieved through the admission of new owners/shareholders who can participate in the decisions made by the organisation itself, as defined in the financing contract.

Crowdfunding offers numerous advantages, as noted in the document "Collective Financing in Detail" developed by the (European Union, 2015). The entrepreneur's main motivation to resort to crowdfunding is due to the desire to raise financial resources. Compared to traditional financing mechanisms, crowdfunding is typically a faster, more flexible and lower-cost financing tool (Yu *et al.*, 2017; Ryu, 2019). Other benefits provided by crowdfunding include easy access to finance, as the match between entrepreneurs who have created a campaign and the funders are done more effectively and efficiently through a CF platform based on the internet (Agrawal et al., 2013; Hommerová, 2020). Also, CF involves low exposure to risk, both for the entrepreneur, especially in non-investment modalities, as well as for investors, who make small investments in each one of the projects. The CF also involves low communication costs with financiers and other economic agents, even those geographically distant.

In addition to the financial benefits that the CF provides in terms of access to financial resources, crowdfunding also offers access to a multitude of people who may be interested in the projects and who can contribute valuable information and vast knowledge inputs. According to the (European Union, 2015), among these contributions beyond the financial benefits is the testing and validation of the concept, since the campaigns launched on the CF platforms receive feedback on the possible acceptance and approval of the product/service in the market.

Thereby, in addition to increasing the financed capital, the CF can also serve as a market test for the product to be launched. Furthermore, according to the (European Union, 2015), the development of a CF campaign allows access to the community, allowing the entrepreneur to interact with a vast audience, facilitating access to information and knowledge at a very low cost. The CF is also a powerful marketing tool, because the CF campaign triggers future clients' desire, even before the product is made.

Another advantage of collaborative financing is the reduction of marketing campaign costs, due to the use of the word-of-mouth effect, which generates confidence and makes it possible to reach potential clients and consolidate the brand (Cumming & Hornuf, 2018). According to Blaseg et al. (2020), the use of CF is influenced by the entrepreneur's profile behind the project, being more common using CF as a source of funding in young teams, with less experience and with female participation.

Despite the critical benefits that the CF is able to provide as a funding source, it also has some limitations. As other funding sources, the CF is not risk-free, leading many entrepreneurs to fear when using collaborative funding platforms. In particular, there is a lack of guarantee that the entrepreneur will reach the funding target defined in the campaign, the intellectual property right is not assured, there is a risk of disclosing information to competitors, legal requirements, violating the law due to lack of knowledge of legal norms, risk of using false crowdfunding platforms, risks related to the responsibility assumed and relationship with investors, underestimating the costs involved, image deterioration, as well as investors who do not honour commitments, among others (European Union, 2015). In addition, the failure of a project may condition the entrepreneur's reputation, who will not have another opportunity to make a "first good impression" (Cumming & Hornuf, 2018; Bukhari *et al.*, 2019).

Another important deterrent to the use of CF is the logistics of the CF campaign preparation and the delays in the campaign completion and achievement of the pledging goal (Agrawal et al., 2013; Maehle, 2020).

Another issue that limits the use of crowdfunding is the time associated with the range of activities to be developed, such as the materials to prepare for the campaign (such as video pitch, prototypes, etc.) and the management of social networks to be used for dissemination (e.g. Facebook, Instagram, LinkedIn and Twitter, among others) (Bernardino & Santos, 2020).

Existing empirical studies are still scarce despite the growing interest crowdfunding has received in recent years and its potential for financing entrepreneurial projects in different fields, including those promoted by immigrants. Nevertheless, a growing number of studies are beginning to focus on the use of CF by immigrants (e.g. Arshad & Berndt, 2021; Butticè & Useche, 2019; Dejean, 2020; Di Pietro,

2021). For instance, the investigation carried out by Butticè and Useche (2019), reveals low usage of this financial mechanism by immigrants, as about one in every ten crowdfundees of the largest reward-based crowdfunding platform worldwide (Kickstarter) are a foreign-born entrepreneur. The investigation performed also indicated that the success attained by immigrant entrepreneurs in crowdfunding campaigns is quite similar to local-born entrepreneurs.

METHODOLOGY

To perform the research, we have used an exploratory research, since it is the more appropriate for those situations where there is little knowledge about the subject being studied (Gil, 2008). The investigation followed a quantitative methodology, through an only questionnaire sent to immigrant entrepreneurs in Portugal.

To collect and analyse the data, it was necessary to build and validate a tool that would allow to identify and gather relevant information to understand the level of knowledge about crowdfunding from Brazilian immigrants in Portugal.

To this purpose, a questionnaire was built up that comprised five groups. The first group intended to collect information on the overall characteristics of the respondents. The second group aimed to assess the knowledge immigrants have about crowdfunding. The level of agreement/disagreement of respondents to different CF definitions was measured through a five-point Likert scale. The third group of the questionnaire, also based on a Likert type scale, sought to understand immigrants' predisposition to the use of CF. In group four and five we sought, respectively, to assess the main benefits and fears perceived by respondents regarding the use CF, based on the use of a Likert type scale. The questionnaire was developed following the literature review and was based on a previously administered and validated questionnaire (Bernardino & Santos, 2020).

For the study, the sample consisted of those individuals coming from other countries and currently residing in Portugal, who attend training courses on entrepreneurship, such as the Program for the Promotion of Immigrant Entrepreneurship, conducted by the Office of Support to Entrepreneurial Migrants held by the Portuguese High Commission for Migration, as well as the Women's Connection Network focused on women's issues, especially female entrepreneurship. Initially, we requested the support of the office of the High Commissioner for Migration, which forwarded the request to the responsible by the Office of Support to Entrepreneurial Migrants, which has collaborated by sending the questionnaire to the immigrants participating in different editions of the Program for the Promotion of Immigrant Entrepreneurship. It was not possible to know precisely the number of contacts to whom the questionnaires was sent. However, the number of replies obtained was low (39 respondents), and only 19 questionnaires were answered entirely. Therefore, due to the advance of the deadline and the few responses obtained, we decided to disseminate the research questionnaire to the Women's Connection Network, which is based on the support to female entrepreneurship. Thus, there was a great concern during the survey period to make the questionnaire reach as many respondents as possible. The questionnaire was made accessible online through the LimeSurvey platform.

The data collection was carried out between March and September 2020. During this period, it was possible to obtain 137 responses, although only 65 responses were considered valid for analysis, after excluding incomplete replies and responses whose respondents indicated other nationalities besides the Brazilian one.

The data were statistically analysed using the SPSS statistical tool, version 26. First, descriptive analysis techniques were used to analyse the data and then inferential statistics were applied.

RESULTS DESCRIPTION AND ANALYSIS

Sample Characterization

Table 1 summarises the characteristics of immigrants that compose the sample of this study. We observe that 63.1% of the respondents are female, and 36.9% are male. The analysis of age reveals that most immigrants in the sample are over 36 years old (67.7%), by contrast with the percentage of respondents who are less than 36 years old (32.3%).

Most respondents have been living in Portugal for at least 3 years (73.8%) and only 3.1% have been living in the country for more than 10 years. The respondents' characteristics indicate that the vast majority of them have higher education (93.8%), while the remaining respondents have secondary education qualifications (6.2%). In order to better understand the profile of immigrant entrepreneurs in Portugal, we sought to ascertain the number of immigrants who had already created an organisation and the probability of creating an enterprise in the future, as well as to know if they have already used any CF platform. As shown in Table 1, slightly over half of the respondents (53.8%) had already created an organisation. Respondents also indicated that the probability of creating an organisation in the future is high, with 62.7 per cent of immigrants considering this possibility as likely or very likely. It was also noted that only a small proportion of respondents had already used collaborative funding (12.3%), with the most common situation being that they had never used a CF platform (87.7%).

Knowledge About Crowdfunding

To evaluate the knowledge of Brazilian immigrants living in Portugal about crowdfunding and its different modalities, respondents were asked to indicate their level of agreement/disagreement regarding different definitions of CF. Some definitions were provided by the Portuguese Securities and Exchange Commission (Comissão do Mercado de Valores Mobiliários - CMVM), and others were based on the different crowdfunding modalities mentioned in the literature review.

As Table 2 reveals, immigrants in general have a basic knowledge of what collaborative financing is. It should be highlighted that the definition with the highest acceptance by respondents is that which indicates that through crowdfunding investment tranches are raised from several single investors. This statement attained the highest average value (average of 4.4 on the 5-point Likert scale), with 84.6% of respondents agreeing or fully agreeing with the definition. Another statement with great acceptance by respondents is the one that considers that crowdfunding consists of financing entities or their activities and projects through electronic platforms accessible on the internet. This definition was accepted by 75.4% of respondents, who agreed or fully agreed with the assertion, and had an average value of 4.3 points. There is greater recognition by respondents of the definitions related to non-investment modalities, since the donation based CF ("the financed entity does not remunerate the financing obtained, since the financing can be provided as a donation") and rewards based CF ("in crowdfunding the financed entity offers some products/services, discounts or another type of gratifications to investors or some of the investors supporting the project") are the models most recognised by the immigrant community

Table 1. Characteristics of the immigrant entrepreneur profile

Variable	Categories	N	%
Gender	Female	41	63.1%
	Male	24	36.9%
Age	< 25 years	3	4.6%
	25-35 years	18	27.7%
	36-45 years	22	33.8%
	46-55 years	16	24.6%
	> 56 years	6	9.2%
Number of Years in Portugal	< 3 years	48	73.8%
	3-5 years	14	21.5%
	5-10 years	1	1.5%
	>10 years	2	3.1%
Educational background	Secondary education	4	6.2%
	Higher education	61	93.8%
Already created any organization	Yes	35	53.8%
	No	30	46.2%
Probability of creating an organisation in the future	Very unlikely	7	11..9%
	Unlikely	5	8.5%
	Neither unlikely nor likely	10	16.9%
	Likely	15	25.4%
	Very likely	22	37.3%
Already used a CF platform	Yes	8	12.3%
	No	57	87.7%

Source: Authors' elaboration

(average value of 3.2 and 4.0, respectively). It should also be noted that the equity-based CF modality receives an average value of 3.1 among respondents. However, with the interest rate being fixed at the time of the funds asking, the loan-based CF modality is only shared by 23.1% of the respondents, who attribute an average valuation of 2.7 on the 5-point Likert scale.

To better understand the results obtained, we performed factor analysis by principal components (APC), through the varimax rotation and the listwise method, which offered the best quality criteria for statistical analysis. The Bartlett sphericity test and the Kaiser-Meyer-Olkin (KMO) measurement confirm the adequacy of the data for factorial analysis.

The factorial analysis excluded two variables that did not meet the standards of significance suggested by (Field, 2005; Hair et al., 1998).

The first component obtained is related to the general knowledge of CF and contains the variables related to raising funds through small amounts from several individual investors, the method of financing using electronic platforms accessible through the internet, as well as the variables that affirm that CF is a form of funding for-profit and non-profit entities.

Table 2. Knowledge about crowdfunding

Code	Definition	(1) %	(2) %	(3) %	(4) %	(5) %	No answer (%)	Average	Standard Deviation
B1	Crowdfunding consists of financing entities, or their activities and projects, through electronic platforms accessible through the Internet;	0.0%	1.5%	16.9%	29.2%	46.2%	6.2%	4.3	0.8
B2	Through crowdfunding, investment parcels are raised from several single investors;	0.0%	1.5%	9.2%	32.3%	52.3%	4.6%	4.4	0.7
B3	Crowdfunding is a financing tool for for-profit entities;	3.1%	3.1%	20.0%	21.5%	43.1%	9.2%	4.1	1.1
B4	Crowdfunding is a financing tool for non-profit entities;	20.0%	12.3%	15.4%	7.7%	32.3%	12.3%	3.2	1.6
B5	In crowdfunding the financed entity remunerates the financing through an equity participation, dividend distribution or profit sharing;	20.0%	6.2%	18.5%	15.4%	18.5%	21.5%	3.1	1.5
B6	In crowdfunding the financed entity remunerates the financing through the payment of an interest rate fixed at the time of the financing solicitation	21.5%	13.8%	12.3%	9.2%	13.8%	29.2%	2.7	1.5
B7	In crowdfunding the financed entity does not remunerate the financing obtained, since the financing can be granted as a donation;	20.0%	4.6%	13.8%	12.3%	23.1%	26.2%	3.2	1.6
B8	In crowdfunding the financed entity offers some products/services, discounts or other type of gratifications to investors or some of the investors who support the project	3.1%	6.2%	16.9%	15.4%	38.5%	20.0%	4.0	1.2

Note: (1) corresponds to disagree totally and (5) corresponds to agree totally;
Source: Authors' elaboration

By constructing the component index through the weighted average of the variables comprised in each principal component, it can be observed that component 1 receives an average valuation of 4.03 among the respondents (Table 3).

Component 2, in turn, refers to specific knowledge of the CF modalities and includes the variables related to donation-based and rewarded based crowdfunding. The average value of the component is 3.67.

The ex-post internal reliability test was done through the Cronbach alpha (Field, 2005).

Predisposition to the use of Crowdfunding

One of the study's main objectives was to understand the predisposition of Brazilian entrepreneurial immigrants to using crowdfunding. The analysis of the results in Table 4 indicates that although there is some predisposition on immigrant entrepreneurs to resort to CF, it is not very high. We observe that only 18.4% of the respondents indicated that they intend to use the CF to finance their entrepreneurship project, having this question received an average value of 2.7 on the five-point Likert scale. The values obtained are higher when asking if they intended to use CF if their own resources (such as goods and

Table 3. Factorial analysis for CF knowledge

Component	Loading factor	Average	Standard Deviation	Eigenvalues	% Var.	%. Accum. Var.	Cronbach's Alpha
Component 1: General knowledge		4.03	0.71	2.43	40.55	40.55	0.54
B2. Through crowdfunding. investment parcels are raised from several single investors;	0.80	4.42	0.74				
B3. Crowdfunding is a financing tool for for-profit entities;	0.70	4.08	1.07				
B4. Crowdfunding is a financing tool for non-profit entities;	0.68	3.23	1.61				
B1. Crowdfunding consists of financing entities, or their activities and projects, through electronic platforms accessible through the internet;	0.61	4.28	0.82				
Component 2: Specific knowledge of the CF modalities		3.67	1.26	1.34	22.25	62.80	0.77
B8. In crowdfunding the financed entity offers some products/services, discounts or another type of gratifications to investors or some of the investors who support the project	0.89	4.00	1.17				
B7. In crowdfunding the financed entity does not remunerate the financing obtained, since the funding can be granted as a donation;	0.88	3.19	1.61				

Note: Extraction method: APC; varimax rotation, KMO measure= 0.655; Bartlett sphericity test, p <0.000.
Source: Authors' elaboration

savings) were insufficient to launch and develop the business (30.8% agreed or fully agreed with the situation, and the average value was 2.9). However, when faced with the insufficiency of other fund sources, the predisposition to resort to CF is lower, as it happens in the case of not obtaining funding through the network (only 13.8% agreed or fully agreed, with an average value of 2.1), not obtaining financing through traditional fund sources (only reported by 15.4% of respondents, with an average value of 2.1) or not obtaining funding through other types of investors (only reported by 9.2% of respondents, with an average value of 2.0).

The majority of respondents indicated they were willing to offer discounts on products/services to people who have supported the project through the CF (61.5% of respondents, average value 4.0) or offer products or services (58.5%, average value 3.9), both related to rewards-based CF. It should also be noted that a significant percentage of respondents mentioned that they do not mind sharing part of the project profits with the potential supporters of the campaign (40.0%, average value of 3.3); the predisposition for the payment of interest on the capital obtained is lower for immigrant entrepreneurs in Portugal (30.8%, average value of 2.9). The analysis of the results also indicates that only 21.5% of the respondents mentioned that they would resort to CF if it did not involve the reimbursement of the capital obtained (average value of 2.4); 44.6% of the respondents disagreed or totally disagreed with this assertion.

Table 4. Predisposition for the use of CF

Code	Definition	(1) %	(2) %	(3) %	(4) %	(5) %	No answer (%)	Average	Standard deviation
C1	In the future I intend to use a CF platform as a means of financing my entrepreneurial project;	23.1%	10.8%	33.8%	9.2%	9.2%	13.8%	2.7	1.3
C2	I only intend to use CF if my own resources (such as assets and savings) are not sufficient to launch/develop my business;	18.5%	12.3%	23.1%	16.9%	13.8%	15.4%	2.9	1.4
C3	I only intend to use CF if I can't raise funds through my network (such as family and friends);	43.1%	9.2%	16.9%	4.6%	9.2%	16.9%	2.1	1.4
C4	I only intend to use CF if I cannot obtain financing through traditional sources of funding (e.g. bank loan);	43.1%	13.8%	12.3%	6.2%	9.2%	15.4%	2.1	1.4
C5	I only intend to use CF if I cannot obtain funding from other types of investors, such as venture capital;	40.0%	13.8%	16.9%	6.2%	3.1%	20.0%	2.0	1.2
C6	I only intend to use CF if I do not have to repay the capital obtained;	38.5%	6.2%	16.9%	12.3%	9.2%	16.9%	2.4	1.5
C7	I don't mind paying an interest rate for the capital I get through the CF campaign;	21.5%	6.2%	24.6%	21.5%	9.2%	16.9%	2.9	1.4
C8	I am willing to offer products/services to the people who support my project through CF;	10.8%	1.5%	12.3%	20.0%	38.5%	16.9%	3.9	1.4
C9	I am willing to offer discounts on products/ services to people who support my project through CF;	10.8%	0.0%	12.3%	20.0%	41.5%	15.4%	4.0	1.3
C10	I am willing to share part of the profits of my project with the people that support my project through CF;	13.8%	12.3%	16.9%	15.4%	24.6%	16.9%	3.3	1.5

Note: (1) corresponds to disagree totally and (5) to agree totally;
Source: Authors' elaboration

After confirming the data's adequacy through Bartlett's sphericity test and KMO measurement, the factorial analysis of the predisposition to the use of CF was then performed, which allowed the extraction of three principal components capable of explaining 68.27% of the total data variance (Table 5).

The first component represents immigrants who are prone to include rewards, i.e. are willing to offer discounts or products/services, and/or share part of the profit with people who have supported the project in the campaign, as well as includes the predisposition to use CF in the future to finance the venture. This component received an average value of 3.58 among respondents. With an average value of 2.26, the second component represents immigrant entrepreneurs with a predisposition to use CF in the absence of financial resources. The third component, in turn, includes only one variable and represents entrepreneurs who are willing to pay interest rates for the capital obtained through the CF campaign.

Table 5. Factorial analysis for predisposition to CF use

Component	Loading factor	Average	Standard Deviation	Eigenvalues	% Var.	%. Accum. Var.	Cronbach's Alpha
Component 1: Predisposition for Including Rewards		3.55	1.05	3.58	35.80	35.80	0.80
C9. I am willing to offer discounts on products/services to people who support my project through CF;	0.87	3.96	1.35				
C8. I am willing to offer products/services to the people who support my project through CF;	0.86	3.89	1.37				
C1. In the future I intend to use a CF platform as a means of financing my entrepreneurial project;	0.73	2.66	1.28				
C10. I am willing to share part of the profits of my project with the people that support my project through CF;	0.69	3.30	1.46				
Component 2: Predisposition driven by lack of financial resources		2.26	1.03	2.16	21.58	57.39	0.80
C4. I only intend to use CF if I cannot obtain financing through traditional sources of funding (e.g. bank loan);	0.80	2.11	1.40				
C5. I only intend to use CF if I cannot obtain funding from other types of investors, such as venture capital;	0.75	1.98	1.18				
C6. I only intend to use CF if I do not have to repay the capital obtained;	0.73	2.37	1.47				
C3. I only intend to use CF if I can't raise funds through my network (such as family and friends);	0.71	2.13	1.40				
C2. I only intend to use CF if my own resources (such as assets and savings) are not sufficient to launch/develop my business;	0.60	2.95	1.38				
Component 3 - Predisposition to the payment of interest rate		2.89	1.36	1.09	10.88	68.27	---
C7. I don't mind paying an interest rate for the capital I get through the CF campaign;	0.92	2.89	1.36				

Note: Extraction method: APC; varimax rotation, KMO measure= 0.678; Bartlett sphericity test, p <0.000.
Source: Authors' elaboration

Benefits Perceived Through the use of Crowdfunding

The analysis of the main benefits that immigrant entrepreneurs attribute to the use of crowdfunding, present in Table 6, indicates the importance attached to the increased visibility of the project provided by the CF platform, which is valued by 60.0% of respondents (average value of 4.1). This is followed by the importance assigned to obtaining feedback (53.8% of respondents, the average value of 4.0). After that, with a very close valuation among entrepreneurial immigrants comes the fact that CF allows easy financing without bureaucracy (49.2%, average value of 3.7), provides access to funding at low cost, does not require the having a collateral in the funding process and allows quick access to financing (in all cases, observed in 43.1% of respondents and with an average value of 3.6).

Table 7 presents the results of the factor analysis that follows a varimax orthogonal rotation. Based on the components' extraction criterion with eigenvalues above one (Field, 2005), two main components were obtained capable of explaining 75.61% of the total data variance. Component 1 corresponds to the variables related to communication and credibility, linked to the project's visibility, feedback from potential clients and the non-obligation to have collaterals in the financing. On the other hand, Component 2 represents the accessibility in which the related variables are easy to access CF at low cost and without bureaucracy.

The computation of the index of the main components, obtained according to the method of the factors loading weight in the principal component (Field, 2005), indicates that the main perceived benefits are essentially the visibility, feedback and not obligatory collateral in the financing (average of 3.9); conversely the fast access with low cost and without bureaucracy are less valued (average of 3.72).

Table 6. Benefits perceived by the use of CF

Code	Definition	(1) %	(2) %	(3) %	(4) %	(5) %	No answer (%)	Average	Standard deviation
D1	Crowdfunding is important because it allows quick access to funding in just a few days;	9.2%	6.2%	20.0%	15.4%	27.7%	21.5%	3.6	1.4
D2	Crowdfunding is important because it allows easy access to financing without bureaucracy;	7.7%	4.6%	16.9%	20.0%	29.2%	21.5%	3.7	1.3
D3	Crowdfunding is important because it allows access to low-cost financing	6.2%	6.2%	23.1%	16.9%	26.2%	21.5%	3.6	1.2
D4	Crowdfunding is important because it does not require the presentation of collateral in the financing (such as a guarantee or mortgage);	6.2%	7.7%	24.6%	13.8%	29.2%	18.5%	3.6	1.3
D5	Crowdfunding is important because it allows to get feedback from potential customers;	1.5%	3.1%	18.5%	24.6%	29.2%	23.1%	4.0	1.0
D6	Crowdfunding is important because it allows increased visibility to the project through the CF platform;	1.5%	4.6%	13.8%	26.2%	33.8%	20.0%	4.1	1.0

Note: (1) corresponds to totally disagree and (5) to totally agree;
Source: Authors' elaboration

Table 7. Factorial analysis for the benefits perceived by the use of CF

Component	Loading factor	Average	Standard Deviation	Eigenvalues	% Var.	%. Accum. Var.	Cronbach's Alpha
Component 1 Communication and credibility		3.90		3.29	54.78	54.78	0.83
D5. Crowdfunding is important because it allows to get feedback from potential customers;	0.90	0.94	0.99				
D6. Crowdfunding is important because it allows increased visibility to the project through the CF platform;	0.86	4.08	1.01				
D4. Crowdfunding is important because it does not require the presence of collateral in the financing (such as a guarantee or mortgage);	0.79	3.64	1.27				
Component 2 Accessibility		3.72		1.25	20.83	75.61	0.80
D1. Crowdfunding is important because it allows quick access to funding in just a few days;	0.90	1.06	1.36				
D3. Crowdfunding is important because it allows access to low-cost financing	0.77	3.65	1.25				
D2. Crowdfunding is important because it allows easy access to financing without bureaucracy;	0.74	3.75	1.29				

Note: Extraction method: APC; varimax rotation, KMO measure= 0.759; Bartlett sphericity test, p <0.000.
Source: Authors' elaboration

Perceived Fears About the use of Crowdfunding

The potential concerns felt in the utilisation of this financial instrument are presented in Table 8, where respondents emphasise, above all, the need to provide information on the business and the fear of not being able to obtain the necessary financing, mentioned as capable of dissuading 52.3% and 49.2% of respondents, respectively (average value of 4.2 in both cases).

Regulatory issues (average value of 3.8), concerns related to administrative matters (average value of 3.6) and difficulties associated with preparing a campaign (average value of 3.5) are also pointed out by respondents as significant deterrents.

For the factorial analysis, the variables whose own correlation in the anti-image matrix did not correspond to the criteria for the use of factor analysis were excluded (Field, 2005). The factorial analysis allowed extracting three variables with eighteen values higher than the unit, explaining 75.13% of the total data variance (Table 9).

The first component concerns the fears related to the costs involved and the campaign's preparation, which obtained an average value of 3.22. With an average value of 3.6, the second component refers to fears related to the external environment, particularly concerning administrative issues, regulation, and lack of knowledge of the campaign funders. On the other hand, the third component comprises the uncertainties related to financial movements – either inflows (ability to obtain the necessary funding) and outflows (ability to pay the costs of financing and repay capital), with an average value of 3.70.

The analysis of the internal reliability of the components obtained was carried out through Cronbach's Alpha.

SOLUTIONS AND RECOMMENDATIONS

The research results indicate that Brazilian immigrant entrepreneurs in Portugal, who are highly educated, have a general knowledge of the concept of crowdfunding, as they know the basic principles of the CF

Table 8. Fears perceived in the use of CF

Code	Definition	(1) %	(2) %	(3) %	(4) %	(5) %	No answer(%)	Average	Standard deviation
E1	There are difficulties related to the preparation of a CF campaign	1.5%	7.7%	29.2%	20.0%	12.3%	29.2%	3.5	1.0
E2	CF has costs related to the preparation of the campaign	6.2%	9.2%	32.3%	9.2%	10.8%	32.3%	3.1	1.1
E3	CF has costs related to obtaining capital (financing)	4.6%	9.2%	24.6%	13.8%	9.2%	38.5%	3.2	1.1
E4	CF generates uncertainty regarding the ability to pay the costs of financing and reimbursement of capital	1.5%	12.3%	29.2%	9.2%	10.8%	36.9%	3.2	1.0
E5	In CF there is a need to provide personal information	6.2%	6.2%	15.4%	23.1%	12.3%	36.9%	3.5	1.2
E6	In CF there is a need to provide information about the business	0.0%	4.6%	15.4%	10.8%	41.5%	27.7%	4.2	1.0
E7	In CF there is a fear of not being able to obtain the necessary financing	0.0%	1.5%	20.0%	9.2%	40.0%	29.2%	4.2	0.9
E8	In CF there are fears related to administrative issues	1.5%	9.2%	24.6%	16.9%	16.9%	30.8%	3.6	1.1
E9	In CF there are fears related to regulatory issues	1.5%	4.6%	23.1%	13.8%	23.1%	33.8%	3.8	1.1
E10	In CF it is not known who will be the funders of the campaign	9.2%	7.7%	23.1%	9.2%	21.5%	29.2%	3.4	1.4

Note: (1) corresponds to totally disagree and (5) to totally agree;
Source: Authors' elaboration

system as exposed in the first two statements of the questionnaire. As stated in the literature (Mollick, 2014; Belleflamme et al., 2015), the respondents agree that through crowdfunding it is possible to raise investment parcels from several individual investors. Respondents also agreed with existing positions in the literature that crowdfunding consists of financing entities, or their activities and projects, using electronic platforms accessible through the internet.

Although the CF represents itself as an essential alternative for mobilising financial resources, which allows raising the resources required to implement the ideas or products, especially in the start-up stage (Pierrakis & Collins, 2012; Cumming & Johan, 2020), the investigation carried out indicates that Brazilian immigrants in Portugal revealed to be more aware of the non-investment CF modalities, linked to donation and reward-based models.

The research reveals that despite all the potential that the CF has for entrepreneurship's dynamisation among immigrants, this is still an instrument under-exploited by this entrepreneurs' niche.

Several authors have reported the need for external financing in new businesses, and the difficulties in accessing funding for new projects (Blaseg et al., 2020), especially for immigrant entrepreneurs (Coutinho *et al.*, 2008; Dabić *et al.*, 2020). However, it is with some surprise we observe that the lack of financial resources does not appear to be one of the major CF funding drivers. It should also be noted that the research suggests that immigrant entrepreneurs are willing to use CF even if it includes some kind of reward.

Table 9. Factorial analysis of perceived fears on the use of CF

Component	Loading factor	Average	Standard Deviation	Eigenvalues	% Var.	%. Accum. Var.	Cronbach's Alpha
Component 1. costs and preparation		3.22	0.96	3.24	40.50	40.50	0.82
E2. CF has costs related to the preparation of the campaign	0.94	3.14	1.13				
E3. CF has costs related to obtaining capital (financing)	0.93	3.23	1.12				
E1. There are difficulties related to the preparation of a CF campaign	0.58	3.48	0.98				
Component 2 Fears related to the external environment		3.60	0.90	1.52	18.98	59.48	0.69
E8. In CF there are fears related to administrative issues	0.85	3.56	1.08				
E9. In CF there are fears related to regulatory issues	0.77	3.79	1.08				
E10. In CF it is not known who will be the funders of the campaign	0.74	3.37	1.37				
Component 3 Uncertainty related to financial flows		3.70	0.86	1.25	15.65	75.13	0.62
E4. CF generates uncertainty regarding the ability to pay the costs of financing and reimbursement of capital	0.82	3.24	1.04				
E7. In CF there is a fear of not being able to obtain the necessary financing	0.80	4.24	0.95				

Note: Extraction method: PCA; varimax rotation, KMO measure= 0.619; Bartlett sphericity test, $p < 0.000$.
Source: Authors' elaboration

Therefore, the research does not allow to confirm the argument of Blaseg et al. (2020), which indicates that the financing difficulty represents one of the main reasons why young ventures are significantly more likely to use crowdfunding.

The research also points out that immigrant entrepreneurs perceive several benefits in the use of crowdfunding. The most valued benefit is the perceived increased visibility of the project provided by the CF platform, which corroborates the position that highlights the importance of CF in terms of marketing, confidence building, reaching potential customers and brand consolidation (Cumming & Hornuf, 2018).

Indeed, the analysis of the perceived benefits of using CF indicates that the dimension related to communication and credibility, linked to the visibility of the project, feedback from potential clients and the non-obligation to have collaterals in the financing, surpasses the attribution given to the component related to accessibility to CF, which comprises the variables of easy access to funding, with low cost and without bureaucracy.

Finally, the investigation highlights the fears related to the use of the CF which focus mainly on the need to provide information on the business and the fear of not being able to obtain the necessary financing, which is recognised as capable of dissuading the use of the CF.

The research carried out has some practical implications. A more precise knowledge of the predisposition of entrepreneurial immigrants for using CF will support the development of more assertive public policies and strategies that might stimulate the use of CF and help to bridge the immigrant entrepreneurs' financing gap. Also, the development of training programs and capacity building programs for the use of the CF among immigrants will also be beneficial for increasing the potential entrepreneurial rate, and alleviate many of the social and economic problems that immigrants face in the new country country. Indeed, the creation of successful new businesses provides a significant improvement in the immigrants' quality of life, fostering their social and economic inclusion in the host society.

FUTURE RESEARCH DIRECTIONS

As a future research, it is worthy of enlarging the sample and include entrepreneurs who have been in the market for a more extended period to perceive better the knowledge and predisposition to the use of CF, as well as the benefits and fears perceived.

Further, other investigations related to crowdfunding and immigrant entrepreneurship are also suggested, due to the still very scarce empirical evidence and especially due to the need for specific knowledge of the immigrant community and the barriers faced in different countries.

CONCLUSION

This investigation aimed to understand the level of knowledge Brazilian immigrant entrepreneurs in Portugal have about crowdfunding and their predisposition to use this funding source.

The research findings indicate that the immigrant entrepreneurs in the study have some knowledge about the general conceptions of crowdfunding, although they demonstrate a lack of knowledge about the existing different financing modalities, especially those related to investment. Although immigrant entrepreneurs have a high propensity to create organisations, only a small percentage indicated having already used CF, and although they have some predisposition to use this financing tool, the likelihood to resort it is not very high.

The research also reveals that immigrant entrepreneurs, despite realising the benefits of using crowdfunding to mobilise resources, mainly value the project's visibility that the CF platform is capable of leverage.

Concerning the fears related to the use of crowdfunding, the study indicates that immigrants entrepreneurs' worries focus mainly on the uncertainties associated with the CF campaign financial flows and the external issues, rather than the preparation of the campaign itself and the costs involved.

The findings of the study suggest that there is a need to focus on the adequate promotion of this important alternative fundraising source among immigrant entrepreneurs in Portugal, a target group that could derive a significant advantage from the use of crowdfunding.

Another aspect that the research signals is the relevance of the benefits linked to marketing and attracting clients for rewarding products or services in the immigrant entrepreneurs' niche.

The research main limitations are related to the sample size, despite all the diligence made to increase the response rate. Thus, due to the recognised limitation, and for being an exploratory study, the results obtained should be analysed in accordance with the specific context in which the empirical research was conducted. Nevertheless, the findings attained strengthen the current knowledge about CF and it is expected that the exploratory study could trigger future researcher's realisation. Another limitation of the study is not considering the different types of immigrats involved, a topic that could be explored in future research.

ACKNOWLEDGMENT

This work is financed by Portuguese national funds through FCT (Fundação para a Ciência e Tecnologia), under the project UIDB/05422/2020. The authors also wish to thank Centre for Social and Organizational Studies (CEOS).

REFERENCES

Agrawal, A., Catalini, C., & Goldfarb, A. (2013). Some Simple Economics of Crowdfunding. In *NBER Chapters* (pp. 63–97). National Bureau of Economic Research, Inc. https://ideas.repec.org/h/nbr/nberch/12946.html

Arshad, N., & Berndt, A. (2021). Expanding understanding of family social capital in crowdfunding of migrant entrepreneurial ventures. *Journal of Enterprising Communities: People and Places in the Global Economy*.

Azmat, F. (2010). Exploring social responsibility of immigrant entrepreneurs: Do home country contextual factors play a role? *European Management Journal*, *28*(5), 377–386. doi:10.1016/j.emj.2009.11.004

Baggio, A., & Baggio, D. (2015). Empreendedorismo: Conceitos e definições. *Revista de Empreendedorismo. Inovação e Tecnologia*, *1*(1), 25–38.

Baycan-Levent, T., & Nijkamp, P. (2010). Migrant Entrepreneurship in a Diverse Europe. In *Search of Sustainable Development. Em Chapters*. Edward Elgar Publishing. https://ideas.repec.org/h/elg/eechap/14043_16.html

Belleflamme, P., Lambert, T., & Schwienbacher, A. (2014). Crowdfunding: Tapping the right crowd. *Journal of Business Venturing*, *29*(5), 585–609. doi:10.1016/j.jbusvent.2013.07.003

Belleflamme, P., Omrani, N., & Peitz, M. (2015). The economics of crowdfunding platforms. *Information Economics and Policy*, *33*, 11–28. doi:10.1016/j.infoecopol.2015.08.003

Belleñamme, P., Lambert, T., & Schwienbacher, A. (2010, Junho 25). *Crowdfunding: An Industrial Organization Perspective*. Digital Business Models: Understanding Strategies, Paris.

Bernardino, S., & Santos, J. F. (2020). Crowdfunding: An Exploratory Study on Knowledge, Benefits and Barriers Perceived by Young Potential Entrepreneurs. *Journal of Risk and Financial Management*, *13*(4), 1–24. doi:10.3390/jrfm13040081

Blaseg, D., Cumming, D., & Koetter, M. (2020). Equity Crowdfunding: High-Quality or Low-Quality Entrepreneurs? *Entrepreneurship Theory and Practice*.

Brzozowski, J., Cucculelli, M., & Surdej, A. (2017). The determinants of transnational entrepreneurship and transnational ties' dynamics among immigrant entrepreneurs in ICT sector in Italy. *International Migration (Geneva, Switzerland)*, *55*(3), 105–125. doi:10.1111/imig.12335

Bukhari, F., Usman, S., Usman, M., & Hussain, K. (2019). The effects of creator credibility and backer endorsement in donation crowdfunding campaigns success. *Baltic Journal of Management*, *15*(2), 215–235. doi:10.1108/BJM-02-2019-0077

Butticè, V., & Useche, D. (2019). Crowdfunding to Overcome Liability of Outsidership: Drivers of Immigrants' Fundraising Performance. *Academy of Management Proceedings*, *2019*(1), 11642. doi:10.5465/AMBPP.2019.11642abstract

Coutinho, A., Oliveira, B., Soares, V., & Sanchez, S. (2008). O empreendedorismo imigrante em Portugal: Factores que influenciam este percurso profissional e actividade da ASI decorrente dos resultados do projecto PEI. *Revista Migrações*, *3*, 263–270.

Cruz, E., & Falcão, R. (2017). Revisão bibliométrica no tema Empreendedorismo Imigrante e Étnico. *Internext*, *11*(3), 78–94. doi:10.18568/1980-4865.11378-94

Cumming, D., & Hornuf, L. (2018). *The Economics of Crowdfunding—Startups, Portals and Investor Behavior*. Palgrave Macmillan.

Cumming, D., & Johan, S. (2020). *Crowdfunding Fundamental Cases, Facts, and Insights* (2nd ed.). Elsevier.

Dabić, M., Vlačić, B., Paul, J., Dana, L.-P., Sahasranamam, S., & Glinka, B. (2020). Immigrant entrepreneurship: A review and research agenda. *Journal of Business Research*, *113*(C), 25–38. doi:10.1016/j.jbusres.2020.03.013

Dejean, S. (2020). The role of distance and social networks in the geography of crowdfunding: Evidence from France. *Regional Studies*, *54*(3), 329–339. doi:10.1080/00343404.2019.1619924

Di Pietro, F. (2021). Leveraging regional immigration and immigration diversity for financing crowdfunding projects. *Regional Studies, Regional Science*, *8*(1), 291–301. doi:10.1080/21681376.2021.1939129

Dresner, S. (2014). *Crowdfunding: A Guide to Raising Capital on the Internet*. Wiley.

European Union. (2015). *O financiamento coletivo em pormenor*. European Union Publications. https://op.europa.eu/pt/publication-detail/-/publication/d5e626ba-d7c8-11e6-ad7c-01aa75ed71a1

Field, A. (2005). Discovering statistics using SPSS (2nd ed.). Sage Publications, Inc.

García-Cabrera, A., Lucía-Casademunt, A. M., & Padilla-Angulo, L. (2020). Immigrants' entrepreneurial motivation in Europe: Liabilities and assets. *International Journal of Entrepreneurial Behaviour & Research*, *26*(8), 1707–1737. doi:10.1108/IJEBR-01-2020-0042

Golob, T., Kleindienst, P., Makarovič, M., & Kildi, J. M. (2020). Challenges of Migrant Entrepreneurship in Selected Regions of Central Europe. *Comparative Sociology*, *19*(4–5), 609–631. doi:10.1163/15691330-BJA10021

Jiang, G., Kotabe, M., Hamilton, I. III, & Smith, S. (2016). Early internationalization and the role of immigration in new venture survival. *International Business Review*, *25*(6), 1285–1296. doi:10.1016/j.ibusrev.2016.04.001

Kuti, M., & Madarász, G. (2014). Crowdfunding. *Public Finance Quarterly*, *59*(3), 355–366.

Lintner, C. (2015). Migrant Entrepreneurship: New Potential Discovered. *Procedia: Social and Behavioral Sciences*, *191*, 1601–1606. doi:10.1016/j.sbspro.2015.04.519

Maehle, N. (2020). Sustainable crowdfunding: Insights from the project perspective. *Baltic Journal of Management*, *15*(2), 281–302. doi:10.1108/BJM-02-2019-0079

Mestres, J. (2010). *Migrant entrepreneurship in OECD countries and its contribution to employment*. Academic Press.

Mollick, E. (2014). The dynamics of crowdfunding: An exploratory study. *Journal of Business Venturing*, *29*(1), 1–16. doi:10.1016/j.jbusvent.2013.06.005

Moura, B. (2017). *Crowdlending (Financiamento Colaborativo por Empréstimos) Perfil dos Early Fundraisers. Estudo de Caso—Plataformas Portuguesas*. Academic Press.

Muchineripi, J., Chinyamurindi, W., & Chimucheka, T. (2019). A narrative analysis of barriers encountered by a sample of immigrant entrepreneurs in the Eastern Cape province of South Africa. *The Journal for Transdisciplinary Research in Southern Africa*, *15*(1), 9. doi:10.4102/td.v15i1.556

OECD. (2019). *The Missing Entrepreneurs 2019 Policies for inclusive Entrepreneurship*. https://www.oecd.org/cfe/leed/2019-ME-Policy-Highlights.pdf

Oliveira, C. (2019). *Empregadores e Empreendedores Imigrantes: Tipologia de Estratégias Empresariais*. Observatório das Migrações, ACM, I.P.

Paço, S., & Ramos, M. (2018). Empreendedorismo em Portugal de imigrantes de países de fora da União Europeia. *HOLOS*, *2*(0), 365–385. doi:10.15628/holos.2018.6924

Pierrakis, Y., & Collins, L. (2012). *The venture crowd: Crowdfunding equity investment into business*. Nesta.

Ryu, S. (2019). Key challenges and drawbacks of crowdfunding. In Beauty of Crowdfunding. Routledge. doi:10.4324/9780429243714-11

Sah, P. (2019). Immigrant and refugee language policies, programs, and practices in an era of change: Promises, contradictions, and possibilities. In *Routledge International Handbook of Migration Studies* (pp. 325–338). Routledge.

Sahin, M., Nijkamp, P., & Baycan, T. (2007). Migrant entrepreneurship from the perspective of cultural diversity. Handbook of Research on Ethnic Minority Entrepreneurship, 99–113.

Shane, S., & Venkataraman, S. (2000). The Promise of Entrepreneurship as a Field of Research. *Academy of Management Review*, *25*(1), 217–226. doi:10.5465/amr.2000.2791611

Shneor, R., & Vik, A. (2020). Crowdfunding success: A systematic literature review 2010–2017. *Baltic Journal of Management*, *15*(2), 149–182. doi:10.1108/BJM-04-2019-0148

Silva, E., & Monteiro, F. (2014). *Empreendedorismo e plano de negócio* (2a ed.). Vida Económica.

Stakanov, R. (2016). Influence of immigrants on the entrepreneurship development in the host countries. *Baltic Journal of Economic Studies*, *2*(4), Article 4.

Stemler, A. (2013). The JOBS Act and crowdfunding: Harnessing the power – and money – of the masses. *Business Horizons*, *56*(3), 271–275. doi:10.1016/j.bushor.2013.01.007

Tengeh, R., & Nkem, L. (2017). Sustaining Immigrant Entrepreneurship in South Africa: The Role of Informal Financial Associations. *Sustainability*, *9*(8), 1396. doi:10.3390u9081396

Ulceluse, M. (2020). Self-employment as a stepping stone to better labor market matching: A comparison between immigrants and natives. *Journal of Demographic Economics*, *86*(4), 479–501. doi:10.1017/dem.2020.1

Van Auken, H., Stephens, P., Fry, F., & Silva, J. (2006). Role model influences on entrepreneurial intentions: A comparison between USA and Mexico. *The International Entrepreneurship and Management Journal*, *2*(3), 325–336. doi:10.100711365-006-0004-1

Wang, W., Chen, W., Zhu, K., & Wang, H. (2020). Emphasizing the entrepreneur or the idea? The impact of text content emphasis on investment decisions in crowdfunding. *Decision Support Systems*, *136*, 113341.

Yu, S., Johnson, S., Lai, C., Cricelli, A., & Fleming, L. (2017). Crowdfunding and regional entrepreneurial investment: An application of the CrowdBerkeley database. *Research Policy*, *46*(10), 1723–1737.

Zolfagharian, M., & Iyer, P. (2020). The effects of intergroup boundary permeability and hierarchy legitimacy on immigrant entrepreneurs' affective states, exchange strategies, and intentions toward suppliers. *Industrial Marketing Management*, *89*, 373–388. doi:10.1016/j.indmarman.2020.02.002

ADDITIONAL READING

Block, J., Fisch, C., & Hirschmann, M. (2021). The determinants of bootstrap financing in crises: Evidence from entrepreneurial ventures in the COVID-19 pandemic. *Small Business Economics*. Advance online publication. doi:10.100711187-020-00445-6

Fonrouge, C. (2017). Crowdfunding and Diasporas: Do Crowdfunding Practices Challenge Players Involved in Project Financing in their Former Homeland? *Innovations*, *1*(1), 211–231. doi:10.3917/inno.052.0211

Malki, B., Uman, T., & Pittino, D. (2020). The entrepreneurial financing of the immigrant entrepreneurs: A literature review. *Small Business Economics*. Advance online publication. doi:10.100711187-020-00444-7

March-Chordà, I., Adame-Sánchez, C., & Yagüe-Perales, R. (2021). Key locational factors for immigrant entrepreneurs in top entrepreneurial ecosystems. *The International Entrepreneurship and Management Journal*, *17*(3), 1049–1066. Advance online publication. doi:10.100711365-021-00746-6

March-Chorda, I., Adame-Sanchez, C., & Yague-Perales, R. M. (2021). Key locational factors for immigrant entrepreneurs in top entrepreneurial ecosystems. *The International Entrepreneurship and Management Journal*, *17*(3), 1049–1066. Advance online publication. doi:10.100711365-021-00746-6

Patler, C., & Saadi, A. (2021). Risk of Poor Outcomes with COVID-19 Among U.S. Detained Immigrants: A Cross-Sectional Study. *Journal of Immigrant and Minority Health*, *23*(4), 863–866. Advance online publication. doi:10.100710903-021-01173-z PMID:33661415

Szczygiel, N., Nunes, C., & Ramos, D. (2020). Social Support in Migrant Entrepreneurship Before and During the Coronavirus Crisis. *European Conference on Innovation and Entrepreneurship*. DOI:10.34190/EIE.20.222

Zahra, S. (2021). International entrepreneurship in the post Covid world. *Journal of World Business*, *56*(1), 101143. doi:10.1016/j.jwb.2020.101143

KEY TERMS AND DEFINITIONS

Crowdfundee: Entrepreneur that use crowdfunding platforms for attracting funds for financing a company or new venture.

Crowdfunder: People that offer funds to support a crowdfunding campaign, that could or not be repaid and rewarded.

Crowdfunding: Fundraising operation through which an organization asks funds through an open call directly to a large number of people (the crowd), who typically contribute with small amounts of money.

Crowdfunding Platforms: Digital platforms that disseminate on their website the projects that pledge for funding (crowdfundees), and collect the offers made by crowdfunders. Crowdfunding platforms also defines the rules to be used in the CF operations.

Entrepreneur: A proactive person that develops a new venture assuming the risks involved.

Entrepreneurship: Process that involves the identification and exploration of opportunities through the development of innovative products, services or business models.

Fundraising: Process of gathering resources to finance a given activity.

Immigrant Entrepreneurship: Entrepreneurial activity that is carried out by an immigrant person in the host foreign country.

Immigrants: People who move from one country to another, which becomes his/her usual place of residence.

Immigration: Process in which people move to a foreigner country, looking for new opportunities for personal and professional development.

Chapter 7
Entrepreneurial Intention and Multidimensional Proverty:
Analysis of the Relationship

Francisco Espasandin-Bustelo
Universidad de Sevilla, Spain

Juan Ganaza Vargas
Universidad de Sevilla, Spain

María del Mar Vaquero Ruiz
Universidad de Sevilla, Spain

ABSTRACT

The authors intend to identify the level of entrepreneurial intention and multidimensional poverty of the population of a Spanish rural municipality; secondly, they want to know the impact of the factors that, according to the theory of planned behavior, determine the entrepreneurial intention; thirdly, they attempt to show the characteristics of the relationship between the entrepreneurial intention and multidimensional poverty; and, fourthly, and in light of previously generated knowledge, strategies, programs, projects, and/or actions that contribute to the reduction of multidimensional poverty will be proposed. This research provides social utility and is original to the extent that it remedies a weakness in the literature consulted: the deficit of studies that contemplate, from both the theoretical and empirical perspective, the relationship between entrepreneurial intention and multidimensional poverty.

INTRODUCTION

Entrepreneurship is a key factor for economic growth and development, and job creation (Habib et al., 2020; Valencia, 2020); and it provides hope to combat poverty (Verspagen, 2005). The entrepreneur plays a central role in the economy since he/she offers innovative goods and services, contributes to increase productivity and combats unemployment (Ibarvo et al., 2018). So, Shane (2009) argues that

DOI: 10.4018/978-1-7998-8925-0.ch007

there tend to be more entrepreneurial activities in poor countries than in developed nations; although according to Chen et al. (2014) perceived poverty and lack of financing determine the probability that people start businesses.

According to Moradi et al. (2020) the scientific literature on knowledge areas "entrepreneurial intention" and "multidimensional poverty" is very broad. However, few studies theorize, analyze or model the influence of entrepreneurship on multidimensional poverty, due to different causes (Bruton et al., 2013). Firstly, entrepreneurship academics do not live or experience conditions of poverty and, therefore, they are not sensitized to the state of poverty and, secondly, the majority of researchers who publish on entrepreneurial intention reside in North America or Europe (where poverty is not a core issue) or they are part of underdeveloped countries relatively rich elite. So Sutter et al. (2019) signal that this area research, although deficient, evolves in an increasing progression. Thus it is beneficial to generate knowledge about entrepreneurship and poverty and to propose strategies, programs and projects that contribute to poverty reduction.

Researchers and management professionals (Si et al., 2020; Sutter et al., 2019) are increasingly entrenched in the idea that entrepreneurship plays a fundamental role in reducing poverty. Rahman et al. (2016) state that the relationship between entrepreneurship and poverty has not been theorized. In this sense, Si et al. (2020) argue that some research could be technically valid, although conceptually flawed and generate misunderstandings. Most of the research that has been carried out on entrepreneurial intention has focused on students (Liñán & Fayolle, 2015), unemployed (Hodzic et al., 2015), teachers and researchers (Miranda et al., 2017), employees (Gast et al., 2017) and former entrepreneurs (Hsu et al., 2017); but there is little research that focuses on people at risk of poverty.

On the other hand, Chen et al. (2014) state that the poor are more likely to start their own business because it is more desirable than their current condition and because they do not have much to lose by becoming entrepreneurs. Furthermore, Venugopal et al. (2015) argue that people in precarious subsistence conditions draw upon entrepreneurial intention as a mechanism to improve their living standards. However, people living in poverty have cognitive limitations (Mullainathan & Shafir, 2013) and lack management skills (Venugopal et al., 2015).

There are several objectives that are pursued with this exploratory, quantitative, descriptive and explanatory research. In the first place, we intend to identify the level of entrepreneurial intention and multidimensional poverty of the population of a Spanish rural municipality; secondly, we want to identify the impact of the factors that, according to the theory of planned behavior (TPB) of Ajzen (1991), determine the entrepreneurial intention; thirdly, we will attempt to show the characteristics of the relationship between entrepreneurial intention and multidimensional poverty; and, fourthly, and in the light of previously generated knowledge, strategies, programs, projects and / or actions will be offered that favor the reduction of multidimensional poverty.

To achieve these objectives, the research has been structured according to the following sections. First, the literature on the two most relevant research topics "multidimensional poverty" and "entrepreneurial intention" is reviewed; second, the data collection and analysis methods are described; third, the results are discussed; and, finally, the final considerations are presented in which the conclusions, implications, limitations and future lines of research are detailed.

LITERATURE REVIEW

Poverty and Its Measurement

Entrepreneurship by necessity versus entrepreneurship by opportunity may be motivated by circumstances related to the loss of a job or an attempt to leave the state of poverty (Shinnar & Zamantili, 2019; Tarapuez et al., 2018); it is recognized as a survival strategy, rather than a profitable economic activity (Moradi et al., 2020). Entrepreneurs driven by necessity present characteristics inherent to poor communities, among which the literature refers to inadequate social capital (Lee et al., 2011), the difficulty of access to material resources (Rhyne and Otero, 1992) or the low level educational (Baxter et al., 2014).

In this sense, Moradi et al. (2020) state that poor people when they want to start their own business face three types of problems: structural problems (lack of resources, education and skills related to business); social and cultural problems (prejudice, discrimination and stigmas related to poverty); and institutional problems (lack of laws and regulations that provide resources to informal entrepreneurs).

Although the most widely used and accepted definition of poverty is that which focuses on income (Moradi et al., 2020), it is widely known that poverty is a multifaceted and multidimensional phenomenon, encompassing social, economic and psychological dimensions (Misturelli & Heffernan, 2008). Valencia (2020) also considers that poverty is a phenomenon of multiple causes, consequences and manifestations.

The multidimensional nature of poverty gives it a characteristic of extreme complexity, enhanced by the vicious circle that poverty itself generates (Rohima et al., 2013). Furthermore, Si et al. (2020) argue that poverty has a dynamic character, since economic, social, and psychological situations and measurement models change over time.

Si et al. (2020) assert that poverty is likely caused by a wide variety of reasons. Rohima et al. (2013) relate these reasons as internal and external in nature. Sumodiningrat (2002) considers internal factors as those related to limitations of poor individuals or society (low motivation, poor work ethic, lack of capital, lack of management control, and technological aspects) and external factors as unfavorable institutional aspects (lack of infrastructure or support).

Among the internal factors that condition the level of poverty identified in the analyzed literature include: educational deficit and lower association capacity (Rohima et al., 2013); work experience and gender (Chen et al., 2014); age, self-efficacy, risk perception and leadership motivation (Arrighetti et al., 2016); and lower business education (Habib et al., 2020).

The scientific community has identified, among others, the following external factors that condition the level of poverty: level of development of the area of residence (Si et al., 2020); culture of poverty (Moradi et al., 2020); entrepreneurship education (Liñan et al., 2013); business education (Habib et al., 2020); university system (Arrighetti et al., 2016); family and friends (Taormina and Lao, 2007); providers of financial resources (Henderson and Robertson, 2000); institutional support for advice or specialized training (Veciana et al., 2005); and perception of economic crises (Arrighetti et al., 2016).

On the other hand, the measurement of poverty is a controversial fact about which there is no consensus, despite having been the object of attention for a long time (Bersisa & Heshmati, 2021). In this area, the scientific literature identifies two approaches: the unidimensional, focused on income and / or expenses, and the multidimensional, which measures the level of poverty considering dimensions such as education, health, or housing, among others.

For some years now, the multidimensional approach has been increasingly accepted by the scientific community, and even politics; and, under this, different methods and models have been developed; among which the Alkire-Foster (AF) method, widely used in the international scientific literature, and the AROPE rate, highly recognized in the European Union, stand out.

AROPE (At Risk of Poverty and / or Exclusion) is a rate designed by the European Commission in the Framework of the European Strategy 2020, which measures the volume of people at risk of poverty and / or exclusion and consists of 11 indicators that are grouped into 3 dimensions: material lack or deprivation, intensity of employment and disposable income. The indicators that define the dimension of material shortage or deprivation can be grouped into three categories (economic difficulties, durable goods and housing) and have a dynamic character. In this sense, the European statistical system has excluded some of the indicators of material shortage or deprivation (absence of washing machine, color television and telephone) because they are outdated and have lost relevance, and has proposed adding new indicators (replacement of damaged furniture, replacement of old clothes with new ones, make accessible two pairs of well-fitting shoes, spending a small amount of money each week on oneself, regular participation in recreational and leisure activities, connecting to the Internet for personal use at home, getting together with friends / family at the table at least once a month).

The intensity of employment is defined as the ratio between the number of months totally worked by all members of the household and the total number of months that, at most, all people of working age in the household could work (Voronov et al., 2020). Finally, disposable income measures the risk of poverty based on disposable income.

Voronov et al. (2020) defines the rate of risk of poverty or social exclusion (AROPE) as a complex and multidimensional indicator, which recognizes as poor people who are below the poverty line in any of its dimensions.

According to AROPE, people at risk of poverty and / or social exclusion are in at least one of these three situations: they suffer severe material deprivation (they do not have 4 of the 9 items defined for this dimension); they reside in households without employment or with low intensity in employment (which means that their members of working age did less than 20% of the total potential to work); and / or have an income below the risk of poverty threshold (set at 60% of the national average equivalent disposable income).

The value of the AROPE rate ranges from 0 to 100%; so that the higher the value of AROPE, the greater the risk of poverty or social exclusion.

Entrepreneurial Intention

On the other hand, intention is central in the entrepreneurship process (Bird, 1988), as it is one of the best predictors of the start-up of new companies (Vinogradov et al., 2013); it is closer to entrepreneurial behavior than traits or demographics (Kautonen et al., 2013); and it has been used as a valid indicator of business behavior (Venugopal et al. (2015). The explanatory power of intention models is notable and presents different values. In the field of entrepreneurial behavior, entrepreneurial intention is the most studied determinant when it is about founding companies because it allows for the explanation of 30% or higher percentages of the behavior variance (Krueger et al., 2000). Jaén (2010) confirms that intention is the best predictor of planned behavior, particularly when this behavior is occasional, difficult to observe, and / or involves unpredictable delays.

Soria-Barrcto et al. (2016) define the entrepreneurial intention as the self-recognition of the conviction to create a business and the conscious planning for its realization in a future time. Also, Thompson (2009) considers intention as the self-recognized conviction that a person has the purpose of establishing a new company and consciously plans to do so at some future time; and Tsordia & Papadimitriou (2015) point out that entrepreneurial intention is that mental state that directs a person's attention and action towards self-employment instead of organizational employment.

The scientific literature offers several models to measure and explain entrepreneurial intention, among which the following stand out: business event model (Shapero & Sokol, 1982), entrepreneurial potential model (Krueger & Brazeal, 1994), interactive model for the implementation of entrepreneurial ideas (Bird, 1988), entrepreneurial support model (Türker & Selçuk, 2009), maximization of expected utility (Douglas & Shepherd, 2002), Davidsson model (Davidsson, 1995), theory of orientation towards entrepreneurial attitudes (Robinson et al., 1991) and the Theory of Planned Behavior (Ajzen, 1991). Research shows that there is little difference between these models; in this sense, Fayolle & Liñán (2014) show that intention-based models are compatible; and in the opinion of Krueger et al. (2000) TPB provides greater flexibility by adopting personal and social factors to explain the differences between individuals in terms of their preference and desire to start their own business.

TPB has been rated by Sampedro et al. (2014) as the ideal framework to measure entrepreneurial intention; since it is a global theory, well elaborated and scientifically tested, and allows a wide explanation of the intention. Furthermore, Fini et al. (2012) consider that TPB is a general, robust, parsimonious and more easily falsifiable framework than others; and Díaz-Casero et al. (2012) argue its utility and solid theoretical framework. According to Ostermann (2020) the theory proposed by Ajzen (1991) is used to measure the intention to carry out a certain behavior and predict it. According to Bereket & Wasihun (2015), it has been applied in different contexts: intention to grow (Kozan et al., 2006), intention to leave (Brigham et al., 2007), intention to internationalize (Sommer & Haug, 2011); corporate entrepreneurial intention (Fini et al., 2012); intention to use new software (Yang, 2013); consumer behavior and participation and voting in elections (Vinogradov et al., 2013); or entrepreneurial potential (Liñán et al., 2013).

TPB was developed 20 years ago; it originated in social psychology and in the Theory of Reasoned Action (Fishbein & Ajzen, 1975); and it has been widely tested, criticized and improved upon by a great deal of interdisciplinary research (Fayolle & Liñán, 2014). TPB's basic idea is that intention predicts behavior; so that the stronger the intention to implement an action, the greater the probability that action will be implemented (Ajzen, 1991). According to this model, entrepreneurial intention determinants are attitude towards starting a new company (the business decision), subjective norms on entrepreneurship behavior and perceived behavioral control on the start of a company (Ajzen, 1991).

According to Roman et al. (2015), the entrepreneurial intention could be expressed as:

$$EI = EA + SN + PBC$$

From which results:

EI = Intention to develop (or not) a business.
EA = Entrepreneurial Attitude
SN = Subjective Norms
PBC = Perceived Behavioral Control.

According to Vinogradov et al. (2013) attitude is a strong predictor of entrepreneurial intention. Attitude (Ajzen, 2002) is defined as the degree to which a person has a favorable or unfavorable evaluation of a behavior; and reflects an individual's perception of the convenience of creating a new business, or the desire to be self-employed (Tsordia & Papadimitriou, 2015). In simple form Vinogradov et al. (2013) define subjective norms (NS) as the perceived social pressure to perform a behavior. According to Soria-Barreto et al. (2016) subjective norms are the formal mechanisms (regulation tools, codes and lack of explicit support) and informal (social norms) that hinder or favor the creation of new businesses.

Perceived behavioral control (PBC) is one of the main components of TPB. According to Ostermann (2020) the PBC refers to the perception of the ease or difficulty to carry out a behavior; and it is associated with individual beliefs about the ability to successfully execute certain behavior (Tarapuez et al., 2018). The PBC is maximized the higher the number of resources and opportunities perceived and the lower the number of anticipated obstacles (Jaén, 2010).

THEORY OF PLANNED BEHAVIOR AND POVERTY RISK

Research on the influence of each of the components of the TPB model on entrepreneurial intention is variable (Krueger et al., 2000; Liñán & Chen, 2006). Tsordia & Papadimitriou (2015) argue that there are no conclusive findings on the relationship between intention and its antecedents; although Gird & Bagraim (2008) argue that perceived control of behavior, subjective norms and attitudes towards entrepreneurship are significant preceptors of entrepreneurial intention.

TPB's component with the weakest influence on entrepreneurial intention is subjective norms (Ajzen, 1991; Armitage & Conner, 2001).

Literature analyzed shows that the relationship between subjective norms (SN) and the entrepreneurial intention (EI) is contradictory: some studies show that there is a significant relationship (Ferreira et al., 2018; Yang, 2013), while other studies conclude that such a relationship does not exist (Fini et al., 2012; Liñán et al., 2011) or its effects are very weak (García-Rodríguez et al., 2015). Santos & Liñán (2006), after a review of nineteen empirical studies applying TPB, discovered that in eleven there was a negative or non-significant relationship. Therefore, we formulate the following hypothesis.

Hypothesis 1: Subjective norms are negatively related to entrepreneurial intention.

There is a broad consensus in the literature regarding the fact that perceived behavioral control has a significant and positive impact on entrepreneurial intention (Ambad et al., 2016; Liñán & Chen, 2011; Usaci, 2015; Varamäki et al., 2015). Furthermore, Jaén (2010) explains that perceived behavioral control and entrepreneurial intention are direct predictors of behavior; and García-Rodríguez et al. (2015) indicate that perceived behavioral control explains 20% of the variance of entrepreneurial intention. In light of this evidence, we formulate the following hypothesis.

Hypothesis 2: Perceived behavioral control is positively related to entrepreneurial intention.

Although part of the research shows that the impact of attitude on entrepreneurial intention is not significant (Yaseen et al., 2018), the majority of research shows the existence of a significant and positive impact of attitude on intention to create a venture (Koe et al., 2012; Varamäki et al., 2015), even being the case that attitude is rated as the most important factor in determining entrepreneurial intention (Gird et al., 2008; Tarapuez et al., 2018) and assessing the impact of the effect of the entrepreneurial attitude on the entrepreneurial intention in 31% of the variance (García-Rodríguez et al., 2015). So, we formulate the following hypothesis.

Hypothesis 3: The attitude towards entrepreneurial behavior will be positively related to entrepreneurial intention.

Scholars and professionals argue that entrepreneurship is a critical means of alleviating extreme poverty (Sutter et al., 2019) and poverty (Bruton et al., 2013); although the size of the impact is still unclear and vague (Moradi et al., 2020). The increase in income as a result of entrepreneurial behavior will have implications for savings and investment and will allow people to free themselves from poverty's vicious circle (Rohima et al., 2013). Studies that address the relationship between entrepreneurial intention and poverty are scarce and provide contradictory results. One part of these studies shows that the situation of poverty stimulates entrepreneurial intention out of necessity, and another part sustains that entrepreneurial intention fades under the pressure of extreme poverty (Moradi et al., 2020). Sutter et al. (2019) state that the literature is fragmented and inconsistent, both in theoretical and practical implications terms. Previous evidence allows the following hypothesis to be formulated.

Hypothesis 4: Entrepreneurial intention is negatively related to the risk of poverty.

To conclude the review of the literature, we highlight that, according to Sutter et al. (2019) and Si et al. (2020), poverty reduction through entrepreneurship can be approached from three perspectives: remediation, reform, and revolution. Remediation perspective considers poverty reduction through entrepreneurship addressing the problem of scarcity of resources, reform approach achieves this through institutional changes, and revolution standpoint focuses on changing capitalist-based assumptions of business. Table 1 highlights different aspects of these perspectives.

Once the hypotheses have been presented and justified, the collection of data and the analysis methods used in this research will be described below.

METHODS

Regarding the data collection method, we highlight, first, that the data necessary for this research are derived from the hypotheses previously raised and synthesized in the conceptual model that is presented in the following figure.

As can be seen in the figure, the proposed model will explain the risk of poverty based on the entrepreneurial intention of the respondents, which in turn will be determined by subjective norms, attitude towards entrepreneurial behavior and perceived behavioral control. Regarding the measures used in the research, subjects' entrepreneurial intention and their determining factors are measured according to the Theory of Planned Behavior (Ajzen, 1991) and the risk of poverty was measured with the AROPE indicator.

The measurement instrument was distributed among the population of the municipality of La Rambla (Córdoba, Spain), which in 2017 had 7,508 inhabitants (3,777 women and 3,731 men).

Table 1. Description of the perspectives on poverty reduction based on entrepreneurship.

		Remediation	Reform	Revolution
Key assumptions		Poverty is a lack of resources.	Poverty is the result of social exclusion.	Poverty is the result of corrupt systems.
		Poverty is alleviated by providing access to resources.	Poverty is addressed as entrepreneurship facilitates inclusion.	Poverty is dealt with by introducing new means of organizing society.
		When the spirit of entrepreneurship among the poor is "unleashed", markets will flourish.	Power plays an important role in the functioning of markets.	The concept of markets needs critical evaluation.
		Alleviation of poverty is a "win-win" situation for everyone involved.	The alleviation of poverty implies economic and social compensations.	Alleviation of poverty must lead to equality.
		Researchers are objective scientists.	Researchers explore subjective perspectives.	Researchers are advocates.
Identification of opportunities.	Main Focus	The role of external agents in providing resources and creating new opportunities for the poor.	The ways in which institutions and social structures facilitate or limit the identification of opportunities, especially among the marginalized.	Criticism of conceptualizations of the identification of opportunities and the role of entrepreneurship.
	Main conclusions	Partnerships are critical to help identify opportunities for the poor, but cross-sector partnerships are complex to implement. Investment in human capital through training influences the identification of opportunities.	Entrepreneurship can change the social or institutional context. It is necessary to stabilize local contributions with resources and the assistance of external actors.	Business empowerment from a neoliberal perspective can be harmful, and many of the opportunities promoted through such efforts are, in fact, delusions; and the recovery of social welfare can lead to new types of opportunities.
Opportunities exploitation	Main focus	The providing of resources for the poor and the relationship with opportunities exploitation.	The relationship between social and institutional contexts and the exploration of opportunities by the poor.	The motivation and the consequences of the exploration of opportunities among the poor.
	Main conlusions	Improve access to financial resources and increase human capital through training and coaching of women can increase the exploration of opportunities. The structure and content of relationships shape the exploration of opportunities.	Entrepreneurship can make the social and institutional context more inclusive. Opportunities exploitation can lead to women empowerment.	Compassion and serving the needs of the poor can be a boost for seizing opportunities.
Growth	Main focus	The role of normalization in contexts of poverty and the elimination of barriers to growth.	The role of business growth in affecting institutional context.	The positive and negative consequences of business growth, as well as criticism and suggestions on how growth should be evaluated.
	Main conclusions	Take advantage of local social networks and relationships among the poor can be critical to growth; most small firms don't grow even when some of the barriers to growth are removed.	Business growth can lead to empowering results, but there is a danger of unintended consequences.	Business growth can be detrimental when it embraces neoliberal discord and perpetuates power differences. One needs a much wider criterion than just economics.

Source: Sutter et al. (2019).

Regarding the data analysis method, we elucidate that after the validation of the correctly completed questionnaires (198), different statistical analysis techniques were applied: descriptive analysis of the variables (frequencies and central measures) and structural equations modeling (SEM), specifically the PLS technique using the SmartPLS software (Ringle et al., 2015).

DISCUSSION OF THE RESULTS

To present the results of our empirical work, we will abide by the following order. In the first place, the main data referring to interviewed characterization are presented, using descriptive statistical data (distribution of frequencies and central measures). Second, data over participants socioeconomic situ-

Figure 1. Conceptual Model.
Source: *The Authors.*

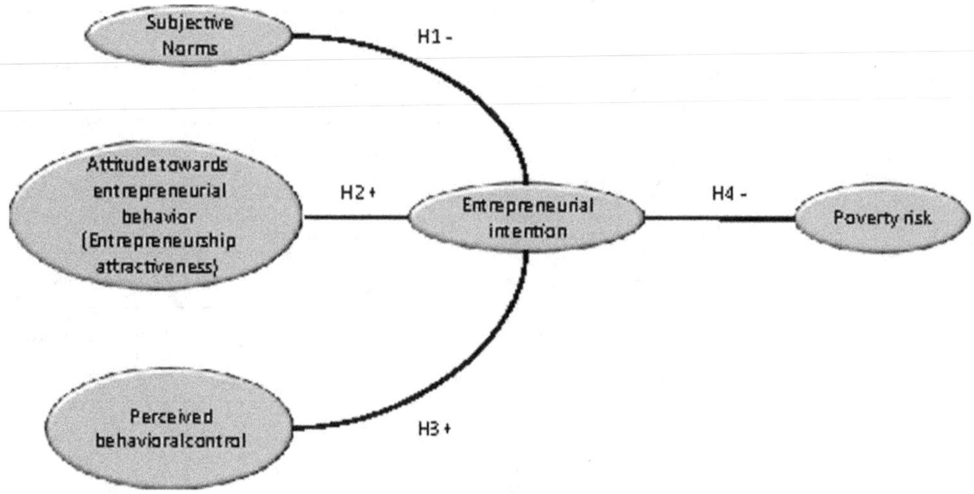

ation are offered, distinguishing between people with and without risk of poverty. Third, the problem of identifying the variables of the theory of planned behavior is addressed, as well as the determination of the values of these variables. Fourth, the results corresponding to the proposed structural equation model are presented. Finally, we analyze sample's entrepreneurial intention results.

Profile of the Participants in the Study

A total of 208 people from the Spanish municipality of La Rambla and its surroundings, a place located in the province of Córdoba (Spain), have participated in this empirical study. In the end, only 198 surveys have been useful, since 10 of them were disregarded due to incorrect answers and / or omission of information. Archetypal profile of the people interviewed is as follows: female population (57.1%) of an average age of around 31 years, performing some professional activity (62.1%), single (79.3%) and being a part of households with 3 members or less (49.5%).

Respondents' Socio-Economic Situation

Following the methodology proposed by the AROPE indicator, mentioned in previous sections, the following aspects will be discussed in this section: lack or severe material deprivation of households, poverty threshold, intensity of household work and, finally, qualification in terms of the AROPE index.

Severe Financial Deficiency

The main shortcomings are found, shown from most relevant to least, in the incapacity to pay big expenses without prior notice, the lack of means to be able to afford a week of vacation and, finally, the difficulties to keep the home at adequate temperature. Consequently, we can say that in the population studied there is no severe material deficiency, since only the variable related to the impossibility of facing large expenses unexpectedly shows a higher rate of recurrence in the affirmative option.

Poverty Threshold

Regarding the poverty threshold (located in our case at a household income level below € 684 per month), it can be stated that the respondents show an almost balanced situation between those who do not exceed this threshold (100 respondents; 50.5% of the total) and those that they do (98 subjects; 49.5%).

Intensity of Employment

This variable of the AROPE index assesses the extent to which the households of the respondents are in precarious employment situations, either because most of their members are unemployed or because they are in a situation of low employment intensity.

Overall results show that in most households it is not possible to speak of a situation of low intensity employment, since, on average, at least 70% of the households have had someone with a job throughout the year.

AROPE Index

Following the AROPE index methodology, we have proceeded to differentiate between households in a situation of poverty and those outside of a situation of poverty. In this sense, it should be noted that this indicator, as explained previously, considers that a household is poor when it is based on any of the indicators indicated in the preceding sections. For this reason, the percentages of the AROPE index coincide with those of the poverty threshold: 50.5% can be considered as households at risk of poverty and 49.5% as households without risk of poverty.

Entrepreneurial Intention Analysis

Table 2 data show the global information on respondents' entrepreneurial intention, as well as the results corresponding to the comparisons of the values of the said variable based on various independent variables: sex, marital status and number of household members. The table shows, firstly, that the level of entrepreneurial intention is moderate (3.9 on a scale of 1 to 8). Second, there are only statistically significant differences based on the number of household members: households with 4 members and those with only one member score higher in entrepreneurial intention than the rest of households (with 2, 3, 5 and more). members).

Analysis of the Relational Model

This model has been evaluated with the PLS technique, specifically through the SmartPLS program (Ringle et al., 2015). For this, the three steps indicated by the specialized literature (Roldán & Cepeda, 2018; Sarstedtet al., 2016) have been followed: global model validation, evaluation of the measurement model and structural model assessment.

Table 2. Entrepreneurial intention of the respondents. ANOVA results.

	N	Average	F	p
Entrepreneurial Intention	**198**	**3.90**		
Gender			0.088	0.766
Man	85	3.86		
Woman	113	3.93		
Marital status			0.178	0.674
Married	*41*	3.80		
Single	157	3.92		
Total number of members in the household			3.244	0.008
One	14	4.64		
Two	28	3.84		
Three	56	3.55		
Four	74	4.26		
Five	18	3.65		
Six and more	8	2.44		

Source: The Authors.

Validation of the Global Model

Estimated model SRMR index (0.083) indicate a relatively adequate fit of the global model, since it is very close to the ideal value of 0.08 and clearly below the critical threshold (0.10).

Measurement Model Assessment

This process consists in turn of two parts: a) evaluation of the global measurement model (determination of goodness of fit) and b) evaluation of the constructs and indicators that are part of the measurement model (individual reliability of the indicators, reliability of the constructs in terms of internal consistency, constructs convergent validity, and latent variables discriminant validity).

About the global measurement model, the situation is similar to global model validation, since the SRMR index is 0.083. Once again, we are in a situation of moderate goodness of fit.

The data regarding validation of individual indicators reliability and different latent variables (subjective norms, entrepreneurship attractiveness, perceived behavioral control and entrepreneurial intention) as well as their convergent validity are shown in Table 3. The results collect all the indicators with factor loadings above the threshold (0.707) as well as highly reliable constructs (Cronbach's alphas and composite reliabilities above 0.707) and of proven convergent validity, since the AVE of each of them is greater than 0.5. The variable "AROPE Index" is not included because it is a construct made up of a single indicator.

Finally, to validate the measurement model, we present in Table 4 both the correlations between the latent variables and the square root of the AVE. The results confirm the existence of discriminant validity between the constructs, that is, each construct is different from the others.

Table 3. Individual reliability, composite reliability and medium variance extracted (AVE) for the model constructs.

Construct and indicator	Load	Cronbach's Alpha	Composite Reliability	AVE
Subjective norms		**0.859**	**0.916**	**0.786**
My friends would approve of my decision to start a business.	0.933			
My immediate family would approve of my decision to start a business	0.769			
My colleagues would approve of my decision to start a business	0.947			
Entrepreneurship attractiveness		**0.776**	**0.870**	**0.690**
If I had the opportunity and the resources, I would love to start a business	0.838			
Being an entrepreneur would give me great satisfaction.	0.852			
Being an entrepreneur implies more advantages than disadvantages to me.	0.803			
Perceived behavioral control		**0.790**	**0.864**	**0.615**
Starting a business and keeping it viable would be easy for me.	0.732			
I am able to control the process of creating a new business.	0.891			
If I tried to start a business, I would very likely be successful.	0.769			
I know all about the practical details needed to start a business.	0.747			
Entrepreneurial Intention		**0.866**	**0.909**	**0.714**
I am willing to do anything to become an entrepreneur.	0.825			
I Will do my best to start and run my business.	0.826			
I am determined to start a business in the future	0.867			
My professional goal is to become an entrepreneur.	0.860			

Source: The Authors.

With all the results having been shown, we can infer that the measurement model is valid.

For this, 5 different stages must be faced: determination of the collinearity problems between the variables that precede the endogenous variables; path coefficients assessment (sign, magnitude and statistical significance); relevance of the coefficient of determination (R^2) and decomposition of the variance; determine the effect sizes (f^2); and, finally, evaluation of predictive relevance (Q^2). Figure 2 offers the basic results of the structural model, which will be discussed in greater depth later.

For the evaluation of the existence or not of multicollinearity between constructs, the values of the variance inflation factor (VIF) between a dependent variable and all the variables that condition it must

Table 4. Values of the Fornell-Larcker criterion of discriminant validity.

Constructs	1	2	3	4	5
1Subjective norms	**0.887**				
2. Entrepreneurship attractiveness	0.389	**0.831**			
3. Perceived control	0.362	0.556	**0.784**		
4. Intention to undertake	0.398	0.760	0.667	**0.845**	
5. AROPE index	0.061	0.105	0.165	0.023	**1**

Elements of the diagonal (in bold) are the square root of shared variance between the constructs and their indicators. Items off the diagonal are the correlations between constructs. Discriminant validity occurs if the elements on the diagonal are greater than the elements outside the diagonal.

Source: The Authors.

Figure 2. Results of the structural model.
Source: The Authors.

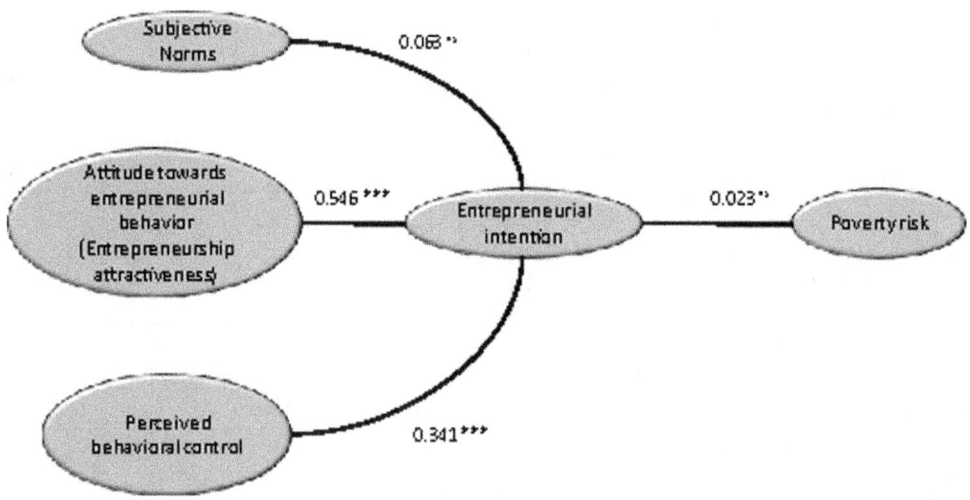

be considered. This model tries to see, firstly, if there is collinearity between the variable "entrepreneurial intention" and its three determinants: "subjective norms", "entrepreneurship attractiveness" and "perceived behavioral control". The VIF values are, respectively, 1.222, 1.537, and 1.501. Secondly, the absence of multicollinearity between the variables "entrepreneurial intention" and "poverty risk" must be verified. In this case, the VIF value is 1. As none of the four values is greater than 3, the non-existence of collinearity in the model can be affirmed. We can move on to the next step.

In Table 5 we present the data related to the beta coefficients of the model. All of them are positive, although not all of them reach statistically significant values. Of the 4 hypotheses raised, only two are confirmed: both the attitude towards entrepreneurship and the degree of perceived behavioral control determines entrepreneurial intention of interviewees. Although the subjective norms variable has a positive effect on entrepreneurial intention, it is not statistically significant. Finally, entrepreneurial intention does not cause significant effects on the poverty risk, as measured by the AROPE methodology.

The values associated to the coefficient of determination, the decomposition of the variance and the predictive relevance of the effects appear in Table 6. The data show that the coefficient of determination

Table 5. Values and significance of the path (beta) coefficients.

Relations between dimensions (Beta values)	Original Sample	Sample Average	Standard Error	T Statistic	Medium
Subjective norms -> Entrepreneurial Intention (H1)	0.063	0.061	0.051	1.223	No
Entrepreneurship attractiveness -> Entrepreneurial Intention (H2)	0.546	0.548	0.051	10.668	Sí
Perceived behavioral control -> Entrepreneurial Intention (H3)	0.341	0.343	0.048	7.056	Sí
Entrepreneurial Intention -> Poverty Risk (H4)	0.023	0.021	0.070	0.323	No

Source: Bootstraping simulation. Resampling (5000 times), p = 0,01

Table 6. Direct effects on endogenous variables.

Endogenous variables	Direct effects	T value (bootstrap)	Confidence interval (95%)	Correlations	Explained variance
Entrepreneurial Intention ($R^2 = 0.662$ / $Q^2 = 0.467$)					
H1: Subjective Norms	0.063^{ns}	1.223	[-0.026; 0.142]	0.398	2.51%
H2: Entrepreneurship attractiveness	0.546***	10.668	[0.455; 0.625] Sig	0.760	41.50%
H3: Perceived behavioral control	0.341***	7.056	[0.563; 0.723] Sig	0.667	22.74%
Poverty Risk ($R^2 = 0.001$ / $Q^2 = 0.011$)					
H4: Entrepreneurial Intention	0.023^{ns}	0.323	[-0.096; 0.136]	0.023	0.05%

Source: Bootstraping simulation. Resampling (5000 times), R^2 adjusted.
***p<0.001, **p<0.01, *p<0.05, ns: not significant.
t (0.05; 4999) = 1.645; t (0.01; 4999) = 2.327; t (0.001; 4999) = 3.092. One-tail test.

for the variable entrepreneurial intention in this model is moderate. Despite this, it is possible to speak of a certain predictive relevance of the model, because of the value of Q^2, clearly higher than zero. However, there is no predictive relevance with respect to the poverty risk variable or an effect that is significant.

Table 7, which includes the values and significance levels of the effect sizes, shows the absence of a significant effect in the case of the relationship between "Subjective norms" and "Entrepreneurial intention", in absolute agreement with what happened with the beta coefficients, as well as between "Entrepreneurial Intention" and "Poverty Risk". On the other hand, the effects of the other two variables (entrepreneurship attractiveness and perceived behavioral control) are significant. The effect of entrepreneurship attractiveness is stronger (large effect) than that of perceived behavioral control (moderate effect).

Table 7. Effect size of beta coefficients.

Relations between dimensions (Beta values)	f^2	f^2 Sample average	Standard error	T Statistic	P
Subjective norms -> Entrepreneurial Intention (H1)	0.010	0.017	0.019	0.495	0.310
Entrepreneurial attractiveness -> Entrepreneurial Intention (H2)	0.583	0.610	0.157	3.717	0
Perceived control -> Entrepreneurial Intention (H3)	0.233	0.245	0.075	3.101	0.001
Entrepreneurial Intention -> Poverty Risk (H4)	0.001	0.005	0.008	0.068	0.473

Source: Bootstraping simulation. Resampling (5000 times).

FINAL CONSIDERATIONS

Below we present conclusions, theoretical and empirical implications, limitations and future lines of research.

The main conclusions of the research are as follows. In the first place, the population interviewed is not in a situation of severe material shortage, since the only aspect of this concept to highlight is the one related to the impossibility of facing large expenses without prior notice.

Second, most households do not experience a situation of low intensity of employment, since at least 70% of households indicate that one of their members has been working throughout the year.

Third, in terms of the monthly income of households, a situation of equilibrium is observed between those located below and those located above.

Fourth, the situation of the multidimensional poverty indicator AROPE can be classified as moderate, since only 50.5% of households can be considered at risk of poverty status.

Fifth, surveyed population entrepreneurial intention is moderate-low, since on a scale of 1 to 8 the mean rises to 3.9, relatively below the intermediate point of the scale (4.5). The population studied does not show, therefore, an excessive entrepreneurial inclination.

Sixth, the proposed explanatory model presents acceptable levels in terms of its goodness of fit (both for the structural and measurement models), moderate predictability in terms of entrepreneurial intention and lack of predictive character regarding poverty risk.

Seventh, the results on the hypotheses reveal the confirmation of hypotheses 2 and 3, which indicate the positive effects of the variables "attitude towards entrepreneurship" and "perceived behavioral control" on entrepreneurial intention. On the other hand, it has not been possible to confirm the existence of a negative relationship between "subjective norms" and "entrepreneurial intention" (hypothesis 1), since it has been positive, although not significant. In addition, the data indicate that entrepreneurial intention is not a determining factor of poverty risk of subjects.

Eighth, the analysis of the data of our model highlights that both "entrepreneurship attractiveness" and "perceived behavioral control" explain the variance of the "entrepreneurial intention", although the most important effect corresponds to attractiveness (41.50%) versus perceived behavioral control (22.74%). Which indicates that the people in our sample feel more driven to entrepreneurship by the attractiveness of said behavior than by confidence in their ability to master the knowledge, skills and attitudes necessary for it.

The previous conclusions and the fact that widespread poverty is affecting many lives makes it necessary to adopt stricter and more fundamental measures to solve this problem (Moradi et al., 2020). In this sense, theoretical and empirical measures are suggested.

The research main theoretical implication is to sensitize social science researchers about the seriousness of poverty problem at the global and local level, and about the urgent need to generate more and better knowledge on this topic. In particular, knowledge is needed on how employment generation through entrepreneurship can contribute to alleviating or abandoning states of poverty; For this, it is necessary to apply different theoretical approaches, among which institutional theory stands out, since institutional factors are easier to manipulate than individual factors (Yurtkoru et al., 2014).

Regarding the empirical implications, it is adopted as a starting point, in line with Sutter et al. (2019) and Si et al. (2020), that poverty reduction through entrepreneurship should be approached with perspectives of remediation (allocation of financial resources) and reform (promoting institutional changes); and that poverty reduction through entrepreneurship must be done from different spheres, among which the following stand out: public administrations, educational system, business system and family and friends of people at risk of poverty.

Public administrations will help people to get out of the "poverty trap" by facilitating access to financial resources, under preferential conditions, which will make it possible to satisfy the primary needs of the population at risk of poverty or by implementing institutional changes that will allow the creation of an environment conducive to business creation (Akinbola, et al., 2013). Such institutional changes will consist, according to Yurtkoru et al. (2014), in making the workforce more flexible, improving communications, opening the market or eliminating bureaucracy. Along the same lines, Liñán et al. (2011) propose promoting more positive business values, which reinforce the social message that business creation is an attractive, valued and feasible career option. This will reinforce perceived behavioral control and raise the level of entrepreneurial intention. Furthermore, Liñán et al. (2013) suggest raising awareness, training, providing technical assistance and stimulating the creation of incubation centers aimed at the population at risk of poverty that is more likely to translate intention into entrepreneurial behavior (Shirokova et al., 2016; Yurtkoru et al., 2014).

Possibly the most relevant institutional reform that can be carried out will be aimed at the educational system and will consist of strengthening entrepreneurship education in schools, vocational training institutions and universities (Usaci, 2015) and even in informal education (Canal, 2015). This implies that changes will have to be made in the educational subsystems that, according to Akınbola et al. (2013) are located in the field of governance and leadership of the educational center, its culture and values, its infrastructure and the commercialization of research and technology. In addition, the integration of the population at risk of poverty in the education system will be stimulated by offering scholarships and a network of people who can provide experience (Saeed et al., 2015; Akinbola et al., 2013) and role models (Saeed et al., 2013). al., 2015).

Of course, changes will also be made in educational programs and projects that will instill an entrepreneurial mentality among the population at risk of poverty (Romero & Petrescu, 2011); provide the necessary knowledge and skills on entrepreneurship (Kadir et al., 2012); positively influence attitudes towards entrepreneurial activity (Yurtkoru et al., 2014); will stimulate creativity, initiative, tenacity, teamwork, understanding of risk and a sense of responsibility (Usaci, 2015); offer the opportunity to conduct feasibility studies, develop business plans, and benefit from business simulation, case studies, or the presence of guest speakers; and that will measure the perception of the influence of the education received on the intention of the entrepreneurial behavior (Saeed et al., 2015).

The business system will provide financial support, for example, through venture capital formulas, and will be an active part in the alliances that are created to carry out the necessary institutional reforms.

Ultimately, family and friends will do their best, according to Akinbola, et al. (2013), in providing adequate moral, professional and financial support for people at risk of poverty to improve their entrepreneurial intention and behavior.

The implementation of these measures contributes to the improvement of perceived behavioral control, subjective norms and attitude towards entrepreneurship and, consequently, entrepreneurial intention of people at poverty risk.

On the other hand, the main limitations of the research focus on the conceptual model, the measures used, the population under study and the cross-sectional nature of the research. To try to alleviate these limitations, the following future lines of research are proposed. First, a more holistic approach will be adopted that incorporates new elements (variables and indicators) and new mediation and / or moderation relationships to the conceptual model.

Second, although the AROPE rate is widely used at the European level to measure multidimensional poverty, other indicators are available to measure multidimensional poverty widely agreed in the international literature; therefore, in future research poverty will be measured with the Alkire-Foster (AF) indicator.

Third, the investigation will be extended to other towns in the Spanish territory; in order to identify, through self-reported measures, the situation of the population of other municipalities in terms of multidimensional poverty and entrepreneurial intention.

Fourth, in line with Moradi et al. (2020) will seek to know if entrepreneurial intention differs between people who come from a poor environment and those who come from a rich environment. Finally, in line with Fayolle & Liñán (2014), the intention-behavior relationship will be studied as soon as possible with longitudinal data; since, as Jaén (2010) indicates, the longer the time elapsed, several factors can intervene in the change of attitudes, subjective norms or perceived behavioral control and modify, in this way, entrepreneurial intention and, consequently, entrepreneurial behavior.

REFERENCES

Ajzen, I. (1991). The theory of planned behaviour. *Organizational Behavior and Human Decision Processes*, *50*(2), 179–211. doi:10.1016/0749-5978(91)90020-T

Ajzen, I. (2002). Perceived behavioral control, self-efficacy, locus of control, and the theory of planned behavior. *Journal of Applied Social Psychology*, *32*(4), 665–683. doi:10.1111/j.1559-1816.2002.tb00236.x

Ajzen, I., & Fishbein, M. (1975). A Bayesian analysis of attribution processes. *Psychological Bulletin*, *82*(2), 261–277. doi:10.1037/h0076477

Akinbola, O. A., Ogunnaike, O. O. & Amaihian, A. B. (2013). *The Influence of Contextual Factors on Entrepreneurial Intention of University Students in Nigeria*. Academic Press.

Ambad, S. N. A., & Damit, D. H. D. A. (2016). Determinants of entrepreneurial intention among undergraduate students in Malaysia. *Procedia Economics and Finance*, *37*, 108–114. doi:10.1016/S2212-5671(16)30100-9

Armitage, C. J., & Conner, M. (2001). Efficacy of the theory of planned behavior: A meta-analytic review. *British Journal of Social Psychology*, *40*(4), 471–499. doi:10.1348/014466601164939 PMID:11795063

Arrighetti, A., Caricati, L., Landini, F., & Monacelli, N. (2016). Entrepreneurial intention in the time of crisis: A field study. *International Journal of Entrepreneurial Behaviour & Research*, *22*(6), 835–859. doi:10.1108/IJEBR-12-2015-0326

Baxter, A., Chapman, D. W., Dejaeghere, J., Pekol, A. R., & Weiss, T. (2014). Youth entrepreneurship education and training for poverty alleviation: A review of international literature and local experiences. *International Perspectives on Education and Society*, *23*(2), 33–58. doi:10.1108/S1479-3679(2013)0000023010

Bersisa, M., & Heshmati, A. (2021). A Distributional Analysis of Uni-and Multidimensional Poverty and Inequalities in Ethiopia. *Social Indicators Research*, *155*(3), 1–31. doi:10.100711205-021-02606-w

Bertrand, M., Mullainathan, S., & Shafir, E. (2006). Behavioral economics and marketing in aid of decision making among the poor. *Journal of Public Policy & Marketing*, *25*(1), 8–23. doi:10.1509/jppm.25.1.8

Bird, B. (1988). Implementing entrepreneurial ideas: The case for intention. *Academy of Management Review*, *13*(3), 442–453. doi:10.5465/amr.1988.4306970

Brigham, K. H., De Castro, J. O., & Shepherd, D. A. (2007). A person-organization fit model of owner-managers cognitive style and organizational demands. *Entrepreneurship Theory and Practice*, *31*(1), 29–51. doi:10.1111/j.1540-6520.2007.00162.x

Bruton, G. D., Ketchen, D. J. Jr, & Ireland, R. D. (2013). Entrepreneurship as a solution to poverty. *Journal of Business Venturing*, *28*(6), 683–689. doi:10.1016/j.jbusvent.2013.05.002

Buli, B. M., & Yesuf, W. M. (2015). Determinants of entrepreneurial intentions: Technical-vocational education and training students in Ethiopia. *Education + Training*, *57*(8/9), 891–907. doi:10.1108/ET-10-2014-0129

Canal, M. N. (2015). *La educación emprendedora en la enseñanza escolar: medidas e indicadores de la situación de España en el contexto europeo* (Doctoral dissertation). Universidad CEU San Pablo.

Chen, S., Shen, Y., Naznin, P., Wang, H., & Wu, S. (2014). Types of poverty and entrepreneurial intention in Bangladesh. *Social Behavior and Personality*, *42*(5), 857–867. doi:10.2224bp.2014.42.5.857

Davidsson, P. (1995). Determinants of Entrepreneurial Intentions. *RENT DC Workshop in Entrepreneurship Research.*

Díaz-Casero, J. C., Ferreira, J. J. M., Mogollón, R. H., & Raposo, M. L. B. (2012). Influence of institutional environment on entrepreneurial intention: A comparative study of two countries university students. *The International Entrepreneurship and Management Journal*, *8*(1), 55–74. doi:10.100711365-009-0134-3

Douglas, E. J., & Shepherd, D. A. (2002). Self-Employment as a Career Choice: Attitudes, Entrepreneurial Intentions, and Utility Maximization. *Entrepreneurship Theory and Practice*, *26*(3), 81–90. doi:10.1177/104225870202600305

Fayolle, A., & Liñán, F. (2014). The future of research on entrepreneurial intentions. *Journal of Business Research*, *67*(5), 663–666. doi:10.1016/j.jbusres.2013.11.024

Ferreira, J., Fernandes, C., & Raposo, M. (2018). Measuring and understanding the psychological effects of entrepreneurial intentions: Multigroup analysis. In A. Tur & D. Ribeiro (Eds.), *Inside the mind of the entrepreneur. Contributions to Management Science* (pp. 17–31). Springer International Publishing. doi:10.1007/978-3-319-62455-6_2

Fini, R., Grimaldi, R., Marzocchi, G. L., & Sobrero, M. (2012). The determinants of corporate entrepreneurial intention within small and newly established firms. *Entrepreneurship Theory and Practice, 36*(2), 387–414. doi:10.1111/j.1540-6520.2010.00411.x

García-Rodríguez, F. J., Gil-Soto, E., Ruiz-Rosa, I., & Sene, P. M. (2015). Entrepreneurial intentions in diverse development contexts: A cross-cultural comparison between Senegal and Spain. *The International Entrepreneurship and Management Journal, 11*(3), 511–527. doi:10.100711365-013-0291-2

Gast, J., Werner, A., & Kraus, S. (2017). Antecedents of the small firm effect: The role of knowledge spillover and blocked mobility for employee entrepreneurial intentions. *The International Entrepreneurship and Management Journal, 13*(1), 277–297. doi:10.100711365-016-0403-x

Gird, A., & Bagraim, J. J. (2008). The theory of planned behaviour as predictor of entrepreneurial intent amongst final-year university students. *South African Journal of Psychology. Suid-Afrikaanse Tydskrif vir Sielkunde, 38*(4), 711–724. doi:10.1177/008124630803800410

Habib, M., Aamir, A., Khan, I., & Ullah, W. (2020). Role of Entrepreneurship Education in Poverty Alleviation: Mediating by Entrepreneurial Intention. *City University Research Journal, 10*(2), 1–24.

Henderson, R., & Robertson, M. (2000). Who wants to be an entrepreneur? Young adult attitudes to entrepreneurship as a career. *Career Development International, 5*(6), 279-287.

Hodzic, S., Ripoll, P., Lira, E., & Zenasni, F. (2015). Can intervention in emotional competences increase employability prospects of unemployed adults? *Journal of Vocational Behavior, 88*, 28–37. doi:10.1016/j.jvb.2015.02.007

Hsu, D., Shinnar, R., Powell, B., & Coffey, B. (2017). Intentions to reenter venture creation: The effect of entrepreneurial experience and organizational climate. *International Small Business Journal, 35*(8), 928–948. doi:10.1177/0266242616686646

Ibarvo Urista, V., Quijano Vega, G. A., & Loya Olivas, E. M. (2018). Actitud hacia el emprendimiento social en los alumnos del Instituto Tecnológico de Chihuahua, como respuesta a una problemática nacional. Universidad Nacional Autónoma de México y Asociación Mexicana de Ciencias para el Desarrollo Regional A.C.

Jaén, I. (2010). *Una revisión teórica de los valores en el estudio de la intención emprendedora.* Universidad de Sevilla. Disponible en institucional.us.es/vie/documentos/resultados/ValoresIntencionEmprendedoraInmaJaen.pdf

Kadir, M. B. A., Salim, M., & Kamarudin, H. (2012). The relationship between educational support and entrepreneurial intentions in Malaysian higher learning institution. *Procedia: Social and Behavioral Sciences, 69*, 2164–2173. doi:10.1016/j.sbspro.2012.12.182

Kautonen, T., Van Gelderen, M., & Tornikoski, E. T. (2013). Predicting entrepreneurial behaviour: A test of the theory of planned behaviour. *Applied Economics*, *45*(6), 697–707. doi:10.1080/00036846.2011.610750

Koe, W. L., Sa'ari, J. R., Majid, I. A., & Ismail, K. (2012). Determinants of entrepreneurial intention among millennial generation. *Procedia: Social and Behavioral Sciences*, *40*, 197–208. doi:10.1016/j.sbspro.2012.03.181

Kozan, M. K., Öksoy, D., & Özsoy, O. (2006). Growth plans of small businesses in Turkey: Individual and environmental influences. *Journal of Small Business Management*, *44*(1), 114–129. doi:10.1111/j.1540-627X.2006.00157.x

Krueger, N. Jr, Reilly, M., & Carsrud, A. (2000). Competing models of entrepreneurial intentions. *Journal of Business Venturing*, *15*(5-6), 5–6, 411–432. doi:10.1016/S0883-9026(98)00033-0

Krueger, N. F. Jr, & Brazeal, D. V. (1994). Entrepreneurial potential and potential entrepreneurs. *Entrepreneurship Theory and Practice*, *18*(3), 91–104. doi:10.1177/104225879401800307

Lee, L., Wong, P. K., Foo, M. D., & Leung, A. (2011). Entrepreneurial intentions: The influence of organizational and individual factors. *Journal of Business Venturing*, *26*(1), 124–136. doi:10.1016/j.jbusvent.2009.04.003

Liñán, F. & Chen, Y. W. (2006). *Testing the entrepreneurial intention model on a two-country sample*. Document de Treball núm. 06/7. Universitat Autònoma de Barcelona.

Liñán, F., & Fayolle, A. (2015). A systematic literature review on entrepreneurial intentions: Citation, thematic analyses, and research agenda. *The International Entrepreneurship and Management Journal*, *11*(4), 907–933. doi:10.100711365-015-0356-5

Liñán, F., Nabi, G., & Krueger, N. (2013). British and Spanish entrepreneurial intentions: A comparative study. *Revista de Economía Mundial*, (33), 73–103.

Liñán, F., Rodríguez-Cohard, J. C., & Rueda-Cantuche, J. M. (2011). Factors affecting entrepreneurial intention levels: A role for education. *The International Entrepreneurship and Management Journal*, *7*(2), 195–218. doi:10.100711365-010-0154-z

Miranda, F., Chamorro, A., & Rubio, S. (2017). Academic entrepreneurship in Spanish universities: An analysis of the determinants of entrepreneurial intention. *European Research on Management and Business Economics*, *23*(2), 113–122. doi:10.1016/j.iedeen.2017.01.001

Misturelli, F., & Heffernan, C. (2012). The shape of change: A memetic analysis of the definitions of poverty from the 1970s to the 2000s. *Journal of International Development*, *24*, S3–S18. doi:10.1002/jid.1770

Moradi, M., Imanipour, N., Arasti, Z., & Mohammadkazemi, R. (2020). Poverty and entrepreneurship: A systematic review of poverty-related issues discussed in entrepreneurship literature. *World Review of Entrepreneurship, Management and Sustainable Development*, *16*(2), 1, 25–152. doi:10.1504/WREMSD.2020.105984

Ostermann, E. (2020). *"Refugee Entrepreneurship": The role of the theory of planned behavior and country of origin on entrepreneurial intention of refugees* (Doctoral dissertation). Universität Linz.

Rahman, S. A., Amran, A., Ahmad, N. H., & Taghizadeh, S. K. (2016). Enhancing the wellbeing of base of the pyramid entrepreneurs through business success: The role of private organizations. *Social Indicators Research, 127*(1), 195–216. doi:10.100711205-015-0951-4

Rhyne, E., & Otero, M. (1992). Financial services for microenterprises: Principles and institutions. *World Development, 20*(11), 1561–1571. doi:10.1016/0305-750X(92)90014-M

Ringle, C. M., Wende, S., & Becker, J. M. (2015). SmartPLS 3. SmartPLS GmbH, Boenningstedt. *Journal of Service Science and Management, 10*(3).

Robinson, P. B., Stimpson, D. V., Huefner, J., & Hunt, H. K. (1991). An attitude approach to the prediction of entrepreneurship. *Entrepreneurship Theory and Practice, 15*(4), 13–31. doi:10.1177/104225879101500405

Rohima, S., Suman, A., Manzilati, A., & Ashar, K. (2013). Vicious Circle Analysis of Poverty and Entrepreneurship. *IOSR Journal of Business and Management, 7*(1), 33–46. doi:10.9790/487X-0713346

Roldán, J. L., & Cepeda, G. (2018). *Curso sobre PLS*. SEM.

Roman, T., Manolica, A., & Voznenko, N. (2015). Study on the Factors that Influence the Development of Entrepreneurship among Romanian Students. In *Proceedings of the International Management Conference (pp.* 198-208). Faculty of Management, Academy of Economic Studies.

Romero, I., & Petrescu, R. M. (2011). Universities as suppliers of entrepreneurship education services. The cases of the University of Seville and the academy of economic studies in Bucharest. *Amfiteatru Economic Journal, 13*(30), 347–361.

Saeed, S., Yousafzai, S. Y., Yani-De-Soriano, M., & Muffatto, M. (2015). The role of perceived university support in the formation of students' entrepreneurial intention. *Journal of Small Business Management, 53*(4), 1127–1145. doi:10.1111/jsbm.12090

Sampedro, I. R., Fernández-Laviada, A., & Crespo, Á. H. (2014). Entrepreneurial intention: Perceived advantages and disadvantages. *Academia (Caracas), 27*(2), 284–315. doi:10.1108/ARLA-09-2013-0144

Santos Cumplido, F. J., & Liñán, F. (2006). La influencia del capital social sobre los empresarios potenciales. *Estudios de Economía Aplicada, 24*(2), 459–489.

Sarstedt, M., Hair, J. F., Ringle, C. M., Thiele, K. O., & Gudergan, S. P. (2016). Estimation issues with PLS and CBSEM: Where the bias lies! *Journal of Business Research, 69*(10), 3998–4010. doi:10.1016/j.jbusres.2016.06.007

Shane, S. (2009). Why encouraging more people to become entrepreneurs is bad public policy? *Small Business Economics, 33*(2), 141–149. doi:10.100711187-009-9215-5

Shapero, A., & Sokol, L. (1982). The social dimensions of entrepreneurship. In C. Kent & D. Sexton (Eds.), *The Encyclopedia of Entrepreneurship* (pp. 72–90). Prentice-Hall.

Shinnar, R. S., & Zamantılı nayır, D. (2019). Immigrant Entrepreneurship in an Emerging Economy: The Case of Turkey. *Journal of Small Business Management, 57*(2), 559–575. doi:10.1111/jsbm.12408

Shirokova, G., Osiyevskyy, O., & Bogatyreva, K. (2016). Exploring the intention–behavior link in student entrepreneurship: Moderating effects of individual and environmental characteristics. *European Management Journal*, *34*(4), 386–399. doi:10.1016/j.emj.2015.12.007

Si, S., Ahlstrom, D., Wei, J., & Cullen, J. (2020). Business, Entrepreneurship and Innovation Toward Poverty Reduction. *Entrepreneurship & Regional Development*, *32*(1-2), 1-20.

Sommer, L. (2011). The Theory of Planned Behaviour and the Impact of Past Behaviour. *International Business & Economics Research Journal*, *10*(1), 1. doi:10.19030/iber.v10i1.930

Soria-Barreto, K., Zuniga-Jara, S., & Ruiz-Campo, S. (2016). Educación e intención emprendedora en estudiantes universitarios: Un caso de estudio. *Formación Universitaria*, *9*(1), 25–34. doi:10.4067/S0718-50062016000100004

Sumodiningrat, G. (2002). Strategi pemberdayaan masyarakat dalam penanggulangan kemiskinan. Materi kuliah umum Program Pasca Sarjana Universitas Brawijaya, Malang.

Sutter, C., Bruton, G. D., & Chen, J. (2019). Entrepreneurship as a solution to extreme poverty: A review and future research directions. *Journal of Business Venturing*, *34*(1), 197–214. doi:10.1016/j.jbusvent.2018.06.003

Taormina, R., & Kin-Mei Lao, S. (2007). Measuring Chinese entrepreneurial motivation, personality and environmental influences. *International Journal of Entrepreneurial Behaviour & Research*, *13*(4), 200–221. doi:10.1108/13552550710759997

Tarapuez, E., Guzmán, B., & Parra, R. (2018). Factores que determinan la intención emprendedora en América Latina. *Suma de Negocios*, *9*(19), 56–67. doi:10.14349umneg/2018.V9.N19.A7

Thompson, E. R. (2009). Individual entrepreneurial intent: Construct clarification and development of an internationally reliable metric. *Entrepreneurship Theory and Practice*, *33*(3), 669–694. doi:10.1111/j.1540-6520.2009.00321.x

Tsordia, C., & Papadimitriou, D. (2015). The Role of Theory of Planned Behavior on Entrepreneurial Intention of Greek Business Students. *International Journal of Synergy and Research.*, *4*(1), 23. Advance online publication. doi:10.17951/ijsr.2015.4.1.23

Turker, D., & Selcuk, S. S. (2009). Which factors affect entrepreneurial intention of university students? *Journal of European Industrial Training*, *33*(2), 142–159. doi:10.1108/03090590910939049

Usaci, D. (2015). Predictors of professional entrepreneurial intention and behavior in the educational field. *Procedia: Social and Behavioral Sciences*, *187*, 178–183. doi:10.1016/j.sbspro.2015.03.034

Valencia Arechiga, A. L. (2020). *La intención emprendedora en población con alto y muy alto grado de marginación en Puerto Vallarta*. Jal. Universidad de Guadalajara, Méjico.

Varamäki, E., Joensuu, S., Tornikoski, E., & Viljamaa, A. (2015). The development of entrepreneurial potential among higher education students. *Journal of Small Business and Enterprise Development*, *22*(3), 563–589. doi:10.1108/JSBED-02-2012-0027

Veciana, J. M., Aponte, M., & Urbano, D. (2005). University students attitudes towards entrepreneurship: A two countries comparison. *The International Entrepreneurship and Management Journal*, *1*(2), 165–182. doi:10.100711365-005-1127-5

Venugopal, S., Viswanathan, M., & Jung, K. (2015). Consumption constraints and entrepreneurial intentions in subsistence marketplaces. *Journal of Public Policy & Marketing*, *34*(2), 235–251. doi:10.1509/jppm.14.181

Verspagen, B. (2005). Innovation and economic growth. In J. Fagerberg, D. C. Mowery, & R. R. Nelson (Eds.), *The Oxford handbook of innovation* (pp. 487–513). Oxford University Press.

Vinogradov, E., Kolvereid, L., & Timoshenko, K. (2013). Predicting entrepreneurial intentions when satisfactory employment opportunities are scarce. *Education + Training*, *55*(7), 719–737. doi:10.1108/ET-06-2012-0067

Voronov, V. V., Ruza, O. P., & Stasane, J. (2020). Multidimensional poverty in the Baltic States in the EU context: theoretical and practical aspects. *Baltic Region*, *12*(3).

Yang, J. (2013). The theory of planned behavior and prediction of entrepreneurial intention among Chinese undergraduates. *Social Behavior and Personality*, *41*(3), 367–376. doi:10.2224bp.2013.41.3.367

Yaseen, A., Abid, M., Zahra, S., & Israr, M. (2018). Precursory effects on entrepreneurial behaviour in the agri-food industry. *Journal of Entrepreneurship in Emerging Economies*, *1*(10), 2–22. doi:10.1108/JEEE-08-2016-0029

Yurtkoru, E. S., Kuşcu, Z. K., & Doğanay, A. (2014). Exploring the antecedents of entrepreneurial intention on Turkish university students. *Procedia: Social and Behavioral Sciences*, *150*, 841–850. doi:10.1016/j.sbspro.2014.09.093

APPENDIX: MEASURING INSTRUMENT

1.-Gender
☐ Man
☐ Woman
2.- Age:
______
3.- Profession:
____
4.- Marital Status:
☐ Married
☐ Single
☐ Widower/Widow
5.- Number of members of the household under the age of 60:
_____
6.- Number of members of the household under the age of 18:
_____
7.-Total number of people in the household:
_____.

The Entrepreneurial Intention (Liñán & Chen, 2006)

Indicate your level of compliance with the following statements on business activity from 1 (total disagreement) to 7 (total agreement).

A01. Starting a company and keeping it viable would be easy for me.	1	2	3	4	5	6	7
A02. A career as an entrepreneur is very unappealing to me.	1	2	3	4	5	6	7
A03. My Friends approve of my decision to start a business.	1	2	3	4	5	6	7
A04. I am willing to do anything to become an entrepreneur.	1	2	3	4	5	6	7
A05. I believe I would be totally unable to start a business.	1	2	3	4	5	6	7
A06. I will do all I possibly can to start and run my business.	1	2	3	4	5	6	7
A07. I am able to control the process of starting a new business.	1	2	3	4	5	6	7
A08. My close family would approve of my decision to start a business.	1	2	3	4	5	6	7
A09. I have serious doubts about starting my own business.	1	2	3	4	5	6	7
A10. If I had the opportunity and the resources, I would love to start a business.	1	2	3	4	5	6	7
A11. My colleagues would approve of my decision to start a business.	1	2	3	4	5	6	7
A12. Among several options, I'd rather be anything either than an entrepreneur.	1	2	3	4	5	6	7
A13. I am determined to start a business in the future.	1	2	3	4	5	6	7

A14. If I were to start a business, I'll have high probabilities of being successful.	1	2	3	4	5	6	7
A15. Being an entrepreneur would give me great satisfaction.	1	2	3	4	5	6	7
A16. It would be very difficult for me to develop a business idea.	1	2	3	4	5	6	7
A17. My professional goal is to be an entrepreneur.	1	2	3	4	5	6	7
A18. Being an entrepreneur implies in more advantages than disadvantages.	1	2	3	4	5	6	7
A19. I have very little intention of starting a business.	1	2	3	4	5	6	7
A20. I know everything about the practical details to start a business.	1	2	3	4	5	6	7
C1. My immediate family values the entrepreneurial activity over other activities and careers.	1	2	3	4	5	6	7
C2. The culture of my country is very favorable to the business activity.	1	2	3	4	5	6	7
C3. The role of entrepreneurs in the economy is generally undervalued in my country.	1	2	3	4	5	6	7
C4. My friends value the business activity over other activities and careers.	1	2	3	4	5	6	7
C5. The majority of the people in my country consider it unacceptable to be an entrepreneur.	1	2	3	4	5	6	7
C6. In my country the business activity is considered beneficial, in spite of the risks.	1	2	3	4	5	6	7
C7. My colleagues value the business activity over other activities and careers.	1	2	3	4	5	6	7
C8. In my country it is believed that entrepreneurs take advantage of the people.	1	2	3	4	5	6	7

Poverty Risk (AROPE)

RP. The net rent of the household is under 684 €/month

- ☐ Yes
- ☐ No

PMS1. There have been delays in paying some bills related to main matters of the home (mortgage, rent, gas, community …) in the last 12 months.

- ☐ Yes
- ☐ No

PMS2. We are unable to maintain suitable temperature in our home.

- ☐ Yes
- ☐ No

PMS3. We cannot go on holidays not even for one week per year.

- ☐ Yes
- ☐ No

PMS4. We cannot eat meat, chicken or fish everyday (likewise with vegetables).

- ☐ Yes
- ☐ No

PMS5. We do not have the capacity to deal with unexpected expenses (for a sum of up to 650 €).

- ☐ Yes
- ☐ No

PMS6. We cannot have a telephone.

- ☐ Yes
- ☐ No

PMS7. We cannot buy a colour T.V.

- ☐ Yes
- ☐ No

PMS8. We cannot buy a washing machine.

- ☐ Yes
- ☐ No

PMS9. We cannot buy a car.

- ☐ Yes
- ☐ No

IT. Number of months the members of the household under the age of 60 worked during the last 12 months. ______

Chapter 8
Ruminating on Microfinance as a Contrivance of Economic Development and Women Upliftment:
A Case of India

Manpreet Arora
Central University of Himachal Pradesh, Dharmashala, India

ABSTRACT

This chapter focuses on the success of microfinance as a tool to create opportunities for women and other deprived sections in the formal financial structure of India. It also aims at focusing on the role of various institutions which play a significant position in providing rural credit through various channels. The author contends that in this pandemic where economies at global level require resilience strategies, microfinance once again can prove to be an effective strategy to bounce back in terms of improving the economic conditions of poor and vulnerable who suffered the most due to lockdowns, especially in developing nations like India. Localization and promotion of local product can help boost entrepreneurial activities at various levels, which can improve the distorted global supply chain slowly and gradually but effectively.

INTRODUCTION

Global challenges due to Covid -19 pandemic are very complex in nature and they require a great deal of research to find out certain innovative solutions to reshape the devastated economies. Entrepreneurship is the backbone of every economy (Karadağ, 2016, Onileowo & Anifowose, 2020). Due to Covid-19 the survival of economies was majorly affected especially because existence of small scale businesses was threatened as they had less resources compared to the larger firms. Microfinance is considered as a significant practice of providing small loans or monetary help to the deprived and the disadvantaged

DOI: 10.4018/978-1-7998-8925-0.ch008

people who are unable to access formal banking services. The financial services comprise of not only facilitating savings and disbursement for providing credit, but also include providing varied other services like insurance, leasing, money transfer, equity transaction, etc . It is the provision of thrift, credit and other financial services as well as products designed especially for poor; enabling them to raise their income level thereby improving their living standards. In this scenario where Covid-19 has hit the world so bad that overseas business is severely affected. Many nations have faced second wave of the pandemic and they are forced to use lockdowns again in 2021, where 2020 was worst hit by closure of international trade at various levels across the globe. Many nations adopted the policy of going local from global to revive their economies. The situation started improving in some nations in the beginning of 2021 but again second wave hit the developing nations like India and developed nations like Europe and Britain. So the supply chain disruptions continue to affect the global trade in one way or another (Arora & Sharma, 2021). Overall to revive the economies promoting entrepreneurship, start ups and small ventures is the only solution, which is to bring back economies back on trail (Arora & Sharma, 2021). It has proved to be significant tool to empower deprived in various nations. Reduction of poverty as an agenda of developing economy is not a new phenomenon and nations had been striving hard before pandemic to reach up to a level of reasonable level of development by using certain intervention programmes. In India also Central Bank has started various intervention programmes which focus on serving poor by triggering the weaker section with the help of microcredit which makes them free from the shackles of poverty and vulnerability. Thereby a SHG Bank linkage programme was initiated by the central bank where providing microfinance to the weaker sections of society is the main priority. This programme facilitates enough flexibility in intervention so as to alter the support activities as per the needs of the poor and unprivileged; focusing especially on women. It also acts as a mediator for bridging the gap between poor and formal financial structure by providing the facilities of credit encourage savings and making credit available to become socially and economically independent (Arora & Singh, 2017).

Talking particularly of India, the worth mentioning fact for provision of microfinance, rural women have proved to be the main stakeholders of microfinance programmes. They have been provided deliberate opportunity to connect with the mainstream financial system through certain flagship programmes of Govt. of India. The basic objective of microfinance programme is to provide women an access to the financial services so that they can engage themselves in income generating activities, become financially independent and contribute to their family income (Arora & Singh, 2015). Investment of credit amounts into income generating activities improves the living standard as well as the empowerment level of the participants by making them financially independent. This helps women to become economically empowered.

When we are talking about empowerment, it is not confined to economic aspects, but it is a process of making women and other deprived sections empowered economically, socially as well as politically empowered (Bakhtiari, 2006). One of the interesting positive effects of microfinance programmes in India is that the women and other deprived sections are getting ample opportunities to establish their independent ventures, they are getting enough credit without collaterals under microfinance initiatives to become self sufficient. This chapter will focus on the success of microfinance as a tool to create opportunities for women and other deprived sections in the formal financial structure of India. It will also aim at focusing on the role of various institutions which play a significant position in providing rural credit through various channels. The author contends that in this pandemic where economies at global level require resilience strategies, microfinance once again can prove to be an effective strategy to bounce back in terms of improving the economic conditions of poor and vulnerable who suffered the most due to lockdowns especially in developing nations like India. Localization and promotion of local product can help boost entrepreneurial activities at various levels, which can improve the distorted global supply chain slowly, gradually but effectively.

WORKING OF MICRO FINANCE ACTIVITIES

In India micro financing gained importance by a scheme initiated by Govt. of India called as SHG bank linkage programme. It has turned out to be one of the important and booming developmental techniques for the growth of the society. Through the SHG Bank Linkage Programe a link between the commercial banks and rural public is created. They created a platform for rural India and linked rural poor with the financial structure. It ultimately is providing an opportunity to become socially and economically empowered. In many countries Micro finance has proved to be a tool of poverty reduction, women empowerment and self employment (Krogh, Hansen, Wendt, & Elkjaer, 2009). Microfinance as a tool to empower deprived sections economically and socially has received extensive recognition in various parts of the world including India. The peculiar feature of microfinance is that it is provided to low income individuals or groups who otherwise are deprived of the financial services (Kyereboah,Coleman & Osei, 2008). The main motive behind providing finance to those people who are engaged in small livelihood earning processes at rural level provides them prospect to start various self sufficiency/ employment generation opportunities.

Micro credit aims at providing opportunities to low income people to help them become self sufficient by providing them credit, saving facilities and other related activities. An important and notable achievement of this programme has been that deprived sections in rural India have been benefitted by this scheme to a large extent and still it has a lot of potential to uplift the weaker sections of society (Arora & Singh, 2018). Especially during and post pandemic such interventions where direct access to credit can be given will help to put the economies back on rail.

The Role of Microfinance has proved to be very relevant in the economic progress of a country when it is linked with the formal players of the financial system (McGuire & Conroy, 2000, Osman, 2020). In India financial system reforms have played a tremendous role in bridging the gap between the service providers and the beneficiaries. The Self Help Group is the best example which helps to link the informal groups with the formal financial sector. In the financial systems Commercial Banks, Regional Rural Banks and Cooperatives Banks are the major players which ultimately link the micro financing activity with the development goals of the country.

Microfinance institutions provide credit to the SHGs through various schemes initiated at the Centre or State level. Microfinance Institutions are the major players in India which boost savings by their intervention in villages, then provide financial services to the poor and rural masses of various underdeveloped areas. There are several reasons which are associated with the emergence of microfinance concept which are: lack of opportunities for poor and vulnerable in the formal financial structure of a country, lack of viable, dependent and adequate financial structure in the rural areas, persistent and continual exclusion of rural poor from the financial structure, difficult to access financial services offered by formal structure and lack of credit support by the credit agencies to rural poor who don't have collaterals. Micro-finance and SHG approach intend to augment the purpose of income generation and savings, self-employment and empowerment of rural poor.

Self Help Group is a deliberately created group of people who come forward voluntarily for doing some business activity in order to achieve self sufficiency. These groups of people pool their resources as well as some seed money and utilize this collective money/ resources to use it further for the group members in the form of loan. If this group is able to sustain for at least six months then the subsequent stride is to link the self help group to a bank of the area which is promoting self help group bank linkage programme. This scheme of SHG's linking with a bank is known as Self Help Group Bank Linkage Programme. NABARD (National Bank for Agriculture and Rural Development) started this programme in the year 1992.

Through this scheme of Self Help Group bank linkages the rural people get an access to financial services without any need for collateral security. The prevalent shortcoming of the commercial banking system is that the credit is provided only by pledging or providing some sort of security/ collateral. The poor or rural clients who do not have any collateral to provide they stay deprived from the benefits of access of credit or other financial services provided by the formal financial structure of a country. Developing economy like India has certain drawbacks in terms of provision of basic needs to every citizen of India. Like developed nations pension, insurance, medical facilities are not absolutely free right of citizens. Though after fifty years of independence much in this regard has been achieved, still much more is required to be done.

Self Help Group bank linkage programme is considered to be a good and successful scheme for providing financial services to the poor. This self help group bank linkage model linked with banks is considered to be of having qualities of both formal and informal financial system. The current scenario of microfinance provided in the last three years is shown in Table 1 below.

It is evident from table 1 that the SHG bank linkage programme for providing microcredit is benefitting women at a larger level. Out of the total SHG's formed the percentage of number of SHG's formed and amount sanctioned as loan to SHG's more than eighty percent in every year is to women.

Most of the members in these self help groups are women of rural areas. It is empowering the women through self employment and making them economically independent. Non government organizations and banks are the important players in encouraging the Self Help Group bank linkage programmes. Non government organizations are playing very important role in the formation and promotion of Self Help Groups and providing full assistance and guidance to rural people about the working and importance of these groups. Reserve Bank of India (RBI) and NABARD are themselves playing developmental, supervisory and regulatory role in the promotion of self help groups and self help group bank linkage programme. NABARD through its policy measures and time to time initiatives is making a huge contribution for growth of microfinance sector by providing new innovative products created for the benefit of poor.

NABARD took initiative and started promoting SHG's in 1992 with the objective of providing credit linked to savings in order to meet the needs of families. This scheme has certain underlying objectives namely it is purely savings oriented, women- centric and the microfinance programmes are self led. This scheme proved out to be the world's largest movement which organized poor especially the women and linked them with commercial banks for credit facilities. In the past twenty five years it has proven to be a successful tool for empowering rural women. The holistic objective of financial inclusion helped to make it a successful tool for poverty alleviation also. Chhay (2011), in his paper highlighted the fact that governments as well as non-governmental organizations have been using microfinance as a tool for enhancing income generation as well as creating employment among the poor. Microfinance is widely recognized as an innovative form of financial assistance for benefitting poor especially the women in rural areas. Many researches confirm that not only economic condition of women improves by micro-

Table 1. No. of SHG's and Amount Sanctioned (Number in lakh/ Amount in Rs. crore)

		2015-16		2016-17		2017-18		2018-19		2019-20		2020-21	
	Criteria	**No. of SHGs**	**Amount**	**No. of SHGs**	**Amount**	**No. of SHGs**	**Amount**	**No. of SHGs**	**Amount**	**No. of SHGs**	**Amount**	**No. of SHGs**	**Amount**
SHG Savings with Banks as on 31st March	Total SHG Nos.	79.03 (2.68%)	13691.39 (23.79%)	85.77 (8.53%)	16114.23 (17.69%)	87.44 (1.95%)	19592.12 (21.59%)	100.14 (14.52%)	23324.48 (19.05%)	102.43 (2.29%)	26152.05 (12.12%)	112.23 (9.57%)	37477.61 (43.31%)
	All women SHGs	67.63 (1.68%)	12035.78 (29.92%)	73.22 (8.26%)	14283.42 (18.67%)	73.90 (0.94%)	17497.86 (22.51%)	85.31 (15.44%)	20473.55 (17.01%)	85.31 (15.44%)	23320.55 (13.91%)	97.25 (10.11%)	32686.08 (40.16%)
	Percentage of Women	85.58	87.91	85.36	88.64	84.51	89.31	85.19	87.78	86.22	89.17	86.65	87.21
	Of which NRLM/ SGSY	34.57 (13.27%)	6244.97 (41.16%)	37.44 (8.30%)	7552.70 (20.94%)	41.84 (11.76%)	10434.03 (38.15%	55.8 (33.37%)	12867.18 (23.32%)	57.89 (3.75%)	14312.7 (11.23%)	64.78 (11.9%)	19353.7 (35.22%)
	% of NRLM/ SGSY Groups	43.74	45.61	43.65	46.87	47.85	53.26	55.72	55.17	56.52	54.73	57.72	51.64
	Of which NULM/ SJSRY	4.46 (3.00%)	1006.22 (6.12%)	5.46 (22.42%	1126.86 (11.99%)	4.25 (-22.10%)	1350.80 (19.87%)	4.39 (3.29%)	1614.42 (19.52%	4.69 (6.83%)	1523.57 (-5.63%	5.29 (12.79%)	1954.09 (28.26%)
	% of NULM/ SJSRY Groups	5.64	7.35	6.36	6.99	4.86	6.89	4.38	6.92	4.58	5.83	4.71	5.21
Loans Disbursed to SHGs during the year	Total No. of SHGs extended loans	18.32 (12.67%)	37286.90 (35.18%)	18.98 (3.60%)	38781.16 (4.01%)	22.61 (19.13%)	47185.88 (21.67%)	26.98 (19.33%)	58317.63 (23.59%)	31.46 (16.60%)	77659.35 (33.17%)	28.87 (-8.23%)	58070.68 (-25.22%)
	All women SHGs	16.29 (12.50%)	34411.42 (40.92%)	17.16 (5.34%)	36103.13 (4.92%	20.75 (20.92%)	44558.74 (23.42%)	23.65 (13.98%	53254.04 (19.51%)	28.84 (21.95%)	73297.56 (37.64%)	25.9 (-10.19%)	54423.13 (-25.75%)
	Percentage of Women Groups	88.92	92.29	90.42	93.09	91.78	94.43	87.66	91.32	91.67	94.38	89.71	93.72

Source: NABARD.com

finance but the status of their family along with the whole community gets better (Chhay, 2011; Amin & Becker, 1998; Khan & Noreen, 2012; Noreen, 2011; McCarter, 2006; Sigalla & Carney, 2012; Swain & Wallentin, 2009; De Aghion, Armendáriz & Morduch, 2007; Aruna & Jyothirmayi, 2011; Nukpezah & Blankson, 2017). Giving access to credit especially to women has shown turnaround positive consequences for whole economies. SHG Bank linkage scheme is a group based scheme which has twin objectives i.e empowerment and upliftment. Javed & Abrar (2015) conducted a regional analysis of 382 MFI's which covered six regions of the world. The results of their study support the fact that if credit is provided to large number of active borrowers as well as women then it would help in reducing the poverty level of the household.

Regional Distribution of Microfinance Credit in India

Microfinance has the ability to balance the regional growths across the nations. The regional distribution of credit under the scheme for various years in India is shown below in Table 2. It is quite obvious that

Table 2. Regional Distribution of Microfinance in India (Amount in Rs. Lakh)

Regions	2015-16			2016-17			2017-18		
	No. of SHGs	Total Loans Disbursed	Average Loan Disbursed	No. of SHGs	Total Loans Disbursed	Average Loan Disbursed	No. of SHGs	Total Loans Disbursed	Average Loan Disbursed
North Eastern	26037	21969	84375	28961	28421	98134	35017	35721	102010
Northern	38106	48298	126746	46567	57414	123294	51800	54038	104320
Central	84282	119067	141272	82012	67958	82864	69295	55943	80732
Western	112525	188632	167636	106825	148819	139311	128973	155099	120257
Eastern	412576	349489	84709	497063	473172	95194	720444	908950	126165
Southern	1158797	3001235	258996	1136692	3102332	272926	1255603	3508834	279454
All India	1832323	3728690	203495	1898120	3878116	204314	2261132	4718587	208683

Source: NABARD.com

the numbers of SHG's are continuously increasing. The total amount of loan distributed is also quite heavy. The western, southern and eastern part of India much more number of SHG's as compared to northern area.

During the pandemic years also the number of SHG's formed and the loan disbursed show a continuous increase. The highest number of loans disbursed is in the southern region of India.

During pandemic also the picture is quite motivating. Provision of credit is monetary but the benefits of the microfinance are far more than the monetary benefits. It often targets the underprivileged and the disadvantaged sections of the society that are unable to get credit from commercial banks and thus remain deprived from the basic amenities of life. Due to lack of financial resources, many women and deprived sections are subject to domestic violence; their psychological and mental health is badly affected; they are deprived of education; they are not socially and economically empowered; and many commit suicides and are vulnerable to heinous crimes such as rapes too. In developing countries like

Table 3. Region-wise Status of Bank Loan Disbursed to SHGs during 2018-19 to 2020-21 (Total loan disbursed in Rs. Lakh/ Average loan disbursed in Rs. per SHG)

Region	2018-19			2019-20			2020-21		
	No. of SHG's	Total loans Disbursed	Average loan disbursed	No. of SHG's	Total loans Disbursed	Average loan disbursed	No. of SHG's	Total loans Disbursed	Average loan disbursed
Northern	55922	62664	112056	62905	84694	134637	67658	94045	139001
North Eastern	27086	29001	107070	37807	57893	153128	68116	103651	152168
Eastern	909375	1197079	131638	1123517	1785075	158883	1124578	1487551	132276
Central	85135	72199	84805	111074	104249	93856	128617	105428	81971
Western	146674	184565	125833	174218	249327	143112	161159	230331	142921
Southern	1474208	4286256	290750	1636481	5484696	335152	1337266	3786063	283120
Total	2698400	5831763	216119	3146002	7765935	246851	2887394	5807068	201118

Source: NABARD.com

Table 4. Region-wise progress of Savings Linked SHGs with Banks (2018-19 to 2020-21)

Sr. No.	Regions	2018-19		2019-20		2020-21	
		No. of SHGs	Savings-Amount	No. of SHGs	Savings-Amount	No. of SHGs	Savings-Amount
1	Northern Region	5,48,624	62,453	5,77,122	59,550	6,09,808	1,74,345
2	North Eastern Region	5,23,469	40,407	5,56,899	48,141	6,33,714	83,126
3	Eastern Region	26,54,358	6,01,155	28,11,130	6,64,333	31,22,424	7,74,912
4	Central Region	10,62,759	1,33,230	11,35,083	1,71,217	13,45,575	2,11,870
5	Western Region	13,88,615	2,05,275	14,73,853	2,01,880	15,50,176	3,74,023
6	Southern Region	38,36,418	12,89,928	36,89,236	14,70,085	39,61,703	21,29,485
	Total	1,00,14,243	23,32,448	1,02,43,323	26,15,205	1,12,23,400	37,47,761

Source: NABARD.com

India, microfinance has been acknowledged as a pro-poor growth intervention as it may focus on various special programs/ models which can fulfill the needs of the poor and vulnerable sections of the society such as women in particular. In addition to this, it also helps achieve the developmental goals. It has emerged as an alternative to the failure of the mainstream financial sector in order to make the services available to the poor. Various microfinance schemes are spread widely across the world because they are considered as one of the effective and flexible strategies to fight against global poverty.

Table 5 shows us a clearer picture from the year 2015-16 to 2019-20. The amount percentage of savings in bank has shown an increase in these years which was 67.63% for all women SHGs in 2015-2016. It grew to 85.31% in 2018-19 to 86.22% in 2019-20. In loans disbursed to SHGs over these years a considerable increase can be seen in total as well as in the loans disbursed to all women SHGs also. In 2015-16 out of the total loan disbursed to SHGs 88.92% of the loan was disbursed to all women SHGs. In 2016-17, it grew to 90.42%, in 2017-18 it was 91.78%, in 2018-19 it was 87.66%, and in 2019-20 it was 91.67%. It gives us a clear indication that microfinance has been used as a development tool in India. It not only connects poor with the mainstream but also helps them grow economically as well as socially.

The picture of microfinance is clear from the data shown above. It has benefitted women to a large extent. Out of the total SHGs formed, the percentage of number of SHGs formed and amount sanctioned as loan to SHGs, more than eighty percent is given is to women every year. Most of the women who are given credit belong to the weaker and deprived sections of society. Many of them also belong to rural areas where women are more vulnerable, excluded and are deprived in many senses. The societal pattern does not give them opportunity to grow and raise their voices against social evils. Various agencies in India have been contributing to make available microfinance services in every part of the country. Savings led SHG-BLP (Self Help Group-Bank Linkage Program) is especially a women-oriented scheme and is considered as "world's largest movement of organizing the poor into groups..." (NABARD 2019-2020, Annual Report). The role of NABARD in microfinance activities cannot be ignored in India. As per the Annual Report of 2019-20 of NABARD, the following facts relating to microfinance are worth mentioning in Table 6:

The progress of SHG-Bank Linkage Programme can be shown as below in Table 7:

Table 5. SHG Savings with Banks and Loans Disbursed (Number in lakh/Rs. in crore)

	Total SHG Nos.	Amount	All women SHGs	Amount	Percentage of Women	Amount
SHG Savings with Banks as on31st March						
2015-16	79.03 (2.68%)	13691.39 (23.79%)	67.63 (1.68%)	12035.78 (29.92%)	85.58%	87.91
2016-17	85.77 (8.53%)	16114.23 (17.69%)	73.22 (8.26%)	14283.42 (18.67%)	85.36%	88.64
2017-18	87.44 (1.95%)	19592.12 (21.59%)	73.9 (0.94%)	17497.86 (22.51%)	84.51%	89.31
2018-19	100.14 (14.52%)	23324.48 (19.05%)	85.31 (15.44%)	20473.55 (17.01%)	85.19%	87.78
2019-20	102.43 (2.29%)	26152.05 (12.12%)	88.32 (3.53%)	23320.55 (13.91%)	86.22%	89.17
2020-21	112.23 (9.57%)	37477.61 (43.31%)	97.25 (10.11%)	32686.08 (40.16%)	86.65	87.21
Loans Disbursed to SHGs during the year						
	Total No. of SHGs extended loans	**Amount**	**All women SHGs**	**Amount**	**Percentage of Women Groups**	**Amount**
2015-16	18.32 (12.67%)	37286.90 (35.18%)	16.29 (12.50%)	34411.42 (40.92%)	88.92%	92.29
2016-17	18.98 (3.60%)	38781.16 (4.01%)	17.16 (5.34%)	36103.13 (4.92%	90.42%	93.09
2017-18	22.61 (19.13%)	47185.88 (21.67%)	20.75 (20.92%)	44558.74 (23.42%)	91.78%	94.43
2018-19	26.98 (19.33%)	58317.63 (23.59%)	23.65 (13.98%)	53254.04 (19.51%)	87.66%	91.32
2019-20	31.46 (16.60%)	77659.35 (33.17%)	28.84 (21.95%)	73297.56 (37.64%)	91.67%	94.38
2020-21	28.87 (-8.23%)	58070.68 (-25.22%)	25.9 (-10.19%)	54423.13 (-25.75%)	89.71%	93.72

Source: NABARD.com

Table 6. Facts

Contribution in Micro finance activities by NABARD
1. "102.43 lakh SHGs are savings linked involving about 12.4 crore poor households. 2. 2.29 lakh SHGs were added during 2019-20 3. The SHG-BLP has traversed more than 25 years of successful journey towards empowering rural poor in general and rural women in particular. It has emerged as a powerful intervention for poverty alleviation through holistic financial inclusion." (Source: 2019-20 Annual Report of NABARD)

Source: NABARD.com

Table 7. Progress of SHG-Bank Linkage Programme

Particulars	2018-19		2019-20		%change	
	No. of SHG's	Amount (Rs. Crore)	No. of SHG's	Amount (Rs. Crore)	No. of SHG's	Amount
Loans Disbursed	26,98,400	58,317	31,46,002	77,659.35	16.59	33.17
Loans Outstanding	50,77,332	87,098	56,77,071	1,08,075.07	11.81	24.08
Savings with Banks	1,00,14,243	23,324	1,02,43,323	26,152.05	2.29	12.12
NPA level (%)	5.19		4.92			
Average Loan disbursed per SHG	Rs 2.16 Lakh		Rs 2.7 Lakh			

Source: NABARD.com

Role of Microfinance Institutions in Promoting Microfinance in India

SHG movement in India has been associated with social empowerment of women at a larger scale(Shinde & Joshi, 2016; Moyle, Dollard & Biswas, 2006; Brody, De Hoop, Vojtkova, Warnock, Dunbar, Murthy & Dworkin, 2015; Bali & Wallentin, 2012; Thorat, 2006; Tesoriero, 2006). But on the same hand the biggest challenge of this system is that it is based on self initiative. Many NGO's in various states of India came forward and took the SHG movement among rural poor and helped them to create SHG's. The role of NGO's in promoting microfinance has been crucial along with commercial banks, regional rural banks and commercial banks. With the help of NGO's these microfinance providers have made it possible for the rural poor to get an access to create their own sources of livelihood. Microfinance is encouraging sustainable development programmes. MYRADA, SEWA, SADHAN, ASSEFA (All are NGO's) are the key players in India working for promoting microfinance activities by helping rural women to first create self help groups and further linking them with the banks for financial assistance. Not only this, they help in training and development of these rural people as and when required. They help them to address various challenges at the market forefront also, in order to sell and market their product. These institutions have basic objectives of eradication of poverty, unemployment, children education and women empowerment. The origin of this SHG model can be traced back to the successful model of Grameen Bank initiated by Prof. Muhammad Yunus in Bangladesh. He along with his students designed an experimental credit programme to serve rural poor in Bangladesh. It rapidly spread to unlimited villages. Through the support of various donors, the Grameen Bank was formed in 1983. According to this model providing credit for agriculture was treated just as other financial service. The financial structure served this need by proving credit through financial institutions who did not demand collateral for activities relating to agriculture and related sector. Micro Credit can be used by poor people to meet their household needs, livelihood support or other expenditures for sustaining their families. The formal financial institutions, banks, co-operative banks, regional rural banks are the major players which help through various schemes to get micro credit to poor or to even start micro enterprises. IRDP (Integrated Rural Development Program), DWACRA (Development of Women and Children in Rural Areas), SGSSY (*Swaranjyanti Gram Swarojgar Yojna*) are some of the other schemes started by Govt. of India in the current scenario to provide microfinance facilities at various levels. There are certain Microfinance Institutions also which have been continuously providing credit as well as financial services to the weaker sections of the society in the form of microcredit. Several types of co-operative societies,

Non Banking Financial Companies which are MFI's are the basic microfinance providers in India. Presently, Govt. of India has restructured SGSY to "National Rural Livelihood Mission". There are other Entrepreneurial schemes of NBCFDC which provide microcredit especially to women. To name a few there are schemes like *New Swarnima* for women, *Saksham, Shilp Sampada, Mahila Samridhi Yojna* (Microfinance schemes for women) and *Krishi Samadan* scheme for agricultural oriented activities.

The role of various active agencies in India for encouraging SHG's can be highlighted with amount disbursed as loans by them and ultimately the amount saved by SHG's in banks. The Table 8 can throw light on this fact

In the SHG bank linkage scheme the major stakeholder is women. More than eighty percent of the loan availed and disbursed is targeted towards women. In order to enhance the flow of credit towards women various promotional measures were taken in India which continue till now. The Government of India established Rashtriya Mahila Kosh in March 1993, it works as a society and since its inception it is supporting NGO's widely so that they can in turn support NGO's for providing financial services to women all over the country. Loans on some nominal interest is provided to NGO's, women oriented corporations and co-operative societies for the promotion of SHG's. It ultimately works on the concept of women empowerment by assisting them in providing loans. Microfinance sector in India has taken a big jump; however, in volume and outreach it may not be comparable to various neighboring countries like Bangladesh. A suitable regulatory framework, innovative products related to microfinance industry, self-regulation by MFIs, suitable governance practices, updated technology to lessen the transaction costs, training, development and provision of adequate marketing facilities to the micro entrepreneurs are the key factors that can contribute to the growth and success of this sector.

How Women are Empowered Through Microfinance?

The origin of microfinance cannot be associated typically to any country as a tool to empower the vulnerable sections of the society especially women. Existence of saving mechanisms can be

Table 8. Progress under Microfinance - Agency-wise status of SHG-BLP in 2020-21 (Amt. Rs. lakh)

Sr. No.	Name of the Agency	Loans disbursed to SHGs by Banks during 2020-21		Total Savings of SHGs with Banks as on 31 March, 2021	
		No. of SHGs	Loans disbursed	No. of SHGs	Savings Amount
1.	Commercial Banks	14,57,333	27,95,251	61,28,387	22,59,633
2.	% Share	50.47	48.14	54.60	60.29
3.	Regional Rural Banks	11,84,775	24,49,430	35,96,731	9,51,168
4.	% Share	41.03	42.18	32.05	25.38
5.	Cooperative Banks	2,45,286	5,62,387	14,98,282	5,36,960
6.	% Share	8.50	9.68	13.35	14.33
	Total	28,87,394	58,07,068	1,12,23,400	37,47,761

Source: NABARD.com

found extensively in South Africa, Mexico, China, India etc. Compelling reasons like poverty and unemployment are the major inducers of schemes associated with micro financing initiated in many countries (Ghosh & Das, 2020). Bangladesh remains pioneer with the contributions of Prof. Yunus in sorting out these economic problems in many countries through Grameen model of providing credit. Empirical investigations done by researchers across the countries have proved that microfinance and microcredit have a strong prospective of alleviating poverty and is in particular associated with socio-economic empowerment of women (Obaidullah, 2008; Quinones & Remenyi, 2014; Miyashita, 2000; Kasali, Ahmad & Lim, 2015; Wright, Kasente, Ssemogerere, & Mutesasira, 1999; Mawa, 2008; Sultana, Jamal, & Najaf, 2017; Nader, 2008; Hietalahti & Linden, 2006 ; Chhay, 2011; Rehman, Moazzam & Ansari, 2020, D'Agostini, 2020). Many studies suggest that the access of women to financial services has grown considerably in the last decade. The fact insists that this access has the ability to benefit them on their social, psychological and economic level. Microfinance schemes have also been regarded as having the capability of transforming power relations. It is an acceptable fact that microfinance does not address to all barriers/ hindrances or issues relating with women empowerment. But it can make considerable, notable, evident and acceptable level of contribution towards empowerment of women. Internationally and at various governmental initiatives from time to time microfinance has been evaluated as a strategy which is capable of targeting women and their vulnerability. According to USAID's annual Microenterprise Results Report for 2000, approximately 70 percent of USAID-supported MFIs' clients were women. Using microfinance for improving income generation activities among poor and vulnerable has been quite prevalent in many countries. When poor families are provided loan with small amounts there is a possibility they invest in micro enterprises. Banks at regional, rural levels help them by giving microcredit and in turn they become empowered to create job opportunities, raise their standard of living and improve the well being of their family. Particularly when women are provided such micro credit facilities they tend to spend a major chunk of their disposable income on improving the condition of family as well as education of their children.

Women in developing nations are seen to save more money than men or they tend to spend more money towards the betterment of whole family and education of children (Campbell, 2010). In countries like South Korea, Taiwan etc evidences are found that micro lending has raised the level of empowerment. Nawaz (2015) in her paper focused on economic and socio-cultural empowerment of women through micro financing. He stressed on the fact that financial literacy is one of the important factor for the success of microfinance programme. It can be used as a tool for improving economic status of women as well as help in improving power relations but only if it is combined with financial literacy. The empirical investigations of various researches in many studies it is stressed and proved that microfinance success can be evaluated and seen in the following manifold dimensions. The SHG bank linkage programme of Govt. of India has visibly shown profound social impacts. The studies reflect clearly that micro financing helped the households to spend more on the education of their children as compared to the non members. The programme has undoubtedly empowered the women lenders as their contribution in household income increased considerably. They also show increase and purchase of new household assets. The control over the use and decision making regarding the assets also reported to be better as compared to the earlier situation of women. Some studies also report reduction in child mortality, better and improved maternal health due to better availability of finance, food and nutrition (Karmakar, 2009).

Microfinance as a Tool of Social Empowerment of Women

Pucchio (2015), in her study on Iranian women studied five aspects of women's life. To quote these were, "possibility to go out, role within the community, participation to social and civil life, involvement in the decision- making process about family expenses and ability to conciliate work and family". The study showed the positive index for all the variables under study thereby clearly indicating the fact that the microfinance program was found to be successful in empowering the clients. However researcher lays thrust on the fact that microfinance is not the ultimate and supreme solution to the problem of poverty but if it is integrated wisely with other initiatives to improve the conditions of the households it can work miraculously.

An important feature of micro financing these days is that it is built upon the existing system of banking in most of the developing nations. In this process a separate bank linkage program was started in India and the financial resources were linked with the existing schemes/initiatives and the regular banking channels acted as a source for channelizing the savings of SHG bank linkage program into the main stream financial system. The micro finance has emerged as an innovation all over the world. It acted as an effective system for the provision of financial services specifically to the poor households and further it led to the development of micro enterprises. The group approach of micro finance helps the entire economy through the financial system. It helps not an individual but the whole group in order to link them with the formal financial structure. All the savings, loans and loan related payments are taken care of at the group level. This leads to a shared responsibility as well as accountability which can be regarded as an important factor for the success of the bank linkage program.

Basically Microfinance is aimed at providing adequate and cheap credit to the vulnerable sections of the society and each section of the society like regional artisans, poor families; women who have persistent problems in the day-to-day lives are especially taken care of. It is very difficult for them to reach to the formal financial institutions like commercial banks and ask for credit. Commercial banks and formal money lending houses have always avoided lending to the weaker sections of the society because of high cost of transactions and high-risk of the repayment. That is why in various developing economies including India the markets for rural credit and urban credit were segmented. The dominance of *sahukars (individual money lenders)* was found in rural areas that used to exploit the vulnerable by charging highest interest rates.SHG bank linkage program proved to be a boom for the society. Rahman (2017), examined the effects of microcredit on women's empowerment in rural Bangladesh by doing empirical investigations. A survey was done by him in four districts of Bangladesh to analyze the improvement in the level of women empowerment after participating in women microfinance program. His study revealed the positive impacts of microfinance on all the selected indicators for women empowerment. The study reveals the fact that largely most of the programs target women as they are globally found to be credit constrained. Women have been marginalized in male dominated society particularly in developing nations. As women constitute around 70 percent of world population many programs orient toward social and economic development of women. Moreover, researches have proved the fact that women have the tendency to support their whole family and if they are provided ample opportunities to grow economically, they uplift the standard of living of whole family. Mohapatra & Sahoo (2016), advocated in their study that in India SHG bank linkage program should be advocated particularly in those social groups or communities where women are discriminated. In their empirical investigations done in the state of Odisha, they found that participation in the microfinance programs lay down a positive as well as significant impact on women empowerment. According to the researchers microfinance acts as a catalyst to develop the status of women in developing or underdeveloped regions. Hassan & Saleem (2017), examined the role of Islamic microfinance business model in eradicating poverty and social-economic well being of women in Bangladesh. Their study revealed that microfinance led to the increase in women's revenue and when they are given credit it ultimately helps in improving their financial freedom. It results in the increase of self –possession. The results of the study revealed the fact that the group members gave preference to education of their children when their living standard increased; health and provision of food were other preferences for them. The process of empowerment has different dimensions and it varies from culture to culture. Several and varied kinds of changes which take place over the period of time are considered to be relevant in wide range of cultures. These changes may even range from clothing and education to spending and investment. It may also be relating to the factors having deep connotations for the society as a whole like increased participation in decision making, equitable status of the women in family and community as a whole, increased participation in power politics relationships in the business scenarios or it may be on a much more deeper sense i.e increased self esteem. Self confidence is yet another crucial area of empowerment, yet it is most difficult to assess or measure. The concept of increase in self confidence is quite complex as it is relating to women's perception of their own capabilities, their learning's and skills. Microfinance has been regarded as a tool to increase the self confidence level of women too (Swain & Wallentin, 2009). Swain & Wallentin argue that women's empowerment takes place when women reach up to a level where they can challenge the existing norms and culture to such a level that they can improve their well being. The results of their study strongly demonstrate that a significant increase in the level of empowerment of women in SHG member group was seen.

Microfinance as a Tool of Economic Empowerment of Women and Reduction of Poverty

Literature gives evidences of relevance of microfinance programs in countries like Tanzania, Iran, Bangladesh, Cambodia, India and much more developing nations. The impact studies done in these studies indicate that microfinance has proved to be an effective tool for the economic empowerment of women. Pucchio (2015), in her study highlighted the working and success of microfinance programmes in Iran. The Iranian government started the implementation of microfinance programs with the help of international organizations in 1990's. Reduction of poverty and development were the main objectives behind starting the programs. The program was inspired again the success of microfinance programs initiated by Yunus in Bangladesh. To meet the needs of poor *muslim* in the country a branch of microfinance was established which developed later into Islamic microfinance. In 1999, a program addressing females headed low income households was initiated and SHG's were made by the efforts of some welfare organizations. The study clearly highlights the fact that when a great deal of independence was given to the self help groups then it led to a process of liberation of women and ultimately leading and paving way towards empowerment. Later, after the success of this plan many new programmes were initiated by the international bodies as well as Iranian government aiming at the development of women. Pucchio in her empirical investigation studied the effects of microfinance programs on the poverty eradication and women empowerment. The results of the study showed that the program had a positive effect on the economic condition of the members. The monthly income of the households remained quite low, but the positive fact was that almost all the members were capable to pay off their loans without difficulties and invested the money for creating or improving any related income generating activity. Out of the sample taken 84% reported an improvement in the living standards.

Mamun, Malarvizhi, Hossain & Tan (2019), examined the effect of microcredit on poverty in Malaysia. The study aimed at analyzing the effects of the microcredit programme. Amaah Ikhtiar Malaysia (AIM) on the hardcore poor households of Malaysia. The findings of the study indicate that the program proved to be quite effective in eradicating poverty. The study highlighted the fact that through AIM nearly 82% of the poor and hardcore poor households were provided support with collateral free microcredit. It helped to bring down the poverty rate significantly. The study mentions that "the poverty rate in Malaysia declined significantly from 16.5 per cent in 1990 to only 3.6 per cent in 2007".

Empirical advances also support the fact that over the globe the average monthly incomes of the household's increases if the microcredit is used effectively in income generating activities. Increases in asset creation and consumer durables including two wheelers are also supported by empirical studies done by researchers. In the year 2011 a study was conducted in Tunisian government which highlighted the fact that 3 million Tunisians were the potential microfinance customers. Not only in Asia but in Latin America also, microfinance has been used as a tool to cure poverty and decrease unemployment. Errais & Miled (2015) analyzed the microfinance initiatives in Tunisia. The Tunisian government encourages all activities to enhance microfinance programs and is working continuously to reach at an appropriate rate of financial inclusion of the deprived, vulnerable and marginalized poor people of Tunisia. They have recognized microcredit to be an effective tool for eradicating poverty.

The situation in many countries changed gradually due to development of SHG's. The rural poor women are the most benefitted with the provision of credit. The development strategies of the groups are team oriented which increases a sense of belongingness as well as accountability towards each other. The SHG group is therefore a representation of a voluntary as well as participatory endeavor. The overall effort of all the activities is devoted towards improving the lives of participants and their families.

Supporting Entrepreneurship

The concept of entrepreneurship and development of micro enterprises is closely associated with microfinance especially in the rural areas. SHG's model is suited to local conditions and the income generating activities are dependent largely on the raw material availability in the local vicinity. The concept is basically for the promotion of self employment and small businesses. The women are regarded as sincere towards their duties and responsibilities. The micro enterprises are the result of SHG's which, with the passage of time sustain and start generating employment beyond the group members. Undoubtedly, this process is slow but the positive effects are long lasting, contributing towards the development of economy as a whole. Various govt. initiatives, NGO's plan of actions etc. are consistently and persistently oriented towards entrepreneurial development at village levels especially in developing nations.

Consequent awareness, training and development, financial support and knowledge of marketing the products are some of the important factors associated with success of start ups. The SHG's get consistent support from NGO's and govt. to move forward in the process of development of micro enterprises. The various stages of business development require sensible decisions and SHG's are trained, sensitized in all respects. Women get an opportunity not only to learn in this process but they also understand the relevance of taking independent decision making. They need to ensure liquidity, profitability and other operational aspects of business, which helps them to learn to grow the business. Entrepreneurship has been recognized as an important force for the development of rural areas. Various developing nations have used the strategy of rural entrepreneurship for improving the social and economic life of the poor and vulnerable sections of the society. SHG programmes of group lending focuses extensively on extending the benefits of development to the poor women who seek livelihood. It not only helps to speed up the economic growth but also helps in creating job opportunities which in turn have the capability of improving the quality of rural life leading way towards sustainability. A wide range of activities which pertains to various aspects of rural life and rural people are covered under these programmes. Skilled and unskilled jobs, rural artisans, rural art and craft are persistently nurtured and saved by the initiatives taken under microfinance progrmmmes.

The, SHGs distribute micro-finance to the rural poor for making them enterprising women and motivating them to go into in to entrepreneurial activities. Credit needs of the rural poor especially women are fulfilled completely through the SHGs. It augments quality of status of women as participants of the schemes, decision makers and beneficiaries in the economic, social and cultural spheres of life. It is assumed that to be in command of their own financial resources can help them in their social, economic and political development.

DISCUSSION

In the broader and technical terms microfinance is providing wide range of financial services which includes micro-loans, channelizing micro savings and provision of micro insurance which is designed as per the needs of poor people who do not have resources and usually are excluded from the formal financial set up of a country. Various microfinance institutions in many developing countries came up with the solution inspired by the success of Grameen bank of Bangladesh. The gap between the poor and the marginalized was very thin as they were deprived of the benefits of the formal financial structure. The concept of microfinance spread out all over the world in 18th and 19th century and then in 20th century the members started reaping the benefits of the initiatives. In order for a woman to be empowered, she needs right to use to the material, human, and social resources which are compulsory/ important for making planned choices in her life. In this global crisis women have been hit very badly. Every day we see the instances where the earnings hands of the families lost their jobs or lives. Moreover, microcredit facilities are available to all sections of societies. Earlier in countries like India the main focus was on India because not only have women been traditionally deprived of access to various material resources like credit, assets, and money, but they had also been excluded from social resources like education, liberation, and much more. Only access to these resources does not ensure automatic translation of a deprived woman into an empowered woman; however they must have the ability and confidence to use these resources to meet their goals. The Self Help Group or group concept of lending in one way or another boosts that confidence to express, to discuss, to give an idea and take initiatives. It helps to shape up the personality of a complete woman, who has some objectives; she has access to money and autonomy to take the decisions. The psychology of a woman is badly affected if she is excluded from decision making. She lacks confidence for whole of her life to define goals and act effectively to achieve the desired goals. So in order to improve the status of women the main impetus was on women. It's a big challenge for the agencies who work for women empowerment to provide them a psychological freedom and ability to take their own decisions. The influence of such programs which are related to consider various factors of a women's life can have a long lasting effect in the society. The availability of adequate money in the hands of a woman ensures much more than just access to credit. It in one way or another is liberation from poverty, access to education, better standard of living, shackling out her from the clutches of poverty and her acceptability in the society. The same is applicable to men and other sections of socities which are now badly hit. The author contends that a little more planned effort to cater the worst hit sectors of society during and after pandemic via microfinance can prove wonders.

The capability or the ability of a woman to make her life better or transform through getting access to finance or financial services is not sole success parameter. Her transformation is dependent on many factors which can be related to her personal life as well as the societal environment in which she operates. Even if women are the main focus they can help whole family to survive and can provide the male counterparts opportunities to grow and revive. Many factors can be pertaining to her individual circumstances. Control on money or capital is just one dimension towards the empowerment of vulnerable. It is an ever changing process in a society in which the excluded or worst hit is evolved over the period of time. In the due course of time when vulnerable or excluded invest, learn to take decisions, become independent and gets mature they start coming out of the cycle of poverty. A large chunk of population is now disadvantaged not only in terms of money, but they are suffering psychologically too due to not having access to basic amenities of life. Even for many sanitation facilities, health facilities and education has become a distant dream. Only by evaluating their needs, their social status, and the level of the disadvantageous position in the society the MFI's should take the decisions regarding the plans or the programs to uplift them in the society. It can help them to maximize their empowerment potential to the maximum if the level of the vulnerability is assessed before hand and the plan of the actions are devised accordingly. The reported positive effects of microfinance by various studies are that it is the most effective way of providing low cost financial services to vulnerable sections of the society. These programs show evidence of development and growth of the local economies, local artisans, or skilled people who otherwise lose their identities with the passage of time. These programs also helped in improving living standards and increasing the disposable income levels of the participants. Not only extreme poverty of the participants was recorded to come down but it has helped them to live with dignity. The peculiar problems of poverty, unemployment, economic inequalities, illiteracy, and gender disparity are addressed with the help of microfinance initiatives. Formation of self help groups undoubtedly have helped to achieve important aspects of rural entrepreneurship also which ultimately is triggered by micro and small ventures which turn into successful start ups or MSME's.

CHALLENGES AHEAD

It is unclear that whether microfinance will help significantly in reducing global poverty or not. Moreover many countries are showing increase in NPA's which an extreme challenge to combat with this issue. The microfinance users have also shown the tendency of landing themselves in to debt traps in some nations. This means to repay one loan they go for taking a new loan. A proper training and development along with financial literacy can only help the deprived sector to use the debt efficiently. They need proper sensitization and updating regarding the understanding of the market to sell their products or to run their ventures effectively. Moreover it is a great challenge to make them understand that they can become input providers of supply chain management practices. if such challenges are well thought off then in the times of global crises many nations can gain the momentum through micro financing activities.

REFERENCES

Al-Mamun, A., Malarvizhi, C., Hossain, S., & Tan, S. (2012). Examining the Effect of Microcredit on Poverty in Malaysia. *ASEAN Economic Bulletin*, *29*(1), 15–28. doi:10.1355/ae29-1b

Amin, R., & Becker, S. (1998). NGO-promoted microcredit programs and women's empowerment in rural Bangladesh: Quantitative and qualitative evidence. *Journal of Developing Areas*, *32*(2), 221–236. PMID:12294125

Arora, M., & Sharma, R. L. (2021). Repurposing the Role of Entrepreneurs in the Havoc of COVID-19. In Entrepreneurship and Big Data (pp. 229-250). CRC Press. doi:10.1201/9781003097945-16

Arora, M., & Sharma, R. L. (2021). Neutralizing Maleficent Effects of COVID-19 Through Entrepreneurship: Peeping Through the Lens of Communication. In Effective Strategies for Communicating Insights in Business (pp. 67-86). IGI Global.

Arora, M., & Singh, S. (2015). An Evaluation of the Non Performing Assets of Public and Private Sector Banks Under the SHG Bank Linkage Programme. *Indian Journal Of Finance*, *9*(6), 41–50. doi:10.17010/ijf/2015/v9i6/71161

Arora, M., & Singh, S. (2016). Disbursement of Credit Under the SGSY Scheme: A Comparison of SHGs' Swarozgaris and Individual Swarozgaris. *Indian Journal Of Finance*, *10*(11), 54–63. doi:10.17010/ijf/2016/v10i11/104918

Arora, M., & Singh, S. (2017). Role of Financial Institutions in Promoting Microfinance through SHG Bank Linkage Programme in India. *Pacific Business Review International*, *10*(4), 50–58.

Arora, M., & Singh, S. (2018). Impact Assessment of Self-Help Group Bank Linkage Programme on Women Empowerment in the State of Himachal Pradesh. Academic Press.

Arora, M., & Singh, S. (2018). The Impact of SHG Bank Linkage Programme on the Members of Self Help Groups: An Empirical Investigation in the State of Himachal Pradesh. *Sumedha Journal of Management*, *7*(1), 34–46.

Aruna, M., & Jyothirmayi, M. R. (2011). The role of microfinance in women empowerment: A study on the SHG bank linkage program in Hyderabad (Andhra Pradesh). *Indian Journal of Commerce & Management Studies ISSN*, *2229*, 5674.

Bakhtiari, S. (2006). Microfinance and poverty reduction: some international evidence. *International Business & Economics Research Journal*, *5*(12).

Bali Swain, R., & Wallentin, F. Y. (2012). Factors empowering women in Indian self-help group programs. *International Review of Applied Economics*, *26*(4), 425–444. doi:10.1080/02692171.2011.595398

Brody, C., De Hoop, T., Vojtkova, M., Warnock, R., Dunbar, M., Murthy, P., & Dworkin, S. L. (2015). Economic Self-Help group programs for improving women's Empowerment: A systematic review. *Campbell Systematic Reviews*, *11*(1), 1–182. doi:10.4073/csr.2015.19

Campbell, G. (2010). Microfinancing the Developing World: How small loans empower local economies and catalyse neoliberalism's endgame. *Third World Quarterly, 31*(7), 1081-1090. Retrieved from https://www.jstor.org/stable/27896601

Chhay, D. (2011). Women's economic empowerment through microfinance in Cambodia. *Development in Practice*, *21*(8), 1122–1137. doi:10.1080/09614524.2011.606891

Chhay, D. (2011). Women's economic empowerment through microfinance in Cambodia. *Development in Practice*, *21*(8), 1122–1137. doi:10.1080/09614524.2011.606891

D'Agostini, D. (2020). Microfinance in the African continent. *Policy*, (1).

De Aghion, B. A., Armendáriz, B., & Morduch, J. (2007). *The economics of microfinance*. Academic Press.

Di Pucchio, Y. (2015). Microfinance in Iran: A Case Study of the Rural Microfinance Support Project. *Oriente Moderno, 95*(1/2), 211-232. Retrieved from https://www.jstor.org/stable/44289942

Errais, E., & Miled, S. (2015). Investing in Microfinance: The Case of Tunisia. *Journal of Private Equity*, *18*(3), 79–96. doi:10.3905/jpe.2015.18.3.079

Ghosh, C., & Das, A. (2020). Drivers of performance of the microfinance institutions in selected South Asian countries. *International Journal of Economics and Accounting*, *9*(2), 155–179. doi:10.1504/IJEA.2020.105207

Hassan, A., & Saleem, S. (2017). An Islamic microfinance business model in Bangladesh: Its role in alleviation of poverty and socio-economic well-being of women. *Humanomics*, *33*(1), 15–37. doi:10.1108/H-08-2016-0066

Hietalahti, J., & Linden, M. (2006). Socio-economic impacts of microfinance and repayment performance: A case study of the Small Enterprise Foundation, South Africa. *Progress in Development Studies*, *6*(3), 201–210. doi:10.1191/1464993406ps138oa

Hussen, S., Wodajo, M. R., & Tasente, T. (2021). The role of microfinance in funding Small & Medium Enterprises: Harekello Town of Goro Dolla District in Focus, Ethiopia. *Technium Soc. Sci. J.*, *17*, 355. doi:10.2139srn.3801885

Javid, A., & Abrar, A. (2015). Microfinance Institutions and Poverty Reduction: A Cross Regional Analysis. *Pakistan Development Review*, *54*(4), 371–387. https://www.jstor.org/stable/43831326. doi:10.30541/v54i4I-IIpp.371-387

Karadağ, H. (2016). The role of SMEs and entrepreneurship on economic growth in emerging economies within the post-crisis era: An analysis from Turkey. *Journal of Small Business and Entrepreneurship Development*.

Karmakar, K. (2009). Emerging Trends in Microfinance. *Economic and Political Weekly*, *44*(13), 21–24. https://www.jstor.org/stable/40278656

Kasali, T. A., Ahmad, S. A., & Lim, H. E. (2015). The role of microfinance in poverty alleviation: Empirical evidence from South-West Nigeria. *Asian Social Science*, *11*(21), 183–192. doi:10.5539/ass.v11n21p183

Khan, R. E. A., & Noreen, S. (2012). Microfinance and women empowerment: A case study of District Bahawalpur (Pakistan). *African Journal of Business Management*, *6*(12), 4514–4521.

Krogh, E., Hansen, T. N., Wendt, S., & Elkjaer, M. (2009). Promoting employment for women as a strategy for poverty reduction. *Promoting Pro-Poor Growth, 133*.

Kyereboah-Coleman, A., & Osei, K. A. (2008). Outreach and profitability of microfinance institutions: The role of governance. *Journal of Economic Studies (Glasgow, Scotland)*, *35*(3), 236–248. doi:10.1108/01443580810887797

Matter, F. (2011). *Development in Practice*, *21*(8). https://www.jstor.org/stable/41413000

Mawa, B. (2008). Impact of micro-finance towards achieving poverty alleviation. *Pakistan Journal of Social Sciences*, *5*(9), 876–882.

McCarter, E. (2006). Women and microfinance: Why we should do more. *U. Md. LJ Race, Religion. Race, Gender, & Class*, *6*, 353.

McGuire, P. B., & Conroy, J. D. (2000). The microfinance phenomenon. *Asia-Pacific Review*, *7*(1), 90–108. doi:10.1080/713650817

Miyashita, Y. (2000). Microfinance and poverty alleviation: Lessons from Indonesia's village banking system. *Pac. Rim L. & Pol'y J.*, *10*, 147.

Mohapatra, S., & Sahoo, B. K. (2016). Determinants of participation in self-help-groups (SHG) and its impact on women empowerment. *Indian Growth and Development Review*, *9*(1), 53–78. doi:10.1108/IGDR-04-2015-0016

Moyle, T. L., Dollard, M., & Biswas, S. N. (2006). Personal and economic empowerment in rural Indian women: A self-help group approach. *International Journal of Rural Management*, *2*(2), 245–266. doi:10.1177/097300520600200207

Nader, Y. F. (2008). Microcredit and the socio-economic wellbeing of women and their families in Cairo. *Journal of Socio-Economics*, *37*(2), 644–656. doi:10.1016/j.socec.2007.10.008

Nawaz, F. (2015). Microfinance, Financial Literacy, and Household Power Configuration in Rural Bangladesh: An Empirical Study on Some Credit Borrowers. *Voluntas*, *26*(4), 1100–1121. doi:10.100711266-015-9585-z

Noreen, S. (2011). Role of microfinance in empowerment of female population of Bahawalpur district. In *International Conference on Economics and Finance Research* (*Vol. 4*, No. 20, pp. 65-71). Academic Press.

Nukpezah, J. A., & Blankson, C. (2017). Microfinance intervention in poverty reduction: A study of women farmer-entrepreneurs in rural Ghana. *Journal of African Business*, *18*(4), 457–475. doi:10.1080/15228916.2017.1336915

Obaidullah, M. (2008). *Role of microfinance in poverty alleviation: Lessons from experiences in selected IDB member countries. In Role of Microfinance in Poverty Alleviation: Lessons from Experiences in Selected IDB Member Countries*. Islamic Development Bank.

Onileowo, T. T., & Anifowose, O. D. (2020). Catalyst and Instrument of National Growth: Interrogating the Significance of Entrepreneurship in Nigerian Economic Development. *Catalyst, 12*(3).

Osman, O. S. (2020). The role of microfinance post trauma: the case of Syria. *Journal of Sustainable Finance & Investment*, 1-15.

Quinones, B., & Remenyi, J. (2014). *Microfinance and poverty alleviation: Case studies from Asia and the Pacific*. Routledge. doi:10.4324/9781315800455

Rahman, M. M., Khanam, R., & Nghiem, S. (2017). The effects of microfinance on women's empowerment: New evidence from Bangladesh. *International Journal of Social Economics*, *44*(12), 1745–1757. doi:10.1108/IJSE-02-2016-0070

Rehman, H., Moazzam, D. A., & Ansari, N. (2020). Role of microfinance institutions in women empowerment: A case study of Akhuwat, Pakistan. *South Asian Studies*, *30*(1).

Shinde, R., & Joshi, A. (2016). Socio-economic Empowerment of Women through Micro-financing: A Study of Self Help Groups in Pune City. *Journal of Commerce and Management Thought*, *7*(4), 633–655. doi:10.5958/0976-478X.2016.00034.3

Sigalla, R. J., & Carney, S. (2012). Poverty reduction through entrepreneurship: Microcredit, learning and ambivalence amongst women in urban Tanzania. *International Journal of Educational Development*, *32*(4), 546–554. doi:10.1016/j.ijedudev.2012.02.011

Sultana, H. Y., Jamal, M. A., & Najaf, D. E. (2017). Impact of microfinance on women empowerment through poverty alleviation: An assessment of socio-economic conditions in Chennai city of Tamil Nadu. *Asian Journal for Poverty Studies, 3*(2).

Swain, R. B., & Wallentin, F. Y. (2009). Does microfinance empower women? Evidence from self-help groups in India. *International Review of Applied Economics*, *23*(5), 541–556. doi:10.1080/02692170903007540

Tesoriero, F. (2006). Strengthening communities through women's self help groups in South India. *Community Development Journal: An International Forum*, *41*(3), 321–333. doi:10.1093/cdj/bsi066

Thorat, U. (2006). Financial inclusion and millennium development goals. *RBI Bulletin*, *50*(2), 239–243.

Wright, G. A., Kasente, D., Ssemogerere, G., & Mutesasira, L. (1999). *Vulnerability, risks, assets and empowerment–the impact of microfinance on poverty alleviation.* Final report. Kampala, Uganda: MicroSave-Africa and Uganda Women's Finance Trust.

Chapter 9
Mobilizing Zakat (Almsgiving) Funds to Support Refugee Microenterprise Pogroms:
A Proposed Conceptual Model

Omar Kachkar
https://orcid.org/0000-0001-7786-8893
Ibn Haldun University, Turkey

Marwa Alfares
Istanbul Sabahattin Zaim University, Turkey

ABSTRACT

This chapter examines the prospects and challenges of using zakah as a source of funding in microenterprise support programs for refugees. According to the literature, lack of funds represents a fundamental obstacle in supporting refugees' livelihood in particular in microenterprises programs. Zakat is one of the five pillars of Islam. All Muslims have to pay 2.5% of their wealth every year to the poor and needy. Refugees represent one of the main beneficiaries of zakah. Recently the UNHCR has established a zakah fund to mobilize zakah funds to help refugees. This chapter argues that instead of assisting refugees with cash money, zakat funds or at least part of the zakat funds can be used to provide microcredit grants to support the refugees and help them to help themselves. Despite all the challenges of microfinance programs in particular in the context of refugees, well-designed microfinance programs can provide a more sustainable solution to refugees in particular those trapped in protracted situations.

INTRODUCTION

The last few years have witnessed an unprecedented rise in the number of refugees worldwide. In 2010, approximately 200,000 new refugees were registered by the UNHCR (UNHCR, 2012). In 2017 the number of newly registered refugees reached 2.7 million, more than thirteen times higher than it was in 2010 (UNHCR, 2018). The UNHCR report (2019) affirms that by the end of 2019 the total number of

DOI: 10.4018/978-1-7998-8925-0.ch009

Figure 1. State-of-art of refugees around the world
Source: UNHCR report 2020 https://www.unhcr.org/figures-at-a-glance.html

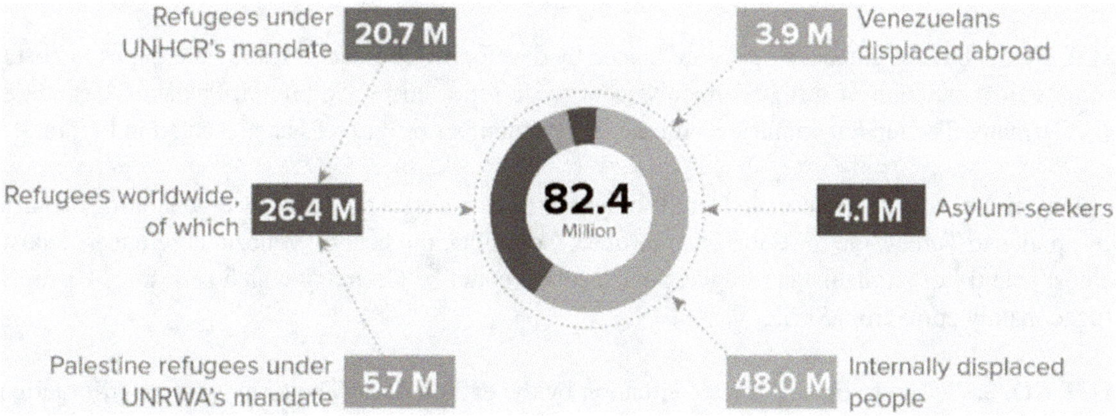

forcibly displaced populations worldwide had hit a new record high of 82.4 million including around 26.4 million refugees. Since 2012, the overall number of refugees under the UNHCR's mandate has nearly doubled (UNHCR, 2019; 2020; 2021).

An examination of this large number of refugees reveals three undeniably facts, these facts will be highlighted as follow:

FACT NO. 1. almost all world refugees come from developing countries and many of them are from the least developing countries. According to the latest UNHCR report issued in June 2020, at the end of the decade, 8 out of 10 people displaced across borders more specifically, 83% are originated from just 10 countries as shown below in figure 2.

Figure 2. Top refugee-generating countries
Source: UNHCR report 2020 https://www.unhcr.org/figures-at-a-glance.html

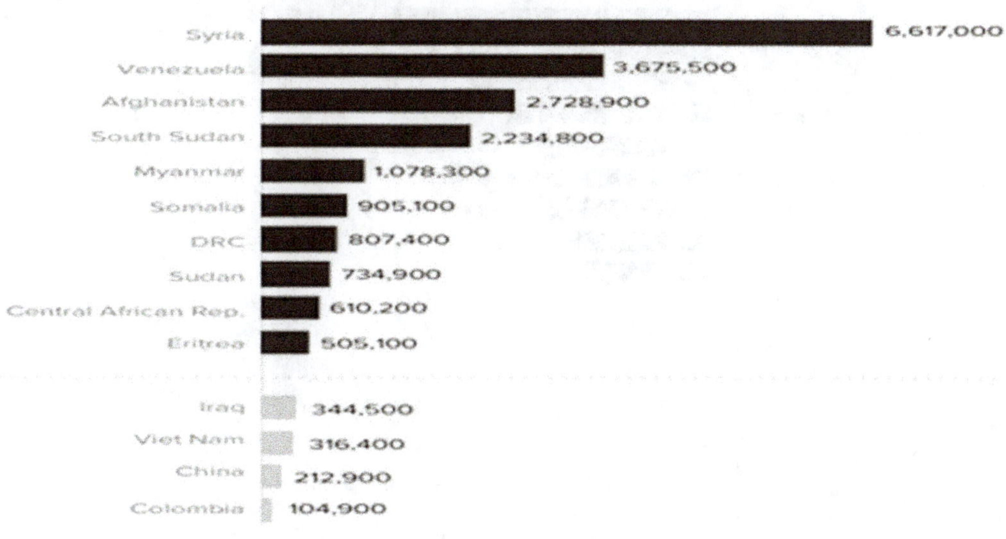

The above figure does not include around 5.6 Palestinian refugees registered under the mandate of the United Nations Relief and Works Agency for Palestine Refugees in the Near East (UNRWA).

FACT NO. 2. 85% of global refugees are hosted by developing countries. Turkey continues to host the largest population of refugees mainly from Syria followed by Colombia, Pakistan, Uganda and Germany. The top ten countries with the highest number of refugees as presented in Figure 3.

Many of the host countries are in fact the neighbouring countries of the refugee-generating countries. This applies to Turkey, the host of Syrian refugee, Colombia, the host of Venezuela refugees, Pakistan the host country of Afghanistan refugee. An exception could be Germany which is hosting 1.1 million refugee mainly come from Syria.

FACT NO. 3. 77% were in a protracted situation by the end of 2019. The term "protracted situations" refers to situations where 25,000 or more refugees of the same nationality have been in exile for five years or longer in a given asylum country. By the end of 2019, it is estimated that approximately 15.7 million refugees are considered in protracted situations. Approximately, 5.8 million of them were in a situation lasting 20 years or more. These refugees are hosted by 27 countries, representing 32 protracted situations. In 2018 NINE additional situations become protracted, and NONE of the previous protracted situations were resolved in the same year (UNHCR, 2019). The Diagram below capture the snapshot of refugees in protracted situations as of December 2018.

The outbreak of coronavirus disease 2019 (COVID-19) with its disastrous impact on public health and global economies, has aggravated the difficulties encountered by refugees and marginalised communities (Action Against Hunger, 2020). This is mainly because 85% of global refugees are hosted by

Figure 3. top ten refugee-host countries
Source: UNHCR report 2020 https://www.unhcr.org/figures-at-a-glance.html

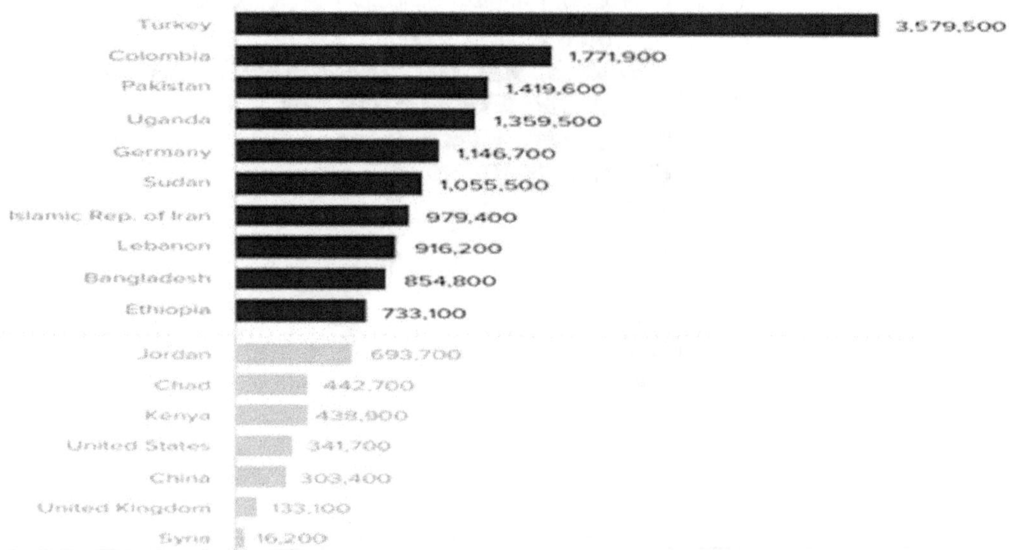

Figure 4. Refugees in protracted situations
Source: https://blogs.worldbank.org/dev4peace/2019-update-how-long-do-refugees-stay-exile-find-out-beware-averages

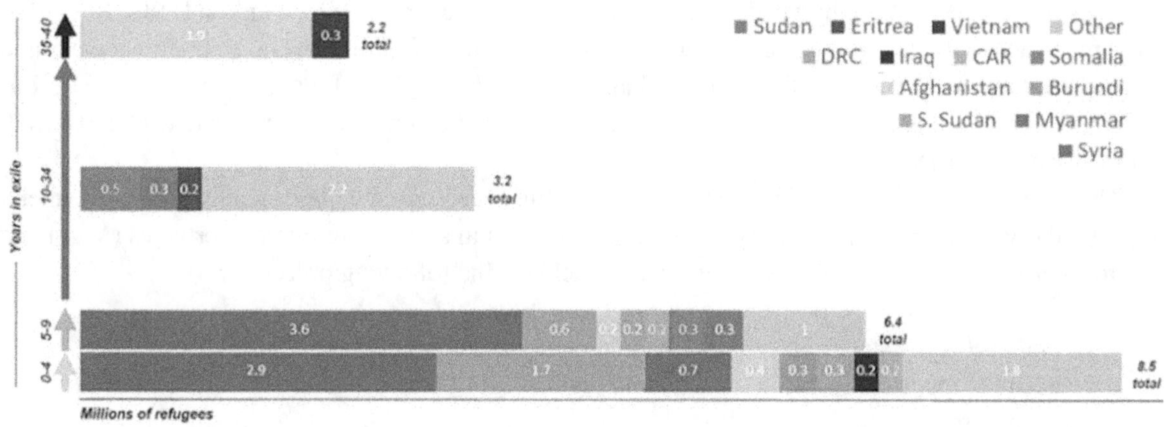

developing countries that in addition to their persistent economic and social problems, were seriously hit by the ongoing pandemic.

Relief International, a development and humanitarian non-profit alliance, and it has been working in Turkey since 2014, in April 2020, the organisation published the results of its rapid needs assessment (RNA) that it conducted to explore the impact of the COVID-19 outbreak on d on its program participants, the survey took place in five provinces: Istanbul, Izmir, Manisa, Gaziantep, Kilis, and Hatay. Participants were asked if they had urgent needs that cannot be accessed during this outbreak. Eighty-one percent reported that they lost access to essential needs since the onset of the outbreak. Of these, 59% reported having lost access to food, 37% to hygiene materials, and 5% to water. The highest percentage across all was recorded in Istanbul (35% food, 32% hygiene materials, and 43% water), and the full distribution of urgent needs among cities is shown below in Figure 5.

Figure 5. Distribution of urgent needs among cities
Source: https://reliefweb.int/sites/reliefweb.int/files/resources/76504.pdf

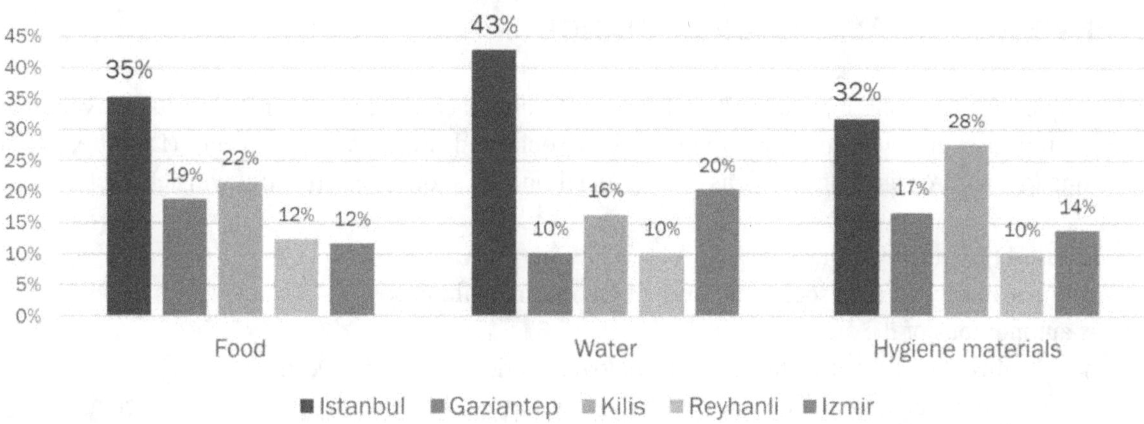

Zakah is the third pillar in Islam, and it is considered one of the fundamental tools in Islamic economic system that plays a remarkable role in poverty alleviation throughout the Islamic history. Estimation of total *zakah* amounts payable by Muslims around the world ranges from US$ 76 billion UNHCR (2019a) to as much as US$600 billion (UNICEF, 2019), in between these figures, several estimations are found in the literature including the estimation of Shaikh al-Qaradaghi, (2014) that reaches about 137.5 billion and the estimation of the Islamic Development Banks that estimated *zakah* at to reach $230 - $560 billion (Modéer, 2018).

This paper is an additional effort in the field of refugee economic engagement and empowerment. It particularly focuses on the viability of using *zakah* funds in supporting microenterprises (MEs) and microfinance programs for refugees. It attempts to achieve the following objectives:

a) To underscore the state of art of refugee microenterprises support programs
b) To examine the latest literature on *zakah* in the context of microfinance and microenterprise support programs,
c) To propose a viable model based on *zakah* funds; and
d) To highlight best practises in offering microenterprise support programs based on *zakah*

To achieve the above-mentioned research objectives, the authors have employed qualitative and descriptive research methods. This method has been used in many disciplines in social sciences. Hence, an intensive literature review has been conducted to survey, identify, and analyse all relevant materials including academic papers, articles, books, and other published materials. According to Bocke at all, (2009) literature reviews play a critical role in scholarship because science remains, first and foremost, a cumulative endeavour. As such, an overview on the existing state-of-art literature has been presented to reflect the recent situations of refugees globally. The analysis of refugees as a potential and eligible beneficiary of *zakah* funds is also provided. The UNHCR program on *zakah* has been highlighted as a case in point and an example of tapping on *zakah* funds for humanitarian actions. To support the argument of this research, two programs have been cited along with a discussion of their practices in using *zakah* funds in microenterprises programs. Building on the cited programs and practices, a conceptual framework is proposed with full explanations of the model flow and steps.

OVERVIEW OF ISLAMIC SOCIAL FINANCE

In its simplest forms social finance can be defined as "An approach to managing investments that generate financial returns while including measurable positive social and environmental impact." (Deloitte, 2019) according to the European Commissions (2016) social finance should have the following characteristics:

- is at least nominally repayable
- pursues an accountable social, cultural, or environmental purpose
- is autonomous of the state
- has the mission of the investee as the principal beneficiary of any investment
- is transparent about assessing, measuring, and reporting the social impact it seeks to create

- is structured to create financial value or organisational or community capacity over time, e.g., by helping the investee invest in growth, acquire an asset, strengthen management, generate income and/or make savings, and by providing wider non-financial support
- is inclusive. (p.11)

Features of social finance are not strange to the Islamic economic system including Islamic financial instruments. In fact, many of them are among the intrinsic components of Islamic economic system. Islamic social finance instruments like *waqf*, *zakah*, *qard al-hasan* and *sadaqah* have played a crucial role in providing for the basic needs of Muslim communities throughout the Islamic history. As such. These roles can be revived to address the increasing budget deficit of humanitarian programs including economic engagement and financial inclusion of refugees. Shaikh Ali al-Qaradaghi estimates that annual *zakah* funds may reach around 400 billion (Al-Taher, 2017). In the same context, the Islamic Development Bank has estimated that figure to reach between $230 and $560 billion globally. (Modéer, 2018).

Juristic Issues in Using *Zakah* Funds in Development Projects

Bearing in mind the great potential of *zakah* funds in relief and humanitarian operations and projects, there is a widespread misconception on the permissibility of using *zakah* funds in development projects, due to the well-known condition of *tamlik* (full entitlement of the funds to the beneficiary and possession by the beneficiary) many scholars believe that *zakah* funds may not be used for development projects. However, this research argues that in microfinance and microenterprise programs, *tamlik* is achieved through two forms:

1. The grand of funds provided to the microenterprises
2. The equipment that is provided to the microentrepreneurs,

At this juncture we might have a Shariah issue in relation to paying *zakah* in kind goods and commodities not in cash which is permissible according to the famous opinion in Malikiyyah *mazheb* (school of thought) and one account in the *Hanabilah mezhab* the permissibility of using *zakah* funds to purchase army tools and equipment and grand them to the military individuals (Al-Uthman, 2012). Additionally, according to imam Abu Hanifah as reported by Ibn 'Abidin in his famous book *Radd al-Muhtar*, in general it is allowed to pay the value of *zakah*, furthermore, the *Hanafiyyah* allowed for the Imam to borrow the money of *zakah* from the *zakah* House, to settle the expenses of the state and to return the money back as a borrower. (Ibn 'Abidin (2/369). Even the *Malikiyyah*, *Shafi'yyah* and *Hanabilah* allowed the sale of *zakah* commodities and goods in the cases of necessity or to convert the *zakah* funds or properties according to the *maslaha* and interest of the poor. Such as in the case of risk on the sheep cattle on the way etc. (Al-Uthman and Hamzah, 2012). Finally, the International Islamic *Fiqh* Academy allowed using *zakah* funds in profit generating projects as early as 1986 in its third session held in Amman, Jordan and issued the resolution that states:

It is permissible, in principle, to put Zakah funds in investment projects which eventually lead to be owned by those who are deserving of Zakah, or which are under the control and administration of the entity which is responsible and has the jurisdiction over collecting and distributing Zakah, provided that it is done after satisfying the basic and immediate needs of the beneficiaries and with proper guar-

antees against loss." (Resolutions and Recommendations of the Council of the Islamic Fiqh Academy 1985-2000, 2000:27).

Refugees as Eligible Beneficiaries of *Zakah* Funds

According to the 1951 Refugee Convention 'refugee' as a term is applicable to: "someone who is unable or unwilling to return to their country of origin owing to a well-founded fear of being persecuted for reasons of race, religion, nationality, membership of a particular social group, or political opinion." (UNHCR, 1951) Thus, the above definition describes a social phenomenon of displacement that may affect individuals due to any of the reasons highlighted in the definition. in other words, the definition is not meant to underline the economic situation of the displaced populations. In contrast, *zakah*, is more of a religious term that implies the obligation of the payment of a certain percentage of one's wealth to the poor and underprivileged people. The Holy Qur'an (9:60) specifies eight categories of *zakah* beneficiaries: *The alms are meant only for the poor and the needy and those who are in charge thereof, those whose hearts are to be reconciled, and to free those in bondage, and to help those burdened with debt, and for expenditure in the Way of Allah and for the wayfarer. This is an obligation from Allah. Allah is All-Knowing, All-Wise."* (Quran 9:60). Now, even though many refugees are potential beneficiaries of *zakah*, it must be asserted that from the juristic point of view, not all refugees are, by definition, eligible to receive *zakah* funds, in fact many of them are neither poor nor needy. Therefore, a robust screening system must be put in place to ensure that only eligible beneficiaries from among the refugees will receive *zakah* payments.

In the report issued by Tabah Foundation on 'The distribution of Muslim alms through UNHCR', Furber, (2017) cites fatwas (legal opinion) of three institution on the issue along with the legal opinion of a number of shariah schools, these institutions are:

- The Fatwa Authorities of Egypt (*Dar al-Ifta' al-Missriyyah*)
- The Senior Scholars' Council of Morocco
- The Fatwa Council of *Tareem, Hadramaut*, Yemen,

Legal opinions (fatwas) of all the above institutions emphasised the following three points:

1. UNHCR can collect and redistribute *zakah* on behalf of Muslims.
2. *Zakah* funds must be given to the categories mentioned in Quran 9:60.
3. *Zakah* funds must not be used to cover expenses or wages (Furber, 2017).

UNHCR *Zakah* Funds

As a result of the increasing interest in Islamic social finance, the UNHCR has launched in late 2016 a *zakah* program with the aim of "expanding the impact of *Zakah* funds to thousands more eligible refugee and internally displaced families who desperately need support worldwide". (https://*zakah*.unhcr.org/en/about-*zakah*) according to the UNHCR refugee *zakah* fund report 2019 "100% of *Zakah* donations goes to those who need it the most" with no fees deducted from the principle *zakah* amount. Donors can select the beneficiaries of their *zakah* from a list of projects including internally displaced populations in Iraq and Yemen, Malian Refugees Rohingya refugees and Syrian refugees. UNHCR piloted the receipt of *Zakah* funds in 2017 and 2018, receiving $14.4M, with which it assisted 6,888 families in Jordan and Lebanon. Based on this, UNHCR launched in 2019 the "Refugee *Zakah* Fund": In the same year it assisted 1,025,014 beneficiaries in eight countries by distributing $43.165 million of *Zakah* funds in addition to $222,907 in *sadaqah* donations and purification funds (UNHCR, 2020). These figures are depicted in Figure 6.

In the first six months of 2020, UNHCR received a total of $55.2 million $46 million in *Zakah* $9.2 million in *sadaqah* funds. The majority of the *zakah* funds were donated from MENA region and from institutional and philanthropists giving as illustrated in Figure 7.

Figure 6. Zakah Funds raised and distributed in 2019
Source: https://zakah.unhcr.org/wp-content/uploads/2020/04/IP-English-Impact-Full-Final.pdf

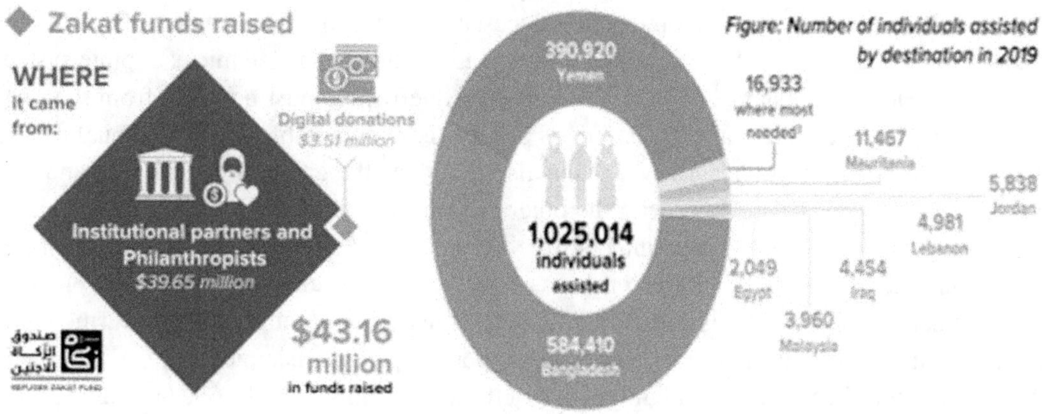

Figure 7. Zakah Funds raised by type and region in 2020
Source: https://zakah.unhcr.org/wp-content/uploads/2020/11/UNHCR-2020-Mid-Year-Islamic Philanthropy Report English-Compressed.pdf

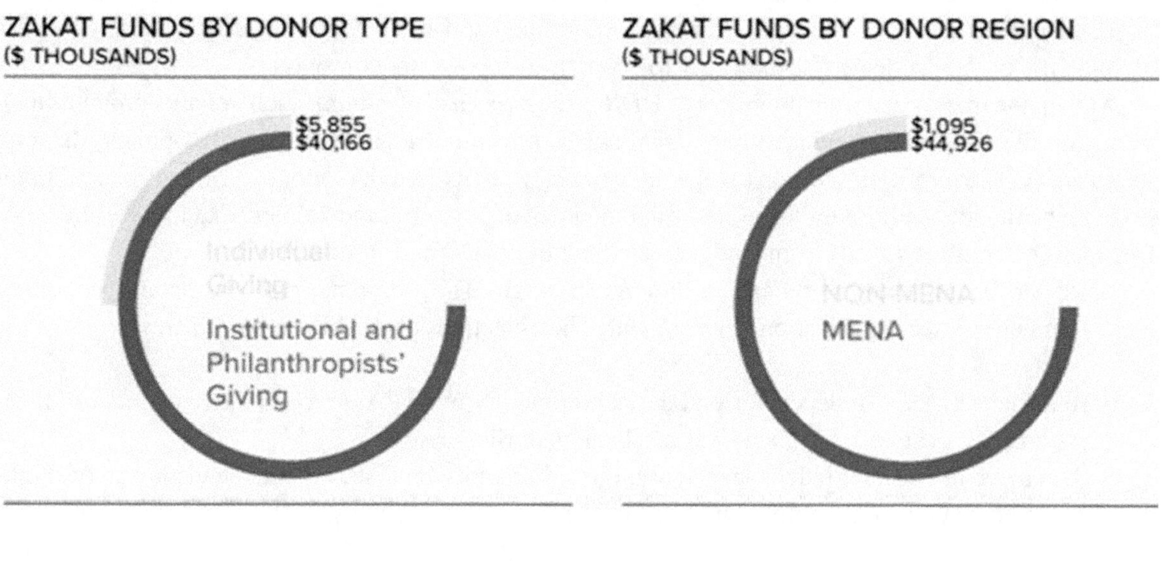

OVERVIEW OF USING *ZAKAH* FUNDS IN MICROFINANCE AND MICROENTERPRISES PROGRAMS

Microfinance has emerged as an important tool for poverty alleviation in the developing countries (Yonis, 2012). The World Bank has highlighted three dimensions of poverty; 1- lack of income and assets 2- voicelessness and powerlessness in the institutions of the state and society and 3-the inability to cope with unexpected shocks such as sudden changes in currency values or market forces (Loescher and Milner, 2005). Needless to assert that majority of refugees suffer from all these conditions of poverty.

Microfinance positive effects include increasing income, economic growth, assets and reducing vulnerability through the provision of microcredit to the poor (Obaidullah, 2008).as a poverty alleviation tool is more appreciated when it is used to improve the socio-economic situations of refugees who suffer the worst forms of poverty (Kachkar, 2019). As rightly put by Antonio Guterres, the former UNHCR Secretary General “When leaving is not an option but a necessity, this is more than poverty.” (UNHCR, 2007).

Zakah is considered one of the key tools in poverty alleviation in the Islamic economic system. According to the teaching of Islam, *zakah* is a compulsory due which must be taken from the rich to be given to the less fortunate on yearly basis. *Zakah* scheme is a remarkable national annual programme which is meant not only to eradicate poverty, but also to reduce the gap between the rich and the poor. (Mohsin and Alhabshi, 2016). Along with the other components of Islamic social finance such as endowment (waqf), charity (*sadaqh*) and interest-free loans (*al-qard al-hasan*), it can play a vital role in closing the funding gaps in humanitarian projects as well as in the socio-economic development. In the literature, numerous success stories can be highlighted for using *zakah* funds in empowerment projects, particularly, in microfinance and microenterprises support programs. (Islamic Commercial Law Report 2018). The following discussion will highlight two of these programs, namely, one program in Indonesia and the other program is implemented in Malaysia.

Case Study One: Dompet Dhuafa Republika, Indonesia

Dompet Dhuafa Republika (DDR) is a philanthropic institution that serves to help the poor using donated assets including *zakah*, *sadaqah* and waqf from individuals, groups, companies, or institutions. On top of the objectives of DDR is to (i) build human values and self-reliance. to this effect, DDR allocated around 10% of total collected *Zakah* funds to economic empowerment programs.

Among the major economic programs of DDR is the *masyarakat mandiri* (self-reliant communities), *pertanian sehat* (health/ organic farming), *kampoeng ternak nusantara* (livestock development), Islamic microfinance (for-profit) in addition to capacity building initiatives under Indonesia Magnificence *Zakah* (IMZ). The first three programs follow a similar model of economic empowerment that involves interest-free loan financing to groups from a pool created out of *zakah* funds (Alim 2013).

Below we focus on the (self-reliance community program. The program focused on income generating and community-based organization development. The objectives of the MM program are:

- To achieve material independence of target community by realizing its productive ability to meet basic needs and to establish survival mechanism during crises.
- To achieve intellectual independence of target community by fostering independent way of thinking and behaviour and ability to make critical judgment.

- To achieve managerial independence of community-based organization by ensuring the community's capability to take collective action in creating a sustainable local institution that can establish equal partnership between multi-stakeholders.

Program Selection Criteria

The program has set up different selection criteria for the regions to operate n as well as for the potential individuals to support. Details of the selection criteria will be presented below.

Selection Criteria for Urban Region

The program announced three criteria for the targeted regions as follows:

1. Densely populated area
2. Potential to be developed into a centre of production and
3. ease of access to transport and marketing facilities and networks.

Selection Criteria for Rural Region

Four criteria have been identified for investing in rural regions, these criteria are listed below:

1. comparative advantages in specific commodities or produce
2. natural resources with access to the same by the poor
3. available human resources both in terms of quality and quantity
4. not witnessing any conflicts or have a high potential for conflict.

Selection Criteria for Individuals

The program identifies its target group of individuals based on three key criteria (table 1):

1. income and ownership,
2. potential for forming partnerships, and
3. quality as human resource.

Program Components

The program has the following key components:

- Building Awareness: The program helps the community to identify its problems and its potential under the assumption that the community itself has the ability to solve the problems. Community organizers from the program are immersed in the target region and share the life of the communities. The program also facilitates a learning process to bring about changes in attitudes.

Table 1. Dompet Dhuafa Republika Program Selection Criteria

Income and Ownership	Potential for forming partnerships,	Quality as human resource
less than 2 dollars a day for rural areas	potential for expansion of their micro-businesses	Those who are between 18 and 60 years of age,
less than 3 dollars a day for suburban and urban areas	past track record in enhancing the scope and scale of business;	able to work with a vision for further expansion of their efforts
conditions of residence and ownership of assets	the availability of raw materials,	must not be currently receiving assistance from other similar programs
local community based on their evaluation of the individual or family	production capacity and market potential;	
	the capacity to absorb labour	
	potential to create further economic opportunities and to utilize local resources	

Source, Alim (2013) developed by author

- Organization: It generates self-help groups as the medium to build bargaining position; helps form a local organization through community initiative.
- Building Cadre: It prepares a local cadre who will develop local self-help and who will take over the "hand-holding" role once the program ends.
- Technical Support: It provides technical training based on locally available and appropriate technology.
- Partnership: The local Community figures out what can be implemented and what support will be needed from external party (the program). The community establishes cooperation based on specific roles for each stakeholder based on mutual trust and transparency.

Services Offered by the Program to Beneficiaries

The program provides the following services to its beneficiaries:

- Developing human resources through various training program, workshops, meetings among members and others.
- Developing institutions with proper documentation of standard operating procedures for each organization or group to be commonly monitored.
- Provision of capital to local businesses through group-based credit, self-help savings.
- Providing business development services for improving production methods.
- Developing markets through sharing of information on business opportunities, building networks and synergies. The program emphasizes building and strengthening of individual and institutional capacity. At an individual level, the focus is on improving perceptions & attitudes, enhancing knowledge & skills and ability to generate income and manage funding of micro enterprises. At an institutional level, the focus is on strengthening organization management, improving access to financial services, information, marketing services and networks.

Performance of the Program

According to the five-year report of the programs, beneficiaries of the empowerment programs reached of the DDR reached 17133. as depicted in Table 2 below, major business segments included organic farming, livestock, fisheries, for profit microfinance and research and in-house and public training.

Case Study Two: LZS Asnaf Entrepreneurship Program (AEP), Selangor, Malaysia

In Malaysia, the Administration of *zakah* funds falls under the State Islamic Religion Councils (SIRCs). A total of 14 SIRCs over Malaysia where 13 of it is belong to the state and one for Wilayah Persekutuan KL (Razimi et al., 2016). Furthermore, *zakah* in Malaysia is under the mandate of the Department of Wakaf, Zakat, and Hajj (JAWHAR). JAWHAR was set up on March 27, 2004 (6 Safar 1425H) by former Prime Minister Tun Abdullah Ahmad Badawi. (JAWHAR, 2020).

Asnaf is the Arabic word to denote the eight categories of *zakah* recipients highlighted in Surah At-Tawba (9:60). Through Asnaf Entrepreneurial Program (AEP), LZS endeavours to aid the poor to become entrepreneurs and to enhance their social and economic life. The program can be divided into four core elements which are (1) entrepreneurship development program, (2) skill development program (3) administrative and monitoring and (4) distribution program. In addition to start-up capital (Shiyuti and Al-Habshi, 2018). To this effect, LZS collaborates with other institutions such as Institute Keusahawanan Negara (INSKEN) and Institute Latihan Islam Malaysia (ILIM) within the scope of training and skill improvements among entrepreneurs (Din et al., 2019). Asnaf program is in line with the core objectives of *zakah* that aims to "empower the productive asnaf to generate income up to the level of graduation from the asnaf status" (Qardawi, 2009). Eligibility criteria taken into account when selecting the eligible asnaf to become entrepreneurs are commitment, hardworking, mental and physical capability, and shows interest in entrepreneurship (Mohamed, et al, 2018). Asnaf program is quite important and has many advantages for many reasons, for instance:

1. The *zakah* institution provides capital assistance to Asnaf entrepreneurs in order to fulfil self-confidence and productivity in running the business.
2. In addition, this capital will add and enhance the social and morale in the societies,
3. Also, it has a positive impact on the economy (Din et al., 2019).

Table 2. Five-year Details on Economic Empowerment Programs by DDR (figures in Indonesian Rupiah IDR)

No.	Field Program	Programs	Funds	Beneficiaries
1.	organic farming	15	4.6	2611
2.	livestock	9	6	997
3.	fisheries	52	11.1	6175
4.	for profit microfinance	6	4.3	2186
5.	research and in-house and public training	150	5.6	5164
Total		**232**	**31.7**	**17133**

Source: Alim 2013

In 2015, *zakah* institutions supported around RM 9,000,0000 to Asnaf who are under this program covered in terms of training, capital and monitoring to become entrepreneurs (Asnaf MAIS, 2015).

Lembaga *Zakah* Selangor (2016) has identified three types of *zakah* receipts under AEP program, first type is Asnaf who has no professional skills and cannot run any type of business; second type is Asnaf who is in need of one-time assistance to cope or get out of the poverty; and the third type is Asnaf which is currently struggling with hardship but has the potential to develop, grow and graduate from Asnaf (Din, et al., 2019).

According to (Din, et al., 2019) the AEP program consists of many processes as follow:

1. Identifying the inputs by selecting the possible entrepreneurs who are complying with Islamic ideas.
2. Transformation process, which is transforming the training and project preparation to the outputs such as goods, services, ideas, and entertainment based on the outputs it will achieve the goals that is rapidly national growth.

LZS Asnaf Entrepreneurship Program (AEP) has two manners of financial assistance granted to recipients. The first is the distribution of start-up financial assistant based on the request made by the recipients to run their own business. Secondly, LZS also offers capital assistance to businesses selected by LZS management. Consequently, two categories are identified, the first category include micro-entrepreneurs of *zakah* beneficiaries who run micro enterprises of value less than RM5,000, such as selling nasi lemak (traditional Malaysian food), fried banana and others. The second category include business with value varies between RM5,000 to RM50,000, such as restaurants, laundry shops and others (Mohamed, et al, 2018).

A PROPOSED REFUGEE MICROENTERPRISE *ZAKAH* SUPPORT MODEL (RMZSM)

Before going into the model few points must be highlighted on any microfinance and microenterprise support program:

1. Microfinance is not a viable tool for all refugees (must differentiate between the types and capabilities of refugees mentally and physically).
2. The second point is part of the first one, in the sense that *zakah* cash assistance is not the right solution for all refugees.
3. Microfinance programs is not all about giving the start-up capital, non-financial services are essential for the success of such programs (micro-Takaful, safety net, substance provision, training, marketing, legal advisory, mentoring and monitoring).

A Conceptual Framework of RMZS Model

The structure of RMZSM model conceptual framework largely focuses on addressing the major challenge of supporting refugee enterprise, i.e., lack of funds. As shown in figure 1 below, the model introduces the use of *zakah* as a source of funds to provide a start-up capital for refugees.

Figure 8. Conceptual Framework of RMZS Model
Source: developed by authors

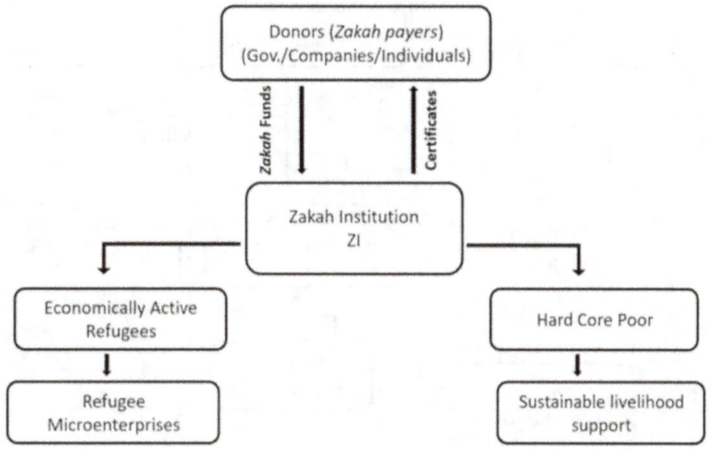

As depicted in the above figure, *zakah* Institution must differentiate between two types of poor refugee, the economically active refugees who potentially the targeted population with the microenterprises program and the other type that cannot participate in such programs such as sick and elderly. As such ZI should divide the available funds to cater for both types of refugees in a proportionate way. In regard to the economically active refugees, *zakah* funds should also be divided into three sub funds, a. micro-takaful fund, b. microcenturies seed capital fund and the subsistence fund these three sub funds are depicted below in Figure 9.

Model Outflow

The detailed outflow of the model is presented in the following discussion, it is depicted in Figure 10 at the end of the discussion.

1. The applicant approaches the Administrative Office (AO) and applies for equipment, raw material or capital to be used in the project
2. AO sends the applicant's application containing all the necessary documents to the Assessment Committee (AC), which assesses the capabilities of the applicant against the eligibility criteria

Figure 9. Distribution of zakah funds on economically active refugees
Source: developed by authors

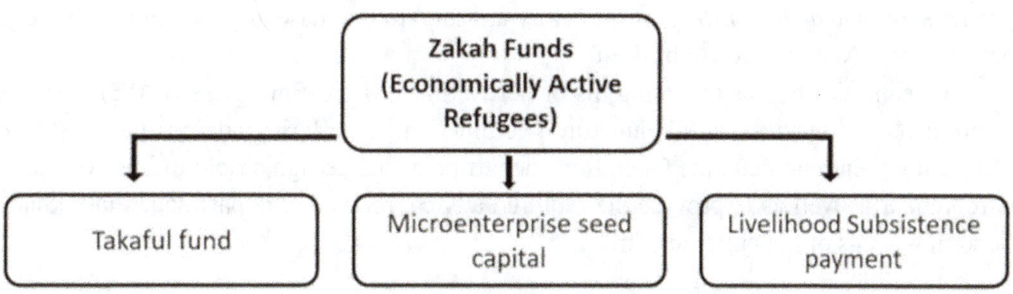

Figure 10. Operational Structure of RMZS Model
Source: developed by authors

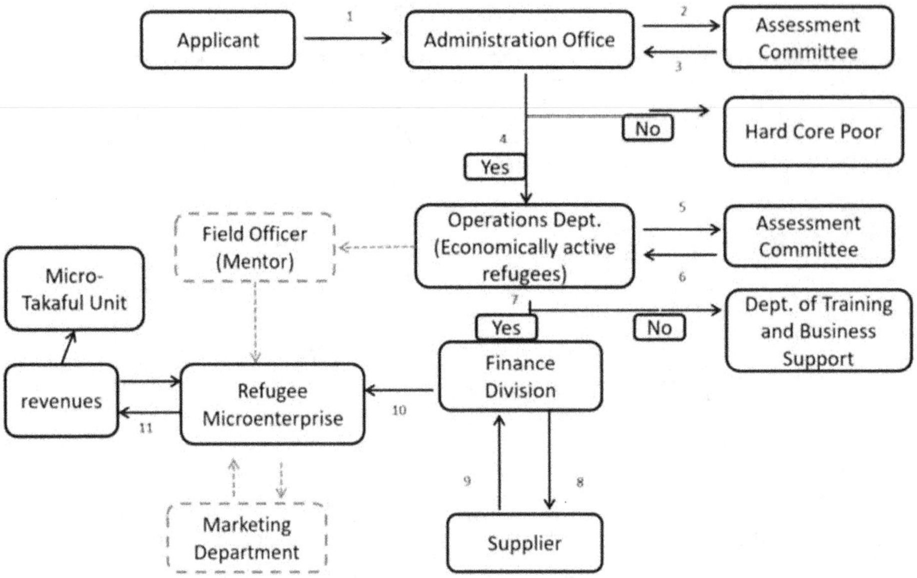

3. The documents are then returned by AC to AO. Hard-core poor are directed to the relevant unit for assistance.
4. Successful applications (economically active candidates) are forwarded to the Operation Department (OD),
5. The Operation Department (OD) send the candidates to the Assessment Committee for a further assessment of professional and business administrative skills and needs.
6. Assessment Committee send the assessment results with their report
7. Based on the report from AC, the applicant is sent by the Operations department either to the Department of Training and Business Support (DTBS) to provide the required training, or would be directly sent to the Finance Division to evaluate and process with the equipment's and financial needs,
8. The applicant is sent to the supplier for the required equipment. It is worth noting that cash money is intentionally avoided to be handled over to refugees. It is feared that needy refugees may spend the cash money on personal needs or for purposes other than income generating activities.
9. The applicant (refugee) acquires the equipment from the supplier as an agent on behalf of the NGO/agency, the applicant must report back to Finance Division to sign a formal low risk Islamic financing contracts such as *Murabahah* (cost-plus sale), *Ijarah*, (lease) Diminishing *Musharakah* (partnership) and *al-Bai' Bithaman Ajil* (forward sale) to purchase and own the equipment or raw material from NGO/agency to himself.
10. The applicant now begins operating his or her Refugee Micro-Enterprise (RME) business to offer products and services, at this juncture two units will be offering advice and assistance to the refugee microentrepreneur, the Operations department shall assign a field officer to supervise the entrepreneur as well as to provide the required advice, marketing department shall advice in the marketing needs of the entrepreneur.

11. The revenue generated from the microenterprise is shared in three portions. Part of it goes to the applicant, another portion to NGO/agency through its Finance Division (FD) and the applicant is encouraged to donate a small third portion to a Micro-Takaful Unit (MTU) or fund.

The MTU is integrated into the model in order to provide guarantee for refugee microenterprises. Each and every interested refugee should join this unit before applying for any financial assistance. This unit is considered essential in the absence of any financial collateral and with the considerable ineffectiveness of social collateral in the refugee camp setting. Members of this unit will actually depend on the recommendation of participants. In the sense that any new individual should have a signed recommendation from a member or more of old members of the MTU. Additional function of MTU will include providing financial assistance for refugees in emergency situations such as illness or unexpected accidents or death of any MTU member.

Suggested Eligibility Criteria of Microentrepreneurs

Considering the size of risky elements in the proposed model of *Zakah* microfinance for refugees, it is suggested that the eligibility criteria for economically active refugees to benefit from the *Zakah* financing must be very strict. These strict criteria are designed to target only potential economically active refugees who meet the minimum level of administrative and professional criteria. Refugees who do not meet these criteria may join other programs offered to refugees such as administrative and professional training. The eligibility criteria for the applicant to participate and become a member of the *Zakah* Fund are elaborated as follows. Applicants must:

1. Be between 25-45 years old.
2. Married with at least two children.
3. Not recipient of any other grand or financial assistance.
4. Have at least three years' working experience in the suggested profession or enterprise.
5. Acquire the basics of accounting and business administration.
6. Provide three recommendation letters from community leaders or religious authorities.
7. Have at least a high school education.
8. Obtain a valid ID such as a passport or to be registered by the UNHCR or the local authorities.
9. Be allowed to operate and own a business in the country.

SOLUTIONS AND RECOMMENDATIONS

Lack of financial resources have always been a serious challenge for the sustainability of microfinance and microenterprise support programs. With the annual obligation to pay 2.5 percentage by wealthy Muslims, *zakah* funds constitute a great potential to address the lack of financial resources. The following list of best practices aims at assisting policy makers and stakeholders in designing and implementing microenterprise support programs for refugees by mobilising *zakah* funds. These practices are mainly deduced from the earlier cited programs of microfinance for refugees and of microenterprise support based on *zakah*.

1. Provision of living allowances to beneficiaries in the early implementation stages.
2. Adoption of group lending as well as individual lending.
3. Careful selection of beneficiaries; not all refugees are ready to receive funds and undertake enterprises.
4. Integration of a mutual, cooperative reserve fund (*micro-takaful*).
5. Provision of non-financial assistance such as professional training and marketing.
6. Collective cooperation among stakeholders including hosting authorities, aid agencies and other supporting institutions.
7. Allocation of a considerable portion of intervention to the hosting community.
8. Supporting short-term enterprises.
9. Linking the program with future engagement after refugee repatriation.
10. Adoption of technology to monitor beneficiaries.
11. Avoidance of direct cash advances to beneficiaries; alternatively, direct communication with suppliers.
12. Usage of different packages/arrangements for different types of beneficiaries.
13. Don't be so much optimistic as the success rate is around 30% (Ibrahim and Ghazali, 2014).

FUTURE RESEARCH DIRECTIONS

The importance and relevance of this book stems from the themes embraced within it. This research contributes to the book by highlighting the latest situations of refugees around the globe. The facts presented in the introductory chapter along with the added factor of COVID-19 and the subsequent variants do not tell a bright story of these situations. Moreover, this research extends the discussion on empowering refugees and supporting them to sustain themselves. Despite the importance of the proposed model conceptualised in this research to support refugee microenterprises with *zakah* funds, future research may take a further practical step by exploring the feasibility of the proposed model by means of communication with key stakeholders i.e., refugee entrepreneurs, agencies operating in the field, policy makers and others.

CONCLUSION

This paper has explored the possibility of using *zakah* funds in microfinance and microenterprise programs for refugees. It argues that despite the importance and effectiveness of using *zakah* funds in cash interventions, such programs are not sustainable and do not offer the best solution for all refugees. This argument is supported by highlighting two microfinance and microenterprise programs that are based on using *zakah* funds. The first one is managed by Dompet Dhuafa Republika Institution from Indonesia, and the second one is implemented by Selangor *Zakah* Board (Lembaga *Zakah* Selangor-LZS) Malaysia. Furthermore, the paper is proposing a model based on *zakah* to mobilise the funds for microenterprise support programs for refugees. The model is comprised of the key elements that most microfinance and microenterprises programs often contain, including the assessment process, training department, microfinance department, marketing, and mentoring departments. Finally, the model also contains a micro-insurance (takaful) unit to assist the refugee microentrepreneurs in difficulties and hardship times. The paper ends with a recommended list of eligibility criteria and a list of best practises in designing microenterprises support programs for refugees based on *zakah* funds.

REFERENCES

Al-Qaradaghi. (2014) رقفلا ءاهنإل طفنلا سمُخو امتاورث ةاكز جارخإل ةيمالسإلا تاموكحلا وعدي يغاد هرقلا https://arabic.cnn.com/middleeast/2014/07/17/ali-qaradahji-islamic-finance

Al-Taher. (2017). بالقنالا ضهجأ اعورشم وحمل رقفلا رصمب, Asnaf MAIS (2015). Bersama kami membantu Asnaf. Selangor: Lembaga Zakah Selangor.

Al-Uthman, M. (2012). Shart al-Tamlik fi al-*Zakah* wa Mada Tathirihi fi 'Amal al-Jam'iyat al-Khayriyyah al-Islamiyyah. *Damascus University Journal for Legal and Economics Sciences, 28*(1). http://damascusuniversity.edu.sy/mag/law/images/stories/1-2012/a/681-699.pdf

Alim, M. (2013). *Photo-Documentation of Successful Development Initiatives in Indonesia: Case Study of Dompet Dhuafa Republika*. https://sadaqaindia.files.wordpress.com/2014/04/dompet_dhuafa_case_study1.pdf

Bocke, J., Niehaves, B., Riemer, K., & Plattfaut, R. (2009). *R*econstructing the giant: on the importance of rigour in documenting the literature search process. *Proceedings of the 17th European Conference on Information Systems (ECIS 2009)*.

David, A. (2017). *Amanah Ikhtiar willing to give more loans to women entrepreneurs*. New Straits Time.

Deloitte. (2019). *Social finance, what is it and why it matters?* Author.

Din, N. M., Rosdi, M. S. M., Ismail, M., Muhammad, M. Z., & Mukhtar, D. (2019). Contributions of Asnaf Entrepreneurs in *Zakah* of Business: A Revisiting Based on Turning over Model. *International Journal of Academic Research in Business and Social Sciences*, *9*(9), 744–752.

European Commission. (2016). *A Recipe Book for Social Finance*. https://publications.jrc.ec.europa.eu/repository/bitstream/JRC111373/jrc111373_jrc-s4p_report_sii-eu_maduro-pasi-misuraca_def_12122018.pdf

Furber, M. (2017). *UNHCR zakah collection and distribution*. https://reliefweb.int/sites/reliefweb.int/files/resources/TR-1-UNHCR-*Zakah*-Collection-And-Distribution-English.pdf

Ibrahim, P., & Ghazali, R. (2014). *Zakah* as an Islamic Micro-Financing Mechanism to Productive *Zakah* Recipients. *Asian Economic and Financial Review, 4*(1), 117-125. https://www.researchgate.net/publication/259478450_*ZAKAH*_AS_AN_ISLAMIC_MICRO-FINANCING_MECHANISM_TO_PRODUCTIVE_*ZAKAH*_RECIPIENTS/link/02e7e52c0e4cbc3773000000/download

Islamic Commercial Law Report. (2018). *ISRA*. Thomson Reuters & IRTI.

Kachkar, O. (2019). Refugee Entrepreneurship: Empirical Quantitative Evidence from Refugee Camps in Turkey. *Journal of Immigrant & Refugee Studies*, *17*(3), 333–352. doi:10.1080/15562948.2018.1479913

Loescher, G., & Milner, J. (2005). *Protracted Refugee Situations: Domestic and International Security Implications*. Routledge.

Modéer. (2018). *Unlocking Islamic Social Finance to Help Communities Address Vulnerability and Inequality*. https://www.undp.org/content/undp/en/home/news-centre/speeches/2018/Unlocking_Islamic_Social_Finance_to_Help_Communities_Address_Vulnerability_and_Inequality.html

Mohamed, N., Mastuki, N., Yusuf, S., & Zakaria, M. (2018). Management Control System in Asnaf Entrepreneurship Development Program by Lembaga *Zakah* Selangor [Sistem Kawalan Dalaman bagi Program Pembangunan Usahawan Asnaf di Lembaga *Zakah* Selangor]. *Jurnal Pengurusan.*, *53*, 13–22.

Mohsin, M., & Alhabshi, S. (2016). Hybrid Model of *Zakah*, Waqf, Qard-Hassan & Islamic Finance for a Just and Sustainable Microfinance. *Sahulat: A Journal of Interest free Microfinance*, *4*(1).

Obaidullah, M. (2008). *Introduction to Islamic Microfinance*. https://www.researchgate.net/publication/228201195_Introduction_to_Islamic_Microfinance

Qardawi, Y. (2009). A comparative study of *Zakah*: Regulations and Philosophy in the light of Qur'an and sunnah. *Fiqh Al Zakah*, *I*, 1–309.

Resolutions and Recommendations of The Council of the Islamic. (2000). *Fiqh* Academy *1985-2000*. https://uaelaws.files.wordpress.com/2012/05/resolutions-and-recommendations-of-the-council-of-the-islamic-fiqh-academy.pdf

Shiyuti, H. (2018). *An Overview of Asnaf Entrepreneurship Program by Lembaga Zakah Selangor, Malaysia*. Paper presented at 6th ASEAN Universities International Conference on Islamic Finance (AICIF), Manila, Philippines.

UNHCR. (1951). *The 1951 Convention: Lasting Cornerstone of Refugee*. http://www.unhcr.ch/issues/asylum/qa000615.htm

UNHCR. (2007). *Opening Statement by Mr. António Guterres*. United Nations High Commissioner for Refugees, at the Fifty-eighth Session of the Executive Committee of the High Commissioner's Programme (ExCom). https://www.unhcr.org/uk/admin/hcspeeches/4700eff54/opening-statement-mr-antonio-guterres-united-nations-high-commissioner.html

UNHCR. (2012). *The State of The World Refugees in Search of Solidarity*. Retrieved March 21, 2014, https://www.refworld.org/pdfid/5100fec32.pdf

UNHCR. (2019). *Refugees: The most in need of Zakah funds*. UNHCR *Zakah* Program: 2019 Launch Report. https://*zakah*.unhcr.org/wp-content/uploads/2019/04/UNHCR-Annual-*Zakah*-Report-2019-En.pdf

UNHCR. (2019b). *Financials*. http://reporting.unhcr.org/financial

UNHCR. (2020). *UNHCR report 2020*. https://www.unhcr.org/figures-at-a-glance.html

UNHCR. (2021). *Figures at a glance*. https://www.unhcr.org/flagship-reports/globaltrends/

UNICEF. (2019a). *UNICEF and the Islamic Development Bank launch first global Muslim philanthropy fund for children*. https://www.unicef.org/press-releases/unicef-and-islamic-development-bank-launch-first-global-muslim-philanthropy-fund

Uthman, M. A., & Hamzah, H. (2012). شرط التمليك في الزكاة ومدى تأثيره في عمل الجمعيات الخيرية الإسلامية. *Damascus University Magazine for Economic and Legal Sciences, 28*(1). http://damascusuniversity.edu.sy/mag/law/images/stories/1-2012/a/681-699.pdf

Yonis. (2012). *Islamic Microfinance System and Poverty Alleviation in Somaliland*. BBA research paper presented to the of Hargeisa.

KEY TERMS AND DEFINITIONS

Dompet Dhuafa Republika, Indonesia: A philanthropic institution that serves to help the poor using donated assets including *zakah*, sadaqah and waqf from individuals, groups, companies, or institutions.

Islamic Social Finance: The Islamic perspective of managing investments that generate financial returns with positive social and environmental impact.

JAWHAR: The Department of Wakaf, *Zakah*, and Hajj in Malaysia.

Lembaga *Zakah* Selangor (LZS): The official authority that oversees managing *zakah* affairs in the state of Selangor in Malaysia.

Microenterprises: Small businesses that are often targeted by microcredit and microfinance programs.

Refugee: Someone who is unable or unwilling to return to their country of origin owing to a well-founded fear of being persecuted for reasons of race, religion, nationality, membership of a particular social group, or political opinion.

***Zakah*:** A religious obligation to contribute a certain portion of one's wealth in support of the poor or needy.

Chapter 10
The Effect of Teleworking on Anxiety During COVID-19:
Turkey Example

Elif Baykal
Istanbul Medipol University, Turkey

ABSTRACT

Turkey is among the countries that the pandemic has affected most profoundly. Many people have been infected, and the pandemic has given way to both physiological and psychological problems. In this study, the effect of teleworking, which has been embraced durng the pandemic, has been tested on the anxiety levels of Turkish participants. The research has been carried out on white-collar employees working in the service sector. The related data has been collected through online surveys. In the related field study, 2,892 online questionnaires have been sent, and 385 usable questionnaires were obtained. Analysis of the study has been carried out with SPSS 20.0 statistics tool. The results of the study revealed that teleworking has a negative effect on anxiety levels of individuals, as predicted in the study.

INTRODUCTION

The Covid-19 pandemic has revealed the lack of business level contingency to respond to crises (e.g., a that has created the need for reorganization in many organizations (Belzunegui-Eraso and Erro-Garcés, 2020). Many sectors had to give Unfortunately, about 8% of people are employed in closed sectors suggesting that they experience considerable wage losses (Duman, 2020). The outbreak of the pandemic has created the requirement for social distancing giving way to remote working (Prin and Bartels, 2020). Unfortunately one of the most important effect of Covid-19 pandemic has come about to be the slowdown, recession and constriction in the economies of almost all countries (Acar, 2020).

Actually, remote working or in other words teleworking has been constantly growing on all over the world in myriad sectors in the last few decades in relation to the digital revolution. However, the pandemic has created a huge necessity for teleworking (Contreras, Baykal and Abid (2020) among the sectors that mostly prefer teleworking, specifically service industry is prominent with the biggest per-

DOI: 10.4018/978-1-7998-8925-0.ch010

centage of workforce working remotely (17%), later comes the health industry (12%) and than comes the finance and banking sectors (10%), manufacturing sector (8.5%) and education sector (7.5%) (He et al., 2020). The Covid-19 example has showed us the fact that individuals with high strength to cope with difficulties and lower levels of anxiety can overcome this test more easily (Baykal, 2020c: 23). Hence in this study, it is atempted to see what properties of teleworkers are important in their tendencies to feel anxious. Factors including age, gender and sector has been investigated in the hypotheses of the study.

Teleworking

Flexible work arrangements are those kind of work practices that helps individuals to work from home, to work outside regular hours or to change contract (Groen, Van Triest, Coers and Wtenweerde, 2018). Teleworking is one of the most prominenet flexible working methods. As Allen et al., (2015) explains teleworking as the concept of performing work-related activities remotely using high technology. It is a new mode of alternative work arrangement developed in the 1970s (Belzunegui-Eraso and Erro-Garcés 2020).

In teleworking, managers can solve the problem of not being able to monitor the actions of teleworkers by giving more importance to output controls (Groen, Van Triest, Coers and Wtenweerde, 2018). As Darics (2020) posits in remote working, management and leadership functions are combined. In this work method managers should maintain a team identity through a trust-based work environment, shared vision, corporate values, and organizational goals. Teleworking is one of the most famous flexible working method. Teleworking is also considered as a way of soothing global warming owing to the fact that it reduces air pollution in relation to peak-time traffic congestion and energy consumption in workplaces (Hook, Sovacool and Sorrell, 2020).

In teleworking, distances are not important. Technical profile and self-discipline of individuals are more significant owing to their effects on efficiency and effectiveness (Galvez et al., 2020). Teleworking is a method for solving mobility problems by decreasing the number of commuting trips (Ravalet and Rérat, 2019). That is why, the use of internet and advanced technologies are significant aspects of teleworking. The transition to digitalized World in business has created a constantly changing work atmosphere with loose boundaries and more flexible organizational designs (Pulley and Sessa, 2001). The successful examples of teleworking model encompasses use of high technology and sincere organizational support (Contreras, Baykal and Abid (2020). According to Ravalet and Rérat (2019) service sector is more plausible for teleworking. For instance The banking and insurance sector are characterized by a higher propensity for partial telework compared to many other sectors. Moreover, Teleworking is more developed in those kind of sectors like trade, mechanical repair, tourism, accommodation and catering, health and similar service sectors.

Teleworker is an employee working in an organization and has a conventional workplace that he/she normally can physically go and work but works outside the office for a certain reason (Aguilera et al., 2016). In this point it should be emphasized that employees who are normally working at home or whose activities are decentralized should not considered among teleworkers (Ravalet and Rérat, 2019). In fact, According to Ravalet and Rérat (2019) flexibility of working hours tend to facilitate teleworking since it gives way to informal teleworking situations. According to the International Labour Organization telework is the use of information and communications technologies (ICTs), such as laptops, desktops, smartphones, tablets and laptops for work that is performed outside the workplace. This working model permits workers to work in diffirent locations via any platform that has the necessary technologies

(Belzunegui-Eraso and Erro Garcés, 2020). In spite of the potential advantages of teleworking in solving problems about commuting time, traffic congestion and vehicle emissions, unfortunately, teleworking is still largely informal. In most companies its still authorized by the employer and rarely the subject of a formal convention (Ravalet and Rérat, 2019). It has so far failed to become a popular practice until the Covid-19 pandemic (Bojovic, Benavides, and Soret (2020).

De Vries Tummers and Bekkers (2019) posits that teleworking is beneficial in boosting organizational commitment, work engagement and professional isolation in employees. Telework is considered a discretionary benefit and contributes to greater work-life balance (Golden, 2006). According to Montgomery et al. (2016), in teleworking, owing to the reduction in the social and interpersonal distance, leaders ought to be more democratic and should encourage open communication. Teleworking is also categorized under the heading od remote working. It is about either working full-time or part-time from home or from other locations (Hook, Sovacool and Sorrell, 2020). Teleworking contributes to greater performance, higher job satisfaction, reduced stress and lower turnover intentions (Contreras, Baykal and Abid, 2020). Moreover, it increases work-life balance Othman et al. (2009), quality of life (Azarbouyeh and Naini, 2014), employee happiness (Kazekami, 2020). Teleworking is beneficial in creating viable solutions to improve the environment and quality of life (Giovanis, 2018).

Withoutdoubt teleworking has also some disadvantages. For instance; teleworking leads to social isolation of employees. Being disconnected from their work environment employees may experience demotivation that lowers their performance (Fedakova and Ištoňová, 2017). Cooper and Kurland (2002) suggest that teleworking reduces the learning opportunities individuals enjoy while they are physically working in the same workplace. Moreover, as Tavares (2017) suggest when the employee does not have a proper office of his own or lacks the necessary skills efficiency of the employee can decrease. On the one hand, Felippe (2018) mentions the lack of coaching, the loss of social connection and the fear of career development among the disadvantages of teleworking.

Teleworking and Covid-19

Telework has gained greater importance as a result of the measures taken to protect individuals from the Covid-19 pandemic (Belzunegui-Eraso and Erro-Garcés, 2020). Daniels, Lamond and Standen (2001) posits three different alternative model for teleworking including; home-based telework where; teleworking from remote offices and mobile telework where work is done by people whose work usually involves travel. During the Covid-19 pandemic most companies have preferred home-based version of teleworking since it permits avoidance from social contact which is significant to prevent dispersion of the illness. Teleworking is adopted owing to the concerns regarding occupational health and safety in terms of both employers and workers (Oğuz, 2021).

In their studies conducted in Portuese context during the COVID-19 pandemic. Tavares et al., (2020) showed that adapting to teleworking was easy for many people. Teleworking utilizes virtual means of communication in maintaining contact between people and in controlling employees and projects (Ramadani et al., 2020). However it has also some basic problems encountered by people during the Covid-19 that worked with teleworking model were the lack of communication with coworkers, the lack of resources regarding technological infrastructure, work-life balance problems, and time management. Many Turkish employees also experienced the same anxiety owing to the transition to this new work model (Tavares et al., 2020).

Teleworking in Turkey

In Turkey during the pandemic, teleworking has inevitably started to be applied in business lines where remote work has not been applied before (Oğuz, 2021). In Article 14 of the Turkish Labor Law numbered 4857 teleworking is explained as a business model based on the principle of fulfilling the work outside the workplace with technological communication tools (Oğuz, 2021). Telework has become legal after the enactment of the 4857 Turkish Labour Law article no-14 (Özen, Grima and Hamarat, 2021). Moreover, after the outbreak of the pandemic additional legal arrangements has been conducted in order to make that remote work feasible. After the outbreak of the pandemic, the regulation 31419 made it possible to work remotely in most of the white collar works which made spread of the disease much slower.

Without doubt, these arrengement have been useful in making work safer and more comfortable especially for white collar workers. Results of Kulak and Tüzüner 's (2020) study conducted in Turkey revealed that flexible working patterns can be in two different forms. One is the employee-friendly approach that provides work-life balance to the employees. These are, flexible working, job sharing, part-time working and compressed workweeks. The other is employer-friendly approach that includes weekend work, shiftwork a nd fixed-term arrangements. According to this study, although Turkish Labor Law permits firms to use different kinds of flexible patterns, employers are still hesitant to use these methods. With COVID-19 pandemic, many firms had to refer flexible working patterns, that can lead the individuals to look working life with different approaches.

Although scarce in numbers, there are some empirical studies showing the effects of teleworking during the pandemic in Turkish context. For instance; In Coban's (2021) study that focused on teleworking in Turkey during the pandemic results revealed that this new working model mostly effected women professionals. After the transition to this new model, women's domestic status during the pandemic has changed a lot both giving flexibility and greater work-life balance but also increasing family-related workload. Results of the study revealed that teleworking created the risks of detaching women from professional work, precarizing their labor, and consolidating their roles as traditional housewives. In another study conducted by Özen, Grima and Hamarat's (2021) study conducted in Turkey, it was revealed that during the pandemic teleworking has gained popularity especially in finance sector. They tested the relationship between teleworking, Covid-19 fear, emotional experience, and affective well-being. Their results showed that increased openness and rumination during Covid-19 increases the positive affective well-being in the remote working.

Easing Anxiety through Teleworking During Covid-19: Turkish Case

Increasing bureaucratization in modern organizations harms human nature and existential realities, bringing an exaggerated uniformity to social life, ignoring the inner world and feelings of employees. In modern world, employees mostly compromise their individuality within the organization and cannot find enough space to express themselves (Baykal, 2019). Moreover, latest develpments in technology contributed to enlightenment of individuals regarding their individual rights and obligations increasing the demands for more sophisticated business models and managerial practices making teleworking attractive for employees (Baykal, 2020). On the one hand, technological developments have contributed to increased efficiency, reduced paperwork, and promoted higher levels of work–life balance (Pollock and Hauseman, 2019).

The modern employee is obliged to bear stress conditions more often compared to previous generations owing to changinging working habits and the use of advanced Technologies (Grönlund, 2007). On the one hand, natural disasters, economic crises, social conflicts and pandemics also change the lives of modern employees. The Covid-19 pandemic is one of these examples we can witness as modern empoyees' dilemmas. The Covid-19 pandemic compelled the companies to implement teleworking on a massive scale. This massive change implies creates a challenge for organziations making them reorganize their business activity around this new model (Belzunegui-Eraso and Erro-Garcés, 2020).

Actually the transition of work life during the pandemic was an obligatory situation rather than a preference. The pandemic necessitated social distancing and made remote work necessary for preventing the transmission of the pandemic (Ahmed, Zviedrite, and Uzicanin, 2018) and has given way to more frequent and widespread use of working models like teleworking. But this does not mean that teleworking ws not eminent before the pandemic. Actually, after 2000s more and more work has been detached from place owing to the transition to knowledge economy, technological developments, new market synamics, demographical changes and demands of workforce (Felstead and Henseke, 2017). Covid-19 has accelerated the transformation to more flexible designs like teleworking by maing it necessary to try more flexible business models. In fact, in the modern World with the help of advanced technology greater flexibility, alternative ways for fitting work around other responsibilitieslower costs for switching between work and non-work roles have occured thus greater control over one's work and higher productivity during work hours have been made possible (Fleck, Cox and Robison, 2015). Hence, employees are prone to feel more comfortable while switching among different domains of life when they feel themselves interdependent among these different domains, when they have high level of integration, and when there is minimal role conflict (Ilies et al. 2009).

When we handle the issue regarding the pandemic with a psychological perspective, it can be suggested that individual level resilience is an important tool for combatting the work related difficulties of the pandemic. In fact, the more psychologically resilient individuals are, the more successful they are in adapting to new situations and they recover much faster (Brooks et al., 2018). According to some researchers, prevention methods like quarantine and remote working deprived many employees of their critic psychological capitals like self-esteem and social support that are usually used as mechanisms for reducing stress (Jesus et al., 2016). During Covid-19, the most noteworthy emotional outcomes of the illness were financial and health-related fears stemming from negative thoughts and communications (Trnka and Lorencova, 2020: 546). Rapid changes and uncertainity that has been experienced in business life triggered panic regarding possible job losses and contributed to greater anxiety (Godinic, Obrenovic and Khudaykulov, 2020:62).

Covid 19 and Anxiety

Anxiety disorder is associated with many mental problems, including mood disorders and psychiatric disorders, and its negative impact on individuals creates a significant global economic burden especially during the pandemic (Baykal, 2020b). Although the number of these traumatic events is quite high, only a relatively small number of people experience severe mental problems (Zehir and Narcıkara, 2018). But this does not change the fact that human nature tend to perceive the bad and the negative faster and more intensely than the good and the positive (Narcıkara, 2017a). Anxiety can be helpful to some degree. But, while arousal due to anxiety affects performance positively in a certain range, ongoing anxiety can decrease the individual's productivity, disrupt social relationships, and decrease the individual's motivation (Baykal, 2020).

According to Conservation of Resources Theory, individuals feel discomfortable when a risk ocurcured endangering their possesions (Hobfoll, Shirom and Golembiewski, 2000). With this approach, during Covid-19 pandemic many people experienced that risk. Their normality has changed. Their routines, habits and daily responsibilities have been manipulated by the pandemic making people irritated about both their existing moment and future. As Mao et al., (2020) suggested that the psychological resources of employees have been seriously depleted during the pandemic. Many people have experienced economic uncertainty stemming from the pandemic created anxiety about money and has given way to negative effects on peoples' mental health (Godinic, Obrenovic and Khudaykulov, 2020:61)

During the Covid-19, people lived the risk of losing their resources in both material and non-material sense (Silahtaroğlu, Baykal and Canbolat, 2020). Corporate COVID-19 responses were important in satisfying employees and creating positive perceptions about their companies' corporate reputations. During the pandemic when companies help their stakeholders, these attempts enhance perceived satisfaction and make employees better cope with this crisis. This enhances the positive evaluations of employees regarding their organizations. In this point, Erdoğdu Koçoğlu and Sevim (2020) examined despair and anxiety experienced by individuals in the Covid-19 pandemic processes in the context of Turkey. Their study revealed that every 4 that show one of anxiety symptoms than participants, and all 3 showed one of despair symptoms than participants. In Baykal's (2020) study in Turkish context, it has been proven that the anxiety experienced during the Covid-19 outbreak will have an impact on the endurance levels of individuals and this will affect their life satisfaction.

Hypotheses

By giving greater access to resources, like physical spaces, digital assets and resource utilization skills organizations can upgrade employee productivity and increase employee confidence (Flammer and Luo, 2017). In the extant literature teleworking is associated with greater autonomy (Gajendran and Harrison, 2007) and well-being (Thompson and Prottas, 2006). Teleworkers can avoid interruptions at work (Haddad, Lyons, and Chatterjee, 2009) that may make them work more peacefully and ease their work related concerns. Baykal (2020d) showed that, during the COVID-19, higher anxiety levels led to lower levels of psychologieal resilience, which in turn led to lower levels of life satisfaction. Hence we can think that all kinds of anxiety soothing practices including teleworking will lead to lower levels of anxiety during the pandemic. Actually, When individuals have the necessary autonomy for designing and organizing their own business, they become more hopeful and confident about their future and feels less anxious (Rhoades and Eisenberger, 2002). All kinds of supportive managerial practices and leadership styles lead to greater autonomy and creates self efficacy on the side of the employees (Narcikara, 2017b). In this study it is assumed that teleworking during the pandemic will make employees less anxious. In this point, Kapoor et al. (2021) revealed the positive impact of teleworking in easing stress of teleworkers during the pandemic. Lizana et al., (2021) also revealed the stress reducing effect of teleworking during the pandemic in their study conducted. In this study it is hypothesized the anxiety levels of teleworkers will be effected by their gender, age and the sector they work in. Hence the following hypotheses have been built;

H1: During the pandemic, anxiety levels of teleworkers are effect by their gender.
H2: During the pandemic, anxiety levels of teleworkers are effect by their ages.

H3: During the pandemic, anxiety levels of teleworkers are effect by the sector they work in.

METHODOLOGY

Sampling and Data Collection

In the field study of our research, a convenience sampling method was used as a data collection method. Surveys belonging to the study were applied on white-collar employees working in both government and public institutions operating in the service sector. The data has been collected through online surveys. In order to test the anxiety levels of individuals Zaleski et al.'s (2019) one dimension, 5 item scale has been used.

Data were collected from 14 May 2020-30 December 2020 in Turkey during the Covid-19 outbreak. The answers to the questionnaire questions were taken with the Five-Point Likert Scale. In the study, 2014 online questionnaires were sent to the participants and 276 usable responses were received. 24% of the participants work in public institutions, others work in private organizations. 36% of the participants are women and the others are men. 11% of the participants are high school graduates, 52% are university graduates, 28% are masters and 9% have a doctorate degree.

Hypothesis Testing

The normality of the data was tested before performing statistical analysis. For this purpose, the skewness of the data was examined first. Statistically, skewness is a measure of the symmetry of the distribution of a data set and is a comparison with a normal distribution. Values between -1 and +1 are accepted as acceptable ranges in social sciences (Hair et al., 2013). The data of this study have skewness values greater than -1 and less than +1, which is suitable for continuing the analysis. Besides, kurtosis values of $\pm$ 1.0 are considered as statistically perfect values (George & Mallery, 2012). The data in our study has kurtosis values between -0.505 and +0.150, which make our sample a reasonable data set for tests. The Kaiser-Meyer-Olkin Sampling Adequacy Measurement was conducted to test whether the data obtained from the research sample were sufficient. The sufficiency coefficient of the sample is 0.873 and the Barlett score is below 0.001 and they are suitable for factor analysis. Explanatory factor analysis was used to test whether the observed variables were loaded into the default dimension of anxiety. In order to see the internal consistency of the measurement tools, Cronbach's alpha coefficients were calculated for the anxiety scale (0, 854) and factor analysis was performed to see whether the items were loaded in the default dimension of anxiety. Results of the factor analysis confirmed that 5 items of the anxiety scale has been loaded as it is assumed.

In order to investigate whether there is a difference between anxiety levels of different genders we have conducted independent t tests. Result of the independent t test revealed that Turkish women are more prone to anxiety during the Covid-19 when compared to men. This was something that was accepted before the results were obtained owing to greater responsibilities that Turkish women Professional hold owing to their dual roles stemming from cultural norms of Turkey.

Moreover, another t-test has been conducted for examining whether anxiety levels of employees working in private sector and public sector are different or not. Results revealed that there is not a significant difference between anxiety levels of public employees and private employees.

Table 1. Factor Analysis

Anxiety 1	.767
Anxiety 2	.784
Anxiety 3	.815
Anxiety 4	.814
Anxiety 5	.796
Extraction Method: Principal Component Analysis.	

Table 2. Group Statistics and T-test for Gender Differences

	SEX	N	Mean	Std. Deviation	Std. Error Mean
Anx	1.00	70	25.743	.98858	.11816
	2.00	192	23.000	.87979	.06349

Table 3. T-Test for Gender Differences and Anxiety Levels

	F	Sig.	t	df	Sig. (2-tailed)	Mean Difference	Std. Error Difference	95% Confidence Interval	
								Lower	Upper
Equal variances assumed	.53	.46	2.1	260	.032	.27429	.12705	.0241	.5244
Equal variances not assumed			2.04	111	.043	.27429	.13414	.0084	.5400

Table 4. Group Statistics and T-test for sector differences

		SECTOR	N	Mean	Std. Deviation	Std. Error Mean
Public	Anx	1.00	68	23.147	.88187	.10694
Private		2.00	194	23.938	.92941	.06673

On the one hand, an Anova test has been applied to see possible differences in anxiety level between different age groups. Results of the Anova test are summarized below. According to the test there are no significant differences between different age groups regarding their anxiety levels.

CONCLUSION

According to our Hypothesis tests H1 Hypothesis, the hypothesis investigating whether there is a difference between different genders regarding their anxiety levels during the pandemic in Turkey, is confirmed. Hence it is revealed that the anxiet levels of women are different from men. They tend to experience

Table 5.Independent Samples t-test

	Levene's Test for Equality of Variances		t-test for Equality of Means						
	F	Sig.	t	df	Sig. (2-tailed)	Mean Difference	Std. Error Difference	95% Confidence Interval of the Difference	
								Lower	Upper
Equal variances assumed	.000	.985	-.612	260	.541	-.07911	.12929	-.33369	.17547
Equal variances not assumed			-.628	122	.531	-.07911	.12605	-.32862	.17041

Table 6.Anova Test for Age Differences

	Sum of Squares	df	Mean Square	F	Sig.	
Between Groups	(Combined)	7.373	2	3.687	4.509	.012
Linear Term	Unweighted	5.780	1	5.780	7.070	.008
Weighted	7.033	1	7.033	8.602	.004	
Deviation	.340	1	.340	.416	.520	
Within Groups	211.759	259	.818			
Total	219.133	261				

higher levels of anxiety that makes the pandemic more difficult to bear creating a more negative mood and attitude. Before conducting the study it was assumed that there can be a difference between anxiety levels of white-collar workers working in private sector and public sector. Owing to the problems related to job security and greater rivalry in private sector may have created greater anxiety among private sector employees. However, results have not confirmed this assumption. Hence, H2 has been rejected. Results make us think that although they enjoy greater job security the pandemic has made problic officers as irritated as private sector employees. Lastly, in H3 hypothesis, it has been attempted to examine whether among different age groups there is a significant difference regarding anxiety levels. But this hypothesis has also been rejected. Results of the study did not confirm our assumption that when age level changes, anxiety level also change. Actually, in the initial phase of the pandemic elderly people were more anxious about being infected due to the information serviced by the authorities about the lethality of the illness for people above 60s.

DISCUSSION

Today, employee empowerment is considered an important tool in terms of adaptation to internal and external factors (Narcıkara, 2017). Empowering leadership boosts hopefulness among employees and contributes to greater satisfaction and higher motivation (Baykal, 2020). Previous research on the impacts of increased computer technologies on telework showed that high technology creates the opportunity of working outside the Office and get use of empowering leadership. Technology-based practices contributes to more flexible work arrangements such as teleworking that leads to greater autonomy (Belzunegui-Eraso and Erro-Garcés 2020). As mentioned before teleworking explains a method for flexible working which is not limited by time and location and utilizes various communication technologies (Contreras, Baykal and Abid, 2020). In other words, teleworking is beneficial in creating empowerment culture. Individuals engaging in teleworking consider their managers as providers of help to manage their work and life balance. Hence, they tend to have greater commitment to stay since they believe this is what is expected of them considering the norm of reciprocity (Golden, 2006) and they feel themselves secure and peaceful in their workplaces. Covid-19 pandemic has made teleworking and advantages of this working model more visible. In this regard, teleworking has become paramount as a response to the Covid-19 crisis since it satisfies the contingency requirements of organizations.

Our study confirmed the positive effect of teleworking on easing the pains of the pandemic through its effect on stress and anxiety reduction. In parallel with our findings in the extant literature we can come accros myriad empirical studies revealing the positive effect of teleworking on anxiety reduction during the pandemic. For example Shi et al. (2020) showed that teleworking contributes to increased productivity owing to better sleep quality, spending less time on social media and more time on personal hobbies. Similarly Fullana et al.'s (2020) study showed that taking the opportunity to pursue hobbies, and staying outdoors or looking outside are the best predictors of lower levels of depressive symptoms during the pandemic which are possible through teleworking. Ipsen et al. (2021) has conducted one of the most widespread study on telework after the outbreak of the pandemic. Their results revealed that among the most significant advantages of teleworking work–life balance, improved work efficiency and lower levels of anxiety stemming from greater work control rank as the top three. There are also studies revealing the negative effects of teleworking on the psychological situations of teleworkers. For instance in their study conducted during the pandemic Afonso et al. (2020) revealed that teleworking leads to high levels of anxiety and depression. Later Nagata et al.,'s study (2021) conducted in Japan revealed that telework leads to musculoskeletal disorders, psychological problems like isolation and stress, and exhaustion owing to long working hours. This study is novel in explaining effects of individual differences among teleworkers during the pandemic regarding their gender, age and regarding the industry they work in. However, previous studies such as Maruyama and Tietze (2012) that were conducted before the pandemic revealed the positive effect of teleworking on decreasing anxiety levels of individuals. Moreover, studies like Asher et al., (2017) and Gao et al., (2020) revealed that gender is an important determinant of higher levels of anxiety and women prone to be more anxious as it is also confirmed with our study. On the one hand, Gold et al., (2020) and Solomou and Constantinidou (2020) had revealed contradicting facts about the tendency of different age groups and their tendency to feel anxiety whereas our study has revealed no relationship between different age groups and anxiety during the Covid-19. However, there is no study observing the difference between the anxiety levels of individuals working in different sectors as in the case with this study.

SOLUTIONS AND RECOMMENDATIONS

The COVID-19 pandemic has provided anopportunity to try an alternative mode of urban and business life that encourages people to rethink telecommuting practices (Bojovic, Benavides, and Soret (2020). Actually, during the pandemic novel methods of working including teleworking has been experienced.

Bojovic, Benavides, and Soret (2020) revealed that COVID-19 pandemic offer insights into the collective social benefits leading to a more peaceful environment. The enhanced competencies and alternative methods to develop and deploy new resources give way to greater organizational resilience. More resilient organizations can overcome environmental risks more conveniently and they can struggle with ther anxiety more easily (Baykal, 2018). Actually, anxiety is a negative mood disorder that disturbs people and makes their distress even more unbearable. Uncertainties, health problems and financial difficulties experienced during the pandemic process have caused many people to reach high levels of anxiety. Many employees had to go through this process even more anxiously for fear of losing their job or having to take a break from work. The teleworking business model, which is one of the flexible working opportunities that has become popular lately, has made the life of white-collar employees much easier during the pandmei period and has been useful in reducing the concerns that may arise from job loss.

FURTHER RESEARCH AND MANAGERIAL IMPLICATIONS

In future studies, the effect of the teleworking business model on other possible psychological reactions can be examined. Other individual factors that may affect anxiety can be examined. A model similar to the one in our study model can be applied in other cultures and empirical studies can be conducted to see the differences between cultures. Our research has shown that female employees are more worried than men during the teleworking period, and in this sense, employers should show extra sensitivity. Gender does make a significant difference, although neither the industry nor the sector makes a difference in worrying. This guides employers to be more careful about the work-life balance and motivation of female employees.

REFERENCES

Acar, A. C. (2020). Effects of COVID-19 Crisis on Employment and Working Arrangements. *Reflections on the Pandemic*, 463.

Afonso, P., Fonseca, M., & Teodoro, T. (2021). Evaluation of anxiety, depression and sleep quality in full-time teleworkers. *Journal of Public Health (Oxford, England)*, fdab164. doi:10.1093/pubmed/fdab164 PMID:34036369

Aguilera, A., Lethiais, V., Rallet, A., & Proulhac, L. (2016). Home-based telework in France: Characteristics, barriers and perspectives. *Transportation Research*, *92*(1), 1–11.

Ahmed, F., Zviedrite, N., & Uzicanin, A. (2018). Effectiveness of workplace social distancing measures in reducing influenza transmission: A systematic review. *BMC Public Health*, *18*(1), 518. doi:10.118612889-018-5446-1 PMID:29669545

Allen, T. D., Golden, T. D., & Shockley, K. M. (2015). How effective is telecommuting? Assessing the status of our scientific findings. *Psychological Science in the Public Interest*, *16*(2), 40–68. doi:10.1177/1529100615593273 PMID:26403188

Asher, M., Asnaani, A., & Aderka, I. M. (2017). Gender differences in social anxiety disorder: A review. *Clinical Psychology Review*, *56*, 1–12. doi:10.1016/j.cpr.2017.05.004 PMID:28578248

Azarbouyeh, A., & Naini, S. (2014). A study on the effect of teleworking on quality of work life. *Manage. Sci. Lett*, *4*(6), 1063–1068. doi:10.5267/j.msl.2014.5.027

Baykal, E. (2018). Promoting resilience through positive leadership during turmoil. *International Journal of Management and Administration*, *2*(3), 34–48. doi:10.29064/ijma.396199

Baykal, E. (2019). Rol-içi ve Rol-üstü Performansın İşyeri Ruhsallığı ile Arttırılması. *Uluslararası Hukuk ve Sosyal Bilim Araştırmaları Dergisi*, *1*(1), 15–25.

Baykal, E. (2020a). Effects of Servant Leadership on Psychological Capitals and Productivities of Employees. *Atatürk Üniversitesi İktisadi ve İdari Bilimler Dergisi*, *34*(2), 273–291. doi:10.16951/atauniiibd.533275

Baykal, E. (2020b). A Model on Authentic Leadership in The Light Of Hope Theory. *Sosyal Bilimler Arastirmalari Dergisi*, *10*(3), 813–827.

Baykal, E. (2020c). Boosting Resilience through Spiritual Well-being: COVID-19 Example. *Bussecon Review of Social Sciences*, *2*(4), 18-25.

Baykal, E. (2020d). Covid-19 Bağlamında Psikolojik Dayanıklılık, Kaygı ve Yaşam Doyum İlişkisi. *International Journal of Social and Economic Sciences*, *10*(2), 68–80.

Belzunegui-Eraso, A., & Erro-Garcés, A. (2020). Teleworking in the Context of the Covid-19 Crisis. *Sustainability*, *12*(9), 3662. doi:10.3390u12093662

Bojovic, D., Benavides, J., & Soret, A. (2020). What we can learn from birdsong: Mainstreaming teleworking in a post-pandemic world. *Earth System Governance*, *5*, 100074. doi:10.1016/j.esg.2020.100074

Brooks, S., Amlôt, R., Rubin, G. J., & Greenberg, N. (2018). Psychological resilience and post-traumatic growth in disaster-exposed organisations: Overview of the literature. *Journal of the Royal Army Medical Corps*. Advance online publication. doi:10.1136/jramc-2017-000876 PMID:29420257

Çoban, S. (2021). Gender and telework: Work and family experiences of teleworking professional, middle-class, married women with children during the Covid-19 pandemic in Turkey. *Gender, Work and Organization*. PMID:34230782

Contreras, F., Baykal, E., & Abid, G. (2020). E-leadership and teleworking in times of COVID-19 and beyond: What we know and where do we go. *Frontiers in Psychology*, *11*, 3484. doi:10.3389/fpsyg.2020.590271 PMID:33362656

Cooper, C. D., & Kurland, N. B. (2002). Telecommuting, professional isolation, and employee development in public and private organizations. *Journal of Organizational Behavior*, *23*(4), 511–532. doi:10.1002/job.145

Daniels, K., Lamond, D., & Standen, P. (2001). Teleworking: Frameworks for organizational research. *Journal of Management Studies*, *38*(8), 1151–1185. doi:10.1111/1467-6486.00276

Darics, E. (2020). E-leadership or "How to be boss in Instant Messaging?". The role of nonverbal communication. *International Journal of Business Communication*, *57*(1), 3–29. doi:10.1177/2329488416685068

de Vries, H., Tummers, L., & Bekkers, V. (2019). The benefits of teleworking in the public sector: Reality or rhetoric? *Review of Public Personnel Administration*, *39*(4), 570–593. doi:10.1177/0734371X18760124

De Vries, H., Tummers, L., & Bekkers, V. (2019). The benefits of teleworking in the public sector: Reality or rhetoric? *Review of Public Personnel Administration*, *39*(4), 570–593. doi:10.1177/0734371X18760124

DumanA. (2020). Wage losses and inequality in developing countries: labor market and distributional consequences of Covid-19 lockdowns in Turkey. Available at SSRN 3645468. doi:10.2139/ssrn.3645468

Fedakova, D., & Ištoňová, L. (2017). Slovak IT-employees and new ways of working: Impact on work-family borders and work-family balance. *Československá Psychologie*, *61*, 68–83.

Felippe, G. (2018). *A internet e as novas tecnologias na relação de trabalho: teletrabalho/home office e a jornada de trabalho* (Dissertação de Mestrado). Pontifícia Universidade Cat olica de São Paulo.

Felstead, A., & Henseke, G. (2017). Assessing the growth of remote working and its consequences for effort, well-being and work-life balance. *New Technology, Work and Employment*, *32*(3), 195–212. doi:10.1111/ntwe.12097

Flammer, C., & Luo, J. (2017). Corporate social responsibility as an employee governance tool: Evidence from a quasi- experiment. *Strategic Management Journal*, *38*(2), 163–183. doi:10.1002mj.2492

Fleck, R., Cox, A. L., & Robison, R. A. (2015). Balancing boundaries: Using multiple devices to manage work-life balance. In *Proceedings of the 33rd Annual ACM Conference on Human Factors in Computing Systems* (pp. 3985-3988). 10.1145/2702123.2702386

Fullana, M. A., Hidalgo-Mazzei, D., Vieta, E., & Radua, J. (2020). Coping behaviors associated with decreased anxiety and depressive symptoms during the COVID-19 pandemic and lockdown. *Journal of Affective Disorders*, *275*, 80–81. doi:10.1016/j.jad.2020.06.027 PMID:32658829

Gajendran, R. S., & Harrison, D. A. (2007). The good, the bad, and the unknown about tele- commuting: Meta-analysis of psychological mediators and individual consequences. *The Journal of Applied Psychology*, *92*(6), 1524–1541. doi:10.1037/0021-9010.92.6.1524 PMID:18020794

Galvez, A., Tirado, F., & Alcaraz, J. M. (2020). 'Oh! Teleworking!' Regimes of engagement and the lived experience of female Spanish teleworkers. *Business Ethics (Oxford, England)*, *29*(1), 180–192. doi:10.1111/beer.12240

Gao, W., Ping, S., & Liu, X. (2020). Gender differences in depression, anxiety, and stress among college students: A longitudinal study from China. *Journal of Affective Disorders*, *263*, 292–300. doi:10.1016/j.jad.2019.11.121 PMID:31818792

Giovanis, E. (2018). The relationship between teleworking, traffic and air pollution. *Atmospheric Pollution Research*, *9*(1), 1–14. doi:10.1016/j.apr.2017.06.004

Godinic, D., Obrenovic, B., & Khudaykulov, A. (2020). Effects of Economic Uncertainty on Mental Health in the COVID-19 Pandemic Context: Social Identity Disturbance, Job Uncertainty and Psychological Well-Being Model. *International Journal of Management Science and Business Administration*, *6*(1), 61–74. doi:10.18775/ijied.1849-7551-7020.2015.61.2005

Gold, A. L., Abend, R., Britton, J. C., Behrens, B., Farber, M., Ronkin, E., Chen, G., Leibenluft, E., & Pine, D. S. (2020). Age differences in the neural correlates of anxiety disorders: An fMRI study of response to learned threat. *The American Journal of Psychiatry*, *177*(5), 454–463. doi:10.1176/appi.ajp.2019.19060650 PMID:32252541

Golden, T. D. (2006). Avoiding depletion in virtual work: Telework and the intervening impact of work exhaustion on commitment and turnover intentions. *Journal of Vocational Behavior*, *69*(1), 176–187. doi:10.1016/j.jvb.2006.02.003

Groen, B. A., Van Triest, S. P., Coers, M., & Wtenweerde, N. (2018). Managing flexible work arrangements: Teleworking and output controls. *European Management Journal*, *36*(6), 727–735. doi:10.1016/j.emj.2018.01.007

Grönlund, A. (2007). Employee control in the era of flexibility: A stress buffer or a stress amplifier? *European Societies*, *9*(3), 409–428. doi:10.1080/14616690701314283

Haddad, H., Lyons, G., & Chatterjee, K. (2009). An examination of determinants influencing the desire for and frequency of part-day and whole-day homeworking. *Journal of Transport Geography*, *17*(2), 124–133. doi:10.1016/j.jtrangeo.2008.11.008

He, S., Lai, D., Mott, S., Little, A., Grock, A., Haas, M. R., & Chan, T. M. (2020). Remote e-work and distance learning for academic medicine: Best practices and opportunities for the future. *Journal of Graduate Medical Education*, *12*(3), 256–263. doi:10.4300/JGME-D-20-00242.1 PMID:32595840

Hobfoll, S. E., Shirom, A., & Golembiewski, R. (2000). Conservation of resources theory. Handbook of organizational behavior, 57-81.

Hook, A., Sovacool, B. K., & Sorrell, S. (2020). A systematic review of the energy and climate impacts of teleworking. *Environmental Research Letters*, *15*(9), 093003. doi:10.1088/1748-9326/ab8a84

Ilies, R., Wilson, K. S., & Wagner, D. T. (2009). The spillover of daily job satisfaction onto employees' family lives: The facilitating role of work-family integration. *Academy of Management Journal*, *52*(1), 87–102. doi:10.5465/amj.2009.36461938

Ipsen, C., van Veldhoven, M., Kirchner, K., & Hansen, J. P. (2021). Six key advantages and disadvantages of working from home in Europe during COVID-19. *International Journal of Environmental Research and Public Health*, *18*(4), 1826. doi:10.3390/ijerph18041826 PMID:33668505

Jesus, S. N., Leal, A. R., Viseu, J. N., Valle, P., Matavelli, R. D., Pereira, J., & Greenglass, E. (2016). Coping as a moderator of the influence of economic stressors on psychological health. *Análise Psicológica*, *34*(4), 365–376. doi:10.14417/ap.1122

Kapoor, V., Yadav, J., Bajpai, L., & Srivastava, S. (2021). Perceived stress and psychological well-being of working mothers during COVID-19: a mediated moderated roles of teleworking and resilience. *Employee Relations: The International Journal.*

Kazekami, S. (2020). Mechanisms to improve labor productivity by performing telework. *Telecommunications Policy*, *44*(2), 101868. doi:10.1016/j.telpol.2019.101868

Kulak, F. A., & Tüzüner, V. L. (2020). A comparative analysis of flexible working patterns in Germany and Turkey. *International Journal of Research in Business and Social Science, 9*(4), 1-14.

Lizana, P. A., & Vega-Fernadez, G. (2021). Teacher teleworking during the covid-19 pandemic: Association between work hours, work–family balance and quality of life. *International Journal of Environmental Research and Public Health*, *18*(14), 7566. doi:10.3390/ijerph18147566 PMID:34300015

Mao, Y., He, J., Morrison, A. M., & Andres Coca-Stefaniak, J. (2020). Effects of tourism CSR on employee psychological capital in the COVID-19 crisis: From the perspective of conservation of resources theory. *Current Issues in Tourism*, 1–19.

Maruyama, T., & Tietze, S. (2012). From anxiety to assurance: Concerns and outcomes of telework. *Personnel Review*, *41*(4), 450–469. doi:10.1108/00483481211229375

Montgomery, V. A., Roman, A., & Pierce, S. (2016). The rise and effect of virtual modalities and functions on organizational leadership: Tracing conceptual boundaries along the e-management and e-leadership continuum. *Transylvanian Review of Administrative Sciences*, *12*, 102–122.

Nagata, T., Ito, D., Nagata, M., Fujimoto, A., Ito, R., Odagami, K., Kajiki, S., Uehara, M., Oyama, I., Dohi, S., Fujino, Y., & Mori, K. (2021). Anticipated health effects and proposed countermeasures following the immediate introduction of telework in response to the spread of COVID-19: The findings of a rapid health impact assessment in Japan. *Journal of Occupational Health*, *63*(1), e12198. doi:10.1002/1348-9585.12198 PMID:33527667

Narcıkara, E. (2017b). *Spiritüel liderlik davranışının algılanan performans üzerine etkisi* (Published Phd Thesis). Yıldız Technical University. Social Sciences Institude.

Narcıkara, E. B. (2017). Örgüt Ortamında Artarak Yükselen Olumluluk: Pozitif Örgüt Okulu Bakış Perpektifi. *İş'te Davranış Dergisi*, *2*(1), 20-33.

Oguz, O. (2021). Teleworking Conditions in Turkish Labour Law. *Mokslas Ir Praktika: Aktualijos Ir Perspektyvos*, *32*.

Othman, N., Yusef, S. A. M., & Osman, W. R. S. (2009). A conflict between professional vs. domestic life? Understanding the use of ICT in teleworking for balance in work and family units. *Comp. Infor. Sci.*, *2*, 3–15.

Özen, E., Grima, S., & Hamarat, B. (2021). *Teleworking and Emotional Experience and Wellbeing: The Case in the Turkish Financial Services Industry During COVID-19*. Scientific Annals of Economics and Business.

Pollock, K., & Hauseman, D. C. (2019). The use of e-mail and principals' work: A double-edged sword. *Leadership and Policy in Schools*, *18*(3), 382–393. doi:10.1080/15700763.2017.1398338

Prin, M., & Bartels, K. (2020). Social distancing: Implications for the operating room in the face of COVID-19. *Canadian Journal of Anaesthesia*, *67*(7), 789–797. doi:10.100712630-020-01651-2 PMID:32291632

Pulley, M. L., & Sessa, V. I. (2001). E-leadership: Tackling complex challenges. *Industrial and Commercial Training*, *33*(6), 225–229. doi:10.1108/00197850110405379

Ramadani, V., Palalic, R., Dana, L.P., Krueger, N., & Caputo, A. (2020). Organizational Mindset of Entrepreneurship. Springer.

Ravalet, E., & Rérat, P. (2019). Teleworking: Decreasing mobility or increasing tolerance of commuting distances? *Built Environment*, *45*(4), 582–602. doi:10.2148/benv.45.4.582

Rhoades, L., & Eisenberger, R. (2002). Perceived organizational support: A review of the literature. *The Journal of Applied Psychology*, *87*(4), 698–714. doi:10.1037/0021-9010.87.4.698 PMID:12184574

Shi, X., Moudon, A. V., Lee, B. H., Shen, Q., & Ban, X. J. (2020). Factors Influencing Teleworking Productivity–a Natural Experiment during the COVID-19 Pandemic. Findings. Silahtaroğlu, G., Baykal, E., & Canbolat, Z. N. Weekly Emotional Changes Amidst Covid-19: Turkish Experience. *Ekonomi İşletme ve Maliye Araştırmaları Dergisi*, *2*(3), 280–304.

Smith, S. A., Patmos, A., & Pitts, M. J. (2018). Communication and teleworking: A study of communication channel satisfaction, personality, and job satisfaction for teleworking employees. *International Journal of Business Communication*, *55*(1), 44–68. doi:10.1177/2329488415589101

Solomou, I., & Constantinidou, F. (2020). Prevalence and predictors of anxiety and depression symptoms during the COVID-19 pandemic and compliance with precautionary measures: Age and sex matter. *International Journal of Environmental Research and Public Health*, *17*(14), 4924. doi:10.3390/ijerph17144924 PMID:32650522

Tavares, A. I. (2017). Telework and health effects review. *International Journal of Healthcare*, *3*(2), 30. doi:10.5430/ijh.v3n2p30

Tavares, F., Santos, E., Diogo, A., & Ratten, V. (2020). *Teleworking in portuguese communities during the COVID-19 pandemic. Journal of Enterprising Communities*. People and Places in the Global Economy.

Thompson, C. A., & Prottas, D. J. (2006). Relationships among organizational family support, job autonomy, perceived control, and employee well-being. *Journal of Occupational Health Psychology*, *11*(1), 100–118. doi:10.1037/1076-8998.10.4.100 PMID:16551178

Trnka, R., & Lorencova, R. (2020). Fear, anger, and media-induced trauma during the outbreak of COVID-19 in the Czech Republic. *Psychological Trauma: Theory, Research, Practice, and Policy*, *12*(5), 546–549. doi:10.1037/tra0000675 PMID:32538654

Zehir, C., & Narcıkara, E. (2016). Effects of resilience on productivity under authentic leadership. *Procedia: Social and Behavioral Sciences*, *235*, 250–258. doi:10.1016/j.sbspro.2016.11.021

KEY TERMS AND DEFINITIONS

Anxiety: Anxiety is the body's natural response to stress. It's a feeling of fear or apprehension about what's to come.

COVID-19: It is an infectious disease caused by a newly discovered coronavirus.

Flexible Working: It is a way of working that suits an employee's needs, for example having flexible start and finish times, or working from home.

Teleworking: The action or practice of working from home, making use of the internet, email, and the telephone.

Chapter 11 Consumer Behavior and Its Impact on Poverty Reduction

Ana Nery Rodrigues Carneiro
FIEMA, Brazil

João Conrado de Amorim Carvalho
https://orcid.org/0000-0001-8121-2539
Centro de Ensino Superior Dom Bosco, Brazil

ABSTRACT

This chapter aims to present the motivational factors that determine the behavior of beer consumers. The research considered the situation before and during the COVID-19 pandemic. The results showed that men consume and spend more on beer than women, including by age group; however, women consume more expensive types of beer, reducing this inequality relatively. It was also found that women are more likely to be influenced by their relatives, friends, and social occasions. As for preference, women showed more interest in light beers than men, especially craft beer. It has also been found that differences in preferences between men and women are narrowing as opportunities to try beer increase. In this sense, younger age groups tend to show fewer differences. It was also observed that, during the period of social isolation, consumption habits were maintained, but purchases took place through a delivery system, which affected the performance of bars and restaurants.

INTRODUCTION

The world is going through a turbulent moment and this moment is reflected in companies. In addition to the usual political, economic, and ideological crises that affect major world economies, society was recently affected by the Covid-19 pandemic. The necessary social isolation, in some cases, the blocking decreed by the authorities, put at risk the success of the companies' operations, especially those that depend heavily on customer visits. Much was invested in techniques to surprise customers, delivering more than promised in terms of products and services. However, suddenly, the clientele was forced to stay

DOI: 10.4018/978-1-7998-8925-0.ch011

at home to avoid the contagion of the coronavirus and the consequent spread of the disease, considered the most crisis since the Spanish flu a century ago.

Before the pandemic, companies sought to strengthen an internal culture in relation to a proactive posture, that is, the company's employees needed to anticipate the needs of customers, understanding their expectations, and providing all the facilities and attributes to surprise and delight those that represent survival. of business and jobs. The ability to react was also needed to adapt to new demands, providing enough innovation not to lose the opportunity to the competitor.

As social distancing was imposed as a necessary rule to reduce Covid-19 cases, it became necessary to understand which elements determine consumer behavior. If, before the pandemic, this activity was already a complex task, movement restrictions implied changes in the purchasing process. In addition to the traditional preferences for consumer satisfaction, aspects related to logistics were incorporated into the concerns of companies, since the product needed to reach consumers.

The consumption of food and beverages is strongly influenced by the purchasing power of people, their preferences, the quality of products and the service involved, and also by the experiences provided in the consumption itself. In this sense, the acquisition of beer in Brazil has undergone a process of evolution, due to the insertion of artisan beers (premium or special) in the market, where the 'income' factor is less significant than the tasting sensations experienced by consumers. In recent years, there has been a considerable increase in the number of scientific publications dealing with wine consumer behavior, but the study of factors influencing beer consumption behavior is more limited (Hajdu, Major, & Lakner, 2007). Considering that beer consumption in Brazil has been increasing, especially in craft beers, and that this growth is strongly influenced by the female audience, the question is: how do consumers relate their consumption preferences to sensory experiences before and during the pandemic?

The interest in this field of study came from the observation of the emergence of several bars in São Luís, capital of the state of Maranhão, Brazil, aimed at a select public, more demanding and adept at the consumption of craft beers. It was initially noticed that the purchase of this type of beer took place in specialized stores and, little by little, sales began to occupy spaces on supermarket shelves and convenience stores. It didn't take long for craft beers (also known as premium) to occupy pub and restaurant menus, competing with industrial beers for consumer preference. During the pandemic, consumers retreated and stopped going to these places, preferring consumption in their homes.

BACKGROUND

Beer is considered the oldest and most consumed alcoholic drink in the world. According to Innovare Pesquisa (2016), the Czech Republic occupies the top of the per capita annual consumption ranking, with 143 liters per inhabitant, followed by Austria (108 liters), Germany (107 liters) and Ireland (94 liters). Brazil, currently home to the world's leading production company, Ambev, occupies only 17th place, with 82 liters per inhabitant.

In this niche, premium beer has been expanding its space with the male and female public. The delicacy receives this name because its production considers aspects related to the tasting, like greater presence of malt in the composition, interfering in the aroma, flavor, and color of the product. The premium beers are more elaborate and slightly sweetened by the addition of hops in their formula, which gives them unique characteristics and awaken the pleasure in the consumption experience, something very close to what happens with the wine. It is for no other reason that consumption has increased, avoiding even the effects of the crisis and establishing a new characteristic of consumption related to lifestyle (Innovare, 2016).

Industrial beer, produced and consumed on a large scale, positions itself to win supporters by offering lower prices and promotions, which attract new consumers. On the other hand, premium or artisan beers, on the other hand, for betting on the development of a consumer experience, very similar to what happens with wine, are positioning themselves by criteria of differentiation, with prices far superior to those of industrial beers. The purchase process is not always easy due to the high potential of risk, promoted by the possibility of not identifying the consumer with the product. Like wine, quality, olfactory aspects, flavor and other attributes will only be known at the time of consumption (Innovare, 2016).

Companies know that for their business to exist it is necessary to win over the consumer. In this way, they define strategies to know their desires and expectations and, thus, be able to retain them. Thus, the importance of studying the subject consumes part of concepts expressed in different areas.

In legal terms, the Consumer Defense Code informs that *the consumer is any natural or legal person who acquires or uses a product or service as the final recipient* (Brazil, 1990.). Tomaz (1999, *apud* Medeiros, & Lima, 2002, p.12) states that the consumer *is the one who uses (consumes) a particular good or service, not necessarily who pays for it. Individuals and groups that purchase products and services for personal use.*

In the globalized and highly competitive market, it is imperative that companies study consumer behavior. Ibdaiwi, Garcia and Lopes (2008) teach that the field of consumer behavior includes the study of processes in which individuals or groups select, buy, use or have products, services, ideas and experiences in order to satisfy your needs. And with regard to services, the above-mentioned authors point out as an alternative the differentiation and the offer of facilities to the consumer in their purchases. Consumer behavior is motivated by the desire to meet genetically programmed needs in your mind or desires aroused by the society in which you live.

Souza, Pontes and Oliveira (2007) affirm that, in the past, companies reigned and imposed on the will of the client. Today, the situation has reversed, companies are searching for clients, seeking to identify their desires and needs to win them. Being essential for the good development of the business, to be attentive to the changes of the market, to know the behavior of the clients, to reassess their operational conducts and to study the best strategies to attract and to conquer.

MAIN FOCUS OF THE CHAPTER

Issues, Controversies and Problems

Based on the aforementioned positions and concepts, the relationship between the variables (consumer profile, consumer behavior and habits, satisfaction with the services provided and sales strategies to attract consumers - marketing) and hypotheses (market, business and business, consumer and its characteristics and marketing) related to this study, using theoretical linearity.

In the design of Silveira, *et al.* (2012), who explain consumer theory, market analysis is done through the microeconomic approach, in three aspects: preferences, budget constraints and choices. Knowing these determinants is crucial so that the entrepreneur who offers some type of product and service is better able to design his business strategies, expand the possibilities of growth and ensure his permanence in the market.

The contributions of Meister (2008), Costa, Santana and Wheat (2015) and Feitosa and Viana (2015), on the importance of the entrepreneur to relate to the client based on their behavior, are based on the need of the market, knowledge of the business about the desires of the consumer, when the consumer proposes to consume something. Emphasizing that, in order to build a good relationship between client and company, it is essential that the market identifies the needs of the customers, to satisfy them and guarantee their loyalty. In addition, it must continually invest in the quality of products and services.

Ibdaiwi, et al. (2008), emphasize that the highly competitive globalized market requires companies to study consumer behavior. And that includes studying the processes by which individuals or groups select, buy, use or own products, services, ideas and experiences in order to meet their needs. The recognition of consumer behavior influences the type of service and products that the enterprise offers, and even its business style and, why not say, the way the product is made available to the customer.

Costa, *et al.* (2015) highlight quality as a concept that must be practiced intensely by companies, because, through this tool, they optimize productivity, survival and growth of the business. Quality must be present in all processes (clean and organized environment, good quality products, well-arranged and good-looking attendants, education in customer care, decorated environment, etc.) and involves all members of the organization, employees must be prepared to provide quality service, investing in the delight and satisfaction of consumer needs, in order to be successfully competitive.

In this perspective, Kotler (1998) contributes, by explaining that the satisfaction or frustration of the customer in face of the service performed in the establishment chosen to consume is a result of the comparison made with the competitors, equating products and services that influence the choice of what best meets their expectations and needs.

Oliveira (2010) concludes that the satisfaction with the products or services and with respect to the physical and structural aspects of the enterprise is perceived by the consumer before the service. The feelings of pleasure or disappointment are the result of the service offered by the company, that is, if the quality of the products and services is not among the organizational principles of the business, the consumer perceives the lack of preparation and the poor quality of the service, and gives up consuming in that environment. Thus, a poor performance of the product or service offer, and that does not meet the need for consumption, will leave the consumer dissatisfied.

Silva (2007) argues that the physical environment is the concrete physical and spatial aspect, in which the consumption activity and even the surrounding space are found. This space is made up of factors such as color, noise, lighting, climate and the position of people and objects in the space. The author reveals that these aspects can influence consumer behavior through sensory mechanisms of vision, hearing, smell, and touch. The environment, in general, must be worked according to the behaviors, attitudes and beliefs of consumers. The physical environment also includes the geographic location, decoration, cleaning and organization of objects and attendants, aromas and disposition of goods or other objects that surround the object of stimulation, meeting consumer expectations.

The new behavioral format of the consumer takes place from his/her relationship with the physical environment in which he/she intends to consume, thus, the companies seek to create an image from this relation, creating a layout that carries the characteristics of the consumer, as was made explicit by Silva (2007). However, the retraction of consumers during the pandemic changed this aspect somewhat, although with the reduction of isolation measures, preferences for physical environments have resumed their course.

Knowledge about the variables that influence purchasing behavior is substantial so that entrepreneurs can create strategies that are more adequate and consistent with their reality. Authors, such as Santos

(2013), explain that products or services must follow the parameters of consumer satisfaction, according to their taste and the market-oriented demand. For when you go to an establishment, people, in general, expect to be well attended and considered important at that moment. The organization - when it acts based on consumer conceptions about its company, products and services - is creating a good tune with the customer/consumer.

Silva (2013) reveals that the new activities attributed to management processes, which are based on the requirement for quality of service, are the result of failures and defects caused by the product or service offered. In order to guarantee the quality of their offerings, organizations implement activities to control and supervise the degree of variation of the product and service, adopting a production standard, according to the original specifications.

As mentioned previously, Cobra (2003) relates critical points that can't occur during the development of the business, namely: apathy, automatism, condescension, dispensation, coldness, attitudes that frustrate the client's expectations and contribute to the client's not wanting to return to the enterprise, and to create a bad reputation for the same. The risks in a business are predictable and can be worked out in advance. If you don't pay attention to them, these bugs can hurt the company and even close your doors.

It is understood, therefore, that a satisfied customer is one who has his/her expectations reached and receives a satisfactory service and quality, without any discrimination or neglect for his needs.

Scholars, such as Pimentel (2013), point out that the internet is becoming the most widely used communication channel for the dissemination of products and services to their respective consumer sectors, because information becomes more accessible to all, and offers are evaluated before they were even acquired. The internet has become an environment that brings a preview of what the consumer wants, and where it selects what they will consume, according to their needs and financial conditions.

In this sense, business marketing must be idealized and concretized to leverage the company's strong points and exclude weaknesses. For Cobra (2003), weaknesses constitute variables such as apathy, automatism, condescension, dispensation, indifference, among others, which threaten the development of the business of any segment.

Faced with the current relationship between customers and companies on the Internet, it is advised prudent to take the utmost care when exposing quality products and services to the consumer, ensuring the fulfillment of what is propagated on the business. Baltzan (2016) points out that the entrepreneur must also keep in mind that the internet is a double-edged sword, while the company can use it to expand its business and facilitate the customer's access, so that the customer wants to consume their products and services, the computer network is also used by the customer to comment, positively or negatively, on the service of the company.

Nowadays, for companies, internet communication implies bringing good and bad impressions about their business, demanding the same knowledge about this tool and monitoring everything that happens and is disclosed, or by the company or the consumer, that can both bring positive, negative, and positive responses about the products and services offered by the enterprise.

Miele, Waquil, and Schultz (2011) emphasize that in competition, it is essential for the company to analyze its management processes and obtain as much information about its consumers as possible for more comprehensive, concrete and coherent decision making, as this will determine the good or bad business results. The combination of variables such as production, marketing, human resources, technology, communication, supply, distribution, investments, etc., consists of careful studies to reduce risks and losses that could lead to a decline in business. As noted, the authors list important relative aspects that enable more assertive sales strategies to attract consumers, drawn on the basis of market knowledge.

Thus, the internet, at that moment, has become another instrument for the expansion and evolution of consumer markets.

Beer, like wine, has become a beverage associated with lifestyle, and women have been rising as buyers and consumers of this item. These increasing consumption rates are associated with premium beverages, taking into account age-related issues, which is why the following hypotheses have been formulated:

H1. Men consume and spend more on beer than women, including by age group.
H2. Women are more likely than men to be influenced in their beer purchases by their relatives, friends and social occasion.
H3. The choice of food to match the beverage is the most important factor in all age groups and gender.
H4. Women's preference for light beer is higher than men's.
H5. Women's preference for craft beers is higher than men's.
H6. Differences in preferences between men and women are declining, as opportunities to try beer are increasing. Therefore, younger age groups will have fewer differences.

SOLUTIONS AND RECOMMENDATIONS

The Method

To reach the objectives, answering the central question of the investigation and testing the hypotheses formulated was adopted a methodology of quantitative approach, having as strategy of data collection the application of a questionnaire, with answers analyzed statistically.

Initially, extensive analysis of the specialized literature was undertaken, based on journals and journals of reference in the area of Administration and Entrepreneurship, as well as scientific articles found in publications indexed and reputed in the academic world.

Once the scope of work was understood, a questionnaire was prepared for data collection, based on the research conducted by Bruwer, Saliba and Miler (2011) on the behavior of wine consumers in Australia. The questionnaire reproduced questions similar to those surveyed by Bruwer, *et al.* (2011), with the necessary adaptation to the beer market, with the exception of the open questions, for not providing conditions of application in the chosen platform.

The sample was calculated statistically, based on the universe of persons comprised in the age group from the age of eighteen. It was not feasible and it was not desirable to identify consumers, so it is not possible to guarantee that all respondents are beer drinkers. The results were worked through descriptive statistics and ANOVA test, seeking to evidence the relationship between the variables and, thus, to test the formulated hypotheses.

The questionnaires were developed and made available on the Google Forms platform, due to its ability to reach a greater number of responses, without the interference of the researcher, and easy tabulation, besides being more dynamic, fast, free access and with voluntary responses. Access to the questionnaires occurred through social networks (Facebook, WhatsApp, Linkedin, Instagram etc.), available in different groups, whose participants could share the link in other networks, increasing access to those who wanted to respond to the questionnaires. The questionnaires were made available and shared during the period from 10 to 18 April 2017.

In the questionnaire, questions were asked about the characteristics of the respondents, as well as their patterns of beer consumption and preferences.

The collected data were submitted to analysis by means of statistical techniques. Initially, they were organized in a spreadsheet extracted from the Google Forms platform, used to collect the questionnaires. In this platform, the data are already organized in columns, each corresponding to each item formulated, accompanied by pie charts and bars on the frequency of responses.

After the selection of the validated questionnaires, the normality test (Kolmogorov-Sminorv Test or KS Test) was carried out, which aimed to explore the relations between variables, when the researcher does not have all the elements of the population parameters (Bussab, & Morettin, 2004, Bruni, 2011). The KS test confirms adherence, since it evaluates the distribution of a set of values observed in the sample and determines the theoretical distribution.

To carry out the KS Test, the SPSS statistical package was used with the whole set of data and variables. The results indicated that the distribution is normal, enabling the data of the sample to analyze the descriptive statistics, since they represent the universe searched.

After extracting the worksheet, the analysis was called 'descriptive statistics', which aims to describe and summarize the data, creating tables with absolute frequency and relative frequency for each class analyzed. As we worked with sample, it became necessary to use inference techniques to make the sample representative of the researched universe (discussed in the previous section). In this stage of the work, Excel software was used, because it is easier and more agile in data analysis, and because it has the ability to interact with the text editor used to compose this research, making data transposition more productive without loss of data quality. The results of this part of the work are demonstrated in frequency frames and self-explanatory graphs. In parallel, we performed a cross-over between variables to understand the preferences of classes and subclasses in relation to the research object.

This information obtained from the crossing of variables is a good indicator for validation or refutation of the hypotheses proposed. However, we also used the ANOVA or Variance Analysis, a statistical procedure capable of comparing the distribution of groups of independent samples. The ANOVA test summarizes a linear regression model, decomposing the sum of the squares to the source of variation in the model, making it possible to test the hypotheses considering that any source of variation in the model is equal to zero.

This work arose from questions about a phenomenon that has been perceived in Brazil, especially in the capital of the State of Maranhão, related to the consumption of beer. It is noted that the demand for craft beers is increasing, even the country faced one of the most serious crises in its history, and that consumption is strongly influenced by the female audience. The work sought to answer how consumers relate their consumption preferences to sensory experiences or to what extent the sensorial experiences are determinant for the choice of the type of beer in the consumer public.

The Results

In this section, we present the profile of beer consumers in São Luís, Maranhão, Brazil, their consumption habits and preferences, and, finally, test the hypotheses that were previously proposed. In the presentation of the profile, we used the descriptive statistics and in the test of hypotheses, the regression and correlation techniques were used. It is important to emphasize that the application of the questionnaires took place two years before the start of the pandemic, which allowed us to understand the consumption habits and preferences of consumers at a time without a health crisis.

Profile of Beer Consumers

Regarding gender, a slightly higher number of women were identified among the respondents (57.39%). Regarding the frequency by age group, a higher concentration was observed in the range of 29 to 34 years (22.16%). However, the cumulative frequency of consumers aged up to 45 years represents more than 85% of respondents.

Analyzing the profile of consumers by level of education, it was found that beer consumers have reached the last stages of formal education. No less than 49.43% of them have a higher education level and 38.07%, graduate studies, totaling 87.5%. Regarding the income range, beer consumers are concentrated in the lower purchasing power sectors. More than 67% earn up to R $ 20 thousand (something less than € 6 thousand, in the current par).

The favorite places to buy beer are bars and restaurants, with almost 45% of the answers, and supermarkets with almost 31%. These two sites account for 75.57% of consumer preferences. It was also possible to identify 9 people who did not answer the question (5.11%). It was also found that beer consumers are strongly influenced by 3 major factors when purchasing the product: the social occasion (46.02%), product label (21.02%) and friends (15.91%). These 3 factors determine almost 83% of the consumption surveyed.

In the original study by Bruwer, *et al.* (2011), with wine consumers in Australia, the authors identified that the size of households was generally small, with an average of less than 3 people, but most adults consumed the beverage. The authors also examined the same question regarding the variables 'income' and 'education'. These points were analyzed in relation to beer and, added still, the variables 'age' and 'gender'. It has been found that the average number of people under the age of 18 in the family nucleus surveyed is 0.89, the average number of people over the age of 18 is 2, of which the average number of those who drink beer is 1.49 people.

The cross-statistic of people who drink beer with age, income and educational level showed that the largest number of beer consumers is housed in families with 1 or 2 people who drink the product (more than 66% of respondents) and that the age group of the highest consumption is that of people between 29 and 34 years of age (more than 22% of respondents are in this age group). Regarding consumption by educational level, 87.5% of consumers have a higher or postgraduate level and the highest incidence is in families with 1 or 2 people (68.18%). Consumption by gender did not reveal significant differences, being concentrated in families with 1 and 2 people.

Hypothesis Test

The hypotheses were tested using the ANOVA or Variance Analysis. The data were extracted from the SPSS system, and analyzed, correlating the variables contained in each of the proposed hypotheses.

The hypothesis H1 correlates the consumption (and expenditure) with beer, with the gender and age group:

H1. Men consume and spend more on beer than women, including by age group.

The ANOVA test indicated that there are at least two items in which the pattern of consumption is significantly different between gender and age group ($p < .05$), which leads to confirm the hypothesis H1. In addition, it was possible to verify that, from the descriptive statistics, the average number of people in the family consuming beer by age group is significantly higher in the age groups of 29 to 34 years. Among those who did not declare their sexual orientation and the male audience, it is higher in the age range of 41 to 45 and 55 to 65 years.

The data show that beer consumption is still higher among men than among women and that the public whose sexual orientation has not been declined in the survey represents almost double the average male audience. It should be noted, however, that the hypothesis contemplates the consumption of beer in general (industrial beer and artisanal beer), obliging to extend the analysis of the other hypotheses to understand if there is a greater preference of consumption in the female gender for other types of beer.

H2. Women are more likely than men to be influenced in their beer purchases by their relatives, friends and social occasion.
H3. The choice of food to match the beverage is the most important factor in all age groups and gender.

The ANOVA test confirms the existence of at least one item in which women are more likely to be influenced than men in beer purchases. In the case, as presented later (descriptive statistics), the influence starts from the husband, confirming the hypothesis H2.

It was observed that the social occasion is the most important factor for women (53.47%), followed by the label / brand (14.85%) and friends (12.87%). Men are also influenced by these same factors, but with different intensity. The social occasion appears with 36.49%, label / brand with 29.73% and friends with 18.92%. The wife was not recorded in any men's response as a factor of importance in influencing beer purchase. The public whose sexual orientation has not been declined is totally influenced by friends.

It is important to emphasize that women and men do not associate beer consumption with food harmonization and are not influenced by waiters and employees of the places where they shop, which leads to a refutation of the hypothesis H3.

H4. Women's preference for light beer is higher than men's.
H5. Women's preference for craft beers is higher than men's.
H6. Differences in preferences between men and women are declining, as opportunities to try beer are increasing. Therefore, younger age groups will have fewer differences.

Hypotheses H4 and H5 speculate whether the preference of women for light beer and craft beer is greater than for men, while hypothesis H6 proposes that younger groups will have less variation in preferences because differences are decreasing over time.

The ANOVA test confirmed the 3 hypotheses, admitting the existence of 3 items in which the preference of consumption is significantly higher. These items were identified through descriptive statistics.

Regarding light beer, by frequency counting, it was possible to verify that 61 women who answered the questionnaire (60.4%) agree partially or totally with the proposition that they prefer light beer more than men. In the same question, 66.22% of the men also confirmed the proposition, which reinforces the validation of the H4 hypothesis. Regarding artisanal beers, 17.82% of women stated that they preferred this type of beer much more than men. The male audience not only confirmed the proposition, but also exceeded the indicator, with 18.91% agreement, reinforcing the validation of the hypothesis H5.

Confirmation of the H6 hypothesis is also reinforced by the frequency of responses. There is a clear perception by the respondents that differences in beer consumption preference have changed over the years. Something around 80% of the respondents of all genders agreed partially and totally with the change. Just over 62% of men and 72% of women agreed that the differences were lower in the younger audience, between 18 and 40 years.

Thus, 5 of the 6 hypotheses released were confirmed in the survey. The only hypothesis refuted concerns the non-finding that beer consumption is influenced by the harmonization with food.

This study was not only limited to demonstrating the results of the research, it was also intended to present some suggestions with respect to certain critical points, that the managers of the establishments dealing with beers, especially the artisanal ones, can develop, aiming at a better performance. It does not directly concern consumer behavior, but can change this behavior for the better and bring changes that can add new values, expand customer base and generate more profit. In addition, and taking into account that Covid-19 can become a permanent disease in society, such as the flu, alternating periods of localized high incidence with periods of low incidence, it is possible to understand how establishment owners can and should act in time of aggravation.

One of the main objectives of this study was to identify differences in the consumption of artisanal beer among men and women, including by age group. Determining factors of these differences or preferences were examined, among them preferences for light and premium beers, from the first contact with the beverage. It is known that in more consolidated markets, beer consumption is influenced by income, which is why demand falls during times of crisis. However, the best quality beers are little affected by this issue and this is due to the fact that the preferences for their consumption are related to a lifestyle that is being constituted by the new generations and by the women, in particular. It was also found, through observations, that during the pandemic period these preferences did not change, but consumption started to be carried out in people's own homes.

As with wine, many factors contribute to the development of this trend, including health issues. Some alcoholic beverages, in small amounts, are beneficial to health and this seems to be the case, both beer and wine. As the consumption of craft beers is given – as was clear from the analysis of the data – due to the higher quality and to the detriment of the quantity consumed, the habit of consuming artisan beers ends up favoring its consumers by dealing with lower volume of the drink. In addition, craft beers also come up with the idea of a certain sophisticated behavior of their consumers, since the price selects the target audience, which is not the case with industrial beers, produced and consumed on a large scale.

It is worth mentioning that the consumption of beer in social events favors another relevant aspect, which concerns the maintenance and expansion of contact networks, friendships and fraternization opportunities. It is no wonder that consumption at such events, almost always held in bars and restaurants, seduce much more young audiences and women, while the older audience prefers to purchase the product in supermarkets and consume alone at home. With the pandemic, household consumption grew at the expense of consumption in bars and restaurants. This is due, at first, to restrictions imposed by the authorities, which did not allow social gatherings in commercial establishments. In a second moment, due to the awareness of the people, who deliberately started to avoid agglomerations.

One of the main findings of this research, which is in line with the findings of Bruwer, *et al.* (2011) is that women drink less beer than men therefore spend less but tend to purchase higher quality, lighter and fruity products. Thus, in relative terms, they buy more expensive products and, as a result, reduce differences and increase the consumption of special beers, while industrial beers experience a drop in sales due to the ongoing economic and sanitary crisis.

Recommendations

It is believed that, from this study, beer producers, distributors, bars, restaurants and retail stores can adopt marketing orientation strategies aimed at consumer preferences. Acting in this way, they will be able to perceive alterations of consumption patterns from the understanding of the factors that motivate consumers to acquire the products. All these agents may perceive that there are sensorial discrepancies between age groups and genders, and that it is no longer possible to induce consumption from the producer to the client. On the contrary, marketers must perceive the needs of customers and induce manufacturers to produce the variety of beer that meets this demand. The great challenge, therefore, is to embrace the opportunities to meet the desires of consumers, and this assistance will only be possible by understanding these needs and by the way the industries will do this in practice.

The findings may even be the subject of the ads' guidance. Since there are differences and these differences are clear, it is possible to direct the messages in such a way that it reaches the specific public (millennial, mainly female). Although artisanal beer made in Brazil does not yet have a variety of labels sufficient for young women to exercise their power of choice, local production along with the variety of imported beers can meet consumers' needs, which would make communication easier and help in the decision-making process.

It is noteworthy that beer suppliers must be aware of crisis manifestations that may determine agglomeration restrictions. In this situation, it is very important to anticipate the facts and strengthen the online sales and home delivery system as a way to keep the customer satisfied while the problem remains. This suggestion may be useful to maintain the performance of commercial establishments, since periods of pandemic tend to reduce sales and cause losses in results.

FUTURE RESEARCH INSTRUCTIONS

The arguments raised in this research reveal the relevance of the subject, which concerns not only academic researchers and marketing science, but also entrepreneurs of different types of establishments, who can know the results of studies on consumer behavior in a city so peculiar, but with prospects of generalization of results.

Among the limitations of the research, the exploratory nature applied to only one region of Brazil stands out. Although São Luís is a state capital with a population of more than one million inhabitants, it still has provincial habits, which in a way inhibits the rise of the consumption of differentiated beers. In addition, because it is also one of the poorest regions of the country, the consumption of artisanal beers is still limited to a limited number of people with higher purchasing power. In this regard, new research contemplating other regions of the country would be welcome to mitigate this limitation, making it possible to make comparisons and broaden the base of respondents.

Another limitation for carrying out this investigation was the sample size. Considering statistical criteria limited to the population of São Luís over the age of eighteen, the sample was considered ideal for the universe. Studies to evolve in this theme should consider a broader sample, taking into account that the universe searched will also be broader.

For further research, it becomes necessary to better understand how beer consumers take into account the sensory aspects such as taste, alcoholic content, lightness, aromas etc. It is recommended that quantitative research be complemented with blind tests, reducing the chances of responses based only on the intuition or expectations that can modify the true perception of the respondents. And, also, understand how sanitary restrictions impacted business performance.

CONCLUSION

The present research had as general objective to study which are the motivating factors that determine the behavior of the beer consumers in São Luís do Maranhão, Brazil, and if such factors take into account the sensorial experiences provided by the drink. In order to achieve the general objective, this research formulated the following specific objectives: to identify the consumption profile by gender; to investigate whether women have a preference for certain types of beer; and if there is any kind of change of preference due to the increase in contact opportunities with more elaborate drinks.

Statistical tests performed showed significant differences in consumption between genders and age groups. These results were even more significant when, in addition to the factors inherent in the different age groups and gender, motivational factors of beer consumption, locations and consumption preferences. It has been noticed, as has been found in previous wine surveys, that there is a trend towards changing consumption patterns, and that this is more noticeable in younger audiences and in women.

Younger respondents, referred to as 'millennials' (generation born since 1977), showed a clear preference for beer consumption in bars and restaurants (about 50%) and this preference is more evident the younger they are. In parallel, the baby boomer generation (born between 1946 and 1964) and the generation X (1965 to 1977) divide their preferences between consumption in bars and restaurants and purchases of beer in supermarkets and convenience stores for residential consumption. Perhaps the explanation for the greater beer consumption of the millennial generation in bars and restaurants is due to its greater mobility, fewer children living in the home, which could restrict participation in social activities outside the home. This behavior was also noticed in the study by Bruwer *et al.* (2011), which guided this study.

In this research, for obvious reasons, no surveys were contemplated in a tasting room. There is no such widespread practice with beers, even artisanal ones, in Brazil and in São Luís, where the research was carried out. Thus, it was not possible to evaluate this factor and compare it with the same measure in relation to wine consumption, in Bruwer, *et al.* (2011). Nevertheless, on the comparative tests between genders in relation to the consumption of artisanal beers, it has been confirmed by both men and women that the female consumption has been increasing in relation to this type of drink, as well as in relation to the lighter beers. In this respect, the consumption of women is similar to that of wine, that is, although they continue to drink less than men, their preferences lie in higher quality products with a higher average price.

It is important to highlight a discordant point between this research with beer consumption and the research on wine consumption. Millennial generation consumes far more light and handmade beers than Generation X, a diametrically opposite fact in wine research, in which older generations spend more on better quality wines. This point reinforces the hypothesis that a change of consumption habit is taking place that is more noticeable in younger generations (H6).

The factors of influence tested in the research revealed small differences between men and women. In order of importance, men and women indicated the social occasion, product label / brand and friends as the most influential factors. What differentiates is the note given to each factor. Social occasion, for example, appears with more than 53% of women's answers and only slightly more than 36% of men's responses. Already the label / mark is frequent in almost 15% of the female answers and in almost 30% of the masculine answers.

The influence of friends is reported in almost 13% of women's responses and in almost 19% of men's responses. It is concluded that the majority of women prefer to consume beers on social occasions, gives medium importance to the label / brand and the influence of friends. Men, however, balance their preferences between social occasions and label / brand, also considering the opinions of friends. Factors such as food harmonization, comments from trade magazines, and spouse's opinion had little influence on beer consumption, although women took the husbands' views a little lightly.

REFERENCES

Baltzan, P. (2016). Tecnologia orientada para gestão (6a ed.). Porto Alegre: AMGH editora Ltda.

Brasil. *Lei nº. 8.078*, de 11 de setembro de 1990. Código de Defesa do Consumidor. Dispõe sobre a proteção do consumidor e dá outras providências. Brasília. Retrieved June 24, 2017, from: <http://www.planalto.gov.br/ccivil_03/Leis/L8078.htm>

Bruni, A. L. (2011). Estatística Aplicada à Gestão Empresarial (3a ed.). São Paulo: Atlas.

Bruwer, J., Saliba, A., & Miler, B. (2011). Consumer behaviour and sensory preference diferences: Implications for wine product marketing. *Journal of Consumer Marketing*, *28*(1), 5–18. doi:10.1108/07363761111101903

Bussab, W. O., & Morettin, P. A. (2004). Estatística básica (5a ed.) São Paulo: Saraiva.

Cobra, M. (2003). *Administração de Marketing no Brasil.* Cobra Editora de Marketing.

Costa, A. S. C., Santana, L. C., & Trigo, A. C. (2015). *Qualidade do atendimento ao cliente: um grande referencial competitivo para as organizações.* Retrieved May 12, 2017, from: https://www.cairu.br/riccairu/pdf/artigos/2/10_qualidade_atend_cliente.pdf

Feitosa, D. R., & Viana, T. A. (2015). *Perfil e grau de satisfação de consumidores de estabelecimentos comerciais do setor alimentício de três cidades do Cariri cearense.* Retrieved May 3, 2017, from: www.fjn.edu.br/revista/index.php/eciencia/article/view/48

Hajdu, I., Major, A., & Lakner, Z. (2007). Consumer behavior in the Hungarian beer market. *Studies in Agricultural Economics (Budapest)*, *106*, 89–104.

Ibdaiwi, T. K., Garcia, F. T., & Lopes, L. F. D. (2008). *Comportamento do consumidor: características de referência dos vestibulandos da cidade de Santa Maria – RS.* Retrieved June 11, 2017, from: www.convibra.org/dwp.asp?id=3846&ev=25

Innovare Pesquisa. (2016). *O consumo de cerveja no Brasil.* Retrieved September 6, 2017, from: https://www.innovarepesquisa.com.br/blog/o-consumo-de-cerveja-brasil/

Kotler, P. (1998). Administração de marketing: análise, planejamento, implementação controle (5a ed.). São Paulo: Atlas.

Medeiros, F. C. L. M., & Lima, V. M. S. (2002). *Consumidor, cliente e paciente: existe alguma diferença? 1*(2). Retrieved May 22, 2017, from: www.revistaunirn.inf.br

Meister, A. P. S. (2008). *Pesquisa de satisfação dos clientes do restaurante Vermelho Grill*. Retrieved May 12, 2017, from: www.lume.ufrgs.br/handle/10183/18040

Miele, M., Waquil, P. D., & Schultz, G. (2011). Mercados e comercialização de produtos agroindustriais. *Ciências Sociais Aplicadas*. Universidade Federal do Rio Grande do Sul. Retrieved March 22, 2017, from: www.lume.ufrgs.br

Oliveira, J. (2010). *Satisfação do cliente*. Retrieved May 22, 2017, from: https://www.administradores.com.br/producao-academica/satisfacao-do-cliente/2859/

Pimentel, G. S. (2013). *A influência das redes sociais na escolha dos consumidores: o caso do bar Botequim Tá Na Hora*. Retrieved May 22, 2017, from: docplayer.com.br/3661987-A-influencia-das-redes-sociais-na-escolha-dos-consumido.

Santos, R. S. (2013). *Fatores influenciadores de consumo de festas sertanejas: um estudo na cidade de Belém – PA*. Retrieved June 28, 2017, from: www.fpl.edu.br/2013/.../dissertacao_ricardo_da_silva_santos_2013.pdf

Silva, K. A. (2007). *O comportamento do consumidor: a influência do ambiente físico na compra em lojas de shopping centers no Distrito Federal*. Retrieved June 22, 2017, from: http://docplayer.com.br/13186861-O-comportamento-do-consumidor-a-influencia-do-ambiente-fisico-na-compra-em-lojas-de-shopping-centers-no-distrito-federal.html#show_full_text

Silva, V. B. (2013). *Gestão da qualidade dos serviços prestados em bares e restaurantes na praia da Rendinha (Natal-RN)*. Retrieved May 22, 2017, from: <https://sigaa.ufrn.br/sigaa/verProducao?idProducao=1940241&key.>

Silveira, L. S., Abdallah, P. R., Hellebrandt, L., Barbosa, M. N., & Feijó, F. T. (2012). *Análise socioeconômica do perfil dos consumidores de pescado no município de Rio Grande*. Retrieved June 28, 2017, from: repositorio.furg.br/.../Análise%20socioeconômica%20do%20perfil%20dos%20consu

Souza, F. S., Pontes, L. M., & Oliveira, F. N. S. (2007). *O marketing e a relação de satisfação com os clientes*. Retrieved May 18, 2017, from: happyslide.org/doc/106249/o-marketing-e-a-relação-de-satisfação-dos-clientes

Chapter 12

The Decisive Role of Intangible Assets in the Development of More Humane and Profitable Organizations in the Post-Pandemic Context

Janiele Queiroz Mendes Caroba
Caixa Econômica Federal, Brazil

ABSTRACT

This chapter aims to describe the role of intangible assets (trust, love, and well-being) in the development of organizations. After a first approach in which the authors point out distortions of the traditional organizational management models and politics in Brazil, they propose solutions adopted by several companies in construing of humanized models. Based on these successful experiences, they highlight several indicators that demonstrate the profitability of these organizations and their differentials in tackling the post-pandemic economic and social crisis.

INTRODUCTION

Large-scale economic development built on unlimited production growth has prioritized the accumulation of money in disregard of human and natural necessities.

The economic and social crisis that has been heightened since the beginning of the pandemic has caused the need to rethink this marginalization of life and health, and requires, also, in an even more urgent manner, shared interventions in the private and public organizations' environments.

In this global context of deep social changes, a scenario arises, in which truths previously proposed as pillars of political and economic development are giving way to new views, perceptions and meanings on what the role of leadership is.

DOI: 10.4018/978-1-7998-8925-0.ch012

Traditional autocratic leaders (whether in the private or public sectors) have been producing results which fall short of desired expectations. Such leadership tends to exponentially reveal insecurity, fear and distrust in a desirable future.

The complexity which emerges from chaos, we can envisage the dawn and strengthening of different models of management and cooperation which not only uncover organizations that are politically and socially more righteous, that are protagonists of new levels of evolution, but express amplified results, steered by sustainability, trust and prosperity.

Throughout this text, it is intended to encourage the reader(s) to enter a new and innovative environment, cantered on businesses that favour the human perspective through more meaningful, productive and clear-purpose work relationships that boil over the traditional measurements of results.

For this purpose, in this article is presented a more practical approach than an academic one, namely: i) methods of measuring results that exceed financial outcomes; ii) the necessary deconstructions to create more balanced, fair and prosperous environments; iii) humanized management models: recognition of the interdependence phenomenon; iv) the decisive role of intangible assets (trust, love and well-being) as factors that enhance organizational development and, v) the importance of social and organizational leadership in the post-pandemic context.

METHODS OF MEASURING RESULTS BEYOND FINANCIAL STATEMENTS

If you want to change reality – one powerful way is to change what you measure, how you measure it, and why you measure it. By measuring and making visible more of reality – we can then enter into a deeper dialogue with reality and thus cultivate greater forms of intimacy with it. To successfully navigate the complexity of the 21st. century we need non-reductive and integrative ways of measuring impact and value exchange between individuals and systems. (n.d.)[1].

The premise that success is based on the binominal profit and growth prevails in most organizations. According to Sisodia and Gelbs,

The dominant narrative about business remains focused narrowly on generating as much profit and growth as possible. This is done by generating as much revenue as possible, which means selling as many products as possible to as many people as possible at as high a price as you can get away with, whether people benefit from these products or not. Since profit equals revenue minus cost, traditional businesses also look to minimize costs. They do that by spending as little as possible on their people, squeezing their suppliers to the extent that they can, externalizing any costs that they can onto society and the environment, and minimizing the taxes they pay. (2019).

Similarly, Sean Esbjorn-Hargens, specialist in integrative theories for organizations and founder of the "MetaCapitals" theory, was inspired in the previous reflection]. According to this author, there are at least another nine other measurable capitals, namely: health, social, manufactured, intellectual, human, cultural, psychological, natural and spiritual, in addition to financial capital, which he defines as follows:

1. Health capital: the total expression of physical health and well-being;

2. Social capital: breadth and variety of social connections that a given group of people can initiate and foster;
3. Manufactured capital: total amount of assets and infrastructure of an organization;
4. Intellectual capital: amount of information, knowledge, understanding and wisdom;
5. Human capital: experiences that have meaning and human development to expand the group's inventory of know-how and skills;
6. Cultural capital: quality of internal and external relationships, in the process of sharing experiences and the group's sense of meaning;
7. Psychological capital: the individuals' ability to think, ponder and have access to multiple psychological resources;
8. Natural capital: the impact the organization has on the environment and the natural resources it currently uses or will need in the future;
9. Spiritual capital: ability to seek, find and access resources that bring meaning to accept the present context and activate its innermost potential.

To penetrate the concept of this new *façade* permits us to transport the traditional perspective of Financial Statements screens, or Gross Domestic Product numbers and analyse the direct influence these capitals exert on the prosperity of organizations.

Professor Sean's methodology is, thus, disruptive in the sense of presenting integrative measurement systems for the capitals indicated above.

The establishment of methodologies such as this expands the vision of management and allows for analysis of how to control each of these resources in the development and prosperity of enterprises.

Surprisingly, studies such as this (or any other alternate means of valuing an organization's input) have little or no importance in corporate governance and in Public Administration.

However, practice has demonstrated that enterprises that base their values on the abovementioned attain better results as they remain in the market for longer and more notably.

The Startup *Humanizada*, in Brazil, co-founded by Pedro Paro, sponsored the first survey on conscious businesses with a multi-stakeholder dimension, in 2019[2].

By using the Integral approach – the research method analyses companies in three distinct dimensions, such as: i) Results: enterprises with the best multi-stakeholder results in the country were researched; ii) Process and Procedures: for each company, the procedures that generate these results were evaluated and, iii) Source of inspiration: in addition to the procedures, dialogues were constructed to understand the founders' and principle leaders of these enterprises source of inspiration, thus establishing extremely rich and valuable composition of raw material. The remarkable results are produced is presented in translated version of the original document:

Most of the research already undertaken ends up being conducted from the point of view of a single group interested in the business (mono-stakeholders). This research considers a more diverse and comprehensive look (multi-stakeholders), collecting and checking information from different sources. The survey systematically considers the perception of value generated by the business through the lens of the founders, c-level, directors, managers, employees, suppliers, partners, customers, investors, environmental impact, partner social entities and society in general. It uses an integrally scientific methodology and a totally impartial approach – free of payments and conflicts of interest on the part of the companies – to choose the outstanding enterprises in the country.

The following measurement criteria were used:

Exceptional Results:

1. Companies that had regular results in the last five years were chosen. For this, different indicators that could promote a multi vision of the business were taken into consideration, distinguishing the perspective of different stakeholders. Examples of indicators were: employee satisfaction, customer satisfaction, response rate to customer complaints, quality of life, well-being, organizational culture, among many others.
2. Legitimacy: Companies with recognized reputation in the Brazilian market and which are hold prominent rankings and certifications in the country were the chosen ones. E.g.: System B, Great Place to Work (GPTW), and several others.
3. Conscious Procedures: Finally, the companies that showed they consistently adopted conscientious humane procedures in their business were chosen. A broad survey of each company's attitude and procedures were undertaken according to the four pillars of the Humanized Companies – higher purpose, orientation to stakeholders, leadership and a culture of consciousness.

After evaluating 1.115 of the biggest and best companies in Brazil (900.000 Consumer Evaluations; 136 thousand Employee Evaluations; 2.394 Stakeholders were heard; 152 Indicators were evaluated; 65 total hours of interviews were held; 12 hours of recording and 1.400 pages of case studies) it is possible to identify the key success factors of organizations that generate shard value and superior results.

They are on a journey of consciousness evolution. They radically created new rules. And they set a new paradigm for the business world. HCBRs (Humanized Companies in Brazil) do not envisage business as a money-making machine, but as a social fabric, with all its interdependencies, and willing to heal the pain of society and the planet.

When compared to the 500 largest companies in Brazil, when evaluating the accumulated profits, it becomes seen that the financial performance of the Humanized Companies in Brazil (HCBR) is six times higher in the long term.

In this original and commendable work, Pedro Paro, Mateus Gerolano and Rodrigo Caetano lead us to the surprising conclusion that employees and leaders of this type of company are 3.2 times more satisfied than the general group of others who do not adopt this type of management; their clients are 3.4. times more engaged with the brand, its Return on Equity (ROE) is 2.2. times higher in the long term and the net margin in the medium and long term is 2.5 times higher.

We foresee that projects like this are seeds for these assessment methods to be disseminated and, in the near future, institutionalized in the majority of organizations.

THE REQUIRED DECONSTRUCTIONS TO ENHANCE ORGANIZATIONAL DEVELOPMENT

"Are we free? Are we aware? (...).

If we are not aware, we are not free. We have a social structure that induces trauma in many people, therefore, it induces diverting and addictive behaviour. And these internal tendencies line up with the external form of society. So, everything seems normal and perfectly natural.

Fundamentally, the message is that we create the world with our minds. If I have the vision that the world is a horrible place, I will live in a world where I have to be aggressive, suspicious, competitive and make myself as big as possible so as not to be devoured. I have to be ambitious and shrewd because this is the world I live in. And these are the people our society rewards with power." – Excerpt from the film, **The Wisdom of Trauma**. *Dr. Gabor Maté.*

There re many unseen problems that ravage our institutions and organizations. Despite the existence of a great deal of information material on irresponsibility in public administration and a considerable number of lawsuits that challenge working conditions, there are structural issues in the public and private spheres that have not yet been addressed.

Socio-emotional distortions in leaders of some enterprises have devastated the lives and dignity of countless laborers, whose motivation is maimed due to excessive working hours, exacerbated control, lack of autonomy and recognition. Stuck within the normality narrative, countless situations of bullying are experienced daily, increasing of ailments at work[i].

Deafened by discourses that understand financial capital as core objective, the basis of organizations is not made audible at its principal level of necessities. With reactive planning, focus on short-term tasks, excessive command and lack of autonomy, there is no room for establishing trustworthy and essential relationships.

To deconstruct models that are so deeply rooted in our society, it is necessary there be collective planning directed at privileging sensitivity, reliability and purpose in a diverse, collaborative and innovative environment.

It is necessary to cultivate a narrative that favours health, social, human, cultural, psychological and spiritual capital, besides the financial and manufactured capital.

The founders of "Evolutionary Organizations", Laloux's object of study,

... use a different metaphor for work environments they aim to create. Surprisingly frequently, they talk about their organizations as living organisms or systems. Life, with all its evolutionary wisdom, organizes ecosystems in an incredibly beautiful way, always evolving towards completeness, intricacy and awareness. In nature, changes occur everywhere and continually, in self-organized impulses emanating from every cell and organism, without the need there be a central command and control to give orders or pull levers. (2017, p.56).

Thus, if organizations and institutions are considered as living systems, it is necessary to look at each cell of this very complex and independent system.

It may sound exceedingly optimistic, but we believe it is possible to reduce the unnecessary hurt caused by the way organizations are managed and give way to places of growth and innovation.

To heal the "cellular systems" of organizations it is necessary to deconstruct fear-based leadership, exponential exploitation of life and work and make room for organizations that are *a place of healing for their employees and their families, a source of healing for customers, communities and ecosystems and a healing force in society, helping to alleviate cultural, economic and political disparities.* (Sisodia and Gelb, 2020, p.82).

HUMANIZED MANAGEMENT MODELS: UNDERSTANDING THE PHENOMENON OF INTERDEPENDENCE

We have developed speed, but we shut ourselves in it; machinery that gives abundance has left us in want. Our knowledge has made us cynical, our cleverness hard and unkind. We think too much and feel too little. More than machinery we need humanity, more than cleverness we need kindness and gentleness[4].

In this section of the chapter the characteristics of "Evolutionary Organizations" are deepened, from the result of Laloux's (2017) research and Humanized companies, classified based on Pedro Paro's academic work. Which are his assumptions? How do they differ? Are they real, or utopian?

The basic assumptions for "Evolutionary Organizations" are:

- Self-management: relationships between employees are built on trust, openness and self-responsibility. Organized via self-managed teams, with decentralized decision making;
- Integrity: develop a consistent set of practices that allow for the employees to recover their innermost selves, in a safe environment in which everyone is the same in worth;
- Evolutionary Purpose: this means that the organization is a system with a soul of its own, energy, identity, creative potential and sense of direction. Individual and organizational purposes go hand in hand.

Such organizations differ due to their innovative perspective on financial results. As Laloux explains, "*Profit is necessary and investors deserve a fair return, but the objective is purpose, not profit. Several of the organizational founders used the same metaphor: profit is like the air we breathe. We need air to live, but we don't live to breathe.*" (2017, p.195).

In his research, the former McKinsey & Company partner quotes enterprises with up to 40.000 employees that operate under these assumptions and present considerable results. They are organizations in the energy, healthcare, technology, clothing and metallurgical sectors[5].

In Brazil there is a similar disruptive study, undertaken by the abovementioned start up, *Humanizada*, which is dedicated to other ways of measuring results. These are companies that

... act in a powerfully positive manner that people admire, value and even love them. These countries make the world a better place because of the way they do business – and the world retorts. (...) These companies, with the country's best results are driven by passion and purpose, not money. They have a superior return on equity precisely because they help all stakeholders, employees, customers, suppliers, investors, partners, communities and society to prosper[6].

Both Frederic Laloux's "evolutionary organization and Pedro Paro's "*Humanizadas*" (Humanized) ones change challenges commonly encountered in traditional organizations as follows:

Additionally, what makes the new organizational models different is the recognition of the interdependence of the entire chain of participation in the production process, which has direct implications on the relationship between employees, customers, suppliers, investors, partners and society, enhancing the intangible assets that make successful and socially responsible companies.

Table 1.

Traditional Organizations	"Evolutionary"/"Humanized" Organizations
Domineering leadership.	Constructive and supporting leaders.
Excessive investment in rules and control.	Trusting relationships built on clear agreements.
Limited information and communication problems.	Clear communication at all levels of the organization.
High risk of failure and lack of support for innovation.	Adaptability, will tolerance to error and learning as a source of innovation.
Centralized decision structures, concentration of power.	Decentralized and cooperative hierarchical models.

THE DECISIVE ROLE OF INTANGIBLE ASSETS (TRUST, LOVE AND WELL-BEING) AS FACTORS FOR ENHANCING ORGANIZATIONAL DEVELOPMENT

"The most exciting breakthroughs of the 21st. century will not occur because of technology but because of an expanding concept of what it means to be human." John Naisbitt.

In the previous sections of this chapter capital that overflow into the financial issue is described, considering the deconstructions that will give rise to more prosperous work places in the intellectual, social, emotional, cultural and natural perspectives with examples of organizations that privilege humanized models and structures.

Now, the attention turns to the intangible assets that serve as solutions, effective alchemies for helping elevate organizations to higher levels of management and results, so that the future of management in Brazil is built not on the Shortcomings presented in the previous section of this chapter, but on small unexplored powers.

According to Zanini and Migueles,

intangible liabilities (everything that drains time, effort and intelligence) we will be able to discover intangible assets (everything that increases the capacity to transform time resources, capacity and human intelligence) into concrete, measurable and perceptible results for customers (via the perceived value of the product or service that affects the price and converts into reputation for the brand) and for society. (2021, p.47)

We will not undertake an in-depth analysis of the concepts contained in accounting standards[7], we will, however, guide ourselves by the logic presented by Zanini and Migueles to examine assets that we consider essential to maximize human capacity and intelligence and to influence the development and performance of organizations. They are: trust, love and well-being.

TRUST

Migueles, quoting Zanini, presents us with the following definitions of the asset "trust":

Mayer, Davis and Schoorman (1995) define trust as the willingness of an individual to place themselves in a vulnerable position in relation to another individual or group of individuals. The propensity to trust is therefore a measure of the property to accept risks in a relationship. According to Zanini (2016), trust reduces the perception of risk derived from the interaction, increasing the performance of organizations as a result of reciprocity and the quality of the relationship between those involved. (2021, p.66).

In the excellent line of argument presented by Migueles, in order to understand this important asset, it is necessary to investigate its absence. That is, how organizations in which one trusts is weaker or non-existent operate.

For the author, such absence excludes the ability to deal with differences and transform them into something new and complementary. These organizational environments become dominated by static individual ideas and highly resistant to change and innovation.

A consequence of trust is psychological safety, a statistically significant asset and positively related to performance[8]. It is accepted as the belief shared by the group that there is safety in taking interpersonal risks.

In this sense, criticism, mockery and rejection are ways to undermine self-confidence in an organization and prevent simple every-day behaviours such as asking for help, making mistakes and presenting new ideas, which leads to the nurturing of feelings of frustration and that the individual's efforts are useless.

Thus, a direct relationship between trust and commitment is established. As employees are frustrated in their ability to contribute, their collaborative potential is less, thus reducing organizational performance on an aggregate scale.

For this asset to be elevated to its adequate level in organizational spheres, there needs to be a greater and closer connection between dialogue and practices, by privileging the quality of interactions, based on the assumption that all people are of equal worth and therefore, have equal rights to present their points of view for the benefit of the organization, without being subject to judgement or constraint.

The conception of a safe environment for meaningful exchange of knowledge and experiences seems the perfect scenario to strengthen the development of collaboration at exponential levels, not only in organizations, but also in political and social relations.

LOVE

To talk about love in ay project that intends to elevate it as a management element is ludicrously challenging. There is a great associative charge involving the concept of the topic, reducing it to interpersonal contexts.

Although science, philosophy and religion present us with different dimensions and meanings, there are very few references that relate it, at least nominally, tom organizational scenarios.

But there is much to be learned from analysing this powerful institutionally driving asset. In Grün *et al.*, (2019), a very consistent definition of love is stated:

This concept encompasses emotions and feelings that make it possible to feel each other and even each other living being not as an object, but as a subject in itself and thus build, on that basis, cooperative relationships and evolutionary processes that are filled with trust. (2019, p.102).

This definition allows us to extract the essence of the asset, which is to appreciate the entire production chain (employees, consumers, suppliers and stakeholders) as living and individualized beings.

In the book **The Healing Organizations** (2020), Sisodia and Gelb explain that:

"The dual systems of democracy and capitalism were meant to generate greater opportunities for everyone to experience life, freedom, prosperity and happiness. When these systems act out of love, which is their function, the result is inclusion, abundance, creativity, joy and fulfilment for all. When these systems are dominated by fear, the result is oppression of minorities, attempts to obstruct the right to vote, vilification of immigrants, greed, exploitation and growing disparity between winners and losers. (2020, p.47).

And, if by practicing love in the organization leads to abundance, joy, creativity and fulfilment, why do we one continues to privilege organizational and institutional systems that cause us to feel fear? For this reason, and notwithstanding the academic challenges of daring to raise love to the status of a business asset, it is proposed to focus on the theme, as a contribution to promoting reflections in the management scenario in Brazil.

In the illustrative transcription of Emotions and language in education and politics (1998), Maturana presents that love is a catalyst for more fruitful professional relationships, as opposed to strictly hierarchical relationships:

I would say that in living together within a human community, there are times when power relations must be accepted, but these relations are not social relations. We know that all relationships within a human community are commonly called social. What I say is that different emotions are involved in relationships, and that these give them different characteristics that are obscured or denied when they are not recognized. So there are those that have to do with our biological history, like love, which is the realm of mutual acceptance. Every time we talk about the social in everyday life, we make reference to this emotion. Saying "Here you don't socialize, here you work" means to say that socializing and working are different activities, and that they are different because they happen under different emotions. So when you say "Work relationships are social relationships", relationships that are impossible to be joined together if we consider the emotions involved. I don't want to do this because different emotions are domains of different actions, and the relationships that are established in them lead to different ways of acting. In other words, I want to separate human relationships according to the emotions on which they are based, because it is the emotion that defines them. If we do not do this, I assert, we cannot understand human communities, because we do not see that they are constituted as networks of different types of systems that must not be confused because they imply different actions. And if we don't understand human communities, we can barely understand the individuals who carry them out and who, like us, live at the intersection of many systems at the same time. (1998, p. 87)

Understanding that organizations are relational phenomena makes room for dedicating time and energy to nurture relationships and encourage environments of collaboration, trust, empathy and creativity.

Continuing the work, concrete situations are presented, taken from the Report "Emerging Business Practices in Response to the Covid-19 Crisis" (2020), available at https://humanizadas.com/praticas-emergentes-dos-negocios-em-resposta-a-crise-do-covid-19/ practices that endorseds this abovementioned asset in the post-pandemic context are exemplified.

Enterprises such as Natura & Co and Danone announced the suspension of dismissal procedures of their employees in the first period of the pandemic. TetraPak has offered a Child Care program for their employees who need to continue working away from their homes, and do not have any other means for their children to be taken care of.

Group Boticário intensified the production of 70% liquid alcohol dispensers and soap to be donated to people who are in a socially vulnerable situation and who are being aided in government and public health networks. In all, 2016 tonnes of products will also be donated to employees.

Cielo published a report mapping the impact that this health crisis will have on Brazilian retail, with the aim of helping businesses in Brazil. By recognizing the value of Brazilian businesses, the company evokes the existence of this referred to asset, through its main outcome, which is generosity.

All these examples show us that organizational cultures based on love are spaces in which mutual acceptance and understanding, cooperation and creativity, tenderness and freedom for all individuals who are directly or indirectly related with the organization occurs.

WELL-BEING

According to the World Health Organization (WHO), mental health is "*a state of well-being in which the individual realizes his or her own abilities, can cope with the normal stresses of life, can work productively and fruitfully, and is able to make a contribution to his or her community*" (2004, p.12).

Likewise, it encompasses a context that allows for the fulfilment of individual skills and characteristics, opening the way for there to be relationships of respect and trust, which allow for coping with any form of suffering and labour fatigue.

Distortions in mental health within the scope of work organizations can cause obstructions in the relationship between the employee and work, with short, medium and long-term effects for the individual (loss of purpose, disconnection and hopelessness) and collectively (impact on the business's results).

Dejours, in his **The Madness of Work**: Labour Psychopathology Study (2000), deals with predatory work patterns and their degrading consequences on the mental composition of employees, generating obstructions in relationships between man and work, occupational and psychosocial diseases.

In the opposite sense, Viegas (2015), in his study, **Social Psychology of Work and Education** presents viewpoints based on recent Spanish literature, quoting Blanch and Cantera (2008), in which he points out that, by comparing "engagement" to that state of illness (Burnout) it is:

... a positive mental state, of accomplishment, related to work, which is characterized as vigour, dedication and absorption. Vigour ... carries high levels of dynamism and resilience and this is the opposite of exhaustion. Dedication ... conveys high involvement, motivation and the assumption of what work entails as it being a source of meaning and challenge, which represents the opposite of scepticism. And Resilience ... is complemented with elevated doses of concentration on work and satisfaction in doing it, thus representing the opposite of lack of accomplishment and work efficiency (2015, p.86). (Author's translation)

The study of this topic does not seem to attract institutional support from companies, despite the alarming numbers (see previous note). It is a by-product of the Human Resources area, with little or no cultural reverberation.

Well-being is an asset useful not only for development, but also for the firms' sustainability. It is an unavoidable tendency, especially when most companies will have their employees working from home, in the post-pandemic scenario.

If, before the pandemic, information from the WHO already showed Brazil as having the highest number of people suffering from anxiety in the world, currently this situation has increased exponentially.

According to a survey led by Workana, 43% of employees felt some symptom of mental damage during the pandemic. Among the people surveyed, 24% felt it difficult to concentrate, 13,2% felt anxiety, 5,8% felt lonely and 0,8% were either depressed or felt claustrophobic[9].

So, an expansion movement commences, besides the successful cases mentioned throughout the text of this chapter. Brazilian companies invest in positions such as: Director of Happiness (Chief Happiness Officer), Director of Purpose, Director of Mental Health, Head of Diversity and Inclusion.

In an interview to the **Exam** magazine, Mariana Holanda, Director of Mental Health at AMBEV (a Brazilian brewing company), says that the company seeks to invest in means to deal with emotional instability at work and also to provide a repertoire regarding mental health:

"It's a battle to end stigma and we need to surpass it. Provide repertoire so that they understand what it's like to experience situations of anxiety, depression or Burnout. And, to deal with it is as important to health as is treating a cold or a broken leg", and she states also that, "We thought that resilience was the power to make an effort, to give that something extra. The more resilient, the more acknowledged a person is. The greater the effort, the greater the recognition. And that goes against our nature when we think about biological aspects. When we talk about resilience, it's not just about the effort, but the recovery time for a person's brain. The brain is our main muscle and we just won't get used to seeing it that way. In this world, which is super volatile and surrounded by uncertainties, the person needs to be minimally safe. When the situation gets difficult and the person is not well, they don't deliver, they just seize-up. In addition, companies are now entering into another phase. Nowadays, companies are being requested to have social participation. To enter into the mental health topic is also about getting into the social participation one. We need to understand how it is we can collaborate to have healthier people[10]".

Thus, to talk about well-being in a broad perspective is to shed light to the individual as a propellant of collective strength. It is looking on self-knowledge as a performance factor, empathy as an essential leadership skill, and human development as a permanent agenda for organizations.

THE IMPORTANCE OF SOCIAL AND ORGANIZATIONAL LEADERSHIP IN THE POST-PANDEMIC CONTEXT

"Evolution is a formidable process that brings forth unfathomable beauty and complexity not through a grand design, but by means of relentless, small-scale, parallel experimentation. It is not a process imposed by the boss on his subordinates. Everyone is summoned and needed to contribute to the whole. Each living entity in the ecosystem of life – each cell, each conscious being – perceives its environment, comes into harmony with others and explores new possibilities." (Frederic Laloux in: **Reinventing Organizations**. *2014).*

Finally, the post-pandemic context is explained as a milestone for the construction of the changes presented, replacing the reactive concept with a self-responsible view of the community.

The damage generated on the world stage allows us to realize that everyone is part of a global community, equated by the same vital needs, interdependent and connected.

Systems are needed that to reveal individual potentials for the benefit of the whole. Foucault (1979) theorizes that power is not found in an institution, but in the foundations of the social fabric:

It is about (...) seizing power at its extremities, in its ultimate ramifications (...) seizing power in its more regional and local forms and institutions, especially at the point in which it exceeds the rule of law that organize and restrict it (...). In other words, seizing power at its extremity less and less justifies exerting it. (1979, p.182)

The task of leaders, in this sense, is to give voice to the "extremities", creating very active spaces of cooperation, in which everyone can benefit from. Tânia Zapata, a Sociologist, who is an associate of the Institute of Assistance for Human Development (IADH), describes this mission with great affection.

"We must galvanize society and mobilize it. Enthusiasm combined with an intelligent will and action, and a creative richness of solid actions that alter the current reality. It is the Neolithic revolution of the Third Millennium. From the informational economy and the knowledge society. From the new understanding of the holistic, systemic and complex view to the apprehension of sociological and anthropological phenomena. In search of building sustainable human development." (Zapata, 2011)

These leaders who are present in multiple scenarios, be it in the political, community or organizational domains (already widely discussed), extract the fullness of the intangible assets mentioned in previous moments in this chapter.

The information reveals that the models are not just theories, much less utopian. These are real experiences in Brazil and in the world.

More than paradigms of the power of love, trust and well-being, they bare living demonstrations of the driving force of the awakening of the individual consciousness in the collective sphere. In these, power surfaces autonomously, guided towards clear purposes, with wide participation of those involved.

A model extracted directly from the Public Administration shows how possible and desirable an institution based on an evolutionary purpose is. The highlight is the city of Santa Rita, in Sapucaí, State of Minas Gerais, under Mayor Wander Chaves, who has an integrated, futuristic and loving vision of local management. Wander Chaves has developed a systematic assembly between knowledge, production and public authorities, with a project called *Cidade Criativa, Cidade Feliz* (*Creative City, Happy City*).

This re-reading of the role of Public Administration made Santa Rita do Sapucaí the stage form grandiose management experiences, with local productions recognized worldwide.

With a well-founded vison of the future and investment in education, for more than 40 years Vale da Eletrônica has been firm in its firm purpose to increasingly implement a long-term government plan to obtain equally long-lasting results that impact and bring prosperity to several generations, becoming an example of growth and innovation in Brazil[11].

Thus, the survival capacity of an institution or organization is increasingly linked to the totality of established cooperation relationships. There is no other way to offer longevity than one that preserves its precious intangible assets.

CONCLUSION

"Our current difficulties do not consist of the fact that we do not have enough knowledge or technical skills: our present difficulties stem from a lack of sensitivity (...), they are a consequence of the loss we suffer because we are forcibly inserted in the discourses of conquest, power, control over life and nature that decisively determine our patriarchal culture." Humberto Maturana.

It is not intended to exhaust the topic, just to compile stories about a topic still in development. An invitation to study and deepen issues so dear to managers, workers, politicians and citizens.

Considering new methods of measuring results, investing energy in creating more balanced, fair and prosperous environments and giving life to management spaces that are increasingly humanized, can influence not only employees and steakholders [stakeholders], but the entire social field.

In the scarcity scenario produced by the pandemic, with bleak economic forecasts, there is much to learn from the leaders presented in the text.

Current change initiatives need to be aligned with the economic, social and environmental reality that the pandemic has opened up. By exploring the power of individual and collective entrepreneurship to co-create new solutions, space is opened up for combating structural problems such as poverty, education and a low level of development.

New communication cultures and new economic models emerge outside the academic context to permeate the cruel reality that devastates Brazil and the world.

It is possible to build new relationships in organizations. The first steps start from accepting the need for major economic, social and cultural changes, through examples that surpass the limiting ideology of current leadership and management.

It is not intended to create magic formulas, but to address fundamental issues for leaders. The sustainability of the productive force depends on the energy spent on building relationships based on trust, love and well-being. These assets generate produce an intrinsic motivation that generates extraordinary results.

Views caused by losses suffered in these last 15 months of the pandemic cannot be forgotten. Rethinking public management, health, environment, interdependence of the human species and self-responsibility are every citizen's obligation.

Using the abundant assets in each organization would, in the logic of Mullainathan and Shafir (2020), would become "scarcity-proof our environment" (2020). How about starting by rethinking the role of each individual in relation to this complex and interconnected ecosystem? With an image of self-responsibility, society can seek directions for the full realization of intangible assets. There is still a lot to do. However, you must get started!

REFERENCES

Chaplin, C. (n.d.). *The Final Speech from The Great Dictator*. Available: https://www.charliechaplin.com/en/articles/29-the-final-speech-from-the-great-dictator-

Dejours, C. (2000). A Loucura do Trabalho: Estudo de psicopatologia do trabalho (5 ed.). São Paulo: Cortez.

Empresas que curam. (2020). Rio de Janeiro: Alta Books.

Focault. (1979). Microfísica do Poder. Organização e tradução de Roberto Machado. Rio de Janeiro: Edições Graal.

Grün, A., Hüther, G., & Hosang, M. (2019). Amar é a única revolução – A força transformadora do amor a partir das ciências, filosofia e da religião. Petrópolis, RJ: Vozes.

Laloux, F. (2017). Reinventando as Organizações. Curitiba: Voo.

Mullainathan. (2020). *Escassez – Uma nova forma de pensar a falta de recursos na vida das pessoas e nas organizações*. Best Business.

Sisodia, R., & Gelb, M. (2019). *Creating a New Myth for Business – The Healing Organization*. Mindful Leader. Available: https://www.mindfulleader.org/blog/30404-creating-a-new-myth-for-business-the

Viegas, M. F. (2015). Psicologia Social do Trabalho e Educação: uma discussão a partir da literatura espanhola recente, em Psicologia Social e Trabalho: perspectivas críticas. Florianópolis: ABRAPSO Editora: Edições do Bosque CFH/UFSC.

World Health Organization. (2004). *Promoting mental health: concepts, emerging evidence, practice* (Summary Report). Geneva: World Health Organization. Available: https://www.who.int/mental_health/evidence/en/promoting_mhh.pdf

Zanini, T., & Miguels, C. (Eds.). (2021). *O elo perdido: cultura, produtividade e coletividade*. FGV Editora.

Zapata, T. (n.d.). *Desenvolvimento Humano*. Disponível em: http://www.iadh.org.br/wp-content/uploads/2011/08/Desenvolvimento-humano-Tania-Zapata.pdf

ENDNOTES

1. Esbjorn-Hargens, Sean. https://www.metaintegral.com/
2. Available: https://humanizadas.com/
3. We have translated from: https://docplayer.com.br/196470381-Humanizadas-resultados-gerais-da-pesquisa-1a-edicao-powered-by.html
4. Chaplin, Charles. *Final speech* from The Great Dictator, *In*: https://www.charliechaplin.com/en/articles/29-the-final-speech-from-the-great-dictator- (2nd. to the 5th. lines of the second paragraph).
5. Organizations included in the survey: AES (Energy sector); BSP/Origin (IT Consulting); Buurtzorg (Health Care); ESBZ (Elementary Education); FAVI (Metallurgy); Heiligennfeld (Mental Health

Hospital); Holacracy (Operational Organizational Model); Morning Star (Food Processing); Patagonia (Clothing); RHD (Humanitarian Services); Sounds True (Media) and Sun Hydraulics (Hydraulic components).

6 As can be read in Relatório 1ª Edição Pesquisa Empresas Humanizadas, 2019 (Report 1st. Edition *Humanizadas* Companies Research, 2019). *In*: https://humanizadas.com/relatorio-1-edicao-pesquisa-empresas-humanizadas/

7 According to the Accounting Pronouncements Committee, in Pronouncement nº 4 (R1), an intangible asset is an identifiable non-monetary asset without physical substance.

8 *Op cit.*, Cultural variables and organizational performance: a journey in search of the relationship between variables.

9 https://exame.com/carreira/estes-graficos-mostram-como-a-saude-mental-virou-prioridade-na-pandemia/

10 https://exame.com/carreira/a-aposta-da-ambev-para-o-futuro-a-nova-diretora-de-saude-mental/

11 https://inovecapacitacao.com.br/exemplo-de-gestao-publica-e-visao-de-futuro-com-o-vale-da-eletronica-brasileiro/

i On the subject, a revealing article by Professors Ricardo Antunes and Luci Praum, in **A** sociedade dos adoecimentos no trabalho (The Society of illnesses at work), to which, as Barreto points out, "Everyone is subjected to" (2013, p.18). Even though most of the times it is directed to a specific employee, harassment affects the whole group. As it is a management tool, its practice, despite being personified on a manager, supervisor or any other individual whose power relation can trigger it, it is aligned with the set of guidelines that ordain collective work at the enterprise (Barreto, 2013; Heloani, 2013; Gaulejac, 2007). Such type of procedures are management tools aimed at guaranteeing, through institutionalized pressure, both the constant increase in productivity and the isolation and exclusion of those who represent 'barriers' to its plain achievement.

Chapter 13
Poverty Plus Pandemic Equal to Lethal Epidemics in Mexico

Amada Hidalgo Gallardo
Universidad Autónoma del Estado de Hidalgo, Mexico

Ruth L. Hidalgo
Universidad Autónoma del Estado de Hidalgo, Mexico

Blanca Josefina García Hernández
Universidad Autónoma del Estado de Hidalgo, Mexico

Eleazar Villegas González
Universidad Autónoma del Estado de Hidalgo, Mexico

Sofía Elizabeth Ávila Hidalgo
SHCP Gobierno de México, Mexico

ABSTRACT

For Mexican society it is relevant to know the prospects of well-being in an environment of instability and social insecurity; therefore, this research has the purpose of publicizing the health, economic, and social situation from COVID-19 in Mexico. The work has a qualitative, analytical, and descriptive research design considering current information from the Bank of Mexico with recent indicators of economic activity, The National Institute of Statistics and Geography (INEGI) with data on occupation and employment, as well as the National Council for the Evaluation of Social Development Policy (CONEVAL) regarding the consequences of poverty in Mexican society and other documents that refer to the problem, all this analysis in order to form an idea of the near future of Mexicans. Currently, there is an increase in poverty and inequality resulting from the mismanagement of government policies and the lack of proposals to improve the social sector.

DOI: 10.4018/978-1-7998-8925-0.ch013

INTRODUCTION

Mexico is a country that stands out for its natural wealth and for a multicultural society derived from a vast territory and population that currently amounts to 126 million inhabitants; which has constituted a social diversity that has been one of the paradigms for Mexican governments. The problems faced by each government are; poverty, extreme poverty, inequality, corruption, insecurity, among others.

To study poverty it is necessary to interlock a whole multifactorial analysis since the subject is chained to other circumstances that society lives; aspects such as the lack of employment, education, opportunities and both political and economic aspects have caused this sector to be divided among the poor themselves, that is to say it is no longer only poverty but now encompasses extreme poverty that generates greater inequality.

The National Development Plan (PND 2018-2024) of the current President Lopez Obrador is based on a government policy in support of the poor, offering new social programs with which real opportunities are sought for people disabled in the labor field and in education mainly, also with the firm purpose of reviewing economic and development policies in which welfare actions can be generated for this sector.

According to these objectives, the beginning of this six-year term generated great expectations in Mexican society, however, we never thought about the calamities that sometimes nature or globalization takes us by surprise, in this peculiar case, two years into management faced the COVID-19 pandemic that has brought global disasters mainly health and economic as well as confinement. If it has been a nightmare for developed countries to face this condition, the more so for underdeveloped countries such as Mexico with such a large population and deep-rooted problems of poverty; turning or rethinking public policies to combat the pandemic has been a complication for the government and Mexican society.

That is why this analysis is focused on making a journey in recent years of the behavior that poverty has had in Mexico, taking into account relevant information from bodies such as INEGI and CONEVAL who work reliable statistical data as well as information that can help to propose recommendations on this controversial area in Mexico.

DEVELOPMENT OF THE THEME

1. The trajectory of poverty and inequality in Mexico in the period 2015-2019

Poverty and inequality in Mexico date back to colonial times, however the development and economic growth of the country has been involved since the last century when government policies focus on addressing poverty.

López E, (2011), Ward mentions that, "*neither the rapid economic growth, between 1940 and 1970, nor the increase in oil production (since the late 70s) modified income inequalities, although both factors generated changes in economic activity.*"

It is from the decade of the 70's that the creation of relevant anti-poverty programs such as: Public Investment Program for Rural Development (PIDER), General Coordination of the National Plan of Depressed and Marginalized Areas (COPLAMAR), Mexican Food System (SAM), all of them with the purpose of creating proposals in support of society that was already divided into rural and urban, the poor amounted to approximately 8 million inhabitants.

These programs did not meet the objective, derived from the lack of a strategic plan for the administration of resources, coupled with the fact that in this decade the import substitution model was implemented, which housed social policy to economic policy. This structure caused shared development, in addition to economic depressions, devaluations and fall in oil prices, leading to the debt crisis and a severe economic recession, events that placed social policy in the background.

For the above, in the decade of the 80's, the National Solidarity Program (PRONASOL), again with the aim of supporting the most disadvantaged only that, in this decade is already counted not only the simple poor but already exist the poor in extreme poverty. The objectives of the program were: a) to channel the benefits directly to the population and b) to give the population the opportunity to make decisions on the benefits to be granted.

However, the evaluation of the programmed showed negative data to minimize the poverty rate on the contrary, contributed to the variable of inequality, in addition to the fact that, the problems of democratization and the interests of society were accentuated. The results of this policy increased the population in poverty, it means, this decade begins with approximately 15 million inhabitants in extreme poverty and ends with approximately 18 million inhabitants in this condition.

For the decade of the 90's the government policy launches, in 1996, the Education, Health and Food Program (PROGRESA), with greater economic resources and with the aim of providing benefits to the population in extreme poverty, despite this, the decade ends with an indicator of 26 million inhabitants in extreme poverty. At this time, Mexico lived an event of opening markets via economic liberalization, shown under its participation in the signing of International Treaties, which implied great challenges in the markets and in the process of globalization. For the country it meant a great opportunity to the external commercialization of goods and services, however, internally, globalization did not bring benefits since it showed greater inequality, that is to say social policy did not apply to the needs of Mexicans nor did it reduce poverty indicators; this is how Mexico faces the new millennium with approx. 40 million people in extreme poverty.

Through this tour of the situation in Mexico in the last century with regard to alleviating poverty, it can be referred that the strategies considered in each program have not been the most successful, since poverty is a multidimensional symptom. The poverty is not only attended con economic resources, but, generating in the poor other ways of orbiteer their well-being considering that people are in a precarious situation that lacks skills and/or opportunities, so, the programs must also offer other alternatives that help them to overcome. In view of this circumstance, in 2003 the General Law on Social Development was created, a broader concept that seeks to institutionalize itself in order to deal with the problem.

In López E, (2011) mentions the application of a questionnaire prepared by the Secretariat of Social Development (SEDESOL) in 2003 named "What the poor say" considering rural and urban areas in the north, center and south of the country in 45 municipalities of 29 states. In general, the results of this survey indicate that poor people require sources of well-paid employment; they no longer accept subsidies or gifts because that does not give them the opportunity to progress.

This means that, the economic does not save at all, in order to have a well-paid salary, people must be offered opportunities, that is, education, quality public health, decent housing, adequate food, non-discrimination; to comment on the main ones, these items are very direct in the answers of this questionnaire; as can be seen they are a series of links united to achieve the well-being of the population in poverty, it is a multifactorial aspect that must be considered in governance and public policies.

The survey also confirmed that there was no change in poverty, despite government programs, the rate of extreme poverty continued to rise. According to (CONEVAL), the behavior of poverty from 2008 to 2014 is as follows:

So if we take into account the one applied by SEDESOL "what the poor say" and relates tables 1 and 2, it is observed that the increase in poor inhabitants is approximately 3 million in every two years. Likewise that social security is the sector with a high percentage of non-care, followed by health services, food and educational lag and in the end housing is outlined.

On the other hand, it is reflected that the increase of inhabitants in poverty at the beginning of the year was approximately 40 million people in 2014 and has the data of 55.3 million an increase of 15.3 million; this makes a percentage of 46.19% according to the population of 2014 being 119,713,204 million inhabitants.

In spite of the Law and programs established to curb poverty, in its wake it will acquire new areas such as: corruption, the democratic process and representativeness of the city, insecurity and homelessness.

It can therefore be expressed that social policy and economic policy go hand in hand, between a series of obstacles that are political groups, accumulation and distribution of wealth and the process

Table 1. Multifactorial Poverty in Mexico 2008-2014

Concept	**Indicators (percentage in M of people)**			
	2008	**2010**	**2012**	**2014**
Poverty	44.4	46.01	45.5	46.2
Social Deprivation				
Educational Lag	21.9	20.7	19.2	18.7
Health Services	38.4	29.2	21.5	18.2
Social security	65.0	60.7	61.2	58.15
Housing	17.7	13.2	13.6	12.3
Feeding	21.7	24.8	23.3	23.4
Welfare				
Population with income below the extreme poverty line by income	16.8	19.4	20.0	20.6
Population with income below the income poverty line	49.0	52.0	51.6	53.2

Source: Own elaboration with information from CONEVAL – Poverty measurement Mexico Series 2008-2018

Table 2. Population in Mexico 2008-2014

Period	**No. of people**	**Increase in M-hb., in poverty related to data of 40 M at the beginning of the millennium.**	
2008	111, 299,015	49,416,762	+ 9,5 M
2010	114,255, 555	52,568,980	+12,5 M
2012	117,053,750	53,259,456	+13,3 M
2014	119,713,204	55,307,500	+15,3 M

Source: Own elaboration with data from INEGI indicators https://www.inegi.org.mx/app/indicadores/#tabMCcollapse-Indicadores

of the international economy; this means that as the country's general economic policy moves, social stability and poverty change.

Within a scheme of parallel evolution of poverty and growth, Mexico has been conceptualized as a producer country then underdeveloped and currently emerging in contrast to the social has moved into: a) poverty b) extreme poverty c) inequality d) insecurity e) corruption and f) lacking capacities and opportunities; this analogy reflects the disparity in both directions.

Social welfare has been hit by general instability by collaborating with a charitable system for sectors holding economic power. However, in parallel the Law of Social Development has been reformed in order to combat the negative items that make poverty grow. Similarly to the last reform of said Law in 2018 are considered issues such as: transparency; gender; the right to decent and decent housing; healthy environment; work; social security; non-discrimination; to benefit from social programs and the liaison of federal, state and municipal governments to exercise public resources honestly; opportunity; transparency and fairness, finally the popular denunciation of any fact, act or omission that threatens the exercise of established rights

This Law also covers the Intersecretarial Commission for Social Development, which is entrusted with the task of specifying strategies linked to the National Health Development Policy and which works in conjunction with Secretaries of State related to anti-poverty. Among the responsibilities of this omission are: a) planning and execution of regional, state and municipal policies and programs, b) proposing items and amounts of social spending, as well as actions and investments, c) mechanisms for financing and distribution of federal resources, d) analyzing and proposing alternative financing schemes, e) commenting on the budgets of the agencies, f) exchange of experiences in the field of development and overcoming poverty, g) revision of the regulatory framework, h) training actions for public servants, i) thematic and regional working groups and rafter activities deemed necessary for the well functioning of the national system.

On the other hand, it is necessary to promote the participation of citizens and organizations to monitor, operate and evaluate actions in government programs as well as to carry out studies and investigations and carryout audits.

All this proposed law has been applied by the bodies involved in governance, contemplating constant measurement both in operation and in social welfare. However, not only the country within the internal evaluations but we are observed by international organizations, in such a way that the application of policies that report indicators favorable to eradicating poverty is appreciated. That is why the Organization for Economic Cooperation and Development (OECD) of which we are members, makes its evaluation of the political reforms in Mexico during the period 2014-2019 (Annex 1) reporting its perception on the reform actions.

According to the analysis carried out by the OECD, it corresponds practically to the presidential term of Enrique Peña Nieto who was governing the country from 2012 to 2018 although some of the actions carried out in 2018 and 2019 already correspond to the current presidency of Andrés Manuel López Obrador. According to the country's trajectory, Peña Nieto receives it with a poverty of 45.5% in addition to the high levels of corruption, insecurity and without formal employment strategies, in addition to characterizing this very precarious period in governance. Despite this, the reform actions that were approved in the Senate were aimed at addressing the various problems in the country as well as adjusting the observations made at the international level to Mexico.

The evaluation report is comprehensive, however, only here the reforms that contribute to the chain that implies the growth of poverty will be announced, according to the information in Annex 1. Therefore, the OECD's evaluation of this presidential period in fiscal matters reports that there were revisions to taxes, mainly the Value Added Tax (VAT), sustainable finances, public design, accountability, transparency, carbon tax for fuel. Also ordered the report of municipalities to the state government, included taxes on sugary and caloric foods for the population to take care of health.

At the same time, it generated competition policies by autonomous authorities, envisioning regulations, criminal sanctions against cartels, and the creation of courts; in relation to telecommunications, the backbone network was promoted to promote the Internet for all. In order to combat informality, a federal body is proposed to monitor the determination of collective agreements.

With reference to education, it is supported with quality and for all, through a new educational model with emphasis on transition-permanence-completion of studies, investment in infrastructure and the analysis of increased practices to improve student learning.

With regard to security, the following actions are determined: a National Code of Criminal Procedure is created, the Federal Prosecutor's Office of the Republic, the National Guard, and presidential immunity, the expansion of crimes and confiscation of property to include corruption and a plan to prevent fuel theft. With regard to transparency, the General Law on Administrative Responsibilities, a national audit plan with competence for anti-corruption and integrity, as well as the Transparency Law, were implemented.

On the other hand, for innovation and technology, the science, technology and innovation body is created, the budget for the National Council of Science and Technology (CONACYT) is increased, spending for research and development is increased, and special economic zones are approved as well as the Shared Network in mobile networks. This is reflected in the agricultural sector with subsidies for irrigation technology, agro parks are created and design, construction and operation are subsidized at the same time that guaranteed minimum prices are installed for five agricultural products for small producers.

On the subject of unemployment, in 2014 the Prospera Social Inclusion Program begins with links in education, training and formal employment, is launched through scholarships and training for young people, the universalization of pensions and increase to double the amount paid, interest-free microcredits for entrepreneurs and cash transfers, scholarships for residents where fuel theft is high.

What is proposed for the health sector is to increase care for the population through the health system, which includes the People's Insurance, in addition to the creation of the National Strategy for the Prevention and Control of Overweight, Obesity, and Diabetes; the universalization of health services is dictated; and the purchases of the health system are improved through the Coordinating Commission for the Negotiation of Prices of Medicines, Supplies, and Medical Equipment for the Institutions coordinated by the Mexican Social Security Institute (IMSS).

Finally, in matters of housing, the National Urban Development and National Programs of Housing are established.

It is worth mentioning that in the course of all this reform, the actions and their implementation to alleviate poverty, in parallel the impact that was had on society was measured. The analysis of poverty in its multifactorial format is shown in table 3 which reflects that the percentage of poverty in 2014 is 46.2% and in 2018 ends at 41.9%, that is to say there is a decrease of 4.3% the vulnerable population of social deprivation increases by 3% the vulnerable population in low income by 0.2%.

The educational lag falls by 2.5%, health services falls by 2%, access to social security falls by 1.2%, housing low by 1.2% and finally in food low by 3%. Therefore, the report on the well-being of the population in extreme income poverty falls by 3.8% and the population of income poverty falls by 4.4%.

According to the CONEVAL statement, it can be deduced that the reforms and actions, in that period, gave good results, except in the social security indicator; in this period it is observed that there were

Table 3. Poverty and Extreme Poverty in Mexico 2014-2018

CONCEPT	M hab 2014	M hab 2018	% of population 2014	% of population 2018
Poverty	55.3	52.4	46.2	41.9
Extreme poverty	11.4	9.3	9.5	7.4
Population vulnerable due to social deprivation	31.5	36.7	26.3	29.3
Vulnerable population by income	8.5	8.6	7.1	6.9
Indicators of social deprivation				
Educational Lag	22.4	21.1	18.7	16.9
Lack of access to health services	21.8	20.2	18.2	16.2
Lack of access to social security	70.1	71.7	58.5	57.3
Lack of quality and housing spaces	14.8	13.8	12.3	11.1
Lack of access to food	28.0	25.5	23.4	20.4
Welfare				
Population with income below the extreme poverty line by income	24.6	21-0	20.6	16.8
Population with income below the income poverty line	63.8	61.1	53.2	48.8

Source: Own elaboration with information from the CONEVAL 10 years of measuring poverty in Mexico, advances and challenges in social policy (Press release No. 10).

workers discharged, which leads to the increase in unemployment. On the other hand, the population with vulnerability to social deprivation is increasing, which means that although there has been a decrease in social deprivation, the vulnerability of the poor in the reception of social benefits remains latent.

The monitoring of the population with incomes below the poverty line, CONEVAL (2014) measures this factor according to the following:

"The poverty measure uses the following two income lines: The income poverty line, formerly the welfare line, is equivalent to the monetary value of one basic consumption food and non-food basket per person per month.

The extreme income poverty line, formerly the minimum welfare line, is the monetary value in a given month of a basic food basket.

- For the purposes of the measurement, the value of the basket for the month of August of each year in which the calculation is made is taken as a reference.
- This line is estimated for rural and urban areas.
- It is updated monthly using the National Consumer Price Index (INPC) calculated and published by INEGI."

Table 4 shows the increase in the basic basket in both the rural and urban a population, although in reality the increase reflected for both sectors is 80.00 pesos. In this regard, it has to be considered

Table 4. Food basket Extreme Poverty 2014 – 2018

Basic Basket	2014	2015	2016	2017	2018	AVERAGE
RURAL	868.00	870.00	950.00	1,100.00	1,180.00	$ 993.60
URBAN	1,227.00	1,380.00	1,400.00	1,500.00	1,580.00	$ 1,417.40

that there are differences in the rural and urban population in social deprivation and opportunities, as detailed in table 5.

In this regard to the above-mentioned indicators, the CONEVAL mentions the population in rural and urban poverty but emphasizing the place of residence, this is a very relevant aspect because it is not the same to have urban poor in the northern part of the country than in the center. Another aspect that is considered is the population in poverty according to ethnicity, which, in the same way, is not the same to speak of ethnic groups in urban areas as in rural areas, therefore and according to the territories, the territorial context of poverty in Mexico is reflected in Table 6 relating the figures to Annex 2.

According to the information above, it can be interpreted that, although there is a decrease in poverty and extreme poverty by region, between the period 2014 and 2018, the approach that throws us are the differences between regions; that is to say the population in poverty in the Center and South is higher than in the North of the country between the north and the south there is a difference of 26.02. While, the data on extreme poverty reports differences between regions but is very marked in the South, with a difference between north and south of 13.59%

Table 5. Poverty and Extreme Poverty in Mexico 2014-2018

Concept	Year	% Rural	% Urban	
Population living in poverty by place of residence	2014	61.1	41.7	
	2018	55.3	37.6	
Population living in poverty by ethnicity		% Indigenous	% Non-Indigenous	
	2014	78.4	43.6	
	2018	74.9	39.4	
Population living in poverty by sex		% Women	% Men	
	2014	46.3	46.0	
	2018	42.4	41.4	
Population living in poverty by age group		% Youth	% Adults	% Under 18s
	2014	47.1	45.9	53.9
	2018	42.4	41.1	29.6
Disabled people living in poverty		% Disabled	% Non-Disabled	
	2014	54.1	45.6	
	2018	48.6	41.4	

Source: Own elaboration with information from the CONEVAL 10 years of measuring poverty in Mexico, advances and challenges in social policy (Press release No. 10).

Table 6. Poverty and Extreme Poverty in Mexico 2014-2018

CONCEPT	Urban Areas	% 2014	% 2018
Population in poverty by territory	North	35.17	28.89
	Center	46.27	40.08
	On	55.15	54.91
Population in extreme poverty by territory	North	4.52	2.51
	Center	7.0	4.46
	On	17.7	16.1

Source: Own elaboration with information from the CONEVAL 10 years of measuring poverty in Mexico, advances and challenges in social policy (Press release No. 10).

As discussed in previous paragraphs, the period strongly analyzed by the OECD corresponded to that of Enrique Peña Nieto, although the years 2018-2019 correspond to the current six-year term of Andrés Manuel López Obrador.

2. The behavior of poverty indicators in the year of pandemic.

SARS-COV-2 was first detected in December 2019 in the city of Wuhan, Hubei province, in China, the lack of knowledge of the scientific community led to its rapid spread, becoming a worldwide pandemic. A month after the virus spread to other countries, this is how in January 2020 the countries affected by this virus were: China; Thailand; Korea; Taiwan; USA. By February, Chile and Brazil have already appeared, that is, they have transmuted to another continent.

The first case that was reported in Mexico was on February 27, 2020; by March 18 there were already 118 cases, with these figures what in other countries are considered the exponential growth of the coronavirus. In the same way it was considered the time to test the capabilities of the State to contain the pandemic that in this case had entered the "phase of other possibilities". In this period the forecast was decreed in that, 80% of the population would be infected and there would be a lethality mainly in older adults, also that it did not depend on standardization, but on the reaction and timely management of the pandemic.

At the end of April Basque Trade & Investment (2020) announces the impact of Covid-19 in Mexico, within the economic aspect they state that the Forecast of the Bank of Mexico is -3.5% in GDP, decline caused mainly by the price of oil and remittances from abroad. The Industrial Production Index fell from 50.3 points in February to 46.9 in March, boosted by the difficulties of demand. A year and a half on, it is clear that the pandemic forecasts far exceeded expectations.

In order to measure the scope of both the new government policies and the pandemic in the country, it is pertinent to analyze the main sectors in which the growth and development of the same falls, which have suffered an incalculable deterioration for Mexican society.

1. The health sector was a key element to combat this disease, however it was minimized in its resources, due to the escases of medicines and infrastructure, causing this disease to have a high cost for users, who regardless of their economic status, disbursed large amounts of money in their health. This situation not only affected Mexico but also worldwide.

Figure 1. Covid-19 Cases, Cumulative and Deaths in Mexico
Source: Ministry of Health

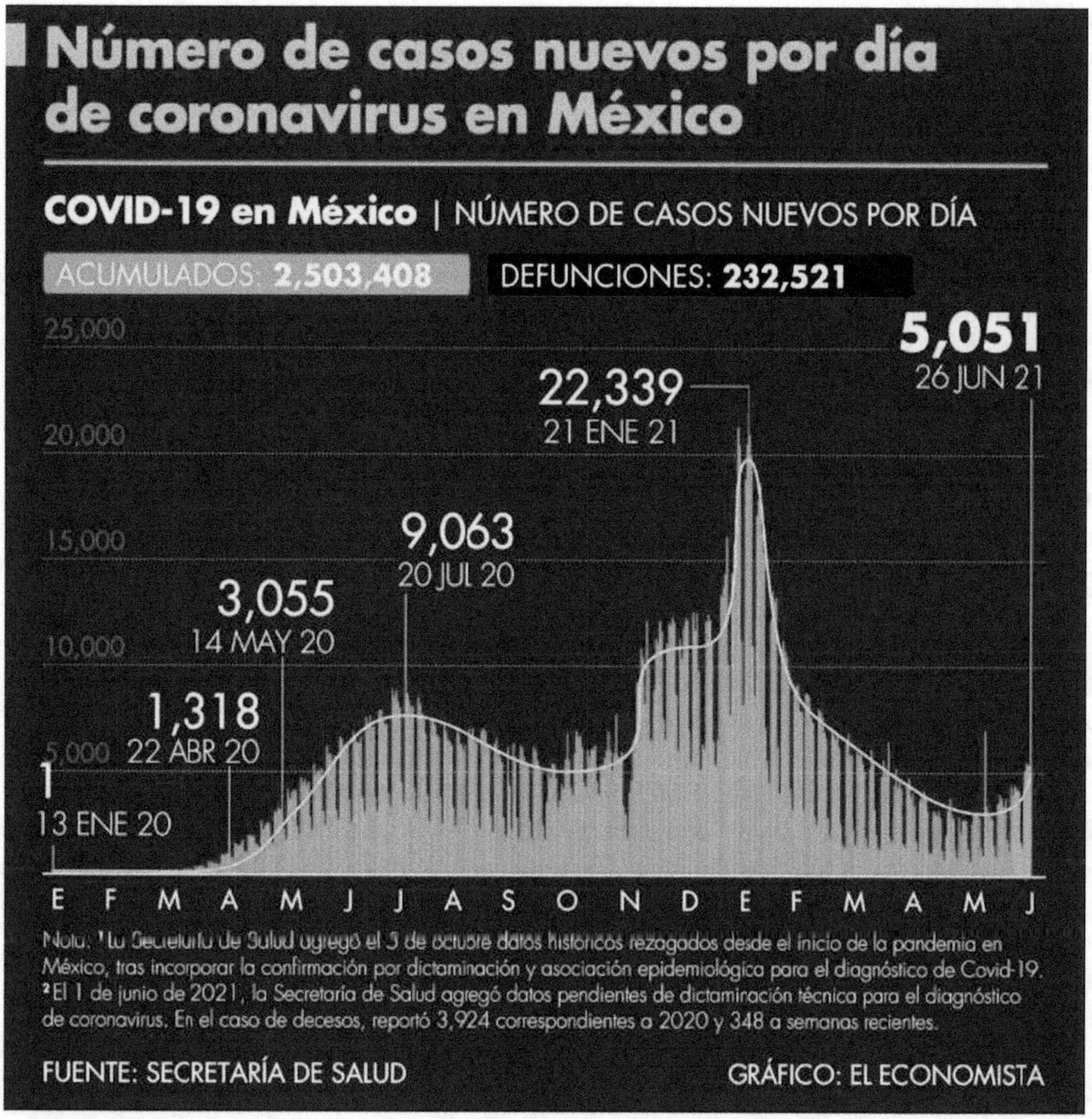

As graph 1 show, the first wave of the virus was reflected in early April 2020, after the health emergency was declared due to the high demand for hospitals in our country. The second wave began at the end of November, reaching the peak as of January 21, 2021; the main causes were the December meetings. The data that the Federal Government reports daily is alarming, this is how this pandemic has been occurring, however in mid-June 2021 marked the beginning of the third wave that according to experts may be more lethal than the previous ones, since the virus has been mutating and more variants are found than in previous months.[1]

This third wave was caused mainly by the announcement of finding most of the states of the Republic in green light, which originated the opening of primary, secondary and tertiary activities, in order to reactivate the economy, even though the percentage of the population with a full vaccination schedule is 15.9% that corresponds to adults over 60 years and over and population from 50 to 59 years. This false trust has caused them to let their guard down and strengthen the virus now affecting young people which is doubly lethal to them[2]. The Government of Mexico has reported by June 6th, 2021 a total of 2,549,862 confirmed cases, as well as 233,958 deaths from Covid-19 (Zamora-Guzmán, 2021).

2. The economic impact of the pandemic at this time is still unqualified. The classification used in Mexico to measure the economy that generates wealth in the country, is divided into three activities: primary (livestock, fishing, hunting, forestry, agriculture, and mining); secondary (manufacturing industries, generation and distribution of water, electricity and gas) and tertiary (government activities, transport and storage, real estate, retail trade, judicial activity, health services, financial services and insurance, media, educational services, telecommunications, hotels and restaurants).

Table 7 clearly reflects the impact that confinement brought about in the country, mainly in the second quarter manifesting a decrease of -18.7% of GDP, mainly the activities that were most affected were rum: the secondary ones, which correspond basically to industry and manufacturing; followed by the tertiary government activities transport, education, hotels and restaurants; and the last one the primary ones related to livestock agriculture and mining.

Even GDP was recovering although with negative figures showing results in the third quarter of up to -9%; in the fourth it decreased by up to -5% and finally in the first quarter of 2021 to -3%. This basically corresponds to the reactivation of activities that were taking place gradually as the color of the traffic light changed, following the instructions that it was permissible or not. However, in these quarters the tertiary and secondary activities are the most affected, the primary one maintains its activity proportionally.

Graph 2 shows the GDP of the period from 2013 to 2021 in Mexico, it is usual in the country that the comparison of growth or decrease of each quarter is made with the quarter of the immediately preceding year, in order to appreciate the variations from one year to another. On the other hand, the bank of Mexico's assessment of GDP growth prospects before the pandemic was: 2013/1.24%; 2014/3.41%; 2015/2.4%; 2016/2.5%; 2017/2. 5%; 2018/3% and 2019/3.2%. According to this information, this graph reflects that, in the six-year period from 2013 to 2018, the rates are positioned from0.6% to 4.1% being insufficient to reactivate the country's economy; the generation of jobs and reduce poverty.

The beginning of the six-year period 2018-2023, proposes a considerable decrease in 2019 being -0.7%; mainly due to the presidential change made at the end of 2018 coupled with structural changes of government and the implementation of a new national policy called the "Fourth Transformation". In

Table 7. Annual Percentage Change Quarterly Gross Domestic Product, seasonally adjusted figures

Denomination	2020				2021
	1T	2T	3T	4T	1T
GDP at market price	**-2.1**	**-18.7**	**-8.6**	**-4.6**	**-2.8**
Primary Activities	-3.0	-3.4	2.9	1.4	2.6
Secondary Activities	-3.1	-25.4	-8.6	-3.4	-2.0
Tertiary Activities	-1.2	-16.3	-8.8	-5.1	-3.4
Source: INEGI. Preliminary figures. Due to the estimation method the series can be modified when new information is incorporated.					

Figure 2. Mexico Quarterly GDP 2013 to 2021. Original figures
Source: INEGI System of National Accounts of Mexico

	2013	2014	2015	2016	2017	2018	2019	2020	2021
1T	0.6	2.8	3.4	2.7	3.4	1.5	1.3	-1.3	-3.6
2T	2.1	2.3	3.1	3	1.7	3.2	-1	-18.7	
3T	1.5	2.9	4.1	1.7	1.6	2.8	-0.2	-8.7	
4T	1.2	3.4	2.6	3.1	1.8	1.3	-0.7	4.5	

addition to these political changes was added the calamity of SARCOV-2 in Mexico, an aspect that is reflected in the year 2020 at a rate of -18.7%.

3. The education sector shows a significant lag, according to the OECD the school suspension causes loss of skills, Mexico is the country that has had a longer school closure, the above is equivalent to 4.5% of GDP. Also due to the absence of skills that had been acquired in that school year, the country will stop producing an approximate amount of 1 trillion 120 billion pesos, which corresponds to 17.79% of the net expenditure of the government of the country. On the other hand, the Mexican Institute for Competitiveness makes the comparison with respect to:

Figure 3. Number of students who dropped out of school as a result of the pandemic, April-August 2020, by educational level
Source: https://es.statista.com/estadisticas/1196796/desercion-escolar-nivel-educativo-covid-mexico

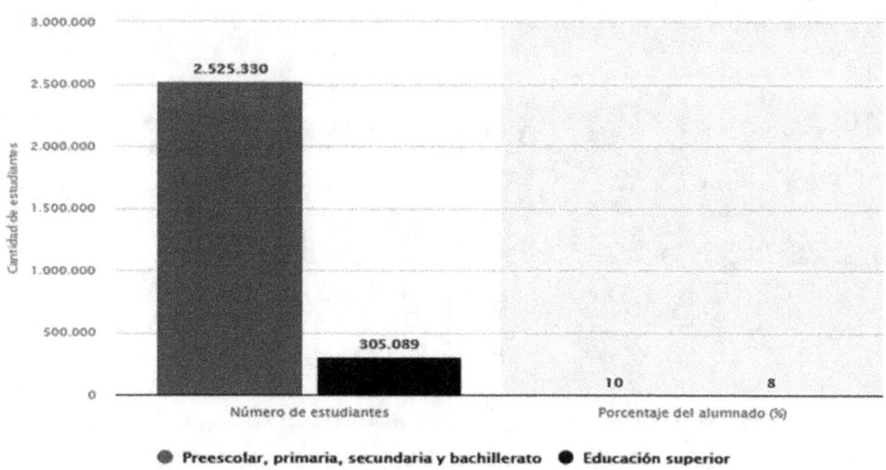

- Before the pandemic, Mexicans reached an average apprenticeship in the third grade of high school and
- Currently, with the loss of 217 face-to-face classes, their knowledge will be equivalent to first year of secondary school, causing with this delay the risk of positioning themselves in a competitive labor market.

Likewise, the Inter-American Development Bank (IDB) contemplates that approximately 628 thousand students between 6 and 17 years old abandoned their studies, the previous due to the lack of technology and efficient internet to access distance education, causing a lag in knowledge as well as affectations of personal maturation in cognitive, emotional and moral dimensions (Hector Aguilar Camín 23.06.2021). Also figure 2 shows the dropout existing in the months of April to August 2020, making a total of 2, 525,330 students in basic education and 305,089 in higher education.

4. Regarding employment in Mexico and according to data from the Ministry of Labor it indicates that the result of the pandemic contributed to the formal unemployment of 346,878 people, which represents less than 25% of the population that contributes to Social Security. The sectors that have been most affected by the paralysis of non-essential activities are: automotive, auto parts, electrical-electronic, clothing, medical equipment, aerospace, metalworking, appliances, furniture and product remanufacturing; leaving only basic medical and pharmaceutical health services; public safety; economy (food industry, gas station, banking, agriculture, agriculture), security services (emergency, funeral homes, transport of cargo and passengers); social programs and critical infrastructure (conservation and maintenance of basic infrastructure for the production and distribution of services such as water, electricity, drainage, sanitation and gas).

Figure 4. Seasonally adjusted series of the national unemployment rate. INEGI, percentage with respect to the PEA
Source: INEGI (Ministry of Labour)

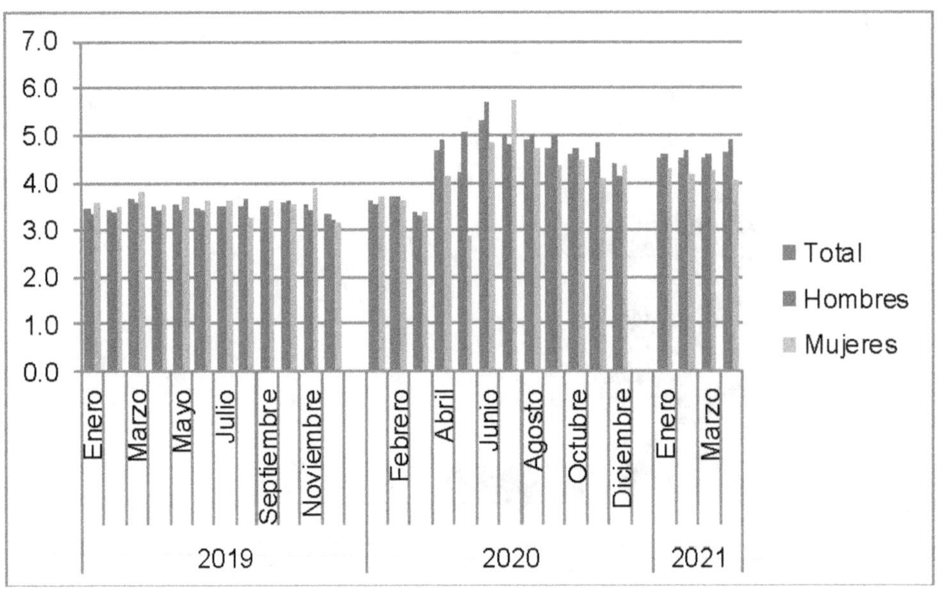

Figure 2 shows the impact of unemployment caused by the pandemic, which can be seen from April 2020, suffering an uptick of 1.7 percentage points compared to March, this data is important because since 2014 this level of unemployment had not occurred. Likewise, in April and May, the unemployment rate continues to fall, becoming more visible in April. It should be mentioned that the rate of 5.5% of the economically active population (EAP) in the month of June 2020 had not been so high for years. The opening of activities make visible the return to the labor force from august 2020, but still the unfavorable economic conditions do not allow employment to be found, which causes that it could rise more than 10% by 2021.(Beam, 2020)

THE STRATEGIES PROPOSED TO FACE POVERTY IN MEXICO FROM 2021

The preceding paragraphs analyze the country's trajectory with respect to the multidimensional factors that gave rise to inequality, poverty, extreme poverty and lack of opportunities for the lagging population, the result of previous government efforts.

The current government of Lopez Obrador, was received by this social deterioration and the catastrophic pandemic (including rich and poor who have suffered the devastating epidemic) as well as the sudden adaptation of government policies to alleviate a little the situation of the country that has been ventilated in deficient sectors, especially the health one. However, the federal government wants to restore to Mexican society what it had already planned for its management.

For the current government, the change of policy is based on "The Fourth Transformation" which means a regime with institutional and legislative changes, greater citizen power, peace and rescue of the social fabric. Within the National Development Plan (2019), the government placed this shift towards "[3]*a country with a spirit transformed for the better, a population aware of its ability to shape history, with a radical improvement in its levels of well-being and security compared to those prevailing in 2018, with healthy, reliable and law-abide scent institutions and with a participatory society involved in the exercise of public power*".

Likewise, the purposes of this change related to opportunities for the people in rescue from poverty were written with phrases such as: "no to the rich Government with poor people"; "economy for welfare"; "to the welfare of all, first the poor" and "no more migration due to hunger or violence". In order to address significant changes in social welfare and eradicate poverty, government policies were based on building social programs that would provide a solution to the entire problem.

This government policy, promoted through the National Development Program (PND) 2019-2024, published in the Official Journal of the Federation (DOF), embodies the most important objective of the current government: that the Mexican population lives in an environment of well-being. In this way, the government of the fourth transformation is committed to promote sustainable development to achieve an environment of well-being for all Mexicans.

In this regard, the Government of Mexico has projects in the areas of education, labor, agriculture, the economy, health, urban development and social welfare.

The 2019-2024 NDP lists the following:

1. Program for the Welfare of the Elderly
2. Pension Program for the Welfare of People with Disabilities:
3. National Scholarship Program for the Welfare Benito Juarez

4. Young People Building the Future
5. Young People Writing the Future
6. Sowing life
7. National Reconstruction Programme
8. Urban Development and Housing
9. Batches for Welfare

In relation to the above, it can be seen that the planning in this government period was dedicated to realizing opportunities for the most disadvantaged people, since its social programs were aimed at national growth.

However, President Lopez Obrador began his government with a decision unfavorable to the Mexican economy: the cancellation of the Mexico's City International Airport, according to the report of Lozano, G. (2021) of the Superior Audit of the Federation, the cancellation it cost 114 million pesos which meant 232% more than the expected in conjunction with the new proposal of the Santa Lucia Airport. The justification for the change was to avert an ecological disaster.

Another decision that has also involved an economic resource is the implementation of another project: "The Mayan Train", according to reports, the cost is now 321 billion pesos since adjustments have been made to the project and have resulted in adjustments that raise it to 30% more than predicted. The justification for this project is to provide the peninsula with an economic diversification.

These two projects are the triumphs considered at the end of the six-year period; they must be completed and activated by 2024. Therefore, all infrastructure operations are at high speed including all the financial resources that are required. The inconsistencies result in one project wanting to avoid ecological disaster while in the other, if there is an ecological disaster, the economy involved in the tourism sector matters more.

In both cases, expensive and complex projects are presented, considering that it does not end up defining the investment or the real-time remuneration of the projects, additionally without considering that they are exaggerated investments for a country with the basic deficiencies that Mexico has.

Definitely this infrastructure planning has not been optimal to generate resources, on the contrary it has been invested, perhaps what is salvageable is for the construction sector generating employment and consumption of raw materials. The strategies to obtain the resource for these construction works were based on allocating federal resources and actions of financial "armor-plating", the truth is that today these projects exceed the initial prospects.

In another perspective, the government of the republic launched the social programs, mentioned above, which also required economic resources to exercise them. One of the most representative is the welfare program for the elderly, consisting of universal financial support for women and men over the age of 68; however, for older adults from the country's indigenous communities, the minimum age is 65 years. The aid is delivered directly (currently $2,250 bimonthly) and has been universally implemented.

Another relevant project has also been the Youth Building the Future (JFC) program; with the aim that young people who do not study or work between 18 and 29 years old receive the amount of $3,600.00 pesos monthly during one year to perform a job within a company. The Benito Juarez Welfare Scholarships are supports for young people with limited resources who wish to have a professional training.

These projects have also not yielded the results, Zuckerman, L. (2021) comments that the reports of the Superior Audit of the Federation document that the young people received two scholarships, those of JCF and the scholarships for higher education; they had no supervision, so it is not found that they worked and learned a trade; some companies do not have RFCs; others are shell companies; contact telephone numbers with fake or untraceable HFCs. Of the resources allocated for this program, almost 24 billion pesos could only be audited, 18.8% that corresponded to Mexico City and the State of Chiapas; a percentage shows to verify that unfortunately the program was not applied as it should.

In relation to the Sowing Life program with the aim of supporting the agroforestry sector with the intention that families have a resource and work it in the field, unfortunately the opportunity has been extinguished since the Ministry of Finance and Public Credit (SHCP) has taken the decision to eliminate the agricultural insurance program by 2022; that is, the rural population has been left helpless for natural disasters, droughts and others that they may face; that's why insurance is important. In this regard, Mexico's agriculture is put at risk and, as a result, the country's food self-sufficiency.

Meanwhile these programs were implemented, the pandemic is facing internationally, consolidating in Mexico at the beginning of 2020, according to the characteristics of the virus and the lack of vaccines anywhere on the planet, the decisions of the government fell on the confinement of the population, closing schools, businesses and any activity that involved mass contagion. The only sector that was working was the health one, all kinds of hospital, doctor and assessment instruments, were at the service of the community.

The complete closure of the country was during the whole 2020, which brought drastic consequences especially when you do not have an economic capacity to withstand the modus vivendi of 127 million inhabitants. Clearly, the actions carried out had an impact on Mexican society, much more so on the poor, who hardly have the opportunity to have social security or access to health care.

Since the pandemic, there are circumstances that happen in the population, mainly in health, the government and the citizenry became aware of the deficiencies of the sector, however attention was offered as far as the conditions were, since they faced not only a few sick but thousands of infected, therefore the facilities were not sufficient in the care.

In addition to health, the population faced economic deprivation resulting from the closure of all business and economic activities; in this regard, the business sector suffered from the lack of support from the government, despite offering several proposals to alleviate the problem.

The Business Coordinating Council (2020), warned that SMEs could not survive the onslaught of closure since they did not have sufficient financial resources to avoid the collapse of SMEs, it is necessary to have an investment to reactivate the economy and avoid unemployment.

In addition to these serious consequences, other situations arising from confinement have worsened, being homeschooling, psychology for people who have disorders due to confinement as well as the care of food as a basis for overcoming a contagion.

All these problems were reflected in the indices marked by CONEVAL in its last publication of 2021 showing the poverty results 2018-2020.

The information in table 8 shows that poverty suffered a major collapse in 2020, rising 2% in that year, which translates into an increase of 3.8 million inhabitants, while extreme poverty increases by 1.5% representing 2.1 million inhabitants. The consequences of the educational lag were minimal compared to the indicator of the lack of health services were framed in the increase of 12% which corresponds to 15.6 Mhabs, which refers to the lack of spaces in hospitals, vaccines, changes of institutions from the Popular Insurance to the Institute of Health for well-being. Moreover, access to social security fell by 1.5% represented by the 0.2 Mhabs this indicator is related to job loss. The items described above influence the acquisition of quality food; this is reflected in a decrease of 0.3% represented in 1.1 Mhabs.

Table 8. Poverty Results 2018-2020

CONCEPT	Population 2018 %	Population 2020 %	Millions of habs 2018	Millions of habs 2020	Results	
					%	Mhabs
Poverty	41.9	43.9	51.9	55.7	2.0	3.8
Extreme Poverty	7.0	8.5	8.7	10.8	1.5	2.1
Population below the extreme poverty line by income	14.0	17.2	17.3	21.9	3.2	4.6
Population with income below the income poverty line	49.9	52.8	61.8	66.9	2.9	5.1
Educational Lag	19.0	19.2	0.2	23.5	24.4	0.9
Lack of access to health services	16.2	28.2	20.1	35.7	12	15.6
Lack of access to social security	53.5	52.0	66.2	66.0	1.5	0.2
Lack of access to nutritious and quality food	22.2	22.5	27.5	28.6	0.3	1.1

Source: Own elaboration with information from CONEVAL Communiqué No. 09 of August 5, 2021.

Regarding the income lower in the extreme poverty line, this population suffered the loss of income of 3.2% which means 4.6 Mhabs while for poverty the income represented the loss of 2.9% with a population of 5.1 Mhabs In this reference the CONEVAL takes information made by the National Survey of Household Income and Expenses (ENIGH); the results show current income per decile I (which are the lowest wages) versus decile X (which are the highest wages).

The measure it provides is that the comparison in salary in 2018 from decile I to X was 24 times higher while for 2020 it was 22 times higher. Total current income per capita declined 6.9% this was caused by all the falls in employment. This demonstrates the inequality that still exists between the resources that enter households.

The income that was sustained in increase at the national level was that of transfers, since they increased by 16.2%, it seams that although the foreign policy towards the United States is to limit the migration of Mexicans in its territory, these resources provide the help in some Mexican households.

In this multifactorial panorama that presents the current problem in Mexico, it can be elucidated that poverty in Mexico not only depends on the aforementioned items but also depends on the corruption and insecurity that the country is experiencing, which makes the situation tenser for the poor sector.

CONCLUSION

The six-year terms have created a series of strategies through social programs, however it is detected that in each period instead of reinforcing the measures, the strategy is distorted by the presumption that each stage demarcated in addition to not offering follow up.

On the other hand, the strategies that have been carried out are not optimal to regenerate the fabric of society, since it is not only with economic resources granted to the poor that the problem will be solved, but it is necessary to take it to a multidimensional phase, that is to say that other opportunities are offered such as, education, employment and decent housing that leads to generating human capital that can develop their skills and knowledge in a context of well-being.

It is also detected that the needs of the poor are supported through informal employment; this informality is already in the country an indispensable economic sector to strengthen public policies.

According to everything described, areas of opportunity are detected that may be feasible in the economic, political and social recomposition; that President Lopez Obrador is in the middle of the six-year term in order to change course. It is necessary to change public policies, mainly in the health sector with attention to people with pandemics, medicines for other chronic diseases in Mexicans. Another strategy can be direct economic support to all households, generating actions to offer formal employment by strengthening the business sector with public and /or private finances, ie seek Foreign Direct Investment (FDI).

It is also necessary to strengthen the programs to avoid the educational lag, this sector has also been very affected since the teaching-learning in times of pandemic has led to low academic competitiveness and desertion. For this purpose, it is necessary to have schools enabled with special protocols to avoid contagion in addition to enabling the spaces to offer hybrid education, that is, both face-to-face and virtual. In this regard, Mexican society is involved in pandemic resilience.

Finally, the government must consolidate its policies regarding reducing the rates of insecurity and corruption that exist in the country so that its management of "the poor first" is true and thus generate well-being in Mexicans.

REFERENCES

Aguilar, L. (2017). Reformas Estructurales en México. *Revista Nueva Época, 11*(42). http://www.apps.buap.mx/ojs3/index.php/tlamelaua/article/view/291)

Basque Trade & Investment. (2020). *México COVID-19: Impacto económico, medidas y restricciones.* https://basquetrade.spri.eus/es/informes-y-estudios/mexico/mexico-covid-19-impacto-economico-medidas-y-restricciones/

Bayón, M. (2012). El "lugar" de los pobres: espacio, representaciones sociales y estigmas en la ciudad de México. Universidad Nacional Autónoma de México-Instituto de Investigaciones Sociales. *Revista Mexicana de Sociología, 74*(1), 133-166.

Cámara de Diputados. (2004). *Ley General de Desarrollo Social y últimas reformas en 2018.* http://www.diputados.gob.mx/LeyesBiblio/pdf/264_250618.pdf

Comunicado, No. 10 de México 5 de Agosto 2019. Disponible en https://www.coneval.org.mx/coordinacion/entidades/Documents/Comunicados_Pobreza_2018/Comunicado_Medicion_Pobreza_2018_Aguascalientes.pdf)

Comunicado, No. 09 de México 5 de Agosto 2021. Disponible en https://www.coneval.org.mx/SalaPrensa/Comunicadosprensa/Documents/2021/Comunicado_009_Medicion_Pobreza_2020.pdf)

CONEVAL. (2019). *Press Release No. 10.* Directorate of Information and Social Communication.

CONEVAL. (2021). *CONEVAL Presenta las estimaciones de pobreza multidimensional 2018 y 2020.* Dirección de Información y Comunicación Social.

CONEVAL. (2021). 10 años de medición de pobreza en México, avances y retos en política social Dirección de Información y Comunicación Social Consejo Nacional de Evaluación de la Política de Desarrollo Social. In Líneas de Ingreso - Metodología para la medición multidimensional de la pobreza en México (2nd ed.). CONEVAL.

El Financiero. (2021). *SHCP gives the coup de grace to the agricultural insurance program.* Available at: https://www.elfinanciero.com.mx/economia/2021/07/13/hacienda-da-el-tiro-de-gracia-al-programa-de-aseguramiento-agropecuario/?outputType=amp

El Financiero–Economía. (2021). *Gobierno de México apoya solo a 7 de cada 100 Pymes, Solo el 7 por ciento de las Pymes en México han podido acceder y combinar el apoyo del gobierno en comparación con el 33.6 por ciento en la OCDE.* Expandir. https://www.elfinanciero.com.mx/economia/2021/06/29/gobierno-de-mexico-apoya-solo-a-7-de-cada-100-pymes/

Expansion Magazine. (2020). *In the absence of government support, companies seek to help each other; Carlos Salazar, President of the CCE.* Available at: https://expansion.mx/empresas/2020/04/06/ante-la-falta-apoyo-gobierno-las-empresas-ayudarse-entre-si

Feix, N. (2020). *Mexico and the COVID-19 crisis in the world of work: answers and challenges.* International Labour Organization. https://www.ilo.org/wcmsp5/groups/public/---americas/---ro-lima/---ilo-mexico/documents/publication/wcms_757364.pdf

Government of Mexico. (2019). *Reasons for the cancellation of the New Airport project in Texcoco Secretariat of Communications and Transport.* https://www.gob.mx/sct/articulos/razones-para-la-cancelacion-del-proyecto-del-nuevo-aeropuerto-en-texcoco

Hernández, L. (2021). *Traicionando el lema, Periódico Reforma del 03 de Agosto 202.* Disponible en: https://www.reforma.com/traicionando-el-lema-2021-08-03/op209623

López, R. (2011). *Políticas para la disminución de la pobreza en México: Consideraciones a partir del Programa Oportunidades Revista COFACTOR.* http://cofactor.edomex.gob.mx/sites/cofactor.edomex.gob.mx/files/files/cofactor3/cofactor_pdf_art5o.pdf

National Council for the Evaluation of Social Development Policy. (2014). *Income Lines. In Methodology for the multidimensional measurement of poverty in Mexico.* CONEVAL.

OECD. (2019). *OECD Economic Studies: México 2019.* OECD Publishing. doi:10.1787/fde7bbbe-es

Presidencia de la República. (2018). *Plan Nacional de Desarrollo 2018-2024.* https://lopezobrador.org.mx/wp-content/uploads/2019/05/PLAN-NACIONAL-DE-DESARROLLO-2018-2024.pdf

Revista Expansión. (2020). *Ante la falta de apoyo del gobierno, las empresas buscan ayudarse entre sí.* https://expansion.mx/empresas/2020/04/06/ante-la-falta-apoyo-gobierno-las-empresas-ayudarse-entre-si

Secretaría de Salud. (2021). *Subsecretaría de Previsión y Promoción de la Salud; Informe técnico diario COVID-19 México.* https://www.gob.mx/cms/uploads/attachment/file/644223/Comunicado_Tecnico_Diario_COVID-19_2021.06.06.pdf)

Ulsa, H. (2021). *Hacienda da el tiro de gracia al programa de aseguramiento agropecuario.* https://www.elfinanciero.com.mx/economia/2021/07/13/hacienda-da-el-tiro-de-gracia-al-programa-de-aseguramiento-agropecuario/?outputType=amp

Zukkermann, L. (2021). *La Auditoría al programa jóvenes construyendo el futuro, Excelsior, 23 de Febrero 2021.* https://www.excelsior.com.mx/opinion/leo-zuckermann/la-auditoria-al-programa-jovenes-construyendo-el-futuro/1434222

ENDNOTES

1 Mutation of the SARS-CoV-2 virus that causes Covid-19: WHO has identified 11 variants as of July 11, 2021: four "worrying variant" (VOC): Alpha, Beta; Gamma Delta and seven "variant of interest" (VOI): Epsilon, Zeta, Eta, Theta, Lota, Kappa and Lambda.

2 Measurement of national mobility.- Determined by the federal government as traffic light colors: GREEN: All activities are allowed even school activities; YELLOW: There are more activities but with caution, public spaces are opened with reduced capacity; ORANGE: Stay home if possible; public spaces are opened with reduced capacity; and RED: Do not go out if it is not strictly necessary. For all types of traffic lights, hygiene and maximum prevention measures are recommended.

3 The three episodes referring before the 4th. Transformation are: The independence of Mexico (1810 to 1821), The Reformation (1858 to 1861) and the Mexican Revolution (1910 and 1917)

APPENDIX

The population in Mexico in 2014 was 119,936,000 million; composed by 58.8 million women and 61.4 million men. While the population in 2018 was 125, 328,000 million; composed by 61,720,822 men and 64,469,986 women. Between those years there was an increase of 5,392,000 million inhabitants.

Table 9. Recent Policy Reforms In Mexico2014-2019

Political Area	Reform Area and Actions
Fiscal policy	Limits were imposed on ISR taxes. Vat was extended, a tax was imposed on caloric foods and sugary drinks. The RIF was implemented. Transportation subsidies were eliminated and a carbon tax for fuel was included. VAT was introduced to digital economy and gig.
Fiscal Federalism	Incentive for municipalities to report to the state government. Unification of VAT in aspects such as sustainable finance, public design, accountability and transparency.
Financial Sector	The CNBV, CONDUSEF, regulation to the Fintech Law, Plan of the financial sector of 8 points is strengthened.
Competition Policy	Autonomous competition authorities were created COFECE and the IFT, regulation for "surprise inspections". Criminal sanctions against cartels, creation of specialized courts. Reduction of salaries for all secretaries and public entities.
Regulatory Reform	Creation of the Daily Justice Program throughout the country to simplify business licenses and building permits, has been making adjustments to its regulation.
Telecommunications and broadcasting	Regulatory reinforcement for the IFT to promote competition in the field. In 2019, the Backbone Network was tendered to promote the internet for all, improve connectivity in disadvantaged locations that do not have the service or that is very low.
Energy Market	Creation of new regulators for CFE and PEMEX; access was opened to domestic and foreign investors for exploration, production and transport of oil, gas, refining and marketing. In 2018, the National Refining Plan was created through the rehabilitation of the 6 refineries and the construction of a new one. In 2019, the fourth renewable energy auction was cancelled.
Labour market and the fight against informality	The 2012 reform establishes hiring and employment, the new minimum age for work is 15 years. Labor matters will be transferred to related labor courts. Proposal for a decentralized federal body for the regulation of collective agreements. There are initiatives to reform secondary legislation.
Electoral System	Reform of 2014 allows the re-election of federal deputies, senators, mayors and local deputies. Proposal to increase gender equality.
Quality of Education	The 2012 reform provides quality education for all. In 2013, 3 laws on evaluation in education were passed. In 2017, a new educational model under competencies was implemented, which would increase coverage at all levels of education with emphasis on transitions, permanence and completion of studies, investment in infrastructure, increase teaching practice and reduce administrative burdens. In 2019, the model of classroom teaching observation and practice analysis is implemented to improve student learning.
Judicial System and Security	Daily Justice is resumed and commercial oral trials are implemented. In 2014, a National Code of Criminal Procedure was created. In 2014 the Federal Prosecutor's Office of the Republic is created, the 1st prosecutor appointed in 2019. The Senate is given the presidential immunity with which presidents protect themselves from criminal prosecution. The reform is passed to expand crime and the government can confiscate property to include corruption and fuel theft, the reforms will be carried out by state legislatures. The National Guard is approved and a plan to combat fuel theft is implemented.
Anti-corruption and transparency	The General Law on Administrative Responsibilities (LGRA) was implemented as well as a national audit system to harmonize anti-corruption and integrity policies and competences. In 2015, the General Transparency Law was published, fulfilling the new requirements.
Innovation System	In 2013, the CIT (science, technology and innovation) was created. In 2014 the budget to CONACYT is increased by approx. 20%. For 2018, spending on research and development is increasing. In 2016 the special economic zones are approved 7 zones are created. Start the Shared Network, wholesale market in mobile networks.
Modernization of Agriculture	In 2013 PROAGRO reformed agricultural subsidies, as well as subsidies for irrigation technology on agricultural land. The National Agroparks System is created to provide subsidies for the design, construction and operation of agroparks in potential areas. In 2019, guaranteed minimum prices for five agricultural products are introduced for small producers.
Unemployment insurance, pensions and social benefits	In 2014 PROSPERA started with links for education, training and formal employment, for self-sufficiency. Social plans are under review. The initiatives reviewed are scholarships and training for young people, the universalization of pensions and double the amount paid, interest-free microcredits for entrepreneurs and cash transfers, scholarships for residents of communities where the incidence of fuel theft is high.
Health system	There is the Social Protection System in health (including the People's Insurance,) increased care in 2013 the National Strategywas created. For the Prevention and Control of Overweight, Obesity and Diabetes. In 2016, the National Agreement towards the Universalization of Health Services was signed. The number of agreements in health services has increased, and there is improvement in the purchasing area of the health system through the Coordinating Commission for the Negotiation of Prices of Medicines and Health Supplies of a monopolistic nature, and the consolidated purchase of medicines and medical equipment for the institutions coordinated by the IMSS.
Urban Planning	The National Urban Development and National Housing Programs 2014-2018 are established

Source: OECD 2019. - OECD Economic Studies – Mexico

Table 10. Percentage of population living in poverty

NORTH	2014	2018	CENTER	2014	2018	ON	2014	2018
BC	28.6	23.3	AGUASCALIENTES	34.8	26.2	CAMPECHE	43.6	46.2
B.R.	30.3	18.1	MEXICO CITY	28.4	30.6	CHIAPAS	76.2	76.4
COAHUILA	30.2	22.5	COLIMA	34.3	30.9	GUERRERO	65.2	66.5
CHIHUAHUA	34.4	26.3	GUANAJUATO	46.6	43.4	OAXACA	66.8	66.4
DURANGO	43.5	37.3	HIDALGO	54.3	43.8	QUINTANA ROO	35.9	27.6
NAYARIT	40.5	34.8	JALISCO	35.4	28.4	TABASCO	49.6	53.6
NEW LEON	20.4	14.5	MEXICO	49.6	42.7	VERACRUZ	58.0	61.8
SINALOA	39.4	30.9	MICHOACAN	59.2	46.0	YUCATAN	45.9	40.8
SONORA	29.4	28.2	MORELOS	52.3	50.8	**AVERAGE**	**55.15**	**54.91**
TAMAULIPAS	37.9	35.1	PUEBLA	64.5	58.9			
ZACATECAS	52.3	46.8	QUERETARO	34.2	27.6			
AVERAGE	**35.17**	**28.89**	SAN LUIS POTOSI	49.1	43.4			
			TLAXCALA	58.9	48.4			
			AVERAGE	**46.27**	**40.08**			

Table 11. Percentage of the population living in extreme poverty

NORTH	2014	2018	CENTER	2014	2018	ON	2014	2018
BC	3.1	1.6	AGUASCALIENTES	2.1	1.2	CAMPECHE	11.1	9.8
B.R.	3.9	1.5	MEXICO CITY	1.7	1.7	CHIAPAS	31.8	28.7
COAHUILA	3.7	1.4	COLIMA	3.4	2.4	GUERRERO	24.5	26.8
CHIHUAHUA	5.4	2.6	GUANAJUATO	5.5	4.2	OAXACA	28.3	23.3
DURANGO	5.3	2.2	HIDALGO	12.3	6.1	QUINTANA ROO	7.0	3.5
NAYARIT	8.5	5.9	JALISCO	3.2	3.0	TABASCO	11.0	12.3
NEW LEON	1.3	0.5	MEXICO	7.2	4.9	VERACRUZ	17.2	17.7
SINALOA	5.3	2.7	MICHOACAN	14.0	6.1	YUCATAN	10.7	6.7
SONORA	3.3	2.6	MORELOS	7.9	7.4	**AVERAGE**	**17.7**	**16.1**
TAMAULIPAS	4.3	3.3	PUEBLA	16.2	8.6			
ZACATECAS	5.7	3.4	QUERETARO	3.9	2.0			
AVERAGE	**4.52**	**2.51**	SAN LUIS POTOSI	9.5	7.3			
			TLAXCALA	6.5	3.1			
			AVERAGE	**7.0**	**4.46**			

Source: datosmacro.com (accessed June 2021_https://datosmacro.expansion.com/demografia/poblacion/mexico?anio=2014)

Chapter 14
Poverty and Crime in Young People From Children Protection Centers

Sonia Castizo Vega
Universidad Pablo de Olavide, Spain

Salvador Cutiño-Raya
Universidad Pablo de Olavide, Spain

Francisco Espasandin-Bustelo
University of Sevilla, Spain

ABSTRACT

Young people who are in a situation of residential care are considered to be in a condition of multidimensional poverty. Research aims to achieve the following general objectives: first, to identify the level of delinquency of young people and its determining factors and, second, to propose strategies and programs. This research will follow a two-stage research process in which different research methods will be applied. Along with the main results, the authors point out that the most frequent crimes refer to these youngsters getting involved in gang fights; alcohol consumption; in attacking classmates, parents, and teachers; they steal money and or other objects from the collaborating family; they consume pornography and go out to discotheques, pubs, and nightclubs. In the educational field, although they are dedicated to their education, they obtain very low grades. They only participate moderately in sports activities and have very low participation in religious services; furthermore, the young men have a moderately high level of belief in the legal system.

1. INTRODUCTION

There are several reasons that justify this research, which can be understood within the criminological, social, academic and personal fields.

From a criminological point of view, Álvarez-Vivar, Bustamante-Cárcamo, & Salazar-Muñoz (2017) show that in various longitudinal studies, it is observed that the majority of recidivist adult offenders

DOI: 10.4018/978-1-7998-8925-0.ch014

begin their criminal career at the end of childhood, increases notably during adolescence and gradually ceases after the age of 20. It is, therefore, in the adolescent period that criminal behavior is enhanced.

From a social point of view, the problem of young people in a residential care situation is, to the same extent, that of their situation. These young people have lived situations of abandonment and suffering, they have difficulties maintaining social relationships, accepting norms and acquiring knowledge or managing emotions, among others. Of the more than 2,000 children who, in the Andalusian case, reside in Child Protection Centers, only a minority has the support of a Collaborating Family (a family that mainly hosts them on weekends and holidays), which is, in the majority of the cases, the only structured family reference that these young people have. These families constitute a restorative experience responding to the affective deficiencies suffered by most of this group, and which influence their emotional, cognitive and behavioral development.

On the other hand, the impact of the Collaborating Families on the child is vital, as it helps the young person to create a feeling of belonging to the family, improve their self-esteem, develop their identity and have suitable models of reference and imitation. We are, therefore, before a social problem (that of young residents in Child Protection Centers) and the solution that the Collaborating Family provides to that reality.

From an academic point of view, Agnew & Brezina (1997) point out that criminal behavior has been the subject of several studies in recent decades and urgently calls for approaches and theories that allow understanding the factors that influence criminal behavior, as well as the recidivism and abandonment of the same. In contrast, Campoy & Summers (2015), citing Wortley (2008), state that the situational factors of crime have received little attention in the criminological literature in the Spanish language.

The purpose of this research is to provide useful knowledge to improve the situation of young people living in Child Protection Centers. More specifically, this research aims at achieving the following general objectives: first, to identify the level of delinquency of young people and its determining factors; and secondly, to propose strategies and programs that allow young people and collaborating families to alleviate or eliminate the level of delinquency of these young people.

This research has a descriptive, explanatory and exploratory nature and is structured according to the following pillars: first, the literature on crime and its determining factors is reviewed; secondly, the data collection and analysis methods are described; third, the main results are discussed; and fourthly, the final considerations are presented, including the conclusions, the theoretical and empirical implications, the limitations and the future lines of research.

2. LITERATURE REVIEW

This section deals with the theoretical framework that supports the research. In the criminological field, there are a large number of theories (the Social Control Theory or the Social Learning Theory, among others) that explain, in a limited way, crime in terms of the individual's social relations (Zhang, Day & Cao, 2012). In order to provide a concise theory about crime and delinquency, Agnew (2005) proposes the General Tension Theory (GST) that is chosen in this research for the following reasons: it surpasses the theoretical and empirical criticisms of their previous theories (Agnew, 1992); it organizes previous theories into an integrated whole (Zhang, Day & Cao, 2012); it is much broader than current theories and complements them, insofar as it offers a synthesis of all the significant variables of the prevailing criminological theories (Zhang, Day & Cao, 2012).

In the words of Redondo (2008), the purpose of this theory is to prevent crime, insofar as it has the potential to provide valuable knowledge about the origins of crime in all social contexts (Blevins, Listwan, Cullen & Jonson, 2010).

The general idea of GST is itemized in that this theory more precisely specifies the relationship between tension and crime and shows that tension has a cumulative effect on crime once a certain threshold is reached (Agnew, 1992).

Agnew (1992) summarizes the existing empirical findings, considers all the variables that potentially explain crime at the individual level, and organizes these variables around three key concepts: restrictions, motivations, and the five domains of life.

According to Zhang, Day & Cao (2012) the domains of life affect, directly or indirectly, the level of crime through motivations (factors that attract or pressure to participate in crime) and restrictions (factors that serve to prevent crime); thus, crime is more likely when the restrictions on crime are low and the motivations for crime are high.

In short, the Agnew GST establishes the relationship between a certain level of stress and crime. The following paragraphs describe the two main elements that support this theory: crime and tension.

Delinquency can be a method of relieving tension, which has been associated (Agnew, 1992) with harmful stimuli such as child abuse and neglect, physical punishment, negative relationships with parents and peers, adverse or negative school experiences, etc. These harmful stimuli can lead to crime when the individual rejects leading norms and values, prioritizes self-interest, and is exempted from the responsibility of meeting seemingly impossible standards (Bao, Haas, Chen & Pi, 2014).

Tension or the causative factor of crime (Agnew, 1992) is defined as negative or aversive relationships with others (Wareham, Cochran, Dembo & Sellers, 2005). Bao, Haas, Chen & Pi (2014) identify three sources of tension that are specified in: not achieving positively valued objectives (good grades, for example), losing stimuli with a positive assessment (customary privileges, for example), and finding incentives negatively valued (physical punishment, for example); and each type of tension generates a predisposition to commit a crime; so that not all types of tension inevitably lead to crime (Blevins, Johnson, Cullen, & Lero, 2010).

On the other hand, empirical research on stress considers the magnitude, timeliness, duration and grouping of stressful events as relevant dimensions.

The relationship between stress and crime is moderated by a series of intermediate variables or domains of life that, according to Agnew (2005), are: the individual, family, school, friends or peers and work. These domains of life, in addition to impacting directly or indirectly (through restrictions or motivations) on crime, also influence each other; Thus, for example, Vitulano, Fite & Rathert (2010) show that poor education in the family increases the probability of association with criminals and negatively affects commitment to education. The domains of life covered in this research are described below.

In relation to the family domain, all the main theories of crime affirm that the family plays a nuclear role in juvenile delinquency; since it has the greatest effect on the magnitude of stress and the reaction of young people (Patterson, DeBaryshe & Ramsey, 1989). Empirical research shows crosswise (Krevans & Gibbs, 1996; Ordoñez Camacho, 2015; Wright and Cullen, 2001) and longitudinally (De Kemp, Scholte, Overbeek & Engels, 2006; Hoffmann and Miller, 1998) that the stress caused by events Negative effects of family life have a significant effect on crime.

The literature on family dominance deals with variables such as punitive discipline, parental supervision, family time or poverty, among others. Regarding punitive discipline, Carpio, García, Cerezo, & Casanova (2016) indicate that it is characterized by excessive control and has negative effects on the social and emotional functioning of the young person. Bao, Haas, Chen & Pi (2014) consider that the harshness of discipline by parents can generate severe tension that can be the cause of criminal behavior.

Regarding parental supervision, Stattin & Kerr (2000) state that it refers to the set of behaviors related to the care of children, the true knowledge of their whereabouts, their activities and the adaptation of activities outside the home and is related to parents' efforts to find out what their children are doing through request/summons and control. In a simplified form, Carrillo, Juárez, González-Forteza, Martínez, Icaza & Elena (2016) sustain that parental supervision is made up of the care for the children, knowledge of their whereabouts and activities and adaptation.

For Barnes & Farrell (1992) it is important that there is a family environment of communication and support that develops freer communication between parents and children, so that family supervision is more easily achieved. The relationship between parents and children based on communication and support, according to Carrillo, Juárez, González-Forteza, Martínez, Icaza & Elena (2016), must operate preventively and be bidirectional. When these circumstances occur, parental supervision limits juvenile delinquency (Wright & Cullen, 2001).

Another of the variables that is most often considered in the field of literature on family dominance is parental attachment, which, among others, generates the following results: more security, more trust and adequate socio-emotional development of the young person, feelings of belonging and well-being emotional and absence of anxiety and fear (Balabanian, Lemos & Rubilar (2015). The quality of attachment is directly related to its impact on the young person (Gordillo, & Carolina, 2017); in the sense that in addition to favoring daily contact with parents, it allows for relationship to be extended to other contexts and to other people (Bowlby, 1973). Bowlby (1969; 2009) himself defines attachment as the affective bond that is established between parent and child and that refers to any of the different forms of behavior to achieve the desired proximity. In the same vein, Chapple, McQuillan & Berdahl (2005) define attachment more broadly as the affective identification that has a person with their parents, teachers and peers. Guevara, Marchena & del Rosario (2017) highlight that a warm, rich and supportive relationship, although it does not have to be omnipresent with at least some of the parents, mitigates the harmful effects of crime.

Another variable that is usually dealt with in the family domain is family time. In relation to this variable, Warr (1993) affirms that the best indicator of family supervision is the real time that parents or other family members spend with young people and Aebi (2003) maintains that the young person attached to the parents, spend more time with them and consequently have fewer opportunities to commit crimes; With this, crime is prevented by keeping young people away from temptations (Felson, 1998).

Finally, the last variable that is dealt with in the family domain is poverty. Regarding this variable, Goode (1960) states that absolute poverty is not necessarily a cause of tension and a consequent and possible crime; however, such as relative poverty that compares the situation of an individual with people of the same or similar origin who are leading a better life, if it is a source of tension and can generate crime. Agnew and Brezina (1997) find that poor peer relationships with their peers are positively associated with juvenile delinquency.

On the other hand, in the field of school domain, the variables commitment to education and academic performance are usually dealt with. Regarding the commitment to education, Cohen (1955) affirms that a lower attachment to the school or the absence of educational goals is associated with increases in delinquency. Regarding academic performance, Agnew (2006) affirms that negative school experiences generate great tensions, which increases motivation towards delinquency. Along the same lines, Sikorski (1996) points out that poor academic performance and school failure pose a risk of incurring in conduct disorders, use of addictive substances and delinquency.

Regarding the domain of peers, we first highlight that criminal peers had the greatest impact on crime (Bao, Haas, Chen & Pi, 2014) and according to Bobbio, Lorenzino, & Arbach (2016) it is one of the most studied in the field of crime. The variables that are usually treated in this domain are: the number of friends [the more delinquent friends a young person has, the greater the probability that an individual will become a delinquent (Agnew, 2005)]; time spent with friends [the more time spent with peers who meet social norms, the greater the likelihood of reducing crime (Costello, 2010)]; the rewards of friends [the greater the importance of the social rewards of delinquent peers, the greater the probability of increasing delinquency (Rebellon, 2006)]; commitment to peers and membership in youth gangs.

Regarding youth gang membership, a study with Swiss students found that young people who belong to a gang are five times more likely to have committed a crime in the last twelve months, compared to non-criminal youth or individuals who do not. they are part of no gang (Schioppa, 2013).

According to Hirschi (1969) the social bond is made up of four elements: attachment, participation, commitment and belief. Attachment and commitment have already been referred to and justified previously; Next, we refer to participation in organizations and belief in the legal system. The participation according to Chapple, McQuillan & Berdahl (2005) represents the time that one dedicates to conventional activities. Hirschi (1969) indicates that participation in conventional activities alone is not sufficient to deter crime.

Finally, belief in the legal system measures the youth's support, in this case, for general social norms and public laws; logically, the more support, the lower the level of crime.

It should be clarified that the domains of life are not constant over time and their direct and indirect effects on crime will also differ. That is why in future research, the degree of change that occurs in the domains and its impact on juvenile delinquency should be known for the sample under study and / or extended. For this, it is necessary to carry out a longitudinal investigation.

In the light of the described evidence, we propose the following hypotheses:

- H1: The greater the punitive discipline of the family domain, the lower the level of delinquency of the young person.
- H2: The greater the supervision of the parents, the lower the level of delinquency of the young person.
- H3: The more time spent by the family, the lower will the youth's level of delinquency be.
- H4: The higher the family's level of poverty, the higher the youth's level of delinquency will be.
- H5: The greater the family attachment, the lower the youth's level of delinquency.
- H6: The greater the commitment to education, the lower the youth's level of delinquency.
- H7: The higher the academic performance, the lower the level of delinquency of the young person.
- H8: The greater the commitment to peers, the lower the youth's level of delinquency.
- H9: Belonging to a youth gang increases the youth's level of delinquency.
- H10: The greater the participation in organizations, the lower the level of delinquency of the young person.
- H11: The greater the belief in the legal system, the lower the youth's level of delinquency.

Figure 1. The Conceptual Model.
Source: *The authors.*

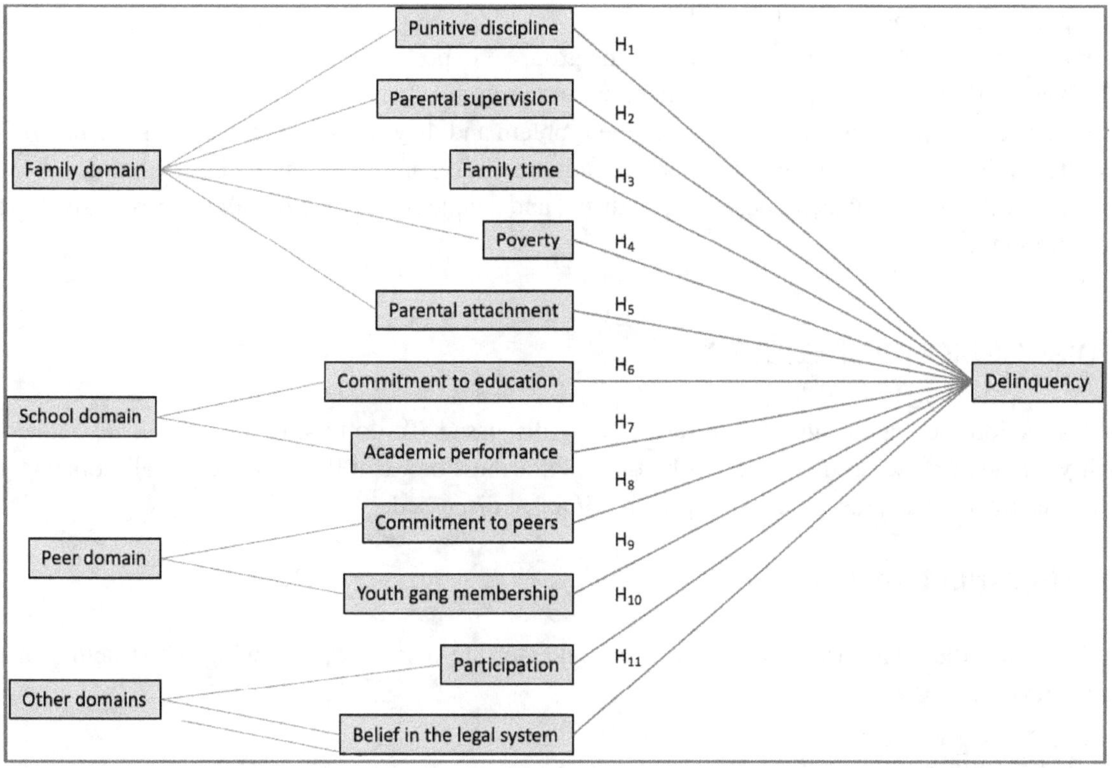

3. RESEARCH METHODS

In this work a two-stage research process is followed. The objective of the first stage of the research is to know the level of delinquency of young people living in a residential care situation and the domains (family, peers, school and other domains). To achieve this objective, we start from the Agnew conceptual model and design a questionnaire (ANNEX No. 2) that consists of 56 questions and is grouped into four blocks. Once the questionnaire has been designed, a pretest is carried out with a collaborating family made up of 2 professors from the Faculty of Psychology at the University of Seville. Once the questionnaire has been corrected, the data is collected from July 1 to July 15, through a personal interview lasting 45 minutes; and later they are coded and tabulated. The unit of this first stage of the research is made up of young beneficiaries of the Collaborating Families Program and Collaborating Families.

The size of the sample amounts to 23 individuals belonging to 15 Collaborating Families and 7 young beneficiaries of this resource.

The data analysis is carried out with IBM SPSS Statistics Version 24. Specifically, a descriptive analysis is carried out that includes a univariate and bivariate analysis, to check if the hypotheses are supported. Motivated by the continuous nature of the variables, a one-way ANOVA is applied.

The second stage of the research aims to propose solutions to the problems identified in the previous stage. The method used for this is a group of experts. The process that is followed in the group of experts includes the following stages:

1. All the experts summoned that are detailed in Annes 1 meet
2. Attendees are informed of the results of the previous investigation, emphasizing the objectives, processes and problems identified.
3. A problem is chosen and clarified with the group of experts.
4. They reflect for 3 minutes on the strategies and programs to solve the problem.
5. Each expert presents their solutions to the problem and they are noted on a concept map.
6. The solutions are discussed as a group in order to clarify and agree on the best solution.
7. The different solutions proposed are analyzed and a table is created with all the proposals that are presented.

4. DISCUSSION OF RESULTS

In this section the main results of the research are discussed. To do this, firstly, the results related to each variable are discussed and, secondly, the relationships between the variables of all domains and identification data and their relationship with crime are discussed.

4.1. Univariant Analysis

At this point, the main results related to each indicator are discussed, following the structure of the questionnaire.

4.1.1. Identification Data

Next, we present the identification data of the respondent and the Collaborating Family; as well as the type of school the young man has attended.

We present the relative information of the respondent's data. By sex, we note that the majority of the people interviewed are women, the least frequent value being men.

The age of the interviewees ranges between 60 and 18 years, with the mean age being 38.09 years and the standard deviation 14.513.

Regarding the training of the people who answer, we highlight that all the interviewees have training that ranges between "Primary Studies" and "Master or Postgraduate"; highlighting that the fashion of the people interviewed is "Diploma, Bachelor or Graduate"; It should also be noted that there is a high percentage of the interviewed population (17.4%) who have "Master's or Postgraduate" degrees.

Regarding the profession, we highlight that 26% of the sample is related to the education sector, 8.6% are administrative personnel and 65.4% are free professionals, being the profession of teacher or student the trend.

On the other hand, the standard of living of the Collaborating Families is "relatively good" or "good" in 73.82% of the cases; being normal that the standard of living is "relatively good" (43.4%). 34.8% of families have a standard of living that amounts to "fair" and there is no "poor" or "almost poor" family.

The Collaborating Families normally reside (34.8%) in Montequinto (Seville); 30.4% reside in the center of Seville, in the Macarena, S. Jerónimo and Sevilla Este area 17.3% of the population reside and 12.9% reside in a town in Seville or Madrid.

The number of members of the Collaborating Family ranges from 1 to 8 members, the most common being that the number of members is 2 and the average is 3.04.

Young people normally attend public schools (73.9%); a small percentage (21.7%) attend subsidized schools and only one young person attends a private school.

4.1.2. The Youngster: Delinquency

In order to calculate the youth's level of delinquency, we have created a new variable that we have called "Delinquency" as an average of the 15 indicators that define the variable. After calculating a frequency analysis of the variable, it is observed that the level of delinquency of young people is very low, close to 0 (0.2638). The most common crimes usually refer to stealing money or other things from the Collaborating Family or other members of the Collaborating Family, involvement in gang fights, hitting classmates, parents or teachers, drinking alcohol, going out to discos, pubs and nightclubs and the consumption of pornography. The lowest incidence of crime occurs in the damage or destruction of property that did not belong to him, theft, the purchase, sale or retention of stolen goods, the attack on someone with the idea of hurting or trying to kill him, the consumption of marijuana, gambling and harassment through mobile or another electronic device. Finally, no young man used force to obtain money or the things of others.

4.1.3. Family Domain

At this point, we discuss the data regarding the domain of the family; in a particular way we refer to: family time, punitive discipline, supervision of the Collaborating Family and parental attachment.

The number of hours per week that the young person spends with the Collaborating Family ranges from a minimum of 3 to a maximum of 168. The trend is for the young person to spend with the Collaborating Family 24 hours a week and the weekly average amounts to 59.48 hours.

Helping Families typically "never" use punitive discipline. In only one case was punitive discipline used "rarely" by completely ignoring the young person and "sometimes" by acting as if they did not care, withdrawing privileges, blaming or criticizing him undeservedly and yelling or teasing him.

In no case was physical violence used as a form of punitive discipline for the Collaborating Family.

The Collaborating Family knows "almost always" (78.3%) where and with whom the young beneficiaries of this resource are. It is not the case that the Collaborating Family "never" know who the young man is with. Only in three cases (13%) is it known "rarely" or "sometimes" where and with whom the young people are.

Young people's attachment to the Collaborating Family seems high to the extent that the trend is for all members of the sample to fully agree that the young person talks about their future plans with the Collaborating Family, share their thoughts and feelings with she perceives that the Collaborating Family understands her; getting to the point that you would like to be the kind of person your Supporting Family is.

In no case was physical violence used as a form of punitive discipline for the Collaborating Family.

4.1.4. Other Domains

At this point we deal with other domains that determine the level of crime. Especially, commitment to education, participation in organizations, belief in the legal system, and commitment to peers (friends).

Young people residing in Protection Centers seem to have a high commitment to education insofar as they usually finish their homework, pay a lot of attention at school, "never or almost never" are late for school or class, "never or almost never" they skip classes and receive an admonishment from the teachers. Despite this, their normal grades only reach the "pass" level.

In relation to participation in organizations, the trend is that these young people played "several times" in an organized sports team and in youth clubs outside of school; however, the normal thing is that they do not attend "never or almost never" religious services; although, on average, a part of them attend religious services "once a month".

The level of belief in the legal system of the young beneficiary of the Collaborating Family seems moderately high; to the extent that there is indecision that in most of the things that people call crime they do not harm anyone, there is a high respect for the police and there is disagreement that the rules were made to be broken and that it is okay to avoid the law if you get what you want.

Regarding the commitment to peers (friends), young people in residential care do not have delinquent peers, since they do not meet with them or belong to any youth gang. However, he is "once a week or more" with his peers without supervision. On the other hand, the level of abuse by their peers is very low, as reflected by the fact that "never or almost never" the young person is mistreated by their peers.

4.2. Anova Analysis Results

In this section the main results related to the hypotheses raised are discussed. The first result obtained is that the ANOVA analysis of a single factor cannot be applied to the hypotheses that relate to the membership of a youth gang and the punitive discipline of the family domain with the level of delinquency, because the distribution of the variables of membership The youth gang and punitive discipline do not allow it. Secondly, we highlight that the results of applying the one-factor ANOVA to the rest of the hypotheses presented in the following table only allow us to conclude that there is a significant relationship between the supervision of the Collaborating Family and the level of crime, since the level of significance is less than 0.05; this means that the relationship between both variables holds.

5. FINAL CONSIDERATIONS

In this section we will refer to the main conclusions, theoretical and empirical implications and limitations and future lines of research.

Regarding the conclusions, we highlight the evidence (problems) identified in the first stage of the investigation, which are detailed below. In the first place, the most frequent crimes refer to the youth getting involved in gang fights; consume alcohol; hits classmates, parents, or teachers; steals money or other things from the Collaborating Family; consumes pornography and goes out to discos, pubs and nightclubs. Second, no problems are identified in the family domain; although if any problem is identified in other domains. As well as in the educational domain, adolescents, although committed to their education, have very low grades; Regarding their participation in organizations, young people present moderate levels in their participation in sports activities and very low in their participation in religious services; Furthermore, the young man believes moderately high in the legal system; and, finally, in the peer domain, the young person is with peers without supervision, more than once a week.

Table 1. Single factor ANOVA.

HYPOTHESIS	F	Sig.
LEVEL OF DELINQUENCY BY FAMILY TIME	0,628	0,544
LEVEL OF DELINQUENCY BY BELIFE IN THE LEGAL SYSTEM	0,269	0,61
LEVEL OF DELINQUENCY BY COMMITMENT TO EDUCATION	0,522	0,478
LEVEL OF DELINQUENCY BY SCHOOL PERFORMANCE	1,598	0,22
LEVEL OF DELINQUENCY BY COLLABORATING FAMILY SUPERVISION	9,13	0,006
LEVEL OF DELINQUENCY BY COMMITMENT TO PEERS	0,761	0,393
LEVEL OF DELINQUENCY BY PARTICIPATION IN ORGANIZATIONS	0,522	0,478
LEVEL OF DELINQUENCY BY DEGREE OF POVERTY	1,478	0,252
LEVEL OF DELINQUENCY BY PARENTAL ATTACHMENT	1,957	0,167
LEVEL OF DELINQUENCY BY PERSON THE YOUNSTER CHALLENGES	1,159	0,334
LEVEL OF DELINQUENCY BY TRAINING	0,936	0,443
LEVEL OF DELINQUENCY BY GENDER	1,319	0,264

Source: The Authors.

Finally, there is only a significant relationship between the degree of supervision of the Collaborating Family, measured from the number of hours that the Collaborating Family spends on average supervising the youth, and the level of delinquency, which means that the greater the supervision of the Collaborating Family, the lower the level of crime. Logically, that only one hypothesis is fulfilled is a weakness of the research, although similar results are obtained by Zhang, Day & Cao (2012) when they show that there are a large number of variables from different domains that do not have a significant effect on crime. (Only 5 out of 11 relationships are sustained). This finding does not imply the existence of a causal relationship; associative only.

This research has theoretical and empirical implications. The main theoretical implication is that evidence, based on data, is provided on GST theory; although we are aware that, along the lines of Zhang, Day & Cao (2012), we provide "fragmented" evidence, which makes it difficult to fully test the theory given the extension of the causal network. In addition, evidence is offered on the level of delinquency of young people in the Spanish context, which did not exist before concluding this investigation.

The empirical implications derive from the second stage of the research and show that this work, according to the experts consulted, has practical implications for the following stakeholders: Junta de Andalucía, Collaborating Families, Educational System, Centers for the Protection of Underaged and Neighborhood Associations.

The regional Administration of the Junta de Andalucía should, in line with House (1981 cited by Agnew, 1992), increase the endowment of resources (greater financial, informative and educational support and psychological support for the young person and the Collaborating Family); increase rigor in law enforcement, sanctioning discos, pubs and nightclubs and alcoholic beverage vendors. In the field of sports and leisure, the regional administration must increase the offer and facilitate access to sports activities, reducing the price; promote leisure activities and a healthy life. Finally, in the sexual sphere, you should include pornography in courses on sexuality.

The Collaborating Families, according to the experts, must: educate in values and citizenship, teaching social skills such as self-esteem, self-control, self-concept, impulse control and consequences of criminal behavior; reduce the overprotection of the young person and gain authority working from affection and not from aggression; provide real and close reference role models (grandparents) and family role models; and, finally, limiting internet access through parental control.

The educational system must: carry out a prior preparation that includes a period of adaptation for the young person and the elimination of the stigma that the "foster youth is not suitable for studying"; Likewise, it must promote education in values and adaptation to the needs of young people; offer the possibility of reinforcing the training of the young person, paying more attention to those who have a poor performance and experience stress at school; finally, in the sports and leisure field, a program must be designed where sport is an essential activity and the leisure offer must be adapted to the demand of young people.

Neighborhood Associations should improve the leisure proposal and promote the creation of Parenting Schools, which, according to Gao, Wong & Yu (2016), help parents learn effective parenting practices and improve their knowledge of parenting. building positive relationships with children.

Finally, the Centers for the Protection of Minors should promote education in social skills.

The limitations of this work are of a different nature and refer to the chosen theoretical approach, the conceptual model, the sample, the data analysis method used and the cross-sectional nature of the research.

In the first place, we are aware, from the beginning of the research, that it has not been possible to fully test the Agnew Theory, due to its complexity; so we have only had to test some "fragments of it" as stated by Agnew (2005).

Secondly, the proposed conceptual model does not include the work domain, it is not easy to operationalize, as stated by Campoy & Summers (2015), the constructs, and furthermore, it does not include mediating variables in causal relationships.

Third, the sample has a small size motivated by the time the data were collected and a certain bias, insofar as the individuals that compose it have been selected by the organization Crecer con Futuro.

Additionally, we have not been able to obtain official data from other provinces, either because they do not exist, as is the case of Huelva, which does not yet have this resource, or as a consequence of the absence of official data.

Fourth, another limitation is due to the method of data analysis. According to Zhang, Day & Cao (2012), the structural equation model provides the best support for Agnew's Theory (2005), however, its application has not been possible due to the limited sample size.

Fifth, the research, like Chapple, McQuillan & Berdahl (2005), is transversal in nature.

The previous limitations suggest the following directions for future research. In the first place, given the open nature of Agnew's General Theory of Crime and Delinquency (Zhang, Day & Cao, 2012) we should include other domains such as self, work, and community domain (Wareham, Cochran, Dembo & Sellers, 2005).

Second, the conceptual model must consider the presence of mediating, moderating and control variables and more refined measures.

Third, the size must be enlarged and sampling bias avoided.

Fourth, the structural equation model that provides the best support for Agnew's Theory should be used as a data analysis method.

Fifth, a longitudinal investigation should be proposed in the same way as Gao, Wong & Yu (2016).

REFERENCES

Aebi, M. (2003). Familia disociada y delincuencia: El caso suizo en los años 1990. *Revista Electrónica de Ciencia Penal y Criminología, 5.*

Agnew, R. (1992). Foundation for a general strain theory of crime and delinquency. *Criminology*, *30*(1), 47–87. doi:10.1111/j.1745-9125.1992.tb01093.x

Agnew, R. (2005). *¿Por qué los delincuentes ofenden?: Una teoría general del crimen y la delincuencia.* Academic Press.

Agnew, R., & Brezina, T. (1997). Relational Problems with Peers, Gender, and Delinquency. *Youth & Society*, *29*(1), 84–111. doi:10.1177/0044118X97029001004

Álvarez-Vivar, L, Bustamante-Cárcamo, Y., & Salazar-Muñoz, M. (2017). Paternidad y su incidencia en el desistimiento delictual: Una revisión teórica. *Revista Criminalidad*, *59*(1), 65–75.

Balabanian, C., Lemos, V., & Rubilar, J. V. (2015). Apego percibido y conducta prosocial en adolescentes. *Revista Colombiana de Ciencias Sociales*, *6*(2), 278–294. doi:10.21501/22161201.1515

Bao, W. N., Haas, A., Chen, X., & Pi, Y. (2014). Repeated strains, social control, social learning, and delinquency: Testing an integrated model of general strain theory in China. *Youth & Society*, *46*(3), 402–424. doi:10.1177/0044118X11436189

Barnes, G. M., & Farrell, M. P. (1992). Parental support and control as predictors of adolescent drinking, delinquency, and related problem behaviors. *Journal of Marriage and Family*, *54*(4), 763–776. doi:10.2307/353159

Blevins, K. R., Johnson Listwan, S., Cullen, F. T., & Lero Jonson, C. (2010). A general strain theory of prison violence and misconduct: An integrated model of inmate behavior. *Journal of Contemporary Criminal Justice*, *26*(2), 148–166. doi:10.1177/1043986209359369

Bobbio, A., Lorenzino, L., & Arbach, K. (2016). Familia, barrio y sociedad: Un estudio comparativo en jóvenes con y sin antecedentes delictivos de Argentina. *Criminalidad*, *58*(1), 81–95.

Bowlby, J. (1969). *Attachment and loss* (Vol. 3). Random House.

Bowlby, J. (1973). Attachment and Loss: Vol. 2. *Separation: Anxiety & Anger*. Hogarth Press.

Bowlby, R. (2009). *Just Looking (Routledge Revivals): Consumer Culture in Dreiser, Gissing and Zola*. Routledge. doi:10.4324/9780203855720

Bracho, A. (2014, Mayo-Agosto). *Revista de Derecho Político nº 90: políticas públicas y marco de protección jurídica del menor en España*. Recuperado de https://www.congreso.es/docu/docum/ddocum/dosieres/sleg/legislatura_10/spl_78/pdfs/31.pdf

Campoy Torrente, P., & Summers, L. (2015). Los precipitadores situacionales del delito: Otra mirada a la interacción persona-ambiente. *Revista Criminalidad*, *57*(3), 41–58.

Carpio, M. D. L. V., García, M. D. L. C., Cerezo, M. T., & Casanova, P. F. (2016). *Perfiles de inteligencia emocional en universitarios y disciplina de los padres*. Academic Press.

Carrillo Amezcua, L., Juárez García, F., González-Forteza, C., Martínez Vélez, N. A., Icaza, M. M., & Elena, M. (2016). Relación entre supervisión parental y conducta antisocial en menores infractores del Estado de Morelos. *Salud Mental, 39*(1), 11–17. doi:10.17711/SM.0185-3325.2015.063

Chapple, C. L., McQuillan, J. A., & Berdahl, T. A. (2005). Gender, social bonds, and delinquency: A comparison of boys' and girls' models. *Social Science Research, 34*(2), 357–383. doi:10.1016/j.ssresearch.2004.04.003

Cohen, A. (1955). Delinquent boys. Academic Press.

Consejería para La Igualdad y Bienestar Social. Junta de Andalucía. (2003). *Decreto 362/2003, de 22 de Diciembre por el que se aprueba el Plan General de Atención a la Infancia de Andalucía.* Recuperado de www.juntadeandalucía.es/boja/2004/18/1 [última consulta el 22 de junio 2018]

Consejería para La Igualdad y Bienestar Social. Junta de Andalucía. (2007). Programa de tratamiento a Familias con Menores. Manual de referencia de los Equipos de Tratamiento Familiar, España.

Consejería para La Igualdad y Bienestar Social. Junta de Andalucía. (2016). *II Plan de Infancia y Adolescencia de Andalucía (2016-2020).* Recuperado de www.juntadeandalucia.es/organismos/igualdadypoliticassociales/areas/infancia-familias/presentacion.html

Costello, B. J. (2010). Peer influencia hacia la conformidad. *Journal of Crime and Justice, 33*(1), 97–116. doi:10.1080/0735648X.2010.9721281

Crecer Con Futuro. (2017). *Memoria anual de actividades.* Recuperado de www.crecerconfuturo.org/wp-content/uploads/2018/07/MEMORIA-CcF-17.pdf

Felson, M. (1998). *Crime and everyday life.* Pine Forge Press.

Furman, W., & Buhrmester, D. (2009). Methods and measures: The network of relationships inventory: Behavioral systems version. *International Journal of Behavioral Development, 33*, 470–478.

Gao, Y., Wong, D. S., & Yu, Y. (2016). Maltreatment and delinquency in China: Examining and extending the intervening process of general strain theory. *International Journal of Offender Therapy and Comparative Criminology, 60*(1), 38–61. doi:10.1177/0306624X14547495 PMID:25145686

Goode, W. J. (1960). A theory of role strain. *American Sociological Review, 25*(4), 483–496. doi:10.2307/2092933

Gordillo, S., & Carolina, M. (2017). *Experiencias tempranas y personalidad en personas en conflicto con la ley estudio piloto con aplicación de cuestionario ETEP* (Bachelor's thesis). Quito: UCE.

Guevara Perez, M., Marchena, S., & del Rosario, A. (2017). *Resilencia y riesgo suicida en Adolescentes de un centro juvenil, Diagnostico y Rehabilitación.* Pimentel 2016.

Hirschi, T. (1969). *Causes of Delinquency.* University of California Press.

Hoffmann, J. P., & Miller, A. S. (1998). A latent variable analysis of general strain theory. *Journal of Quantitative Criminology, 14*(1), 83–110. doi:10.1023/A:1023048509438

Krevans, J., & Gibbs, J. C. (1996). Parents' use of inductive discipline: Relations to children's empathy and prosocial behavior. *Child Development, 67*(6), 3263–3277. doi:10.2307/1131778 PMID:9071781

López Azcona, M.A (2016). Luces y sombras del nuevo marco jurídico en materia de acogimiento y adopción de menores a propósito de la Ley Orgánica 8/2015 y la Ley 26/2015 de modificación del sistema de protección a la infancia y adolescencia. *Boletín del Ministerio de Justicia, 2185*.

Moreno-Torres Sánchez, J. (2015). *Modificación del sistema de protección a la infancia ya la adolescencia. Guía para profesionales y agentes sociales*. Málaga: Save the Children. Recuperado de: www. savethechildren.es/sites/default/files/imce/docs/modificacion_del_sistema_de_proteccion_a_la_infancia_y_a_la_adolescencia.pdf

O´Donell, D. (1990). *Instituto Interamericano del niño, la niña y adolescentes*. Academic Press.

Ordoñez Camacho, J. G. (2015). Consideraciones metodológicas sobre el estudio del comportamiento antisocial en la teoría de curso de vida de sampson y laub. *Anuario de Derecho, 32*(32).

Patterson, G. R., DeBaryshe, B., & Ramsey, E. (1989). *A developmental perspective*. Academic Press.

Rebellon, C. J. (2006). Do adolescents engage in delinquency to attract the social attention of peers? An extension and longitudinal test of the social reinforcement hypothesis. *Journal of Research in Crime and Delinquency, 43*(4), 387–411. doi:10.1177/0022427806291259

Redondo, S. (2008). Individuos, sociedades y oportunidades en la explicación y prevención del delito: Modelo del Triple Riesgo Delictivo. *Revista Española de Investigación Criminológica, 7*(6), 1–53.

Schioppa, M. (2013). Influence of the group of delinquent couples in the involvement of the adolescent in delinquency. *Justicia Juris, 9*(1), 93-111.

Sikorski, J. B. (1996). Academic underachievement and school refusal. In *Handbook of adolescent health risk behavior* (pp. 393–411). Springer. doi:10.1007/978-1-4899-0203-0_15

Stattin, H., & Kerr, M. (2000). Parental monitoring: A reinterpretation. *Child Development, 71*(4), 1072–1085. doi:10.1111/1467-8624.00210 PMID:11016567

Vitulano, M. L., Fite, P. J., & Rathert, J. L. (2010). "Delinquent peer influence on childhood delinquency": The moderating effect of impulsivity. *Journal of Psychopathology and Behavioral Assessment, 32*(3), 315–322. doi:10.100710862-009-9160-2

Wareham, J., Cochran, J. K., Dembo, R., & Sellers, C. S. (2005). Community, Strain, and Delinquency: A Test of a Multi-Level Model of General Strain Theory. *Western Criminology Review, 6*(1).

Warr, M. (1993). Parents, peers, and delinquency. *Social Forces, 72*, 247–264.

Wells, L. E., & Rankin, J. H. (1991). Families and Delinquency: A Meta-Analysis of the Impact of Broken Homes. *Social Problems, 38*(1), 71–93. doi:10.2307/800639

Wortley, R. (2008). Situational precipitators of crime. In R. Wortley & L. Mazerolle (Eds.), *Environmental criminology and crime analysis* (pp. 48–69). Willan.

Wright, J. P., & Cullen, F. T. (2001). Parental efficacy and delinquent behavior: Do control and support matter? *Criminology*, *39*(3), 677–706. doi:10.1111/j.1745-9125.2001.tb00937.x

Zhang, Y., Day, G., & Cao, L. (2012). A partial test of Agnew's general theory of crime and delinquency. *Crime and Delinquency*, *58*(6), 856–878. doi:10.1177/0011128712461738

APPENDIX 1

Table 2. List of experts who collaborated in the research.

Name	Position	Schooling	Experience
Antonio Molina Serrano. antonio.molina.serrano@gmail.com	• Director of the Addiction Center	• Diploma in Social Education • Socio-Cultural Animation and Community Dynamization • Councilor Mairena del Aljarafe.	4 years
Clara Luisa Garrido Garrucho. Claluga_13@hotmail.com	• Educator at el Polígono Sur in Fundación Atenea with homeless people.	• Double diploma in Social Education and Social Work. • Master's Degree in Development, Social Awareness and Culture of Peace. • Upper Cycles. • Sign Language Interpretation Technician. • Communicative Mediation Technician.	6 years
Cristina Gómez Gómez. psicologia.crecerconfuturo@gmail.com	• Residential Technician for the Protection of the Underaged. • Psychologist at the CCF in the Child Protection Program	• Degree in Psychology • Master's Degree in Clinical, Legal and Forensic Psychology. • Master's Degree in Intervention and Mediation with Underaged in a Situation of Vulnerability and or Social Conflict	14 years
Germán Venegas Díaz. german@consultores.supercable.es	• Coordinator of the Underaged Shift of the Seville Bar Association. • Associate Professor at the Universidad Pablo de Olavide (Criminal Law Area). • Member of the Juvenile Commission of the Andalusian Council of the Bar Association	• Degree in Law. • Master's Degree in Business Administration and Management. • Juvenile Delinquency Specialist.	18 years
Cristina Vega Iglesias lavega12@gmail.com	• Founder and Coordinator of the NGO Crecer con Futuro (Grow with a Future).	• Diploma in Hispanic Philology.	14 years
Manuel Bruno Rivera Borrego aprome.se.pol@juntadeandalucia.es	• Police of the Group for the Protection of the Underaged (APROME)	• Electronic Higher Degree Training Cycle. • Electronic Engineering	6 years

APPENDIX 2. FORM YOUNG RESIDENTS IN PROTECTION CENTRES

The objective of this form is to collect data from the members of the legal age of Collaborating Families and from the young people of legal age who are beneficiaries of the Program.
Indicate how often, during the last 12 months, the young beneficiary of the Collaborating Families Program carried out some of the following actions, being 0 = never, 1 = a few times a year, 2 = a few times a month, 3 = once or twice per week, and 4 = almost every day.

Table 3. Identification Data

Variables and Indicators		Scale	Answer
Survey data	Gender	1=Man.	
		2=Woman.	
	Age (years)		
	Schooling	1=No studies	
		2=Primary education	
		3=Bachellor / MUBD o UOC	
		4=Diploma, Degree o Graduate	
		5= Master o Postgrado	
	Profession		
Collaborating Family Data	Standard of Living	1 = Poor	
		2 = Almost Poor	
		3 = Fair	
		4 = Relatively good	
		5 = Good	
	Post Code of The Residence of the Collaborating Family		
	Number of Members of the Collaborating Family		
School data	Type of Centre that the Young person assisted or was assisted by.	1= Public school	
		2= Concerted school	
		3= Private school	

APPENDIX 3

Table 4. Youth: Delinquency

Indicator	Scale					Answer
	0	1	2	3	4	
1. Damaged or destroyed property that did nor belong to you						
2. Stole (or tries to steal) something.						
3. You knowingly bought, sold or retained stolen property (or attempted to do any of these things).						
4. You stole Money or Other things from your parents or Other members of the Collaborating Family.						
5. You stole (or tried to) something at school like someone's coat in the classroom, locker or cafeteria, or a book from the library.						
6. You attacked someone with the intention of hurting or killing the person.						
7. You were involved in gang fights.						
8. You struck (or threatened to do so) classmates, parents or teachers.						
9. You used force to obtain money or things from others.						
10. You drank alcoholic beverages (beer, wine or hard liquor).						
11. You went out to discotheques, pubs or nightclubs.						
12. You consumed marijuana.						
13. You played games of chance.						
14. You watched or heard pornographic products.						
15. You harassed a person using a mobile phone or any Other electronic device.						

Table 5. Family Domain

Variables e indicadores						Answer
Average Weekly hours that the young person spends with the Collaborative Family						
Variables e indicadores	Escala					
	1 = never	2 = rarely	3 = sometimes	4 = often	5 = almost always	
Completely ignored the Young person						
They acted like They didn't care about the young person						
They slapped the young person						
They beat the young person with an object						
Privileges were taken from the young man						
They undeservedly blamed or criticised the young person						
They yelled and teased the young person						
How often does the Collaborative Family know where the young person is and who he/she's with?						
	(1) Totally agree	(2) I agree	(3) Undecided. I'm not sure	(4) I disagree	(5) Strongly disagree	
Discuss future plans with the Collaborative Family						
Share your thoughts and feeling with your Collaborative Family						
Your Collaborative Family seems to understand you						
You would like the kind of person your Collaborative family is.						

Table 6. Other Domains

Variables and indicators			Scale					Answer
			(1) Totally agree	**(2) Agree**	**(3) Undecided. I'm not sure**	**(4) In disagreement**	**(5) Strongly disagree**	
Commitment to education	The Young person usually finishes homework							
	Pay close attention at school							
	How frequently		Escala					Answer
			(1) Once a week or more	(2) Two or three times a month	(3) Once a month	(4) A few times a year	(5) Never or hardly ever.	
	How often	Arrive late at school						
		Arrive late to class						
		Skip class						
		Receive punishment or reprimand from teachers						
			Escala					A nswer
			Outstanding	Notable	Approved	Suspensions	Not presented	
	What kind of grades do you normally get?							
Variables and indicators			**Escala**					**Answer**
			(1) Never	**(2) Once or twice**	**(3) Repeatedly**	**(4) Many times.**		
Participation in Organizations	Have you ever played for an organized sports team?							
	Have you ever participated in youth clubs outside of school?							
	Variables and indicators		Scale					A nswer
			(1) Once a week or more	(2) Two or three times a month	(3) Once a month	(4) A few times a year	(5) Never or hardly ever.	
	On average, how often do you attend religious services?							
Variables and indicators			**Escala**					**Answer**
			(1) Totally agree	**(2) Agree**	**(3) Undecided. I'm not sure**	**(4) In disagreement**	**(5) Strongly disagree.**	
Faith in the legal system	Most of the things people call crime don't really hurt anyone							
	I have a lot of respect for the police							
	Rules were made to be broken							
	It's okay to avoid the law if you get what you want							
Variables and indicators			**Escala**					**Answer**
			(1) Once a week or more	**(2) Two or three times a month**	**(3) Once a month**	**(4) A few times a year**	**(5) Never or hardly ever..**	
Commitment to peers (friends)	How often	Spend time with peers unsupervised						
		Meets with criminals						
		Mistreated by his peers						
	Indicators		Scale					Answer
			Yes			No		
	Belongs to a Youth band							

*Collaborating Family: any person of legal age, couple or family.

Table 7. Solutions provided by experts

Problem	Solution to the Problem	Responsible Interest Group to Apply It
Get involved in gang fights	• Education in values.	Collaborative family.
	• Real and close references of children.	
	• Education in social skills (self-esteem, self-control and self-concept).	
	• Education in social skills (self-esteem, self-control and self-concept).	Child Protection System.
	• Education in social skills (self-esteem, self-control and self-concept).	Education System.
	• Psychological support for the young person and the collaborative family.	Junta de Andalucía.
	• Financial support.	
	• Information and training support.	
Consumption of alcohol.	• Education in values.	Collaborative family.
	• Real and close references of children.	
	• Education in social skills (self-esteem, self-control and self-concept).	
	• Education in social skills (self-esteem, self-control and self-concept).	Child Protection System.
	• Education in social skills (self-esteem, self-control and self-concept).	Education System.
	• Psychological support for the young person and the collaborative family.	Junta de Andalucía.
	• Financial support.	
	• Information and training support.	
	• Improve the leisure proposal.	Neighborhood associations.
Was struck by classmates, parents or teachers.	• School for parents.	Collaborative families.
	• Education in values (self-control).	
	• Gain authority by working with love, not agressively.	
	• Recognize an authority figure.	
Consumption of pornography.	• Include pornography in courses on sexuality.	Junta de Andalucía.
	• Limit internet access through parental control.	Collaborative families.
Stealing money or other things from parents or other members of the foster family..	• Education in values.	Collaborative families.

Chapter 15
Foreign Direct Investment and Poverty in Mexico:
Regional Imbalances, Following NAFTA

Ruth Ortiz Zarco
Universidad Autónoma del Estado de Hidalgo, Mexico

Eusebio Ortiz Zarco
Universidad Autónoma del Estado de Hidalgo, Mexico

Amada Hidalgo Gallardo
Universidad Autónoma del Estado de Hidalgo, Mexico

ABSTRACT

In this chapter, the authors want to analyze the regional imbalance of foreign direct investment (FDI) in Mexico and its relation with poverty levels for the 32 states that make up the country. The period studied covers from 1994 to 2020, taking as a temporary starting point the entry into force of the North American Free Trade Agreement (NAFTA); from the beginning of the 1980s until the beginning of the 1990s, FDI in Mexico maintained a tenuous growth, and from 1994, there was a considerable increase. Currently, developing countries, including Mexico, have positioned themselves as receiving entities of large flows of FDI. The research is based on an econometric scrutiny under the panel data methodology, which allows the authors to conclude that poverty is a factor that hinders a symmetrical distribution of FDI throughout the Mexican territory.

INTRODUCTION

In the period before to the 1980s in Latin America, most of the countries in the region adopted an economic protectionist model, assisted by large current account deficits in their balance of payments, a situation that triggered the debt crisis; One of the measures taken by governments to deal with the situation was to initiate a process of opening and liberalization of trade, financial and Foreign Direct

DOI: 10.4018/978-1-7998-8925-0.ch015

Investment (FDI) regimes; from this moment on, FDI legislation, rather than regulating FDI flows, has focused on foment them.

From the beginning of the 80's until the early 90's, FDI in Mexico maintained a tenuous growth, it was from 1994, with the entry into force of the North American Free Trade Agreement (NAFTA), when there was a considerable increase; currently developing countries, including Mexico, have positioned themselves as attractive entities for FDI, Latin America in particular has established itself as a recipient entity of strong FDI flows.

The Secretariat of the United Nations Conference on Trade and Development (UNCTAD) identifies the determinants of FDI flows as the following: a) the general policy framework for foreign investment, b) the costs and availability of factors of production, and c) business facilitation measures (UNCTAD, 2009); however, each country has structural characteristics that define and differentiate it from the rest, and in the case of Mexico, these in turn generate particular conditions for each state. This research document identifies the relationship between FDI inflows and poverty in different states, considering that there are factors in Mexico that have led to a regionalization of FDI inflows after NAFTA came into force.

The implementation of NAFTA as of January 1, 1994, shaped the dynamics of the financing of productive projects in Mexico, making FDI inflows substantial for the Mexican economy, which in 2017 amounted to US$ 29,695 million, representing an increase of 11% compared to 2016; 46. 79% came from the United States, of that total, 38.49% fell under the heading of new investments, 32.46% in reinvestment of profits and 29.05% corresponded to intercompany accounts, (Ministry of Economy, 2017).

The advantages of FDI inflows to Mexico cannot be generalized to all of the country's states, since FDI flows gravitate around the manufacturing industry, which attracted 45.26% of the total, followed by the transportation industry, which attracted 10.82%, and the construction sector with 10.28%; added to this, 70% of FDI is focused in five federal entities: Mexico City, State of Mexico, Coahuila, Nuevo León and Chihuahua, (Ministry of Economy, 2017)., 2017). Taking up the finding of Suanes and Roca (2015), who state that although FDI causes an increase in inequality, from certain levels of FDI as a percentage of Gross Domestic Product (GDP) it induces greater equity; there are states that require economic policies that strengthen the attraction of FDI, as a means to reduce their lag compared to the rest of the country, as well as inequality within the same states.

The Annual Reports of Poverty Situation and Social Gap of the different states, prepared by the Undersecretary of Planning, Evaluation and Regional Development (SEDESOL, 2020), based on data issued by the National Council for the Evaluation of Social Development Policy (CONEVAL), highlight as states with the greatest social gap: Chiapas, Guerrero, Oaxaca, Veracruz, Puebla, Tabasco, Morelos, Tlaxcala, Zacatecas, Campeche, Michoacán and Hidalgo. The first is a brief review of the literature on the subject, the second details the behavior of the variables that explain the regional differences in the attraction of FDI and its link with poverty, the third refers to the methodology used and the results that show the regional imbalance in attracting FDI, and finally the conclusions are presented.

Background

The rise of the international movement of capital (export of productive capital) from developed economies to developing economies has been the scenario that has motivated the emergence of a vast literature on the subject, with the central objectives of study being the effect of FDI on economic growth and the determinants of FDI; while research on the regionalization of FDI and its effects on inequality is less.

Some of the works that analyze the differentiated impact of FDI on Mexico's 32 states include: García, 2001; Aguayo, 2004; Mejía, 2005; Calderón, 2007; Ángeles and Ortiz, 2010; Germán and Ríos, 2011; Medina, 2013; Torres, Polanco and Tinoco, 2015; Rosas, 2016; Almonte, Morales and Carbajal, 2018; among others. García (2001), after a study of the evolution and prospects of the Mexican manufacture industry, as well as its implications for the 32 federative entities in the years from 1965 to 2001; affirms that measures are needed to promote stronger links between the manufacure industry, potential local suppliers and local educational centers.

An evaluation of the economic divergence caused by the rapid growth of the entities of Baja California Norte, Quintana Roo and the Federal District, during the period from 1990 to 2000, was carried out by Aguayo (2014), who after a statistical analysis found no evidence that the northern border states have attracted more educated workers than the rest of the country, in other words no relatively higher increase in wages to skilled labor in the northern border region is visualized. Mejía (2005) analyzes the evolution of FDI in Mexico for the period 1989-2001, and after determining the statistical correlation between FDI flows to the country's states, he suggests that market potential has been the determining factor in attracting FDI, while other factors have played a modest role.

Calderón (2007), using a panel data model, corroborated the hypothesis of β-absolute convergence to the Barro, of FDI inflows to the 32 for the Mexican states in the years from 1994 to 2002, concludes that the states in the southern region of Mexico have higher convergence speeds than the more developed and industrialized states. Ángeles and Ortiz (2010) later determined the effects of FDI on growth and economic inequality for the period 1994-2006, and using a panel data model showed that in Mexico FDI flows tend to increase economic inequality between states but improve income distribution within them.

German and Ríos (2011), analyzing the connection between FDI and wage inequality in Mexico and its 32 states from 1994 to 2002, estimate that with a 1% increase in per-capita FDI, wage inequalities widen by six percent, while for the states with the highest levels of investment the effect is negative and close to 12%. Medina (2013), by means of a spatial concentration analysis, determines the impact of FDI by state for the 1999-2012 period, and obtains evidence that suggests the existence of negative effects, although FDI is located in states where the Manufacturing and Export Services Industry (IMMEX) model is found, it is also located in states with high international tourism, in a context of high raw material prices.

A study focused on spatial distribution corresponds to Torres, Polanco y Tinoco (2015), who, based on spatial Markov chains, explore the evolution of the spatial and temporal distribution of FDI in Mexico's states between 1994 and 2013; their finding suggests that regional divergence in FDI attraction is a process that seems to become more entrenched when different time slices are analyzed.

To the previous works are added contributions on specific determinants of FDI dynamics, Rosas (2016), explored the impact of educational level on FDI attraction for the 32 federal entities in the period 1994-2013, concludes that the higher the educational level the less FDI inflows, due to the fact that multinational companies require a greater amount of labor with few skills and training. More recently Almonte, Morales and Carbajal (2018) analyzed using panel data the effects of FDI on manufacturing employment generation in the entities of Brazil, Argentina, Mexico (32 federative entities), during the period 2007-2014, they found no consistent evidence that FDI accumulation is a factor influencing manufacturing employment generation. Carrada (1998), after analyzing the annual evolution of FDI in the Mexican maquiladora industry from 1980 to 1996, asserts that the Mexican government's tendency to deregulate maquiladora operations, given the imposition of regulations governing exports to Mexico, makes it difficult for companies from non-NAFTA countries to export tax-free to that market, and the combined effect of the two trends is fundamental in the prediction of higher levels of FDI in Mexico.

Mendoza (2011), with the estimation of a panel data econometric model at the level of the 9 manufacturing subsectors of the Mexican economy, provides empirical evidence of the impact of FDI on the growth of the manufacturing sector from 1999 to 2008, his results, although they denote a positive effect of the opening of the manufacturing sector, the effect of FDI is not statistically conclusive. Vergara, Almonte and Carbajal (2015), evaluated the effect that FDI has had on employment generation in the four large divisions that make up the industrial sector in the northern region of the country using a panel data model, for the years 2004-2013, the result is limited to demonstrating a positive and significant relationship between FDI and employment in the electrical industry.

Chiatchoua, Neme and Valderrama (2018), through cointegration and time series methodologies, provide evidence of the effect of FDI on sectoral employment in the Mexican economy for the period from 1980 to 2015, concluding that domestic private investment and public spending play a more prominent role in the three sectors of the Mexican economy than foreign capital. Thus, it is evident that the role of the government is a determining factor in the dynamics of FDI inflows and outflows. In this regard, Guevara (2002) refers that FDI flows to Mexico have increased as a result of the economic policies implemented; however, specific sectoral policies and specific microeconomic policies have not been implemented simultaneously.

De la Mora (2007), after analyzing the Mexican government's policies since the 1970s to promote local capacity building, technology transfer, job creation and foreign trade, affirms that Mexico urgently requires a proactive policy to attract FDI with a better articulation between the country's development needs and the interests of foreign companies. León and Mercedes (2016), proved the social impact of FDI which is not seen as a parameter that defines success as a state or country, consequently they suggest working on small and medium enterprises as a support for their beneficial growth.

Drawing on the research papers that precede this one, the following section contains stylized facts about the dependence of Mexico's economic growth on FDI inflows, due in part to the country's low domestic savings.

FDI IN MEXICO: A DRIVING FORCE FOR ECONOMIC GROWTH AND POVERTY ERADICATION

The empirical economic literature that studies the connection between FDI and economic growth is generally supported by two strands: the endogenous growth theory that argues that FDI promotes economic growth, and the neoclassical theory that states that the effect of FDI on an economy's economic growth is minimal. This paper adopts the planning that productive investment is a necessary element to underpin a country's growth and development, (Morales, 2010; Romero, 2012; Suanes and Roca, 2015; Rivas and Puebla, 2016; De la Cruz and Núñez, 2016; Among others), a prior step to investment is savings, domestic savings (IA) in Mexico, which is converted into national private investment, is not enough to cover the demand for resources by the industry, hence the need to implement economic policies that encourage the arrival of FDI, making it a necessary complement.

Figure 1 compares the evolution of FDI inflows with the dynamics of the percentage of population (in relation to the total population) in a situation of poverty in Mexico, for the period 1994-2020; it is

Figure 1. Comparison of FDI and the percentage of poverty at the national level, period 1994-2020.
Source: Own elaboration with data from the World Bank, (2021).
https://databank.bancomundial.org/source/world-development-indicators

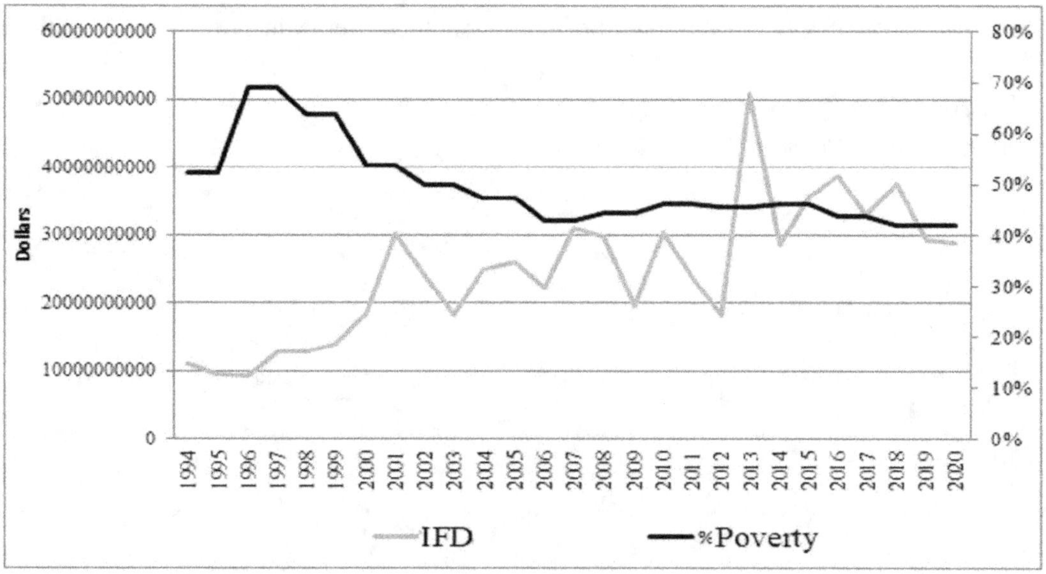

observed that FDI flows are highly unstable and sensitive to the imbalances of the national and international economy, a clear example of this are the crises that have been experienced during the study period: Tequila crisis (1994), dotcom crisis (2001), global financial crisis (2007), and the current crisis due to the Coronavirus pandemic (COVID) initiated in 2020; the effect of economic imbalances negatively impact FDI inflows to the country, causing in turn an increase in poverty (measured by the percentage of people living in poverty, in relation to the total population of the country).

At the national level, despite fluctuations derived from internal and external factors, there is a growing trend in FDI inflows, with 2013 being a historic year for Mexico in terms of incoming FDI, a situation justified by the acquisition of Grupo Modelo by the multinational company AB Inbev; in addition to this, there is a long-term downward trend in the level of poverty in Mexico; however, the situation within the country is unequal for the different states. The entry into force of the North American Free Trade Agreement (NAFTA), which allowed the participation of FDI in previously protected sectors, boosting the manufacturing sector and economic dynamism, accentuating unequal economic growth in the country, marking a clear regionalism.

At the national level, despite fluctuations derived from internal and external factors, there is a growing trend in FDI inflows, with 2013 being a historic year for Mexico in terms of incoming FDI, a situation justified by the acquisition of Grupo Modelo by the multinational company AB Inbev; in addition to this, there is a long-term downward trend in the level of poverty in Mexico; however, the situation within the country is unequal for the different states. The entry into force of the North American Free Trade Agreement (NAFTA), which allowed the participation of FDI in previously protected sectors, boosting the manufacturing sector and economic dynamism, accentuating unequal economic growth in the country, marking a clear regionalism.

In figure 2 visualizes the total amount of FDI inflows by federative entity, for the period 1994-2018; the gap between states is clear, Mexico City leads FDI uptake with US$ 150,497 million, followed by Nuevo Leon (US$ 56,629 million), State of Mexico (US$ 54,446 million), Chihuahua (US$ 35,559 million), and Jalisco (US$ 31,341 million) in fifth place; at the extreme the five entities with the lowest

Figure 2. FDI inflows by State, accumulated 1994-2018.
Source: Own elaboration with data from BANXICO (2021).

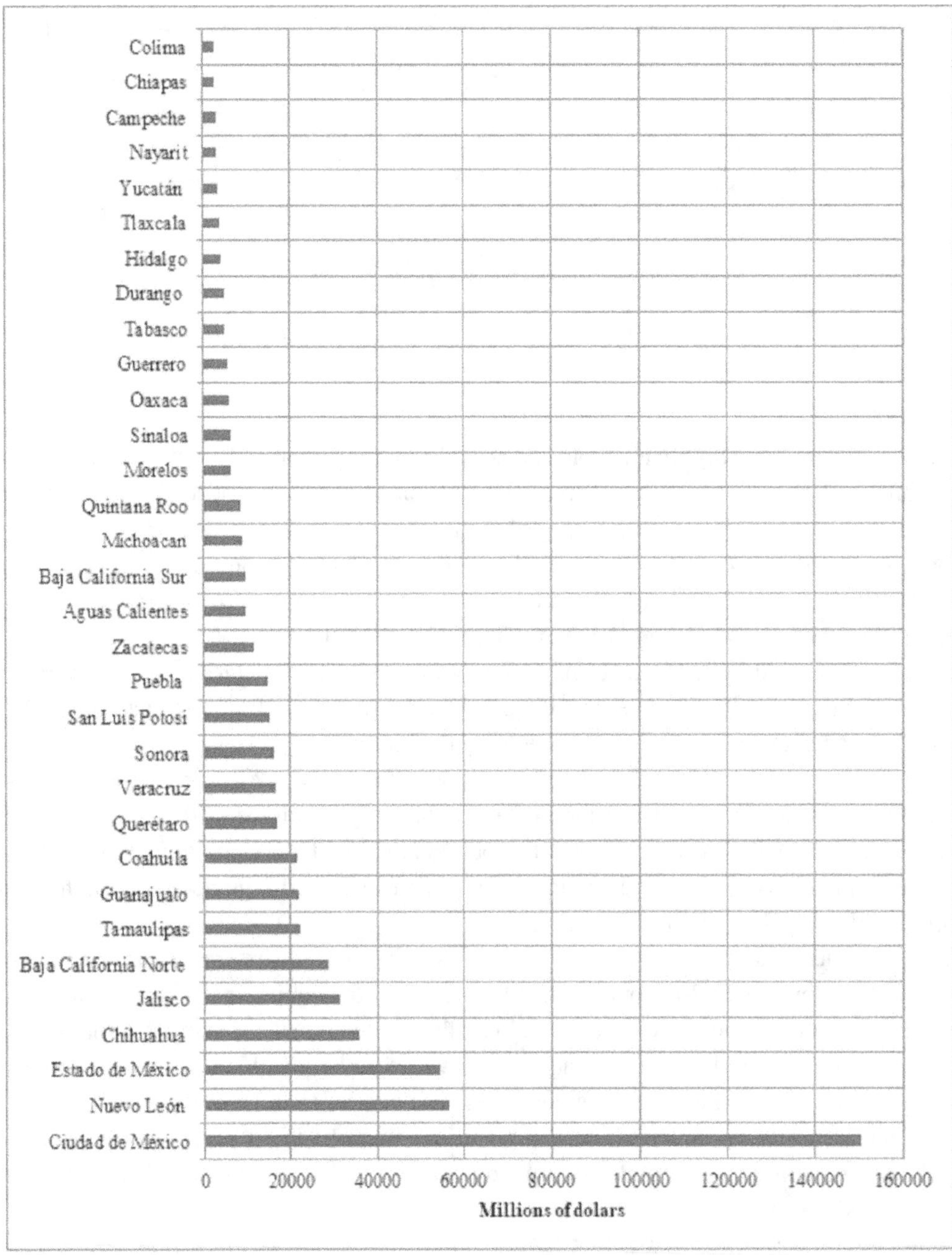

FDI inflows were: Colima (US$ 2,564 million), Chiapas (US$ 2,709 million), Campeche (US$ 3,012 million), Nayarit (US$ 3098 million).

Taking the proposition of Álvarez et. al. (2009) that FDI has a positive effect on economic growth, a determinant of regionalization in Mexico is the differentiated flows of FDI throughout the national territory, which deepen the gaps in various indicators, including: poverty, employment, quality of life, wages and productivity. Figure 3 contrasts the positions of the federative entities around the average HDI for the period 1994-2018, the HDI is an indicator that allows contextualizing the quality of life of the

Figure 3. Human Development Index (HDI), average by state, period 1994-2018.
Source: Own elaboration with data from the United Nations Development Program (UNDP Bulletin, 2020).

population; for some federative entities high FDI inflows coincide with high HDI, or low FDI inflows with low levels for HDI

In Mexico, the CONEVAL, a decentralized public organization, is in charge of measuring poverty, using statistical information provided by the National Institute of Statistics and Geography (INEGI). Poverty in Mexico, is seen as a multidimensional phenomenon, therefore, its measurement, based on Title Three, Chapter VI, Article 36 of the General Law of Social Development (2018), considers at least the following indicators:

- Average educational lag in the household;
- Access to health services;
- Access to social security;
- Quality and spaces of decent and dignified housing;
- Access to basic services in decent and dignified housing;
- Access to nutritious and quality food;
- Degree of social cohesion;
- Degree of accessibility to paved road; (General Law of Social Development, 2018)

Table 1 shows the evolution of the main indicators for measuring poverty in Mexico; it can be observed that poverty is decreasing in the long term, but at a very slow pace. Improvements are observed in access to health services, basic housing services, the quality and space of decent and dignified housing, access to food and educational backwardness; however, social security, social deprivation and income vulnerability are elements that demand the attention of public policies.

Table 1. Evaluation of poverty indicators in Mexico, 2008 - 2018. (Percentage in relation to the total population).

Indicator	2008	2010	2012	2014	2106	2018
Population living in poverty	44.4	46.1	45.5	46.2	43.6	41.9
Population living in moderate poverty	33.3	34.8	35.7	36.6	35.9	34.5
Population living in extreme poverty	11	11.3	9.8	9.5	7.6	7.4
Population vulnerable by social deprivation	32.3	28.1	28.6	26.3	26.8	29.3
Population vulnerable by income	4.7	5.9	6.2	7.1	7	6.9
Non-poor and non-vulnerable population	18.7	19.9	19.8	20.5	22.6	21.9
Population with at least one social deprivation	76.6	74.2	74.1	72.4	70.4	71.2
Population with at least three social deprivations	31.7	28.2	23.9	22.1	18.7	18.8
Educational backwardness	21.9	20.7	19.2	18.7	17.4	16.9
Deprivation due to access to health services	38.4	29.2	21.5	18.2	15.5	16.2
Deprivation due to lack of access to social security	65	60.7	61.2	58.5	55.8	57.3
Deprivation due to housing quality and space	17.7	15.2	13.6	12.3	12	11.1
Deprivation due to lack of access to basic services in housing	22.9	22.9	21.2	21.2	19.3	19.8
Deprivation due to lack of access to food	21.7	24.8	23.3	23.4	20.1	20.4

Source: own elaboration with data from CONEVAL (2021).

Table 2 is a comparison of the 10 states with the lowest and highest percentage of population living in poverty; in the first case are those states close to the northern border and those in the Bajío region, which coincides with the boom in FDI inflows; after the implementation of NAFTA, FDI began to position itself in the north of the country, and once a certain level of growth was reached in the area, investments were dispersed in the Bajío region (mainly Guanajuato and Jalisco).

Table 3 is a comparison of the states with the lowest and highest FDI inflows, for the period 1994-2018; when interpreting the data in tables 2 and 3 together, it can be seen that the states with lower percentages of poverty have higher FDI inflows, and vice versa, the lower the FDI inflows, the higher the percentage of population living in poverty. The determinants of poverty are many and varied, ranging from climate change, the type of economic policies applied, to the political and military conflicts faced by the country in question; this analysis allows us to observe a clear relationship between the dynamics of FDI and poverty in Mexico, under a regionalization pattern.

METHODOLOGY FOR THE DIAGNOSIS OF FDI REGIONALIZATION AND POVERTY IN MEXICO.

Globalization acted as a detonator of FDI flows worldwide, touching an all-time high in 2017, the moment prior to the outbreak of the subprime financial crisis, an event from which, the world economy and therefore the dynamics of FDI have not recovered; to this must be added the tax reforms of late 2017 in the United States which, by encouraging the repatriation of profits obtained by multinational companies with U.S. capital, had a negative impact on the mobilization of FDI, according to the most recent UNCTAD report (2019), in 2018 global FDI flows decreased by 13%, hitting developed economies the hardest, where FDI flows fell to their lowest point since 2004, after registering a 27% reduction, while flows to developing countries remained stable, with a slight increase.

Table 2. Comparison: States with the lowest and highest percentage of population living in poverty, average: 1994-2018.

Lower Percentage		Higher Percentage	
Federal entity	**Average poverty**	**Federal entity**	**Average poverty**
Nuevo León	19.12	Hidalgo	51.89
Baja California Sur	25.48	Zacatecas	52.11
Baja California	26.96	Tabasco	52.44
Coahuila	27.65	Michoacán	54.19
Ciudad de México	28.59	Tlaxcala	56.50
Sonora	29.13	Veracruz	57.22
Colima	32.56	Puebla	62.23
Chihuahua	32.90	Oaxaca	65.70
Quintana Roo	33.23	Guerrero	66.96
Aguascalientes	33.78	Chiapas	76.64

Source: Own elaboration with data from the Ministry of Economy (2020).

Table 3. Comparison: States with the lowest and highest FDI inflows, average: 1994-2018.

Lower inflow		Higher inflows	
Federal entity	**Foreign Direct Investment**	**Federal entity**	**Foreign Direct Investment**
Colima	133.43	Veracruz	1099.30
Chiapas	141.37	Tamaulipas	1154.23
Tlaxcala	155.62	Baja California	1258.63
Yucatán	158.88	Coahuila	1358.65
Nayarit	171.91	Guanajuato	1369.88
Campeche	190.52	Jalisco	1676.16
Hidalgo	272.53	Chihuahua	1789.03
Durango	273.04	Nuevo León	2473.20
Tabasco	314.32	Estado de México	2863.61
Morelos	335.04	Ciudad de México	5785.90

Source: own elaboration with data from CONEVAL (2021).

In the particular case of Mexico, international trade and FDI inflows were essential to emerge from the 1994 crisis, however the distribution of FDI throughout the national territory has been characterized by its asymmetry, 5 states enjoy the technological transfer of multinational companies that represent 70% of FDI inflows in Mexico, Pedraza, García and Armperas (2011). Government strategies to attract FDI in Mexico, based on the FDI regulatory framework and the specific programs of the Ministry of Economy, have not been able to attenuate the regional imbalances derived from the asymmetric settlement of FDI, and in turn this asymmetric distribution seems to have an impact on the poverty levels of the 32 states.

This section presents a proposal that adds to the comprehensive diagnosis of the problem, for which a measurement is proposed based on the methodology of analysis of a gravitational econometric model or gravity model, based on the "Law of universal gravitation" by Isaac Newton (1687), developed in the work "Mathematical principles of natural philosophy", which affirms that the force of attraction between two bodies is directly proportional to the square of the distance between them; by transferring this theory to the economic field, specifically to the analysis of FDI flows between two countries, it is possible to affirm that the value of FDI flows between two regions is directly proportional to the size of their economies, measured in terms of Gross Domestic Product (GDP) and inversely proportional to the distance, which for the purposes of this document we propose to add to the geographic distance two indicators representative of the distance or economic gap reflected in the quality of the population; the first indicator is the percentage of the total population of the federative entity that according to the CENEVAL lives in a situation of poverty, and the second is the entity's Human Development Index.

The basis of the proposal is that the most developed countries place FDI in countries with less development and less expensive labor, but the destination of FDI depends on several elements, among them: laws regulating FDI flows, taxes, social and political stability, abundance of natural resources, infrastructure, characteristics of human capital, etc.; in the specific case of Mexico, there is evidence that the states with higher HDI and less poverty are those that receive more FDI, therefore poverty is assumed to be an obstacle to the attraction of FDI.

Jan Tinbergen (1962), is the predecessor in the adaptation and application of physical postulates to economic modeling, specifically to the modeling of bilateral trade flows; in 1978, Anderson, proposes a gravity econometric model, with a cross-sectional structure, which can be estimated by means of ordinary least squares or as a panel data model. Considering the objective of this paper, the specification of the model to be estimated has the structure of the panel data methodology, capturing the heterogeneity of cross-sectional and longitudinal data, for the time period 1994-2020.

$$\ln\left(IED_{ijt}\right)=\beta_0+\beta_1\ln\left(GDP_{ijt}\right)+\beta_1\ln\left(D_{ijt}\right)+\beta_3\ln\left(POB_{ijt}\right)+\beta_4\ln\left(IDH_{ijt}\right)$$

where IED_{ijt}, expresses the volume of FDI inflows in millions of dollars to each of the federative entities (FDI flows from i to j) between countries i and j; GDP_{it}*GDP_{jt}, is an approximation of the size of the economies (real GDP of the United States, multiplied by the real GDP of the FDI recipient federative entity, amounts expressed in millions of dollars); D_{ijt}, is the distance between the capital of the United States and the capital of the corresponding state, measured in kilometers; POB_{ijt}, represents the percentage of population living in poverty in each of the states; finally, HDI_{it}, represents the human development index of each of the states. Subindex i refers to the United States, due to the fact that the Ministry of Economy in its Statistical Information Folder Foreign Direct Investment in Mexico and the World, states that the United States is the main investor in Mexico, contributing 42.3% of the total FDI inflow in 2019, and 40.2% as of June 2020, (SE, 2020). According to the above, the variables of analysis are described in Table 4.

The estimation of the model was carried out in STATA, and two regressions were obtained, the first consisted of a panel data estimation with fixed effects (MEF), which groups the statistical data to explore the behavior and independent effects for each cross-sectional unit (each of the states), and the second is a panel data estimation with random effects (MEA), which estimates an intercept for each of the states, which is assumed as a random variable with a mean value, and a random deviation with respect to that mean value. The results of both estimations are summarized in Table 5.

The results of the MEF and MEA estimates are contrasted by means of the Hausman test (see Table 6), which allows validating the most adequate estimate.

Now, the estimation of a dynamic panel is justified by the presence of autocorrelation, identified in the Baltagi –WuLBI test:

Table 4. Variables used in the model

Variable	Description	Unit of measurement	Source
IED_{ij}	Inflows of foreign direct investment by state	Millions of dollars	BANXICO
GDP_i	Gross Domestic Product of the United States	Millions of dollars	FRED
GDP_j	Gross Domestic Product of each of the 32 states	Millions of dollars	INEGI
D_{ijt}	Distance between the capital of the United States and the capital of the state	Kilometers	Google maps
POB_{ijt}	Percentage of the population living in poverty	Porcentage	CONEVAL
IDH_{ijt}	Human Development Index	Index (Values from 0 a 1)	Boletín PNUD

Source: own elaboration.

Table 5. Estimation results: FEM and MEA.

	MEF	MEA
Constant β_0	-459.3242	-1100.498
Probability	0.707	0.495
$GDP_{it}*GDP_{jt}$	.1310704	.1571495
Probability	0.376	0.286
D_{ijt}	--------	-.0299699
Probability	--------	0.927
POB_{ijt}	-16.46868	-16.16491
Probability	0.000	0.000
IDH_{ijt}	2818.888	3796.65
Probability	0.074	0.013

Source: Own elaboration with data obtained in the estimations.

Table 6. Hausman's test

Methods to compare	Hypotheses	Result	Interpretation
EF vs EA	Ho. Random-effects and fixed-effects estimators do not differ systematically	chi2(2) = (b-B)'[(V_b-V_B)^(-1)](b-B) = 11.62 Prob>chi2 = 0.0030	The difference between the coefficients is systematic, estimation by fixed effects is preferable.

Source: Own elaboration with data obtained from estimations.

F test that all u_i=0:
F(31,605) = 39.31
Prob > F = 0.0000
Modified Bhargava et al. Durbin-Watson = 1.9454852
Baltagi-Wu LBI = 2.1347724

As we can see in Table 7, the cross-sectional or group effects are expressed below. Each of the 4 variables is segmented by state of the republic to observe the specific group effects, among the most important conclusions are the following.

The impact of GDP is general, it is positive for foreign direct investment, however, the individual results are indistinct, negative cases such as Aguascalientes, Baja California, Campeche y Yucatán stand out, on the other hand those that have a positive difference, highlight that This result expresses the impact that investment in infrastructure has to contribute to foreign direct investment. Positive are the cases of Chihuahua, Guerrrero and Oaxaca.

The relationship between the distance of each of the states with respect to the center of the country has positive implications in general with respect to direct foreign investment; Chiapas, Chihuahua, Mexico City and Michoacán, highlighting that said variable expresses that the distance from the The country is not decisive in attracting foreign direct investment.

Table 7. Estimation of group effects

Variable	Parameter	Parameter	Parameter	Parameter
Constant β_0	-15853.69*	-1076.446	-898.7312	-4085.35
$GDP_{it}*GDP_{jt}$		.1310704	.0915783	.1180065
D_{ijt}	.09708		-.1558692	1.051771
POB_{ijt}	7.293789	-16.46868*		-16.02671*
IDH_{ijt}	22165.82*	2818.888***	4275.552*	
E1	-4.595715*	.0050914	-36.98706*	2514.034
E2	-.9520464	.173408*	-21.22661	2689.581***
E3	-19.21995*	-.0485421	-49.8471*	1642.125
E4	-11.89953*	-.0257249	-33.70185*	3195.431
E5	1.10585	.1110197*	-12.53245	-324.894
E6	2.967069*	.3982091*	-3.376691	4309.344**
E7	-.8948724	.191468**	-28.13468*	3689.745**
E8	-25.87987*	-.1004663***	-44.53193*	1630.857
E9		1.673829*	85.61416*	8725.027*
E10	-3.143144**	.0176989	-30.22767*	2516.135
E11	1.570157*	.7435666*	17.13158*	5588.446*
E12	2.94793**	.2975733*	-13.15609**	3771.854**
E13	6.014051*	.2207418*	-14.6459*	3259.491***
E14	-1.817348	.0567428	-26.94871*	2899.785***
E15	1.71829	.351615*	-6.169402	3808.211**
E16	.7921089	.1321889 **	-21.08879*	2922.589***
E17	-1.629609	.0469941	-28.30152*	2663.2
E18	-7.902235*	-.0248248	-34.49944*	2088.173
E19	2.335495*	.6888483*	21.73358	5426.877*
E20	1.119556***	.1735122**	-18.38378*	3222.582***
E21	.6090785	.280407*	-14.57472*	3758.538**
E22	-1.372663	.133896**	-26.75639*	3108.983***
E23	-5.706333*	-.0208718	-43.10796*	3176.179
E24	.8785249	.2241123*	-18.66081*	3587.065**
E25	-3.814602*	-.040468	-39.38495*	2073.804
E26	-2.299466*	.0555439	-33.39215*	2444.661***
E27	-6.267737**	.0744595	-26.7379*	3146.012***
E28	-.3978543	.2153776*	-23.37023*	3823.561**
E29	-8.689704*	.0396713	-28.00694*	2785.717***
E30	.8743541	.314121*	-13.80751*	4039.974**
E31	-13.12975**		-33.02937*	3548.517
E32	1.711719	.1668515*	-20.84436*	3281.902***

Source: Own elaboration with data obtained from estimations.

The variable poverty expresses a negative impact on the capture of foreign direct investment, since clearly a state that does not have a high capture of foreign direct investment is a state in which there could be poverty, note that the states of Nayarit, Quintana Roo, Sinaloa, Sonora, Baja California Norte, Campeche and Colima are states in which the impact is clearly negative.

The variable that is notoriously significant is the Human Development Index, highlighting that the states in which the Human Development Index most impacts as a determinant of attracting foreign direct investment are the states of Zacatecas, Yucatan, Oaxaca, Michoacán, Guanajuato, State of Mexico and Coahuila. This variable is significant positive in all the estimates made.

On the other hand, on table 8 below presents the results of estimates that seek to identify the temporal effects of the four independent variables, for this case the period to be examined is from 2000 to 2021. The conclusions in this regard are subsequently shown.

Table 8. Estimation of temporally effects

Variable	Parameter	Parameter	Parameter	Parameter
Constant β_0	-12431.44*	-12803.07*	-12685.57*	-12787.72*
GDP_{it}*GDP_{jt}		1.025715*	.9949251*	1.039317*
D_{ijt}	.0715842		.0833574	.0898192
POB_{ijt}	-.637125	8.094748***		7.988161**
IDH_{ijt}	17161.94*	17565.46*	17426.99*	
T2000	.0568659	-.0057446	2.161204	17189.34*
T2001	2.792797**	.1751568***	11.14146**	17956.63*
T2002	2.079771***	.1142118	8.575523	17657.85*
T2003	1.413924	.0552534	6.0951	17383.62*
T2004	2.343265**	.1239588	9.504269***	17683.56*
T2005	2.124555**	.1241351	9.213869	17725.42*
T2006	.7873255	.0651489	5.898309	17433.69*
T2007	1.475524**	.1602311	10.97754***	17868.73*
T2008	.9359707***	.1282158	11.70021***	17717.24*
T2009	-.1412644	-.0410852	.6941722	16951.77*
T2010	.617386	.021083	3.679961	17244.02*
T2011	.3531764	.0222891	5.160528	17255.88*
T2012	.8099104	-.0149653	2.649415	17050.89*
T2013	3.21697*	.235551**	20.15342*	18158.61*
T2014	1.024376**	.0501007	6.466537	17373.52*
T2015	1.79195**	.125999	11.13963**	17712.89*
T2016	1.038164	.1021617	9.002816	17609.76*
T2017	2.438186*	.1379787	11.97012***	17750.96*
T2018	1.537686***	.1266917	11.0299***	17724.12*
T2019	2.458796**	.1487557	13.39843 **	17816.18*
T2020	1.27026	.0147697	3.855194	17182.23*

Source: own elaboration with data obtained from estimations.

In general, the variables investment in GDP, distance, poverty, and Human Development are variables that have generally positive results when making the estimates. It should be noted that, unlike the past estimate of group effects, it shows a change in the poverty variable; highlighting that investment in infrastructure, the Human Development index and the distance from the center of the country have a positive impact on foreign direct investment.

Regarding the temporal observations, it is highlighted that in the periods 2001-2002, 2004-2005 and 2017-2019 are the periods in which the investment in infrastructure has had the most positive impact in determining foreign direct investment. In the distance variable, there is no noticeable change in the significance of the variables, it is even noted that only in 2 periods the variable is significant, 2013 and 2001. In the poverty variable, an interesting result stands out that in the periods of the financial crisis of 2007 and 2008 it was highly significant in a positive way, the result indicates that high levels of poverty attracted or required foreign direct investment, as well as in the 2017 periods to 2019.

The Human Development Index variable is undoubtedly the most significant, being significant and positive in all periods separately, from 2000 to 2021, with 2013 being the year with the greatest impact on FDI and 2009 with the least.

CONCLUSION

Mexico is a country that has historically been characterized by regional inequality and polarization in economic and social terms; Regional inequality must be considered as a structural problem in Mexico, established by events such as NAFTA, whose implementation has established polarization among the states that make up the country. Since 1994, the inflows of FDI to Mexico have increased abruptly, the above has brought with it advantages and disadvantages (widely analyzed by various authors), one of the effects is the regionalization of FDI flows.

The advantages of the entry of FDI to Mexico have not been generalized in all the states, nor for all economic sectors, has just under 50% of the FDI been positioned in the manufacturing industry, while 70% of the IED is focused on five states: Mexico City, State of Mexico, Coahuila, Nuevo León and Chihuahua. The figures show a correspondence between the states with the lowest inflow of FDI and the highest level of poverty. Apparently, the inflow of FDI has benefited the receiving entities, helping to reduce poverty; In this sense, in Mexico, both theoretical aspects are combined around the study of the link between FDI and economic growth, in the states with the highest inflow of FDI, the endogenous growth theory is verified that maintains that FDI promotes economic growth, while in the rest of the entities the neoclassical theory seems to be displayed, which affirms that the effect of FDI on the economic growth of an economy is minimal.

In Mexico, government strategies to attract FDI, and the specific programs of the Ministry of Economy, have not counteracted the asymmetric distribution of FDI, and the impact of this behavior on the degree of poverty of the 32 states. This document estimated a gravitational econometric model, which sought to verify that FDI flows between two regions are directly proportional to the size of the economies, (measured in terms of GDP), and inversely proportional to distance, in this model they were used as representative values of this gap: geographic distance, poverty and HDI. The econometric results allowed corroborating a differentiated behavior among the 32 states, a positive impact was observed between the GDP of the host state and the GDP of the United States (main investor in Mexico), with regard to geographic distance, only 4 entities obtain a positive parameter (Chiapas, Chihuahua, Mexico City and Michoacán), in such a way that distance is not a determining variable in the positioning of FDI in Mexico.

Poverty and the HDI were included as representative variables of the social gap between states, the results reflect that poverty has a negative impact on attracting FDI, that is, states with greater poverty will attract less FDI, a situation that generates a circle vicious if we consider FDI as a strategy to combat poverty; On the contrary, a high HDI promotes the arrival of FDI to the federal entity.

In Mexico, uneven regional development and high poverty rates are persistent problems since before the conquest, although this reflects a structural problem, the evidence shows that the attraction of FDI is an element that, combined with other economic policy measures, is effective in combating poverty; Thus, a task of the Mexican government is to search for strategies to diversify FDI flows.

REFERENCES

Aguayo, E. (2004). Divergencia Regional en México, 1990-2000. *Ensayos. Revista de economía, 23*(2), 30–42.

Álvarez, A., Barraza, S., & Legato, A. M. (2009). Inversión Extranjera Directa y Crecimiento Económico en Latinoamérica. *Información Tecnológica, 20*(6), 115–124.

Angeles, G., & Ortiz, J. (2010). La inversión extranjera directa en México y su efecto en el crecimiento y la desigualdad económica. *Eseconomia, 0*(26), 95–123.

Calderón, C., & Tykhonenko, A. (2007). Convergencia regional e inversión extranjera directa en México en el contexto del TLCAN, 1994-2002. *Investigacion Economica, 66*(259), 15–41.

Carbajal, Y. & Almonte, L. de J. (2017). Manufacturing labor in the Central Region of Mexico. An estimation by great division, 1985-2008. *Contaduría y Administración, 62*, 902-923.

Carrada, F. (1998). Inversión Extranjera Directa e industria maquiladora en México. *Comercio Exterior, 48*(4), 273–282.

Chiatchoua, C., Neme, O., & Valderrama, A. L. (2016). Inversión Extranjera Directa y empleo en México: Análisis sectorial. *Economía Informa, 398*, 40–59. doi:10.1016/j.ecin.2016.04.004

De la Cruz, J. L., & Núñez, J. A. (2006). Comercio internacional, crecimiento económico e inversión extranjera directa. *Revista de Economía Mundial, 15*, 181–202.

De la Mora, L. M. (2007). *Políticas para la atracción de inversión extranjera directa como impulsora de la creación de capacidades locales y del cambio estructural El caso de México*. CEPAL.

Fernández, A. M., & Ladrón de Guevara, R. (2002, january). *Elasticidad de la Inversión Extranjera Directa (IED) ante las variaciones de política fiscal en México* [Paper presentation]. *VI congreso Nacional de Investigación en Ciencias Económico Administrativas, Retos de las ciencias administrativas desde las economías emergentes: Evolución de sociedades*, Ciudad de México, México.

García, R. (2001). La maquila y la inversión extranjera directa en México. *ICE: Revista de Economía, 795*, 127–140.

Germán, V., & Ríos, M. (2001). El vínculo Inversión Extranjera Directa y desigualdad salarial en los estados mexicanos, Equilibrio Económico. *Revista de Economía. Política y Sociedad*, *7*(2), 119–149.

Instituto Nacional de Estadística y Geografía. (2015). *Mujeres y hombres en México 2015, Censo de población*. Instituto Nacional de Estadística y Geografía, México. http://internet.contenidos.inegi.org.mx/contenidos/Productos/prod_serv/contenidos/espanol/bvinegi/productos/nueva_estruc/702825075019.pdf

León, M. A., & León, M. M. (2016). Impacto de la Inversión Extranjera Directa en el desarrollo económico - social de la región. *Jóvenes en la ciencia Revista de Divulgación Científica, 2*(1), 697-701.

Ley General de Desarrollo Social. (2018). *Diario Oficial de la Federación*. http://www.diputados.gob.mx/LeyesBiblio/pdf/264_250618.pdf

Medina, S. (2013). Inversión Extranjera Directa por entidad. *Comercio Exterior*, *63*(2), 3–7.

Mejía, P. (2005). La inversión extranjera directa en los estados de México: evolución reciente y retos futuros. Economía, Sociedad y Territorio, (99), 185-236.

Mendoza, J. E. (2011). Impacto de la inversión extranjera en el crecimiento manufacturero en México. *Revista Problemas del Desarrollo*, *167*(42), 69–45. doi:10.22201/iiec.20078951e.2011.167.27720

Morales, J. (2010). Inversión extranjera directa y desarrollo en América Latina. *Revista Problemas del Desarrollo*, *41*(163), 141–156.

Newton, I. (1687). *Philosophiae Naturalis Principia Mathematica*. Pincipia. doi:10.5479il.52126.39088015628399

Rivas, S. y Puebla A. D. (2016). Inversión Extranjera Directa y Crecimiento Económico. *Revista Mexicana de Economía y Finanzas, 11*(2), 51-75.

Romero, J. (2012). Inversión extranjera directa y crecimiento económico en México: 1940-2011. *Investigacion Economica*, *71*(282), 109–147.

Rosas, B. (2016). Atracción de inversión extranjera directa en México: El efecto del nivel educativo. *Hitos de Ciencias Económico Administrativas*, *22*(62), 27–36. doi:10.19136/hitos.a0n62.1743

Secretaría de Desarrollo Social. (2020). *Informe anual sobre la situación de pobreza y rezago social 2020*. Subsecretaría de Planeación, Evaluación y Desarrollo Regional, Hidalgo. https://www.gob.mx/cms/uploads/attachment/file/288955/Hidalgo.pdf

Secretaría de Economía. (2018). *Inversión Extranjera Directa en México y en el mundo*. Carpeta de información estadística. https://www.gob.mx/cms/uploads/attachment/file/332558/Carpeta_IED.pdf

Secretaría de Economía. (2020). *Inversión Extranjera Directa en México y en el mundo*. Carpeta de información estadística. https://www.gob.mx/cms/uploads/attachment/file/575327/Carpeta_IED_2020-2T.pdf

Suanes, M., & Roca Sagalés, O. (2015). Inversión Extranjera Directa, crecimiento económico y desigualdad en América Latina. *El Trimestre Economico*, *82*(3), 675–706. doi:10.20430/ete.v82i327.180

Tinbergen, J. (1962). *Shaping the World Economy: Suggestions for an International Economic Policy*. The Twentieth Century Fund.

Torres, V. H., Polanco, M., & Tinoco, M. Á. (2014). Technological innovation and regional economic growth in Mexico: A spatial perspective. *The Annals of Regional Science*, *52*(1), 183–200. doi:10.100700168-013-0581-1

UNCTAD. (2009). *El papel de los acuerdos internacionales de inversión en la atracción de inversión extranjera directa hacia los países en desarrollo*. Colección de publicaciones de la UNCTAD sobre las políticas internacionales de inversión para el desarrollo, Nueva York y Ginebra.

UNCTAD. (2019). *Informe sobre las Inversiones en el Mundo 2019*. https://unctad.org/es/paginas/PressRelease.aspx?OriginalVersionID=514

Chapter 16
Sustainable Development Goals (SDG) and Economic Results in the Economic Sector of the Colombian Caribbean

Francisco Espasandín-Bustelo
University of Sevilla, Spain

Lourdes Osorio Bayter
ASIBEAM, Colombia

ABSTRACT

This research is important for several reasons. First, companies are being pressured by different interest groups to contribute to the achievement of the SDGs; second, a very high percentage of companies are not even sensitive to the fact that the SDGs are important for their sustainability; thirdly, researchers, especially those in the social sciences, have not generated knowledge about the state of the SDGs in companies; and fourth, the tourism sector is important for the achievement of the SDGs. The data collection method focuses on the material object "hotel companies" and uses secondary data available in different sources. Among the most relevant results of the research, the authors highlight the following: first, the companies in the sample, although they do not seem to have a formal plan, implement one or more SDGs; in second place, the SDG implemented in the largest number of companies is gender equality; thirdly, the least implemented SDGs are quality education, clean water and sanitation, affordable and non-polluting energy, and reduction of inequalities.

INTRODUCTION

In the words of Bowen et al. (2017) an unprecedented international policy window to address issues of sustainability and human development at the global level through the United Nations 2030 agenda and its central element, the "Sustainable Development Goals" (SDG), which were signed in 2015, has been opened.

DOI: 10.4018/978-1-7998-8925-0.ch016

The Sustainable Development Goals (SDGs), agreed on by the Heads of 193 countries, represent an important multilateral effort to move the world towards more sustainable and resilient pathways (Caiado et al., 2018).

According to Fleming et al. (2017), this allows for a much broader vision of sustainability, never before achieved, focused on environmental and human development achievements until 2030 (Salvia et al., 2019).

The SDGs have been acknowledged in many different ways, among which we highlight the following: the largest consultation in the history of the UN (Reyers et al., 2017); the means to reduce global and long-term existential and catastrophic risks to humanity (Cernev & Fenner, 2020); the opportunity for systemic (Costanza et al., 2016) and transformative change on a global scale (Bowen et al., 2017); the key global (Hák et al., 2016), broad, complex (Salvia et al., 2019) and ambitious challenges of humanity (Biermann et al., 2017); the new approach to global governance (Biermann et al., 2017); the shared goals of all humanity (Costanza et al., 2016); or an important step to build global consensus on what kind of world is desirable (Costanza et al., 2016).

Achieving the SDGs is a gigantic task that requires all stakeholders on Earth to work together (Fleming et al., 2017); since none, separate from the others has sufficient resources or capabilities to provide all the solutions necessary to achieve them (Sullivan et al., 2018).

Companies are being pressured by organizations such as the United Nations Global Reporting Initiative to report on their contribution to the SDGs (Moldavska & Welo, 2019).

According to a report by PricewaterhouseCoopers (2020), 71% of companies say they are already planning how they will interact with the SDGs; 41% say they will integrate the SDGs into their strategy and the way they do business within 5 years and 13% have identified the tools they need to assess their impact against the SDGs. By 2020, only 30% expect to have identified the tools they need to assess their impact and 40% think they have not even identified which SDGs are relevant to their business; And reassuringly, only 9% say they will do nothing.

Jones et al. (2015) suggested that business commitment to the SDGs generates unknown demands and will effectively improve the license to operate.

Companies are also subject to increasing pressure from global markets to support and align with the SDGs (Fleming et al., 2017) and from institutional investors to drive corporate transparency regarding the company's contribution to the SDGs (Cernev & Fenner, 2020).

Multinational companies can use the SDGs as a guideline to invest in sustainable development while pursuing their own business interests (Grover et al. (2019).

On the other hand, the academy has intensified its interest in the SDGs (Moldavska & Welo, 2019) and plays a key role in the achievement of the SDGs (Salvia et al., 2019) regarding the measurement of genuine progress and the alignment of the SDGs with existing governance arrangements (Biermann et al., 2017).

Despite this, there is a lack of publications on the extent to which the SDGs are being achieved worldwide (Salvia et al., 2019). As Bramwell et al. (2017) that same lack of studies occurs in the field of the tourism sector.

Research related to the SDGs has emerged in various disciplines in the academic world (Bebbington & Unerman, 2018); and according to Leal et al. (2018) is an opportunity to promote sustainability research.

According to Salvia et al. (2019), there are 3 SDGs preferred by researchers, and they are the following: (Quality education), 11 (Sustainable cities and communities) and 13 (Climate action).

The tourism academy perceives the SDG agenda as an ideal opportunity for criticism and to apply more radical and transformative approaches; although the commitment to the SDGs of tourism courses is limited (Boluk et al., 2019).

According to Fleming et al. (2017), the SDGs cover all aspects of sustainability in all sectors.

In the case of the tourism sector, the United Nations General Assembly determined 2017 as the International Year of Sustainable Tourism for Development and positions tourism as an instrument to advance the 2030 universal agenda, the 17 SDGs and the 169 goals that they envision (Boluk et al., 2019; Kimbu & Tichaawa, 2018); ranking perhaps better than any other sector in contributing to the achievement of the SDGs (Jones et al. (2017).

The reason the tourism sector is important to the achievement of the SDGs is that it is one of the driving forces in the global economy and has a significant range of environmental and social impacts (Jones et al., 2017). In this sense, and according to data from the World Travel and Tourism Council (Hosteltur, 2021), in 2019 the tourism sector generated 10.4% of world GDP and created 1 in 10 jobs worldwide; and, in 2020, it contributed 5.5% to world GDP and generated 1 in 11 jobs.

In the international tourism sector, Colombia is a country recognized worldwide for being one of the tourist destinations with the greatest impact worldwide due to its ecological, cultural, climatic and historical diversity. Tourism is the most dynamic and thriving economic activity in Colombia as evidenced by the fact that, in 2019, it registered a growth of 10.6% (DANE, 2018) and generated 27% of the country's total employment (COTELCO, 2019).

According to Aguilera-Díaz (2016), Cartagena and Santa Marta could be the boomer of the tourism sector, since the Colombian Caribbean has established itself as the tourist region par excellence due to the attractiveness of its resources, its trajectory and the different types of tourism it offers; among which, the following stand out: historical tourism; the tourism of beaches and / or rivers and the tourism of nature reserves, flora and fauna. The impact of the tourist sector of Cartagena and Santa Marta on GDP is very significant, since it amounts to 1.9%, which represents an income of 28 million pesos (Cartagena Como Vamos, 2018). On the other hand, the tourism sector of Cartagena and Santa Marta, in addition to being the one that generates the most income in the Colombian tourism sector, is at the forefront of technology and has substantial hotel infrastructure, although it also has several structural weaknesses.

The objectives of this descriptive and exploratory research are to generate knowledge about the situation of the SDGs in companies in the Colombian hotel sector and propose strategies for this group to progress towards the achievement of the SDGs.

To achieve these objectives, this work is structured on the following pillars. First, the literature on the SDGs and their relationship with the tourism sector is reviewed. Second, the data collection and analysis methods are described. Third, the main results are presented and discussed. Fourth, the final considerations are presented, which include the theoretical and empirical implications, the conclusions, the limitations and the future lines of research.

LITERATURE REVIEW

The SDGs, which entered into effect as of January 1, 2016 (Sullivan et al., 2018), are the cornerstones of the United Nations 2030 Agenda for Sustainable Development (Sullivan et al., 2018); Góssling & Hall, 2019). They were agreed on in a public and complex political process (Costanza et al., 2016), which involved contributions from at least 70 governments and numerous representatives of civil society

(Biermann et al., 2017). In the words of Tomás et al. (2016), the SDGs should be aspirational, action-oriented, concise, easy to communicate, limited in number, global in nature and universally applicable.

The SDGs expand on the previous Millennium Development Goals (MDGs) in many ways, but particularly by trying to deeply link social, economic and environmental aspects (Reyers et al., 2017); with a much broader vision of sustainability (Fleming et al., 2017) and in a more participatory and collaborative way (Hák et al., 2016).

In its simplest form, the SDGs refer to different conceptions: a new approach to governance (Biermann et al., 2017); an ambitious and demanding set of challenges (Jones et al., 2017); a global agreement (Moyer & Bohl, 2019); commitments to reduce poverty, hunger, poor health, gender inequality, environmental degradation and lack of access to safe water and sanitation (Zhang et al., 2016); shared goals for all humanity (Costanza et al., 2016); an ambitious step towards sustainable development (Fleming et al., 2017).

The fusion of the definitions proposed by Sullivan et al. (2018) and (Hák et al., 2016) make it possible to define, in a more complex and precise way, the SDGs as: "a set of measurable and responsible objectives, aimed at guiding the development, policy and priorities of the Member States of the United Nations in promoting sustainable development, which frames its agendas and policies for the next 15 years".

The purpose of the SDGs is to transform our world (Caiado et al. (2018); placing all the countries of the world on a common path towards sustainable development (Dang & Serajuddin, 2019; Orzes et al., 2018; Jones et al., 2017; Nash et al., 2020) and achieving a balance between the three dimensions of sustainable development - social, economic and environmental - and its institutional and governance aspects (Costanza et al., 2016).

This general purpose is specified in the 17 SDGs and 169 targets, mostly qualitative (Biermann et al., 2017).

Cernev & Fenner (2020) classify the 17 SDGs into four groups: results objectives -ODS 1 (No poverty), SDG 3 (Good Health and Well-being), SDG 14 (Life under Water) and SDG 15 (Life on land) ; input targets - SDG 2 (Zero Hunger), SDG 4 (Quality Education), SDG 5 (Gender Equality), SDG 10 (Reduction of inequality), SDG 13 (Climate Action) SDG 16 (Peace, Justice and Institutions) -; physical asset targets (SDG 6 (Water and Sanitation), SDG 7 (Affordable and Clean Energy), SDG 9 (Industry, Innovation and Infrastructure), SDG 11 (Sustainable Cities) and SDG 12 (Responsible Consumption and Production) - and targets enablers SDG 8 (Decent Work and Economic Growth) and SDG 17 (Partnership for the Goals).

Achieving the SDGs requires the participation of different interest groups, among which the following stand out: companies (Góssling & Hall, 2019; Sullivan et al., 2018; Jones et al. 2017), which can commit to the SDGs even without the requirement of governments and social expectations (Fleming et al., 2017); industry along with the informal sector (Bowen et al., 2017); national (Bowen et al., 2017), local and regional governments (Chams & García-Blandón, 2019; Jones et al., 2017); non-governmental organizations (Jones et al., 2017; Chams & García-Blandón, 2019); international organizations (Caiado et al., 2018); civil society organizations (Caiado et al., 2018); public or private actors (Bowen et al., 2017; Chams & García-Blandón, 2019); individuals (Chams & García-Blandón, 2019) and civil society (Caiado et al., 2018).

These interest groups must dialogue (Fontana & Oldekop (2020), establish relationships of trust (Bowen, et al., 2017) and assume political, strategic and financial commitments.

The SDGs have the following characteristics, among others: they are voluntary (Fleming et al., 2017; Bowen et al., 2017), they are not legally binding (Biermann et al., 2017; Sims et al., 2019; Sullivan et al., 2019; Sullivan et al. al. (2018) and they do not generate sanctions (Bowen et al., 2017); they are universal (Bowen et al., 2017; Grover et al, 2019); they accommodate different world views (Schleicher et al., 2018); they are ambitious (Dang & Serajuddin, 2019; Brende & Høie, 2015); they are simple and clear (Brende & Høie, 2015); they are realistic (Dang & Serajuddin, 2019; Brende & Høie, 2015); they adapt to the context (Schleicher et al., 2018) and are integrative and transformative (Bowen et al., 2017).

Progress towards achieving the SDGs is not linear (Cernev & Fenner, 2020). Moyer & Hedden (2020) state that progress will be faster to achieve the SDGs related to extreme poverty, the completion of primary school, access to drinking water and access to electricity; and it will be slower when it comes to reducing infant mortality, reducing secondary school completion and accessing sanitation.

At the continental level, Europe (Salvia et al., 2019) has focused more on the SDGs related to education and Latin America and the Caribbean (Moyer & Hedden, 2020) will significantly increase access to water, achieve school completion primary education and infant mortality rates will improve.

At the country level, the world will make limited progress towards achieving the SDGs. Moyer & Hedden (2020) state that in 2030, 15% of the countries will not achieve any of the SDGs and the rest of the countries will only achieve 53% of the planned goals. Sweden, Denmark and Norway are the countries closest to achieving the SDGs in 2030 (Bali Swain & Yang-Wallentin, 2020). Dang & Serajuddin (2019) point out that it is urgent for developing countries to reduce absolute poverty and guarantee economic growth.

On the other hand, the scientific literature identifies that the tourism sector is relevant to achieve the SDGs. Although there is no known research that describes the situation of the SDGs, it is known that research has been generated on some of the SDGs in the tourism industry. Along these lines, the works of Ferguson (2011) on gender equality and Saarinen & Rogerson (2014) on the contribution of the sector to poverty reduction stand out.

Regarding the situation of the SDGs at the business level, Rosati & Faria (2019) state that only 67 out of 408 companies consulted (16%) include the SDGs in their sustainability reports. Along this line, Sajjad et al. (2018) highlight that the place of origin of the BRICS multinational companies conditions the emphasis and effort made by the company to achieve the SDGs; Furthermore, SDGs 5 (Quality education), 13 (Climate action) and 14 (Life under the sea) are not very relevant for multinational companies in the BRICS, and SDGs 16 (Peace, justice and strong institutions) and 8 (Decent work and economic growth) are the most prominent and adopted SDGs.

On the other hand, there are numerous causal or determining factors that influence the progress and achievement of the SDGs (Cernev & Fenner, 2020) and it is necessary to identify those that are key (Hák et al., 2016). The literature consulted allows us to identify two main types of causal factors: those related to the company and those related to its environment.

We have grouped the set of causal elements related to the company into factors of awareness, structure, support / interest of the CEOs, management (approach, financial management, human resources management and accountability) and results.

Among the sensitization factors Fleming et al. (2017) highlight the access and availability of information; personal and corporate values; knowledge; understanding and awareness; the commitment to sustainability; and the external guarantee (Rosati & Faria, 2019).

Among the structural factors, Rosati & Faria (2019) mention the size, intangible assets and the average age of the employees.

Regarding CEO support, Grover et al. (2019) uphold that it can improve the awareness of the SDGs of different interest groups.

Table 1. Determining factors of the SDGs identified in the consulted literature.

Company		Environment
Sensitization	Access to and availability of information	Complexity, magnitude and scope of the SDG
	Personal and corporate values	Governance
	Knowledge	R&D community support.
	Understanding and awareness	Alliances
	Sustainability commitment	ICT
	External guarantee	Social networks
Structure	Size	Country
	Intangible assets	
	Average age of employees	
	CEO support	
CEOs support/interest		
Management	Management approach	
	Financial management	
	Human resources management	
	Accountability	
Results		

Source: The Authors.

Regarding management, we highlight, first, that the management approach that maximizes success in the implementation of the SDGs requires dialogue and consideration of the needs of multiple stakeholders, including academia, national, regional and regional governments. local, private sector, civil society and international organizations (Salvia et al., 2019).

Second, and regarding financial management, it is evident that the lack of financing is one of the most relevant barriers to achieving the SDGs. Salvia et al. (2019) state that the investment must be large and of a public and private nature; and Caiado et al. (2018) argue that it is essential to mobilize and raise sufficient financial resources.

Third, Chams & García-Blandón (2019) state that human resource management is one of the areas that can contribute the most to achieving the SDGs. In this sense, Rosati & Faria (2019) refer to gender equality as an element of crucial importance to successfully implement the SDGs.

Fourth, Bowen et al. (2017) argue that organizations that implement the SDGs need accountability mechanisms that guarantee their compliance; For this, a system of indicators based on conceptual models and rigorous scientific methods is necessary, as well as having global and integrated scientific information (Hák et al., 2016).

The last group of factors related to the company refers to results and shows that organizations with higher economic performance (Rosati & Faria (2019) and profits (Fleming et al, 2017) are more likely to address the SDGs in their sustainability reports.

The environmental factors identified in the literature consulted are related to the SDGs, international governance, support from the R&D community, alliances, ICT and the country. The first factor resides in the complexity, magnitude and scope of the SDGs (Fleming et al, 2017). The need to improve international governance (Joshi et al., 2015) is the second environmental factor that has been identified in the literature. The third factor refers to the fact that the support of a prepared R&D community that supports the industries is essential for the progress towards the SDGs to be evident (Fleming et al, 2017). The fourth factor refers to the fact that the interaction between stakeholders and the development of alliances is a factor widely recognized by the scientific community (Caiado et al, 2018; Bowen et al, 2017; Salvia et al, 2019; Góssling & Hall, 2019). The fifth factor considers technology crucial to achieve the SDGs (Jones et al, 2017); In particular, social networks provide an unparalleled opportunity to solve global problems (Caiado et al, 2018). And finally, the economic, social and environmental situation of each country and national priorities can also be a facilitating factor or a barrier to achieving the SDGs (Schleicher et al, 2018; Salvia et al, 2019; Joshi et al., 2015).

We conclude this section by recognizing that Colombia, and therefore Cartagena, is one of the countries promoting the SDGs and in 2018 it committed to achieving the quantitative commitments presented in the following table in 2030.

METHODS

In this section we will describe the collection of data and analysis methods used in the research. Regarding the data collection method, we point out in the first place, that the object of this research is the hospitality industry based in the Colombian Caribbean.

Secondly, we inform that we chose the 20 companies that were researched randomly, among those that operate in the hotel sector in the cities of Cartagena and Santa Marta.

Third, it becomes clear that the data necessary to carry out the research is of a secondary nature and is collected from different sources. In this sense, the data necessary to know the level of involvement of companies with the SDGs are located on the web pages of government regulatory bodies of the tourism sector at the national (Ministry of Industry, Commerce and Tourism of Colombia) and regional (Ministry of Industry, Commerce and Tourism of Colombia). Ministry of Tourism) and on the websites of companies in the Colombian Caribbean tourism sector. On the other hand, the data necessary to know the economic results of these companies are obtained from the information available in the Superintendency of Companies of Colombia, which reports on the financial situation of about 26,000 commercial companies.

To conclude the explanation of the data collection method, we state that, once the necessary data was obtained, they were coded and tabulated in an Excel sheet.

Subsequently, the method followed to analyze the data comes from descriptive statistics and focuses on the analysis of each of the variables under study: the implementation of the SDGs and the economic results of the companies that make up the sample.

DISCUSSION OF THE RESULTS

In this section, the most relevant results of the research regarding the implementation of the SDGs and the financial results of the companies that make up the sample are presented and discussed. In relation to the implementation of the SDGs, the following graph shows the following evidence. First, the companies in the hotel sector under study show a certain degree of interest in implementing the SDGs.

Table 2. Commitment to the SDGs of Colombia and Cartagena, calculated in 2018 to 2030.

No	OBJECTIVES	NUMBERS	
		COLOMBIA	CARTAGENA
1	End poverty in all its forms throughout the world	Monetary poverty in Colombia is 26.9%. For the period 2010-2017, 3,5 million people were brought out of poverty, 1.3 million from rural and 2.2 million from urban areas	55.1% of the homes in the insular area of Cartagena are in a condition of poverty.
2	End hunger, achieve food security and improved nutrition, and promote sustainable agriculture	An estimated 3.5 million Columbians suffered from undernourishment in 2016.	I/S
3	Guarantee healthy life and promote well-being for all, of all ages.	In 2017, 95.6% was insured for health, but there are shortcomings in the quality and timelines of health services that cloud this service.	In Cartagens, although the percentage of affiliation to the health system is high (104%), there is ony one affiliate to the contributory program for each subsidized affiliate.
4	Assure inclusive, equitable and quality education to promote lifelong learning opportunities for all.	Desite considerable progress in school enrollment, a portion of the population still does not attend school, especially in early childhood (51%), middle school (22%) and higher or tertiary education (62%) (DANE – Quality of life survey, 2017).	In 2018 there were 231,010 students connected at a general level, 89% were urban and 11% equalled urban population. Preschool education has 10%, Basic Primary Education 43%, Basic secondary education was 34%, Secondary Education13%
5	Achieve gender equality and empower all women and girls.	Employment by gender reveales a significant gap in the participation of women in the labor force. Percentage (12.3%) which is 70% higher than the previous (7.2%).	Women continue to be those who participate the least in the labor market, who suffer the most unemployment and reveal less employment rates.
6	Guarantee the availability of water and its sustainable management as well as sanitation for all.	In 2016, 72.8% of the population received this service continuously so, even with a high coverage, there is still 27.2% of the population who do not plainly enjoy this public home service	The population without conduit coverage in Cartagena is concentrated in the rural area, where it is estimated that around 25,898 people do not have access to drinking wáter.
7	Guarantee access to affordable, safe, sustainable and modern energy for all.	Colombia has placed emphasis on the production of electric energy with a 97% coverage for its users, even though around 70% of its energy matrix depends on hydroelectric plants.	The coverage ratio of the electricity service in the city is 100%.
8	Promote sustained, inclusive and sustainable economic growth, full and productive employment and decent work for all.	By 2010, 47% of the employed population had a formal job, by 2017 this number rose by 4,5%.	Compared to the country's labor occupancy rate, Cartagena is below average, being it that Colombia is 64.0% and 56.7% for the city. The tourism sector clusters 51% of the companies in Cartagens, but they only contribute for 30% of employment generated in the city.
9	Build resilient infrastructure, promote inclusive and sustainable industrialization and stimulate innovation.	On average, 42% of small and medium-sized companies requested **loans** in 2016, 3% less than in 2015, which is consistent with the rise in interest rates, consistent with the contradictory money policy. In the country, in 2018, the entrepreneural composition was: Large = 35%; Medium = 36%; Small = 16% and micro = 12%.	Cartagena's business structure in 2018 was composed of 34.699 productive units, in which 97% of the city's companies were small or micro * 91% Microenterprises (31.682 – with less than 10 workers); * 6% were small enterprises (employing between 10 and 50 workers); * 2% were medium and, * 1% was large.
10	Reduce inequality within and between countries	By income deciles, there is elevated inequality. The Colombian Palma ratio shows that while in 2010, the richest 10% of the population had 4.6 times the income of the poorest 40%, in 2017 this ratio dropped to 3.4, which shows that there has been reduction of inequalities in the last few years. In urban areas it dropped from 4.0 to 3.0. In the rural area it dropped from 2.7 to 2.5 Gini coefficient.	29.9% of the population, i.e.: 268.359 people in Cartagena do not manage to obtain a minum monthly income of $257.433 (pesos) to purchase housing, public services, transportation and food. Cartagena is the city with the highest level of poverty among the main capital cities of Columbia.
11	Make cities and human settlements inclusive, safe, resilient and sustainable.	Colombia has 14 million households and had a quantitative housing deficit of 6.7% in 2015. The qualitative déficit accepted by government for 2015 was 10.7%. On the other hand, of the 1.119 municipalities in which there were housing déficits, 816, (which corresponds to 72.8%) have a higher qualitative deficit rather than a quantitative one and in only 22.2% of them is the quantitative deficit higher than the qualitative deficit.	In Cartagena, strata 1 and 2 homes represent 72%. * Stratum 1 (39%) corresponds to 89.645; * Stratum 2 (33%) corresponds to 75.852; * Stratum 3 (19%), corresponds to 40.318; * Stratum 4 (4%) corresponds to 8.504; * Stratum 5 (3%) corresponds to 6.436; *Stratum 6 (2%) corresponds to 5.750.

continued on following page

Table 2. Continued

No	OBJECTIVES	NUMBERS	
		COLOMBIA	CARTAGENA
12	Guarantee sustainable consumption and production patterns.	Colombia wastes 9,8 million tons of food per year and the recycling rate does not exceed 10%. Colombia produces 13.8 million tons of solid waste annually, and it is estimated that this generation of waste could reach 18.74 million tons in 2030, which would mean about 321 kilograms per person, per year.	S/I
13	Take urgent measures to combat climate change and its effects.	In the period 1990-2012, it is estimated that emissions and this generation of waste could reach up to 18.74 million tons in 2030, which would mean about 321 kilograms per person, per year. Although there was a reduction in deforestation between 2000 and 2015 (315 hectars/year in 2000, and an average of 124 thousand hectares/ year in 2015, with a positive impact on emissions from the sector in this period, unfortunately there has been an increase in deforestation in the recent years, with an average for 2016 of 178 thousand hectares.	Solid waste prduction in tons: * Tons 2013 = 352,284; * Tons 2014 = 378,984; * Tons 2015 = 406,417; * Tons 2016 = 436,259; * Tons 2017 = 462,177; * Tons 2018 = 352,284. Year after year, the KG of solid waste that each Cartagena resident produces daily has increased. This LCA indicates that the monitoring periodicity is incomplete, since it is not permanent, as is required by the IDEAM guidelines.
14	Preserve and use in a sustainable manner, oceans, seas and marine resources, for sustainable development.	Colombia has an approximate total area of 2,070,408Km^2, and its jurisdictional waters spread out over 3.531 Kms. of coastline in the Pacific Ocean and the Caribbean Sea.	The strategic ecosystems of the city coincide with the areas in which there are the worst living conditions.
15	Manage forests sustainably, combat desertification, stop and reverse degradation of land and stop the loss of biodiversity.	The Unique National Register of Protected Areas (RUNAP) has approximately 29 million hectares of protected area, of which 16 million correspond to Protected Areas of the National Natural Parks System. Additionally, RUNAP has registered 111.000 hectares that are a part of Civil Societies's Natural Reserves (RNSC), where scientifc research and efforts undertaken by the private sector and NGOs, to preserve speccies, stand out	Trees planted for compensation in 2018, 6,500 trees in compensation for felling. Most of these were planted in the industrial and towns and bays areas. * 17.568 hectares of wetlands (31% of the territory), and 3.457 hectares of mangroves (6% of the city's área).
16	Promote peaceful, inclusive and just societies.	Since February 2018, 282 social leaders and defenders of human rights have been murdered. HRDs, being it that the majority of them ocurred in the pacified areas (119 deaths), according to the Ombundsman's Office. In recent years Colombia has experienced an increase in the number of hectares cultivated with coca (48.000 hectares in 2012, and 146.000 in 2016).	The lack of citizen coexistence between the natives of Cartagena was the cause of 55% homicides, that is, 126 deaths, followed by deaths caused by hitmen, totalizing 51 cases. In 2018, the number os sex crimes increased by 60 cases, when compared to 2017, with 574 crimes carried out against underaged people. The main victims were between 12 and 17 years of age.
17	Strengthen the means to implement and revitalize global partnership for sustainable development.	In the year 2017, 48% of all cooperation received was used for Peacebuilding issues and another 30% for Sustainable Rural Development and environmental protection.	With a medium-low level of social progress, Cartagena is the fifth city with the lowest social progress, attaining only 56.8 points out of a possible 100. Cartagena shows low performance in the dimension of fundamentals of well-being, where components such as education and health are included.

Source: The Authors (2021).

Second, the SDG that interests a greater number of companies is 5 (Gender Equality), which means that the companies in the sample do not discriminate based on gender.

Third, the least interesting SDGs for the companies in the sample are: 4 (Quality education), since they support educational institutions or human capital training; 6 (Clean Water and Sanitation), which reveals that companies do not make efficient use of the water they use; 7 (Affordable and non-polluting energy), which indicates that energy consumption is not efficient either; and 10 (Reduction of inequalities), which indicates that there are cases where the company is not equitable in dealing with all personnel.

Regarding the financial results of the companies in the sample, presented in the following table, we conclude that, according to their volume of total assets, the company with the greatest financial muscle

Table 3. Companies under study.

Aviatur S.A.	Cartagena
Servincluidos Ltda	Cartagena
Hotel Santa Clara S.A.-En Reestructuración	Cartagena
Hoteles Decamerón Colombia S.A.S. Sigla Hodecol S.A.S	Cartagena
Promotora Turística Del Caribe S.A. Protucaribe S.A.	Cartagena
Aparta Hotel Don Blas S.A.	Cartagena
Grupo Hotelero Mar Y Sol S.A.	Cartagena
Compañía Comercial El Dorado Ltda.	Cartagena
Inversiones Turísticas Del Caribe Ltda. & Cia S. C. A.	Cartagena
Hoteles Vía Del Mar S.A.S.	Cartagena
Cardona Agudelo Martha Lucia.	Cartagena
Bantu Hotel S.A.S.	Cartagena
Gente De Mar Resort S.A.S.	Cartagena
Inversiones Calle Del Cuartel S.A.S.	Cartagena
Santa Marta Real S.A.S.	Santa Marta
F.C. Holding S.A.S.	Santa Marta
Bureche S.A.S.	Santa Marta
Hotel Arhuaco S.A.	Santa Marta
Vargas Castro & Compañía S en C	Santa Marta
Hotel Santorini Ltda	Santa Marta

Source: The Authors, 2020.

is Decamerón, evidently dominating the sector; followed by Promotora Turística el Caribe, Servincluidos Ltda., Aviatur and Mar y Sol hotel group.

In addition, the dominant companies in the ROE indicator are Bureche S.A.S. followed by Hotel Santorini and Aparta Hotel Don Blas; which means that they are the ones that obtained the highest profitability in the sector, according to the investment made compared to Hotel Decamerón, which although it dominates with economic assets, attained losses, since it did not meet the goal proposed by investors. On the other hand, the ROA indicator is higher in the Aparta Hotel Don Blas y Bureche S.A.S.; which indicates that the company is profitable with respect to investment, otherwise the Hotel Decamerón, where this indicator confirms that the company is not profitable despite its great assets.

FINAL CONSIDERATIONS

Based on the literature consulted and the results of the empirical research, the conclusions, the theoretical and empirical implications, and the limitations if future lines of research are presented.

In the first place, the main conclusions of the research show that the topic "Sustainable Development Goals" is an emerging field of research in the scientific literature to which, according to Constanza et al (2016), only the door has been opened.

Figure 1. SDGs implemented in companies.
Source: *The Authors.*

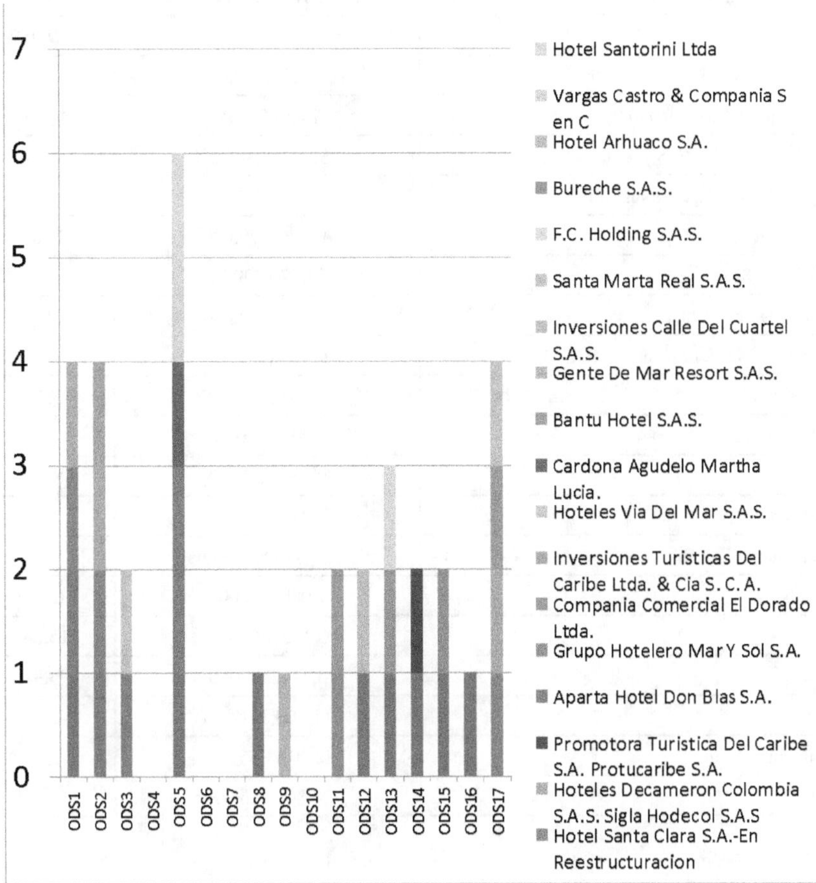

In addition, public administrations, economic sectors and companies, among other interest groups, are increasingly sensitive to the importance of the SDGs to guarantee their sustainability and that of the planet; and they need financial and human resources, knowledge and skills to implement them successfully.

On the other hand, the empirical research allows highlighting, by way of conclusion, the following evidence: the companies in the Colombian hotel sector under study do not develop a formal planning process focused on compliance with the SDGs, although they do implement one or more SDGs; the SDG implemented in the largest number of companies is Gender Equality; the least implemented SDGs are Quality Education, Clean Water and Sanitation, Affordable and clean energy and Reduction of inequalities; According to its total asset volume, the company with the greatest financial muscle is Decamerón; the most profitable company is Bureche S.A.S. and the companies that present a higher value of the ROA indicator are Aparta Hotel Don Blas and Bureche S.A.S.

Second, and in relation to the empirical implications, it is highlighted that there are several interest groups on which this research can potentially influence: the tourism industry, tourism companies and the Colombian public administration.

On the one hand, the Colombian tourism sector must be aware of the potential of the SDGs to transform the industry and contribute to a more sustainable, equitable and just future. In addition, it should

Table 4. Companies' Financial results

Colombian Companies	Total assests (in pesos)	ROE	ROA
Aviatur S.A.	175,325,493,000	19.95%	1.55%
Servincluidos Ltda	224,101,602,000	12.18%	4.11%
Hotel Santa Clara S.A.-En Reestructuraci6n	77,833,579,000	14.81%	5.27%
Hoteles Decamer6n Colombia S.A.S. Sigla Hodecol S.A.S	2,380,284,385,000	-104.13%	-7.59%
Promotora Turística Del Caribe S.A. Protucaribe S.A.	294,842,387,000	0.52%	0.29%
Aparta Hotel Don Blas S.A.	46,757,679,000	27.37%	13.87%
Grupo Hotelero Mar Y Sol S.A.	131,270,799,000	2.20%	1.75%
Compañía Comercial El Dorado Ltda.	13,486,342,000	10.55%	2.78%
Inversiones Turisticas Del Caribe Ltda. & Cia S. C. A.	19,282,930,000	-0.63%	-0.11%
Hoteles Vía Del Mar S.A.S.	6,482,384,000	6.34%	2.60%
Cardona Agudelo Martha Lucia.	851,000,000	0%	0%
Bantu Hotel S.A.S.	9,053,420,000	8.61%	7.18%
Gente De Mar Resort S.A.S.	2,017,042,331	0%	0%
Inversiones Calle Del Cuartel S.A.S.	21,850,655,000	3.14%	2.89%
Santa Marta Real S.A.S.	7,080,145,000	0.17%	0.16%
F.C. Holding S.A.S.	3,132,993,674	15.84%	3.74%
Bureche S.A.S.	3,711,294,000	93.81%	10.04%
Hotel Arhuaco S.A.	11,300,331,000	-2.89%	-2.40%
Vargas Castro & Compañía S en C	11,018,856,000	-2.13%	-2.02%
Hotel Santorini Ltda.	20,361,126,000	34.43%	3.62%

Source: The Authors.

stimulate the connection between the theory and practice of sustainable tourism (Boluk et al., 2017), dialoguing with different stakeholders to develop a coherent, coordinated and proactive approach towards the SDGs, and successfully communicate this approach to all interested parties.

On the other hand, the main implications are focused on the material object of this research: companies in the tourism sector which, together with the rest of the private sector, are an active and fundamental part of the successful implementation of the SDGs (Caiado et al., 2018). These companies must commit, operate responsibly and take advantage of the opportunities associated with the SDGs (Annan-Diab & Molinari (2017). In addition, they must change business attitudes towards new practices, technologies and sustainable business models (Rosati & Faria, 2019). In this sense, Caiado et al. (2018) propose a collaborative management model, which follows a cyclical process for the implementation, monitoring and continuous improvement of the 17 SDGs globally.

This collaborative management model begins with a planning process, which many companies have already started (Pricewaterhouse Cooper, 2020), but which does not establish ambitious objectives for the next five years. Costanza et al. (2016) argue that this planning process needs an ambitious general objective with clear metrics and harmonized specific objectives (Waage et al., 2015).

To achieve these objectives, it is necessary to assign resources to professionals from different departments, adequately managing risks and taking advantage of opportunities to promote sustainable development (Annan-Diab & Molinari, 2017). The implementation of the plan presents risks that can be derived from: subjectivity in the interpretation of the SDGs (Merino-Saum et al., 2018); the language differences between the SDGs and the business world (Fleming et al, 2017); the adoption of an excessively technocratic approach (Schleicher et al, 2018) or that struggles, and power gaps do not allow to secure the SDG agenda. Finally, for the implementation of the SDGs to be successful, it is necessary that companies are accountable to their stakeholders (Bowen et al, 2017) and that, previously, they know how their activities correlate with the SDGs and provide open access and transparent data (Pricewaterhouse Cooper, 2020). However, the reality is that companies have no intention of assessing the impact on the SDGs; aim to analyze the easiest, most obvious and positive results relevant to your business (Pricewaterhouse Cooper, 2020).

Finally, this research has implications for public policy designers, who must move towards an ambitious sustainability agenda (Biermann et al., 2017); for which it is necessary that they adopt a holistic approach to economic development (Sullivan et al., 2018) and develop a framework of political reforms and social changes that make the achievement of the SDGs possible. Stafford-Smith et al. (2017) consider that this is achieved by promoting links between sectors, guaranteeing integration at all educational levels, financing technological innovation of sustainable products or services and committing to sustainable development at the highest levels of government; without forgetting the legislative and regulatory incentives proposed by Caiado et al. (2018) and the cooperation of interested groups (Sajjad et al., 2018).

Third, the theoretical implications of the research are as follows. The scientific community plays a key role in the early stages of the SDG implementation process; since it is necessary for science to serve politics (Caiado et al., 2018) to successfully integrate the economic, social and environmental dimensions of the SDGs (Fleming et al., 2017); it also plays a fundamental role in reducing the ambiguity about the structure and content that differentiates the 17 SDGs (Merino-Saum, et al. 2018) and in monitoring commitment to them (Caiado et al., 2018). For this, it is necessary to create interdisciplinary teams (Annan-Diab & Molinari, 2017) made up of multiple internal and external stakeholders, and scientists from different fields (physics, biology, social sciences, etc.). and use theoretical approaches that explain the reasons why sustainability practices are implemented (Rosati & Faria, 2019); In this sense, Hahn & Kuhnen (2013) propose the theory of legitimacy and the theory of stakeholders as theoretical references to be used. Regarding the type of research that is demanded on the SDGs in the tourism sector; Boluk et al. (2017) make a call in the Journal of Sustainable Tourism for the publication of exploratory, empirical and / or theoretical / conceptual works related to the SDGs.

Fourth, although we consider that this research adds value to different interest groups, it also has a series of limitations that are detailed below. On the one hand, the deficit of scientific knowledge in the social sciences, motivated by the youth of the topic and by the scarce presence of the SDGs in the field of organizations, poses difficulties to support the research in a theoretical approach and in a justified conceptual model; It is for this reason that this exploratory research only deals with "inventorying" the situation of the 17 SDGs in hotels in Colombia.

In addition, the work has limitations since secondary data is collected that is available on the web pages of a reduced sample of Colombian hotels; the data are analyzed only with descriptive statistical methods; and the research is transversal and is limited to the Colombian tourism sector.

To overcome these limitations, future research in this area will be based on institutional theory and / or stakeholder theory; will use a justified conceptual model based on scientific evidence from the social sciences, with valid and reliable indicators and measurement scales; will capture the necessary data through the snowball method (Salvia, 2019; Kimbu & Tichaawa, 2018) and / or personal interviews (Fleming, 2017); will analyze the data with multivariate statistical methods; initially it will have a transversal character that, over time, will be longitudinal; and it will be applied in the Colombian and Spanish territorial scope.

REFERENCES

Annan-Diab, F., & Molinari, C. (2017). Interdisciplinarity: Practical approach to advancing education for sustainability and for the Sustainable Development Goals. *International Journal of Management Education, 15*(2), 73–83. doi:10.1016/j.ijme.2017.03.006

Bali Swain, R. & Yang-Wallentin, F. (2020) Achieving sustainable development goals: predicaments and strategies. *International Journal of Sustainable Development & World Ecology, 27*(2), 96-106.

Bebbington, J., & Unerman, J. (2018). Achieving the United Nations Sustainable Development Goals: An enabling role for accounting research. *Accounting, Auditing & Accountability Journal, 31*(1), 2–24. doi:10.1108/AAAJ-05-2017-2929

Biermann, F., Kanie, N., & Kim, R. E. (2017). Global governance by goal-setting: The novel approach of the UN Sustainable Development Goals. *Current Opinion in Environmental Sustainability, 26–27*, 26–31. doi:10.1016/j.cosust.2017.01.010

Boluk, K. A., Cavaliere, C. T. & Higgins-Desbiolles, F. (2019). *A critical framework for interrogating the United Nations Sustainable Development Goals 2030 Agenda in tourism.* Academic Press.

Bowen, K. J., Cradock-Henry, N. A., Koch, F., Patterson, J., Häyhä, T., Vogt, J., & Barbi, F. (2017). Implementing the "Sustainable Development Goals": Towards addressing three key governance challenges-collective action, trade-offs, and accountability. *Current Opinion in Environmental Sustainability, 26–27*(February), 90–96. doi:10.1016/j.cosust.2017.05.002

Bramwell, B., Higham, J., Lane, B., & Miller, G. (2017). Twenty-five years of sustainable tourism and theJournal of Sustainable Tourism: Looking back and moving forward. *Journal of Sustainable Tourism, 25*(1), 1–9. doi:10.1080/09669582.2017.1251689

Brende, B., & Høie, B. (2015). Towards evidence-based, quantitative Sustainable Development Goals for 2030. *Lancet, 385*(9964), 206–208. doi:10.1016/S0140-6736(14)61654-8 PMID:25242038

Caiado, R. G. G., Leal Filho, W., Quelhas, O. L. G., de Mattos Nascimento, D. L., & Ávila, L. V. (2018). A literature-based review on potentials and constraints in the implementation of the sustainable development goals. *Journal of Cleaner Production, 198*, 1276–1288. doi:10.1016/j.jclepro.2018.07.102

Cartagena de Indias. (2018). *Cómo vamos Cartagena, Turismo (S/F). Turismo en Cartagena.* Disponible en: https://www.cartagenacomovamos.org/nuevo/turismo-en-cartagena/

Cernev, T., & Fenner, R. (2020). The importance of achieving foundational Sustainable Development Goals in reducing global risk. *Futures, 115*, 102492. doi:10.1016/j.futures.2019.102492

Chams, N. & García-Blandón, J. (2019). On the importance of sustainable human resource management for the adoption of sustainable development goals. *Resources, Conservation and Recycling*, *141*(September), 109–122.

Costanza, R., Daly, L., Fioramonti, L., Giovannini, E., Kubiszewski, I., Mortensen, L. F., & Wilkinson, R. (2016). Modelling and measuring sustainable wellbeing in connection with the UN Sustainable Development Goals. *Ecological Economics*, *130*, 350–355. doi:10.1016/j.ecolecon.2016.07.009

Emis, B. (2020). *Bureche S.A.S.* Obtenido de https://www-emis-com.hemeroteca.lasalle.edu.co/php/companies?pc=CO&cmpy=4873743

Emis, F. C. Holding. (2018). *F. C. Holding S.A.S.* Obtenido de https://www-emis-com.hemeroteca.lasalle.edu.co/php/companies/index?pc=CO&cmpy=4960081

Emis, G. D. M. R. (2020). *Gente De Mar Resort S.A.S.* Obtenido de https://www-emis-com.hemeroteca.lasalle.edu.co/php/companies/index?pc=CO&cmpy=8161791

Emis, H. A. (2020). *Hotel Arhuaco S.A.* Obtenido de https://www-emis-com.hemeroteca.lasalle.edu.co/php/companies/index?pc=CO&cmpy=1197861

Emis, H. S. (2020). *Hotel Santorini Ltda.* Obtenido de https://www-emis-com.hemeroteca.lasalle.edu.co/php/companies/index?pc=CO&cmpy=2654254

Emis, I. C. D. C. (2020). *Inversiones Calle Del Cuartel S.A.S.* Obtenido de https://www-emis-com.hemeroteca.lasalle.edu.co/php/companies/index?pc=CO&cmpy=3404415

Emis, S. M. R. (2020). *Santa Marta Real S.A.S.* Obtenido de https://www-emis-com.hemeroteca.lasalle.edu.co/php/companies/index?pc=CO&cmpy=4873453

Emis & Decameron. (2020). *Emis*. Obtenido de Hoteles Decameron Colombia S.A.S. Sigla Hodecol S.A.S.: https://www-emis-com.hemeroteca.lasalle.edu.co/php/companies/index?pc=CO&cmpy=1197916

Emis; Aparta Hotel Don Blas S.A. (2020). *EMIS. Obtenido de Aparta Hotel Don Blas S.A.*: Https://Www-Emis-Com.Hemeroteca.Lasalle.Edu.Co/Php/Companies/Index?Pc=CO&Cmpy=1182500

Emis; Aviatur. (2020). *EMIS*. Obtenido de Turismo: https://www-emis-com.hemeroteca.lasalle.edu.co/php/companies/index?pc=CO&cmpy=1180755

Emis; Bantu Hotel S.A.S. (2020). *Emis*. Obtenido de Bantu Hotel S.A.S.: https://www-emis-com.hemeroteca.lasalle.edu.co/php/companies/index?pc=CO&cmpy=4055087

Emis; Cardona Agudelo Martha Lucia. (2020). *Emis*. Obtenido de Cardona Agudelo Martha Lucia.: https://www-emis-com.hemeroteca.lasalle.edu.co/php/companies/index?pc=CO&cmpy=8156342

Emis; Compania Comercial El Dorado Ltda. (2020). *Emis*. Obtenido de Compania Comercial El Dorado Ltda.: https://www-emis-com.hemeroteca.lasalle.edu.co/php/companies/index?pc=CO&cmpy=1186657

Emis; Grupo Hotelero Mar y Sol S.A. (2020). *Emis*. Obtenido de Grupo Hotelero Mar y Sol S.A.: https://www-emis-com.hemeroteca.lasalle.edu.co/php/companies/index?pc=CO&cmpy=1196930

Emis; Hotel Santa Clara. (2020). *Emis*. Obtenido de Hotel Santa Clara S.A.-En Reestructuracion: https://www-emis-com.hemeroteca.lasalle.edu.co/php/companies/index?pc=CO&cmpy=1197897

Emis; Promotora Turística Del Caribe. (2020). *Emis*. Obtenido de Promotora Turística Del Caribe S.A. Protucaribe S.A.: https://www-emis-com.hemeroteca.lasalle.edu.co/php/companies/index?pc=CO&cmpy=1210652

Emis; Servincluidos. (2020). *Emis*. Obtenido de Servicluidos: https://www-emis-com.hemeroteca.lasalle.edu.co/php/companies/index?pc=CO&cmpy=1213692

Emis; Turisticas del caribe. (2020). *Emis*. Obtenido de Inversiones Turisticas Del Caribe Ltda. & Cia S. C. A.: https://www-emis-com.hemeroteca.lasalle.edu.co/php/companies/index?pc=CO&cmpy=1202559

Emis, Vargas Castro & Compania. (2020). *Vargas Castro & Compania S en C*. Obtenido de https://www-emis-com.hemeroteca.lasalle.edu.co/php/companies/index?pc=CO&cmpy=1217686

Emis;Hoteles Via Del Mar S.A.S. (2020). *Emis*. Obtenido de Hoteles Via Del Mar S.A.S.: https://www-emis-com.hemeroteca.lasalle.edu.co/php/companies/index?pc=CO&cmpy=3906534

Fayomi, O. S. I., Okokpujie, I. P., Fayom, G. U., & Okolie, S. T. (2019). The challenge of Nigeria researcher in meeting up with the challenge of Nigeria researcher in meeting up with sustainable development goal in 21st century. *Energy Procedia*, *157*, 393–404. doi:10.1016/j.egypro.2018.11.204

Ferguson, L. (2011). Promoting gender equality and empowering women? Tourism and the third Millennium Development Goal. *Current Lssues In Tourism*, *14*(3), 235–249. doi:10.1080/13683500.2011.555522

Fleming, A., Wise, R. M., Hansen, H., & Sams, L. (2017). The sustainable development goals: A case study. *Marine Policy*, *86*, 94–103. doi:10.1016/j.marpol.2017.09.019

Fontana, L. B., & Oldekop, J. A. (2020). The sustainable development goals: The bumpy road ahead. *World Development*, *127*, 127. doi:10.1016/j.worlddev.2019.104770

Góssling, S., & Hall, C. M. (2019). Sharing versus collaborative economy: How to align ICT developments and the SDGs in tourism? *Journal of Sustainable Tourism*, *27*(1), 74–96. doi:10.1080/09669582.2018.1560455

Grover, P., Kar, A. K., & Ilavarasan, P. V. (2019). Impact of corporate social responsibility on reputation—Insights from tweets on sustainable development goals by CEOs. *International Journal of Information Management*, *48*, 39–52. doi:10.1016/j.ijinfomgt.2019.01.009

Hahn, R., & Kühnen, M. (2013). Determinants of sustainability reporting: A review of results, trends, theory, and opportunities in an expanding field of research. *Journal of Cleaner Production*, *59*, 5–21. doi:10.1016/j.jclepro.2013.07.005

Hák, T., Janoušková, S., & Moldan, B. (2016). Sustainable Development Goals: A need for relevant indicators. *Ecological Indicators*, *60*, 565–573. doi:10.1016/j.ecolind.2015.08.003

Hosteltur. (2021). *La aportación del turismo al PIB mundial cae a la mitad por la pandemia*. Disponible en https://www.hosteltur.com/143169_la-aportacion-del-turismo-al-pib-mundial-cae-a-la-mitad-por-la-pandemia.html

Jones, P., Hillier, D., & Comfort, D. (2017). The sustainable development goals and the tourism and hospitality industry. *Athens Journal of Tourism*, *4*(1), 7–18. doi:10.30958/ajt.4.1.1

Joshi, D. K., Hughes, B. B., & Sisk, T. D. (2015). Improving Governance for the Post-2015 Sustainable Development Goals: Scenario Forecasting the Next 50years. *World Development*, *70*, 286–302. doi:10.1016/j.worlddev.2015.01.013

Kimbu, A. N., & Tichaawa, M. T. (2018). Sustainable development goals and socio-economic development through tourism in central africa: Mith or realiit? *Geo Journal of Tourism and Geosites*, *23*(3), 780–796. doi:10.30892/gtg.23314-328

Leal Filho, W., Brandli, L. L., Becker, D., Skanavis, C., Kounani, A., Sardi, C., Papaioannidou, D., Azeiteiro, U., de Sousa, L., Raath, S., Pretorius, R., Vargas, V. R., Shiel, C., Trencher, G., & Marans, R. W. (2018). Sustainable development policies as indicators and pre-conditions for sustainability efforts at universities: Fact or fiction? *International Journal of Sustainability in Higher Education*, *25*(2), 131–142. doi:10.1108/IJSHE-01-2017-0002

Merino-Saum, A., Baldi, M. G., Gunderson, I., & Oberle, B. (2018). Articulating natural resources and sustainable development goals through green economy indicators: A systematic analysis. *Resources, Conservation and Recycling*, *139*, 90–103. doi:10.1016/j.resconrec.2018.07.007

Moldavska, A. & Welo, T. (2019). A Holistic approach to corporate sustainability assessment: Incorporating sustainable development goals into sustainable manufacturing performance evaluation. *Journal of Manufacturing Systems*, *50*(November), 53–68.

Moyer, J. D., & Bohl, D. K. (2019). Alternative pathways to human development: Assessing trade-offs and synergies in achieving the Sustainable Development Goals. *Futures*, *105*, 199210. doi:10.1016/j.futures.2018.10.007

Moyer, J. D., & Hedden, S. (2020). Are we on the right path to achieve the sustainable development goals? *World Development*, *127*(104749), 1 13. doi:10.1016/j.worlddev.2019.104749

Nash, K. L., Blythe, J. L., Cvitanovic, C., Fulton, E. A., Halpern, B. S., Milner-Gulland, E. J., Addison, P. F. E., Pecl, G. T., Watson, R. A., & Blanchard, J. L. (2020). To Achieve a Sustainable Blue Future, Progress Assessments Must Include Interdependencies between the Sustainable Development Goals. *One Earth*, *2*(2), 161–173. doi:10.1016/j.oneear.2020.01.008

Orzes, G., Moretto, A. M., Ebrahimpour, M., Sartor, M., Moro, M., & Rossi, M. (2018). United Nations Global Compact: Literature review and theory-based research agenda. *Journal of Cleaner Production*, *177*, 633–654. doi:10.1016/j.jclepro.2017.12.230

Pacto Mundial de la Red Española. (2021). *Implementación de herramientas del Pacto Mundial en la actividad empresarial, como contribución para canalizar los ODS*. Consultado en: https://www.pactomundial.org/herramientas/

Price-waterhouse Cooper. (2020). *Make it your business, engaging with the sustainable development goals*. Disponible en https://www.pwc.com/sdg

Revista El Universal. (2016, Febrero 10). *Turismo continúa siendo el sector que genera más ingresos a Cartagena.* https://www.eluniversal.com.co/economica/turismo-continua-siendo-el-sector-que-genera-mas-ingresos-cartagena-218767-CREU323023

Reyers, B., Stafford-Smith, M., Erb, K. H., Scholes, R. J., & Selomane, O. (2017). Essential Variables help to focus Sustainable Development Goals monitoring. *Current Opinion in Environmental Sustainability*, *26–27*(May), 97–105. doi:10.1016/j.cosust.2017.05.003

Rosati, F., & Faria, L. G. D. (2019). Business contribution to the Sustainable Development Agenda: Organizational factors related to early adoption of SDG reporting. *Corporate Social Responsibility and Environmental Management*, *26*(3), 588–597. doi:10.1002/csr.1705

Saarinen, J., & Rogerson, C. M. (2014). Tourism and the Millennium Development Goals: Perspectives beyond 2015. *Tourism Geographies*, *16*(1), 23–30. doi:10.1080/14616688.2013.851269

Sajjad, A., Talib, H., Guoliang, Z., Mohammad, N., & Benqian, L. (2018). The implementation of sustainable development goals in "BRICS" countries. *Sustainability*, *10*(7).

Salvia, A. L., Leal Filho, W., Brandli, L. L., & Griebeler, J. S. (2019). Assessing research trends related to Sustainable Development Goals: Local and global issues. *Journal of Cleaner Production*, *208*, 841–849. doi:10.1016/j.jclepro.2018.09.242

Schleicher, J., Schaafsma, M., & Vira, B. (2018). Will the Sustainable Development Goals address the links between poverty and the natural environment? *Current Opinion in Environmental Sustainability*, *34*, 43–47. doi:10.1016/j.cosust.2018.09.004

Sims, N. C., England, J. R., Newnham, G. J., Alexander, S., Green, C., Minelli, S., & Held, A. (2019). Developing good practice guidance for estimating land degradation in the context of the United Nations Sustainable Development Goals. *Environmental Science & Policy*, *92*, 349–355. doi:10.1016/j.envsci.2018.10.014

Stafford-Smith, M., Griggs, D., Gaffney, O., Ullah, F., Reyers, B., Kanie, N., & O'Connell, D. (2017). Integration: The key to implementing the Sustainable Development Goals. *Sustainability Science*, *12*(6), 911–919. doi:10.100711625-016-0383-3 PMID:30147763

Sullivan, K., Thomas, S., & Rosano, M. (2018). Using industrial ecology and strategic management concepts to pursue the Sustainable Development Goals. *Journal of Cleaner Production*, *174*, 237–246. doi:10.1016/j.jclepro.2017.10.201

Waage, J., Yap, C., Bell, S., Levy, C., Mace, G., Pegram, T., & Poole, N. (2015). Governing the UN Sustainable Development Goals: Interactions, infrastructures, and institutions. *The Lancet. Global Health*, *3*(5), e251–e252. doi:10.1016/S2214-109X(15)70112-9 PMID:25833663

Zhang, Q., Prouty, C., Zimmerman, J. B., & Mihelcic, J. R. (2016). More than Target 6.3: A Systems Approach to Rethinking Sustainable Development Goals in a Resource-Scarce World. *Engineering*, *2*(4), 481–489. doi:10.1016/J.ENG.2016.04.010

APPENDIX

Data of the Analyzed Companies

Aviatur, S.A.

Company was founded on February 6, 1957, employs 1895 people, of which 1143 are women and 752 men, it is located in 6 countries. It generates an asset of $ 175,325,493,000 only in Colombia. Located in the market as one of the most important companies in the sector. It should be noted that the company obtained a net profit of 2,709,131; an ROE of 19.95% that indicates the return on the investment made by the company, in this case it was a well-paid response by the market. For its part, the ROA obtained 1.55% which indicates that the company is not making adequate use of the company's assets. In addition, it allocated 6% of its profits to the area of Corporate Social Responsibility. (EMIS; Aviatur, 2020).

The SDGs for which the company works are:

- Poverty: carrying out social initiatives to support families displaced by violence.
- Responsible production and consumption: responsibly using the natural resources necessary for the activity they carry out.
- Life of terrestrial ecosystems: control over the felling of trees by not cutting down 170 trees.
- Gender equality: where there is no discrimination based on gender, on the other hand, the level of performance at work is seen and this is shown by the number of members.
- Decent work and economic fulfillment: from the fulfillment of dates the remuneration for the work will be according to this.
- Peace, justice and strong institutions: implements measures to combat corruption and bribery in all its forms within our Organization.
- Underwater life: taking tours without affecting marine life, an example of which is the visit on boats in whale season.
- Climate action: reducing the environmental impact generated by the company (EMIS; Aviatur, 2020).

Servincluidos Ltda.

Company was founded on June 2, 1994 and has 169 employees, generating an asset of $ 224,101,602,000. The company obtained a net profit of 9,221,425,000; an ROE of 12.18% reveals the profitability on the investment made by the company, in this case it was a well-paid response by the market; For its part, the ROA obtained 4.11%, which indicates that it is making good use of the assets. In addition, the company allocates 5% of its profits to the area of corporate social responsibility. (Emis; Servincluidos, 2020).

The SDGs for which the company works are:

- Poverty: through associations or foundations.
- Zero Hunger: providing support to foundations.
- Gender equality: it is not a requirement to be a specific gender to belong to the company. (Emis; Servincluidos, 2020).

Hotel Santa Clara S.A.-En Reestructuración.

Company was founded on November 23, 1987 and has 302 employees, generating assets of $ 77,833,579,000. From the above, the company obtained a net profit of $ 4,100,358,000; an ROE of 14.81%; and an ROA of 5.27%, stating that the company makes adequate and consistent use of the company's assets for a greater benefit of the same. In addition, it allocated 3.2% of its profits to the area of Corporate Social Responsibility. (Emis; Hotel Santa Clara, 2020).

The SDGs for which the company works are:

- Poverty: carrying out social initiatives to support families displaced by violence
- Alliance to achieve other objectives: supporting foundations so that they can have a greater probability of success in their objectives
- Zero Hunger: where the organization periodically donates lunches to foundations (Emis; Hotel Santa Clara, 2020).

Hoteles Decamerón Colombia S.A.S. Sigla Hodecol S.A.S.

Company was founded on March 13, 2014, has 1622 employees, generates an asset of $ 2,380,284,385,000 and is positioned in the market as one of the important companies in the sector. The company obtained a net profit of - $ 180,622,342,000; an ROE of -104.81%, indicates that in this case there was no response from the market, generating a negative percentage in the profitability of the investment made; on the other hand, the ROA obtained -7.59% which indicates that the company is not making an adequate use of the assets, negatively affecting it. It also allocated 3% of its profits to the Corporate Social Responsibility area. (Emis & Decameron, 2020).

The SDGs for which the company works are:

- End of Poverty: through associations or foundations.
- Zero hunger: support community kitchens or passing through.
- Alliance to achieve other objectives: supports foundations so that they can have a greater probability of success in their objectives (Emis & Decameron, 2020).

Promotora Turística Del Caribe S.A. Protucaribe S.A.

Company was founded on April 11, 1983, has 901 employees and generates an asset of $ 294,842,387.00, obtained a net profit of $ 862,180,000; an ROE of 0.52% and indicates that the return on the investment made by the company was slightly covered by the market; For its part, the ROA obtained 0.29%, which shows a very regular use of its assets, so management must take action in this case. Also, it allocated 2.7% of its profits to the area of Corporate Social Responsibility. (Emis; Promotora Turística Del Caribe, 2020).

The SDGs for which the company works are:

- Underwater life: supports foundations that care about marine life (Emis; Promotora Turística Del Caribe, 2020).

Aparta Hotel Don Blas S.A.

Company was founded on August 1, 1977 and has 319 employees, generates assets of $ 46,842,387,000 and obtained a net profit of $ 6,486,883,000; an ROE of 27.37% that indicates the profitability on the investment made in this case was a well-paid response by the market; For its part, the ROA obtained 13.87% which indicates that the company is making adequate and consistent use of the assets for a greater benefit of the company. In addition, it allocated 2.5% of its profits to the Corporate Social Responsibility area. (Emis; Aparta Hotel Don Blas S.A., 2020).

The SDGs for which the company works are:

- Health and wellness: cares about the well-being of employees and sends them annually for medical check-ups.
- Gender Equality: it is not a requirement to be a specific gender to belong to the company. (Emis; Aparta Hotel Don Blas S.A., 2020).

Grupo Hotelero Mar Y Sol S.A.

Company was founded on July 27, 1983 has 269 employees operating and generates an asset of $ 131,270,799,000, obtained a net profit of $ 2,293,411,000 and an ROE of 2.20%, showing that the return on the investment made by the company was covered narrowly in response to the market and population; For its part, the ROA obtained 1.75% which means that it is making regular use of the assets and it is to be taken into account by the management. In addition, it allocated 2.2% of its profits to the Corporate Social Responsibility area. (Emis; Grupo Hotelero Mar y Sol S.A., 2020).

The SDGs for which the company works are:

- Sustainable cities and communities: where communities benefit from the tours that the company does in their cities or towns.
- Life of terrestrial ecosystems: respecting the habitat of animals near the company's headquarters (Emis; Grupo Hotelero Mar y Sol S.A., 2020).

Compañía Comercial El Dorado Ltda.

Company was founded on January 31, 1983 with 295 employees operating, generates an asset of $ 13,486,342,000, obtained a net profit of $ 375,525,000; an ROE of 10.55% that indicates the profitability on the investment made in this case was a well-paid response by the market; On the other hand, the ROA obtained 2.78% which means, it is making adequate use of the assets for a greater benefit of the company, although it could improve and have a greater remuneration, also, it allocated 2% for the area of Corporate Social Responsibility of your profits. (Emis; Compania Comercial El Dorado Ltda., 2020).

The SDGs for which the company works are:

- Sustainable cities and communities: where communities benefit from the tours that the company does in their cities or towns.

- Alliances to achieve objectives: Make alliances with suppliers to reduce costs (Emis; Compania Comercial El Dorado Ltda., 2020).

Inversiones Turísticas Del Caribe Ltda. & Cia S. C. A.

Company was founded on February 21, 1973 has 164 employees and generates assets of $ 19,282,930,000 and obtained a net profit of - $ 21,066,000; an ROE of -0.63% that indicates the profitability on the investment made in this case the market did not respond and strategies must be adopted to obtain a greater profit; For its part, the ROA obtained -0.11%, indicating that the company is not making adequate use of the company's assets and therefore is no longer benefiting. 2% of its profits was allocated to the CSR area. (Emis; Turisticas del caribe, 2020).

The SDGs for which the company works are:

- Zero hunger: supporting community kitchens or passing through (Emis; Turisticas del caribe, 2020).

Hoteles Vía Del Mar S.A.S.

Company was founded on April 19, 2011 has 150 employees operating and generates an asset of $ 6,482,384,000, obtained a net profit of $ 168,406,000; an ROE of 6.34% that indicates the profitability on the investment made in this case was a well-paid response by the market; For its part, the ROA obtained 2.60% evidence that the company is making adequate and consistent use of the assets for a greater benefit of the company, although it can improve if a better strategy is implemented in the use of the asset. In addition, it allocated 1.5% of its profits to the CSR area. (Emis; Hoteles Via Del Mar S.A.S., 2020).

The SDGs for which the company works were not made known through the WEB page and no response was received from the company.

Cardona Agudelo Martha Lucia.

Company was founded on June 1, 1989 and has 14 employees operating, generating an asset of $ 851,000,000 and obtained a net profit of 0 reaching a point of equilibrium and depending on the following year so as not to fall into a crisis or balance in the red. The ROE and ROA of 0% also and indicates the return on the investment made by the company was covering the market without any profit in this regard and that it is making adequate use of the assets but without obtaining profits and this can be a warning indicator for take decisions. (Emis; Cardona Agudelo Martha Lucia., 2020).

The SDGs for which the company works are:

- Gender equality: It is not a requirement to be a specific gender to belong to the company. (Emis; Cardona Agudelo Martha Lucia., 2020).

Bantu Hotel S.A.S.

Company was founded on October 26, 2006 and has 27 employees generating assets of $ 9,053,420,000. He obtained a net profit of $ 650,041,000; an ROE of 8.61% that indicates the profitability on the investment made was a well-paid response by the market; For its part, the ROA obtained 7.18% which indicates that an adequate and consistent use is being made of the company's assets for a greater benefit of the company and the strategies implemented are giving positive results to the company. (Emis; Bantu Hotel S.A.S., 2020).

The SDGs for which the company works were not made known through the WEB page and no response was received from the company.

Gente De Mar Resort S.A.S.

Company was founded on January 31, 201, has 39 employees operating and has generated an asset of $ 2,017,042,331, obtained a net profit of 0 which leaves the company in equilibrium and at risk since the market has a high percentage of competition, being a factor; an ROE of 0% that indicates the profitability on the investment made was covered, but no benefit was obtained on the investment made; For its part, the ROA obtained a 0% which indicates that it is not making an adequate and consistent use of the assets for a greater benefit of the company and the implemented strategies do not generate the expected results. Also, 3.2% of its profits was allocated to the CSR area. (Emis, Gente De Mar Resort, 2020).

The SDGs for which the company works are:

- Industry innovation and infrastructure: always wants to stand out for innovation, for example in the hotel you have a private beach and they offer you leisure and tourist plans taking advantage of this space (Emis, Gente De Mar Resort, 2020).

Inversiones Calle Del Cuartel S.A.S.

Company was founded on January 17, 2007 and has 35 employees, generates an asset of $ 21,850,655,000 and obtained a net profit of $ 630,476,000; an ROE of 3.14% that indicates the profitability on the investment made in this case was effectively covered by the company, obtaining a percentage that generates profitability for the investors who contributed to the project. The ROA that it obtained was 2.89% and although it obtained a positive percentage, it is not making an adequate and consistent use of the assets for a greater benefit of the company and also, the implemented strategies are not giving the expected results for the company. Destiny 2.8% for the CSR area of its profits. (Emis, Inversiones Calle Del Cuartel, 2020).

The SDGs for which the company works are:

- Responsible production and consumption: Acquire the amount of raw material to be used in order not to waste the material (Emis, Inversiones Calle Del Cuartel, 2020).

Santa Marta Real S.A.S.

Company was founded on May 5, 2010 with assets of $ 7,080,145,000 and obtained a net profit of $ 11,504,000; an ROE of 0.17% which indicates the profitability on the investment made has been effectively covered by the company, obtaining a percentage that generates profitability for the investors who contributed to the project; On the other hand, the ROA obtained 0.16% which indicates that the company, although it obtained a positive percentage, is not making an adequate and consistent use of the assets for a greater benefit of the company and the strategies implemented are not giving the expected results . In addition, it allocated 2.5% of its profits to the CSR area. (Emis, Santa Marta Real, 2020).

The SDGs for which the company works are:

- Health and wellness: perform medical exams at the beginning of the year to be sure that the staff can provide the service.
- Alliances to achieve objectives: it is part of alliances with other companies in order to provide a complete service and that all companies benefit (Emis, Santa Marta Real, 2020).

F.C. Holding S.A.S.

Company was founded on April 20, 2009 and has 7 employees, generating an asset of $ 3,132,993,674 and obtained a net profit of $ 117,222,693; an ROE of 15.84%, therefore, the profitability on the investment made by the company was covered and with a great return on the part of the company, obtaining a percentage that generates profitability for the investors who contributed to the project; For its part, the ROA obtained 3.74%, which indicates that the company, although it obtained a positive percentage, is not making adequate and consistent use of the company's assets for a greater benefit of the company and the strategies implemented. (Emis, F.C. Holding, 2018).

The SDGs for which the company works were not made known through the WEB page and no response was received from the company.

Bureche S.A.S.

Company was founded on May 3, 2011 has generated assets of $ 3,711,294,000 and obtained a net profit of $ 372,769,000; an ROE of 93.81%, which means the profitability on the investment made was effectively covered by the company, obtaining a percentage of profitability that is very satisfactory for the investors who contributed to the project, since the company fully exploited the investment made; For its part, the ROA obtained a 10.04% that indicates a positive percentage and adequate and consistent use is being made of the company's assets for a greater benefit of the company and the implemented strategies are giving the expected results to use all its human capital and tangible asset for greater benefit. Also, the company allocated 3% of its profits to the CSR area. (Emis, Bureche, 2020).

The SDGs for which the company works are:

- Climate action: Minimizing the impact on the environment (Informacionempresas Colombia, 2020).

Hotel Arhuaco S.A.

Company was founded on March 6, 1998 has 30 employees operating and generates an asset of $ 11,300,331,000, obtained a net profit of - $ 271,436,000; an ROE of -2.89% indicates that the return on the investment made did not obtain a response from the market, generating a negative percentage; for its part, the ROA obtained a -2.4% which indicates that it is not making adequate use of the company's assets, negatively affecting it. (Emis, Hotel Arhuaco, 2020).

The SDGs for which the company works were not known through the WEB page and no response was received from the company.

Vargas Castro & Compania S. C.

Company was founded on December 4, 1979, has 25 employees operating generating an asset of $ 11,018,856,000 and obtained a net profit of - $ 222,224,000; an ROE of -2.13% indicates that the return on the investment made did not obtain a response from the market, generating a negative percentage; For its part, the ROA obtained a -2.02%, indicating that by obtaining a negative percentage it is not making adequate and consistent use of the assets for the greater benefit of the company and the strategies implemented are not giving the expected results. Also, 1.1% of its profits was allocated to the CSR area. (Emis, Vargas Castro & Compania, 2020)

The SDGs for which the company works are:

- Gender equality: It is not a requirement to be a specific gender to belong to the company. (Emis; Cardona Agudelo Martha Lucia., 2020).

Hotel Santorini Ltda.

Company was founded on May 5, 2010 generates an asset of $ 20,361,126,000 and obtained a net profit of $ 736,060,000; an ROE of 34.43% that indicates the profitability on the investment made by the company, which in this case was effectively covered by the company, obtaining a percentage that generates profitability for the investors who contributed to the project; For its part, the ROA obtained 3.62%, which indicates that despite obtaining a positive percentage, it is not making adequate and consistent use of the assets. The company allocated 3.5% of its profits to the CSR area. (Emis, Hotel Santorini, 2020).

The SDGs for which the company works are:

- Gender Equality: it is not a requirement to be a specific gender to belong to the company.
- Climate action: the company tries to reduce the impact on the environment by carrying out the garbage separation process, saving a step for the company that recycles it (Emis, Hotel Santorini, 2020).

Compilation of References

Acar, A. C. (2020). Effects of COVID-19 Crisis on Employment and Working Arrangements. *Reflections on the Pandemic*, 463.

Acedo, F. J., Barroso, C., Casanueva, C., & Galán, J. L. (2006). Co-authorship in management and organizational studies: An empirical and network analysis. *Journal of Management Studies*, *43*(5), 957–983. doi:10.1111/j.1467-6486.2006.00625.x

Aebi, M. (2003). Familia disociada y delincuencia: El caso suizo en los años 1990. *Revista Electrónica de Ciencia Penal y Criminología, 5.*

Afonso, P., Fonseca, M., & Teodoro, T. (2021). Evaluation of anxiety, depression and sleep quality in full-time teleworkers. *Journal of Public Health (Oxford, England)*, fdab164. doi:10.1093/pubmed/fdab164 PMID:34036369

Agnew, R. (2005). *¿Por qué los delincuentes ofenden?: Una teoría general del crimen y la delincuencia*. Academic Press.

Agnew, R. (1992). Foundation for a general strain theory of crime and delinquency. *Criminology*, *30*(1), 47–87. doi:10.1111/j.1745-9125.1992.tb01093.x

Agnew, R., & Brezina, T. (1997). Relational Problems with Peers, Gender, and Delinquency. *Youth & Society*, *29*(1), 84–111. doi:10.1177/0044118X97029001004

Agrawal, A., Catalini, C., & Goldfarb, A. (2013). Some Simple Economics of Crowdfunding. In *NBER Chapters* (pp. 63–97). National Bureau of Economic Research, Inc. https://ideas.repec.org/h/nbr/nberch/12946.html

Aguayo, E. (2004). Divergencia Regional en México, 1990-2000. *Ensayos. Revista de economía*, *23*(2), 30–42.

Aguilar, L. (2017). Reformas Estructurales en México. *Revista Nueva Época, 11*(42). http://www.apps.buap.mx/ojs3/index.php/tlamelaua/article/view/291)

Aguilera, A., Lethiais, V., Rallet, A., & Proulhac, L. (2016). Home-based telework in France: Character- istics, barriers and perspectives. *Transportation Research*, *92*(1), 1–11.

Aguirre, B. (2010). La multidimensionalidad de la pobreza: Una revisión de la literatura. *Revista Finanzas y Política Económica*, *2*(2), 101–113.

Ahmed, F., Zviedrite, N., & Uzicanin, A. (2018). Effectiveness of workplace social distancing measures in reducing influenza transmission: A systematic review. *BMC Public Health*, *18*(1), 518. doi:10.118612889-018-5446-1 PMID:29669545

Ajzen, I. (1991). The theory of planned behaviour. *Organizational Behavior and Human Decision Processes*, *50*(2), 179–211. doi:10.1016/0749-5978(91)90020-T

Ajzen, I. (2002). Perceived behavioral control, self-efficacy, locus of control, and the theory of planned behavior. *Journal of Applied Social Psychology*, *32*(4), 665–683. doi:10.1111/j.1559-1816.2002.tb00236.x

Ajzen, I., & Fishbein, M. (1975). A Bayesian analysis of attribution processes. *Psychological Bulletin*, *82*(2), 261–277. doi:10.1037/h0076477

Akinbola, O. A., Ogunnaike, O. O. & Amaihian, A. B. (2013). *The Influence of Contextual Factors on Entrepreneurial Intention of University Students in Nigeria*. Academic Press.

Alim, M. (2013). *Photo-Documentation of Successful Development Initiatives in Indonesia: Case Study of Dompet Dhuafa Republika*. https://sadaqaindia.files.wordpress.com/2014/04/dompet_dhuafa_case_study1.pdf

Alkire, S., & Santos, M. E. (2011). Acute Multidimensional Poverty: A New Index for Developing Countries. *Proceedings of the German Development Economics Conference, Berlin 2011, No. 3, ZBW - Deutsche Zentralbibliothek für Wirtschaftswissenschaften*. Leibniz-Informationszentrum Wirtschaft, Kiel und Hamburg.

Alkire, S., & Seth, S. (2016). *Identifying destitution through linked subsets of multidimensionally poor: An ordinal approach*. OPHI Working Paper 99. University of Oxford.

Alkire, S., Chatterjee, M., Conconi, A., Seth, S. & Vaz, A. (2014). *Global multidimensional poverty index 2014*. Academic Press.

Alkire, S., & Foster, J. (2011). Counting and multidimensional poverty measurement. *Journal of Public Economics*, *95*(7), 476–487. doi:10.1016/j.jpubeco.2010.11.006

Alkire, S., Oldiges, C., & Kanagaratnam, U. (2021). Examining multidimensional poverty reduction in India 2005/6–2015/16: Insights and oversights of the headcount ratio. *World Development*, *142*, 105454. doi:10.1016/j.worlddev.2021.105454

Alkire, S., Roche, J. M., & Vaz, A. (2017). Changes over time in multidimensional poverty: Methodology and results for 34 countries. *World Development*, *94*, 232–249. doi:10.1016/j.worlddev.2017.01.011

Alkire, S., & Santos, M. E. (2013). A multidimensional approach: Poverty measurement & beyond. *Social Indicators Research*, *112*(2), 239–257. doi:10.100711205-013-0257-3

Alkire, S., & Seth, S. (2015). Multidimensional poverty reduction in India between 1999 and 2006: Where and how? *World Development*, *72*, 93–108. doi:10.1016/j.worlddev.2015.02.009

Allen, T. D., Golden, T. D., & Shockley, K. M. (2015). How effective is telecommuting? Assessing the status of our scientific findings. *Psychological Science in the Public Interest*, *16*(2), 40–68. doi:10.1177/1529100615593273 PMID:26403188

Al-Mamun, A., Malarvizhi, C., Hossain, S., & Tan, S. (2012). Examining the Effect of Microcredit on Poverty in Malaysia. *ASEAN Economic Bulletin*, *29*(1), 15–28. doi:10.1355/ae29-1b

Al-Qaradaghi. (2014) رقفلا ءاهنإل طفنلا سمُخو اهتاورث ةاكز جارخإل ةيمالسإلا تاموكحلا وعدي يغاد هرقلا https://arabic.cnn.com/middleeast/2014/07/17/ali-qaradahji-islamic-finance

Al-Taher. (2017). رصمب رقفلا وحمل اعورشم ضهجأ بالقنالا, Asnaf MAIS (2015). Bersama kami membantu Asnaf. Selangor: Lembaga Zakah Selangor.

Al-Uthman, M. (2012). Shart al-Tamlik fi al-*Zakah* wa Mada Tathirihi fi 'Amal al-Jam'iyat al-Khayriyyah al-Islamiyyah. *Damascus University Journal for Legal and Economics Sciences, 28*(1). http://damascusuniversity.edu.sy/mag/law/images/stories/1-2012/a/681-699.pdf

Álvarez, A., Barraza, S., & Legato, A. M. (2009). Inversión Extranjera Directa y Crecimiento Económico en Latinoamérica. *Información Tecnológica*, *20*(6), 115–124.

Álvarez-Vivar, L, Bustamante-Cárcamo, Y., & Salazar-Muñoz, M. (2017). Paternidad y su incidencia en el desistimiento delictual: Una revisión teórica. *Revista Criminalidad*, *59*(1), 65–75.

Ambad, S. N. A., & Damit, D. H. D. A. (2016). Determinants of entrepreneurial intention among undergraduate students in Malaysia. *Procedia Economics and Finance*, *37*, 108–114. doi:10.1016/S2212-5671(16)30100-9

Ambel, A. A., Mugera, H. K., & Bain, R. E. (2020). Accounting for drinking water quality in measuring multidimensional poverty in Ethiopia. *PLoS One*, *15*(12), e0243921. doi:10.1371/journal.pone.0243921 PMID:33320919

Amin, R., & Becker, S. (1998). NGO-promoted microcredit programs and women's empowerment in rural Bangladesh: Quantitative and qualitative evidence. *Journal of Developing Areas*, *32*(2), 221–236. PMID:12294125

Anderson, M. (2018). Fair trade and consumer social responsibility: Exploring consumer citizenship as a driver of social and environmental change. *Management Decision*, *56*(3), 634–651. doi:10.1108/MD-01-2017-0013

Andorfer, V. A., & Liebe, U. (2015). Do information, price, or morals influence ethical consumption? A natural field experiment and customer survey on the purchase of fair trade coffee. *Social Science Research*, *52*, 330–350. doi:10.1016/j.ssresearch.2015.02.007 PMID:26004466

Angeles, G., & Ortiz, J. (2010). La inversión extranjera directa en México y su efecto en el crecimiento y la desigualdad económica. *Eseconomia*, *0*(26), 95–123.

Annan-Diab, F., & Molinari, C. (2017). Interdisciplinarity: Practical approach to advancing education for sustainability and for the Sustainable Development Goals. *International Journal of Management Education*, *15*(2), 73–83. doi:10.1016/j.ijme.2017.03.006

Argade, A., & Singh, S. (2016). Seeking Markets in Production Fields: An Assessment of the Potential for Fair Trade in India. *Millennial Asia*, *7*(2), 131–152. doi:10.1177/0976399616655028

Argenti, P. A. (2004). 'Collaborating with activists: How Starbucks works with NGOs'. *California Management Review*, *47*(1), 91–115. doi:10.2307/41166288

Ari, I. R. D., Hariyani, S., & Waloejo, B. S. (2019, October). Neighbourhood Relationship among Villages in Gedangan District: Multidimensional Poverty Approach. *IOP Conference Series. Earth and Environmental Science*, *328*(1), 012043. doi:10.1088/1755-1315/328/1/012043

Armitage, C. J., & Conner, M. (2001). Efficacy of the theory of planned behavior: A meta-analytic review. *British Journal of Social Psychology*, *40*(4), 471–499. doi:10.1348/014466601164939 PMID:11795063

Arora, M., & Sharma, R. L. (2021). Neutralizing Maleficent Effects of COVID-19 Through Entrepreneurship: Peeping Through the Lens of Communication. In Effective Strategies for Communicating Insights in Business (pp. 67-86). IGI Global.

Arora, M., & Sharma, R. L. (2021). Repurposing the Role of Entrepreneurs in the Havoc of COVID-19. In Entrepreneurship and Big Data (pp. 229-250). CRC Press. doi:10.1201/9781003097945-16

Arora, M., & Singh, S. (2018). Impact Assessment of Self-Help Group Bank Linkage Programme on Women Empowerment in the State of Himachal Pradesh. Academic Press.

Arora, M., & Singh, S. (2015). An Evaluation of the Non Performing Assets of Public and Private Sector Banks Under the SHG Bank Linkage Programme. *Indian Journal Of Finance*, *9*(6), 41–50. doi:10.17010/ijf/2015/v9i6/71161

Arora, M., & Singh, S. (2016). Disbursement of Credit Under the SGSY Scheme: A Comparison of SHGs' Swarozgaris and Individual Swarozgaris. *Indian Journal Of Finance*, *10*(11), 54–63. doi:10.17010/ijf/2016/v10i11/104918

Arora, M., & Singh, S. (2017). Role of Financial Institutions in Promoting Microfinance through SHG Bank Linkage Programme in India. *Pacific Business Review International*, *10*(4), 50–58.

Arora, M., & Singh, S. (2018). The Impact of SHG Bank Linkage Programme on the Members of Self Help Groups: An Empirical Investigation in the State of Himachal Pradesh. *Sumedha Journal of Management*, *7*(1), 34–46.

Arrighetti, A., Caricati, L., Landini, F., & Monacelli, N. (2016). Entrepreneurial intention in the time of crisis: A field study. *International Journal of Entrepreneurial Behaviour & Research*, *22*(6), 835–859. doi:10.1108/IJEBR-12-2015-0326

Arshad, N., & Berndt, A. (2021). Expanding understanding of family social capital in crowdfunding of migrant entrepreneurial ventures. *Journal of Enterprising Communities: People and Places in the Global Economy*.

Aruna, M., & Jyothirmayi, M. R. (2011). The role of microfinance in women empowerment: A study on the SHG bank linkage program in Hyderabad (Andhra Pradesh). *Indian Journal of Commerce & Management Studies ISSN*, *2229*, 5674.

Asher, M., Asnaani, A., & Aderka, I. M. (2017). Gender differences in social anxiety disorder: A review. *Clinical Psychology Review*, *56*, 1–12. doi:10.1016/j.cpr.2017.05.004 PMID:28578248

Aslam, M., Kumar, S., & Sorooshian, S. (2019). Social Versus Financial Performance of Microfinance: Bangladesh Perspective. *Review of World Economics*, *10*(3), 263–272.

Asselin, L. M. (2009). *Analysis of multidimensional poverty: Theory and case studies* (Vol. 7). Springer Science & Business Media. doi:10.1007/978-1-4419-0843-8

Azarbouyeh, A., & Naini, S. (2014). A study on the effect of teleworking on quality of work life. *Manage. Sci. Lett*, *4*(6), 1063–1068. doi:10.5267/j.msl.2014.5.027

Azmat, F. (2010). Exploring social responsibility of immigrant entrepreneurs: Do home country contextual factors play a role? *European Management Journal*, *28*(5), 377–386. doi:10.1016/j.emj.2009.11.004

Bacon, C. M., Mendez, V. E., & Gliessman, S. R. (2008). *Confronting the Coffee Crisis: Fair Trade, Sustainable Livelihoods and Ecosystems in Mexico and Central America*. MIT Press. doi:10.7551/mitpress/9780262026338.001.0001

Baggio, A., & Baggio, D. (2015). Empreendedorismo: Conceitos e definições. *Revista de Empreendedorismo. Inovação e Tecnologia*, *1*(1), 25–38.

Bakar, A. A., Hamdan, R., & Sani, N. S. (2020). Ensemble Learning for Multidimensional Poverty Classification [Pembelajaran Ensembel untuk Pengelasan Kemiskinan Pelbagai Dimensi]. *Sains Malaysiana*, *49*(2), 447–459. doi:10.17576/jsm-2020-4902-24

Bakhtiari, S. (2006). Microfinance and poverty reduction: some international evidence. *International Business & Economics Research Journal, 5*(12).

Balabanian, C., Lemos, V., & Rubilar, J. V. (2015). Apego percibido y conducta prosocial en adolescentes. *Revista Colombiana de Ciencias Sociales*, *6*(2), 278–294. doi:10.21501/22161201.1515

Balestrin, A. (2016). *Redes de Cooperação Empresarial: Estratégias de Gestão na Nova Economia*. Bookman Editora.

Bali Swain, R. & Yang-Wallentin, F. (2020) Achieving sustainable development goals: predicaments and strategies. *International Journal of Sustainable Development & World Ecology, 27*(2), 96-106.

Bali Swain, R., & Wallentin, F. Y. (2012). Factors empowering women in Indian self-help group programs. *International Review of Applied Economics*, *26*(4), 425–444. doi:10.1080/02692171.2011.595398

Baltzan, P. (2016). Tecnologia orientada para gestão (6a ed.). Porto Alegre: AMGH editora Ltda.

Banco Mundial. (2019). *La pobreza y la prosperidad compartida 2020. Un cambio de suerte*. Retrieved from https://www.un.org/es/global-issues/ending-poverty

Bao, W. N., Haas, A., Chen, X., & Pi, Y. (2014). Repeated strains, social control, social learning, and delinquency: Testing an integrated model of general strain theory in China. *Youth & Society*, *46*(3), 402–424. doi:10.1177/0044118X11436189

Barnes, G. M., & Farrell, M. P. (1992). Parental support and control as predictors of adolescent drinking, delinquency, and related problem behaviors. *Journal of Marriage and Family*, *54*(4), 763–776. doi:10.2307/353159

Barrena-Martínez, J., López-Fernández, M., Márquez-Moreno, C., & Romero-Fernández, P. (2015). Corporate social responsibility in the process of attracting college graduates. *Corporate Social Responsibility and Environmental Management*, *22*(6), 408–423. doi:10.1002/csr.1355

Basque Trade & Investment. (2020). *México COVID-19: Impacto económico, medidas y restricciones.* https://basquetrade.spri.eus/es/informes-y-estudios/mexico/mexico-covid-19-impacto-economico-medidas-y-restricciones/

Baxter, A., Chapman, D. W., Dejaeghere, J., Pekol, A. R., & Weiss, T. (2014). Youth entrepreneurship education and training for poverty alleviation: A review of international literature and local experiences. *International Perspectives on Education and Society*, *23*(2), 33–58. doi:10.1108/S1479-3679(2013)0000023010

Baycan-Levent, T., & Nijkamp, P. (2010). Migrant Entrepreneurship in a Diverse Europe. In *Search of Sustainable Development. Em Chapters.* Edward Elgar Publishing. https://ideas.repec.org/h/elg/eechap/14043_16.html

Baykal, E. (2020c). Boosting Resilience through Spiritual Well-being: COVID-19 Example. *Bussecon Review of Social Sciences*, *2*(4), 18-25.

Baykal, E. (2018). Promoting resilience through positive leadership during turmoil. *International Journal of Management and Administration*, *2*(3), 34–48. doi:10.29064/ijma.396199

Baykal, E. (2019). Rol-içi ve Rol-üstü Performansın İşyeri Ruhsallığı ile Arttırılması. *Uluslararası Hukuk ve Sosyal Bilim Araştırmaları Dergisi*, *1*(1), 15–25.

Baykal, E. (2020a). Effects of Servant Leadership on Psychological Capitals and Productivities of Employees. *Atatürk Üniversitesi İktisadi ve İdari Bilimler Dergisi*, *34*(2), 273–291. doi:10.16951/atauniiibd.533275

Baykal, E. (2020b). A Model on Authentic Leadership in The Light Of Hope Theory. *Sosyal Bilimler Arastirmalari Dergisi*, *10*(3), 813–827.

Baykal, E. (2020d). Covid-19 Bağlamında Psikolojik Dayanıklılık, Kaygı ve Yaşam Doyum İlişkisi. *International Journal of Social and Economic Sciences*, *10*(2), 68–80.

Bayón, M. (2012). El "lugar" de los pobres: espacio, representaciones sociales y estigmas en la ciudad de México. Universidad Nacional Autónoma de México-Instituto de Investigaciones Sociales. *Revista Mexicana de Sociología*, *74*(1), 133-166.

Bebbington, J., & Unerman, J. (2018). Achieving the United Nations Sustainable Development Goals: An enabling role for accounting research. *Accounting, Auditing & Accountability Journal*, *31*(1), 2–24. doi:10.1108/AAAJ-05-2017-2929

Belleflamme, P., Lambert, T., & Schwienbacher, A. (2014). Crowdfunding: Tapping the right crowd. *Journal of Business Venturing*, *29*(5), 585–609. doi:10.1016/j.jbusvent.2013.07.003

Belleflamme, P., Omrani, N., & Peitz, M. (2015). The economics of crowdfunding platforms. *Information Economics and Policy*, *33*, 11–28. doi:10.1016/j.infoecopol.2015.08.003

Belleñamme, P., Lambert, T., & Schwienbacher, A. (2010, Junho 25). *Crowdfunding: An Industrial Organization Perspective.* Digital Business Models: Understanding Strategies, Paris.

Beltrán, R. M. & Galvis, S. C. (2003). Definición de un modelo de redes de conocimiento como soporte a la transferencia del conocimiento generado en clusters de investigación. *Revista GTI*, *2*(2).

Belzunegui-Eraso, A., & Erro-Garcés, A. (2020). Teleworking in the Context of the Covid-19 Crisis. *Sustainability*, *12*(9), 3662. doi:10.3390u12093662

Benckendorff, P. (2009). Themes and trends in Australian and New Zealand tourism research: A social network analysis of citations in two leading journals (1994–2007). *Journal of Hospitality and Tourism Management*, *16*(1), 1–15. doi:10.1375/jhtm.16.1.1

Benckendorff, P., & Zehrer, A. (2013). A network analysis of tourism research. *Annals of Tourism Research*, *43*, 121–149. doi:10.1016/j.annals.2013.04.005

Bérenger, V. (2019). The counting approach to multidimensional poverty. The case of four African countries. *The South African Journal of Economics*, *87*(2), 200–227. doi:10.1111aje.12217

Bernardino, S., & Santos, J. F. (2020). Crowdfunding: An Exploratory Study on Knowledge, Benefits and Barriers Perceived by Young Potential Entrepreneurs. *Journal of Risk and Financial Management*, *13*(4), 1–24. doi:10.3390/jrfm13040081

Bersisa, M., & Heshmati, A. (2021). A Distributional Analysis of Uni-and Multidimensional Poverty and Inequalities in Ethiopia. *Social Indicators Research*, *155*(3), 1–31. doi:10.100711205-021-02606-w

Bertrand, M., Mullainathan, S., & Shafir, E. (2006). Behavioral economics and marketing in aid of decision making among the poor. *Journal of Public Policy & Marketing*, *25*(1), 8–23. doi:10.1509/jppm.25.1.8

Bhattacharya, C. B., & Sen, S. (2004). Doing better at doing good: When, why and how consumers respond to corporate social initiatives. *CA Management Review*, *47*(1), 9–24. doi:10.2307/41166284

Biermann, F., Kanie, N., & Kim, R. E. (2017). Global governance by goal-setting: The novel approach of the UN Sustainable Development Goals. *Current Opinion in Environmental Sustainability*, *26–27*, 26–31. doi:10.1016/j.cosust.2017.01.010

Bird, B. (1988). Implementing entrepreneurial ideas: The case for intention. *Academy of Management Review*, *13*(3), 442–453. doi:10.5465/amr.1988.4306970

Biswal, S. N., Mishra, S. K. & Sarangi, M. K. (2020). Feminization of multidimensional poverty in rural Odisha. *Rupkatha Journal on Interdisciplinary Studies in Humanities*, *12*(5).

Blaseg, D., Cumming, D., & Koetter, M. (2020). Equity Crowdfunding: High-Quality or Low-Quality Entrepreneurs? *Entrepreneurship Theory and Practice*.

Blevins, K. R., Johnson Listwan, S., Cullen, F. T., & Lero Jonson, C. (2010). A general strain theory of prison violence and misconduct: An integrated model of inmate behavior. *Journal of Contemporary Criminal Justice*, *26*(2), 148–166. doi:10.1177/1043986209359369

Bobbio, A., Lorenzino, L., & Arbach, K. (2016). Familia, barrio y sociedad: Un estudio comparativo en jóvenes con y sin antecedentes delictivos de Argentina. *Criminalidad*, *58*(1), 81–95.

Bocke, J., Niehaves, B., Riemer, K., & Plattfaut, R. (2009). *R*econstructing the giant: on the importance of rigour in documenting the literature search process. *Proceedings of the 17th European Conference on Information Systems (ECIS 2009).*

Bojovic, D., Benavides, J., & Soret, A. (2020). What we can learn from birdsong: Mainstreaming teleworking in a post-pandemic world. *Earth System Governance*, *5*, 100074. doi:10.1016/j.esg.2020.100074

Boluk, K. A., Cavaliere, C. T. & Higgins-Desbiolles, F. (2019). *A critical framework for interrogating the United Nations Sustainable Development Goals 2030 Agenda in tourism.* Academic Press.

Bossle, M. B., & Pedrozo, E. A. (2012). Comércio Justo: Em que estágio estamos? *Revista de Gestão Social e Ambiental*, *6*(2), 33–44. doi:10.24857/rgsa.v6i2.428

Bourguignon, F., & Chakravarty, S. R. (2003). The measurement of multidimensional poverty. *The Journal of Economic Inequality*, *1*(1), 25–49. doi:10.1023/A:1023913831342

Bowen, K. J., Cradock-Henry, N. A., Koch, F., Patterson, J., Häyhä, T., Vogt, J., & Barbi, F. (2017). Implementing the "Sustainable Development Goals": Towards addressing three key governance challenges-collective action, trade-offs, and accountability. *Current Opinion in Environmental Sustainability*, *26–27*(February), 90–96. doi:10.1016/j.cosust.2017.05.002

Bowlby, J. (1969). *Attachment and loss* (Vol. 3). Random House.

Bowlby, J. (1973). Attachment and Loss: Vol. 2. *Separation: Anxiety & Anger*. Hogarth Press.

Bowlby, R. (2009). *Just Looking (Routledge Revivals): Consumer Culture in Dreiser, Gissing and Zola*. Routledge. doi:10.4324/9780203855720

Bracho, A. (2014, Mayo-Agosto). *Revista de Derecho Político nº 90: políticas públicas y marco de protección jurídica del menor en España*. Recuperado de https://www.congreso.es/docu/docum/ddocum/dosieres/sleg/legislatura_10/spl_78/pdfs/31.pdf

Bramwell, B., Higham, J., Lane, B., & Miller, G. (2017). Twenty-five years of sustainable tourism and theJournal of Sustainable Tourism: Looking back and moving forward. *Journal of Sustainable Tourism*, *25*(1), 1–9. doi:10.1080/09669582.2017.1251689

Brasil. *Lei nº. 8.078*, de 11 de setembro de 1990. Código de Defesa do Consumidor. Dispõe sobre a proteção do consumidor e dá outras providências. Brasília. Retrieved June 24, 2017, from: <http://www.planalto.gov.br/ccivil_03/Leis/L8078.htm>

Brende, B., & Høie, B. (2015). Towards evidence-based, quantitative Sustainable Development Goals for 2030. *Lancet*, *385*(9964), 206–208. doi:10.1016/S0140-6736(14)61654-8 PMID:25242038

Brida, J. G., Osti, L., & Faccioli, M. (2011). Residents' perception and attitudes towards tourism impacts. *Benchmarking*, *18*(3), 359–385. doi:10.1108/14635771111137769

Brigham, K. H., De Castro, J. O., & Shepherd, D. A. (2007). A person-organization fit model of owner- managers cognitive style and organizational demands. *Entrepreneurship Theory and Practice*, *31*(1), 29–51. doi:10.1111/j.1540-6520.2007.00162.x

Brody, C., De Hoop, T., Vojtkova, M., Warnock, R., Dunbar, M., Murthy, P., & Dworkin, S. L. (2015). Economic Self-Help group programs for improving women's Empowerment: A systematic review. *Campbell Systematic Reviews*, *11*(1), 1–182. doi:10.4073/csr.2015.19

Brooks, S., Amlôt, R., Rubin, G. J., & Greenberg, N. (2018). Psychological resilience and post-traumatic growth in disaster-exposed organisations: Overview of the literature. *Journal of the Royal Army Medical Corps*. Advance online publication. doi:10.1136/jramc-2017-000876 PMID:29420257

Brown, T. J., & Dacin, P. A. (1997). The company and the product: Corporate associations and consumer product responses. *Journal of Marketing*, *61*(1), 68–84. doi:10.1177/002224299706100106

Bruni, A. L. (2011). Estatística Aplicada à Gestão Empresarial (3a ed.). São Paulo: Atlas.

Brunner, T. A. (2014). Applying neutralization theory to fair trade buying behaviour. *International Journal of Consumer Studies*, *38*(2), 200–206. doi:10.1111/ijcs.12081

Brunton, M., Eweje, G., & Taskin, N. (2017). *Communicating corporate social responsibility to internal stakeholders: walking the walk or just talking the talk? Business Strategy and the Environment*. Early View.

Bruton, G. D., Ketchen, D. J. Jr, & Ireland, R. D. (2013). Entrepreneurship as a solution to poverty. *Journal of Business Venturing*, *28*(6), 683–689. doi:10.1016/j.jbusvent.2013.05.002

Bruwer, J., Saliba, A., & Miler, B. (2011). Consumer behaviour and sensory preference diferences: Implications for wine product marketing. *Journal of Consumer Marketing*, *28*(1), 5–18. doi:10.1108/07363761111101903

Brzozowski, J., Cucculelli, M., & Surdej, A. (2017). The determinants of transnational entrepreneurship and transnational ties' dynamics among immigrant entrepreneurs in ICT sector in Italy. *International Migration (Geneva, Switzerland)*, *55*(3), 105–125. doi:10.1111/imig.12335

Bukhari, F., Usman, S., Usman, M., & Hussain, K. (2019). The effects of creator credibility and backer endorsement in donation crowdfunding campaigns success. *Baltic Journal of Management*, *15*(2), 215–235. doi:10.1108/BJM-02-2019-0077

Buli, B. M., & Yesuf, W. M. (2015). Determinants of entrepreneurial intentions: Technical-vocational education and training students in Ethiopia. *Education + Training*, *57*(8/9), 891–907. doi:10.1108/ET-10-2014-0129

Bussab, W. O., & Morettin, P. A. (2004). Estatística básica (5a ed.) São Paulo: Saraiva.

Butticè, V., & Useche, D. (2019). Crowdfunding to Overcome Liability of Outsidership: Drivers of Immigrants' Fund-raising Performance. *Academy of Management Proceedings*, *2019*(1), 11642. doi:10.5465/AMBPP.2019.11642abstract

Caiado, R. G. G., Leal Filho, W., Quelhas, O. L. G., de Mattos Nascimento, D. L., & Ávila, L. V. (2018). A literature-based review on potentials and constraints in the implementation of the sustainable development goals. *Journal of Cleaner Production*, *198*, 1276–1288. doi:10.1016/j.jclepro.2018.07.102

Calderón, C., & Tykhonenko, A. (2007). Convergencia regional e inversión extranjera directa en México en el contexto del TLCAN, 1994-2002. *Investigacion Economica*, *66*(259), 15–41.

Cámara de Diputados. (2004). *Ley General de Desarrollo Social y últimas reformas en 2018*. http://www.diputados.gob.mx/LeyesBiblio/pdf/264_250618.pdf

Camargo. (2012). *Capacidades Dinâmicas. o que são e como identificá las? XXXVI Encontro da ANPAD*. Setembro de.

Campbell, G. (2010). Microfinancing the Developing World: How small loans empower local economies and catalyse neoliberalism's endgame. *Third World Quarterly*, *31*(7), 1081-1090. Retrieved from https://www.jstor.org/stable/27896601

Campoy Torrente, P., & Summers, L. (2015). Los precipitadores situacionales del delito: Otra mirada a la interacción persona-ambiente. *Revista Criminalidad*, *57*(3), 41–58.

Canal, M. N. (2015). *La educación emprendedora en la enseñanza escolar: medidas e indicadores de la situación de España en el contexto europeo* (Doctoral dissertation). Universidad CEU San Pablo.

Carbajal, Y. & Almonte, L. de J. (2017). Manufacturing labor in the Central Region of Mexico. An estimation by great division, 1985-2008. *Contaduría y Administración*, *62*, 902-923.

Carpio, M. D. L. V., García, M. D. L. C., Cerezo, M. T., & Casanova, P. F. (2016). *Perfiles de inteligencia emocional en universitarios y disciplina de los padres*. Academic Press.

Carrada, F. (1998). Inversión Extranjera Directa e industria maquiladora en México. *Comercio Exterior*, *48*(4), 273–282.

Carrillo Amezcua, L., Juárez García, F., González-Forteza, C., Martínez Vélez, N. A., Icaza, M. M., & Elena, M. (2016). Relación entre supervisión parental y conducta antisocial en menores infractores del Estado de Morelos. *Salud Mental, 39*(1), 11–17. doi:10.17711/SM.0185-3325.2015.063

Cartagena de Indias. (2018). *Cómo vamos Cartagena, Turismo (S/F). Turismo en Cartagena.* Disponible en: https://www.cartagenacomovamos.org/nuevo/turismo-en-cartagena/

Casanova, L., & Dumas, A. (2010). Corporate Social Responsibility and Latin American Multinationals: ¿Is Poverty a Business Issue? *Universia Business Review, 25*, 132–145.

Castaldo, S., Perrini, F., Misani, N., & Tencati, A. (2009). The missing link between corporate social responsibility and consumer trust: The case of fair trade products. *Journal of Business Ethics, 84*(1), 1–15. doi:10.100710551-008-9669-4

Castro Duran, L. I., & Cano Gonzalez, R. (2013). Poverty and vulnerability: Risk factors in the education of the borough. *Contextos Educativos-Revista de Educacion*, (16), 55–72.

Catalán, H. E. N., Fifita, V. K., & Faingaanuku, W. (2019). Small-Area Multidimensional Poverty Estimates for Tonga 2016: Drawn from a Hierarchical Bayesian Estimator. *Applied Spatial Analysis and Policy*, 1–24.

Cernev, T., & Fenner, R. (2020). The importance of achieving foundational Sustainable Development Goals in reducing global risk. *Futures, 115*, 102492. doi:10.1016/j.futures.2019.102492

Chams, N. & García-Blandón, J. (2019). On the importance of sustainable human resource management for the adoption of sustainable development goals. *Resources, Conservation and Recycling, 141*(September), 109–122.

Chaplin, C. (n.d.). *The Final Speech from The Great Dictator*. Available: https://www.charliechaplin.com/en/articles/29-the-final-speech-from-the-great-dictator-

Chapple, C. L., McQuillan, J. A., & Berdahl, T. A. (2005). Gender, social bonds, and delinquency: A comparison of boys' and girls' models. *Social Science Research, 34*(2), 357–383. doi:10.1016/j.ssresearch.2004.04.003

Chen, S., & Ravallion, M. (2013). More relatively- poor people in a less absolutely- poor world. *Review of Income and Wealth, 59*(1), 1–28. doi:10.1111/j.1475-4991.2012.00520.x

Chen, S., Shen, Y., Naznin, P., Wang, H., & Wu, S. (2014). Types of poverty and entrepreneurial intention in Bangladesh. *Social Behavior and Personality, 42*(5), 857–867. doi:10.2224bp.2014.42.5.857

Chesbrough, H., Vanhaverbeke, W., & West, J. (2008). *Open innovation: researching a new paradigm*. Oxford University Press.

Chhay, D. (2011). Women's economic empowerment through microfinance in Cambodia. *Development in Practice, 21*(8), 1122–1137. doi:10.1080/09614524.2011.606891

Chiatchoua, C., Neme, O., & Valderrama, A. L. (2016). Inversión Extranjera Directa y empleo en México: Análisis sectorial. *Economía Informa, 398*, 40–59. doi:10.1016/j.ecin.2016.04.004

Ciambotti, G., Sottini, A., & Sydow, A. (2019). *Scaling strategies of social enterprises in fair-trade markets: Meru herbs in Kenya*. SAGE Publications.

Ciani, M., Gagliardi, F., Riccarelli, S., & Betti, G. (2019). Fuzzy measures of multidimensional poverty in the Mediterranean Area: A focus on financial dimension. *Sustainability, 11*(1), 143. doi:10.3390u11010143

Çoban, S. (2021). Gender and telework: Work and family experiences of teleworking professional, middle-class, married women with children during the Covid-19 pandemic in Turkey. *Gender, Work and Organization*. PMID:34230782

Cobra, M. (2003). *Administração de Marketing no Brasil*. Cobra Editora de Marketing.

Codes, L. (2008). A trajetória do pensamento científico sobre a pobreza: em direção a uma visão complexa. Brasília, DF: Ipea.

Cohen, A. (1955). Delinquent boys. Academic Press.

Comunicado, No. 09 de México 5 de Agosto 2021. Disponible en https://www.coneval.org.mx/SalaPrensa/Comunicadosprensa/Documents/2021/Comunicado_009_Medicion_Pobreza_2020.pdf)

Comunicado, No. 10 de México 5 de Agosto 2019. Disponible en https://www.coneval.org.mx/coordinacion/entidades/Documents/Comunicados_Pobreza_2018/Comunicado_Medicion_Pobreza_2018_Aguascalientes.pdf)

CONEVAL. (2019). *Press Release No. 10*. Directorate of Information and Social Communication.

CONEVAL. (2021). 10 años de medición de pobreza en México, avances y retos en política social Dirección de Información y Comunicación Social Consejo Nacional de Evaluación de la Política de Desarrollo Social. In Líneas de Ingreso - Metodología para la medición multidimensional de la pobreza en México (2nd ed.). CONEVAL.

CONEVAL. (2021). *CONEVAL Presenta las estimaciones de pobreza multidimensional 2018 y 2020*. Dirección de Información y Comunicación Social.

Consejería para La Igualdad y Bienestar Social. Junta de Andalucía. (2003). *Decreto 362/2003, de 22 de Diciembre por el que se aprueba el Plan General de Atención a la Infancia de Andalucía*. Recuperado de www.juntadeandalucía.es/boja/2004/18/1 [última consulta el 22 de junio 2018]

Consejería para La Igualdad y Bienestar Social. Junta de Andalucía. (2007). Programa de tratamiento a Familias con Menores. Manual de referencia de los Equipos de Tratamiento Familiar, España.

Consejería para La Igualdad y Bienestar Social. Junta de Andalucía. (2016). *II Plan de Infancia y Adolescencia de Andalucía (2016-2020)*. Recuperado de www.juntadeandalucia.es/organismos/igualdadypoliticassociales/areas/infancia-familias/presentacion.html

Contreras, F., Baykal, E., & Abid, G. (2020). E-leadership and teleworking in times of COVID-19 and beyond: What we know and where do we go. *Frontiers in Psychology*, *11*, 3484. doi:10.3389/fpsyg.2020.590271 PMID:33362656

Cooper, C. D., & Kurland, N. B. (2002). Telecommuting, professional isolation, and employee development in public and private organizations. *Journal of Organizational Behavior*, *23*(4), 511–532. doi:10.1002/job.145

Correia-Loureiro, S. (2014). The role of the rural tourism experience economy in place attachment and behavioral intentions. *International Journal of Hospitality Management*, *40*, 1–9. doi:10.1016/j.ijhm.2014.02.010

Costa & Porto. (2015). Capacidade dinâmica de cooperação nas multinacionais Brasileiras e seus fatores gerenciais determinantes. *Revista Eletrônica de Negócios Internacionais, 10*(1), 57-69.

Costa, A. S. C., Santana, L. C., & Trigo, A. C. (2015). *Qualidade do atendimento ao cliente: um grande referencial competitivo para as organizações*. Retrieved May 12, 2017, from: https://www.cairu.br/riccairu/pdf/artigos/2/10_qualidade_atend_cliente.pdf

Costanza, R., Daly, L., Fioramonti, L., Giovannini, E., Kubiszewski, I., Mortensen, L. F., & Wilkinson, R. (2016). Modelling and measuring sustainable wellbeing in connection with the UN Sustainable Development Goals. *Ecological Economics*, *130*, 350–355. doi:10.1016/j.ecolecon.2016.07.009

Costello, B. J. (2010). Peer influencia hacia la conformidad. *Journal of Crime and Justice*, *33*(1), 97–116. doi:10.1080/0735648X.2010.9721281

Coutinho. (1994). *Estudo da competitividade da indústria brasileira* (4th ed.). Papirus.

Coutinho, A., Oliveira, B., Soares, V., & Sanchez, S. (2008). O empreendedorismo imigrante em Portugal: Factores que influenciam este percurso profissional e actividade da ASI decorrente dos resultados do projecto PEI. *Revista Migrações, 3*, 263–270.

Crecer Con Futuro. (2017). *Memoria anual de actividades*. Recuperado de www.crecerconfuturo.org/wp-content/uploads/2018/07/MEMORIA-CcF-17.pdf

Cross, R., Borgatti, S. P., & Parker, A. (2002). Making invisible work visible: Using social network analysis to support strategic collaboration. *California Management Review, 44*(2), 25–46. doi:10.2307/41166121

Cross, R., & Prusak, L. (2002). The people who make organizations go–or stop. *Networks in the Knowledge Economy, 80*(6), 248–260. PMID:12048992

Cruz, E., & Falcão, R. (2017). Revisão bibliométrica no tema Empreendedorismo Imigrante e Étnico. *Internext, 11*(3), 78–94. doi:10.18568/1980-4865.11378-94

Cumming, D., & Hornuf, L. (2018). *The Economics of Crowdfunding—Startups, Portals and Investor Behavior*. Palgrave Macmillan.

Cumming, D., & Johan, S. (2020). *Crowdfunding Fundamental Cases, Facts, and Insights* (2nd ed.). Elsevier.

D'Agostini, D. (2020). Microfinance in the African continent. *Policy*, (1).

Dabić, M., Vlačić, B., Paul, J., Dana, L.-P., Sahasranamam, S., & Glinka, B. (2020). Immigrant entrepreneurship: A review and research agenda. *Journal of Business Research, 113*(C), 25–38. doi:10.1016/j.jbusres.2020.03.013

Dalmasso, M. B. E. (2008). Las ausencias en las producciones teóricas sobre la pobreza. ¿Una intervención Biopolítica? *Intersticios. Revista Sociológica de Pensamiento Crítico, 2*(2).

Daniels, K., Lamond, D., & Standen, P. (2001). Teleworking: Frameworks for organizational research. *Journal of Management Studies, 38*(8), 1151–1185. doi:10.1111/1467-6486.00276

Darics, E. (2020). E-leadership or "How to be boss in Instant Messaging?". The role of nonverbal communication. *International Journal of Business Communication, 57*(1), 3–29. doi:10.1177/2329488416685068

Datt, G. (2019). Distribution-sensitive multidimensional poverty measures. *The World Bank Economic Review, 33*(3), 551–572. doi:10.1093/wber/lhx017

David, A. (2017). *Amanah Ikhtiar willing to give more loans to women entrepreneurs*. New Straits Time.

David, C. B., & Kim, H. S. (2016). Developing Markets, Building Networks: Promoting Fair Trade in Asia. In *Fair Trade, Corporate Accountability and Beyond*. Routledge.

Davidsson, P. (1995). Determinants of Entrepreneurial Intentions. *RENT DC Workshop in Entrepreneurship Research*.

Davila. (2016). *Relações Entre Práticas de Gestão do Conhecimento, Capacidade Absortiva e Desempenho*. Evidências do Sul do Brasil. Tese de Doutorado Universidade Federal de Santa Catarina. Centro Tecnológico. Programa de Pós Graduação em Engenharia e Gestão do Conhecimento.

De Aghion, B. A., Armendáriz, B., & Morduch, J. (2007). *The economics of microfinance*. Academic Press.

De la Cruz, J. L., & Núñez, J. A. (2006). Comercio internacional, crecimiento económico e inversión extranjera directa. *Revista de Economía Mundial, 15*, 181–202.

De la Mora, L. M. (2007). *Políticas para la atracción de inversión extranjera directa como impulsora de la creación de capacidades locales y del cambio estructural El caso de México*. CEPAL.

De Pelsmacker, P., & Janssens, W. (2007). A model for fair trade buying behaviour: The role of perceived quantity and quality of information and of product-specific attitudes. *Journal of Business Ethics*, *75*(4), 361–380. doi:10.100710551-006-9259-2

de Vries, H., Tummers, L., & Bekkers, V. (2019). The benefits of teleworking in the public sector: Reality or rhetoric? *Review of Public Personnel Administration*, *39*(4), 570–593. doi:10.1177/0734371X18760124

Decancq, K., & Lugo, M. A. (2008). *Setting weights in multidimensional indices of well-being*. Oxford Poverty & Human Development Initiative OPHI Working Paper 18.

Dejean, S. (2020). The role of distance and social networks in the geography of crowdfunding: Evidence from France. *Regional Studies*, *54*(3), 329–339. doi:10.1080/00343404.2019.1619924

Dejours, C. (2000). A Loucura do Trabalho: Estudo de psicopatologia do trabalho (5 ed.). São Paulo: Cortez.

Della Corte, V., & Aria, M. (2016). Coopetition and sustainable competitive advantage. The case of tourist destinations. *Tourism Management*, *54*, 524–540. doi:10.1016/j.tourman.2015.12.009

Deloitte. (2019). *Social finance, what is it and why it matters?* Author.

Deutsch, J., & Silber, J. (2005). Measuring multidimensional poverty: An empirical comparison of various approaches. *Review of Income and Wealth*, *51*(1), 145–174. doi:10.1111/j.1475-4991.2005.00148.x

Di Pietro, F. (2021). Leveraging regional immigration and immigration diversity for financing crowdfunding projects. *Regional Studies, Regional Science*, *8*(1), 291–301. doi:10.1080/21681376.2021.1939129

Di Pucchio, Y. (2015). Microfinance in Iran: A Case Study of the Rural Microfinance Support Project. *Oriente Moderno*, *95*(1/2), 211-232. Retrieved from https://www.jstor.org/stable/44289942

Dias, Á., González-Rodríguez, M. R., & Patuleia, M. (2020). Developing poor communities through creative tourism. *Journal of Tourism and Cultural Change*, 1–21. doi:10.1080/14766825.2020.1775623

Dias, Á., Silva, G. M., Patuleia, M., & González-Rodríguez, M. R. (2020). Developing sustainable business models: Local knowledge acquisition and tourism lifestyle entrepreneurship. *Journal of Sustainable Tourism*, 1–20. doi:10.1080/09669582.2020.1835931

Díaz, A. (1993). *Restructuring and the New Working Classes in Chile: Trends in Waged Employment, Informality and Poverty, 1973-1990*. UNRIS Discussion Paper No. DP47. Geneva: United Nations Research Institute for Social Development.

Díaz-Casero, J. C., Ferreira, J. J. M., Mogollón, R. H., & Raposo, M. L. B. (2012). Influence of institutional environment on entrepreneurial intention: A comparative study of two countries university students. *The International Entrepreneurship and Management Journal*, *8*(1), 55–74. doi:10.100711365-009-0134-3

Dieguez-Castrillon, M. I., Gueimonde-Canto, A., & Sinde-Cantorna, A. (2009). Rural Tourism as diversification strategy: Determinants and performance in Galicia. *Cuadernos de Gestión*, *9*(2), 31–54.

Din, N. M., Rosdi, M. S. M., Ismail, M., Muhammad, M. Z., & Mukhtar, D. (2019). Contributions of Asnaf Entrepreneurs in *Zakah* of Business: A Revisiting Based on Turning over Model. *International Journal of Academic Research in Business and Social Sciences*, *9*(9), 744–752.

Doh, J., Howton, S., Howton, S., & Siegel, D. (2010). Does the market respond to an endorsement of social responsibility? The role of institutions, information and legitimacy. *Journal of Management*, *36*(6), 1461–1485. doi:10.1177/0149206309337896

Douglas, E. J., & Shepherd, D. A. (2002). Self-Employment as a Career Choice: Attitudes, Entrepreneurial Intentions, and Utility Maximization. *Entrepreneurship Theory and Practice*, *26*(3), 81–90. doi:10.1177/104225870202600305

Dresner, S. (2014). *Crowdfunding: A Guide to Raising Capital on the Internet*. Wiley.

Driouchi, A., Zouag, N., & Boboc, C. (2009). Interdependencies of health, education and poverty: The case of South Mediterranean Economies. *Estudios de Economía Aplicada*, *27*(2), 523–543. doi:10.25115/eea.v27i2.4928

Duclos, J. Y., Sahn, D. E., & Younger, S. D. (2006). Robust multidimensional poverty comparisons. *Economic Journal (London)*, *116*(514), 943–968. doi:10.1111/j.1468-0297.2006.01118.x

DumanA. (2020). Wage losses and inequality in developing countries: labor market and distributional consequences of Covid-19 lockdowns in Turkey. Available at SSRN 3645468. doi:10.2139/ssrn.3645468

Duryea, S., Jaramillo, O., & Pagés, C. (2002). *Los mercados de trabajo en América Latina en los noventa: Descifrando la década*. Inter-American Development Bank.

El Financiero. (2021). *SHCP gives the coup de grace to the agricultural insurance program*. Available at: https://www.elfinanciero.com.mx/economia/2021/07/13/hacienda-da-el-tiro-de-gracia-al-programa-de-aseguramiento-agropecuario/?outputType=amp

El Financiero–Economía. (2021). *Gobierno de México apoya solo a 7 de cada 100 Pymes, Solo el 7 por ciento de las Pymes en México han podido acceder y combinar el apoyo del gobierno en comparación con el 33.6 por ciento en la OCDE*. Expandir. https://www.elfinanciero.com.mx/economia/2021/06/29/gobierno-de-mexico-apoya-solo-a-7-de-cada-100-pymes/

Emis & Decameron. (2020). *Emis*. Obtenido de Hoteles Decameron Colombia S.A.S. Sigla Hodecol S.A.S.: https://www-emis-com.hemeroteca.lasalle.edu.co/php/companies/index?pc=CO&cmpy=1197916

Emis, B. (2020). *Bureche S.A.S.* Obtenido de https://www-emis-com.hemeroteca.lasalle.edu.co/php/companies?pc=CO&cmpy=4873743

Emis, F. C. Holding. (2018). *F.C. Holding S.A.S.* Obtenido de https://www-emis-com.hemeroteca.lasalle.edu.co/php/companies/index?pc=CO&cmpy=4960081

Emis, G. D. M. R. (2020). *Gente De Mar Resort S.A.S.* Obtenido de https://www-emis-com.hemeroteca.lasalle.edu.co/php/companies/index?pc=CO&cmpy=8161791

Emis, H. A. (2020). *Hotel Arhuaco S.A.* Obtenido de https://www-emis-com.hemeroteca.lasalle.edu.co/php/companies/index?pc=CO&cmpy=1197861

Emis, H. S. (2020). *Hotel Santorini Ltda.* Obtenido de https://www-emis-com.hemeroteca.lasalle.edu.co/php/companies/index?pc=CO&cmpy=2654254

Emis, I. C. D. C. (2020). *Inversiones Calle Del Cuartel S.A.S.* Obtenido de https://www-emis-com.hemeroteca.lasalle.edu.co/php/companies/index?pc=CO&cmpy=3404415

Emis, S. M. R. (2020). *Santa Marta Real S.A.S.* Obtenido de https://www-emis-com.hemeroteca.lasalle.edu.co/php/companies/index?pc=CO&cmpy=4873453

Emis, Vargas Castro & Compania. (2020). *Vargas Castro & Compania S en C.* Obtenido de https://www-emis-com.hemeroteca.lasalle.edu.co/php/companies/index?pc=CO&cmpy=1217686

Emis; Aparta Hotel Don Blas S.A. (2020). *EMIS. Obtenido de Aparta Hotel Don Blas S.A.*: Https://Www-Emis-Com.Hemeroteca.Lasalle.Edu.Co/Php/Companies/Index?Pc=CO&Cmpy=1182500

Emis; Aviatur. (2020). *EMIS*. Obtenido de Turismo: https://www-emis-com.hemeroteca.lasalle.edu.co/php/companies/index?pc=CO&cmpy=1180755

Emis; Bantu Hotel S.A.S. (2020). *Emis*. Obtenido de Bantu Hotel S.A.S.: https://www-emis-com.hemeroteca.lasalle.edu.co/php/companies/index?pc=CO&cmpy=4055087

Emis; Cardona Agudelo Martha Lucia. (2020). *Emis*. Obtenido de Cardona Agudelo Martha Lucia.: https://www-emis-com.hemeroteca.lasalle.edu.co/php/companies/index?pc=CO&cmpy=8156342

Emis; Compania Comercial El Dorado Ltda. (2020). *Emis*. Obtenido de Compania Comercial El Dorado Ltda.: https://www-emis-com.hemeroteca.lasalle.edu.co/php/companies/index?pc=CO&cmpy=1186657

Emis; Grupo Hotelero Mar y Sol S.A. (2020). *Emis*. Obtenido de Grupo Hotelero Mar y Sol S.A.: https://www-emis-com.hemeroteca.lasalle.edu.co/php/companies/index?pc=CO&cmpy=1196930

Emis; Hotel Santa Clara. (2020). *Emis*. Obtenido de Hotel Santa Clara S.A.-En Reestructuracion: https://www-emis-com.hemeroteca.lasalle.edu.co/php/companies/index?pc=CO&cmpy=1197897

Emis; Promotora Turística Del Caribe. (2020). *Emis*. Obtenido de Promotora Turística Del Caribe S.A. Protucaribe S.A.: https://www-emis-com.hemeroteca.lasalle.edu.co/php/companies/index?pc=CO&cmpy=1210652

Emis; Servincluidos. (2020). *Emis*. Obtenido de Servicluidos: https://www-emis-com.hemeroteca.lasalle.edu.co/php/companies/index?pc=CO&cmpy=1213692

Emis; Turisticas del caribe. (2020). *Emis*. Obtenido de Inversiones Turisticas Del Caribe Ltda. & Cia S. C. A.: https://www-emis-com.hemeroteca.lasalle.edu.co/php/companies/index?pc=CO&cmpy=1202559

Emis;Hoteles Via Del Mar S.A.S. (2020). *Emis*. Obtenido de Hoteles Via Del Mar S.A.S.: https://www-emis-com.hemeroteca.lasalle.edu.co/php/companies/index?pc=CO&cmpy=3906534

Empresas que curam. (2020). Rio de Janeiro: Alta Books.

Errais, E., & Miled, S. (2015). Investing in Microfinance: The Case of Tunisia. *Journal of Private Equity*, *18*(3), 79–96. doi:10.3905/jpe.2015.18.3.079

Espasandin-Bustelo, F., Palacios-Florencio, B., & García, J. S. R. (2020). CSR intellectual structure in management and tourism. *The TQM Journal*, *32*(3), 521–541. doi:10.1108/TQM-06-2019-0173

European Commission. (2016). *A Recipe Book for Social Finance*. https://publications.jrc.ec.europa.eu/repository/bitstream/JRC111373/jrc111373_jrc-s4p_report_sii-eu_maduro-pasi-misuraca_def_12122018.pdf

European Union. (2015). *O financiamento coletivo em pormenor*. European Union Publications. https://op.europa.eu/pt/publication-detail/-/publication/d5e626ba-d7c8-11e6-ad7c-01aa75ed71a1

Expansion Magazine. (2020). *In the absence of government support, companies seek to help each other; Carlos Salazar, President of the CCE*. Available at: https://expansion.mx/empresas/2020/04/06/ante-la-falta-apoyo-gobierno-las-empresas-ayudarse-entre-si

Fayolle, A., & Liñán, F. (2014). The future of research on entrepreneurial intentions. *Journal of Business Research*, *67*(5), 663–666. doi:10.1016/j.jbusres.2013.11.024

Fayomi, O. S. I., Okokpujie, I. P., Fayom, G. U., & Okolie, S. T. (2019). The challenge of Nigeria researcher in meeting up with the challenge of Nigeria researcher in meeting up with sustainable development goal in 21st century. *Energy Procedia*, *157*, 393–404. doi:10.1016/j.egypro.2018.11.204

Fedakova, D., & Ištoňová, L. (2017). Slovak IT employees and new ways of working: Impact on work-family borders and work-family balance. *Československá Psychologie*, *61*, 68–83.

Feitosa, D. R., & Viana, T. A. (2015). *Perfil e grau de satisfação de consumidores de estabelecimentos comerciais do setor alimentício de três cidades do Cariri cearense.* Retrieved May 3, 2017, from: www.fjn.edu.br/revista/index.php/eciencia/article/view/48

Feix, N. (2020). *Mexico and the COVID-19 crisis in the world of work: answers and challenges.* International Labour Organization. https://www.ilo.org/wcmsp5/groups/public/---americas/---ro-lima/---ilo-mexico/documents/publication/wcms_757364.pdf

Felippe, G. (2018). *A internet e as novas tecnologias na relação de trabalho: teletrabalho/home office e a jornada de trabalho* (Dissertação de Mestrado). Pontifícia Universidade Cat olica de São Paulo.

Felson, M. (1998). *Crime and everyday life.* Pine Forge Press.

Felstead, A., & Henseke, G. (2017). Assessing the growth of remote working and its consequences for effort, well-being and work-life balance. *New Technology, Work and Employment*, *32*(3), 195–212. doi:10.1111/ntwe.12097

Feres, J. C. & Villatoro, P. (2012). La viabilidad de erradicar la pobreza: un examen conceptual y metodológico. *CEPAL - Serie Estudios estadísticos y prospectivos*, 76.

Ferguson, L. (2011). Promoting gender equality and empowering women? Tourism and the third Millennium Development Goal. *Current Lssues In Tourism*, *14*(3), 235–249. doi:10.1080/13683500.2011.555522

Fernández, A. M., & Ladrón de Guevara, R. (2002, january). *Elasticidad de la Inversión Extranjera Directa (IED) ante las variaciones de política fiscal en México* [Paper presentation]. *VI congreso Nacional de Investigación en Ciencias Económico Administrativas, Retos de las ciencias administrativas desde las economías emergentes: Evolución de sociedades*, Ciudad de México, México.

Ferreira, F. H., & Lugo, M. A. (2013). Multidimensional poverty analysis: Looking for a middle ground. *The World Bank Research Observer*, *28*(2), 220–235. doi:10.1093/wbro/lks013

Ferreira, J., Fernandes, C., & Raposo, M. (2018). Measuring and understanding the psychological effects of entrepreneurial intentions: Multigroup analysis. In A. Tur & D. Ribeiro (Eds.), *Inside the mind of the entrepreneur. Contributions to Management Science* (pp. 17–31). Springer International Publishing. doi:10.1007/978-3-319-62455-6_2

Ferri, L., Oelze, N., Habish, A., & Molteni, M. (2016). Implementation of responsible procurement management: An institutional perspective. *Business Strategy and the Environment*, *25*(4), 261–276. doi:10.1002/bse.1870

Field, A. (2005). Discovering statistics using SPSS (2nd ed.). Sage Publications, Inc.

Fini, R., Grimaldi, R., Marzocchi, G. L., & Sobrero, M. (2012). The determinants of corporate entrepreneurial intention within small and newly established firms. *Entrepreneurship Theory and Practice*, *36*(2), 387–414. doi:10.1111/j.1540-6520.2010.00411.x

Flammer, C. (2013). Corporate social responsibility and shareholder reaction: The environmental awareness of investors. *Academy of Management Journal*, *56*(3), 758–781. doi:10.5465/amj.2011.0744

Flammer, C., & Luo, J. (2017). Corporate social responsibility as an employee governance tool: Evidence from a quasi-experiment. *Strategic Management Journal*, *38*(2), 163–183. doi:10.1002mj.2492

Fleck, R., Cox, A. L., & Robison, R. A. (2015). Balancing boundaries: Using multiple devices to manage work-life balance. In *Proceedings of the 33rd Annual ACM Conference on Human Factors in Computing Systems* (pp. 3985-3988). 10.1145/2702123.2702386

Fleming, A., Wise, R. M., Hansen, H., & Sams, L. (2017). The sustainable development goals: A case study. *Marine Policy*, *86*, 94–103. doi:10.1016/j.marpol.2017.09.019

Flores-Hernández, A., Cambra-Fierro, J., & Vázquez-Carrasco, R. (2020). Sustainability, brand image, reputation and financial value: Manager perceptions in an emerging economy context. *Sustainable Development*, *28*(4), 935–945. doi:10.1002d.2047

Focault. (1979). Microfísica do Poder. Organização e tradução de Roberto Machado. Rio de Janeiro: Edições Graal.

Fontana, L. B., & Oldekop, J. A. (2020). The sustainable development goals: The bumpy road ahead. *World Development*, *127*, 127. doi:10.1016/j.worlddev.2019.104770

Foster, J., Greer, J., & Thorbecke, E. (1984). A class of decomposable poverty measures. *Econometrica*, *52*(3), 761–766. doi:10.2307/1913475

Fosu, A. K. (2017). Growth, inequality, and poverty reduction in developing countries: Recent global evidence. *Research in Economics*, *71*(2), 306–336. doi:10.1016/j.rie.2016.05.005

Fotiadis, A., Vassiliadis, C., & Piper, L. (2013). Measuring dimensions of business effectiveness in Greek rural tourism areas. *Journal of Hospitality Marketing & Management*, 1–28.

Fotiadis, A., Yeh, S., & Huan, T. C. (2016). Applying configural analysis to explaining rural-tourism success récipes. *Journal of Business Research*, *69*(4), 1479–1483. doi:10.1016/j.jbusres.2015.10.128

Freyre, M. L. (2013). Labour Market and Career Paths in Contexts of Poverty. Challenges for Social Policy. *Gestión y Análisis de Políticas Públicas*, 10.

Fullana, M. A., Hidalgo-Mazzei, D., Vieta, E., & Radua, J. (2020). Coping behaviors associated with decreased anxiety and depressive symptoms during the COVID-19 pandemic and lockdown. *Journal of Affective Disorders*, *275*, 80–81. doi:10.1016/j.jad.2020.06.027 PMID:32658829

Furber, M. (2017). *UNHCR zakah collection and distribution.* https://reliefweb.int/sites/reliefweb.int/files/resources/TR-1-UNHCR-*Zakah*-Collection-And-Distribution-English.pdf

Furman, W., & Buhrmester, D. (2009). Methods and measures: The network of relationships inventory: Behavioral systems version. *International Journal of Behavioral Development*, *33*, 470–478.

Gajendran, R. S., & Harrison, D. A. (2007). The good, the bad, and the unknown about tele- commuting: Meta-analysis of psychological mediators and individual consequences. *The Journal of Applied Psychology*, *92*(6), 1524–1541. doi:10.1037/0021-9010.92.6.1524 PMID:18020794

Gallardo, M. (2020). Measuring vulnerability to multidimensional poverty. *Social Indicators Research*, *148*(1), 67–103. doi:10.100711205-019-02192-y

Gallego Duque, L. M. (2014). *Mecanismos causales de la educación y la pobreza. Aplicación a los casos de Medellín (Colombia) y BeloHorizonte (Brasil)* (Unpublished doctoral dissertation). Universitat Autònoma de Barcelona.

Galvez, A., Tirado, F., & Alcaraz, J. M. (2020). 'Oh! Teleworking!' Regimes of engagement and the lived experience of female Spanish teleworkers. *Business Ethics (Oxford, England)*, *29*(1), 180–192. doi:10.1111/beer.12240

Galvez, M. O., Valdés, B. C., & Castillo, V. P. (2019). Pobreza y autopercepción de salud: Contraste entre pobreza multidimensional y pobreza por ingresos. *Atencion Primaria*, *51*(8), 513–514. doi:10.1016/j.aprim.2018.07.013 PMID:30992153

Gao, W., Ping, S., & Liu, X. (2020). Gender differences in depression, anxiety, and stress among college students: A longitudinal study from China. *Journal of Affective Disorders*, *263*, 292–300. doi:10.1016/j.jad.2019.11.121 PMID:31818792

Gao, Y., Wong, D. S., & Yu, Y. (2016). Maltreatment and delinquency in China: Examining and extending the intervening process of general strain theory. *International Journal of Offender Therapy and Comparative Criminology*, *60*(1), 38–61. doi:10.1177/0306624X14547495 PMID:25145686

García del Junco, J., & Espasandín Bustelo, F. (2018). La pobreza: estado de la cuestión y situación en latinoamérica. *Proceedings I workshop internacional de ASIBEAM.*

Garcia Sainz, C. (2017). The impact of the economic crisis on time poverty and gender inequalities. *Arbor-Ciencia Pensamiento y Cultura, 193*(784).

García-Cabrera, A., Lucía-Casademunt, A. M., & Padilla-Angulo, L. (2020). Immigrants' entrepreneurial motivation in Europe: Liabilities and assets. *International Journal of Entrepreneurial Behaviour & Research*, *26*(8), 1707–1737. doi:10.1108/IJEBR-01-2020-0042

García, R. (2001). La maquila y la inversión extranjera directa en México. *ICE: Revista de Economía, 795*, 127–140.

García, R. E. D., Pupiales, A. F. H., & Espitia, M. E. O. (2013). Relación entre la educación y los componentes del índice de pobreza de Amartya Sen: Un análisis en Colombia. *Revista CIFE: Lecturas de Economía Social*, *15*(23), 23–48. doi:10.153322248-4914.2013.0023.02

García-Rodríguez, F. J., Gil-Soto, E., Ruiz-Rosa, I., & Sene, P. M. (2015). Entrepreneurial intentions in diverse development contexts: A cross-cultural comparison between Senegal and Spain. *The International Entrepreneurship and Management Journal*, *11*(3), 511–527. doi:10.100711365-013-0291-2

Gast, J., Werner, A., & Kraus, S. (2017). Antecedents of the small firm effect: The role of knowledge spillover and blocked mobility for employee entrepreneurial intentions. *The International Entrepreneurship and Management Journal*, *13*(1), 277–297. doi:10.100711365-016-0403-x

Gendron, C., Bisaillon, V., & Rance, A. I. (2009). The institutionalization of fair trade: More than just a degraded form of social action. *Journal of Business Ethics*, *86*(1), 63–79. doi:10.100710551-008-9758-4

Gentilini, U., & Sumner, A. (2012). What do national poverty lines tell us about global poverty? *IDS Working Papers, 2012*(392), 1-48.

Germán, V., & Ríos, M. (2001). El vínculo Inversión Extranjera Directa y desigualdad salarial en los estados mexicanos, Equilibrio Económico. *Revista de Economía. Política y Sociedad*, *7*(2), 119–149.

Geysmans, R., de Krom, M. P., & Hustinx, L. (2017). "Fairtradization": A performative perspective on fair trade markets and the role of retail settings in their enactment. *Consumption Markets & Culture*, *20*(6), 539–558. doi:10.1080/10253866.2017.1331909

Ghosh, C., & Das, A. (2020). Drivers of performance of the microfinance institutions in selected South Asian countries. *International Journal of Economics and Accounting*, *9*(2), 155–179. doi:10.1504/IJEA.2020.105207

Gillani, A., Kutaula, S., Leonidou, L. C., & Christodoulides, P. (2019). The impact of proximity on consumer fair trade engagement and purchasing behavior: The moderating role of empathic concern and hypocrisy. *Journal of Business Ethics*, 1–21.

Giovanis, E. (2018). The relationship between teleworking, traffic and air pollution. *Atmospheric Pollution Research*, *9*(1), 1–14. doi:10.1016/j.apr.2017.06.004

Gird, A., & Bagraim, J. J. (2008). The theory of planned behaviour as predictor of entrepreneurial intent amongst final-year university students. *South African Journal of Psychology. Suid-Afrikaanse Tydskrif vir Sielkunde*, *38*(4), 711–724. doi:10.1177/008124630803800410

Godinic, D., Obrenovic, B., & Khudaykulov, A. (2020). Effects of Economic Uncertainty on Mental Health in the COVID-19 Pandemic Context: Social Identity Disturbance, Job Uncertainty and Psychological Well-Being Model. *International Journal of Management Science and Business Administration*, *6*(1), 61–74. doi:10.18775/ijied.1849-7551-7020.2015.61.2005

Gold, A. L., Abend, R., Britton, J. C., Behrens, B., Farber, M., Ronkin, E., Chen, G., Leibenluft, E., & Pine, D. S. (2020). Age differences in the neural correlates of anxiety disorders: An fMRI study of response to learned threat. *The American Journal of Psychiatry*, *177*(5), 454–463. doi:10.1176/appi.ajp.2019.19060650 PMID:32252541

Golden, T. D. (2006). Avoiding depletion in virtual work: Telework and the intervening impact of work exhaustion on commitment and turnover intentions. *Journal of Vocational Behavior*, *69*(1), 176–187. doi:10.1016/j.jvb.2006.02.003

Golob, T., Kleindienst, P., Makarovič, M., & Kildi, J. M. (2020). Challenges of Migrant Entrepreneurship in Selected Regions of Central Europe. *Comparative Sociology*, *19*(4–5), 609–631. doi:10.1163/15691330-BJA10021

Gong, Z., Kong, Q., & Tan, J. (2020). Analysis on multidimensional poverty reduction of industrial structure upgrading based on provincial panel data and spatial Durbin model. *International Journal of Sustainable Development and Planning*, *15*(8), 1197–1204. doi:10.18280/ijsdp.150806

Goode, W. J. (1960). A theory of role strain. *American Sociological Review*, *25*(4), 483–496. doi:10.2307/2092933

Gordillo, S., & Carolina, M. (2017). *Experiencias tempranas y personalidad en personas en conflicto con la ley estudio piloto con aplicación de cuestionario ETEP* (Bachelor's thesis). Quito: UCE.

Góssling, S., & Hall, C. M. (2019). Sharing versus collaborative economy: How to align ICT developments and the SDGs in tourism? *Journal of Sustainable Tourism*, *27*(1), 74–96. doi:10.1080/09669582.2018.1560455

Government of Mexico. (2019). *Reasons for the cancellation of the New Airport project in Texcoco Secretariat of Communications and Transport*. https://www.gob.mx/sct/articulos/razones-para-la-cancelacion-del-proyecto-del-nuevo-aeropuerto-en-texcoco

Groen, B. A., Van Triest, S. P., Coers, M., & Wtenweerde, N. (2018). Managing flexible work arrangements: Teleworking and output controls. *European Management Journal*, *36*(6), 727–735. doi:10.1016/j.emj.2018.01.007

Grönlund, A. (2007). Employee control in the era of flexibility: A stress buffer or a stress amplifier? *European Societies*, *9*(3), 409–428. doi:10.1080/14616690701314283

Grover, P., Kar, A. K., & Ilavarasan, P. V. (2019). Impact of corporate social responsibility on reputation—Insights from tweets on sustainable development goals by CEOs. *International Journal of Information Management*, *48*, 39–52. doi:10.1016/j.ijinfomgt.2019.01.009

Grün, A., Hüther, G., & Hosang, M. (2019). Amar é a única revolução – A força transformadora do amor a partir das ciências, filosofia e da religião. Petrópolis, RJ: Vozes.

Guevara Perez, M., Marchena, S., & del Rosario, A. (2017). *Resilencia y riesgo suicida en Adolescentes de un centro juvenil, Diagnostico y Rehabilitación*. Pimentel 2016.

Gunn, C. A. (1988). *Tourism Planning* (2nd ed.). Taylor and Francis.

Gupta, M., & Hodges, N. (2012). Corporate social responsibility in the apparel industry: An exploration of Indian consumer perceptions and expectations. *Journal of Fashion Marketing and Management, 16*(2), 216–233. doi:10.1108/13612021211222833

Gutiérrez, J. P. (2013). Brechas en cobertura efectiva por nivel socioeconómico y condición de pobreza. *Salud Pública de México, 55*(Supl.2), s106–s111. doi:10.21149pm.v55s2.5105 PMID:24626685

Habib, M., Aamir, A., Khan, I., & Ullah, W. (2020). Role of Entrepreneurship Education in Poverty Alleviation: Mediating by Entrepreneurial Intention. *City University Research Journal, 10*(2), 1–24.

Habtewold, T. M. (2021). Impact of climate-smart agricultural technology on multidimensional poverty in rural Ethiopia. *Journal of Integrative Agriculture, 20*(4), 1021–1041. doi:10.1016/S2095-3119(21)63637-7

Haddad, H., Lyons, G., & Chatterjee, K. (2009). An examination of determinants influencing the desire for and frequency of part-day and whole-day homeworking. *Journal of Transport Geography, 17*(2), 124–133. doi:10.1016/j.jtrangeo.2008.11.008

Hahn, R., & Kühnen, M. (2013). Determinants of sustainability reporting: A review of results, trends, theory, and opportunities in an expanding field of research. *Journal of Cleaner Production, 59*, 5–21. doi:10.1016/j.jclepro.2013.07.005

Hainmueller, J., Hiscox, M. J., & Sequeira, S. (2015). Consumer demand for fair trade: Evidence from a multistore field experiment. *The Review of Economics and Statistics, 97*(2), 242–256. doi:10.1162/REST_a_00467

Hajdu, I., Major, A., & Lakner, Z. (2007). Consumer behavior in the Hungarian beer market. *Studies in Agricultural Economics (Budapest), 106*, 89–104.

Hák, T., Janoušková, S., & Moldan, B. (2016). Sustainable Development Goals: A need for relevant indicators. *Ecological Indicators, 60*, 565–573. doi:10.1016/j.ecolind.2015.08.003

Hansen, D. L., Shneiderman, B., & Smith, M. (2010, August). *Visualizing threaded conversation networks: mining message boards and email lists for actionable insights.* In *International Conference on Active Media Technology* (pp. 47-62). Springer. 10.1007/978-3-642-15470-6_7

Hassan, A., & Saleem, S. (2017). An Islamic microfinance business model in Bangladesh: Its role in alleviation of poverty and socio-economic well-being of women. *Humanomics, 33*(1), 15–37. doi:10.1108/H-08-2016-0066

Healy, N., Van Riper, C., & Boyd, S. W. (2016). Low versus high intensity approaches to interpretive tourism planning: The case of the Cliffs of Moher, Ireland. *Tourism Management, 52*, 574–583. doi:10.1016/j.tourman.2015.08.009

Helgadóttir, G., & Dashper, K. (2021). 20 years of Nordic rural tourism research: A review and future research agenda. *Scandinavian Journal of Hospitality and Tourism, 21*(1), 60–69. doi:10.1080/15022250.2020.1823246

Henderson, R., & Robertson, M. (2000). Who wants to be an entrepreneur? Young adult attitudes to entrepreneurship as a career. *Career Development International, 5*(6), 279-287.

Hernández, L. (2021). *Traicionando el lema, Periódico Reforma del 03 de Agosto 202*. Disponible en: https://www.reforma.com/traicionando-el-lema-2021-08-03/op209623

Hernández, A. J. (2008). Estudio de la progresividad del gasto público social y su impacto sobre la distribución del ingreso en Venezuela para los años 1997 y 2005. *Revista Venezolana de Análisis de Coyuntura, 14*(2), 69–91.

He, S., Lai, D., Mott, S., Little, A., Grock, A., Haas, M. R., & Chan, T. M. (2020). Remote e-work and distance learning for academic medicine: Best practices and opportunities for the future. *Journal of Graduate Medical Education, 12*(3), 256–263. doi:10.4300/JGME-D-20-00242.1 PMID:32595840

Hickle, G. (2017). Extending the boundaries: An assessment of the integration of extended producer responsibility within corporate social responsibility. *Business Strategy and the Environment*, *26*(1), 112–124. doi:10.1002/bse.1908

Hietalahti, J., & Linden, M. (2006). Socio-economic impacts of microfinance and repayment performance: A case study of the Small Enterprise Foundation, South Africa. *Progress in Development Studies*, *6*(3), 201–210. doi:10.1191/1464993406ps138oa

Hirschi, T. (1969). *Causes of Delinquency*. University of California Press.

Hobfoll, S. E., Shirom, A., & Golembiewski, R. (2000). Conservation of resources theory. Handbook of organizational behavior, 57-81.

Hodzic, S., Ripoll, P., Lira, E., & Zenasni, F. (2015). Can intervention in emotional competences increase employability prospects of unemployed adults? *Journal of Vocational Behavior*, *88*, 28–37. doi:10.1016/j.jvb.2015.02.007

Hoffmann, J. P., & Miller, A. S. (1998). A latent variable analysis of general strain theory. *Journal of Quantitative Criminology*, *14*(1), 83–110. doi:10.1023/A:1023048509438

Homburg, C., Krohmer, H., & Workman, J. Jr. (1999). Strategic Consensus and Performance: The Role of Strategy Type and Market-Related Dynamism. *Strategic Management Journal*, *20*(4), 356–357. doi:10.1002/(SICI)1097-0266(199904)20:4<339::AID-SMJ29>3.0.CO;2-T

Hook, A., Sovacool, B. K., & Sorrell, S. (2020). A systematic review of the energy and climate impacts of teleworking. *Environmental Research Letters*, *15*(9), 093003. doi:10.1088/1748-9326/ab8a84

Hosteltur. (2021). *La aportación del turismo al PIB mundial cae a la mitad por la pandemia*. Disponible en https://www.hosteltur.com/143169_la-aportacion-del-turismo-al-pib-mundial-cae-a-la-mitad-por-la-pandemia.html

Howard, P. H., & Jaffee, D. (2013). Tensions between firm size and sustainability goals: Fair trade coffee in the United States. *Sustainability*, *5*(1), 72–89. doi:10.3390u5010072

Hsu, D., Shinnar, R., Powell, B., & Coffey, B. (2017). Intentions to reenter venture creation: The effect of entrepreneurial experience and organizational climate. *International Small Business Journal*, *35*(8), 928–948. doi:10.1177/0266242616686646

Human & Provan. (1997). An emergent theory of structure and outcomes in small-firm strategic manufacturing network. Academy of Management Journal, 40(2), 368-403.

Hurghis, R. (2017). Integrated reporting and board features. *Audit Francier*, *15*(1), 21–30.

Hussen, S., Wodajo, M. R., & Tasente, T. (2021). The role of microfinance in funding Small & Medium Enterprises: Harekello Town of Goro Dolla District in Focus, Ethiopia. *Technium Soc. Sci. J.*, *17*, 355. doi:10.2139srn.3801885

Ibarvo Urista, V., Quijano Vega, G. A., & Loya Olivas, E. M. (2018). Actitud hacia el emprendimiento social en los alumnos del Instituto Tecnológico de Chihuahua, como respuesta a una problemática nacional. Universidad Nacional Autónoma de México y Asociación Mexicana de Ciencias para el Desarrollo Regional A.C.

Ibdaiwi, T. K., Garcia, F. T., & Lopes, L. F. D. (2008). *Comportamento do consumidor: características de referência dos vestibulandos da cidade de Santa Maria – RS*. Retrieved June 11, 2017, from: www.convibra.org/dwp.asp?id=3846&ev=25

Ibrahim, P., & Ghazali, R. (2014). *Zakah* as an Islamic Micro-Financing Mechanism to Productive *Zakah* Recipients. *Asian Economic and Financial Review, 4*(1), 117-125. https://www.researchgate.net/publication/259478450_*ZAKAH*_AS_AN_ISLAMIC_MICRO-FINANCING_MECHANISM_TO_PRODUCTIVE_*ZAKAH*_RECIPIENTS/link/02e7e52c0e4cbc3773000000/download

Ignacio-González, F. A., & Santos, M. E. (2020). Multidimensional poverty in urban Argentina: Reduction of disparities between the Norte Grande Argentino and Centro-Cuyo-Sur? (2003-2016). *Cuadernos de Economía (Santiago, Chile), 39*(81), 795–822. doi:10.15446/cuad.econ.v39n81.76486

Ilies, R., Wilson, K. S., & Wagner, D. T. (2009). The spillover of daily job satisfaction onto employees' family lives: The facilitating role of work-family integration. *Academy of Management Journal, 52*(1), 87–102. doi:10.5465/amj.2009.36461938

Innovare Pesquisa. (2016). *O consumo de cerveja no Brasil.* Retrieved September 6, 2017, from: https://www.innovarepesquisa.com.br/blog/o-consumo-de-cerveja-brasil/

Instituto Nacional de Estadística y Geografía. (2015). *Mujeres y hombres en México 2015, Censo de población.* Instituto Nacional de Estadística y Geografía, México. http://internet.contenidos.inegi.org.mx/contenidos/Productos/prod_serv/contenidos/espanol/bvinegi/productos/nueva_estruc/702825075019.pdf

Ipsen, C., van Veldhoven, M., Kirchner, K., & Hansen, J. P. (2021). Six key advantages and disadvantages of working from home in Europe during COVID-19. *International Journal of Environmental Research and Public Health, 18*(4), 1826. doi:10.3390/ijerph18041826 PMID:33668505

Islamic Commercial Law Report. (2018). *ISRA*. Thomson Reuters & IRTI.

Jaén, I. (2010). *Una revisión teórica de los valores en el estudio de la intención emprendedora.* Universidad de Sevilla. Disponible en institucional.us.es/vie/documentos/resultados/ValoresIntencionEmprendedoraInmaJaen.pdf

Jaffee, D. (2014). Brewing Justice: Fair Trade Coffee, Sustainability, and Survival. University of California Press. doi:10.1525/9780520957886

Javid, A., & Abrar, A. (2015). Microfinance Institutions and Poverty Reduction: A Cross Regional Analysis. *Pakistan Development Review, 54*(4), 371–387. https://www.jstor.org/stable/43831326. doi:10.30541/v54i4I-IIpp.371-387

Jesus, S. N., Leal, A. R., Viseu, J. N., Valle, P., Matavelli, R. D., Pereira, J., & Greenglass, E. (2016). Coping as a moderator of the influence of economic stressors on psychological health. *Análise Psicológica, 34*(4), 365–376. doi:10.14417/ap.1122

Jiang, G., Kotabe, M., Hamilton, I. III, & Smith, S. (2016). Early internationalization and the role of immigration in new venture survival. *International Business Review, 25*(6), 1285–1296. doi:10.1016/j.ibusrev.2016.04.001

Jindra, C., & Vaz, A. (2019). Good governance and multidimensional poverty: A comparative analysis of 71 countries. *Governance: An International Journal of Policy, Administration and Institutions, 32*(4), 657–675. doi:10.1111/gove.12394

Jones, E., Tiffen, P., Balfour, S., & Mayo, E. (2019). Celebrating the life and work of Fair Trade pioneer, Robin Murray, 1940–2017. *Journal of Fair Trade, 1*(1), 6–12. doi:10.13169/jfairtrade.1.1.0006

Jones, P., Hillier, D., & Comfort, D. (2017). The sustainable development goals and the tourism and hospitality industry. *Athens Journal of Tourism, 4*(1), 7–18. doi:10.30958/ajt.4.1.1

Joshi, D. K., Hughes, B. B., & Sisk, T. D. (2015). Improving Governance for the Post-2015 Sustainable Development Goals: Scenario Forecasting the Next 50years. *World Development, 70*, 286–302. doi:10.1016/j.worlddev.2015.01.013

Kachkar, O. (2019). Refugee Entrepreneurship: Empirical Quantitative Evidence from Refugee Camps in Turkey. *Journal of Immigrant & Refugee Studies, 17*(3), 333–352. doi:10.1080/15562948.2018.1479913

Kadir, M. B. A., Salim, M., & Kamarudin, H. (2012). The relationship between educational support and entrepreneurial intentions in Malaysian higher learning institution. *Procedia: Social and Behavioral Sciences, 69*, 2164–2173. doi:10.1016/j.sbspro.2012.12.182

Kapoor, V., Yadav, J., Bajpai, L., & Srivastava, S. (2021). Perceived stress and psychological well-being of working mothers during COVID-19: a mediated moderated roles of teleworking and resilience. *Employee Relations: The International Journal.*

Karadağ, H. (2016). The role of SMEs and entrepreneurship on economic growth in emerging economies within the post-crisis era: An analysis from Turkey. *Journal of Small Business and Entrepreneurship Development.*

Karmakar, K. (2009). Emerging Trends in Microfinance. *Economic and Political Weekly, 44*(13), 21–24. https://www.jstor.org/stable/40278656

Kasali, T. A., Ahmad, S. A., & Lim, H. E. (2015). The role of microfinance in poverty alleviation: Empirical evidence from South-West Nigeria. *Asian Social Science, 11*(21), 183–192. doi:10.5539/ass.v11n21p183

Kautonen, T., Van Gelderen, M., & Tornikoski, E. T. (2013). Predicting entrepreneurial behaviour: A test of the theory of planned behaviour. *Applied Economics, 45*(6), 697–707. doi:10.1080/00036846.2011.610750

Kazekami, S. (2020). Mechanisms to improve labor productivity by performing telework. *Telecommunications Policy, 44*(2), 101868. doi:10.1016/j.telpol.2019.101868

Khalid, R. U., Seuring, S., Beske, P., Land, A., Yawar, S. A., & Wagner, R. (2015). Putting sustainable supply chain management into base of the pyramid research. *Supply Chain Management, 20*(6), 681–696. doi:10.1108/SCM-06-2015-0214

Khan, R. E. A., & Noreen, S. (2012). Microfinance and women empowerment: A case study of District Bahawalpur (Pakistan). *African Journal of Business Management, 6*(12), 4514–4521.

Kimbu, A. N., & Tichaawa, M. T. (2018). Sustainable development goals and socio-economic development through tourism in central africa: Mith or realiit? *Geo Journal of Tourism and Geosites, 23*(3), 780–796. doi:10.30892/gtg.23314-328

Kim, Y., Park, M. S., & Wier, B. (2012). Is earnings quality associated with corporate social responsibility? *The Accounting Review, 8*(3), 761–796. doi:10.2308/accr-10209

Klammer, J., & van den Anker, F. W. (2018). A Platform to Connect Swiss Consumers of Fair Trade Products with Producers in Developing Countries*: Needs and Motivations. In International Conference of Design, User Experience, and Usability* (pp. 664-681). Springer. 10.1007/978-3-319-91806-8_52

Kocken, M. (2006). Introduction. In A. Osterhaus (Ed.), Business Unusual: Success and Challenges of Fair Trade (pp. 5–6). Academic Press.

Koe, W. L., Sa'ari, J. R., Majid, I. A., & Ismail, K. (2012). Determinants of entrepreneurial intention among millennial generation. *Procedia: Social and Behavioral Sciences, 40*, 197–208. doi:10.1016/j.sbspro.2012.03.181

Kotler, P. (1998). Administração de marketing: análise, planejamento, implementação controle (5a ed.). São Paulo: Atlas.

Kozan, M. K., Öksoy, D., & Özsoy, O. (2006). Growth plans of small businesses in Turkey: Individual and environmental influences. *Journal of Small Business Management, 44*(1), 114–129. doi:10.1111/j.1540-627X.2006.00157.x

Krevans, J., & Gibbs, J. C. (1996). Parents' use of inductive discipline: Relations to children's empathy and prosocial behavior. *Child Development, 67*(6), 3263–3277. doi:10.2307/1131778 PMID:9071781

Krogh, E., Hansen, T. N., Wendt, S., & Elkjaer, M. (2009). Promoting employment for women as a strategy for poverty reduction. *Promoting Pro-Poor Growth, 133.*

Krueger, N. F. Jr, & Brazeal, D. V. (1994). Entrepreneurial potential and potential entrepreneurs. *Entrepreneurship Theory and Practice, 18*(3), 91–104. doi:10.1177/104225879401800307

Krueger, N. Jr, Reilly, M., & Carsrud, A. (2000). Competing models of entrepreneurial intentions. *Journal of Business Venturing*, *15*(5-6), 5–6, 411–432. doi:10.1016/S0883-9026(98)00033-0

Kulak, F. A., & Tüzüner, V. L. (2020). A comparative analysis of flexible working patterns in Germany and Turkey. *International Journal of Research in Business and Social Science, 9*(4), 1-14.

Kumar, K., Boesso, G., & Michelon, G. (2016). How do strengths and weaknesses in corporate social performance across different stakeholder domains affect company performance? *Business Strategy and the Environment*, *25*(4), 277–292. doi:10.1002/bse.1874

Kuti, M., & Madarász, G. (2014). Crowdfunding. *Public Finance Quarterly*, *59*(3), 355–366.

Kyereboah-Coleman, A., & Osei, K. A. (2008). Outreach and profitability of microfinance institutions: The role of governance. *Journal of Economic Studies (Glasgow, Scotland)*, *35*(3), 236–248. doi:10.1108/01443580810887797

Lai, C., Chiu, C., Yang, C., & Pai, D. (2010). The effects of corporate social responsibility on brand performance: The mediating effect of industrial brand equity and corporate reputation. *Journal of Business Ethics*, *95*(3), 457–469. doi:10.100710551-010-0433-1

Laloux, F. (2017). Reinventando as Organizações. Curitiba: Voo.

Lanau, A., Mack, J., & Nandy, S. (2020). Including services in multidimensional poverty measurement for SDGs: Modifications to the consensual approach. *The Journal of Poverty and Social Justice: Research, Policy, Practice*, *28*(2), 149–168. doi:10.1332/175982720X15850580703755

Lane, B. (1994). What is rural tourism? *Journal of Sustainable Tourism*, *2*(1), 7–21. doi:10.1080/09669589409510680

Lanfranchi, M., Giannetto, C., & De Pascale, A. (2014). Rural tourism: A kind of sustainable tourism in the face of global economic crisis. *International Journal for Responsible Tourism*, *3*(2), 15–28.

Larroza, C. A. (2016). Pobreza en Paraguay: Contribución de la educación media en el acceso a las oportunidades para superar la pobreza. *Población y Desarrollo*, (43), 25–34.

Leal Filho, W., Brandli, L. L., Becker, D., Skanavis, C., Kounani, A., Sardi, C., Papaioannidou, D., Azeiteiro, U., de Sousa, L., Raath, S., Pretorius, R., Vargas, V. R., Shiel, C., Trencher, G., & Marans, R. W. (2018). Sustainable development policies as indicators and pre-conditions for sustainability efforts at universities: Fact or fiction? *International Journal of Sustainability in Higher Education*, *25*(2), 131–142. doi:10.1108/IJSHE-01-2017-0002

Lee, L., Wong, P. K., Foo, M. D., & Leung, A. (2011). Entrepreneurial intentions: The influence of organizational and individual factors. *Journal of Business Venturing*, *26*(1), 124–136. doi:10.1016/j.jbusvent.2009.04.003

León, M. A., & León, M. M. (2016). Impacto de la Inversión Extranjera Directa en el desarrollo económico - social de la región. *Jóvenes en la ciencia Revista de Divulgación Científica, 2*(1), 697-701.

Leu, C. H., Chen, K. M., & Chen, H. H. (2016). A multidimensional approach to child poverty in Taiwan. *Children and Youth Services Review*, *66*, 35–44. doi:10.1016/j.childyouth.2016.04.018

Ley General de Desarrollo Social. (2018). *Diario Oficial de la Federación*. http://www.diputados.gob.mx/LeyesBiblio/pdf/264_250618.pdf

Li-Chan, Ch., Shang-Ping, L., & Chun-Min, K. (2013). Rural tourism: Marketing strategies for the bed and breakfast industry in Taiwan. *International Journal of Hospitality Management*, *32*, 278–286. doi:10.1016/j.ijhm.2012.07.005

Liñán, F. & Chen, Y. W. (2006). *Testing the entrepreneurial intention model on a two-country sample*. Document de Treball núm. 06/7. Universitat Autònoma de Barcelona.

Liñán, F., & Fayolle, A. (2015). A systematic literature review on entrepreneurial intentions: Citation, thematic analyses, and research agenda. *The International Entrepreneurship and Management Journal, 11*(4), 907–933. doi:10.100711365-015-0356-5

Liñán, F., Nabi, G., & Krueger, N. (2013). British and Spanish entrepreneurial intentions: A comparative study. *Revista de Economía Mundial*, (33), 73–103.

Liñán, F., Rodríguez-Cohard, J. C., & Rueda-Cantuche, J. M. (2011). Factors affecting entrepreneurial intention levels: A role for education. *The International Entrepreneurship and Management Journal*, *7*(2), 195–218. doi:10.100711365-010-0154-z

Lin, H.-H., Wang, Y. S., & Chang, L. K. (2011). Consumer responses to online retailer's service recovery after a service failure. *Managing Service Quality*, *21*(5), 511–534. doi:10.1108/09604521111159807

Lintner, C. (2015). Migrant Entrepreneurship: New Potential Discovered. *Procedia: Social and Behavioral Sciences*, *191*, 1601–1606. doi:10.1016/j.sbspro.2015.04.519

Liu, Y., & Xu, Y. (2016). A geographic identification of multidimensional poverty in rural China under the framework of sustainable livelihoods analysis. *Applied Geography (Sevenoaks, England)*, *73*, 62–76. doi:10.1016/j.apgeog.2016.06.004

Lizana, P. A., & Vega-Fernadez, G. (2021). Teacher teleworking during the covid-19 pandemic: Association between work hours, work–family balance and quality of life. *International Journal of Environmental Research and Public Health*, *18*(14), 7566. doi:10.3390/ijerph18147566 PMID:34300015

Loaiza Quintero, O. L., Muñetón Santa, G., & Vanegas López, J. G. (2018). An exploratory assessment of the relationship between multidimensional poverty and armed conflict: The case of Antioquia, Colombia. *Desarrollo y Sociedad*, (80), 11–51. doi:10.13043/DYS.80.1

Loescher, G., & Milner, J. (2005). *Protracted Refugee Situations: Domestic and International Security Implications*. Routledge.

López Azcona, M.A (2016). Luces y sombras del nuevo marco jurídico en materia de acogimiento y adopción de menores a propósito de la Ley Orgánica 8/2015 y la Ley 26/2015 de modificación del sistema de protección a la infancia y adolescencia. *Boletín del Ministerio de Justicia, 2185*.

López, R. (2011). *Políticas para la disminución de la pobreza en México: Consideraciones a partir del Programa Oportunidades Revista COFACTOR*. http://cofactor.edomex.gob.mx/sites/cofactor.edomex.gob.mx/files/files/cofactor3/cofactor_pdf_art5o.pdf

López-Pérez, M., Melero-Polo, I., & Sesé, J. (2017). Management for Sustainable Development and Its Impact on Firm Value in the SME Context: Does Size Matter? *Business Strategy and the Environment*, *26*(7), 985–999. doi:10.1002/bse.1961

López-Pérez, M., Melero-Polo, I., Vázquez, R., & Cambra-Fierro, J. (2018). Sustainability and Business Outcomes in the Context of SMEs: Comparing Family Firms vs. Non-Family Firms. *Sustainability*, *10*(11), 4080–4090. doi:10.3390u10114080

Low, W., & Davenport, E. (2005). Postcards from the edge: Maintaining the 'alternative' character of fair trade. *Sustainable Development*, *13*(3), 143–153. doi:10.1002d.275

Lozares Colina, C. (1996). La teoría de redes sociales. *Papers: Revista de Sociologia*, (48), 103–126.

Lu, L. Y. Y., & Liu, J. S. (2014). The knowledge diffusion paths of corporate social responsibility – From 1970 to 2011. *Corporate Social Responsibility and Environmental Management*, *21*(2), 113–128. doi:10.1002/csr.1309

Lund-Thomsen, P., & Nadvi, K. (2010). Global value chains, local collective action and corporate social responsibility: A review of empirical evidence. *Business Strategy and the Environment*, *19*(1), 1–13. doi:10.1002/bse.670

Luo, Y. (2005). Toward coopetition within a multinational enterprise: A perspective from foreign subsidiarie. *Journal of World Business*, *40*(1), 71–90. doi:10.1016/j.jwb.2004.10.006

Maaya, L., Meulders, M., Surmont, N., & Vandebroek, M. (2018). Effect of environmental and altruistic attitudes on willingness-to-pay for organic and fair trade coffee in Flanders. *Sustainability*, *10*(12), 4496–4510. doi:10.3390u10124496

Maehle, N. (2020). Sustainable crowdfunding: Insights from the project perspective. *Baltic Journal of Management*, *15*(2), 281–302. doi:10.1108/BJM-02-2019-0079

Mahrt, K., Rossi, A., Salvucci, V., & Tarp, F. (2020). Multidimensional poverty of children in Mozambique. *Child Indicators Research*, *13*(5), 1675–1700. doi:10.100712187-019-09696-6

Maia, F. S., & Maia, T. S. T. (2011). Network training and strategic alliances in the civil construction sector. *Espacios Magazine.*, *32*, 38.

Maksimović, M., Urošević, S., & Mihajlović, D. (2015). The effects of the development of rural tourism on stara planina. *ЕКОНОМИКА*, *61*(2), 83–91. doi:10.5937/ekonomika1502083M

Mao, Y., He, J., Morrison, A. M., & Andres Coca-Stefaniak, J. (2020). Effects of tourism CSR on employee psychological capital in the COVID-19 crisis: From the perspective of conservation of resources theory. *Current Issues in Tourism*, 1–19.

Maqueda, A. (2021). *La pandemia elevó la pobreza en 2020 al mayor nivel desde la Gran Recesión*. Disponible en https://elpais.com/economia/2021-07-15/la-pandemia-elevo-la-pobreza-en-2020-al-mayor-nivel-desde-la-gran-recesion.html

Marcón, O. A. (2011). De la pobreza a la exclusión: Implicancias teórico-prácticas pensadas desde Argentina. *Prospectiva*, (15), 207–234. doi:10.25100/prts.v0i15.1110

Marmolejo, A. M. (2012). Reflexiones Sobre Competitividad, Educación y Pobreza. *Revista Xihmai*, *1*(2).

Maruyama, T., & Tietze, S. (2012). From anxiety to assurance: Concerns and outcomes of telework. *Personnel Review*, *41*(4), 450–469. doi:10.1108/00483481211229375

Matter, F. (2011). *Development in Practice*, *21*(8). https://www.jstor.org/stable/41413000

Mawa, B. (2008). Impact of micro-finance towards achieving poverty alleviation. *Pakistan Journal of Social Sciences*, *5*(9), 876–882.

Ma, Z., Lee, Y., & Yu, K. H. (2008). Ten years of conflict management studies: Themes, concepts and relationships. *International Journal of Conflict Management*, *19*(3), 234–248. doi:10.1108/10444060810875796

McCarter, E. (2006). Women and microfinance: Why we should do more. *U. Md. LJ Race, Religion. Race, Gender, & Class*, *6*, 353.

McGuire, P. B., & Conroy, J. D. (2000). The microfinance phenomenon. *Asia-Pacific Review*, *7*(1), 90–108. doi:10.1080/713650817

Medeiros, F. C. L. M., & Lima, V. M. S. (2002). *Consumidor, cliente e paciente: existe alguma diferença? 1*(2). Retrieved May 22, 2017, from: www.revistaunirn.inf.br

Medina, S. (2013). Inversión Extranjera Directa por entidad. *Comercio Exterior*, *63*(2), 3–7.

Meister, A. P. S. (2008*). Pesquisa de satisfação dos clientes do restaurante Vermelho Grill.* Retrieved May 12, 2017, from: www.lume.ufrgs.br/handle/10183/18040

Mejía, P. (2005). La inversión extranjera directa en los estados de México: evolución reciente y retos futuros. Economía, Sociedad y Territorio, (99), 185-236.

Melo, T., & Garrido-Morgado, A. (2012). Corporate reputation: A combination of social responsibility and industry. *Corporate Social Responsibility and Environmental Management*, *19*(1), 11–31. doi:10.1002/csr.260

Méndez, J. N. (2002). *Determinantes de la pobreza en Colombia: años recientes*. CEPAL.

Mendoza, J. E. (2011). Impacto de la inversión extranjera en el crecimiento manufacturero en México. *Revista Problemas del Desarrollo*, *167*(42), 69–45. doi:10.22201/iiec.20078951e.2011.167.27720

Merino-Saum, A., Baldi, M. G., Gunderson, I., & Oberle, B. (2018). Articulating natural resources and sustainable development goals through green economy indicators: A systematic analysis. *Resources, Conservation and Recycling*, *139*, 90–103. doi:10.1016/j.resconrec.2018.07.007

Messner, M., Becker, C., Schäffer, U., & Binder, C. (2008). Legitimacy and identity in Germanic management accounting research. *European Accounting Review*, *17*(1), 129–159. doi:10.1080/09638180701819808

Mestres, J. (2010). *Migrant entrepreneurship in OECD countries and its contribution to employment*. Academic Press.

Mideros, A. (2012). Ecuador: definición y medición multidimensional de la pobreza, 2006-2010. *Revista Cepal*.

Miele, M., Waquil, P. D., & Schultz, G. (2011). Mercados e comercialização de produtos agroindustriais. *Ciências Sociais Aplicadas*. Universidade Federal do Rio Grande do Sul. Retrieved March 22, 2017, from: www.lume.ufrgs.br

Miguel González, L. J., Candial Torres, A., Domenech Llorente, E., Ortega Salvador, Á., Pérez Miguel, L., Rodríguez Fernández, J. M., & Rodríguez López, F. (2011). *Microcréditos para combatir la pobreza: una introducción a los conceptos básicos de microfinanzas como instrumento alternativo para la financiación del desarrollo*. Retrieved from https://uvadoc.uva.es/bitstream/handle/10324/47443/MicrocreditosParaCombatirLaPobreza.pdf?sequence=1&isAllowed=y

Minkler, L., & Prakash, N. (2017). The role of constitutions on poverty: A cross-national investigation. *Journal of Comparative Economics*, *45*(3), 563–581. doi:10.1016/j.jce.2017.03.002

Mintzberg, H., & Ahlstrand, B. (2000). LAMPEL, J. Safári de estratégia. Porto Alegre. *The Bookman*.

Miranda, F., Chamorro, A., & Rubio, S. (2017). Academic entrepreneurship in Spanish universities: An analysis of the determinants of entrepreneurial intention. *European Research on Management and Business Economics*, *23*(2), 113–122. doi:10.1016/j.iedeen.2017.01.001

Misturelli, F., & Heffernan, C. (2012). The shape of change: A memetic analysis of the definitions of poverty from the 1970s to the 2000s. *Journal of International Development*, *24*, S3–S18. doi:10.1002/jid.1770

Miyashita, Y. (2000). Microfinance and poverty alleviation: Lessons from Indonesia's village banking system. *Pac. Rim L. & Pol'y J.*, *10*, 147.

Möckel, B. (2019). Dilemmas of Moral Markets: Conflicting Narratives in the West German Fair Trade Movement. In *Moralizing Capitalism* (pp. 267–292). Palgrave Macmillan. doi:10.1007/978-3-030-20565-2_12

Modéer. (2018). *Unlocking Islamic Social Finance to Help Communities Address Vulnerability and Inequality*. https://www.undp.org/content/undp/en/home/news-centre/speeches/2018/Unlocking_Islamic_Social_Finance_to_Help_Communities_Address_Vulnerability_and_Inequality.html

Mohamed, N., Mastuki, N., Yusuf, S., & Zakaria, M. (2018). Management Control System in Asnaf Entrepreneurship Development Program by Lembaga *Zakah* Selangor [Sistem Kawalan Dalaman bagi Program Pembangunan Usahawan Asnaf di Lembaga *Zakah* Selangor]. *Jurnal Pengurusan.*, *53*, 13–22.

Mohapatra, S., & Sahoo, B. K. (2016). Determinants of participation in self-help-groups (SHG) and its impact on women empowerment. *Indian Growth and Development Review*, *9*(1), 53–78. doi:10.1108/IGDR-04-2015-0016

Mohsin, M., & Alhabshi, S. (2016). Hybrid Model of *Zakah*, Waqf, Qard-Hassan & Islamic Finance for a Just and Sustainable Microfinance. *Sahulat: A Journal of Interest free Microfinance*, *4*(1).

Moldavska, A. & Welo, T. (2019). A Holistic approach to corporate sustainability assessment: Incorporating sustainable development goals into sustainable manufacturing performance evaluation. *Journal of Manufacturing Systems*, *50*(November), 53–68.

Mollick, E. (2014). The dynamics of crowdfunding: An exploratory study. *Journal of Business Venturing*, *29*(1), 1–16. doi:10.1016/j.jbusvent.2013.06.005

Montgomery, V. A., Roman, A., & Pierce, S. (2016). The rise and effect of virtual modalities and functions on organizational leadership: Tracing conceptual boundaries along the e-management and e-leadership continuum. *Transylvanian Review of Administrative Sciences*, *12*, 102–122.

Mora, C., Yahevh, O., Villafuerte, L. F., & Sinforoso Martinez, S. (2020). Factors Derived from Multidimensional Poverty That Affect the Usability of E-Government in Mexico. *Braz. J. Pub. Pol'y*, *10*, 69.

Moradi, M., Imanipour, N., Arasti, Z., & Mohammadkazemi, R. (2020). Poverty and entrepreneurship: A systematic review of poverty-related issues discussed in entrepreneurship literature. *World Review of Entrepreneurship, Management and Sustainable Development*, *16*(2), 1, 25–152. doi:10.1504/WREMSD.2020.105984

Morales, J. (2010). Inversión extranjera directa y desarrollo en América Latina. *Revista Problemas del Desarrollo*, *41*(163), 141–156.

Moreno, J. A. D. (2011). *Informalidad laboral y pobreza urbana en Colombia*. CIDSE.

Moreno-Torres Sánchez, J. (2015). *Modificación del sistema de protección a la infancia ya la adolescencia. Guía para profesionales y agentes sociales*. Málaga: Save the Children. Recuperado de: www. savethechildren.es/sites/default/files/imce/docs/modificacion_del_sistema_de_proteccion_a_la_infancia_y_a_la_adolescencia.pdf

Moura, B. (2017). *Crowdlending (Financiamento Colaborativo por Empréstimos) Perfil dos Early Fundraisers. Estudo de Caso—Plataformas Portuguesas*. Academic Press.

Moyer, J. D., & Bohl, D. K. (2019). Alternative pathways to human development: Assessing trade-offs and synergies in achieving the Sustainable Development Goals. *Futures*, *105*, 199210. doi:10.1016/j.futures.2018.10.007

Moyer, J. D., & Hedden, S. (2020). Are we on the right path to achieve the sustainable development goals? *World Development*, *127*(104749), 1–13. doi:10.1016/j.worlddev.2019.104749

Moyle, T. L., Dollard, M., & Biswas, S. N. (2006). Personal and economic empowerment in rural Indian women: A self-help group approach. *International Journal of Rural Management*, *2*(2), 245–266. doi:10.1177/097300520600200207

Muchineripi, J., Chinyamurindi, W., & Chimucheka, T. (2019). A narrative analysis of barriers encountered by a sample of immigrant entrepreneurs in the Eastern Cape province of South Africa. *The Journal for Transdisciplinary Research in Southern Africa*, *15*(1), 9. doi:10.4102/td.v15i1.556

Mullainathan. (2020). *Escassez – Uma nova forma de pensar a falta de recursos na vida das pessoas e nas organizações*. Best Business.

Murphy, P. E. (1985). *Tourism: A Community Approach*. Methuen.

Nader, Y. F. (2008). Microcredit and the socio-economic wellbeing of women and their families in Cairo. *Journal of Socio-Economics*, *37*(2), 644–656. doi:10.1016/j.socec.2007.10.008

Nagata, T., Ito, D., Nagata, M., Fujimoto, A., Ito, R., Odagami, K., Kajiki, S., Uehara, M., Oyama, I., Dohi, S., Fujino, Y., & Mori, K. (2021). Anticipated health effects and proposed countermeasures following the immediate introduction of telework in response to the spread of COVID-19: The findings of a rapid health impact assessment in Japan. *Journal of Occupational Health*, *63*(1), e12198. doi:10.1002/1348-9585.12198 PMID:33527667

Nájera Catalán, H. E., & Gordon, D. (2020). The importance of reliability and construct validity in multidimensional poverty measurement: An illustration using the multidimensional poverty index for Latin America (MPI-LA). *The Journal of Development Studies*, *56*(9), 1763–1783. doi:10.1080/00220388.2019.1663176

Narcıkara, E. (2017b). *Spiritüel liderlik davranışının algılanan performans üzerine etkisi* (Published Phd Thesis). Yıldız Technical University. Social Sciences Institude.

Narcıkara, E. B. (2017). Örgüt Ortamında Artarak Yükselen Olumluluk: Pozitif Örgüt Okulu Bakış Perpektifi. *İş'te Davranış Dergisi*, *2*(1), 20-33.

Nash, K. L., Blythe, J. L., Cvitanovic, C., Fulton, E. A., Halpern, B. S., Milner-Gulland, E. J., Addison, P. F. E., Pecl, G. T., Watson, R. A., & Blanchard, J. L. (2020). To Achieve a Sustainable Blue Future, Progress Assessments Must Include Interdependencies between the Sustainable Development Goals. *One Earth*, *2*(2), 161–173. doi:10.1016/j.oneear.2020.01.008

National Council for the Evaluation of Social Development Policy. (2014). *Income Lines. In Methodology for the multidimensional measurement of poverty in Mexico*. CONEVAL.

Navrátilová, M., Abrhám, J., Beranová, M., & Brož, D. (2019). Fair Trade Products And Sustainable Consumer Behaviour. *Journal of Security & Sustainability. Issues (Chicago, Ill.)*, *8*(4), 34–43.

Nawaz, F. (2015). Microfinance, Financial Literacy, and Household Power Configuration in Rural Bangladesh: An Empirical Study on Some Credit Borrowers. *Voluntas*, *26*(4), 1100–1121. doi:10.100711266-015-9585-z

Naylor, L. (2018). Fair trade coffee exchanges and community economies. Environment and Planning A. *Economy and Spaoo*, *50*(5), 1027 1046.

Neri, M., Oleas, S., Torrado, M. P., Vargas, C. P., Perticara, M., Lomelí, L. I. R., & Trujillo, J. D. (2012). *Pobreza, Desigualdad de Oportunidades y Políticas Públicas en América Latina*. Rio de Janeiro: Konrad-Adenauer-Stiftung Retrieved from https://scholar.google.es/scholar?hl=es&as_sdt=0%2C5&q=Pobreza%2C+Desigualdad+de+Oportunidades+y+Poli%CC%81ticas+Pu%CC%81blicas+en+Ame%CC%81rica+Latina&btnG=

Newton, I. (1687). *Philosophiae Naturalis Principia Mathematica*. Pincipia. doi:10.5479il.52126.39088015628399

Noreen, S. (2011). Role of microfinance in empowerment of female population of Bahawalpur district. In *International Conference on Economics and Finance Research* (*Vol. 4*, No. 20, pp. 65-71). Academic Press.

Nukpezah, J. A., & Blankson, C. (2017). Microfinance intervention in poverty reduction: A study of women farmer-entrepreneurs in rural Ghana. *Journal of African Business*, *18*(4), 457–475. doi:10.1080/15228916.2017.1336915

O'Donell, D. (1990). *Instituto Interamericano del niño, la niña y adolescentes*. Academic Press.

Obaidullah, M. (2008). *Introduction to Islamic Microfinance*. https://www.researchgate.net/publication/228201195_Introduction_to_Islamic_Microfinance

Obaidullah, M. (2008). *Role of microfinance in poverty alleviation: Lessons from experiences in selected IDB member countries. In Role of Microfinance in Poverty Alleviation: Lessons from Experiences in Selected IDB Member Countries.* Islamic Development Bank.

OECD. (2019). *OECD Economic Studies: México 2019.* OECD Publishing. doi:10.1787/fde7bbbe-es

OECD. (2019). *The Missing Entrepreneurs 2019 Policies for inclusive Entrepreneurship.* https://www.oecd.org/cfe/leed/2019-ME-Policy-Highlights.pdf

Ogutu, S. O., Ochieng, D. O., & Qaim, M. (2020). Supermarket contracts and smallholder farmers: Implications for income and multidimensional poverty. *Food Policy*, *95*, 101940. doi:10.1016/j.foodpol.2020.101940

Oguz, O. (2021). Teleworking Conditions in Turkish Labour Law. *Mokslas Ir Praktika: Aktualijos Ir Perspektyvos*, *32*.

Ohe, Y. (2020). *Community-based rural tourism and entrepreneurship.* Springer. doi:10.1007/978-981-15-0383-2

Oliveira, C. (2019). *Empregadores e Empreendedores Imigrantes: Tipologia de Estratégias Empresariais.* Observatório das Migrações, ACM, I.P.

Oliveira, J. (2010). *Satisfação do cliente.* Retrieved May 22, 2017, from: https://www.administradores.com.br/producao-academica/satisfacao-do-cliente/2859/

Onileowo, T. T., & Anifowose, O. D. (2020). Catalyst and Instrument of National Growth: Interrogating the Significance of Entrepreneurship in Nigerian Economic Development. *Catalyst, 12*(3).

Oosterveer, P., Rossing, G., Hendriksen, A., & Voerman, K. (2014). Mainstreaming fair trade: the role of retailers. *Sustainability: Science, Practice and Policy*, *10*(2), 4–13.

Ordoñez Camacho, J. G. (2015). Consideraciones metodológicas sobre el estudio del comportamiento antisocial en la teoría de curso de vida de sampson y laub. *Anuario de Derecho, 32*(32).

Orlitzky, M., Siegel, D., & Waldman, D. (2011). Strategic corporate social responsibility and environmental sustainability. *Business & Society*, *50*(1), 6–27. doi:10.1177/0007650310394323

Orzes, G., Moretto, A. M., Ebrahimpour, M., Sartor, M., Moro, M., & Rossi, M. (2018). United Nations Global Compact: Literature review and theory-based research agenda. *Journal of Cleaner Production*, *177*, 633–654. doi:10.1016/j.jclepro.2017.12.230

Osman, O. S. (2020). The role of microfinance post trauma: the case of Syria. *Journal of Sustainable Finance & Investment*, 1-15.

Ostermann, E. (2020). *"Refugee Entrepreneurship": The role of the theory of planned behavior and country of origin on entrepreneurial intention of refugees* (Doctoral dissertation). Universität Linz.

Othman, N., Yusef, S. A. M., & Osman, W. R. S. (2009). A conflict between professional vs. domestic life? Understanding the use of ICT in teleworking for balance in work and family units. *Comp. Infor. Sci.*, *2*, 3–15.

Overbeek, A. (2019). Examining the Efficacy of Fair Trade and Alternative Consumption on Environmental Sustainability and Human Rights in Developing Countries. *Consilience*, (21), 158–171.

Özen, E., Grima, S., & Hamarat, B. (2021). *Teleworking and Emotional Experience and Wellbeing: The Case in the Turkish Financial Services Industry During COVID-19.* Scientific Annals of Economics and Business.

Paço, S., & Ramos, M. (2018). Empreendedorismo em Portugal de imigrantes de países de fora da União Europeia. *HOLOS*, *2*(0), 365–385. doi:10.15628/holos.2018.6924

Pacto Mundial de la Red Española. (2021). *Implementación de herramientas del Pacto Mundial en la actividad empresarial, como contribución para canalizar los ODS*. Consultado en: https://www.pactomundial.org/herramientas/

Pascual, A. S. (2013). Marcos interpretativos de lo social en la vivencia de la «nueva pobreza» [Interpretative frameworks of the social in the living of the «new poverty»]. *Cuadernos de Relaciones Laborales*, *31*(2), 337–382.

Pasha, A. (2017). Regional perspectives on the multidimensional poverty index. *World Development*, *94*, 268–285. doi:10.1016/j.worlddev.2017.01.013

Patterson, G. R., DeBaryshe, B., & Ramsey, E. (1989). *A developmental perspective*. Academic Press.

Pelham, A. M. (1997). Mediating Influences on the Relationship between Market Orientation and Profitability in Small Industrial Firms. *Journal of Marketing Theory and Practice*, *5*(3), 55–77. doi:10.1080/10696679.1997.11501771

Pérez, A., & de los Salmones, M. D. (2018). Information and knowledge as antecedents of consumer attitudes and intentions to buy and recommend fair-trade products. *Journal of Nonprofit & Public Sector Marketing*, *30*(2), 111–133. doi:10.1080/10495142.2017.1326358

Pieck, E. (2005). Work-related adult education: Challenges and possibilities in poverty areas. *International Journal of Lifelong Education*, *24*(5), 419–429. doi:10.1080/02601370500169798

Pierrakis, Y., & Collins, L. (2012). *The venture crowd: Crowdfunding equity investment into business*. Nesta.

Pilkington, A., & Teichert, T. (2006). Management of technology: Themes, concepts and relationships. *Technovation*, *26*(3), 288–299. doi:10.1016/j.technovation.2005.01.009

Pimentel, G. S. (2013). *A influência das redes sociais na escolha dos consumidores: o caso do bar Botequim Tá Na Hora*. Retrieved May 22, 2017, from: docplayer.com.br/3661987-A-influencia-das-redes-sociais-na-escolha-dos-consumido.

Pinilla-Roncancio, M., Mactaggart, I., Kuper, H., Dionicio, C., Naber, J., Murthy, G. V. S., & Polack, S. (2020). Multidimensional poverty and disability: A case control study in India, Cameroon, and Guatemala. *SSM - Population Health*, *11*, 100591. doi:10.1016/j.ssmph.2020.100591 PMID:32405529

Piquer, D. C., & Ordovás, J. M. (2015). Relación entre el estado socioeconómico, la educación y la alimentación saludable. *Mediterráneo Económico*, (27), 283–306.

Polanco, Y. (2013). ¿Contribuyen las prácticas empresariales responsables a la reducción de la pobreza? [¿Do responsible business practices contribute to poverty reduction?]. *Contabilidad y Negocios*, *8*(15), 43–56.

Pollock, K., & Hauseman, D. C. (2019). The use of e-mail and principals' work: A double-edged sword. *Leadership and Policy in Schools*, *18*(3), 382–393. doi:10.1080/15700763.2017.1398338

Ponce, M. G. (2018). Medición de pobreza multidimensional de la iniciativa en pobreza y desarrollo humano. *Revista de Ciencias Sociales*, *24*, 98–113.

Portales, L. (2019). Reducción de la pobreza multidimensional y fortalecimiento de la inclusión social a través de un programa municipal El caso de la evaluación de impacto del programa «Un Solo San Pedro». *Revista Iberoamericana de Estudios de Desarrollo*, *8*(2), 108–139. doi:10.26754/ojs_ried/ijds.327

Porter, M., & Kramer, M. (2006). Strategy and society: The link between competitive advantage and CSR. *Harvard Business Review*, *84*, 78–92. PMID:17183795

Porter, M., & Kramer, M. (2011). Creating shared value. *Harvard Business Review*, *89*, 62–77.

Poverty & Human Development Initiative. (2016). *Chad Multidimensional Deprivation and Vulnerability Survey*. OPHI Working Papers.

Presidencia de la República. (2018). *Plan Nacional de Desarrollo 2018-2024*. https://lopezobrador.org.mx/wp-content/uploads/2019/05/PLAN-NACIONAL-DE-DESARROLLO-2018-2024.pdf

Price-waterhouse Cooper. (2020). *Make it your business, engaging with the sustainable development goals*. Disponible en https://www.pwc.com/sdg

Prin, M., & Bartels, K. (2020). Social distancing: Implications for the operating room in the face of COVID-19. *Canadian Journal of Anaesthesia*, *67*(7), 789–797. doi:10.100712630-020-01651-2 PMID:32291632

Prodanov, C. C., & Freitas, E. C. (2013). *Metodologia do trabalho científico: Métodos e técnicas da pesquisa e do trabalho acadêmico* (2nd ed.). Universidade Feevale.

Pulley, M. L., & Sessa, V. I. (2001). E-leadership: Tackling complex challenges. *Industrial and Commercial Training*, *33*(6), 225–229. doi:10.1108/00197850110405379

Qardawi, Y. (2009). A comparative study of *Zakah*: Regulations and Philosophy in the light of Qur'an and sunnah. *Fiqh Al Zakah*, *I*, 1–309.

Quinones, B., & Remenyi, J. (2014). *Microfinance and poverty alleviation: Case studies from Asia and the Pacific*. Routledge. doi:10.4324/9781315800455

Racherla, P., & Hu, C. (2010). A social network perspective of tourism research collaborations. *Annals of Tourism Research*, *37*(4), 1012–1034. doi:10.1016/j.annals.2010.03.008

Rahman, M. M., Khanam, R., & Nghiem, S. (2017). The effects of microfinance on women's empowerment: New evidence from Bangladesh. *International Journal of Social Economics*, *44*(12), 1745–1757. doi:10.1108/IJSE-02-2016-0070

Rahman, S. A., Amran, A., Ahmad, N. H., & Taghizadeh, S. K. (2016). Enhancing the wellbeing of base of the pyramid entrepreneurs through business success: The role of private organizations. *Social Indicators Research*, *127*(1), 195–216. doi:10.100711205-015-0951-4

Ramadani, V., Palalic, R., Dana, L.P., Krueger, N., & Caputo, A. (2020). Organizational Mindset of Entrepreneurship. Springer.

Ramasamy, B., & Yeung, M. (2009). "Chinese consumers" perception of corporate social responsibility (CSR). *Journal of Business Ethics*, *88*(1), 119–132. doi:10.100710551-008-9825-x

Ramírez, J. M., Díaz, Y., & Bedoya, J. G. (2017). Property tax revenues and multidimensional poverty reduction in Colombia: A spatial approach. *World Development*, *94*, 406–421. doi:10.1016/j.worlddev.2017.02.005

Ravalet, E., & Rérat, P. (2019). Teleworking: Decreasing mobility or increasing tolerance of commuting distances? *Built Environment*, *45*(4), 582–602. doi:10.2148/benv.45.4.582

Ravallion, M. (2011). Mashup indices of development. *The World Bank Research Observer*, *27*(1), 1–32. doi:10.1093/wbro/lkr009

Raynolds, L. T., & Greenfield, N. (2015). Fair trade: movement and markets. Handbook of research on Fair Trade, 24-41.

Raynolds, L. T. (2012). Fair trade: Social regulation in global food markets. *Journal of Rural Studies*, *28*(3), 276–287. doi:10.1016/j.jrurstud.2012.03.004

Rebellon, C. J. (2006). Do adolescents engage in delinquency to attract the social attention of peers? An extension and longitudinal test of the social reinforcement hypothesis. *Journal of Research in Crime and Delinquency*, *43*(4), 387–411. doi:10.1177/0022427806291259

Redondo, S. (2008). Individuos, sociedades y oportunidades en la explicación y prevención del delito: Modelo del Triple Riesgo Delictivo. *Revista Española de Investigación Criminológica*, *7*(6), 1–53.

Rehman, H., Moazzam, D. A., & Ansari, N. (2020). Role of microfinance institutions in women empowerment: A case study of Akhuwat, Pakistan. *South Asian Studies*, *30*(1).

Resolutions and Recommendations of The Council of the Islamic. (2000). *Fiqh* Academy *1985-2000*. https://uaelaws.files.wordpress.com/2012/05/resolutions-and-recommendations-of-the-council-of-the-islamic-fiqh-academy.pdf

Retana, C. S. (2015). Evaluación de impacto de la educación sobre la pobreza en Costa Rica (un análisis para educación secundaria y post-secundaria). *Revista de Ciencias Económicas*, *33*(2), 9-23.

Revista El Universal. (2016, Febrero 10). *Turismo continúa siendo el sector que genera más ingresos a Cartagena.* https://www.eluniversal.com.co/economica/turismo-continua-siendo-el-sector-que-genera-mas-ingresos-cartagena-218767-CREU323023

Revista Expansión. (2020). *Ante la falta de apoyo del gobierno, las empresas buscan ayudarse entre sí.* https://expansion.mx/empresas/2020/04/06/ante-la-falta-apoyo-gobierno-las-empresas-ayudarse-entre-si

Reyers, B., Stafford-Smith, M., Erb, K. H., Scholes, R. J., & Selomane, O. (2017). Essential Variables help to focus Sustainable Development Goals monitoring. *Current Opinion in Environmental Sustainability*, *26–27*(May), 97–105. doi:10.1016/j.cosust.2017.05.003

Rhoades, L., & Eisenberger, R. (2002). Perceived organizational support: A review of the literature. *The Journal of Applied Psychology*, *87*(4), 698–714. doi:10.1037/0021-9010.87.4.698 PMID:12184574

Rhyne, E., & Otero, M. (1992). Financial services for microenterprises: Principles and institutions. *World Development*, *20*(11), 1561–1571. doi:10.1016/0305-750X(92)90014-M

Ribotta, S. (2010). Pobreza, hambre y justicia en América Latina y el Caribe. Debatiendo sobre la justicia mientras 53 millones de latinoamericanos sufren hambre. *REIB: Revista Electrónica Iberoamericana*, *4*(1), 144–180.

Rimoldi, S. M., Arcagni, A., Fattore, M., & di Belgiojoso, E. B. (2020). Targeting policies for multidimensional poverty and social fragility relief among migrants in Italy, using F-FOD analysis. *Social Indicators Research*, 1–19.

Ringle, C. M., Wende, S., & Becker, J. M. (2015). SmartPLS 3. SmartPLS GmbH, Boenningstedt. *Journal of Service Science and Management*, *10*(3).

Rios, K., Finkelstein, S. R., & Landa, J. (2015). Is there a "fair" in fair-trade? Social dominance orientation influences perceptions of and preferences for fair-trade products. *Journal of Business Ethics*, *130*(1), 171–180. doi:10.100710551-014-2221-9

Rivas, S. y Puebla A. D. (2016). Inversión Extranjera Directa y Crecimiento Económico. *Revista Mexicana de Economía y Finanzas, 11*(2), 51-75.

Robinson, P. B., Stimpson, D. V., Huefner, J., & Hunt, H. K. (1991). An attitude approach to the prediction of entrepreneurship. *Entrepreneurship Theory and Practice*, *15*(4), 13–31. doi:10.1177/104225879101500405

Rohima, S., Suman, A., Manzilati, A., & Ashar, K. (2013). Vicious Circle Analysis of Poverty and Entrepreneurship. *IOSR Journal of Business and Management*, *7*(1), 33–46. doi:10.9790/487X-0713346

Roldán, J. L., & Cepeda, G. (2018). Curso sobre PLS-SEM (6ª ed.) Universidad de Sevilla.

Roldán, J. L., & Cepeda, G. (2018). *Curso sobre PLS*. SEM.

Roman, T., Manolica, A., & Voznenko, N. (2015). Study on the Factors that Influence the Development of Entrepreneurship among Romanian Students. In *Proceedings of the International Management Conference (pp.* 198-208). Faculty of Management, Academy of Economic Studies.

Romero, I., & Petrescu, R. M. (2011). Universities as suppliers of entrepreneurship education services. The cases of the University of Seville and the academy of economic studies in Bucharest. *Amfiteatru Economic Journal*, *13*(30), 347–361.

Romero, J. (2012). Inversión extranjera directa y crecimiento económico en México: 1940-2011. *Investigacion Economica*, *71*(282), 109–147.

Rosas, B. (2016). Atracción de inversión extranjera directa en México: El efecto del nivel educativo. *Hitos de Ciencias Económico Administrativas*, *22*(62), 27–36. doi:10.19136/hitos.a0n62.1743

Rosati, F., & Faria, L. G. D. (2019). Business contribution to the Sustainable Development Agenda: Organizational factors related to early adoption of SDG reporting. *Corporate Social Responsibility and Environmental Management*, *26*(3), 588–597. doi:10.1002/csr.1705

Rúbies, I. P., & Mendizábal, E. (2002). Pobreza y exclusión social en España. Una visión geográfica de las poblaciones de riesgo. *Revija za Geografijo*, 79–103.

Ryu, S. (2019). Key challenges and drawbacks of crowdfunding. In Beauty of Crowdfunding. Routledge. doi:10.4324/9780429243714-11

Saarinen, J. (2007). Contradictions of Rural Tourism Initiatives in Rural Development Contexts: Finnish Rural Tourism Strategy Case Study. *Current Issues in Tourism*, *10*(1), 96–105. doi:10.2167/cit287.0

Saarinen, J., & Rogerson, C. M. (2014). Tourism and the Millennium Development Goals: Perspectives beyond 2015. *Tourism Geographies*, *16*(1), 23–30. doi:10.1080/14616688.2013.851269

Sachs, J. (2005). *The end of poverty: How we can make it happen in our life time*. Penguin Books.

Saeed, S., Yousafzai, S. Y., Yani-De-Soriano, M., & Muffatto, M. (2015). The role of perceived university support in the formation of students' entrepreneurial intention. *Journal of Small Business Management*, *53*(4), 1127–1145. doi:10.1111/jsbm.12090

Sahin, M., Nijkamp, P., & Baycan, T. (2007). Migrant entrepreneurship from the perspective of cultural diversity. Handbook of Research on Ethnic Minority Entrepreneurship, 99–113.

Sah, P. (2019). Immigrant and refugee language policies, programs, and practices in an era of change: Promises, contradictions, and possibilities. In *Routledge International Handbook of Migration Studies* (pp. 325–338). Routledge.

Sajjad, A., Talib, H., Guoliang, Z., Mohammad, N., & Benqian, L. (2018). The implementation of sustainable development goals in "BRICS" countries. *Sustainability*, *10*(7).

Salecker, L., Ahmadov, A. K., & Karimli, L. (2020). Contrasting monetary and multidimensional poverty measures in a low-income Sub-Saharan African Country. *Social Indicators Research*, *151*(2), 547–574. doi:10.100711205-020-02382-z

Salvia, A. L., Leal Filho, W., Brandli, L. L., & Griebeler, J. S. (2019). Assessing research trends related to Sustainable Development Goals: Local and global issues. *Journal of Cleaner Production*, *208*, 841–849. doi:10.1016/j.jclepro.2018.09.242

Sama, C., Crespo-Cebada, E., Díaz-Caro, C., Escribano, M., & Mesías, F. J. (2018). Consumer Preferences for Foodstuffs Produced in a Socio-environmentally Responsible Manner: A Threat to Fair Trade Producers? *Ecological Economics*, *150*, 290–296. doi:10.1016/j.ecolecon.2018.04.031

Sampedro, I. R., Fernández-Laviada, A., & Crespo, Á. H. (2014). Entrepreneurial intention: Perceived advantages and disadvantages. *Academia (Caracas)*, *27*(2), 284–315. doi:10.1108/ARLA-09-2013-0144

Santos Cumplido, F. J., & Liñán, F. (2006). La influencia del capital social sobre los empresarios potenciales. *Estudios de Economía Aplicada*, *24*(2), 459–489.

Santos, M. E. (2013). *Measuring multidimensional poverty in Latin America: Previous experience and the way forward.* OPHI Working Paper 66.

Santos, R. S. (2013). *Fatores influenciadores de consumo de festas sertanejas: um estudo na cidade de Belém – PA.* Retrieved June 28, 2017, from: www.fpl.edu.br/2013/.../dissertacao_ricardo_da_silva_santos_2013.pdf

Santos, M. E. (2014). *Measuring multidimensional poverty in Latin America: previous experience and the way forward. Oxford Poverty & Human Development Initiative*. OPHI. doi:10.35648/20.500.12413/11781/ii040

Santos, M. E., & Villatoro, P. (2020). The importance of reliability in the multidimensional poverty index for Latin America (MPI-LA). *The Journal of Development Studies*, *56*(9), 1784–1789. doi:10.1080/00220388.2019.1663177

Sanz, R., Peris, J. A., & Escámez, J. (2017). Higher education in the fight against poverty from the capabilities approach: The case of Spain. *Journal of Innovation & Knowledge*, *2*(2), 53–66. doi:10.1016/j.jik.2017.03.002

Sarstedt, M., Hair, J. F., Ringle, C. M., Thiele, K. O., & Gudergan, S. P. (2016). Estimation issues with PLS and CBSEM: Where the bias lies! *Journal of Business Research*, *69*(10), 3998–4010. doi:10.1016/j.jbusres.2016.06.007

Schioppa, M. (2013). Influence of the group of delinquent couples in the involvement of the adolescent in delinquency. *Justicia Juris, 9*(1), 93-111.

Schleicher, J., Schaafsma, M., & Vira, B. (2018). Will the Sustainable Development Goals address the links between poverty and the natural environment? *Current Opinion in Environmental Sustainability*, *34*, 43–47. doi:10.1016/j.cosust.2018.09.004

Scott, J. (1991). *Social Network Analysis: A Handbook.* Sage.

Secretaría de Desarrollo Social. (2020). *Informe anual sobre la situación de pobreza y rezago social 2020.* Subsecretaría de Planeación, Evaluación y Desarrollo Regional, Hidalgo. https://www.gob.mx/cms/uploads/attachment/file/288955/Hidalgo.pdf

Secretaría de Economía. (2018). *Inversión Extranjera Directa en México y en el mundo*. Carpeta de información estadística. https://www.gob.mx/cms/uploads/attachment/file/332558/Carpeta_IED.pdf

Secretaría de Economía. (2020). *Inversión Extranjera Directa en México y en el mundo*. Carpeta de información estadística. https://www.gob.mx/cms/uploads/attachment/file/575327/Carpeta_IED_2020-2T.pdf

Secretaría de Salud. (2021). *Subsecretaría de Previsión y Promoción de la Salud; Informe técnico diario COVID-19 México.* https://www.gob.mx/cms/uploads/attachment/file/644223/Comunicado_Tecnico_Diario_COVID-19_2021.06.06.pdf)

Sen, A. (1976). Poverty: An ordinal approach to measurement. *Econometrica*, *44*(2), 219–231. doi:10.2307/1912718

Sen, A. (2000). A decade of human development. *Journal of Human Development*, *1*(1), 17–23. doi:10.1080/14649880050008746

Sen, A. (2001). *Desigualdade reexaminada*. Record.

Seth, S., & Alkire, S. (2014). Did poverty reduction reach the poorest of the poor? Assessment methods in the counting approach (No. ophiwp077). Queen Elizabeth House, University of Oxford.

Shane, S. (2009). Why encouraging more people to become entrepreneurs is bad public policy? *Small Business Economics, 33*(2), 141–149. doi:10.100711187-009-9215-5

Shane, S., & Venkataraman, S. (2000). The Promise of Entrepreneurship as a Field of Research. *Academy of Management Review, 25*(1), 217–226. doi:10.5465/amr.2000.2791611

Shapero, A., & Sokol, L. (1982). The social dimensions of entrepreneurship. In C. Kent & D. Sexton (Eds.), *The Encyclopedia of Entrepreneurship* (pp. 72–90). Prentice-Hall.

Shinde, R., & Joshi, A. (2016). Socio-economic Empowerment of Women through Micro-financing: A Study of Self Help Groups in Pune City. *Journal of Commerce and Management Thought, 7*(4), 633–655. doi:10.5958/0976-478X.2016.00034.3

Shinnar, R. S., & Zamantılı nayır, D. (2019). Immigrant Entrepreneurship in an Emerging Economy: The Case of Turkey. *Journal of Small Business Management, 57*(2), 559–575. doi:10.1111/jsbm.12408

Shirokova, G., Osiyevskyy, O., & Bogatyreva, K. (2016). Exploring the intention–behavior link in student entrepreneurship: Moderating effects of individual and environmental characteristics. *European Management Journal, 34*(4), 386–399. doi:10.1016/j.emj.2015.12.007

Shi, X., Moudon, A. V., Lee, B. H., Shen, Q., & Ban, X. J. (2020). Factors Influencing Teleworking Productivity–a Natural Experiment during the COVID-19 Pandemic. Findings. Silahtaroğlu, G., Baykal, E., & Canbolat, Z. N. Weekly Emotional Changes Amidst Covid-19: Turkish Experience. *Ekonomi İşletme ve Maliye Araştırmaları Dergisi, 2*(3), 280–304.

Shiyuti, H. (2018). *An Overview of Asnaf Entrepreneurship Program by Lembaga Zakah Selangor, Malaysia.* Paper presented at 6th ASEAN Universities International Conference on Islamic Finance (AICIF), Manila, Philippines.

Shneor, R., & Vik, A. (2020). Crowdfunding success: A systematic literature review 2010–2017. *Baltic Journal of Management, 15*(2), 149–182. doi:10.1108/BJM-04-2019-0148

Si, S., Ahlstrom, D., Wei, J., & Cullen, J. (2020). Business, Entrepreneurship and Innovation Toward Poverty Reduction. *Entrepreneurship & Regional Development, 32*(1-2), 1-20.

Sigalla, R. J., & Carney, S. (2012). Poverty reduction through entrepreneurship: Microcredit, learning and ambivalence amongst women in urban Tanzania. *International Journal of Educational Development, 32*(4), 546–554. doi:10.1016/j.ijedudev.2012.02.011

Sikorski, J. B. (1996). Academic underachievement and school refusal. In *Handbook of adolescent health risk behavior* (pp. 393–411). Springer. doi:10.1007/978-1-4899-0203-0_15

Silva, E., & Monteiro, F. (2014). *Empreendedorismo e plano de negócio* (2a ed.). Vida Económica.

Silva, K. A. (2007). *O comportamento do consumidor: a influência do ambiente físico na compra em lojas de shopping centers no Distrito Federal.* Retrieved June 22, 2017, from: http://docplayer.com.br/13186861-O-comportamento-do-consumidor-a-influencia-do-ambiente-fisico-na-compra-em-lojas-de-shopping-centers-no-distrito-federal.html#show_full_text

Silva, V. B. (2013). *Gestão da qualidade dos serviços prestados em bares e restaurantes na praia da Rendinha (Natal-RN).* Retrieved May 22, 2017, from: <https://sigaa.ufrn.br/sigaa/verProducao?idProducao=1940241&key.>

Silva. (2017). *A influência do pluralismo relacional nas estratégias coletivas de responsabilidade social corporativa de uma rede de pequenas empresas do setor hoteleiro. Tese (doutorado) na Universidade do Vale do Rio dos Sinos (Unisinos).* Programa de Pós-Graduação em Administração.

Silva, J. J. D., Bruno, M. A. P., Silva, D. B., & Nascimento, D. (2020). Multidimensional poverty in Brazil: Analysis of the period 2004-2015. *Brazilian Journal of Political Economy*, *40*(1), 138–160. doi:10.1590/0101-31572020-2924

Silveira, L. S., Abdallah, P. R., Hellebrandt, L., Barbosa, M. N., & Feijó, F. T. (2012). *Análise socioeconômica do perfil dos consumidores de pescado no município de Rio Grande.* Retrieved June 28, 2017, from: repositorio.furg.br/.../Análise%20socioeconômica%20do%20perfil%20dos%20consu

Sims, N. C., England, J. R., Newnham, G. J., Alexander, S., Green, C., Minelli, S., & Held, A. (2019). Developing good practice guidance for estimating land degradation in the context of the United Nations Sustainable Development Goals. *Environmental Science & Policy*, *92*, 349–355. doi:10.1016/j.envsci.2018.10.014

Sisodia, R., & Gelb, M. (2019). *Creating a New Myth for Business – The Healing Organization.* Mindful Leader. Available: https://www.mindfulleader.org/blog/30404-creating-a-new-myth-for-business-the

Smith, S. A., Patmos, A., & Pitts, M. J. (2018). Communication and teleworking: A study of communication channel satisfaction, personality, and job satisfaction for teleworking employees. *International Journal of Business Communication*, *55*(1), 44–68. doi:10.1177/2329488415589101

Solomou, I., & Constantinidou, F. (2020). Prevalence and predictors of anxiety and depression symptoms during the COVID-19 pandemic and compliance with precautionary measures: Age and sex matter. *International Journal of Environmental Research and Public Health*, *17*(14), 4924. doi:10.3390/ijerph17144924 PMID:32650522

Sommer, L. (2011). The Theory of Planned Behaviour and the Impact of Past Behaviour. *International Business & Economics Research Journal*, *10*(1), 1. doi:10.19030/iber.v10i1.930

Soria-Barreto, K., Zuniga-Jara, S., & Ruiz-Campo, S. (2016). Educación e intención emprendedora en estudiantes universitarios: Un caso de estudio. *Formación Universitaria*, *9*(1), 25–34. doi:10.4067/S0718-50062016000100004

Souza, F. S., Pontes, L. M., & Oliveira, F. N. S. (2007). *O marketing e a relação de satisfação com os clientes.* Retrieved May 18, 2017, from: happyslide.org/doc/106249/o-marketing-e-a-relação-de-satisfação-dos-clientes

Stafford-Smith, M., Griggs, D., Gaffney, O., Ullah, F., Reyers, B., Kanie, N., & O'Connell, D. (2017). Integration: The key to implementing the Sustainable Development Goals. *Sustainability Science*, *12*(6), 911–919. doi:10.100711625-016-0383-3 PMID:30147763

Stakanov, R. (2016). Influence of immigrants on the entrepreneurship development in the host countries. *Baltic Journal of Economic Studies, 2*(4), Article 4.

Stattin, H., & Kerr, M. (2000). Parental monitoring: A reinterpretation. *Child Development*, *71*(4), 1072–1085. doi:10.1111/1467-8624.00210 PMID:11016567

Stemler, A. (2013). The JOBS Act and crowdfunding: Harnessing the power – and money – of the masses. *Business Horizons*, *56*(3), 271–275. doi:10.1016/j.bushor.2013.01.007

Stenn, T. (2013). Fair Trade and Justice: An examination of fair trade. *The Review of Radical Political Economics*, *20*(10), 1–12.

Stiglitz, J. E. (2015). *New theoretical perspectives on the distribution of income and wealth among individuals: Part IV: Land and credit (No. w21192).* National Bureau of Economic Research.

Suanes, M., & Roca Sagalés, O. (2015). Inversión Extranjera Directa, crecimiento económico y desigualdad en América Latina. *El Trimestre Economico*, *82*(3), 675–706. doi:10.20430/ete.v82i327.180

Sullivan, K., Thomas, S., & Rosano, M. (2018). Using industrial ecology and strategic management concepts to pursue the Sustainable Development Goals. *Journal of Cleaner Production*, *174*, 237–246. doi:10.1016/j.jclepro.2017.10.201

Sultana, H. Y., Jamal, M. A., & Najaf, D. E. (2017). Impact of microfinance on women empowerment through poverty alleviation: An assessment of socio-economic conditions in Chennai city of Tamil Nadu. *Asian Journal for Poverty Studies, 3*(2).

Sumner, A. (2012). Where do the poor live? *World Development*, *40*(5), 865–877. doi:10.1016/j.worlddev.2011.09.007

Sumodiningrat, G. (2002). Strategi pemberdayaan masyarakat dalam penanggulangan kemiskinan. Materi kuliah umum Program Pasca Sarjana Universitas Brawijaya, Malang.

Sutter, C., Bruton, G. D., & Chen, J. (2019). Entrepreneurship as a solution to extreme poverty: A review and future research directions. *Journal of Business Venturing*, *34*(1), 197–214. doi:10.1016/j.jbusvent.2018.06.003

Swain, R. B., & Wallentin, F. Y. (2009). Does microfinance empower women? Evidence from self-help groups in India. *International Review of Applied Economics*, *23*(5), 541–556. doi:10.1080/02692170903007540

Taormina, R., & Kin-Mei Lao, S. (2007). Measuring Chinese entrepreneurial motivation, personality and environmental influences. *International Journal of Entrepreneurial Behaviour & Research*, *13*(4), 200–221. doi:10.1108/13552550710759997

Tarapuez, E., Guzmán, B., & Parra, R. (2018). Factores que determinan la intención emprendedora en América Latina. *Suma de Negocios*, *9*(19), 56–67. doi:10.14349umneg/2018.V9.N19.A7

Tavares, A. I. (2017). Telework and health effects review. *International Journal of Healthcare*, *3*(2), 30. doi:10.5430/ijh.v3n2p30

Tavares, F., Santos, E., Diogo, A., & Ratten, V. (2020). *Teleworking in portuguese communities during the COVID-19 pandemic. Journal of Enterprising Communities*. People and Places in the Global Economy.

Teece, D. J. (2009). *Dynamic capabilities & strategic management*. Oxford University Press.

Tengeh, R., & Nkem, L. (2017). Sustaining Immigrant Entrepreneurship in South Africa: The Role of Informal Financial Associations. *Sustainability*, *9*(8), 1396. doi:10.3390u9081396

Tesoriero, F. (2006). Strengthening communities through women's self help groups in South India. *Community Development Journal: An International Forum*, *41*(3), 321–333. doi:10.1093/cdj/bsi066

Thompson, C. A., & Prottas, D. J. (2006). Relationships among organizational family support, job autonomy, perceived control, and employee well-being. *Journal of Occupational Health Psychology*, *11*(1), 100–118. doi:10.1037/1076-8998.10.4.100 PMID:16551178

Thompson, E. R. (2009). Individual entrepreneurial intent: Construct clarification and development of an internationally reliable metric. *Entrepreneurship Theory and Practice*, *33*(3), 669–694. doi:10.1111/j.1540-6520.2009.00321.x

Thorat, A., Vanneman, R., Desai, S., & Dubey, A. (2017). Escaping and falling into poverty in India today. *World Development*, *93*, 413–426. doi:10.1016/j.worlddev.2017.01.004 PMID:28966435

Thorat, U. (2006). Financial inclusion and millennium development goals. *RBI Bulletin*, *50*(2), 239–243.

Tidd. (2008). *Gestão da Inovação. 3*. Bookman.

Tinbergen, J. (1962). *Shaping the World Economy: Suggestions for an International Economic Policy*. The Twentieth Century Fund.

Torres Penagos, M. F. (2018). Índice de pobreza multidimensional oculta para la localidad de Teusaquillo (Bogotá): Propuesta metodológica a partir de percepciones ciudadanas. *Cuadernos de Economía (Santiago, Chile)*, *37*(74), 555–588. doi:10.15446/cuad.econ.v37n74.56164

Torres, A., Bijmolt, T., Tribó, J., & Verhoef, P. (2012). Generating global brand equity through corporate social responsibility to key stakeholders. *International Journal of Research in Marketing*, *29*(1), 13–24. doi:10.1016/j.ijresmar.2011.10.002

Torres, V. H., Polanco, M., & Tinoco, M. Á. (2014). Technological innovation and regional economic growth in Mexico: A spatial perspective. *The Annals of Regional Science*, *52*(1), 183–200. doi:10.100700168-013-0581-1

Torugsa, N., O'Donohue, W., & Hecker, R. (2012). Capabilities, proactive CSR and financial performance in SMEs: Empirical evidence from an Australian manufacturing industry sector. *Journal of Business Ethics*, *109*(4), 483–500. doi:10.100710551-011-1141-1

Tovernić, I. (2017). *Fair trade in response to the problems of agricultural production of developing countries* (Doctoral dissertation). Ekonomski fakultet, Sveučilište u Zagrebu.

Townsend, P. (1979). *Poverty in the United Kingdom*. Allen Lane and Penguin Books. doi:10.1525/9780520325760

Trnka, R., & Lorencova, R. (2020). Fear, anger, and media-induced trauma during the outbreak of COVID-19 in the Czech Republic. *Psychological Trauma: Theory, Research, Practice, and Policy*, *12*(5), 546–549. doi:10.1037/tra0000675 PMID:32538654

Tsordia, C., & Papadimitriou, D. (2015). The Role of Theory of Planned Behavior on Entrepreneurial Intention of Greek Business Students. *International Journal of Synergy and Research.*, *4*(1), 23. Advance online publication. doi:10.17951/ijsr.2015.4.1.23

Turker, D., & Selcuk, S. S. (2009). Which factors affect entrepreneurial intention of university students? *Journal of European Industrial Training*, *33*(2), 142–159. doi:10.1108/03090590910939049

Ulceluse, M. (2020). Self-employment as a stepping stone to better labor market matching: A comparison between immigrants and natives. *Journal of Demographic Economics*, *86*(4), 479–501. doi:10.1017/dem.2020.1

Ulsa, H. (2021). *Hacienda da el tiro de gracia al programa de aseguramiento agropecuario*. https://www.elfinanciero.com.mx/economia/2021/07/13/hacienda-da-el-tiro-de-gracia-al-programa-de-aseguramiento-agropecuario/?outputType=amp

UNCTAD. (2009). *El papel de los acuerdos internacionales de inversión en la atracción de inversión extranjera directa hacia los países en desarrollo*. Colección de publicaciones de la UNCTAD sobre las políticas internacionales de inversión para el desarrollo, Nueva York y Ginebra.

UNCTAD. (2019). *Informe sobre las Inversiones en el Mundo 2019*. https://unctad.org/es/paginas/PressRelease.aspx?OriginalVersionID=514

UNCTAD. (2021). *Covid-19 and tourism an update. Assessing the economic consequences*. Consultado en julio de 2021 en la siguiente direccion de internet: https://unctad.org/system/files/official-document/ditcinf2021d3_en_0.pdf

UNHCR. (1951). *The 1951 Convention: Lasting Cornerstone of Refugee*. http://www.unhcr.ch/issues/asylum/qa000615.htm

UNHCR. (2007). *Opening Statement by Mr. António Guterres*. United Nations High Commissioner for Refugees, at the Fifty-eighth Session of the Executive Committee of the High Commissioner's Programme (ExCom). https://www.unhcr.org/uk/admin/hcspeeches/4700eff54/opening-statement-mr-antonio-guterres-united-nations-high-commissioner.html

UNHCR. (2012). *The State of The World Refugees in Search of Solidarity*. Retrieved March 21, 2014, https://www.refworld.org/pdfid/5100fec32.pdf

UNHCR. (2019). *Refugees: The most in need of Zakah funds*. UNHCR *Zakah* Program: 2019 Launch Report. https://*zakah*.unhcr.org/wp-content/uploads/2019/04/UNHCR-Annual-*Zakah*-Report-2019-En.pdf

UNHCR. (2019b). *Financials*. http://reporting.unhcr.org/financial

UNHCR. (2020). *UNHCR report 2020*. https://www.unhcr.org/figures-at-a-glance.html

UNHCR. (2021). *Figures at a glance*. https://www.unhcr.org/flagship-reports/globaltrends/

UNICEF. (2019a). *UNICEF and the Islamic Development Bank launch first global Muslim philanthropy fund for children*. https://www.unicef.org/press-releases/unicef-and-islamic-development-bank-launch-first-global-muslim-philanthropy-fund

Usaci, D. (2015). Predictors of professional entrepreneurial intention and behavior in the educational field. *Procedia: Social and Behavioral Sciences*, *187*, 178–183. doi:10.1016/j.sbspro.2015.03.034

Uthman, M. A., & Hamzah, H. (2012). شرط التمليك في الزكاة ومدى تأثيره في عمل الجمعيات الخيرية الإسلامية. *Damascus University Magazine for Economic and Legal Sciences, 28*(1). http://damascusuniversity.edu.sy/mag/law/images/stories/1-2012/a/681-699.pdf

Valencia Arechiga, A. L. (2020). *La intención emprendedora en población con alto y muy alto grado de marginación en Puerto Vallarta*. Jal. Universidad de Guadalajara, Méjico.

Valenzuela, E., Hertel, T., Ivanic, M., & Nin-Pratt, A. (2004). *Evaluating poverty impacts of globalization and trade policy changes on agricultural producers*. Working Paper, Purdue University.

Van Auken, H., Stephens, P., Fry, F., & Silva, J. (2006). Role model influences on entrepreneurial intentions: A comparison between USA and Mexico. *The International Entrepreneurship and Management Journal*, *2*(3), 325–336. doi:10.100711365-006-0004-1

Varamäki, E., Joensuu, S., Tornikoski, E., & Viljamaa, A. (2015). The development of entrepreneurial potential among higher education students. *Journal of Small Business and Enterprise Development*, *22*(3), 563–589. doi:10.1108/JSBED-02-2012-0027

Varela Llamas, R., & Ocegueda Hernández, J. M. (2020). Multidimensional poverty and the labor market in Mexico. *Cuadernos de Economía (Santiago, Chile)*, *39*(79), 139–165.

Veciana, J. M., Aponte, M., & Urbano, D. (2005). University students attitudes towards entrepreneurship: A two countries comparison. *The International Entrepreneurship and Management Journal*, *1*(2), 165–182. doi:10.100711365-005-1127-5

Venugopal, S., Viswanathan, M., & Jung, K. (2015). Consumption constraints and entrepreneurial intentions in subsistence marketplaces. *Journal of Public Policy & Marketing*, *34*(2), 235–251. doi:10.1509/jppm.14.181

Verschoore, J. R. (2010). Programa Redes de Cooperação: Uma análise da política pública gaúcha de formação de redes. *Revista Pós Ciências Sociais.*, *7*, 101–116.

Verspagen, B. (2005). Innovation and economic growth. In J. Fagerberg, D. C. Mowery, & R. R. Nelson (Eds.), *The Oxford handbook of innovation* (pp. 487–513). Oxford University Press.

Verspagen, B. (2007). Mapping technological trajectories as patent citations networks: A study on the history of fuel cell research. *Advances in Complex Systems*, *10*(1), 99–115. doi:10.1142/S0219525907000945

Viegas, M. F. (2015). Psicologia Social do Trabalho e Educação: uma discussão a partir da literatura espanhola recente, em Psicologia Social e Trabalho: perspectivas críticas. Florianópolis: ABRAPSO Editora: Edições do Bosque CFH/UFSC.

Villanueva-Álvaro, J. J., Mondéjar-Jiménez, J., & Sáez-Martínez, F. J. (2017). Rural tourism: Development, management and sustainability in rural establishments. *Sustainability*, *9*(5), 818. doi:10.3390u9050818

Vinogradov, E., Kolvereid, L., & Timoshenko, K. (2013). Predicting entrepreneurial intentions when satisfactory employment opportunities are scarce. *Education + Training*, *55*(7), 719–737. doi:10.1108/ET-06-2012-0067

Vitulano, M. L., Fite, P. J., & Rathert, J. L. (2010). "Delinquent peer influence on childhood delinquency": The moderating effect of impulsivity. *Journal of Psychopathology and Behavioral Assessment*, *32*(3), 315–322. doi:10.100710862-009-9160-2

Voronov, V. V., Ruza, O. P., & Stasane, J. (2020). Multidimensional poverty in the Baltic States in the EU context: theoretical and practical aspects. *Baltic Region*, *12*(3).

Voronov, V.V., Ruza, O.P. & Stasane, S. J. (2020). Multidimensional poverty in the Baltic States in the EU context: theoretical and practical aspects. *Baltic Region*, *12*(3).

Waage, J., Yap, C., Bell, S., Levy, C., Mace, G., Pegram, T., & Poole, N. (2015). Governing the UN Sustainable Development Goals: Interactions, infrastructures, and institutions. *The Lancet. Global Health*, *3*(5), e251–e252. doi:10.1016/S2214-109X(15)70112-9 PMID:25833663

Wang, C. L., & Ahmed, P. K. (2007). Dynamic capabilities: A review and research. *International Journal of Management Reviews, Oxford*, *9*(1), 31–51. doi:10.1111/j.1468-2370.2007.00201.x

Wang, K., Gan, C., Chen, L., & Voda, M. (2020). Poor Residents' Perceptions of the Impacts of Tourism on Poverty Alleviation: From the Perspective of Multidimensional Poverty. *Sustainability*, *12*(18), 7515. doi:10.3390u12187515

Wang, W., Chen, W., Zhu, K., & Wang, H. (2020). Emphasizing the entrepreneur or the idea? The impact of text content emphasis on investment decisions in crowdfunding. *Decision Support Systems*, *136*, 113341.

Wareham, J., Cochran, J. K., Dembo, R., & Sellers, C. S. (2005). Community, Strain, and Delinquency: A Test of a Multi-Level Model of General Strain Theory. *Western Criminology Review*, *6*(1).

Warr, M. (1993). Parents, peers, and delinquency. *Social Forces*, *72*, 247–264.

Wells, L. E., & Rankin, J. H. (1991). Families and Delinquency: A Meta-Analysis of the Impact of Broken Homes. *Social Problems*, *38*(1), 71–93. doi:10.2307/800639

Wilson, S., Fesenmaier, D., Fesenmaier, J., & Van Es, J. (2001). Factors for Success in Rural Tourism Development. *Journal of Travel Research*, *40*(1), 132–138. doi:10.1177/004728750104000203

World Health Organization. (2004). *Promoting mental health: concepts, emerging evidence, practice* (Summary Report). Geneva: World Health Organization. Available: https://www.who.int/mental_health/evidence/en/promoting_mhh.pdf

Wortley, R. (2008). Situational precipitators of crime. In R. Wortley & L. Mazerolle (Eds.), *Environmental criminology and crime analysis* (pp. 48–69). Willan.

Wright, G. A., Kasente, D., Ssemogerere, G., & Mutesasira, L. (1999). *Vulnerability, risks, assets and empowerment–the impact of microfinance on poverty alleviation.* Final report. Kampala, Uganda: MicroSave-Africa and Uganda Women's Finance Trust.

Wright, J. P., & Cullen, F. T. (2001). Parental efficacy and delinquent behavior: Do control and support matter? *Criminology*, *39*(3), 677–706. doi:10.1111/j.1745-9125.2001.tb00937.x

Xu, H., Wang, C., Wu, J., Liang, Y., Jiao, Y., & Nazneen, S. (2018). Human poverty alleviation through rural women's tourism entrepreneurship. *Journal of China Tourism Research*, *14*(4), 445–460. doi:10.1080/19388160.2018.1507860

Yang, J. (2013). The theory of planned behavior and prediction of entrepreneurial intention among Chinese undergraduates. *Social Behavior and Personality*, *41*(3), 367–376. doi:10.2224bp.2013.41.3.367

Yang, Y., & Fu, C. (2019). Inclusive financial development and multidimensional poverty reduction: An empirical assessment from rural China. *Sustainability*, *11*(7), 1900. doi:10.3390u11071900

Yaseen, A., Abid, M., Zahra, S., & Israr, M. (2018). Precursory effects on entrepreneurial behaviour in the agri-food industry. *Journal of Entrepreneurship in Emerging Economies*, *1*(10), 2–22. doi:10.1108/JEEE-08-2016-0029

Yim, S., Bae, Y. H., Lim, H., & Kwon, J. (2019). The role of marketing capability in linking CSR to corporate financial performance: When CSR gives positive signals to stakeholders. *European Journal of Marketing*, *53*(7), 1333–1354. Advance online publication. doi:10.1108/EJM-08-2017-0526

Yonis. (2012). *Islamic Microfinance System and Poverty Alleviation in Somaliland.* BBA research paper presented to the of Hargeisa.

Yurtkoru, E. S., Kuşcu, Z. K., & Doğanay, A. (2014). Exploring the antecedents of entrepreneurial intention on Turkish university students. *Procedia: Social and Behavioral Sciences*, *150*, 841–850. doi:10.1016/j.sbspro.2014.09.093

Yu, S., Johnson, S., Lai, C., Cricelli, A., & Fleming, L. (2017). Crowdfunding and regional entrepreneurial investment: An application of the CrowdBerkeley database. *Research Policy*, *46*(10), 1723–1737.

Zahra, S. A., & George, G. (2002, April). Absorptive capacity: A review, reconceptualization, and extension. *Academy of Management Review*, *27*(2), 185–203. doi:10.2307/4134351

Zampetakis, L., & Kanelakis, G. (2010). Opportunity entrepreneurship in the rural sector: Evidence from Greece. *Journal of Research in Marketing and Entrepreneurship*, *12*(2), 122–142. doi:10.1108/14715201011090594

Zanini, T., & Miguels, C. (Eds.). (2021). *O elo perdido: cultura, produtividade e coletividade*. FGV Editora.

Zapata, T. (n.d.). *Desenvolvimento Humano*. Disponível em: http://www.iadh.org.br/wp-content/uploads/2011/08/Desenvolvimento-humano-Tania-Zapata.pdf

Zavaleta, D. (2017) *¿Cuáles son las dimensiones y los indicadores más usados por los países en sus IPM nacionales?* Disponible en https://mppn.org/es/what-are-the-dimensions-and-indicators-most-commonly-used-by-countries-in-their-national-mpis/

Zehir, C., & Narcıkara, E. (2016). Effects of resilience on productivity under authentic leadership. *Procedia: Social and Behavioral Sciences*, *235*, 250–258. doi:10.1016/j.sbspro.2016.11.021

Zhang, Q., Prouty, C., Zimmerman, J. B., & Mihelcic, J. R. (2016). More than Target 6.3: A Systems Approach to Rethinking Sustainable Development Goals in a Resource-Scarce World. *Engineering*, *2*(4), 481–489. doi:10.1016/J.ENG.2016.04.010

Zhang, Y., Day, G., & Cao, L. (2012). A partial test of Agnew's general theory of crime and delinquency. *Crime and Delinquency*, *58*(6), 856–878. doi:10.1177/0011128712461738

Zolfagharian, M., & Iyer, P. (2020). The effects of intergroup boundary permeability and hierarchy legitimacy on immigrant entrepreneurs' affective states, exchange strategies, and intentions toward suppliers. *Industrial Marketing Management*, *89*, 373–388. doi:10.1016/j.indmarman.2020.02.002

Zukkermann, L. (2021). *La Auditoría al programa jóvenes construyendo el futuro, Excelsior, 23 de Febrero 2021*. https://www.excelsior.com.mx/opinion/leo-zuckermann/la-auditoria-al-programa-jovenes-construyendo-el-futuro/1434222

Zuluaga, I. A. (2009). Educación y pobreza. *Sotavento MBA*, (14), 72–79.

Zupic, I., & Čater, T. (2015). Bibliometric methods in management and organization. *Organizational Research Methods*, *18*(3), 429–472. doi:10.1177/1094428114562629

Zurdo, Á., & López de la Nieta, M. (2013). Estrategias e imágenes sobre la crisis en el espacio social de la «nueva pobreza». Representaciones sociales y atribuciones causales. *Cuadernos de Relaciones Laborales*, *31*(2), 383–433.

About the Contributors

Joao Conrado de Amorim Carvalho is a PhD in Business Administration and Sociology from the University of Extremadura (Spain) and pos-doc in Economy and Management from the Universidade da Beira Interior (Portugal), Master in Business Management from the Getulio Vargas Foundation (Brazil) and a degree in Accounting from the CEUMA (Brazil). Professor, researcher, auditor and business consultant.

* * *

Marwa Alfares is currently a Ph.D. candidate at Istanbul Sabahattin Zaim University in Islamic Economics and Finance. She holds a Master's degree from the University of Malaya in Kuala Lumpur. She has an excellent background in Islamic law with excellent command of the Arabic and English languages. Marwa is equipped with excellent research skills. Her research interests include *Waqf, Zakah*, Social Finance, Green Sukuk, Alternative Finance, and Credit Guarantee.

Manpreet Arora is Senior Assistant Professor of Management in the School of Commerce and Management Studies, Central University of Himachal Pradesh Dharamshala, India. With around nineteen years of teaching experience she has varied interest areas. A Gold medalist at undergraduate and distinction holder at postgraduate level, she obtained her Ph.d in International Trade from Himachal Pradesh University, Shimla, India. Her areas of research interest include Accounting and Finance, Strategic Management, Entrepreneurship, Qualitative Research, Case Study Development, Communication Skills and Microfinance. She has been guiding research at the doctoral level and has worked in the area of Microfinance. As an active seminarian, she has attended more than hundred seminars/ conferences, and has visited several universities and colleges to deliver invited talks on Finance, Strategic Management, Qualitative Research, Business Communication, Interpersonal skills, Entrepreneurship and Skill Development. She is a motivational speaker and conducts workshops on communication and motivation. Having published more than 25 papers in various journals of national and international repute (including SCOPUS, WOS and Category Journals), she has also worked as content developer of MHRD 'e-PG Pathshala' Project and OER's for IGNOU. She has written forty book chapters in national as well as international books/handbooks/volumes published with IGI, Taylor and Francis etc. She has published in category Journals including Scopus and WoS. With four edited books in her credit she is a persistent researcher in the field of Management. She is an active social worker also and is working towards the protecting the rights of women.

Elif Baykal is an associate professor of management and strategy. She is a graduate of Boğaziçi University, Political Science and International Relations. She has completed her master's degree in Istanbul Bilgi University and her doctorate in management and organization at Yıldız Technical University. She has more than 12 years of industry experience. She worked as a human resources manager and project manager in Turkey's leading participation banks. She is still the head of the Department of Business Administration, MBA and PhD coordinator at Istanbul Medipol University. She works in the fields of positive psychology, strategy, family businesses and organizational behavior.

Juan Manuel Berbelpineda is an associate professor of Marketing at the Spanish Pablo Olavide University. He is a member of research group REINTUR (Spanish-Portuguese Network of Researchers on Tourism). He has authored papers published in outlets such as Tourism Economics, Journal of Hospitality Marketing & Management, Tourism and Management Studies, Journal of Retailing and Consumer Services, Journal of Business Economics and Management, International Journal of Business and Social Sciences; e.g. His main research interests are in the fields of Tourism Management, Internationalization Strategy, Franchises and Consumer Behavior. He heads the "Chair of internationalization of Companies Extenda".

Susana Bernardino is an adjunct professor of Management at the Polytechnic of Porto - Institute of Accounting and Administration (ISCAP), S. Mamede de Infesta, Portugal, and researcher at CEOS.PP/ISCAP. She completed her under-graduation degree in Management at the Faculty of Economics of the University of Porto, where also obtained the curricular part of the master's course in Finance. She got her PhD in Management in 2014 from the Portucalense University. Her research interests focus on social entrepreneurship, entrepreneurship, social and solidarity economy, smart cities, urban and regional development. and crowdfunding.

Janiele Queiroz Caroba is a lawyer, manager and researcher of humanized forms of leadership. She has worked for 17 years in Financial Institutions, having worked in the areas of Governance, Logistics, Marketing and Legal Consulting. She is dedicated to studies of human reliability, connection design, psychological safety, U theory and evolutionary leadership.

Salvador Cutiño-Raya is a professor in the Criminal Law Area of the Pablo de Olavide University of Seville. Law degree from the University of Seville in 1999, Expert Tittle in Criminology from the University of Seville in 2002 and Doctor of Criminal Law from the Pablo de Olavide University of Seville in 2013, in the program "Current problems of criminal law and criminology" with the doctoral thesis "Sobre el fin de la pena de prisión. Análisis del principio de resocialización en el sistema penitenciario español". He has been teaching at the Pablo de Olavide University since 2003 in the degrees of Law, Political Science and Administration and Criminology, and in the double degrees of Political Science and Law, Law and Business Administration and Law and Criminology. He also teaches in the Master in Human Rights, Interculturality and Development and in the Master in Criminology and Forensic Sciences. Within this teaching activity, he has tutored a multitude of final degree thesis at the UPO Faculty of Environmental Sciences and in the degree of Criminology and the double degree of Criminology and Law. In addition, during the 2015-2016 academic year he was Academic Director of the Course of Expert in Criminal Law.. He is currently the Quality Manager of the Degree in Criminology at the Pablo de Olavide University and coordinator of the Master in Criminology and Forensic Sciences. His priority lines of research are penitentiary law and the empirical investigation of the prison, Criminal Policy and crimes against public order and religious feelings, topics on which he has presented papers at various conferences and published articles in recognized journals. He is a member of the Spanish Society for Criminological Research (SEIC) and a member of the CIPEC-Research Group in Criminal Sciences and Criminology of the UPO.

Sergio de la Piedra-Vindola is an assistant professor of marketing and management in Unviersity de Lima (Perú). His main research interests are in the Strategic Management field, especially in economies of emerging countries. He is a doctoral student at the University Pablo de Olavide in Seville. The main theme of his doctoral thesis is Fair Trade.

Julio del Junco is a University Professor in Business Organization in the Department of Business Administration and Marketing, University of Seville. Author and co-author of more than 28 books, more than 100 articles in scientific journals. He has directed 25 doctoral theses Visiting Professor at European and American Universities. Main researcher of the groups: Andalusian Research Plan (PAI): "Andalusian SMEs: Management and competitiveness"; National Research Plan (R + D + i) "Creation of Human and Social Capital; and was Coordinator of the Consortium Agreement "The Impact of Knowledge Based Entrepreneurs on the Economic and Social Development of the European Union". He has 4 Erasmus scholarships from the European Economic Community, and a scholarship from the Real Colegio Complutense of Harvard University. Member of the Scientific and Editorial Board of national and international publications. Full Member of the European Academy of Management and Business Economics. Member of the IEAL (Institute for Latin American Studies). President of ASIBEAM (Ibero-American Association of Economy, Administration and Marketing).

Elena García-de-Soto-Camacho's main research interests are business internationalization, environmental management and corporate social responsibility, tourism satisfaction models, management of tourist destinations, cross-border tourism and the valuation of intangible heritage assets. At present, she is a lecturer at the University of Huelva, where she has served in several positions. In addition, she is a member of the Spanish-Portuguese Network of Researchers on Tourism (REINTUR) and the Iberian Circle of Business Economics (CIBECEM). Author of several scientific publications (articles, books and book chapters), she has also presented various papers at international and national congresses. She has been a researcher in several research projects funded in public call.She is a member of different scientific associations and has participated in different scientific committees of national and international congresses, as well as processes of evaluation of scientific articles, highlighting several indexed in the Q1 of SCOPUS or JCR.

Jaime Gutierrez is a Professor at the University of Seville for more than 20 years. He is a professor at the University of Seville and has taught several doctoral courses and Spanish and Ibero-American universities. His main research topics are SDG, Happiness, Poverty and Hunger.

Omar Kachkar is currently an assistant professor at Ibn Haldun University in Istanbul, he holds a PhD in Business Administration (Islamic Finance) from the International Islamic University Malaysia IIUM, an MA in Islamic Banking, Finance and Management from Loughborough University UK, and a B.A (Islamic Law) from Al-Azhar University (Cairo). He has an Excellent background on Islamic Law,

Islamic Economics, Banking & Finance in both academic and industry. Omar is a Registered Shariah Advisor at Securities Commission Malaysia and an Associate of Association of Shariah Advisors In Islamic Finance – ASAS. He has a Long experience lecturing in universities in Damascus, Kuala Lumpur and Turkey. Omar has presented a number of papers in local and international conferences on Islamic microfinance, cash waqf and micro enterprises. He has also published papers in international journals. Main interests include Islamic finance, Shari'ah Standards, microfinance, micro enterprises and cash waqf.

Eusebio Ortiz Zarco has a degree in Administration from the Metropolitan Autonomous University, Master and PhD in Economic Sciences from the National Polytechnic Institute, Member of the National System of Researchers at the candidate level. He has some publications, courses, downdrafts, congresses on national and international economic and financial issues. 7 years of teaching experience, currently full-time professor of the Bachelor of Business Creation and Development educational program at the Autonomous University of the State of Hidalgo.

Beatriz Palacios-Florencio is an assistant professor of marketing at University Pablo de Olavide at Seville. She is a member of research group REINTUR (Spanish-Portuguese Network of Researchers on Tourism) and coordinator of area Corporate Social Responsibility of the European Academy of Management and Business Economics. His main research is developed through two main lines: Corporate Social Responsibility and tourism. She has published in prestigious journal such as Journal of Business Research, Total Quality Management & Business Excellence, Management Decision, Internet Research, e.g. on these and related topics, and she is author and co-author of several scholarly books.

Juan Ganaza-Vargas is a professor at the University of Seville for more than 30 years. He is a professor of Social Responsibility and Business Ethics in the Finance and Accounting degree at the University of Seville and has taught several doctoral courses and Spanish and Ibero-American universities. His main research topics are: Social Responsibility and business ethics, Business Innovation, Academic Networks, Social Capital, Youth Entrepreneurship, SDG, Happiness, Poverty and Hunger.

Sonia Vega is Interim Administration and Services Personnel at Pablo de Olavide University, specifically in the Area of Enrollment Management and Undergraduate Academic Record and Criminology Graduate at Pablo de Olavide University.

Ruth Ortiz Zarco is a Research Professor of the Academic Area of Foreign Trade, at the Institute of Economic-Administrative Sciences at Autonomous University of Hidalgo State; she got her PhD in Economic Sciences from the National Polytechnic Institute, Mexico. Is currently a Member of the National System of Researchers at Level I, and has the Recognition of the Desirable Profile of the Program for Teacher Professional Development. PhD. Ortiz is the coordinator of the bachelor´s degree in Foreign Trade at Autonomous University of Hidalgo State; her publications fall within the following lines of research: Monetary Policy, Foreign Direct Investment and Foreign Trade.

Index

J

L

M

N

P

R

S

T

U

W

Y

Z

www.ingramcontent.com/pod-product-compliance
Lightning Source LLC
LaVergne TN
LVHW080017210926
848481LV00011B/3045